STUDY GUIDE

PRICE THEORY AND APPLICATIONS

STUDY GUIDE

William V. Weber
Eastern Illinois University

PRICE THEORY AND APPLICATIONS

Steven E. Landsburg
University of Rochester

THE DRYDEN PRESS
Chicago New York San Francisco
Philadelphia Montreal Toronto
London Sydney Tokyo

ISBN 0-03-020592-1
Printed in the United States of America
890-018-987654321

Cover source: © 1988 Amcal: <u>Timberline Jack's</u> from an original
painting by Charles Wysocki

Address orders:
6277 Sea Harbor Drive
Orlando, FL 32821

Address editorial correspondence:
908 N. Elm
Hinsdale, IL 60521

The Dryden Press
Holt, Rinehart and Winston
Saunders College Publishing

Contents

Introduction

This study guide has been prepared to accompany Steven E. Landsburg's *Price Theory and Applications*. When properly used in conjunction with the textbook, the study guide can be a valuable supplement in your learning of microeconomic theory. In particular, you should find the 450 completely-solved problems and questions to be extremely helpful.

On the other hand, if you try to use the study guide as a replacement for your work with the textbook and your participation in the classroom, you (a) won't succeed, (b) will have wasted your money, and (c) will probably write me a nasty letter about your experience. Please look through and consider the following recommendations on using the study guide and on drawing effective graphs so that you can get the maximum benefit from your efforts.

Using the Study Guide

Each chapter of the study guide contains five sections to help you with the material covered in the textbook: a chapter summary, a "working through the graphs" section, a selection of multiple choice questions, supplemental review questions, and a section of problems for analysis. The following are some suggestions on how to successfully use each of these features of the study guide.

Chapter Summary. Detailed, section-by-section chapter summaries begin each chapter of the study guide. By no means are these intended to be a substitute for the material in the textbook. If you try to learn the material from the chapter summaries instead of the textbook, you are certainly doomed to failure. A chapter summary is simply too condensed to be used in this manner.

Instead you should use the chapter summaries *after* you feel you have mastered the material in the textbook. By doing this, you can use the chapter summary to check your knowledge of the material. If you read through the summary and say, "Yes, that's easy. Yes, I know that," then you can feel comfortable that you know all the major points of the section or chapter. But instead if you read something in the chapter summary and go, "Huh? Say what?" then that's a clue that you may have overlooked something important. In that case, you should go back to the appropriate section in the textbook and reread that material, paying close attention to the in-text exercises and the "dangerous curve" signals.

Working Through the Graphs. One of the biggest mistakes students make when they study for an economics exam is that they fail to prepare for graphical analysis. No doubt you will be asked on exams to read graphs, label and complete graphs, sketch graphs representing a certain situation, and perform original graphical analysis. You cannot prepare for such questions by simply staring at the graphs in the text and your notes. You must practice using graphs to be adequately prepared for an exam.

Each chapter contains a "working through the graphs" section which builds the most important graphs of the chapter step by step. By completing the graphs yourself, you will see how the graph breaks down into its individual components and what each part of the graph represents. This will give you valuable practice in reading, drawing, and labelling graphs.

Multiple Choice Questions. A selection of 15 multiple choice questions has been included with each chapter. Even if your instructor chooses not to use multiple choice questions on exams, these can be worth going through. The multiple choice questions give you a quick and easy quiz over the key definitions, results, and graphs of the chapter. By spending a relatively small amount of time on these questions, you can identify any problem areas in advance. Also, the solutions include a short one to three sentence explanation in addition to the letter of the correct answer. These explanations will help you see how to approach the problem when you are unsure of the answer.

Questions for Review. A set of 7 review questions, similar to those appearing in the textbook, along with fully written solutions are provided for each chapter. These questions are designed to help prepare you for essay questions on an exam.

Do not simply read through a review question and answer it in your head—that will not help you learn to write using the economist's language. Instead, sit down with a piece of paper and try to write out a complete paragraph in response to the review question. Then check your answer against the one provided in the study guide to see if you've provided enough detail or missed any major points.

You'll find that putting your ideas into words is easier said than done. Too often students believe that they know the material really well, only to discover on the exam that they can't put what they know down on paper. The writing skills that you need for an essay exam, like any other skills, are only developed with practice. Be sure to get the practice you need by **writing out** the answers to review questions.

Problems for Analysis. Each chapter concludes with 3 problems that require a more advanced level of economic analysis than the multiple choice and review questions. Sometimes these will ask you to combine the material you've learned to discover new facts, other times you will be asked to do numerical exercises which show the mathematics behind the material you've learned, and yet other times you will have to apply the material you've learned to new situations. You will not be able to simply "look up the answers" in the textbook—these problems will require you to think on your own as an economist.

The *Problems for Analysis* are designed to help you with the problem sets in the textbook and analytical problems on exams. When confronting a complex economic puzzle, the answer is not immediately obvious. You may frequently wonder, "How do I get started? What do I do next?" To be able to work one of the text's analytical problems, you need to learn how to break a big problem up into several smaller parts.

For this reason, unlike the textbook, the study guide breaks down a problem into several short parts. By seeing step by step how we approach problems in the study guide, this will help you figure out how to break down and analyze the economic problems and puzzles posed by the textbook.

Acknowledgements

Thanks should properly go to a multitude of family, friends, and colleagues, past and present, but space limitations permit me to mention only a selected few. Becky Ryan, Karen Steib, Liz Widdicombe, and the rest of the fine staff at the Dryden Press have done a superlative job of seeing this project through to completion. My colleagues Jannett Highfill (Bradley University), Mark Walbert (Illinois State University), and John Leadley (Illinois State University) deserve special thanks for their moral support, professional advice, and emergency computer use. I also wish to thank the staff of the *Post Amerikan* newspaper who tremendously helped my writing and are the best group of people I know. Finally, I could not have completed this project without Robert Funk, who gave me more strength and support than I ever dreamed possible.

William V. Weber
November, 1988

Drawing Effective Graphs

As you already know, graphical analysis is a major part of economics. Whether you're taking lecture notes involving graphs, working through one of the graphs in the study guide, or drawing a graph on an exam, there are four basic rules you can follow that will make your life easier.

1. **Draw large graphs!** The U.S. Postal Service has never introduced a set of stamps honoring economic graphs, and you should not be trying to design one. If you draw your graphs too small, they will be difficult to label, difficult to correct when you make an error, and impossible to read later when you're studying for an exam (or even worse, impossible for your instructor to read when you're being graded). Save yourself these headaches by starting with a large enough set of axes—a big graph never hurts.

2. **Use pencil when drawing graphs.** You can't always draw a graph right the first time. It can be difficult to draw a curve through precisely the point you desire or to get a tangent point precisely where you want it. After you've completed a graph, you may find that it doesn't really show what you wanted it to. Be prepared to erase.

   I had one student that insisted on doing his graphs in ink. For lecture and for exams, he always brought his bottle of white-out. You can imagine how much valuable time he wasted in exams by using this procedure.

3. **Use several colors and use them consistently.** We use graphs in economics to show cause and effect, action and reaction. It is not easy to see these relationships when you are staring at a fully completed graph. Colors can be an effective way of clarifying the causal relationships we are trying to illustrate.

   In addition to a regular pencil, have two or three colored pencils ready when you take lecture notes, take an exam, or work problems. By using your colors consistently, you can keep track of the order in which things happen in the graph.

   For example, suppose you have a blue pencil and a red pencil in addition to your regular pencil. Always use your regular pencil to draw the axes and the initial situation shown in the graph. Then to show the first thing that changes on your graph (e.g., for the first shift in a curve or the first area identified), always use your blue pencil. Your red pencil will be reserved to show the second change in your graph. By using your colors in a consistent order, you can easily see how the graph was built up step by step to show economic cause and effect.

4. **Use adequate labels on your graphs.** Everything on your graph should be labelled. The last thing you want to see when you're studying the night before an exam is a mysterious curve wandering through your graphs. The curves in your graphs represent specific relationships between economic variables, and you need to know precisely what relationships are being shown. Effective use of labels will help you to keep track of what is happening in your graphs. When you use abbreviations in your labels, be sure you know what the abbreviations stand for. Also, don't hesitate to put additional explanatory notes in the margin beside and beneath your graphs.

Chapter One

Supply, Demand, and Equilibrium

Chapter Summary

No matter how complicated economic models get, they still rest on the fundamental ideas of supply and demand. This chapter reviews the basic facts concerning supply and demand and shows how these ideas can be applied to the analyze the effects of taxation.

Section 1.1. Demand

For any given price, *demand* shows the quantity of a good that consumers are willing and able to purchase, assuming all other relevant factors remain unchanged. Notice that the term demand as used by economists refers to a set of price-quantity pairs, not just a single number. By plotting the relationship between price (placed on the vertical axis) and quantity (placed on the horizontal axis) shown by demand, we can obtain a graph known as a *demand curve*.

The *law of demand* states that price and quantity demanded are inversely related, again assuming that all other relevant factors are unchanged. In other words, a rise in price will cause a fall in the quantity demanded (assuming no other factors are also working to alter the situation), and *vice versa*. The law of demand is shown graphically by drawing the demand curve downward sloping.

Economists make a careful distinction between the terms quantity demanded and demand. *Quantity demanded* refers to a specific amount of a good that individuals have chosen to consume at a particular price. In other words, quantity demanded refers to a specific place on the demand curve. The word demand is reserved for referring to the entire price-quantity relationship that describes the consumers' desires to purchase a good. So a change in price leads to a change in quantity demanded but not a change in demand—this is because the price-quantity relationship that is demand has not changed, only where we are on the demand curve is different when the price of the good changes.

There are several factors underlying the relationship described by the demand curve. Consumers' preferences, consumers' incomes, and the prices of other related goods all influence the decision on how much to purchase at a given price. To get a meaningful relationship between price and quantity demanded, these factors are assumed to be unchanging when we draw a demand curve. Should any of these factors change, then we would get an entirely new price-quantity relationship and a new demand curve. A *fall* (or decrease) *in demand* results when consumers decide to purchase less of a good at each and every possible price; this is illustrated by a shift down and to the left in the demand curve. A *rise* (or increase) *in demand* results when consumers choose to purchase more of a good at each given price; this is shown by a shift up and to the right in the demand curve. A change in any of the above underlying factors that determine demand will cause a rise or fall in demand. But as we noted above, a change in price does *not* cause a rise or fall in demand.

It is often important to know how sensitive quantity demanded is to changes in price. Does quantity demanded rise by a lot or by just a little bit if the price goes down? To answer this question economists calculate the *elasticity of demand*, which measures the percentage rise in quantity demanded resulting from a one percent fall in price. Let Q stand for quantity, P stand for price, and the symbol Δ stand for the phrase "change in." To calculate the elasticity of demand, we take the ratio between the percentage change in quantity (given by the formula $100 \cdot \Delta Q/Q$) and the percentage change in price (given by the formula $100 \cdot \Delta P/P$). This ratio representing elasticity simplifies to the formula $(P \cdot \Delta Q)/(Q \cdot \Delta P)$. Although economists would probably never have the complete information describing a demand curve, a family of statistical techniques known as *econometrics* can be used to get good estimates of elasticities.

Notice that the law of demand tells us that the terms ΔQ and ΔP will have different signs, so our elasticity calculation will always give a negative number. If this number has a magnitude greater than 1, we say demand is *elastic*. When demand is elastic, quantity demanded is rather sensitive to changes in price—a one percent fall in price will cause a larger percentage increase in quantity demanded. Similarly, when the elasticity calculation gives a number with magnitude smaller than 1, we say demand is *inelastic*. In this case, quantity demanded is relatively insensitive to changes in price—a one percent fall in price will cause a smaller percentage increase in quantity demanded.

Section 1.2. Supply

The development of the supply side of a market parallels that of the demand side. *Supply* is a set of price-quantity pairs that shows the quantity that suppliers are willing and able to provide at each and every price, assuming other related factors are held constant. The *law of supply* describes the relationship between price and quantity supplied, stating that a rise in price will result in an increase in quantity supplied, again assuming other related factors are unchanged. The law of supply is illustrated by an upward sloping supply curve. Notice the difference between quantity supplied and supply; the latter term is reserved for the entire supply schedule, while *quantity supplied* refers to the specific quantity provided at some specific price.

Generally speaking, the factors underlying the supply curve are those factors which influence the costs of production, such as the prices of resources, technology, and the number of firms. A change in any of these factors will result in a rise or fall in supply. When such a change causes suppliers to provide more of a good at each and every price, there is a *rise in supply* and the supply curve shifts down and to the right. When a change in an underlying factor causes suppliers to provide less of a good at each possible price, there is a *fall in supply* and the supply curve shifts up and to the left. (Notice that the terms "rise" and "fall" are referring to the direction that the quantity supplied on the horizontal axis is changing.) Of course, a change in price will only change quantity supplied and will *not* cause a rise or fall in supply.

The *elasticity of supply* gives the percentage increase in quantity supplied resulting from a one percent increase in price. The elasticity of supply essentially tells us how sensitive quantity supplied is to changes in price. We calculate the elasticity of supply in the same way we calculate the elasticity of demand, using the formula $(P \cdot \Delta Q)/(Q \cdot \Delta P)$. This number will be positive as long as the law of supply holds since ΔQ and ΔP will have the same sign.

Section 1.3. Equilibrium

When supply and demand are placed on the same graph, there will a single point of intersection that we call the equilibrium point. This equilibrium point is important for two reasons: it shows the only price where the quantity supplied and the quantity demanded are equal and the competitive behavior of demanders and suppliers will cause the price and quantity exchanged in the market to head toward the equilibrium price.

To see why markets frequently reach the equilibrium price and quantity, first consider a price above the equilibrium price where the quantity supplied is larger than the quantity demanded. In this situation, the demanders are *satisfied*—they are able to purchase the quantity they wish at the given price. The suppliers are not satisfied—they cannot sell as much of the good as they would like at the given price. Competition between these unsatisfied suppliers would cause them to lower the price to attract more demanders. This process would continue as long as quantity supplied is larger than quantity demanded, causing the price to fall to the equilibrium price.

We can tell a similar story whenever the price is below the equilibrium price and quantity demanded is larger than quantity supplied. In this case suppliers are satisfied but demanders are not.

The demanders will compete to obtain the good, causing the price to be bid up. The price will continue to rise until it hits the equilibrium price and quantity demanded no longer exceeds quantity supplied.

For most economic problems we can assume that the market has reached its equilibrium point. We can then use the supply/demand model to predict how equilibrium price and quantity change when various market conditions change. To see how an event affects the equilibrium, first determine how supply and/or demand are changed by the event, then find how the resulting shift in supply and/or demand will affect the equilibrium point.

The analysis of taxation provides one interesting application of the supply/demand model. The *legal incidence* of a tax indicates the legal requirements on demanders and suppliers to pay a tax. For example, the legal incidence of a *sales tax* (a per unit tax that demanders are required to pay when purchasing a good) falls entirely on the demanders. At the other extreme, the legal incidence of an *excise tax* (a per unit tax that suppliers are required to pay when selling a good) falls entirely on suppliers. The supply/demand model reveals that the legal incidence of a tax is very different from the *economic incidence*—the amounts of the tax actually paid by suppliers and demanders.

A sales tax will shift the demand curve down vertically by precisely the amount of the tax; this is because the price demanders are willing to pay for any given quantity of the good will be reduced by the amount of the tax. The effect of this change is a lower equilibrium quantity and a lower equilibrium price for the good. Producers now receive a lower price and demanders (after paying the tax) are paying a higher price in total than before the tax was imposed. The economic incidence of the sales tax is split between demanders and suppliers, even though the legal incidence was entirely on demanders.

Similarly, an excise tax will shift the supply curve up vertically by precisely the amount of the tax. Surprisingly the new equilibrium quantity, the new price paid by consumers, and the post-tax price kept by suppliers are the same as if we had imposed a sales tax of the same amount. Even though the legal incidence was on the suppliers this time, the economic incidence was identical. We summarize this idea by saying that **the economic incidence of a tax is independent of (i.e., is not affected by) the legal incidence of the tax.**

Working Through the Graphs—The Economic Incidence of a Tax

Do the following steps to complete Figure 1-1 and show that the economic incidence of a tax is independent of its legal incidence.

Step 1. Two identical graphs of the supply and demand for a market are provided in Figure 1-1. Some specific points on the supply and demand curves are summarized in the tables provided. Verify that the supply and demand curves are correctly graphed. Also verify that the equilibrium for this market occurs at a price of 6 dollars per unit where quantity supplied and quantity demanded are equal to 6 units of the commodity.

Step 2. We will use the top graph to show the effects of a $3 per unit sales tax. Since the legal incidence falls on demanders, the sales tax will affect the demand in the market. Also notice that the net amount demanders are willing to pay for any given quantity of the good has not changed. This implies that the price consumers are now willing to pay for the good itself must be adjusted downward to account for the sales tax. For example, before the tax consumers were willing to pay $8 per unit for 4 units of the good; to make up for the $3 per unit sales tax consumers are now only willing to pay $5 per unit for this same quantity.

To show the effects of the sales tax in the top graph, first complete the table to show the post-tax demand curve. Second, use these points to graph this new demand curve. Finally, find the new equilibrium quantity, equilibrium price received by suppliers, and post-tax price paid by demanders. If you've done this correctly, you should find that 4 units of the good are exchanged, with demanders paying a total of $8 per unit and suppliers receiving $5 per unit.

Figure 1-1 The Economic Incidence of a Tax

Analysis of a Sales Tax

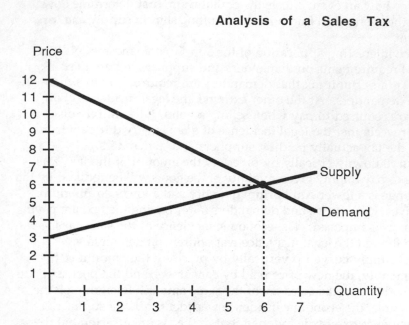

Supply	
Q	P
0	3
1	3.5
2	4
3	4.5
4	5
5	5.5
6	6
7	6.5

Demand		Demand after sales tax	
Q	P	Q	P
0	12	0	
1	11	1	
2	10	2	
3	9	3	
4	8	4	
5	7	5	
6	6	6	
7	5	7	

Analysis of an Excise Tax

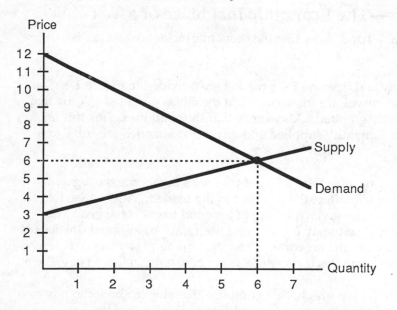

Demand	
Q	P
0	12
1	11
2	10
3	9
4	8
5	7
6	6
7	5

Supply		Supply after excise tax	
Q	P	Q	P
0	3	0	
1	3.5	1	
2	4	2	
3	4.5	3	
4	5	4	
5	5.5	5	
6	6	6	
7	6.5	7	

Step 3. Use the lower graph to show the effects of a $3 per unit excise tax. In this case the legal incidence falls on suppliers. Since suppliers must now receive a higher price to provide any given quantity in order to cover the new cost of the tax, this tax shifts the supply curve upward.

As in Step 2, complete the table to find points on the new supply curve, graph the new supply curve, and find the new equilibrium quantity, price paid by demanders, and post-tax price received by suppliers.

If you've done this step correctly, you should find that the equilibrium quantity and prices under the excise tax are the same as the equilibrium under the sales tax. This shows a major result in the theory of taxation—the group legally required to pay the tax did not affect the final burden that demanders and suppliers have in paying the tax. We summarize this result by saying that the economic incidence of the tax is independent of the legal incidence.

Multiple Choice Questions

1. The immediate effect of a decrease in the price of American automobiles is a decrease in the _____ for American automobiles.
   A. demand
   B. quantity demanded
   C. supply
   D. quantity supplied

2. The immediate effect of a decrease in the price of Japanese automobiles is a decrease in the _____ for American automobiles.
   A. demand
   B. quantity demanded
   C. supply
   D. quantity supplied

3. If the demand for a good is inelastic, then a 4% rise in the price of the good will result in quantity demanded _____ by _____ than 4%.
   A. falling; less
   B. falling; more
   C. rising; less
   D. rising; more

4. Suppose a $10/unit fall in price causes quantity demanded to increase by 20 units. Then
   A. the law of demand is violated.
   B. demand is elastic.
   C. demand is inelastic.
   D. we do not have enough information to determine if demand is elastic or inelastic.

5. The law of supply states that
   A. quantity exchanged will always increase whenever price increases.
   B. quantity exchanged will always decrease whenever price increases.
   C. quantity supplied will increase when price increases, provided other factors remain unchanged.
   D. quantity supplied will decrease when price increases, provided other factors remain unchanged.

6. Suppose the price of a good is $5/unit. At that price consumers wish to purchase 4,000 units weekly and producers wish to sell 5,000 units weekly. Assuming this market heads towards its equilibrium point, competition between _____ will force the price _____.
    A. consumers; up
    B. consumers; down
    C. producers; up
    D. producers; down

7. Suppose the current market price is below the equilibrium price. Then
    A. suppliers are satisfied but demanders are not.
    B. demanders are satisfied but suppliers are not.
    C. neither demanders nor suppliers are satisfied.
    D. both demanders and suppliers are satisfied.

Figure 1a

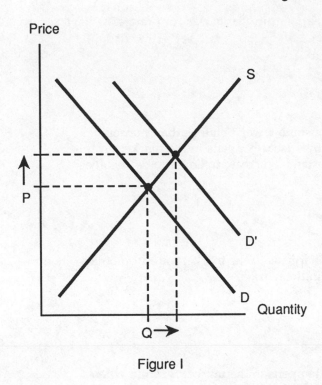

Figure I

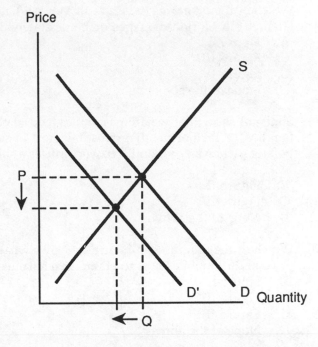

Figure II

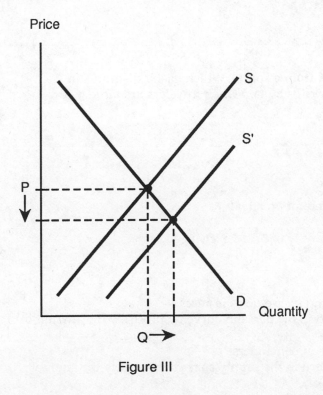

Figure III

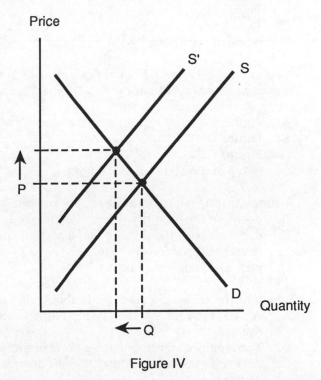

Figure IV

8. Which of the diagrams in Figure 1a shows what happens in the market for oranges when a severe late frost in Florida damages orchards statewide?
   A. Figure II.
   B. Figure III.
   C. Figure IV.
   D. None of the above

9. Statistics show that wealthier families tend to consume fewer potatoes than poorer families. Which of the diagrams in Figure 1a shows what happens in the market for potatoes when an economic recovery causes a substantial increase in households' incomes?
   A. Figure I.
   B. Figure II.
   C. Figure IV.
   D. None of the above

10. Which of the diagrams in Figure 1a shows what happens in the market for automobiles when the price of automobiles falls to eliminate a surplus in the market?
    A. Figure I.
    B. Figure II.
    C. Figure III.
    D. None of the above

11. Which of the diagrams in Figure 1a shows what happens in the market for milk when improvements in cattle feed result in higher milk yields from dairy cows?
    A. Figure I.
    B. Figure III.
    C. Figure IV.
    D. None of the above

12. Airplane travelers take frequent taxi trips to and from airports. Which of the diagrams in Figure 1a shows what happens in the market for trips by taxi when travelers are faced with rising airline prices?
    A. Figure I.
    B. Figure II.
    C. Figure IV.
    D. None of the above

13. A simultaneous fall in both the supply and demand for bread *must*
    A. decrease the quantity of bread exchanged.
    B. decrease both the price of bread and the quantity of bread exchanged.
    C. decrease the price of bread.
    D. increase the price of bread.

14. Which of the following statements about sales and excise taxes is *false?*
    A. A sales tax causes a parallel shift downward in the demand curve by precisely the amount of the tax.
    B. The legal incidence of a sales tax is entirely on demanders.
    C. An excise tax causes a parallel shift downward in the supply curve by precisely the amount of the tax.
    D. The legal incidence of an excise tax is entirely on suppliers.

15. What do we mean when we say that the economic incidence of a tax is independent of its legal `incidence?
    A. The economic incidence and legal incidence of a tax are always the same.
    B. The economic incidence will be the same no matter who bears the legal incidence of the tax.
    C. The economic incidence of a tax will be divided equally between demanders and suppliers no matter who bears the legal incidence of the tax.
    D. Since suppliers can "pass on" a tax to demanders, the economic incidence of a tax will always be on demanders even when the legal incidence is on suppliers.

Solutions

1. D. Applying the laws of demand and supply, a fall in price will increase the quantity demanded and decrease the quantity supplied. There is no change in either the demand or supply schedules.

2. A. No matter what the price of American automobiles is, the fall in the price of Japanese automobiles will cause demanders to substitute away from American automobiles to Japanese automobiles. Hence there is a fall in demand for American automobiles.

3. A. Quantity demanded will fall when price rises according to the law of demand. When demand is inelastic, the percentage change in quantity demanded will be smaller than the percentage change in price.

4. D. To calculate elasticity, we need to know the *percentage* changes in price and quantity demanded.

5. C. This is simply the definition of the law of supply.

6. D. Producers are not satisfied in this situation and will bid the price down to attract demanders.

7. A. Demanders cannot purchase all that they wish at the going market price, so they are not satisfied.

8. C. The frost will increase the cost of producing oranges, so suppliers will be able to bring fewer oranges to the market no matter what the current price. The resulting fall in supply will increase price and lower quantity exchanged.

9. B. Households will switch away from potatoes to other foods as their incomes increase. The resulting decrease in demand will lower both the price and the quantity exchanged.

10. D. There is no change in demand, supply, or the equilibrium point when the price of the good changes.

11. B. The lower costs of producing any given quantity of milk will cause suppliers to provide more milk to the market no matter what the going market price is. The resulting increase in supply will lower the price and increase the quantity exchanged.

12. B. Higher airline prices will lower the amount of travelling by air according to the law of demand. No matter what the going price is, travellers will require fewer trips by taxi. The resulting fall in demand will lower both the price and the quantity exchanged.

13. A. The fall in supply puts downward pressure on quantity and upward pressure on price. The fall in demand puts downward pressure on both quantity and price. Combining these two, we can be sure that quantity exchanged will fall, but the overall effect on price is uncertain.

14. C. The excise tax increases producers' costs and hence causes a fall in supply, shown by the supply curve shifting up and to the left. There will be a parallel shift upward in the supply curve by precisely the amount of the tax.

15. B. It does not matter who is legally obliged to pay the tax—the final division of the burden of the tax between demanders and suppliers will not be affected.

Questions for Review

1. Distinguish between demand and quantity demanded. Distinguish between supply and quantity supplied. Why are these distinctions important?

2. List some situations which would cause a rise in demand. List some situations which would cause a rise in supply.

3. What does elasticity attempt to measure? Why does elasticity provide a better description of the supply or demand schedule than slope?

4. When would a supply curve have a zero elasticity? When would a supply curve have an infinite elasticity?

5. What is the equilibrium point and what is its significance?

6. When would a surplus situation where quantity supplied is larger than quantity demanded be likely to occur? Why is it unlikely that such a situation would prevail in a market for very long?

7. Compare and contrast the effects of a sales tax and an excise tax.

Solutions

1. Demand and supply both refer to an entire set of price-quantity pairs showing how demanders and suppliers adjust their quantities to changes in price, assuming all other relevant factors are held constant. Quantity demanded and quantity supplied refer to the specific amounts to buy and sell desired by demanders and suppliers at some particular price; quantity demanded and quantity supplied refer to particular horizontal coordinates on the demand and supply curves. These terms allow us to distinguish between the determinants of price (demand and supply) and the effects of price (changes in quantity demanded and quantity supplied).

2. Changes in consumers' preferences or consumers' incomes could increase demand. An increase in the price of a substitute good (one used in place of the good in question) or a decrease in the price of a complement good (one used in conjunction with the good in question) would also cause a rise in demand. A fall in the costs of resources, a cost-effective improvement in technology, or an increase in the number of firms would increase supply.

3. Elasticity measures the percentage change in quantity supplied or quantity demanded resulting from a one percent change in price. By looking at percentage changes, elasticity does not depend on the choice of the units used for quantity and price. On the other hand, slope considers absolute changes in price and quantity, and so would give different results when different units are chosen.

4. Recall that the formula to calculate elasticity is given by $P \cdot \Delta Q / Q \cdot \Delta P$. If supply were vertical, then there would be no change in quantity when price changes, so ΔQ and elasticity would be zero. If supply were horizontal, then there would be no change in price when quantity changes, so ΔP would be zero and elasticity would be infinite.

5. The equilibrium point is the point where the demand and supply curves intersect. The equilibrium point gives the only price where demanders' and suppliers' desires agree in the sense that quantity demanded equals quantity supplied. Since this is also the only price where both demanders and suppliers are satisfied, competitive behavior will drive the price to the equilibrium price.

6. When the going market price is above the equilibrium price, the quantity supplied will be larger than the quantity demanded. In this situation, demanders are satisfied but suppliers are not. To avoid being stuck with unsold goods, suppliers will compete and cause the price to be bid down.

7. The legal incidence of a sales tax is entirely on demanders, so the sales tax will cause a parallel shift in demand downward by the amount of the tax. The legal incidence of an excise tax is entirely on suppliers, so the excise tax causes a parallel shift in the supply curve downward by the amount of the tax. The sales and excise taxes are similar in that they have the same economic incidence. The quantity exchanged, the net price paid by the demanders, and the net price received by suppliers will all be the same under the sales and excise taxes.

Problems for Analysis

1. The markets diagrammed in Figure 1b have identical supply curves but different demand curves.

Figure 1b

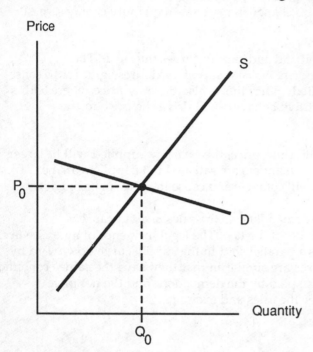

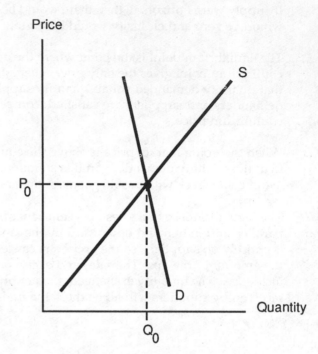

(i)   At the point (Q_0, P_0), which demand curve is the more elastic? Explain.
(Hint—Use the elasticity formula and the fact that the slope of demand is
given by $\Delta P / \Delta Q$.)

(ii) Suppose that an excise tax of the same size is placed on both markets.
Complete the diagrams in Figure 1b to show this situation. The following should be
labelled:

   a.   the new equilibrium quantity and price (Q_1, P_1),
   b.   the net price suppliers pay after the tax (P_S), and
   c.   the size of the excise tax (t).

(iii)   Based on your diagrams, how does the elasticity of demand affect the economic incidence of the excise tax?

2.   (i)   Let Q represent the quantity per week of a good and P represent the price measured in dollars per unit. Suppose demand is given by the formula $P = 200 - (1/2)Q$ and supply is given by the equation $P = 50 + (1/4)Q$. Find the equilibrium price and quantity for this market.

(ii)   Suppose the government imposes a sales tax of $9 per unit on this good. Find the new formula for the demand curve, the new equilibrium price and quantity, and the new post-tax price for the demanders of this good.

(iii)   What fraction of the economic burden of the tax is borne by demanders? By suppliers?

3.   When the government gives demanders or suppliers financial assistance to purchase or produce a good, we say the government has given a subsidy.

(i)   Suppose the government gives demanders a fixed subsidy for each unit of the good purchased. In the diagram on the left in Figure 1c, show the effects of this subsidy. The following should be labeled:

   a.   the new equilibrium quantity (Q_1),
   b.   the post-subsidy price paid by demanders (P_D),
   c.   the post-subsidy price received by suppliers (P_S), and
   d.   the size of the per unit subsidy (s).

(ii)   In the diagram on the right of Figure 1c, repeat part (i) for the case where the government gives the same subsidy to suppliers for each unit of the good sold.

Figure 1c

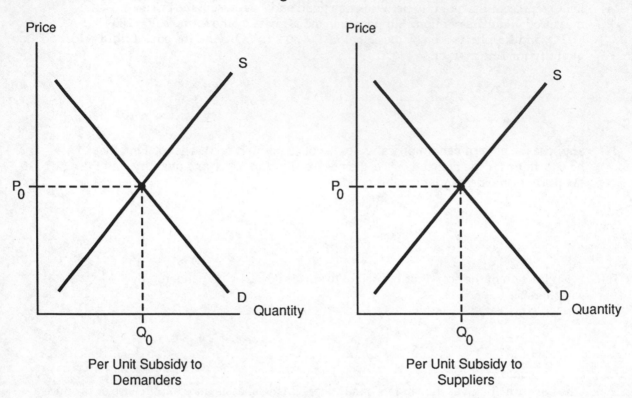

Per Unit Subsidy to
Demanders

Per Unit Subsidy to
Suppliers

(iii)   Using the diagrams in Figure 1c, what can you conclude about the economic incidence of a per unit subsidy?

Solutions

1. (i) Since elasticity equals $P \cdot \Delta Q/Q \cdot \Delta P$ and the slope of the demand curve equals $\Delta P/\Delta Q$, we have the following:

$$
\begin{aligned}
\text{elasticity} &= P \cdot \Delta Q/Q \cdot \Delta P \\
&= (P/Q) \cdot (\Delta Q/\Delta P) \\
&= (P/Q) \cdot [1/(\Delta P/\Delta Q)] \\
&= (P/Q) \cdot (1/\text{slope}).
\end{aligned}
$$

Using this formula we see that the smaller the slope, the larger the elasticity. So the flatter demand curve is the more elastic.

Notice that does *not* say we can simply determine elasticity by slope. Only when we are comparing demand curves that pass through the same point can we use slope to determine when one demand curve is more elastic than another.

(ii)

Figure 1d

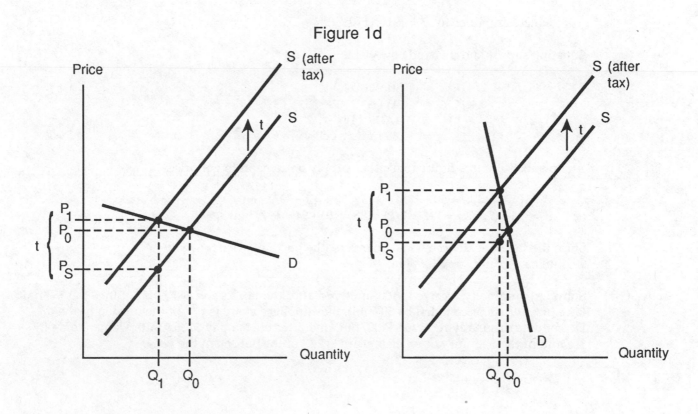

(iii) As shown by the diagrams in Figure 1d, the more inelastic demand is, the greater the demanders' share in the economic burden of the tax.

2. (i) First equate supply and demand to find the equilibrium quantity:

$$50 + (1/4)\,Q \;=\; 200 - (1/2)Q$$
$$3/4)\,Q \;=\; 150$$
$$Q \;=\; (4/3) \cdot 150$$
$$\;=\; 200 \text{ units weekly.}$$

Substitute this into either supply or demand to get price:

$$P = 50 + (1/4)Q = 50 + (1/4) \cdot 200 = 50 + 50 = \$100/\text{unit}$$
or $\quad P = 200 - (1/2)Q = 200 - (1/2) \cdot 200 = 200 - 100 = \$100/\text{unit}.$

(ii) We have:

the new price demanders are willing to pay	=	the old price demanders were willing to pay	-	the tax

so now $\qquad P \;=\; 200 - (1/2)Q \qquad - \quad 9$

which simplifies to $P = 191 - (1/2)Q$.

Equating supply and demand now yields

$$50 + (1/4)\,Q \;=\; 191 - (1/2)Q$$
$$(3/4)\,Q \;=\; 141$$
$$Q \;=\; (4/3) \cdot 141$$
$$\;=\; 188 \text{ units weekly.}$$

Again substitute this figure into either supply or demand to get price:

$$P = 50 + (1/4)Q = 50 + (1/4) \cdot 188 = 50 + 47 = \$97/\text{unit}$$
or $\quad P = 191 - (1/2)Q = 191 - (1/2) \cdot 188 = 191 - 94 = \$97/\text{unit}.$

Since the legal incidence is on demanders, the post-tax price they pay is $97/unit + $9/unit or $106/unit.

(iii) Suppliers originally received $100/unit and after the tax receive $97/unit. Since the $9/unit tax caused their price to fall by $3/unit, the suppliers' share is 1/3 of the burden of the tax. Demanders originally received $100/unit and after the tax pay $106/unit. Demanders pay $6/unit of the $9/unit tax, so their share is 2/3 of the burden of the tax.

3.(i),(ii)

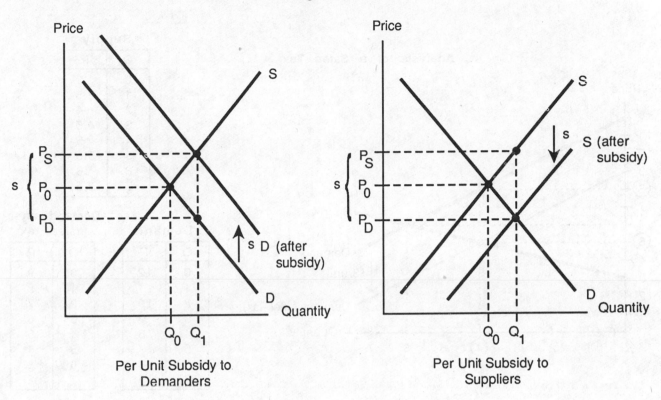

Per Unit Subsidy to
Demanders

Per Unit Subsidy to
Suppliers

(iii)   Just like a per unit tax, the economic incidence of a per unit subsidy is
        independent of the legal incidence.

Solutions to Working Through the Graphs

Figure 1-1   The Economic Incidence of a Tax

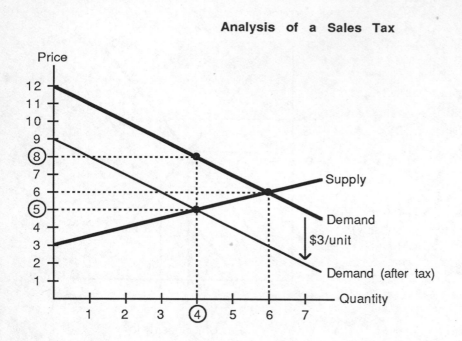

Analysis of a Sales Tax

Supply	
Q	P
0	3
1	3.5
2	4
3	4.5
4	5
5	5.5
6	6
7	6.5

Demand	
Q	P
0	12
1	11
2	10
3	9
4	8
5	7
6	6
7	5

Demand after sales tax	
Q	P
0	9
1	8
2	7
3	6
4	5
5	4
6	3
7	2

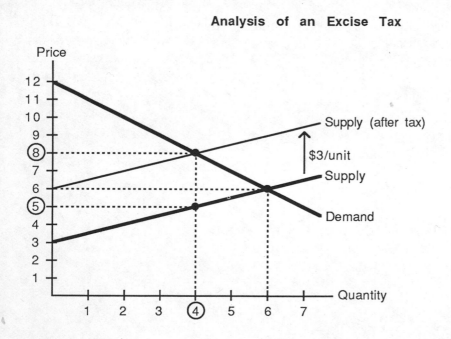

Analysis of an Excise Tax

Demand	
Q	P
0	12
1	11
2	10
3	9
4	8
5	7
6	6
7	5

Supply	
Q	P
0	3
1	3.5
2	4
3	4.5
4	5
5	5.5
6	6
7	6.5

Supply after excise tax	
Q	P
0	6
1	6.5
2	7
3	7.5
4	8
5	8.5
6	9
7	9.5

Chapter Two

Prices, Costs, and the Gains from Trade

Chapter Summary

The desire to benefit from trade underlies the supply and demand curves introduced in the previous chapter. This chapter focuses on the reasons people wish to trade. We begin by discussing the meanings of prices and costs in greater detail, and then show how differences in costs create opportunities for people to benefit from trade.

Section 2.1. Prices

There are two types of prices to consider in economics: absolute prices and relative prices. The *absolute price* of a commodity is the amount of *money* that can be exchanged for a specific quantity of that commodity; these are the prices you and I see posted on various goods every day. The *relative price* of a commodity is the amount of *some other good* that can be exchanged for a specific quantity of the commodity. Put another way, the absolute price tells us the rate of exchange at which we can trade for a good in terms of currency, while the relative price expresses this rate of exchange in terms of other goods.

If we know the absolute prices of goods, we can always calculate the relative prices. Suppose bread costs $1 per loaf and wine costs $5 per bottle—these are the absolute prices of bread and wine. The relative price of wine is the amount of bread that must be sacrificed to obtain more wine. Since a bottle of wine is 5 times as expensive as a loaf of bread, the relative price of wine is 5 loaves of bread per bottle of wine. Similarly, the relative price of bread is 1/5 bottle of wine per loaf of bread since this is the amount of wine you must sacrifice to get a loaf of bread.

Simply knowing that absolute prices have changed tells us nothing about the effect on relative prices. If absolute prices all increase, then relative prices may increase, decrease, or stay the same. For example, return to the bread and wine example and suppose the absolute prices of bread and wine both increase. If they increase by the same percentage, there will be no change in relative prices. If the absolute price of wine increases by a larger percentage than the absolute price of bread, then the relative price of wine is larger and the relative price of bread is smaller. If the absolute price of wine increases by a smaller percentage than the price of bread, then the relative price of wine has fallen and the relative price of bread has risen.

In microeconomics we study relative prices. The term "price" will then always refer to the relative price. Although we will often express the price of a commodity in terms of "dollars per unit," we assume that the word "dollar" in this context means some basket of goods that can be exchanged for the commodity and not simply currency.

Section 2.2. Costs, Efficiency, and the Gains from Trade

Economists use the term *cost* to mean sacrificed alternatives or forgone opportunities. So for example, the cost of a resource is not the amount of money paid for that resource, but the value of the other alternative uses for that resource. The term "opportunity cost" is often used to emphasize this idea of sacrificed alternatives, so "cost" as used by economists always means "opportunity cost." When calculating costs it is important not to double-count; if there are mutually exclusive forgone opportunities, the cost is the more valuable of the alternatives.

When a person's (opportunity) cost to perform a task is lower than anyone else's, we say he has a *comparative advantage* or is *more efficient* in performing the task. The importance of this idea is shown by a basic and essential result in microeconomic theory—**everyone in society can be made better off if each person specializes in the area where he has a comparative advantage (i.e., where he is most efficient) and then trades for the goods he wants to have.**

A simple example should suffice to show the benefits of specialization and trade. Consider a boyfriend and girlfriend (living separately) who both need to mow the lawn and clean the house once a week. The girlfriend is very good at performing these household chores. She can mow the lawn in 3 hours and clean the house in 2 hours, so she spends a total of 5 hours per week on these chores. The boyfriend is distracted rather easily and takes more time to do both chores. He can mow the lawn in 4 hours and clean the house in 5 hours, resulting in a total of 9 hours weekly. Since the girlfriend uses fewer resources to perform both chores, we say she has an *absolute advantage* over her boyfriend in both activities.

Let's calculate their costs in this situation. The cost of mowing the lawn is the sacrificed cleaning that could have been done. Since in the 3 hours she needs to mow the lawn she could have cleaned the house 1 1/2 times, the girlfriend's cost of mowing the lawn is 1 1/2 houses cleaned per lawn mowed. In the 4 hours the boyfriend spends mowing the lawn, he could have instead cleaned 4/5 of the house—his cost of mowing the lawn is 4/5 house cleaned per lawn mowed. Since the boyfriend sacrifices less (i.e., has the lower cost) to mow the lawn, we say he is more efficient or he has a comparative advantage in lawn mowing.

The costs of cleaning the house (i.e., the sacrificed mowing) can be calculated in a similar way. The girlfriend's cost of cleaning the house is 2/3 lawn mowed per house cleaned, and the boyfriend's cost of cleaning the house is 1 1/4 lawns mowed per house cleaned. Since the girlfriend has the lower cost in this area, she is more efficient than her boyfriend and has the comparative advantage in cleaning the house.

Recall that the girlfriend spends 5 hours weekly and the boyfriend spends 9 hours weekly when both do their own chores. Now consider what happens when they specialize in the area of their comparative advantage and trade. The girlfriend offers to clean her boyfriend's house in exchange for him mowing her lawn. Now the girlfriend spends a total of 4 hours cleaning two houses, saving her 1 hour weekly. The boyfriend mows both lawns in a total of 8 hours weekly, saving him 1 hour. By specializing in the area of their comparative advantage and trading, both the boyfriend and girlfriend are made better off. They still have their clean houses and well-kept lawns, but now they have an additional hour of free time every week to spend with each other.

The idea behind this simple example still holds true in complex economies—specialization in the area of one's comparative advantage followed by trade to get the goods one desires makes everyone better off.

Multiple Choice Questions

1. The amount of currency needed to purchase a unit of a commodity is referred to as the _____ price, while the amount of other goods sacrificed to purchase a unit of the commodity is called the _____ price. The _____ term is what microeconomists mean by price.
    A. absolute, relative; former
    B. absolute, relative; latter
    C. relative, absolute; former
    D. relative, absolute; latter

2. The absolute price of food is 4,000 yen per unit and the absolute price of clothing is 20,000 yen per unit. The relative price of food is
    A. 4,000 yen.
    B. 16,000 yen.
    C. 5 units of clothing per unit of food.
    D. 1/5 unit of clothing per unit of food.

3. Suppose there are only two goods: food and clothing. If the price of food is 3 units of clothing per unit of food, then the price of clothing
    A. is 3 units of food per unit of clothing.
    B. is 1/3 unit of food per unit of clothing.
    C. is 1/3 unit of clothing per unit of food.
    D. cannot be calculated from the given information.

4. Suppose there are only two goods: food and clothing. If the price of food rises, then
    A. the price of clothing must also rise.
    B. the price of clothing must fall.
    C. the price of clothing is not affected.
    D. we cannot make any prediction about changes in the price of clothing.

5. When a microeconomist says the price of a commodity is $5 per unit,
    A. he means that a person must spend $5 in currency to purchase one unit of the good.
    B. he is referring to the absolute price of the commodity.
    C. the dollars he is referring to are a collection of goods in the economy.
    D. Both A and B

6. Suppose inflation caused the absolute prices of all goods to rise. Then the price of any particular good
    A. must have also risen.
    B. must have remained constant.
    C. must have fallen.
    D. could have risen, fallen, or remained constant.

7. According to economists' use of the term "cost," which of the following best describes the cost of producing a commodity?
    A. The time and raw materials used in the production.
    B. The monetary value of the time and raw materials used in the production.
    C. The alternative uses of the time and raw materials used in the production.
    D. All of the above represent different types of cost used by economists.

8. When can the phrase "more efficient at producing food" be properly applied?
   A. When the quantity of resources required to produce food is smaller than the amount required to produce any other good.
   B. When the cost of producing food is smaller than the cost of producing any other good.
   C. When the quantity of resources required to produce food is smaller than the amount anyone else requires to produce food.
   D. When the cost of producing food is smaller than anyone else's cost of producing food.

***Questions 9-13 refer to the following table which shows the abilities of two countries to produce food and clothing. Food and clothing are the only two commodities in the world and their production requires only labor. The amounts of labor required to produce one unit of these commodities in the two countries are shown in the table below.

	Country A	Country B
One Unit of Food	6 hours	20 hours
One Unit of Clothing	2 hours	10 hours

9. The cost of producing food in Country A is
   A. 6 hours of labor.
   B. 3 units of food per unit of clothing.
   C. 3 units of clothing per unit of food.
   D. 1/3 units of clothing per unit of food.

10. The cost of producing clothing in Country B is
    A. 2 units of food per unit of clothing.
    B. 1/2 unit of food per unit of clothing.
    C. 2 units of clothing per unit of food.
    D. 1/2 unit of clothing per unit of food.

11. Which country has an absolute advantage in food production and which country has an absolute advantage in clothing production?
    A. Country A has an absolute advantage in the production of both goods.
    B. Country B has an absolute advantage in the production of both goods.
    C. Country A has an absolute advantage in food production, and Country B has an absolute advantage in clothing production.
    D. Country A has an absolute advantage in clothing production, and Country B has an absolute advantage in food production.

12. _____ is the most efficient in food production, and _____ is the most efficient in clothing production.
    A. Country A; Country A
    B. Country A; Country B
    C. Country B; Country A
    D. Country B; Country B

13. When can trade benefit both Country A and Country B?
    A. When Country A specializes in food and Country B specializes in clothing.
    B. When Country A specializes in clothing and Country B specializes in food.
    C. The countries cannot gain from trade since Country A has the lowest costs for producing both goods.
    D. The countries cannot gain from trade since Country B has a comparative advantage for producing both goods.

14. Which of the following does *not* guarantee that specialization and trade will be beneficial to society?
    A. Specialization in the area where one has a comparative advantage.
    B. Specialization in the area where one has a lower cost than others.
    C. Specialization in the area where one uses fewer resources than others.
    D. Specialization in the area where one is more efficient than others.

15. When would people find it beneficial to trade?
    A. When they have different abilities.
    B. When they have different tastes.
    C. Either different abilities or different tastes would be a sufficient reason to pursue trade.
    D. Only when people have both different abilities and different tastes is trade beneficial; just one of these reasons is not enough.

Solutions

1. B. These are the definitions of absolute and relative price. Since microeconomics focuses on trade, it is concerned with the relative price of a commodity and the term "price" is reserved to refer to this definition.

2. D. The 4,000 yen used to purchase a unit of food could have been used to purchase 1/5 unit of clothing. It is this amount of sacrificed clothing that gives the price of food.

3. B. Since 3 units of clothing can be traded for 1 unit of food, 1 unit of clothing can be traded for 1/3 unit of food and *vice versa*.

4. B. For example, if the price of food rises from 3 to 4 units of clothing per unit of food, then the price of clothing falls from 1/3 to 1/4 unit of food per unit of clothing.

5. C. Since "price" means the relative price, we are referring to the amounts of other goods sacrificed even when we use the term "dollars."

6. D. Rising absolute prices are consistent with rising, falling, and constant relative prices.

7. C. Cost always means "opportunity cost" and refers to forgone opportunities.

8. D. This is the definition of the phrase "most efficient." The costs of production (not absolute quantities of resources) are compared across individuals (not activities).

9. C. The 6 hours required to produce one unit of food could have been used to produce 3 units of clothing. So 3 units of clothing are sacrificed for every unit of food produced.

10. B. The 10 hours required to produce one unit of clothing could have been used to produce 1/2 unit of food.

11. A. To determine absolute advantage, we compare the physical amounts of resources needed for production. Country A needs less labor than Country B to produce either food or clothing, so it has the absolute advantage in production of both goods.

12. C. Country A's cost of producing food is 3 units of clothing per unit of food, and Country B's cost of producing food is 2 units of clothing per unit of food. Since Country B has the lower cost, it is the most efficient in food production. Country A's cost of producing clothing is 1/3 unit of food per unit of clothing, and Country B's cost of producing clothing is 1/2 unit of food per unit of clothing. Since Country A has the lower cost, it is the most efficient in clothing production.

13. B. Each country should specialize in producing the good for which it has a comparative advantage (i.e., produces at a lower cost than the other country).

14. C. The absolute levels of resource use do not reflect the true costs of production (i.e., the forgone opportunities), and so do not indicate efficient production or comparative advantage.

15. C. This chapter has shown that differing abilities give sufficient reason for trade. The next chapter shows that different tastes also give a sufficient reason for trade.

Questions for Review

1. Compare and contrast the absolute price and the relative price of a commodity. Which is studied in microeconomics?

2. Suppose there are only two goods: bread and wine. Suppose the absolute price of bread doubles and the absolute price of wine triples. Did the price of bread rise or fall? The price of wine?

3. Generally we say that the price of a commodity is measured in "dollars per unit." Explain precisely what we mean by this phrase.

4. What is cost? If you can produce a good using fewer resources than anyone else, does this imply that you produce the good at the lowest cost?

5. An electrician can rewire a house in 12 hours and can panel a room in 15 hours. His teenage son can rewire a house in 18 hours and can panel a room in 16 hours. Who is more efficient in rewiring a house? Who is more efficient in panelling a room?

6. Compare and contrast absolute advantage and comparative advantage. Which is more important from an economic viewpoint and why?

7. Under what conditions is specialization advantageous for members of society?

Solutions

1. Absolute price shows the amount of currency that must be sacrificed for a unit of a commodity, while relative price shows the amount of other goods that must be sacrificed for that unit. Microeconomics studies relative prices because these are the ones that motivate trade between individuals.

2. The price of bread falls because the currency spent on a loaf of bread can now purchase less wine than before. The price of wine has risen because an individual must now sacrifice more bread to purchase a bottle of wine than before the increase in absolute prices.

3. Price always refers to relative price—the amounts of other goods sacrificed in order to obtain the commodity in question. We frequently use the term "dollar" as a shorthand to represent a basket of other goods being sacrificed to obtain the commodity.

4. Cost is forgone opportunities or sacrificed alternatives. The absolute levels of resource use do not imply anything about cost, because in and of themselves they do not measure the sacrificed alternatives of the production undertaken. Only when the absolute levels of resource use are ompared to the resources required for other production activities can anything about cost be determined.

5. The electrician's cost of rewiring a house is the sacrificed alternative—the 12 hours used could have panelled 12/15 or 4/5 of a room. So the electrician's cost of rewiring a house is 4/5 panelled room per rewired house. Similarly, his son's cost is 18/16 or 1 1/8 panelled rooms per rewired house. Since the electrician's cost is the lowest, he is the more efficient in rewiring a house.
Simply reverse the argument to find who is the most efficient in panelling a room. The electrician's cost of panelling a room is 15/12 or 1 1/4 rewired houses per panelled room. The son's cost of panelling a room is 16/18 or 8/9 rewired house per panelled room. Since the son has the lower (opportunity) cost, he is the more efficient in panelling a room.

6. Absolute advantage compares the *physical amounts* of time and raw materials that different people use to complete a task. Comparative advantage compares different people's *forgone opportunities* for the time and resources used when completing a task. Comparative advantage is the more important for economics because it is the concept that truly represents cost and shows how gains from trade can be obtained.

7. People should specialize in the area of their comparative advantage (i.e., the area where they have lower costs than other people, the area where they are more efficient than other people) and then trade to get the commodities they desire. As compared to the situation where each person produces the goods he chooses to consume, such specialization and trade will make everyone better off.

Problems for Analysis

1. Let P_W denote the absolute price of wine and P_B denote the absolute price of bread. Let p_W be the relative price of wine in terms of bread.

   (i) Show that $p_W = P_W/P_B$.

   (ii) Suppose the absolute price of wine increases by x percent and the absolute price of bread increases by y percent. Use part (i) to show that the price of wine increases if x > y, the price of wine decreases if x < y, and the price of wine is unchanged if x = y.

(iii)   What conclusion can we draw from part (ii) about the relation between inflation and relative prices?

2. Suppose there are three people: an electrician, his teenage son, and their neighbor Mr. Crisp. There are two jobs to do: rewiring houses and panelling rooms. The amount of time each person needs to do each of these two tasks is summarized in the following table.

	Electrician	Son	Mr. Crisp
Rewiring	10 hours	21 hours	16 hours
Panelling	15 hours	18 hours	16 hours

(i)   Calculate the cost for each person to rewire a house.

(ii)   If only Mr. Crisp and the electrician specialize and trade, who will specialize in what activity?

(iii)   If only Mr. Crisp and the electrician's son specialize and trade, who will specialize in what activity?

(iv)   If all three specialize and trade, who will specialize in what activity? (Hint—There is not enough information to provide a definite answer for one of the three.)

3. Suppose there are two countries, call them A and B. Food and clothing are the only two commodities in the world and their production requires only labor. The amounts of labor required to produce one unit of these commodities in the two countries are shown in the table.

	Country A	Country B
One Unit of Food	12 hours	8 hours
One Unit of Clothing	6 hours	2 hours

(i) Calculate the costs of producing food in each of the two countries. When the two countries specialize and trade, which country should specialize in which commodity?

(ii) Suppose that Country A offers to give Country B one unit of food in exchange for every five units of clothing received. (In other words, Country A is offering to trade at a rate of 5 units of clothing per unit of food.) Show that Country B will turn down this offer.

(iii) Suppose that Country B offers to give Country A one unit of clothing for every unit of food received. (So now Country B is offering to trade at a rate of 1 unit of clothing per unit of food.) Explain why Country A will turn down this offer.

(iv) Find the rates of exchange that would be agreeable to both countries. (Hint—There are three possibilities you should consider: rates of exchange larger than Country B's cost of producing food, rates of exchange smaller than Country A's cost of producing food, and rates of exchange between their two costs.)

Solutions

1. (i) Let the currency used be "dollars." Since the absolute price of bread is P_B dollars per loaf, 1 dollar will purchase $1/P_B$ loaves. (For example, if bread is \$2 per loaf, \$1 would purchase 1/2 a loaf.) So each dollar spent on wine implies a sacrifice of $1/P_B$ loaves of bread. Since we sacrifice P_W dollars to purchase a bottle of wine, we are sacrificing $P_W \cdot (1/P_B)$ or P_W/P_B loaves of bread to make this purchase. So the relative price of wine in terms of bread (p_W) equals P_W/P_B loaves of bread per bottle of wine. (Note—If this argument is unclear to you, try substituting in specific numbers for the absolute prices P_B and P_W.)

   (ii) The new absolute price of wine is $(1 + x)P_W$ and the new absolute price of bread is

   $(1 + y)P_B$. So the new price of wine equals $\quad \dfrac{(1 + x)}{(1 + y)} \cdot \dfrac{P_W}{P_B}$

   If $x > y$, then $\dfrac{(1 + x)}{(1 + y)} > 1$, so the price of wine has increased. If $x < y$, then

   $\dfrac{(1 + x)}{(1 + y)} < 1$, so the price of wine has decreased. Finally if $x = y$, then

   $\dfrac{(1 + x)}{(1 + y)} = 1$ and so the price of wine is unchanged.

   (iii) Inflation can either increase, decrease, or not affect the prices of commodities.

2. (i) Simply find the amount of panelling each person sacrifices to rewire a house. Doing so shows that the costs of rewiring a house are 2/3 panelled room per rewired house for the electrician, 1 1/6 panelled rooms per rewired house for the son, and 1 panelled room per rewired house for Mr. Crisp.

   (ii) Notice from part (i) that the electrician has the lowest cost of rewiring a house. Also notice that Mr. Crisp has a lower cost of panelling a room than the electrician (1 rewired house per panelled room as opposed to 1 1/2 rewired house per panelled room for the electrician). So the electrician should specialize in rewiring houses and Mr. Crisp should specialize in panelling rooms when these two trade.

   (iii) From part (i) we know that Mr. Crisp has a lower cost of rewiring a house than the son. Also notice that the son has the lowest cost of panelling a room (6/7 rewired house per panelled room as opposed to 1 rewired house per panelled room for Mr. Crisp.) So Mr. Crisp should specialize in rewiring houses and the son should specialize in panelling rooms when these two trade.

(iv) The electrician should specialize in rewiring houses since he has the lowest cost of the three. The son should specialize in panelling rooms since his cost to perform this task is the lowest of the three. As shown in parts (ii) and (iii), Mr. Crisp could specialize in either activity. The actual result depends on the preferences of the three to have rewiring and panelling done, and on the rate of exchange established for trading rewiring for panelling.

3. (i) As always, to calculate cost we need to find the sacrificed alternatives. In Country A the cost of producing food is 2 units of clothing per unit of food, and in Country B this cost is 4 units of clothing per unit of food. Since Country A has the lowest cost of producing food, it should be the one to specialize in this activity. Country B should specialize in clothing production since its cost is 1/4 unit of food per unit of clothing as compared to 1/2 unit of food per unit of clothing for Country A.

(ii) If Country B purchases food from Country A under this deal, the cost will be 5 units of clothing per unit of food. But from part (i), Country B's cost of producing its own food is only 4 units of lothing per unit of food. Country B will choose the option with the lowest cost and turn down Country A's offer.

(iii) If Country A purchases clothing from Country B under this deal, the cost of clothing will be 1 unit of food per unit of clothing. But from part (i), we know that Country A can produce its own clothing at a cost of only 1/2 unit of food per unit of clothing. Country A will choose the option with the lowest cost and turn down the trade offered by Country B. (Alternatively, we could argue that Country A will not sell food at the price of 1 unit of clothing per unit of food because this is less than its cost to produce food.)

(iv) The rates of exchange agreeable to both are those in between their costs—any rate of exchange between 2 and 4 units of clothing per unit of food will benefit both countries. As shown in part (ii) a rate of exchange larger than Country B's cost of producing food will be turned down by Country B; this is because Country B could then produce its own food at a cost lower than that incurred by purchasing food from Country A. As shown in part (iii) Country A will turn down a rate of exchange smaller than its cost of producing food; in this case Country A could then produce its own clothing at a lower cost than it would incur from purchasing clothing from Country B. (Alternatively, we could say that Country A would refuse to sell its food at a rate of exchange below its cost.) If the rate of exchange is between their costs, then Country B can purchase food from Country A at a price lower than B's cost of producing its own food, and Country A can purchase clothing from Country B at a price lower than A's cost of producing its own clothing. So when the rate of exchange is between 2 and 4 units of clothing per unit of food, both countries will benefit from specialization in the area of their comparative advantage and trade to get the goods they wish to consume.

Chapter Three

The Behavior of Consumers

Chapter Summary

This chapter begins a two-chapter unit investigating the factors which determine demand. The first two sections of the chapter introduce the basic indifference curve/budget line model of consumer choice. The chapter ends with some applications to further develop your familiarity with this economic model.

Section 3.1. Tastes

There are two parts to the consumer's decision to purchase goods: his tastes and his budget. In this section we show how we can draw a picture of the consumer's tastes.

Consider a graph on which we can plot the amounts of two commodities: X (on the horizontal axis) and Y (on the vertical axis). Any point we plot on these axes represents a basket containing some given quantities of the commodities X and Y—the horizontal coordinate of the point represents the quantity of X in the basket, and the vertical coordinate represents the quantity of Y in the basket. An *indifference curve* shows the various combinations of X and Y that a consumer would find equally desirable. In other words, the consumer is "indifferent" between having the two baskets represented by any two points on the same indifference curve. By drawing several of these indifference curves, we can develop a picture of the consumer's tastes or preferences for the commodities X and Y.

We will assume that commodities X and Y are both *goods*—commodities of which the consumer prefers having more to less. This assumption implies that for any fixed basket (i.e., for any fixed point on our graph), the consumer will prefer all baskets to the northeast (since these contain more of both goods). Also the consumer will prefer the fixed basket to all baskets lying to the southwest (since they contain less of both goods).

There are four basic properties of indifference curves showing the consumer's preferences for two goods: the indifference curves fill the plane, never cross, are downward sloping, and are convex (i.e., begins relatively steep and gets flatter and flatter as we move left to right).

The first three of these properties are easy to see. We could start with any basket on the graph and find other baskets that the consumer likes equally well, so we can draw an indifference curve through any point we choose. As shown by Exhibit 3-3 of the textbook, crossing indifference curves would imply that a basket is equally preferred to other baskets to the northeast, which contradicts our assumption that both commodities are goods. The downward slope of an indifference curve is also due to the assumption that we are dealing with two goods. When we start at a specific basket, the indifference curve cannot head northeast because those baskets are strictly preferred to the starting point. Similarly, the indifference curve cannot head southwest because the basket is strictly preferred to those points. So to find equally preferred baskets, we must head northwest and southeast, resulting in a downward sloping indifference curve.

To see why indifference curves are convex, we need another definition. For any given basket of goods, the *marginal rate of substitution (MRS) between X and Y* is the amount of good Y the consumer can substitute for one unit of good X and still remain indifferent. Put another way, the MRS is the rate at which the consumer can substitute good Y for good X while remaining indifferent. The MRS is shown geometrically as the magnitude of the slope of the indifference curve at the given basket.

Now consider two points on the same indifference curve—suppose the first basket has a lot of good Y and only a little good X and the second basket has only a little good Y and a lot of good X. Given the relative scarcity of good X in the first basket, it would be natural for the consumer to place a relatively higher value on the last unit of X in the first basket than in the second basket. This tells us that the MRS for the first basket is larger than that for the second—it would take much more of good Y to compensate the consumer for the last unit of X in the first basket than in the second basket. So as we move from left to right along the indifference curve (i.e., as we move from the first basket to the second), we expect the MRS to get smaller and smaller. This tells us that the indifference curve is getting flatter and flatter as we move left to right, giving us the convex shape for the indifference curve.

Our model of consumer preferences can be generalized to the case of several goods. In this situation, we place the commodity of interest (call it good X) on the horizontal axis. For the vertical axis we group all other goods together and measure them in a single unit such as dollars. This use of the "all other goods" classification for the commodity on the vertical axis is called the *composite-good convention*. We also have a special name for the MRS in this case. The *marginal value* of good X is the marginal rate of substitution between good X and all other goods; usually we measure the marginal value of X in dollars per unit of good X.

Section 3.2. The Budget Line and the Consumer's Choice

The *budget line* is the set of all baskets that the consumer can afford, given his income and the prices he faces. A simple linear equation can be used to describe the consumer's budget line. Let P_X denote the price of good X, P_Y denote the price of good Y, and I represent the consumer's income. Also let x and y denote the quantities of goods X and Y contained in any given market basket. Notice that P_X, P_Y, and I are constants—they represent information faced by the consumer—while x and y are variables—they are chosen by the consumer. The set of all baskets that the consumer can afford given the prices and his income is represented by the equation $P_X \cdot x + P_Y \cdot y = I$; this equation simply says that the amount spent on good X ($P_X \cdot x$) plus the amount spent on good Y ($P_Y \cdot y$) equals the total amount spent by the consumer (his income I).

To get a picture of the consumer's budget, we simply graph the equation of the budget line, putting x on the horizontal axis and y on the vertical axis. This results in a downward sloping line with slope $-P_X/P_Y$, vertical intercept I/P_Y, and horizontal intercept I/P_X. Notice that the magnitude of the budget line's slope represents the relative price of good X in terms of good Y, and the horizontal and vertical intercepts represent the maximum amounts of goods X and Y respectively that the consumer can purchase and stay within his budget.

To model the consumer's economic behavior, we superimpose the diagrams representing the consumer's preferences and his budget. The resulting indifference curve/budget line diagram shows that **the consumer's *optimum*—the most preferred basket from the choices within the consumer's budget—is located where the budget line is tangent to one of the indifference curves.** Using the economic interpretations of the slopes of the budget line and indifference curves, an immediate consequence of this fact is that **the relative price of X in terms of Y equals the consumer's marginal rate of substitution between X and Y at the optimum.**

Be sure to notice the interplay between the relative price (the rate at which good X can be exchanged for good Y in the market) and the MRS (the rate at which the consumer is just willing to exchange good X for good Y). There are three possibilities.

The first possibility is shown by baskets above the optimum where the budget line is flatter than the indifference curve. In this case the relative price is smaller than the MRS. The consumer can make himself better off by sacrificing Y and purchasing X in the market. Since the price of good X (P_X/P_Y) is smaller than the value that the consumer places on the last unit of good X (the MRS), purchasing more X (and consequently less Y) is clearly a good deal for the consumer.

A second possibility occurs where the budget line is steeper than the indifference curve. For these baskets below the optimum, the relative price is larger than the MRS. Here the price of good X (P_X/P_Y) is larger than the amount the consumer is willing to pay (the MRS), so the last unit of X purchased by the consumer was a poor buy. So the consumer can benefit from purchasing less X in the market and accepting more Y.

The third possibility is that the relative price equals the MRS and the budget line is tangent to the indifference curve. Here the cost of good X to the consumer (P_X/P_Y) is just offset by the value he places on the last unit of X (the MRS), so the consumer was indifferent about the purchase of the last unit. In this situation no further trades in the market in either direction can benefit the consumer, and so this equality between the relative price and the MRS signals the optimum basket.

There is one exception to this rule that the optimum occurs where the relative price and the MRS are equal. The relative price may be larger than the MRS when it is optimum for the consumer to purchase only good X. The inequality $P_X/P_Y < MRS$ generally indicates that the consumer can benefit from purchasing more X and less Y, but here the consumer cannot take advantage of this situation because he cannot purchase less than zero units of Y. Similarly, if it is optimum for the consumer to purchase only good Y, the MRS may be smaller than the relative price. Although this inequality signals that the consumer can benefit from purchasing less X and more Y, this is not an option when the consumer is purchasing zero units of X. These exceptions are called *corner solutions*—optimums which occur at one of the axes and where there is no tangency between the budget line and an indifference curve.

Section 3.3.A. Price Indices

To measure inflation, we generally use a *price index*; we develop a price index by seeing how the cost of a fixed market basket of goods purchased by the "average" consumer changes as prices change. The most commonly used price index is the *consumer price index* (*CPI*). As shown by the accompanying diagram, there is unfortunately no "best" price index to use.

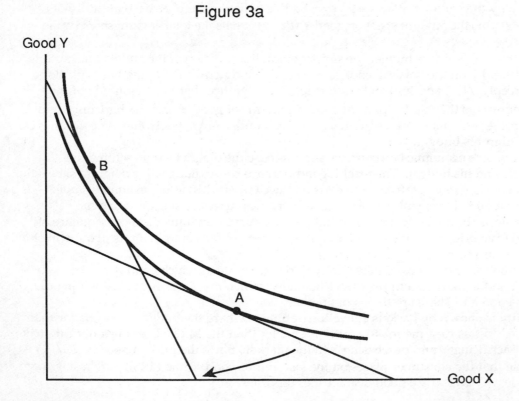

Figure 3a

In Figure 3a, the flatter budget line shows the consumer's budget under this year's prices with the optimum at point A. Next year, the price of X rises and the price of Y falls, resulting in a new steeper budget line and a new optimum at point B. The problem is: Which market basket, A or B, should we use to form the price index?

If we use basket A, we will report that there has been inflation. Your income could purchase basket A under the old prices, but under the new prices you can no longer purchase basket A since it is outside the new budget line. The price change has eaten away at your purchasing power, so we report inflation—even though the price change has made you better off! When we use the basket consumed in the earlier period to form the price index, we have calculated a *Laspeyres price index.* In general, Laspeyres price indices make price changes look worse for consumers than they really are. The CPI used by the U.S. Department of Labor is a Laspeyres price index.

If we instead use basket B to form a price index, we will report that there has been deflation. Under the old prices your income was insufficient to purchase this basket of goods since point B lies outside the old budget line. But after the prices change you can now afford basket B, so your purchasing power has increased which implies deflation. A *Paasche price index* is one where we use the basket purchased in the later period to form the price index, and it always makes price changes seem better for consumers than they really are.

Section 3.3.B. Differences in Tastes

Another question that the indifference curve/budget line model can be used to investigate is whether people's tastes change over time.

Figure 3b

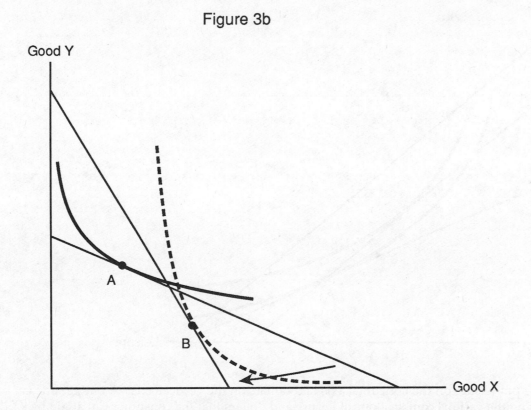

In Figure 3b, suppose that the flatter budget line represents the consumer's budget under this year's prices. Next year the price of X rises and the price of Y falls, resulting in a new steeper budget line as shown.

If this year's optimum is at point A and next year's optimum is at point B, we can conclude that the consumer's preferences have changed. Because indifference curves are convex, the indifference curve tangent at point A must remain flatter than the original budget line to the right of A and the indifference curve tangent at point B must remain steeper than the new budget line to the left of B. Simple geometry then leads us to the conclusion that the two indifference curves must cross. Since a family of indifference curves representing a consumer's preferences cannot contain crossing indifference curves, we must conclude that the two indifference curves shown must belong to different families representing different tastes. So if we ever observe a situation like this one, we can conclude that the consumer's tastes have changed.

Surprisingly the question as to whether or not consumers' tastes change over time is still an open one. In an extensive study done by the author of the textbook, no situation like one shown in Figure 3b was ever found.

Section 3.3.C. Head Taxes versus Income Taxes

Two basic types of taxes are income taxes and head taxes. Under an *income tax* the government takes a certain percentage of your wages, and under a *head tax* it takes a specific dollar amount of total income regardless of wages earned. As shown by the accompanying diagram, when your total tax bill is held constant you will prefer the head tax to the income tax.

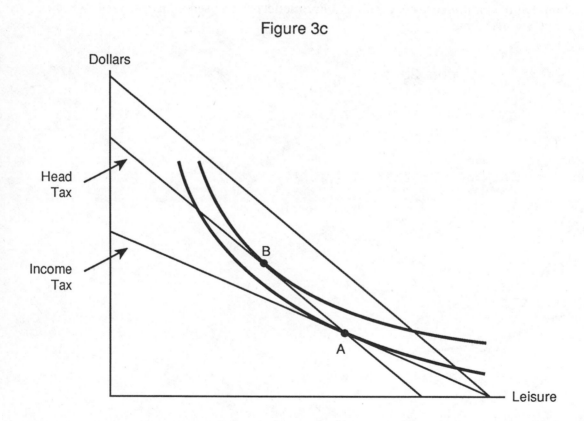

Figure 3c

In this model we put leisure on the horizontal axis and dollars on the vertical axis. A budget line is derived by considering the various combinations of leisure and dollars that the consumer can attain by selling his leisure time at the going wage rate. The magnitude of the slope of this budget line is the wage rate.

An income tax will lower the effective wage rate, and so will make the budget line flatter. The optimum is at point A, and the tax paid is the vertical distance between the old and new budget lines at the optimum.

34

A head tax does not affect the consumer's wage, and so this type of tax does not affect the slope of the budget line. The consumer gets to keep less of his income, and this is shown by the parallel shift inward of the budget line. Again the tax paid is the vertical distance between the old and new budget lines. (Since the lines are parallel, it is not necessary to compare the distance only at the optimum as with the income tax.) Since the budget line for the head tax goes through point A, the consumer pays government the same amount under both taxes.

Notice that the optimum for the head tax is at point B, on a higher indifference curve than point A. Since the head tax does not lower the marginal value of the consumer's leisure like the income tax does, we see that the consumer is better off under the head tax than under the income tax when both result in the same total tax bill.

Working Through the Graphs—Analysis of Income and Head Taxes

A basic result in the theory of taxation is that a tax which distorts relative prices—such as an income tax—makes consumers worse off than a lump sum tax payment of the same total amount—such as a head tax. Figures 3-1 and 3-2, when completed, illustrate this analysis.

Step 1. Figure 3-1 illustrates the situation facing a consumer who has 24 hours of leisure time per day and can receive a wage $10 per hour. Verify that the consumer's budget line is correctly drawn and that the consumer chooses to work 10 hours daily.

Step 2. Suppose the government imposes an income tax of 50% on this consumer. Draw in the consumer's new budget line and locate the new optimum, noticing that this tax lowers his effective wage to $5 per hour. If you've done this correctly, you should find that the consumer now enjoys 16 hours of leisure daily and works 8 hours per day.

Step 3. Use the graph to calculate the tax bill for the consumer under the income tax. To do this, first use the original budget line to find out how much money the consumer earns from his 8 hours of work before the tax. Then use the new budget line to find out how much money the consumer gets to keep from his 8 hours of work after he's paid the tax. The difference between these is the tax bill, which you should find to be $40 per day. Notice that the pre-tax optimum plays no role in determining the tax bill.

Step 4. Let's now suppose that the consumer pays the same $40 in taxes, but now he pays this amount in one lump sum that is not affected by his wages. We will illustrate this head tax in Figure 3-2, in which we've plotted the optimum under the income tax for reference. First draw the new budget line when the consumer must surrender $40 per day no matter how long he works, and then locate the new optimum. If you've done this correctly, you should find that there was a parallel shift in the budget line with the new optimum being to work 12 hours per day.

Notice that the optimum under the income tax lies on the budget line for the head tax. This is because the head tax budget line shows all the possible combinations of leisure and dollars that the consumer can choose from when he pays a tax of $40, and the optimum from the income tax is one such combination.

Step 5. Compare Figures 3-1 and 3-2. Notice that the consumer reached a higher indifference curve and worked more hours under the head tax than under an income tax that collected the same revenue for the government. This is because the income tax, unlike the head tax, distorted the wage received.

At the optimum under the income tax, the marginal value of the consumer's leisure time is below the (pre-tax) wage paid. Suppose the consumer is initially at this optimum, but now he can now pay the $40 as a head tax and still receive the original wage. Then the consumer could benefit from working more hours since the offered wage is greater than the marginal value of his time. So by leaving the wage unaffected, the head tax causes the consumer to provide more hours of work and be better off than under the income tax.

Figure 3-1 Analysis of an Income Tax

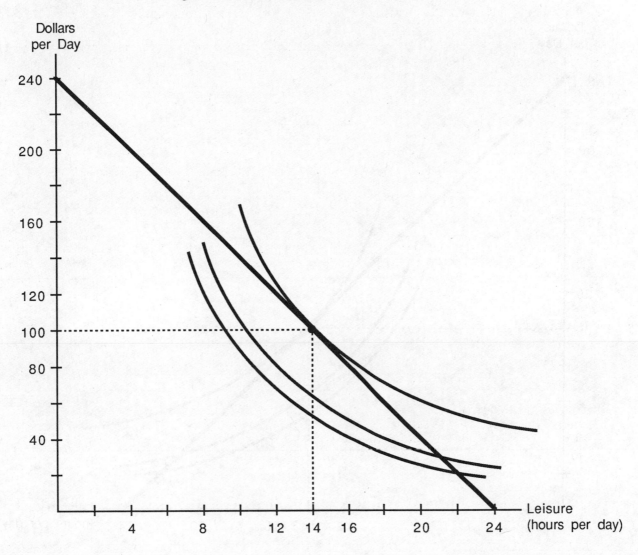

Figure 3-2 Analysis of a Head Tax

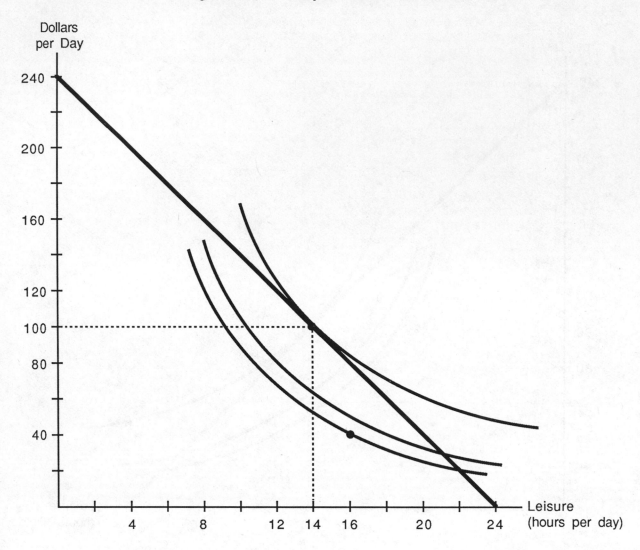

Multiple Choice Questions

1. Which of the following is the same for all points on an indifference curve?
   A. The level of satisfaction obtained from consumption.
   B. The prices faced by the consumer.
   C. The consumer's income.
   D. All of the above

2. Which of the following is *not* a property of the family of indifference curves representing a consumer's preferences between two goods?
   A. Every basket is on one and only one indifference curve.
   B. No two indifference curves can cross.
   C. The indifference curves are all downward sloping.
   D. The indifference curves are all concave.

3. What would upward sloping indifference curves represent?
   A. Both commodities are goods.
   B. One of the commodities is a "bad" instead of a good.
   C. Both commodities are "bads."
   D. Both A and C

4. Which of the following statements about the marginal rate of substitution between X and Y is *false?*
   A. The MRS gives the amount of good Y the consumer can substitute for the last unit of good X and remain indifferent.
   B. The MRS is measured in units of X per unit of Y.
   C. The MRS equals the magnitude of the slope of the indifference curve at the given basket.
   D. As we move from left to right along an indifference curve, the MRS is diminishing.

***For Questions 5-8, assume that good X is on the horizontal axis and good Y is on the vertical axis in the indifference curve/budget line diagram.

5. The slope of the budget line is given by
   A. $-P_X/P_Y$.
   B. $-P_Y/P_X$.
   C. I/P_X.
   D. I/P_Y.

6. Which of the following does *not* change when the price of good Y increases?
    A. The slope of the budget line.
    B. The vertical intercept of the budget line.
    C. The horizontal intercept of the budget line.
    D. All of the above indeed change when the price of good Y increases.

7. Which of the following represents the relative price of good X in terms of good Y?
    A. The intercepts of the budget line.
    B. The magnitude of the slope of the budget line.
    C. The magnitude of the slope of the indifference curve.
    D. Both B and C

8. Suppose the consumer is spending all his income and is purchasing positive amounts of goods X and Y. If the relative price of X in terms of Y exceeds the consumer's marginal rate of substitution, then
    A. the consumer will be better off if he purchases more of good X and less of good Y.
    B. the consumer will be better off if he purchases less of good X and more of good Y.
    C. the consumer will be better off if he purchases more of good X and more of good Y.
    D. the consumer cannot make himself better off with any change in his purchases.

***Question 9 refers to the accompanying indifference curve/budget line diagram.

Figure 3d

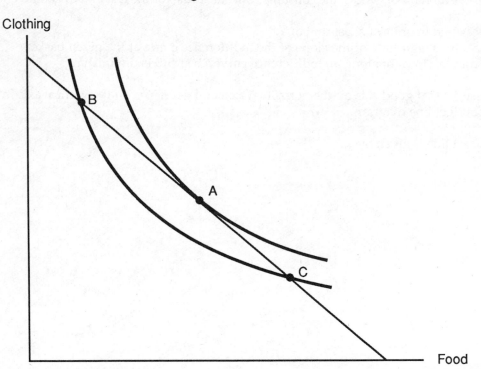

9. At what basket in Figure 3d is the relative price of food in terms of clothing smaller than the consumer's marginal rate of substitution between food and clothing?
    A. Basket A.
    B. Basket B.
    C. Basket C.
    D. Both basket B and basket C.

10. Consider a corner solution in which the consumer buys no food (on the horizontal axis) and only clothing (on the vertical axis). Then the relative price of food in terms of clothing _____ the consumer's marginal rate of substitution.
   A. is less than or equal to
   B. is equal to
   C. is greater than or equal to
   D. can be less than, greater than, or equal to

11. Suppose a consumer's indifference curves are downward sloping but concave (i.e., bowed away from the origin) instead of convex. Which of the following statements is *false*?
   A. The two commodities under consideration cannot both be goods.
   B. The MRS is increasing as we move from left to right along an indifference curve.
   C. The consumer's optimum does not occur where the MRS is equated to the relative price.
   D. The consumer's optimum is always at a corner solution.

12. Which of the following statements about price indices is *false*?
   A. Price indices are based on the changes in the cost of some fixed basket of goods.
   B. A Laspeyres price index is based on the basket consumed in the earlier period, while a Paasche price index is based on the basket consumed in the later period.
   C. A Laspeyres price index makes price changes seem better for consumers than they really are, while a Paasche price index makes price changes seem worse for consumers than they really are.
   D. The consumer price index (CPI) is a Laspeyres price index.

***Question 13 refers to the accompanying diagram where last year's budget is shown by the steeper budget line and this year's budget is shown by the flatter budget line.

Figure 3e

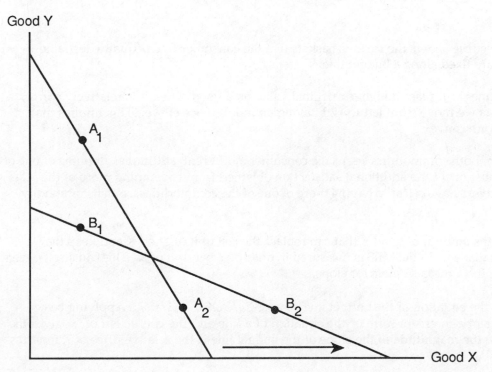

41

13. The consumer's tastes *must* have changed from last year to this year if last year's optimum is at _____ and this year's optimum is at _____.
    A. point A_1; point B_1
    B. point A_1; point B_2
    C. point A_2; point B_1
    D. point A_2; point B_2

14. Consider the indifference curve/budget line model showing the consumer's choice between leisure (on the horizontal axis) and dollars (on the vertical axis). What type of tax will lower the marginal value of the consumer's leisure time at the optimum?
    A. An income tax.
    B. A head tax.
    C. Both the income and head tax cause the marginal value of leisure time to be lowered.
    D. Neither the income tax nor the head tax cause the marginal value of leisure time to be lowered.

15. Which of the following statements about the comparison between income and head taxes is *false*?
    A. Only the income tax lowers the effective wage that the consumer is paid for sacrificing leisure.
    B. For both the income and head taxes, the tax bill paid is given by the vertical distance between the new and old budget lines at the post-tax optimum.
    C. When the tax bill is the same under an income and a head tax, the consumer will be better off under the head tax.
    D. When the tax bill is the same under an income and a head tax, the consumer will work more hours under the income tax.

Solutions

1. A. An indifference curve shows the various baskets that the consumer finds equally desirable. Prices and income are fixed along a budget line.

2. D. Since the consumer will place a higher marginal value on a good when it is relatively scarce, the MRS is falling as we move from left to right along an indifference curve. This implies that indifference curves are convex.

3. B. If having more of both commodities keeps the consumer indifferent, additional amounts of one of the commodities must offset the additional satisfaction obtained from consuming more of the other. So the consumer prefers having less to having more of one of the commodities, so that commodity must be a "bad."

4. B. The MRS gives the amount of good Y that can replace the last unit of good X and keep the consumer equally satisfied. So the MRS is measured in units of Y per unit of X. This can also be seen by looking at the units of measurement for slope.

5. A. We can rewrite the equation of the budget line as $y = (-P_X/P_Y) \cdot x + (I/P_Y)$. Applying basic algebra, this is the slope-intercept form of the equation of a line and the coefficient of x gives the slope. Furthermore the magnitude of the slope of the budget line is the relative price of X in terms of Y, which equals P_X/P_Y.

6. C. The horizontal intercept shows the maximum amount of good X that the consumer can purchase. This quantity is determined by the consumer's income and the price of good X but is not affected by the price of good Y.

7. B. The MRS gives the amount of good Y that the consumer can substitute for the last unit of good X and remain indifferent. It is only *equated* to the relative price of X in terms of Y (i.e., the magnitude of the slope of the budget line) *at the optimum*.

8. B. The consumer has insufficient income to buy more of both goods. Since the amount of good Y sacrificed to obtain the last unit of X (i.e., the relative price) outweighs the additional value that the consumer receives from the last unit of X (i.e., the MRS), the last unit of X was a poor buy. The consumer will benefit from purchasing less X and more Y.

9. B. $P_X/P_Y < $ MRS where the budget line is flatter than the indifference curve.

10. C. As shown by Exhibit 3-10 of the textbook, the budget line can be steeper than the indifference curve at this optimum.

11. A. When both commodities are goods, the indifference curves must be downward sloping but could be either convex or concave.

12. C. The Laspeyres price index overstates and the Paasche price index understates the effect of price increases on consumers.

13. C. An indifference curve tangent at A_2 and an indifference curve tangent at B_1 must cross, so they cannot belong to the same family of indifference curves.

14. A. The marginal value of leisure time (i.e., the MRS between leisure and dollars) is equated to the wage at the optimum. The income tax lowers the effective wage and hence lowers the marginal value of the consumer's leisure time at the optimum, while the head tax does not.

15. D. Since the effective wage is higher under the head tax than under the income tax, the consumer will benefit from selling more leisure time under the head tax (assuming the tax bill is the same under the two taxes).

Questions for Review

1. Why are indifference curves downward sloping? Why are indifference curves convex?

2. Provide a geometric interpretation and an economic interpretation for each of the following terms: (a) P_X/P_Y, (b) I/P_X, and (c) I/P_Y.

3. Compare and contrast the marginal rate of substitution between X and Y and the relative price of X in terms of Y. Why must these two be equated at the consumer's optimum?

4. Show that the consumer's optimum when we use the composite-good convention occurs where the marginal value of good X equals the price of good X.

5. Give a diagram similar to Exhibit 3-10 showing a corner equilibrium where the consumer purchases only good X (on the horizontal axis) and none of good Y (on the vertical axis). What relationship holds between the relative price of X in terms of Y and the marginal rate of substitution between X and Y at this optimum?

6. In what ways are a Laspeyres price index and a Paasche price index different? In what ways are they similar?

7. In what ways do the effects of an income tax and a head tax differ?

Solutions

1. Indifference curves are downward sloping when we assume both commodities are goods. In this case the consumer must substitute one good for another in order to remain indifferent, so the resulting indifference curve must slope downward. Indifference curves are convex when we assume that the MRS is decreasing as we move from left to right along an indifference curve. This is a reasonable assumption to make since the consumer is likely to place a high marginal value on the last unit of the good consumed when it is relatively scarce and a low marginal value on the last unit when the good is relatively abundant.

2. (a) P_X/P_Y is the magnitude of the slope of the budget line and represents the relative price of good X in terms of good Y.
   (b) I/P_X is the horizontal intercept of the budget line and represents the maximum amount of good X that the consumer can purchase with his given income.
   (c) I/P_Y is the vertical intercept of the budget line and represents the maximum amount of good Y that can be purchased with the consumer's income.

3. Both terms represent rates of exchange—the MRS shows the rate at which the consumer is *just willing* to trade X for Y, while the relative price shows the rate at which the consumer *can* trade X for Y *in the market*. Both terms are represented graphically as slopes—the MRS is the magnitude of the slope of the indifference curve at the basket in question, the relative price is the magnitude of the slope of the budget line.
   When these two rates of exchange are different, the consumer can benefit from trade. When the MRS is larger than the relative price, the last unit of X consumed has a higher value for the consumer than its cost in the market. Further purchases of good X would then benefit the consumer. When the MRS is smaller than the relative price, the last unit of X consumed cost the consumer more than what he thought it was worth. So the last unit of good X purchased was a poor buy, and the consumer would benefit from reducing his purchases of good X. Only when the two rates of exchange are equated is the consumer unable to benefit from further trade in the market.

4. The marginal value of good X is the marginal rate of substitution between good X and all other goods (with the latter measured in dollars). So the marginal value of good X is geometrically shown as the magnitude of the slope of the indifference curve when we use the composite-good convention.
   The magnitude of the slope of the budget line gives the relative price of good X in terms of the good on the vertical axis. Since we have "dollars" on the vertical axis when we use the composite-good convention, this slope is simply the price of good X.
   At the optimum, the budget line is tangent to an indifference curve, so the two slopes are equated. Hence the price of X must equal the marginal value of X at the optimum.
   An argument similar to the one used for the previous question can also be used to prove this result.

44

5.

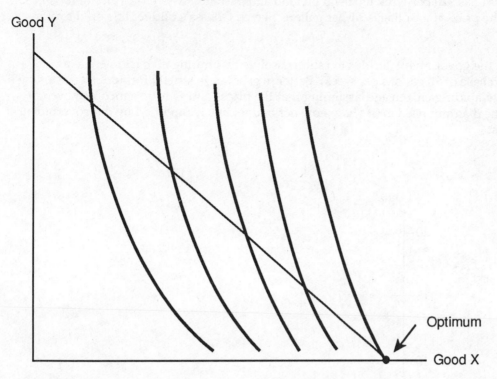

Figure 3f

Since the indifference curve is steeper than the budget line at this optimum, we have $MRS \geq P_X / P_Y$.

6. Both price indices attempt to measure changes in the cost of living based on the changes in the cost of the market basket consumed. A Laspeyres price index is based on the basket of goods consumed in the earlier period and makes the subsequent price changes seem worse than they really are for consumers when relative prices are altered. A Paasche price index is based on the basket of goods consumed in the later period and makes the previous price changes seem better than they really are for consumers when relative prices are altered. If the price changes do not affect relative prices, the Laspeyres and Paasche price indices will be identical.

7. Since an income tax requires the consumer to pay the government a certain percentage of his wages, it will lower the effective wage rate and make the budget line showing the tradeoff between leisure and dollars flatter. A head tax is paid in a single lump sum independent of the wages earned, so it does not affect the wage or the slope of the budget line. (A head tax does shift the budget line inward however.) When the total amount paid is the same under the two taxes, the consumer will provide more labor and will be better off under the head tax than under the income tax.

Problems for Analysis

1. (i) Suppose Odessa has $20 per week to spend on food and gasoline, where the price of food is $2 per unit and the price of gasoline is $1 per gallon. Sketch Odessa's budget line on the axes below.

   (ii) During a war, the government decides to ration gasoline by limiting all customers to a maximum purchase of 10 gallons per week. Barter in gasoline is strictly forbidden. Assuming Odessa is a law-abiding citizen and assuming that the prices and Odessa's income have not changed, on the diagram used in (i) show how her budget line is modified by the government's rationing plan.

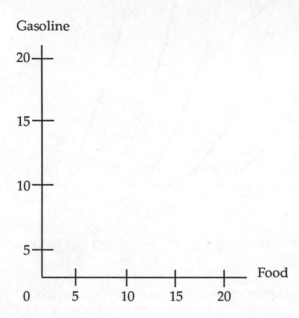

46

(iii)   Provide sketches on the axes below to show that there are two possible cases for Odessa's optimum under the rationing plan:

(a)   Odessa's consumption is unaffected by the rationing plan,
(b)   Odessa's level of satisfaction is lowered by the rationing plan.

For each case, indicate whether the marginal rate of substitution between food and clothing is ≥, ≤, or = the relative price of food in terms of clothing at the optimum under rationing.

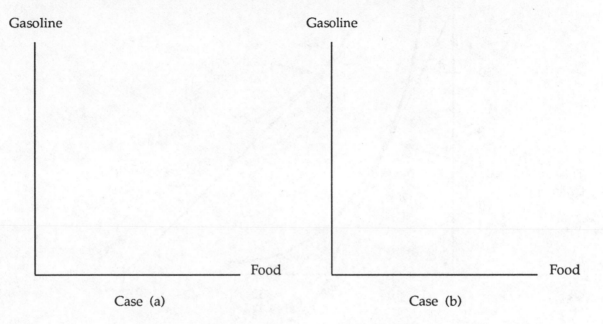

2.   Suppose there are only two goods: bread and wine. Last year the consumer had an income of $100 and his budget is shown by the budget line furthest away from the origin in the diagrams below. This year the consumer again has an income of $100, but higher prices have shifted his budget line closer to the origin. The consumer's optimum for both years is shown.

(i)   Calculate last year's and this year's prices.

(ii)   Show that the Laspeyres price index gives an inflation rate of 75%.

(iii) Suppose the consumer is given a 75% increase in this year's income to compensate him for the price increase. Complete Figure 3g to show the effect of this compensation. Did this scheme over- or undercompensate the consumer for the inflation?

Figure 3g

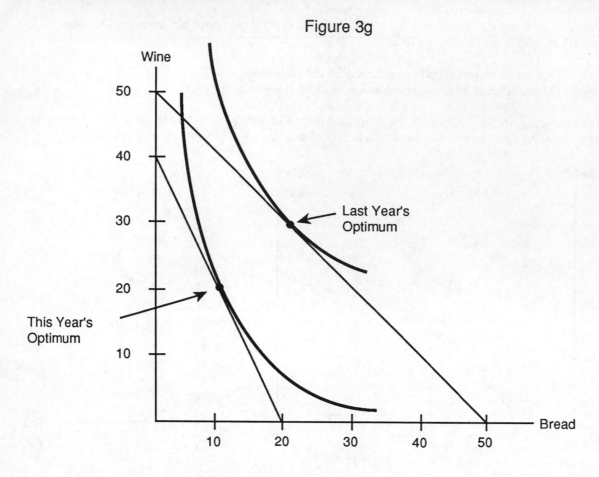

(iv) Prove the Paasche price index would show that last year's prices are 40% lower than this year's prices.

(v) Suppose that instead of the price increase, the consumer must this year accept a 40% reduction in income from last year. Complete Figure 3h to show the effect of this income reduction. Is the consumer better off under the price change or the income reduction?

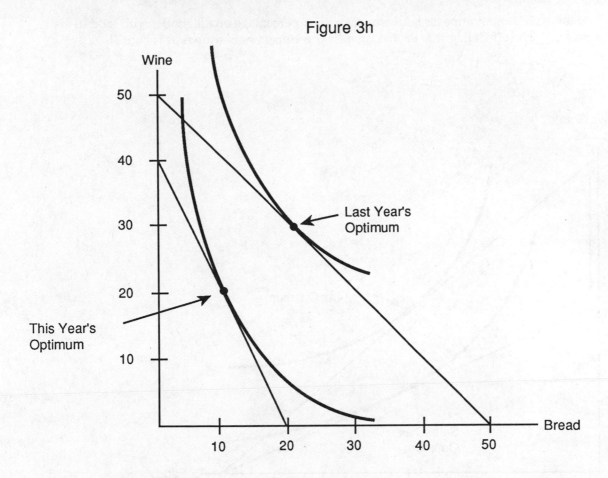

Figure 3h

(vi) What general facts about the interpretations of Laspeyres and Paasche price indices can be deduced from your answers to parts (iii) and (v)?

3. Suppose the government imposes a sales tax at a fixed percentage on all goods, with food items being exempt. The effect that this tax has on a typical consumer is shown in Figure 3i.

Figure 3i

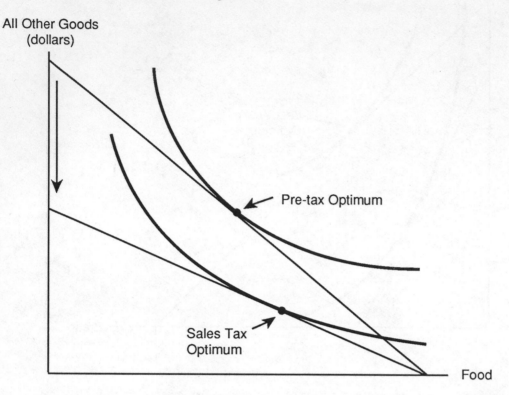

(i) Explain why the budget line would rotate as shown when this sales tax is imposed.

(ii) On Figure 3i, label the amount of revenue (measured in dollars) that the government collects from the sales tax.

(iii) Suppose the government considers replacing the sales tax with a head tax that raises the same amount of revenue. On Figure 3i, show the consumer's budget line and optimum under this head tax.

(iv) Suppose you are a government official interested in protecting the consumer's welfare. Which tax would you support and why?

(v) Suppose you are a government official interested in preserving high levels of agricultural production. Which tax would you support and why?

Solutions

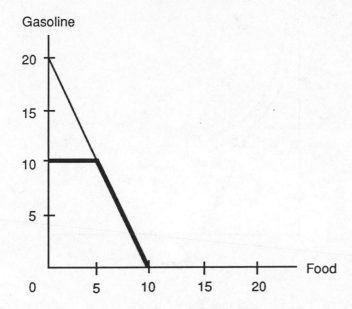

Figure 3j

1.

(i),(ii) Since prices have not changed under the rationing scheme, the slope of the budget line has not changed. The only effect of the rationing scheme is to forbid Odessa from consuming baskets with more than 10 gallons of gasoline. So the rationing plan has "chopped off" the budget line at this level, leaving the other possible purchases (those with less than 10 gallons of gasoline) still available.

(iii) Common sense tells us that Odessa will be unaffected by the gasoline rationing if she was already consuming less than the 10 gallon per week limit. On the other hand, she would be affected if she was originally consuming more than this amount. This is verified in Figure 3k.

Figure 3k

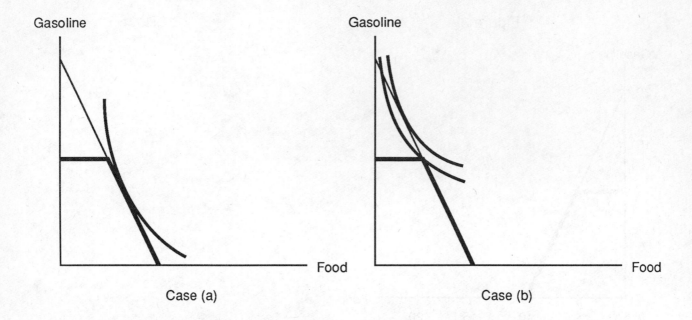

Case (a)   Case (b)

Since the indifference curve and budget line are tangent in case (a), the MRS is equal to the relative price. In case (b) the indifference curve is flatter than the budget line, so the MRS is less than the relative price. Notice the similarity between case (b) and the corner equilibrium.

2. (i) Using the intercepts of the budget line, last year $100 could purchase either 50 loaves of bread or 50 bottles of wine. So bread cost $2 per loaf and wine cost $2 per bottle. This year the same $100 can purchase either 20 loaves of bread or 40 bottles of wine, so bread now costs $5 per loaf and wine costs $4 per bottle.

(ii) We need to calculate the costs of last year's basket, which from the graph contains 20 loaves of bread and 30 bottles of wine. Using the price from past (i), last year this basket cost $100 and this year it costs $175—a 75% increase.

Figure 3l

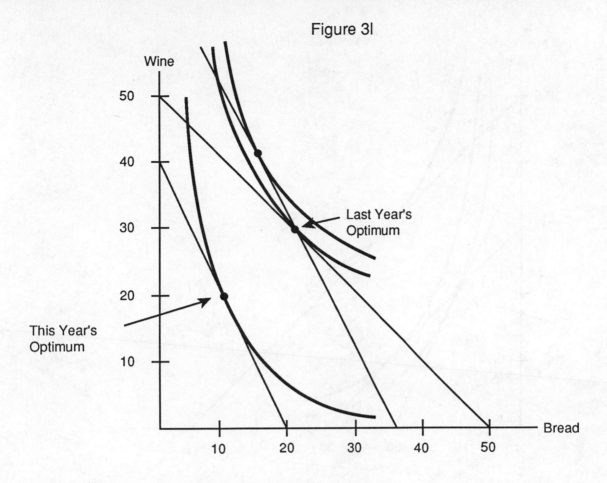

(iii) Since this increase in income allowed the consumer to reach a higher indifference curve, it overcompensates him for the price increase.

(iv) Using the graph in Figure 3l, the basket consumed this year contains 10 loaves of bread and 20 bottles of wine. Using the prices in part (i), this basket cost $60 last year and $100 this year. So last year's prices are 40% lower than this year's prices. (Be sure to start from this year's cost to calculate this. If we begin from last year's cost, we find that this year's prices are 66 2/3 % higher than last year's.)

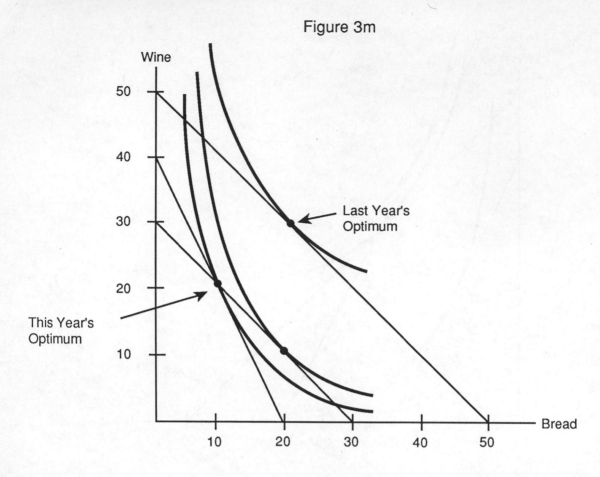

Figure 3m

(v) Comparing the indifference curves reached under the two situations, the income reduction does not hurt the consumer as much as the price increase.

(vi) Part (iii) shows that the Laspeyres price index makes price changes seem worse than they really are, since a 75% increase in income overcompensated the consumer for the "75%" price increase. Part (v) shows that the Paasche price index makes price changes seem better than they really are, since a 40% income reduction would not harm the consumer as much as the price increase (with "40%" lower prices last year) actually does.

3. (i) The consumer will pay no tax if he purchases only food, so the horizontal intercept of the budget line is unchanged. The maximum amount of other goods that can be purchased falls due to the tax, so the vertical intercept shifts downward. The tax has also lowered the price of food relative to other goods, so the budget line becomes flatter.

Figure 3n

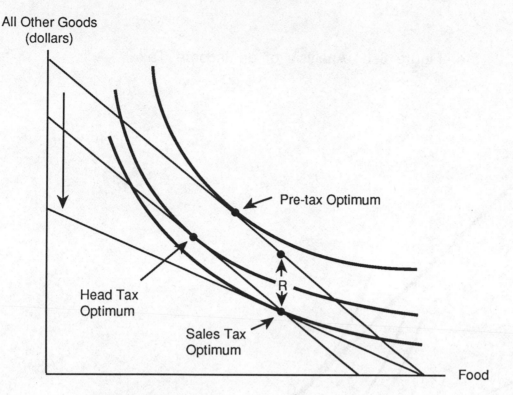

All Other Goods
(dollars)

Pre-tax Optimum

Head Tax
Optimum

Sales Tax
Optimum

R

Food

(ii),(iii)   To find the amount of revenue collected under the sales tax (labelled R in Figure 3n), use the vertical distance between the new and old budget lines *at the post-tax optimum.*

     The head tax will not affect the relative price of food, so it does not change the slope of the budget line. Since the head tax is assumed to collect the same total revenue as the sales tax, it must pass through the sales tax optimum. This causes the optimum for the head tax to lie on a higher indifference curve than the optimum for the sales tax.

(iv)   The head tax allows the consumer to reach a higher indifference curve. So you should support the head tax because it makes the consumer better off.

(v)   The head tax makes the consumer better off because it does not artificially increase the price of non-food items. Because of this, the consumer desires to purchase less food and more of other goods under the head tax than under the sales tax. If you are interested in promoting production of agricultural goods, you would choose the sales tax because consumers purchase more food under the sales tax than under the head tax.

55

Figure 3-1   Analysis of an Income Tax

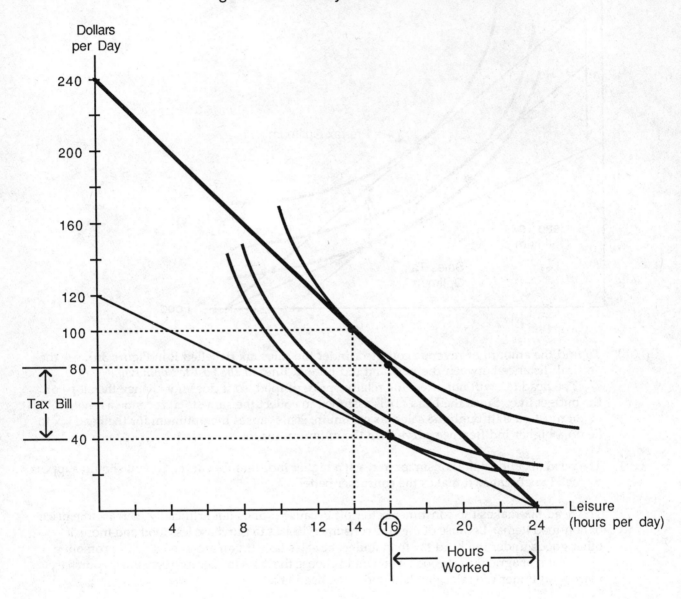

Figure 3-2 Analysis of a Head Tax

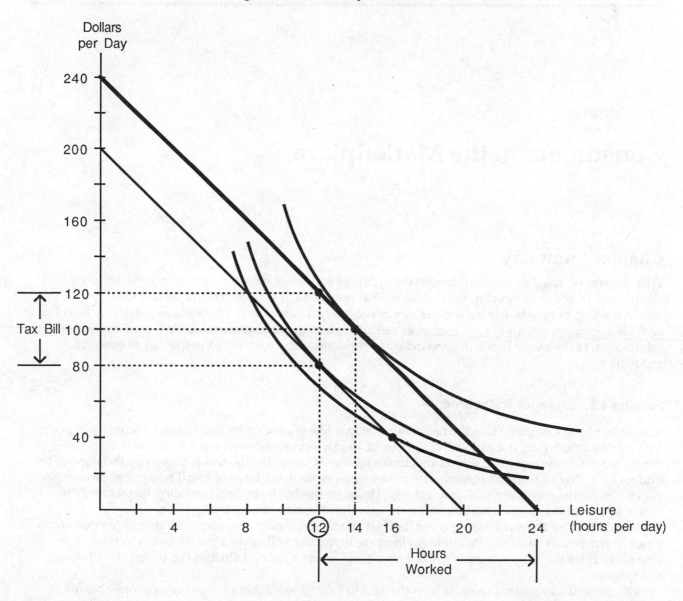

Chapter Four

Consumers in the Marketplace

Chapter Summary

This chapter establishes the foundations for applying consumer choice theory to a wide variety of situations. In order to develop these advanced applications, it is important to have a solid understanding of how to use the indifference curve/budget line model. We begin this study by learning how changes in prices and in the consumer's income affect quantity demanded. We then apply this information to develop a better understanding of the demand curves used so frequently in economic analysis.

Section 4.1. Changes in Income

Remember from Chapter 3 that the consumer's budget line is affected by two factors: income and prices. The *relative prices* (i.e., the ratio of the prices of the two goods) determine the rate at which the consumer can trade one good for another in the market. Geometrically, this is shown by the slope of the budget line. The consumer's income determines whether there is a large or small number of possible purchases for the consumer to choose among. This is shown by the budget line being further away or closer to the origin. Notice that income does *not* affect the slope of the budget line.

So when using the indifference curve/budget line model, there's only one basic rule to remember when the consumer's income changes. **An increase in income will cause a parallel shift in the budget line away from the origin; a decrease in income will cause a parallel shift in the budget line towards the origin.**

Of course it's important to know how changes in income will affect consumers' economic behavior. During recessions, consumers' incomes will be falling and during economic recoveries consumers' incomes will be rising. These will cause significant changes in the demand for goods. Two basic ways that economists summarize these effects of income on demand are *Engel curves* and the *income elasticity of demand.*

An Engel curve simply shows the quantity demanded of a good (on the vertical axis) at each and every income level (on the horizontal axis), assuming prices and preferences are held fixed. To get the information we need to derive an Engel curve, we look at the equilibrium points for a number of income levels in the indifference curve/budget line diagram. An upward-sloping Engel curve would show a good for which quantity demanded rises as the consumer's income rises; we classify these types of goods as *normal goods*. Engel curves can also be downward sloping. In this case, quantity demanded falls as income rises; goods that follow this pattern are classified as *inferior goods.*

The income elasticity of demand tells us the degree to which changes in income affect quantity demanded. To be more precise, the income elasticity gives the percentage change in quantity demanded per one percent change in income. The formula for calculating income elasticity is

$$(\Delta Q/Q)/(\Delta I/I) \text{ or } I \cdot \Delta Q / Q \cdot \Delta I.$$

So if the income elasticity is 2.0, a 1% increase in the consumer's income will cause a 2% increase in the consumer's quantity demanded. Similarly, if the income elasticity is -0.5, a 2% increase in the consumer's income will cause a 1% decrease in quantity demanded. Notice that a positive income elasticity indicates a normal good and a negative income elasticity indicates an inferior good.

Section 4.2. Changes in Price

Price is the other basic factor that affects the consumer's budget. The easiest way to see how price changes affect the budget line is to consider the consumer's possible purchases of only one good. Suppose the price of good X (on the horizontal axis) goes up while the price of good Y (on the vertical axis) and the consumer's income are unchanged. If the consumer chooses to purchase only good Y, the amount of good Y the consumer can buy is unaffected. So the vertical intercept of the budget line is also unaffected. But if the consumer chooses to purchase only good X, the consumer cannot afford as much due to the higher price. Hence the horizontal intercept of the budget line swings inward.

From this analysis we see that changes in the price of a good cause rotations in the budget line. **An increase in the price of good X will cause the budget line to become steeper and rotate inward; a decrease in the price of good X will cause the budget line to become flatter and rotate outward. The vertical intercept is unchanged in both instances.** Notice that the change in the budget line's slope tells us how the relative price which dictates the terms of trade in the market changes. When the budget line gets steeper (flatter), it shows that good X has become relatively more (less) expensive as compared to good Y.

Obviously the effect of price changes on quantity demanded is of overwhelming importance for economic analysis. You should already be familiar with the two tools economists use to describe these price effects: the *demand curve* and the *price elasticity of demand*.

A demand curve shows the quantity demanded of a good (on the horizontal axis) at each and every price (on the vertical axis), assuming income and preferences are fixed. Like the Engel curve, each point on the demand curve corresponds to an equilibrium point from our indifference curve/budget line diagram. This time, however, we use the various equilibrium points that occur when we rotate the budget line in order to get the quantity demanded at several different price levels. Notice that both demand curves and Engel curves are simply different ways of expressing the information contained in the indifference curve/budget line model of the consumer.

The price elasticity of demand measures how sensitive quantity demanded is to changes in price. (As always with elasticities, we compare the percentage changes of these two variables.) The formula for this elasticity is

$$(\Delta Q/Q)/(\Delta P/P) \text{ or } P \cdot \Delta Q / Q \cdot \Delta P.$$

Notice that the format of the formula is the same as for the income elasticity of demand. The only thing that has changed is the variable we wish to relate. For income elasticity of demand we use income and quantity demanded; for price elasticity of demand we use price and quantity demanded.

Also notice that since price and quantity demanded move in opposite directions (according to the law of demand), this elasticity must be a negative number. If you are not comfortable with using the elasticity of demand, you should now go back to Chapter 1 and review this topic.

Section 4.3. Income and Substitution Effects

When the price of a good changes, quantity demanded changes for two distinct reasons. These are called the *substitution effect* and the *income effect* of the price change.

Suppose the price of the good rises. Since that good has become relatively more expensive, you try to get the same utility from your purchases by *substituting* away from this good into other goods that are now relatively less expensive. This is called the substitution effect.

Unfortunately, you cannot keep the same level of utility when the price of the good rises. This is because your purchasing power has been eroded; you can't buy the same amounts of goods as you used to be able to. (We say that your *real income* has been lowered.) In effect, you have been made poorer by the higher price, so you must readjust your purchases to rebalance your budget. This change in quantity demanded to account for the new lower purchasing power of your income is called the income effect.

Income and substitution effects frequently arise in microeconomic analysis. If the two affect quantity in the same way, we can make unambiguous predictions. However, often the substitution and income effects affect quantity in different ways (e.g., one is putting downward pressure and the other is putting upward pressure on quantity demanded). Generally when we get an ambiguous result in microeconomic theory, it is because the income and substitution effects are in opposite directions.

This problem even affects something as basic as the law of demand! When price increases for a normal good, both substitution and income effects put downward pressure on quantity demanded, so there is no problem. But when the price of an inferior good rises, the substitution effect puts downward pressure on quantity demanded and the income effect puts upward pressure on quantity demanded. The law of demand will hold in this case only if the substitution effect is larger than the income effect.

One tool based on substitution and income effects that economists frequently use is the *compensated demand curve*. The ordinary demand curve shows how quantity demanded changes when price changes; it includes both the substitution and income effects. A compensated demand curve is a demand curve purged of its income effects. In other words, the compensated demand curve shows how the quantity demanded changes with respect to price when only substitution effects are considered. Since the substitution effect always supports the law of demand, compensated demand curves must be downward sloping. They are often used to represent the "average consumer" when we study economy-wide phenomena (when the income effects of consumers are expected to average out to zero).

Working Through the Graphs—Substitution and Income Effects

To better understand substitution and income effects, complete the graphs in Figures 4-1 and 4-2 by following the steps below. Your finished products should resemble Exhibits 4-8 and 4-10 in the textbook.

Figure 4-1.

Step 1. Initially the consumer has an income of $24, the price of good X is $2/unit, and the price of good Y is $3/unit. Verify that the budget line for this consumer has been drawn correctly in Figure 4-1. Also verify that the consumer's equilibrium is at (6 units of X, 4 units of Y), which has been labelled "A."

Step 2. Now suppose that the price of good X rises to $6/unit. Draw the consumer's new budget line, and label the new equilibrium "B." If you have done this correctly, you will find the new equilibrium to be at about (1 unit of X, 6 units of Y). We see that when the price of X rises from $2/unit to $6/unit, quantity demanded falls from 6 units to 1 unit. In other words, these two equilibrium points have given us two points on the demand curve for good X, assuming income is fixed at $24 and the price of good Y is fixed at $3/unit.

Step 3. Let's now decompose the effect of the price increase into two separate parts: the substitution effect and the income effect. To do this, you take the *new* budget line (the one you drew in Step 2) and slide it parallel until it's tangent to the *old* indifference curve (the one with the initial equilibrium A). Do this in Figure 4-1. You should find a tangency at about (2 units of X, 8 units of Y); label this point "C."

Figure 4-1 Substitution and Income Effects for a Normal Good

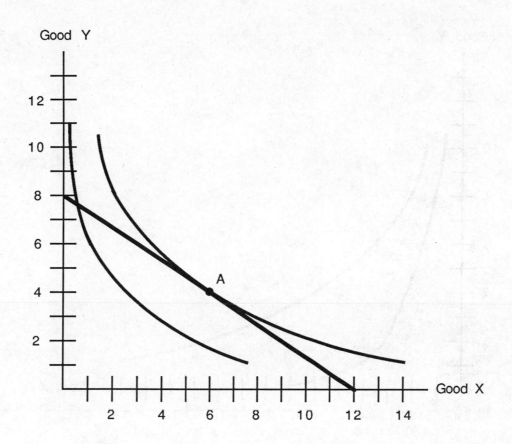

Figure 4-2   Substitution and Income Effects for an Inferior Good

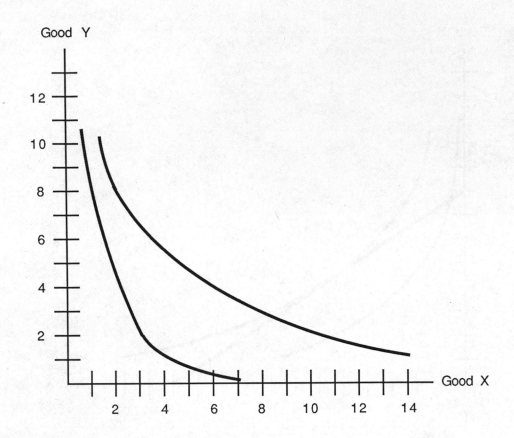

When the price of good X increased causing the equilibrium to move from A to B, the consumer received a lower level of utility. By shifting the new budget line parallel until we're back to the original indifference curve, we've given the consumer enough extra income to *compensate* for the higher price. So the budget line we've drawn in this step is called the *compensated budget line*.

Remember that whether you are doing the case of a price increase or a price decrease, you always shift the *new* budget line parallel until it's tangent to the *old* indifference curve to get the compensated budget line. In other words, the compensated budget line is always tangent to the indifference curve with the initial equilibrium and parallel to the budget line corresponding to the final equilibrium. So for a decrease in the price of good X, the compensated budget line would be below, not above, the final budget line.

Step 4. We use the compensated budget line and point C to separate the effect of a price change into substitution and income effects. We break up the change from the initial equilibrium A to the final equilibrium B by pretending we first move from A to C and then move from C to B.

In our exercise, good X has become more expensive relative to good Y. We say that the *relative price* of X has risen, and this is shown by the budget line getting steeper. To adjust to the higher relative price of X, the consumer tries to keep the same level of utility by substituting good Y for good X. This is shown by the movement from A to C and is called the *substitution effect*. In the diagram, you should verify that substitution effect caused the quantity demanded of X to fall from 6 to 2 units when the relative price of X increased.

The increase in the price of good X also eroded the consumer's purchasing power; he doesn't have enough income to keep the same level of utility. So it's not enough for the consumer to adjust to the change in relative prices (shown by the substitution effect from A to C); the consumer must also rebalance his budget. This is shown by the movement from C to B and is called the income effect. Verify that the income effect in Figure 4-1 lowered the quantity demanded of good X from 2 units to 1 unit.

It is the income effect that tells us that Figure 4-1 shows us a normal good. From C to B, we see income has gone down since the final budget line is closer to the origin than and parallel to the compensated budget line. Also from C to B, quantity demanded of good X has fallen. Since income and quantity demanded are moving in the same direction, good X is classified as a normal good.

Figure 4-2.

Step 1. Draw the consumer's initial budget line when income is $24, the price of good X is $2/unit, and the price of Y is $3/unit. Label this initial equilibrium "A." If you've done this correctly, point A should be at about (6 units of X, 4 units of Y).

Step 2. Find the new equilibrium when the price of X rises to $6/unit and label it "B." If you've done this correctly, point B should be at about (3 units of X, 2 units of Y).

Step 3. Find the compensated budget line and label the tangency point "C." If you've done this correctly, point C should be at about (2 units of X, 8 units of Y).

Step 4. Verify that the substitution effect lowered quantity demanded of X from 6 to 2 units when the relative price of X increased. (Notice that in both diagrams, the substitution effect supported the law of demand.) Verify that the income effect increased quantity demanded of X from 2 to 3 units when the consumer's real income fell. Verify that from C to B, income and quantity demanded are moving in opposite directions, indicating an inferior good. (Notice that the income effect supported the law of demand for a normal good, but works against the law of demand for an inferior good.)

Multiple Choice Questions

1. If the consumer's income and all prices simultaneously double, then
   A. the budget line will shift parallel away from the origin.
   B. the budget line will shift parallel towards the origin.
   C. the budget line will shift unpredictably.
   D. the budget line will be unchanged.

2. Which of the following is/are held constant when we construct an Engel curve?
   A. The consumer's preferences.
   B. The prices faced by the consumer.
   C. The consumer's income.
   D. All of the above
   E. Choices A and B only

***Question 3 refers to Figure 4a, which shows the Engel curve for good X.

Figure 4a

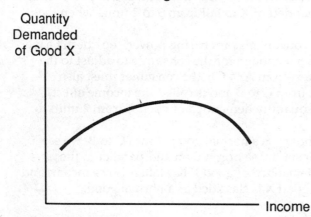

3. From the shape of the Engel curve, we may conclude that good X
   A. is a normal good.
   B. is an inferior good.
   C. is normal for low income levels and inferior for high income levels.
   D. is inferior for low income levels and normal for high income levels.

4. Two points on the Engel curve for good X are ($100, 20 units of X) and ($110, 21 units of X). The income elasticity of demand between the income levels $100 and $110 is calculated to be
   A. 10.
   B. 1/10.
   C. 2.
   D. 1/2.

5. The income elasticity of demand for a good is negative. We may conclude that
   A. the good is normal.
   B. the good is inferior.
   C. demand for this good obeys the law of demand.
   D. the law of demand is violated for this good.

6. Consider a budget line where good X is on the horizontal axis and good Y is on the vertical axis. If the price of good Y falls, then the horizontal intercept of the budget line will _____ and the vertical intercept of the budget line will _____.
   A. shift left; remain unchanged
   B. shift right; remain unchanged
   C. remain unchanged; shift up
   D. remain unchanged; shift down

7. Which of the following is *not* held constant when we use the indifference curve/budget line diagram to derive the demand curve for good X?
   A. The price of good X.
   B. The price of good Y.
   C. The consumer's income.
   D. The consumer's preferences.

8. When the price of a good is $5/unit, a consumer's quantity demanded is 20 units weekly. If the price rises to $6/unit, the consumer decreases her quantity demanded to 19 units weekly. For the price range $5/unit to $6/unit, what is the price elasticity of the consumer's demand?
   A. -1.
   B. -4.
   C. -1/4.
   D. $14.00.

9. The price elasticity of demand for automobiles is -2. If the price of automobiles falls from $10,000/auto to $9,500/auto, we can expect the quantity demanded of automobiles to increase by
   A. 2%.
   B. 5%.
   C. 10%.
   D. 1,000 automobiles.

10. Suppose consumers demand 300 million packs of cigarettes weekly at current prices. The price elasticity of demand for cigarettes is estimated to be -0.5. A 4% price increase would reduce the quantity demanded of cigarettes to
    A. 299.5 million packs weekly.
    B. 298 million packs weekly.
    C. 294 million packs weekly.
    D. 288 million packs weekly.

11. The substitution effect
    A. always supports the law of demand.
    B. supports the law of demand only for normal goods.
    C. supports the law of demand only for inferior goods.
    D. supports the law of demand only for Giffen goods.

12. If the demand for an inferior good is downward sloping,
    A. the substitution and income effects move in the same direction.
    B. the substitution and income effects move in opposite directions with the substitution effect being larger.
    C. the substitution and income effects move in opposite directions with the income effect being larger.
    D. Either B or C is possible

13. Suppose the substitution and income effects both put downward pressure on quantity demanded when there is a price increase. Which of the following statements is *false?*
    A. The good must be normal.
    B. The law of demand must hold for this good.
    C. The income elasticity of demand must be positive for this good.
    D. Demand for this good must be inelastic.

14. A compensated demand curve
    A. is derived assuming the consumer is income-compensated for price changes.
    B. shows the substitution effects of price changes, but does not include the income effects caused by price changes.
    C. always obeys the law of demand.
    D. All of the above

15. Consider the ordinary and compensated demands for a normal good. If the price of the good falls,
    A. the increase in quantity demanded will be larger for the ordinary demandthan for the compensated demand.
    B. the increase in quantity demanded will be larger for the compensated demand than for the ordinary demand.
    C. the increase in quantity demanded will be the same for the ordinary and compensated demands.
    D. Any of the above are possible

Solutions

1. D. The relative prices have not changed, so the slope of the budget line is unchanged. The maximum amounts of the goods the consumer can buy are also unchanged, so the budget line does not shift towards or away from the origin.

2. E. When we derive an Engel curve, we see how the equilibrium changes as income changes, leaving the indifference curves and the slope of the budget line unchanged.

3. C. The Engel curve shown is upward sloping for low income levels indicating a normal good and is downward sloping for high income levels indicating an inferior good.

4. D. Income increased by 10%, causing a 5% increase in quantity demanded. So the income elasticity is 5%/10% = 1/2.

5. B. A negative income elasticity indicates that income and quantity demanded move in opposite directions. Goods of this type are classified as inferior.

6. C. Since the price of X is unchanged, the maximum amount of X that can be purchased with the consumer's income is also unchanged. Since the price of Y has fallen, the maximum amount of Y that can be purchased has increased.

7. A. The demand curve for good X is derived by seeing how the consumer's equilibrium changes as the price of good X changes.

8. C. Price has increased by 20%, causing a 5% decline in quantity demanded. So the price elasticity of demand is -5%/20% = -1/4.

9. C. A price elasticity of -2 says that a 1% increase in price will cause a 2% decrease in quantity demanded. Since the price fell by 5%, quantity demanded rises by -2 X -5% = 10%.

10. C. Quantity demanded will change by -0.5 X 4% = -2%. Two percent of 300 million packs is 6 million packs, so the new quantity demanded is 294 million packs.

11. A. When the price of X rises making the budget line steeper, the tangency between the indifference curve and the compensated budget line will always be at a smaller quantity of X since indifference curves are downward sloping and convex.

12. B. For inferior goods, the substitution effect supports the law of demand and the income effect works against the law of demand. Since the law of demand holds in this case, the substitution effect must have been the larger of the two.

13. D. Since the substitution effect and income effect move in the same direction, the good is normal, which implies statements B and C. Whether the good has elastic or inelastic demand will depend on the size of the price change (in percentage terms) relative to the size of the change in quantity demanded (in percentage terms).

14. D. A compensated demand curve results from removing the income effects from the ordinary demand curve. So a compensated demand curve includes only substitution effects (obtained by income-compensating the consumer) which always support the law of demand.

15. A. For a normal good, when the price falls, both the substitution and income effects put upward pressure on quantity demanded. Since the ordinary demand curve includes both of these effects, but the compensated demand curve reflects only substitution effects, we will see a larger quantity response from the ordinary demand curve.

Questions for Review

1. Under what circumstances will the slope of the budget line become steeper? Under what circumstances will the slope of the budget line become flatter? Under what circumstances will there be a parallel shift in the budget line?

2. How are Engel curves and (ordinary) demand curves similar? How are they different?

3. What would an income elasticity of demand of -0.75 indicate? What would a price elasticity of demand of -0.75 indicate?

4. Give three different ways that a good can be recognized as being normal. Give three different ways that a good can be recognized as inferior.

5. Explain what the substitution and income effects of a price change represent.

6. Why does the substitution effect always support the law of demand? Why does the income effect sometimes support the law of demand and other times work against the law of demand?

7. What is a compensated demand curve? Why do compensated demand curves always obey the law of demand?

Solutions

1. The budget line becomes steeper when the relative price of good X rises; this happens when the price of X rises or the price of Y falls. The budget line becomes flatter when the relative price of good X falls; this happens when the price of X falls or the price of Y rises. Parallel shifts in the budget line are caused by changes in the consumer's income.

2. Engel curves and demand curves both summarize information about consumer equilibria in the indifference curve/budget line model. Engel curves show how the consumer's equilibrium purchases change as *income* changes. Demand curves show how the consumer's equilibrium purchases change as *price* changes.

3. An income elasticity of -0.75 indicates that there will be a 0.75% fall in quantity demanded for every 1% increase in income (so the good would be classified as inferior). A price elasticity of -0.75 indicates that there will be a 0.75% fall in quantity demanded for every 1% increase in price.

4. Normal goods have upward sloping Engel curves, positive income elasticities, and income effects that support the law of demand. Inferior goods have downward sloping Engel curves, negative income elasticities, and income effects that work against the law of demand.

5. A price change affects both relative prices and real income. The substitution effect shows how quantity demanded changes when relative prices change, assuming the consumer has a fixed real income (i.e., a fixed utility level). The income effect shows how quantity demanded changes when real income changes, assuming fixed relative prices.

6. For the substitution effect, the convexity of indifference curves implies that quantity demanded will fall when the budget line is made steeper by a higher relative price. When a higher price causes a lower real income, the income effect may move in either direction. If the good is a normal good, quantity demanded will fall further due to the fall in real income, supporting the substitution effect and the law of demand. If the good is an inferior good, quantity demanded will rise due to the fall in real income, working against the substitution effect and the law of demand.

7. A compensated demand curve is a demand curve showing only substitution effects; any income effects have been removed. The only time ordinary demand curves violate the law of demand is when income effects are sufficiently large in opposition to the substitution effect. Since compensated demand curves have no income effects, this possibility cannot occur.

Problems for Analysis

1. Suppose a consumer's Engel curve for coffee is horizontal.

   (i) What is the income elasticity of demand for coffee for this consumer?

(ii) Give an indifference curve/budget line diagram with coffee on the horizontal axis and good Y (representing all other goods the consumer purchases) on the vertical axis showing how the consumer's equilibrium changes when income changes.

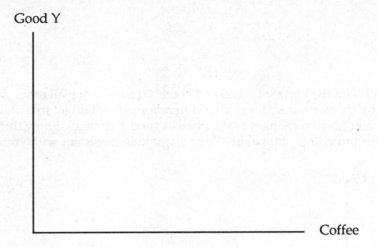

Good Y

Coffee

(iii) Give an indifference curve/budget line diagram showing the substitution and income effects when the price of coffee falls. Be sure to place points B and C so your diagram is consistent with your answers to parts (i) and (ii).

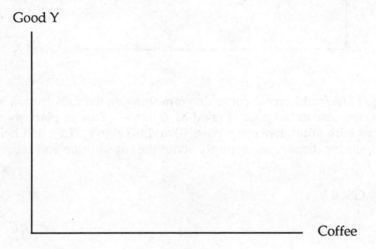

Good Y

Coffee

(iv) Will the consumer's demand for coffee be downward sloping? How will the consumer's ordinary demand curve for coffee compare with the compensated demand curve? Explain.

2. Suppose a consumer's demand for good X is perfectly inelastic.

   (i) How will the consumer's quantity demanded for good X change if its price increases by 5%? By 10%? Give an example of a commodity that you might expect to have perfectly inelastic demand.

   (ii) Putting good X on the horizontal axis and good Y (representing all other goods the consumer purchases) on the vertical axis, use an indifference curve/budget line diagram to show how the consumer's equilibrium changes as the price of good X changes. Show three price levels and three equilibrium points. Make sure your diagram is consistent with your answer to part (i).

   (iii) Give a budget line/indifference curve diagram showing the substitution and income effects caused by a decrease in the price of good X. (Hint—Be sure to place the equilibria so that they are consistent with your answers to parts (i) and (ii) above. This will help you figure out what a perfectly inelastic demand must imply about the substitution and income effects.)

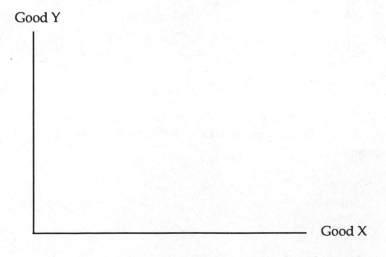

(iv) Use your answer to part (iii) to determine if good X is normal or inferior. Explain your answer.

3. (i) In Figure 4b, label the substitution and income effects that would occur when the price falls from P_0 to P_1. Also indicate whether the diagram shows a normal or inferior good.

Figure 4b

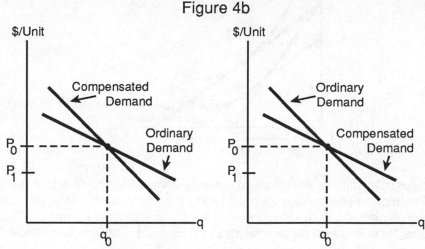

(ii) For a normal good, will the compensated demand curve be more or less elastic than the ordinary demand curve? For an inferior good, will the compensated demand curve be more or less elastic than the ordinary demand curve? Explain.

Solutions

1. (i) Since the Engel curve is horizontal, there will be a zero change in quantity demanded for a given change in income. Letting $\Delta Q = 0$ in the income elasticity formula $(\Delta Q/Q)/(\Delta I/I)$, we find the income elasticity of coffee for this consumer must equal zero.

(ii)

Figure 4c

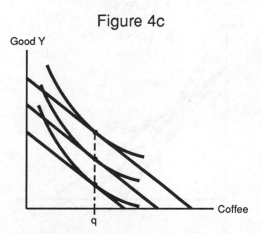

As income changes, the quantity demanded of coffee remains constant. So the equilibrium points must be lined up vertically when there are parallel shifts in the budget line as shown in Figure 4c.

(iii)

Figure 4d

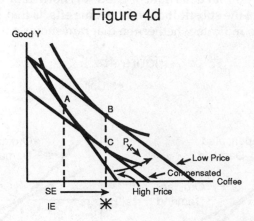

Since changes in income do not affect the quantity demanded of coffee, points B and C in our substitution/income effects diagram must be at the same quantity. In other words, the income effect is zero for a good with zero income elasticity as shown in Figure 4d. Notice that this is the case directly in between the normal and inferior good cases we diagrammed in Figures 4-1 and 4-2.

(iv) Yes, the law of demand will hold for coffee. The substitution effect, as always, supports the law of demand. In this case, the income effect is zero; it neither supports nor works against the law of demand. Combining the two effects, we see the law of demand will hold. The compensated and ordinary demand curves are identical in this case, since the substitution effect is the only effect that changes quantity demanded in this case.

2. (i) When demand is perfectly inelastic (i.e., vertical), quantity demanded remains unchanged when price changes. Commodities that have no substitutes and that the consumer must use in fixed quantities, such as heroin or a life-saving drug like insulin, are the most likely to have perfectly inelastic demand.

(ii)

Figure 4e

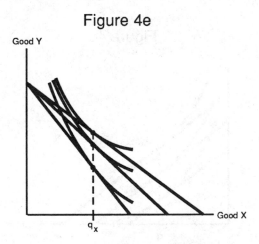

Since quantity demanded does not change as price changes, the equilibrium points must line up vertically when we rotate the budget line as shown in Figure 4e. Notice that this is the case in between the inferior good (where the equilibrium moves to the right as price falls) and the Giffen good (where the equilibrium moves to the left as price falls).

(iii)

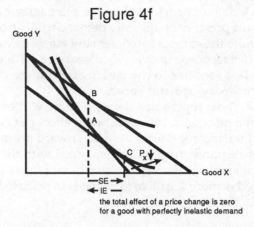

Figure 4f

the total effect of a price change is zero
for a good with perfectly inelastic demand

Again notice that the case of perfectly inelastic demand is in between the inferior good and Giffen good cases. With an inferior good where the Law of Demand holds, the substitution effect outweighs the income effect. With a Giffen good, the income effect outweighs the substitution effect. For this case of perfectly inelastic demand, the substitution and income effects exactly offset each other as shown in Figure 4f.

(iv) To determine if a good is normal or inferior, we must look at the income effect. In part (iii) from B to C, we see that an increase in income causes quantity demanded to decrease. Alternatively, note that the income effect is moving in the opposite direction of the substitution effect. This tells us that a good with perfectly inelastic demand must be inferior.

3. (i)

Figure 4g

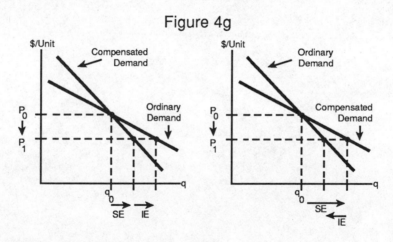

The compensated demand curve shows only substitution effects; the ordinary demand curve shows the combined effect of substitution and income effects. The graph on the left in Figure 4g shows a normal good since the substitution and income effects are moving in the same direction. The graph on the right of Figure 4g shows an inferior good since the substitution and income effects are moving in opposite directions.

(ii) As shown by the graph on the left in Figure 4g, the compensated demand curve will be less elastic than the ordinary demand curve. When the price falls, both the substitution and income effects put upward pressure on quantity demanded. The ordinary demand curve includes both effects, while the compensated demand curve includes only the substitution effect. So we see a smaller response in quantity demanded with the compensated demand curve. Since quantity is less sensitive to changes in price for the compensated demand curve, it is less elastic than the ordinary demand curve.

For an inferior good, the compensated demand curve will be more elastic than the ordinary demand curve. When the price falls, the substitution effect puts an upward pressure on quantity demanded and the income effect puts a downward pressure on quantity demanded. So we will observe a larger response in quantity demanded with the compensated demand curve— this is because it does not include the income effect that offsets part of the substitution effect. Since quantity demanded is more sensitive to changes in price for the compensated demand curve, it is the more elastic.

Solutions to Working Through the Graphs

Figure 4-1 Substitution and Income Effects for a Normal Good

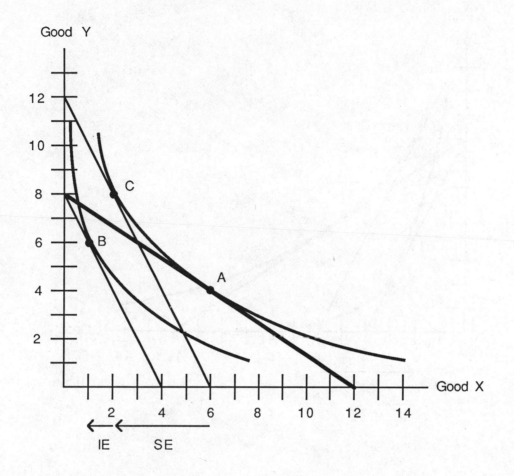

Figure 4-2 Substitution and Income Effects for an Inferior Good

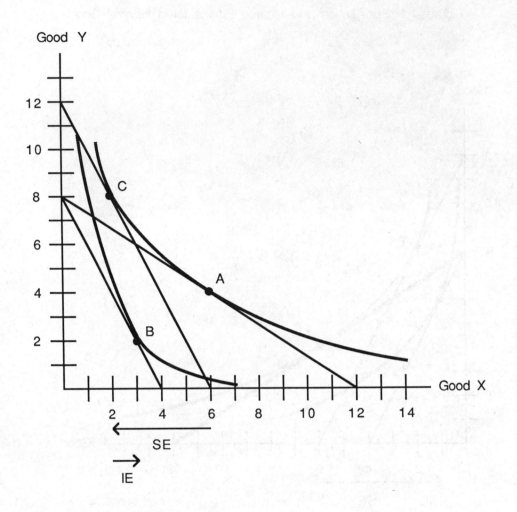

Chapter Five

The Behavior of Firms

Chapter Summary

This chapter begins a three-chapter unit studying the supply side of the goods market, starting with the economic decision making of an individual firm. To discover what factors do and do not influence the production and pricing decisions of a firm, we must learn how to compare a firm's benefits and costs.

Section 5.1. Weighing Benefits and Costs

As always in microeconomic analysis, a careful comparison of benefits and costs is required to determine the proper course of action. However, there are several ways that we could describe or calculate the benefits and costs. The method most commonly used by economists is to calculate the *marginal benefit* and *marginal cost* of an activity.

Marginal benefit is defined as the additional benefit received from the last unit of some economic activity. It tells us how fast the benefits we receive from the activity are increasing. Generally, we measure marginal benefit in dollars per unit of the activity. For example, consider the economic activity of drinking beer. If your marginal benefit from drinking beer is $3/beer, this says that you thought the last beer was worth an extra $3 to you. Put another way, your benefits from beer drinking were increasing at the rate of $3 per additional beer.

Marginal cost is defined as the additional cost incurred from the last unit of some economic activity, which tells us the rate at which your costs are increasing as you pursue the activity. Like marginal benefit, we usually measure marginal cost in dollars per unit of the activity. Suppose your marginal cost of drinking beer was $1/beer. Then you incurred additional costs of $1 from your last beer, and so your costs of beer drinking were increasing at the rate of $1 per additional beer.

Let's turn to a more practical, less frivolous example of using marginal benefit and marginal cost than beer drinking. A city trucks in its water supply from outlying mountain areas. You are the city manager faced with the problem of determining if the city needs to truck in additional water. After extensive surveying of the needs of industries and households, you estimate the residents' marginal benefit of water is 10¢/gallon. You then investigate the costs charged by the trucking firms and by the neighboring regions willing to supply water, learning that the marginal cost of trucking in water is 6¢/gallon. Armed with this information, what do you recommend to the city council?

If you understand what marginal benefit and marginal cost represent, you should recommend that the city truck in more water from outlying areas. You found that the last gallon of water was worth 10¢ to the city, but that same gallon only cost 6¢. Clearly that last gallon was a good deal since it was worth more to the city than what had to be paid for it. Since the city is still receiving more value than what it's paying out, it should continue trucking in more water. Put another way, the city's benefits from trucking in water are still increasing faster than the city's costs (10¢ per additional gallon as opposed to 6¢ per additional gallon), so the city is getting a net gain of 4¢ per gallon.

If the city follows your recommendation, you should not expect the marginal benefits and marginal costs to remain the same. As the basic household and industrial needs of drinking, washing, and cooling are met, the city's residents will likely place lower value on having even more water. In other words, the marginal benefit of water will be falling. You should also expect the marginal costs of trucking in more water to be rising. This is because you will have to drive further or drill deeper as you exhaust the readily available sources of water. **Generally speaking, marginal benefits and marginal costs do not remain constant—marginal benefits usually fall and marginal costs usually rise as more and more of an economic activity is undertaken.**

Looking at marginal benefit and marginal cost also makes it easy to see when to stop pursuing an activity. In our water trucking example, the actual values of marginal benefit and marginal cost are irrelevant. As long as the marginal benefit of the last gallon of water exceeds its marginal cost, the city is receiving additional net gains (albeit smaller and smaller ones) from having additional water. When the additional benefit from the last gallon exactly offsets the additional cost of trucking it in (i.e., when the marginal benefit exactly equals the marginal cost), this is the signal to the city to stop—there are no further net gains for the city to receive.

The fundamental idea behind this example is known as the *equimarginal principle*—**if an activity is worth pursuing at all, it should be pursued up to the point where its marginal benefit equals its marginal cost in order to get the greatest net total benefit from the activity.**

One important implication of the equimarginal principle is that past costs are past and should not influence present economic decision making. This is often summarized by saying, "Sunk costs are sunk." That is, sunk costs—costs that can no longer be avoided—cannot affect marginal cost and hence are not a factor when we apply the equimarginal principle to make economic decisions.

Section 5.2. Firms in the Marketplace

We now want to apply the equimarginal principle to the problem of a firm attempting to maximize its profits. Although in reality firms pursue other goals in addition to profits, the analysis of profit-maximizing behavior provides us with many important conclusions about the way goods are supplied in a market economy.

Profits are simply the difference between revenues (the money the firm takes in from the sale of its product) and costs (the value that has been sacrificed for not using the firm's resources in some other activity). Let's begin with the firm's costs.

We should expect a firm's marginal costs usually to be increasing for most activities. This is because the firm must deal with the scarcity of its resources. As the firm produces more and more of its product, it may be forced to use less talented labor, less efficient machinery, and raw materials of poorer quality, forcing up its marginal costs. We will discuss this in more detail in the next chapter, but for now we will assume the firm's marginal costs are increasing.

It is important to realize that **not all costs affect the firm's marginal cost.** Some costs are what economists call *fixed costs*—these are costs the firm must pay regardless of the level of its production. Fixed costs include insurance, interest payments on loans, and rental payments for its building; these costs must be paid whether the firm is producing 0, 1, 10, or 100,000 units of its product. Since marginal costs only deal with the additional cost imposed from producing the last unit, fixed costs cannot influence marginal costs. Only those factors that influence the cost of the last unit produced—like the technology and the prices of labor and raw materials—can influence marginal cost.

(Do not fall into the trap of thinking fixed costs cannot change. The word "fixed" here only means "fixed with respect to the firm's production." So fixed costs can change for many reasons, they just stay "fixed" when the firm changes the level of its production.)

The other side of profits is revenues—the amount of money the firm takes in from selling its product. Revenues can be simply calculated by multiplying the price the firm charges for its product by the number of units sold. Do not believe, however, that the firm can choose both the price *and* quantity; the demand for the firm's product will limit the amount that can be sold at any given price. So in effect the firm can choose *either* the price to charge *or* the amount sold; once one is chosen, demand will dictate the other.

Marginal revenue is the additional revenue generated by the last unit sold; it tells us how fast the firm's revenues are increasing as its sales volume increases. (We can think of marginal revenue as the firm's marginal benefit from selling its product.) Marginal revenue can be negative—if demand is inelastic, the firm will have had to lower its price so much to sell the last unit that its total revenues will have fallen. Since the firm's revenues are dictated by the demand for the firm's product, marginal revenue comes from demand and any changes in demand will affect the firm's marginal revenue.

With the definitions of marginal cost and marginal revenue in hand, it is straightforward to apply the equimarginal principle to the firm's problem. **To maximize profits, the firm should choose the level of output where marginal revenue equals marginal cost.** If the firm is producing an amount where marginal revenue exceeds marginal cost, then the last unit produced and sold is still adding to the firm's profits, so production should continue to be increased. In this situation, the firm's profits are still increasing because its revenues are increasing faster than its costs. When marginal revenue becomes equal to marginal cost, the last unit fails to contribute any increase to the firm's profits, and so production should not be further increased.

An important prediction we can make from this analysis is that anything that affects the firm's marginal cost or marginal revenue will change the firm's production and pricing decisions. So if the costs of labor or raw materials rise, marginal cost will increase and the firm will respond by producing less and/or charging more. Similarly, if demand changes, marginal revenue will change and the firm reacts by changing its production and pricing decisions.

An equally important prediction is that if marginal cost and marginal revenue remain unchanged, then we should expect no change in the firm's output and price. So if there is an increase in fixed costs, the firm will continue to produce the same quantity of goods and charge the same price, since there has been no change in marginal cost. The higher fixed costs will come totally out of the firm's profits. There is one exception to this rule—if fixed costs increase so much that the firm becomes too unprofitable, the firm will shut down its operations.

Working Through the Graphs—The Firm's Profit-Maximization Problem

Figure 5-1 shows the information typically available to a firm—the demand for its product and the total cost of producing any given level of output. From this information, the firm must determine what level of output to produce and sell in order to make as large of profits as possible. By completing the following steps, you will learn how economists view the profit-maximization problem faced by the firm.

Step 1. Profits are simply total revenue minus total cost. We already have the information on total costs summarized in the second graph, so we need to calculate total cost. To do this, we can use the information in the demand curve in the first graph. This is because total revenue is simply the price per unit times the number of units sold; both of these are summarized in the demand for the firm's product.

Using the points on the demand curve, complete the total revenue column for the second graph and plot these points. For example, you should find that the total revenue received from selling 3 units of output is $30 ($10/unit X 3 units). If you've plotted the points on the total revenue graph correctly, you should see that it increases for the first four units and decreases after that.

Step 2. Compare the total revenue and total cost in the second graph to find the level of output where the firm's profits (the vertical difference between the two graphs) are the largest. You should find that total revenue exceeds total cost by the greatest amount at both two and three units of output. As discussed in the text, we always assume the firm chooses the larger of these two possibilities. (This ambiguity could be resolved by using more advanced mathematics.)

Step 3. Although we've solved the firm's problem of maximizing its profits, economists prefer to analyze this problem in terms of marginal cost and marginal revenue. To calculate these, use the information in the second graph to find the cost/revenue generated by the last unit produced/sold and

Figure 5-1 The Firm's Profit-Maximization Problem

Demand

Q	P
0	16
1	14
2	12
3	10
4	8 6
5	4
6	

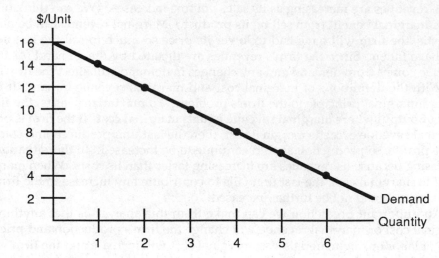

Total Cost and Total Revenue

Q	TC	TR
0	8	
1	10	
2	14	
3	20	
4	28	
5	38	
6	50	

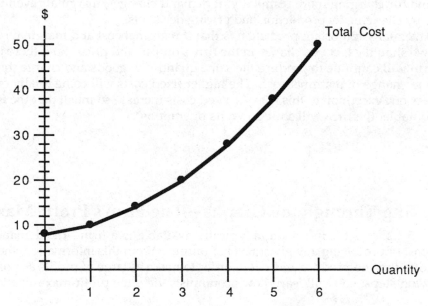

Marginal Cost and Marginal Revenue

Q	MC	MR
0	---	---
1		
2		
3		
4		
5		
6		

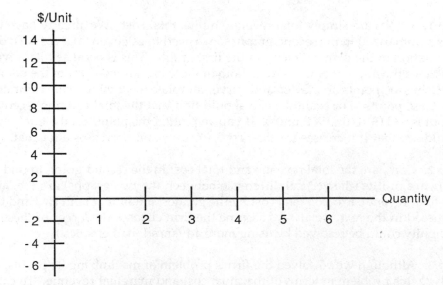

complete the marginal cost and marginal revenue columns in the third graph. Plot the points you find to get the marginal cost and marginal revenue curves. If you've done this correctly, marginal cost and marginal revenue should cross at 3 units of output (both equal $6 per unit since total costs increased from $14 to $20 and total revenue increased from $24 to $30).

Step 4. Compare the second and third graphs. Both summarize the same cost and revenue information in different ways. Marginal cost and marginal revenue simply tell us how fast the firm's total cost and total revenue are increasing.

For less than 3 units of output, marginal revenue is greater than marginal cost. This tells us that the firm's total revenues are increasing faster than its total costs (since the former is the steeper of the two curves in the second graph), so the firm's profits must still be increasing.

Beyond 3 units of output, it is the firm's total costs that are increasing the fastest (since in the second graph, the total cost curve is steeper than the total revenue curve). This indicates that the firm's profits are beginning to fall. But as shown in the third graph, this is precisely what is being described when marginal cost is larger than marginal revenue.

To summarize, the demand for the firm's product can be used to calculate marginal revenue, and the firm's total costs of production can be used to calculate marginal cost. Profits must at first be increasing where marginal revenue exceeds marginal cost. Profits then fall when marginal revenue becomes smaller than marginal cost. We can conclude that profits must be maximized where marginal revenue equals marginal cost. Our third graph gives us a visualization of the equimarginal principle as applied to the firm's economic decision making.

Why do economists prefer to analyze the firm's behavior by comparing marginal cost and marginal revenue instead of total cost and total revenue? Because marginal cost and marginal revenue are closely related to the basic economic concepts of supply and demand. We'll study this further in later chapters, but for now notice that the axes for the marginal cost/marginal revenue graph are the same as the axes we use for supply and demand.

Multiple Choice Questions

1. You spent $15 on a compact disc, only to discover that you hated the music and will never play it again. You can either keep the disc or sell it for $3 to a used record store. Assuming you will have no other options, you should
   A. keep the disc because it cost far more than $3.
   B. keep the disc because its marginal cost of $15 exceeds the marginal benefit of selling it.
   C. sell the disc because its marginal cost of $15 exceeds the marginal benefit of selling it.
   D. sell the disc because the $15 you spent are sunk.

2. The government has spent $200 million to build a new hydroelectric dam. An additional $5 million in funding is needed to complete the project, but due to budget cuts the government is considering the possibility of abandoning the project. Under what conditions should the government *not* complete the dam?
   A. When the additional benefits from completing the dam are projected to be under $205 million.
   B. When the additional benefits from completing the dam are projected to be under $195 million.
   C. When the additional benefits from completing the dam are projected to be under $5 million.
   D. The government should complete the dam under any circumstances to avoid wasting the $200 million investment.

3. A power company has spent $10 million to date on a nuclear power plant, which can be completed for an additional $1 million. However, a new study shows that the electricity generated by the plant will bring in only $3 million in additional revenues. The company
   A. should accept the $10 million loss and not complete the plant.
   B. should not complete the plant since the marginal cost outweighs the marginal benefit.
   C. should complete the plant since the marginal cost outweighs the marginal benefit.
   D. should complete the plant since the marginal benefit outweighs the marginal cost.

4. When should an activity no longer be undertaken?
   A. When its total costs, past and present, exceed its total benefits, past and present.
   B. When its total costs, past and present, exceed its total present benefits.
   C. When its marginal cost begins to exceed its marginal benefit.
   D. When its marginal benefit becomes zero.

5. Marginal costs tend to _____ and marginal benefits tend to _____ as more and more of an activity is pursued.
   A. increase; decrease
   B. increase; increase
   C. decrease; decrease
   D. decrease; increase

6. Using the adjoining table, the marginal cost of producing the third unit is
   A. $10.
   B. $10 per unit.
   C. $8.
   D. $8 per unit.

Number of Units Produced	Total Cost
0	$ 0
1	$ 6
2	$14
3	$24

7. Using the adjoining table, the total cost of producing the third unit is
   A. $10.
   B. $23.
   C. $39.
   D. Cannot be determined from the given information.

Number of Units Produced	Marginal Cost
0	-
1	$ 3/unit
2	$ 7/unit
3	$13/unit

8. The demand for a firm's good is shown in the adjoining table. The firm's marginal revenue received from selling the second unit is
   A. $10 per unit.
   B. $20 per unit.
   C. $25 per unit.
   D. $50.

Price	Number of Units Sold
$30/unit	1 unit
$25/unit	2 units
$20/unit	3 units
$15/unit	4 units
$10/unit	5 units

9. Again refer to the above table showing a firm's demand for its product. When is marginal revenue no longer positive?
   A. For the third, fourth, and fifth units.
   B. For the fourth and fifth units.
   C. For the fifth unit only.
   D. Never—marginal revenue is always positive.

10. If marginal revenue exceeds marginal cost,
   A. the firm is making positive economic profits.
   B. the firm should shut down.
   C. profits will increase if the firm increases its output.
   D. profits will increase if the firm decreases its output.

11. Assuming it does not shut down, an increase in the firm's fixed costs
   A. will not affect the price the firm charges.
   B. will not affect the quantity the firm produces.
   C. will be paid for out of the firm's profits.
   D. All of the above

12. Under a new union contract, a firm now must pay more for its labor. We can predict that the firm will now produce less and/or charge more because
   A. its marginal costs have risen.
   B. its marginal costs have fallen.
   C. its marginal revenues have risen.
   D. its marginal revenues have fallen.

13. A decrease in the firm's marginal costs would cause the firm to
   A. produce more and/or charge more for its product.
   B. produce more and/or charge less for its product.
   C. produce less and/or charge more for its product.
   D. produce less and/or charge less for its product.

14. Which of the following will *not* affect a firm's pricing and production decisions?
   A. An increase in the price of the raw materials it uses in its production.
   B. An increase in the price of the skilled labor it hires.
   C. An increase in the prices charged by its competition.
   D. An increase in the price of the insurance required by government regulations.

15. Which of the following could cause the firm to increase both the quantity it produces and the price it charges?
   A. An increase in the price of the raw materials it uses in its production.
   B. An increase in the price of the skilled labor it hires.
   C. An increase in the price charged by its competition.
   D. An increase in the price of the insurance required by government regulations.

Solutions

1. D. The $15 you spent on the disc are sunk and cannot be recovered. It is better to take the $3 than keep the worthless disc.

2. C. The $200 million are sunk and should not affect the government's decision. The project should be scrapped only if the projected benefits are smaller than the marginal cost of $5 million.

3. D. It is better for the power company to complete the plant and get a net gain of $2 million to in part offset the sunk $10 million than simply write off this loss.

4. C. This is the equimarginal principle. Past total costs are sunk and do not affect the decision.

5. A. Increasing marginal costs are a result of scarcity. Decreasing marginal benefits result as the uses of a good or resource are increasingly exhausted.

6. B. Producing 2 units cost $14 and producing 3 units cost $24, so the third unit contributed an additional $10. We measure marginal cost in "dollars per unit" to indicate we are looking at the additional cost *per* additional unit produced.

7. B. The first unit cost $3, the second cost $7, and the third cost $13, giving us a total of $23.

8. B. The total revenue from selling 1 unit is $30/unit X 1 unit = $30, and the total revenue from selling 2 units is $25/unit X 2 units = $50. So selling the second unit added $20 to the firm's revenues.

9. B. Selling 3 units gives a total revenue of $60 and selling 4 units also gives a total revenue of $60, so the marginal revenue of the fourth unit is $0/unit. Selling a fifth unit will lower total revenue to $50, so the marginal revenue of the fifth unit is -$10/unit.

10. C. The firm's revenues are increasing faster than the firm's costs, so its profits are still increasing and the firm should pursue further production.

11. D. Higher costs imply lower profits, and fixed costs have no influence on the marginal costs on which a profit-maximizing firm will base its decisions.

12. A. Since additional labor will be needed for the firm to produce additional output, this change in costs will affect marginal cost.

13. B. The intersection of marginal revenue and marginal cost will move to the right, indicating the firm will increase its quantity produced. The law of demand implies that to sell more, the firm will have to lower price.

14. D. The required insurance does not change as the firm's production level changes, so it is a fixed cost and does not affect the marginal cost and marginal revenue which determine the firm's production and pricing decisions.

15. C. An increase in the price of a substitute good will increase the demand for the firm's product. The higher demand would allow the firm to charge a higher price. Also, it will likely increase marginal revenue, moving the intersection of marginal revenue and marginal cost to the right, indicating a higher output.

Questions for Review

1. Distinguish between the terms "total benefit" and "marginal benefit." Why might the total benefit of an activity be increasing while its marginal benefit is decreasing? Explain, using an example.

2. State the equimarginal principle. What course of action would you recommend if it were discovered that the marginal cost of an activity currently outweighs it marginal benefit?

3. What is a sunk cost? Why should sunk costs have no effect on economic decision making?

4. What pattern do we generally observe in the marginal costs of production and why does it occur?

5. How do we calculate a firm's profits? Use the equimarginal principle to solve the firm's problem of maximizing profits.

6. When will a firm's marginal cost remain unaffected by a change in its total costs of production? How would such a situation affect the firm's production and pricing decisions?

7. What factors can change a firm's marginal costs? What factors can change a firm's marginal revenues? How are the firm's production and pricing decisions affected by such changes?

Solutions

1. Total benefit shows the total or gross level of benefits received (usually measured in dollars) from an economic activity. Marginal benefit shows the additional benefit received from the last unit of the activity. It is measured in "dollars per unit" and shows how fast the total benefits are increasing. As more and more of an activity is undertaken, the last unit still yields additional benefits (meaning that our total benefits are increasing). However, these additional benefits are getting smaller and smaller (meaning that marginal benefits are decreasing) since there are fewer and fewer wants remaining that the activity can still adequately satisfy.

2. For any economic activity that is worth undertaking, the equimarginal principle states that it should be pursued up to the point that its marginal benefit equals its marginal cost. Doing this will make the net total benefits we receive from the activity as large as possible. If the marginal cost were larger than the marginal benefit, then the last unit of the activity cost us more than what we received from it. So the last unit of the activity should not be undertaken in this case. (Note that this does *not* say that the activity should be totally abandoned, only that it should be cut back.)

3. Sunk costs are costs that can no longer be avoided, such as costs paid in the past. Since these costs cannot be recovered whether or not we continue to pursue an activity, they do not influence the marginal benefits and marginal costs of the activity we consider when applying the equimarginal principle.

4. Marginal costs of production tend to increase as more and more of a good is produced. This results from the scarcity of resources. For example, land and machinery can become less and less effective in production as they begin to get overused. Also, the most efficient resources may no longer be available as we continue to increase production, forcing us to rely on less efficient resources.

5. Profits are the firm's total revenues minus the firm's total costs. Using the equimarginal principle, the firm should pursue the production and sale of its output up to the point where the marginal revenue received from selling its output equals the marginal cost of producing its output. The exception to this rule is that the firm may shut down and produce no output when profits are inadequate at all production levels.

6. Some costs—called fixed costs—are sunk the instant a firm chooses to produce its product. These costs must be paid no matter how much output the firm produces. So any changes in fixed costs cannot affect the cost of producing the last unit of output, which is marginal cost. Applying the equimarginal principle, any changes in these fixed costs will not affect the firm's production and pricing decisions, unless the fixed costs affect profits so adversely they force the firm to shut down.

7. Any change that affects the cost of the last unit produced—such as a change in the cost of labor, the cost of raw materials, or technology—will affect marginal cost. Any change that affects the demand for the firm's product—such as the price and availability of competing products—will affect marginal revenue. These both affect the application of the equimarginal principle, and hence the firm's production and pricing decisions. The exact nature of the changes depends on the exact change in marginal cost, marginal revenue, and demand.

Problems for Analysis

1. (i) A firm's costs and the demand for its product are summarized in the table below. Complete the table and use the equimarginal principle to determine the firm's level of output, price charged, and maximum profits.

COSTS				REVENUES		
Quantity Produced	Total Cost	Marginal Cost	Price	Quantity Demanded	Total Revenue	Marginal Revenue
0	$ 0	--				
1	$ 70		$200/unit	1		
2	$142		$180/unit	2		
3	$217		$160/unit	3		
4	$297		$140/unit	4		
5	$385		$120/unit	5		
6	$485		$100/unit	6		
7	$603		$ 80/unit	7		

(ii) Suppose the firm signs a contract with an advertising firm, agreeing to pay $150 for its efforts. Suppose the effect of the advertising is to increase the price consumers are willing to pay for the firm's product by $100/unit at each and every quantity. Complete the table below to show the new situation that the firm faces. Again use the equimarginal principle to determine the firm's level of output, price charged, and maximum profits.

	COSTS			REVENUES		
Quantity Produced	Total Cost	Marginal Cost	Price	Quantity Demanded	Total Revenue	Marginal Revenue
0		--				
1				1		
2				2		
3				3		
4				4		
5				5		
6				6		
7				7		

(iii) Suppose instead that the advertising is totally ineffective and does not change the demand for the firm's good. How will this change the firm's level of output, price charged, and maximum profits from part (i)? Explain.

2. Suppose that x books can be produced for a total cost of $x^2 + x$ dollars. (So 1 book can be produced for $1^2 + 1 = 2$ dollars; 2 books can be produced for $2^2 + 2 = 6$ dollars; and so forth.)

   (i) Find and simplify an algebraic formula for the marginal cost of production when x books are produced.

   (ii) Suppose the book company has agreed to pay an author a flat fee of $100 for the right to use her material. Will this agreement increase, decrease, or not change the firm's marginal cost? Prove your answer by finding and simplifying an algebraic formula to represent this situation.

(iii) Suppose instead that the cost of producing the cover for each book has risen by $2 per cover. Will this change in the firm's costs increase, decrease, or not change marginal cost? Again prove your answer by finding and simplifying an algebraic formula to represent the situation.

3. Suppose the government is considering two different policies for stimulating steel production in the U.S. The first policy is to give firms in the steel industry an excise (or per unit) subsidy of $10 per ingot. (In other words, the government will give the firm $10 for every ingot it produces.) The second policy is to grant each firm in the steel industry an annual lump sum subsidy of $1,000.

(i) Describe in detail and graphically illustrate how each of these policies will affect the output of a steel-producing firm.

(ii) If you were a government advisor, which policy would you recommend? Why?

Solutions

1. (i)

	COSTS			REVENUES		
Quantity Produced	Total Cost	Marginal Cost	Price	Quantity Demanded	Total Revenue	Marginal Revenue
0	$ 0	--				
1	$ 70	$ 70/unit	$200/unit	1	$200	$200/unit
2	$142	$ 72/unit	$180/unit	2	$360	$160/unit
3	$217	$ 75/unit	$160/unit	3	$480	$120/unit
4	$297	$ 80/unit	$140/unit	4	$560	$ 80/unit
5	$385	$ 88/unit	$120/unit	5	$600	$ 40/unit
6	$485	$100/unit	$100/unit	6	$600	$ 0/unit
7	$603	$118/unit	$ 80/unit	7	$560	-$ 40/unit

Applying the equimarginal principle, marginal revenue equals marginal cost at 4 units of output. Using the demand schedule, the firm should charge $140/unit. The firm's profits will equal its total revenues minus its total costs, which is $560 - $297 = $263.

(ii)

	COSTS				REVENUES		
Quantity Produced	Total Cost	Marginal Cost	Price	Quantity Demanded	Total Revenue	Marginal Revenue
0	$150	--				
1	$220	$ 70/unit	$300/unit	1	$ 300	$300/unit
2	$292	$ 72/unit	$280/unit	2	$ 560	$260/unit
3	$367	$ 75/unit	$260/unit	3	$ 780	$220/unit
4	$447	$ 80/unit	$240/unit	4	$ 960	$180/unit
5	$535	$ 88/unit	$220/unit	5	$1,100	$140/unit
6	$635	$100/unit	$200/unit	6	$1,200	$100/unit
7	$753	$118/unit	$180/unit	7	$1,260	$ 60/unit

Once the contract is signed, the advertising becomes a fixed cost that must be paid no matter how much output the firm produces. So all entries in the total cost column have risen by $150; notice that this leaves marginal cost unchanged. The entries in the price column have increased by $100/unit, indicating that consumers are now willing to pay $100/unit more at any quantity due to the advertising. Notice that since demand has changed, marginal revenue has also changed, affecting the application of the equimarginal principle. The firm will increase its output to 6 units (where marginal revenue equals marginal cost), charge $200/unit, and make $565 in profits.

(iii) If the advertising does not affect demand, then neither marginal cost nor marginal revenue will have changed from part (i). Applying the equimarginal principle, the firm's level of output and price charged will be unchanged. The fixed cost of advertising will come totally out of the firm's profits, lowering them to $113.

2. (i) Producing x books requires a total cost of $x^2 + x$ dollars. Using this formula, producing (x-1) books must require a total cost of $(x-1)^2 + (x-1) = (x^2 - 2x + 1) + (x - 1)$
$$= x^2 - x \text{ dollars.}$$

Marginal cost, the cost of the last unit produced (i.e., the cost of the xth book), must be the difference between these two formulas. So marginal cost equals

(the total cost of producing x books) - (the total cost of producing (x - 1) books)
$= (x^2 + x) - (x^2 - x) = 2x$ dollars per book.

(Note—If we made the units infinitesimally small, the formula for marginal cost would become $2x + 1$ dollars per book.)

(ii) This cost must be paid no matter how many books are produced, so it is a new fixed cost. So marginal cost should be unchanged. To show this, the new total cost of producing x books is

$x^2 + x + 100$ dollars. Following the procedure in part (i), the total cost of producing $(x - 1)$ books is

$$(x-1)^2 + (x-1) + 100 \quad = \quad (x^2 - 2x + 1) + (x - 1) + 100$$
$$= \quad x^2 - x + 100 \text{ dollars.}$$

So marginal cost equals

(the total cost of producing x books) - (the total cost of producing $(x - 1)$ books)
$= (x^2 + x + 100) - (x^2 - x + 100) = 2x$ dollars per book.

We have proven algebraically that this new fixed cost has not affected marginal cost. (Note—If we made the units infinitesimally small, the formula for marginal cost would again become $2x + 1$ dollars per book.)

(iii)   The more expensive cover will increase the cost of the last produced, so we should expect marginal cost to increase. Since each book costs 2 dollars more to produce, x books will cost $2x$ dollars more to produce. So the total cost of producing x books is now $x^2 + x + 2x = x^2 + 3x$ dollars. Using this formula, the total cost of producing $(x - 1)$ books is now

$$(x-1)^2 + 3(x-1) \quad = \quad (x^2 - 2x + 1) + (3x - 3)$$
$$= \quad x^2 + x - 2 \text{ dollars.}$$

So marginal cost equals

(the total cost of producing x books) - (the total cost of producing $(x - 1)$ books)
$= (x^2 + 3x) - (x^2 + x - 2) = 2x + 2$ dollars per book.

We have proven algebraically that when the cost of producing each book increases by \$2, the marginal cost of production increases by \$2/book.
(Note—If we made the units infinitesimally small, the formula for marginal cost would now be $2x + 3$ dollars per book.)

3. (i) The excise subsidy will lower a firm's marginal cost since the government is paying the firm $10 for *each* ingot produced. The firm's cost of producing the last ingot is lowered by $10 (since the government subsidy is now picking up part of the cost), so the marginal cost curve shifts down by precisely $10/ingot. Applying the equimarginal principle, this will increase the quantity produced by the firm as shown by the graph below.

Figure 5a

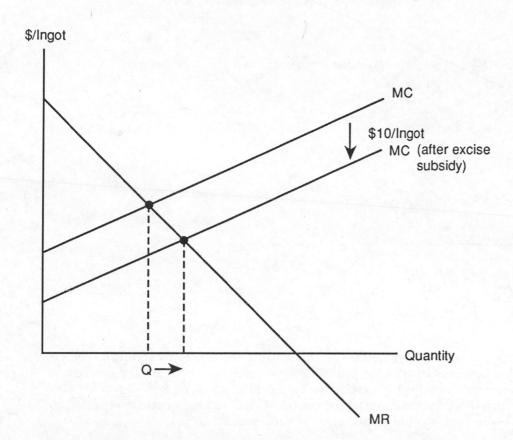

The annual lump sum subsidy will not affect the firm's marginal cost since the government pays the firm $1,000 no matter how much the firm produces. The firm's cost of producing the last ingot is unchanged, so marginal cost does not shift, and by the equimarginal principle the firm's quantity produced will be unchanged as shown below. The lump sum subsidy will help to pay the firm's fixed costs and simply increase the firm's profits by $1,000.

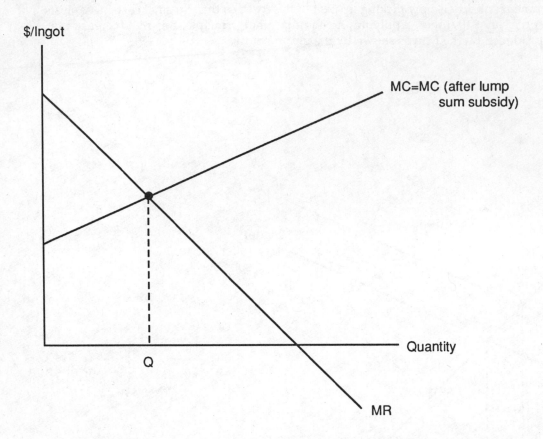

(ii) If the government's goal is to increase steel production, the excise subsidy should be chosen. As seen in part (i), it induces existing steel producers to increase their output. The immediate effect of the lump sum subsidy is to increase the firm's profit, not its output. It would only stimulate steel production after a substantial period of time, as new firms are attracted to the steel industry by the higher profits created by the lump sum subsidy.

Solutions to Working Through the Graphs

Figure 5-1   The Firm's Profit-Maximization Problem

Demand

Q	P
0	16
1	14
2	12
3	10
4	8 6
5	4
6	

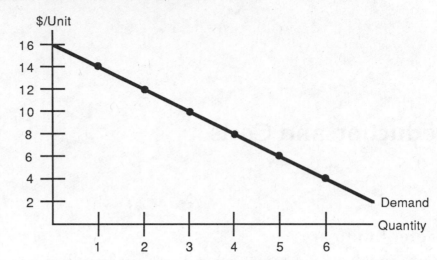

Total Cost and
Total Revenue

Q	TC	TR
0	8	0
1	10	14
2	14	24
3	20	30
4	28	32
5	38	30
6	50	24

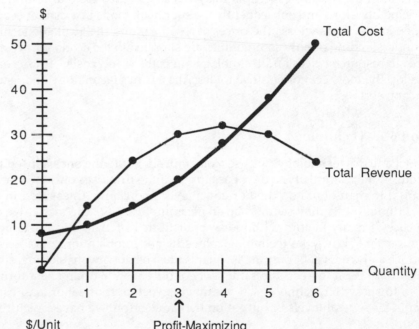

Marginal Cost and
Marginal Revenue

Q	MC	MR
0	---	---
1	2	14
2	4	10
3	6	6
4	8	2
5	10	-2
6	12	-6

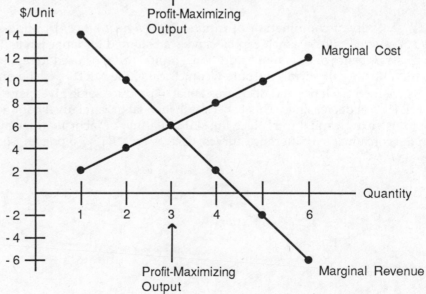

93

Chapter Six

Production and Costs

Chapter Summary

We have seen that costs—especially marginal costs—are essential to understanding a firm's production and pricing decisions and subsequently the supply of goods in a market economy. The firm's costs, in turn, depend on two factors: the prices of resources and the available technology. So in order to have a good understanding of how commodities are supplied in the economy, we must be able to predict how changes in resource prices and technology affect the firm's costs. To this end, our goal for this chapter is to develop the tools economists use to describe a firm's technology and learn about the relation between production and cost.

Section 6.1. Technology

To model a firm's technology, we use a diagram similar to the one we used to describe a consumer's preferences. For simplicity, we will assume that the firm uses only two factors of production: labor (measured in man-hours on the horizontal axis) and capital (measured in machine-hours on the vertical axis). Although this may seem to be an oversimplification, the model we develop could be generalized to the case of many factors with more sophisticated mathematical techniques.

An *isoquant* shows the technologically efficient combinations of labor and capital that can be used to produce a given level of output. Isoquants must be downward sloping, since we must exchange labor for capital or *vice versa* to keep the same level of output. We often use a formula, called a *production function*, to show the technological relation between output, labor, and capital. By showing the isoquants for several levels of output on the same graph, we have a picture of the firm's production function.

For any given combination of inputs, the *marginal rate of technical substitution of labor for capital* ($MRTS_{LK}$) is the rate at which capital can be substituted for labor while keeping output constant. This gives us a measure of how much additional capital could be used to replace the last unit of labor used without affecting the firm's output. Geometrically, the $MRTS_{LK}$ is shown by the slope of the isoquant.

As we increase labor and decrease capital to produce some given level of output, we would find that the $MRTS_{LK}$ is decreasing. This is because when labor is relatively abundant, it is far easier for the firm to use extra capital to replace the skills of a unit of labor than when labor is relatively scarce. As with the consumer's indifference curves, decreasing $MRTS_{LK}$ along an isoquant implies that the isoquant is convex.

To study the supply of goods in a market economy, we must be concerned with the firm's response to changing economic conditions. This requires us to be able to model the changes a firm makes in the production process it uses. If the firm's planning horizon is relatively long, it can make substantial changes in its use of labor and capital—the *long run* is defined to be a situation where the firm can adjust the levels of all factors when it changes its production process. Over a short time frame, the firm's ability to change the use of one or more factors may be limited—the *short run* is a situation in which the usage of some but not all factors can be adjusted. For concreteness we will assume that capital is fixed and labor is variable in the short run.

Section 6.2. Production and Costs in the Short Run

Since the use of capital is fixed in the short run, the only method that a firm can change its output level in our model is by changing the amount of labor it uses. The isoquant diagram defines the precise relationship between labor and output in the short run, known as the *total product curve* or the *short run production function.* Total product is graphed with labor (the independent variable) on the horizontal axis and output (the dependent variable) on the vertical axis. From this technological relationship we can also calculate the marginal product of labor (MP_L)—the additional output generated by the last unit of labor used—which tells us the rate at which output increases as labor use increases.

The existence of a fixed factor imposes a restriction on the firm's short-run production possibilities known as *diminishing marginal returns to labor.* At low levels of output, there may be too little labor to efficiently work the fixed capital. The last units of labor added can contribute increasingly larger additions to production as the possibilities of specialization of labor can be realized. So total product is increasing rapidly as more and more labor is used—we say there are *increasing marginal returns to labor.* But eventually, these possibilities become exhausted and the fixed capital begins to be overused. Output increases less and less rapidly as more labor is used since there becomes too little capital available for the labor to work efficiently. This is called diminishing marginal returns—the last unit of labor provides less and less additional output. This pattern of first increasing and then diminishing marginal returns is shown by the marginal product curve first rising then falling.

The restrictions imposed by diminishing marginal returns are also reflected in the firm's short-run marginal cost curve. Recall from Chapter 5 that *marginal cost* shows the increase in cost required to produce the last unit of output. The pattern of short-run production implies that marginal cost may first be falling but must eventually become rising. For low output levels, greater labor use causes increasingly efficient use of the fixed capital—it takes less and less additional expenditures on labor to produce the last unit of output. But as more output is needed, eventually there is too little capital available for the added labor to use and production becomes less efficient. So beyond the point of diminishing marginal returns, labor expenditures for additional units of output increase and marginal cost is rising.

In addition to this U-shaped marginal cost, there are several other ways of describing the cost structure that arises from the diminishing marginal returns typical of short-run production. These are summarized in Table 6a. Don't just try to memorize all this information; instead try to discover the pattern in the terminology and calculations.

In the short run, the firm is given the wage rate P_L, the rental rate P_K, and a fixed level of capital K_0. Using this information, the firm can choose labor L and output Q as dictated by the short-run production possibilities from the isoquant diagram and calculate the following costs in addition to marginal cost.

Type of Cost	Meaning	Formula for Calculation	Comments
Fixed Cost (FC)	Shows total expenditure on fixed factors required to produce any given level of output.	$FC = P_K \cdot K_0$	FC does not influence MC.
Variable Cost (VC)	Shows total expenditure on variable factors required to produce any given level of output	$VC = P_L \cdot L$	
Total Cost (TC)	Shows total expenditure required to produce any given level of output	$TC = P_L \cdot L + P_K \cdot K_0$	$TC = FC + VC$.
Average Variable Cost (AVC)	Shows total per unit expenditure on variable factors required to produce any given level of output	$AVC = VC/Q$	U-shaped. MC crosses at minimum point of AVC.
Average Cost (AC)	Shows total per unit expenditure required to produce any given level of output	$AC = TC/Q$	U-shaped. MC crosses at minimum point of AC.

Section 6.3. Production and Costs in the Long Run

For given factor prices, an *isocost* shows the various combinations of labor and capital that yield the same total cost. The slope of an isocost is given by the ratio of the factor prices P_L/P_K, where P_L is the wage rate and P_K is the rental rate. (Notice that this parallels the situation with the consumer's budget line.) The set of labor/capital combinations where an isocost is tangent to an isoquant is called the *expansion path*. At these points and no others, the equations $MRTS_{LK} = P_L/P_K$ and $MP_L/P_L = MP_K/P_K$ hold true. (MP_K stands for the marginal product of capital, which is defined analogously to the marginal product of labor.)

By comparing MP_L/P_L (which represents the additional output produced by the last dollar spent on labor) and MP_K/P_K (which represents the additional output produced by the last dollar spent on capital), we find another application of the equimarginal principle. **In the long run a firm will restrict its production to those combinations of factors on the expansion path because these production processes (1) provide the greatest output for specified levels of total cost and (2) provide the lowest total cost required to produce specified levels of output.** (See the textbook for the details of this argument.)

Since the isoquant diagram (via the expansion path) tells us the firm's long-run production possibilities, by using the factor prices we can calculate the firm's long-run total costs. As in the short-run case, it is then straightforward to calculate the long-run average cost and long-run marginal cost of production.

Long-run costs follow a pattern similar to short-run costs. But while marginal returns to labor determine the pattern of short-run costs, the pattern of long-run costs is determined by a very different reason called *returns to scale*. We say there are constant, increasing, or decreasing returns to scale if a 1% increase in *all* factors of production will increase output by exactly, more than, or less than 1%, respectively.

For low levels of output, we should expect that there are many possible technological advantages for the firm to exploit by expanding the scale of its operations—for example, mass production techniques, recycling of by-products, and increased specialization of labor and capital. As production becomes more efficient, we should expect to find increasing returns to scale. Since output would increase by a greater percentage than factor use (and hence total cost), long-run average cost must be falling. However for large levels of output, the advantages of expanding the firm's scale of operations are exhausted. Firm bureaucracy and organizational difficulties take their toll causing diminishing returns to scale, so rising long-run average costs eventually dominate.

Working Through the Graphs—From Production to Cost

A firm's costs depend on its technology, the prices of resources, and its ability to change the amounts of the resources it uses. This basic information for a particular firm has been summarized in Figure 6-1. By completing the following steps, you will calculate the firm's costs from this data and develop a better understanding of the relationship between production and cost.

Step 1. The top graph summarizes the technology available to a firm. Recall that economists use the short run to model the situation where a firm does not have sufficient time to fully vary all of its inputs. Suppose that the firm's use of capital is limited to 20 machine-hours daily in the short run in our example. On the graph, illustrate the production possibilities available to the firm in the short run—your illustration should resemble Exhibit 6-4 of the text. Check your answer by verifying that the points in the accompanying table are on your graph.

Figure 6-1 From Production to Cost

The Firm's Short-Run
Production Choices
(Capital fixed at K = 20)

Q	L	K
0	0 8	20
1	10	20
2	20	20
3	80	20
4		20

The Firm's Long-Run
Production Choices
(Wage = $1 per man-hour ;
Rental = $2 per
machine-hour)

Q	L	K
0	0	0
1	10	10
2	13	16
3	20	20
4	40	25
5	70	40

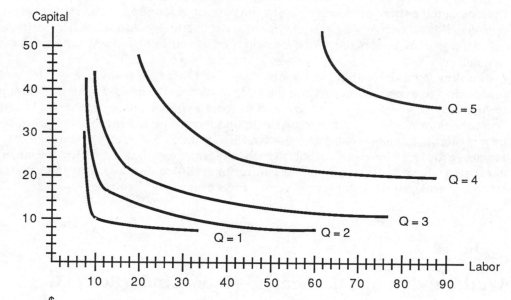

Short-Run and Long-Run
Total Costs
(Wage = $2 per man-hour;
Rental = $1 per machine-hour)

Q	SRTC	LRTC
0		
1		
2		
3		
4		
5		

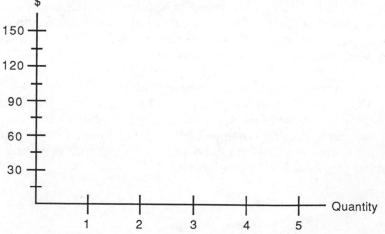

Step 2. The second graph shows the same technology. However, this time suppose we are in the long run where the levels of both labor and capital can be changed. In this case, it is the prices of inputs that limit the firm's production possibilities by determining which combinations of labor and capital are cost-efficient. Recall that these cost-efficient levels of labor and capital are determined by the tangencies of isocosts and isoquants. Also recall that the set of all these isocost/isoquant tangencies are called the expansion path.

Suppose that the wage rate is $1 per man-hour and the rental rate is $2 per machine-hour. Graph the isocosts corresponding to total costs of $30, $45, $60, $90, and $150, find the cost-efficient combinations of labor and capital, and sketch the expansion path. Your result should resemble Exhibit 6-12 of the textbook. Check your answer by verifying that the points in the accompanying table are on your expansion path.

Step 3. Use the firm's short-run production possibilities from Step 1 along with the wage and rental rates to calculate the firm's short-run total costs. Summarize your results in the appropriate column of the table provided, and graph the short-run total cost curve on the bottom set of axes. Similarly, use your results from Step 2 to calculate and graph the long-run total cost curve. If you've done this correctly, your graphs should resemble Exhibit 6-13 of the textbook.

Step 4. Compare the short-run and long-run situations. They are different in several ways.

First notice how the firm's choices of labor and capital are limited. Unlike the consumer, there is no budget constraint that limits the firm. Instead, in the short run it is a fixed factor of production (in this instance capital) that restricts the firm's production possibilities. The only way the firm can increase its output in the short run is to increase its use of labor. In the long run, it is the prices of resources that restrict the production possibilities by determining which labor/capital combinations are cost-efficient.

Second, notice that any short-run total cost curve lies above and is tangent to the long-run total cost curve. This reflects the difference between the use of resources in the short run to the long run. Suppose that it would take the firm one month to retool and adjust the availability of machines in its factory. In our example, the firm has decided that on average it will need to produce 3 units of output daily during the current month; it should use 20 man-hours and 20 machine-hours to minimize the cost of producing this output as shown in the second graph. So the firm commits to using 20 machine-hours daily for this month.

As long as it produces 3 units of output daily, the firm is using the cost-efficient method of production; this corresponds to the tangency between the short-run and long-run total cost curves. But should the firm need to increase or decrease its output during this month, it will still be forced to use the 20 machine-hours and can only change its labor usage. The firm cannot choose the cost-efficient level of production and will have higher costs than if it could adjust its use of capital. Hence the short-run total cost curve must be above the long-run total cost curve at all other levels of output.

Finally, notice in the third graph that both short-run and long-run total costs first increase at slower and slower rates (the total cost curves are getting flatter, indicating that marginal cost is falling), then increase at faster and faster rates (the total costs curves are getting steeper, indicating that marginal cost is rising). Although both follow the same pattern, they do so for different reasons.

In the short run, diminishing marginal returns to labor eventually set in due to the fixed level of capital. Although some specialization of labor can cause marginal costs to fall, eventually the fixed capital gets overused. This causes extra labor to provide less and less additional output, causing increasing marginal costs.

In the long run, this is not a problem since both labor and capital can be increased. The firm can take advantage of mass production techniques, specialization of both labor and capital, recycling of the by-products of production, and organizational advantages to size—these cause increasing returns to scale, meaning that percentage increases in all inputs yield greater percentage increases in output. However, as the size of the firm grows, so does the firm bureaucracy, meaning less organized and more time-consuming decision making. The firm's ability to adjust its output to changing conditions may collapse under its own weight, resulting in decreasing returns to scale and causing total costs to accelerate.

To summarize, both short-run and long-run total costs follow the same pattern but for different reasons—increasing then decreasing marginal returns to labor imposed by fixed capital determine the pattern of short-run costs; increasing then decreasing returns to scale determine the pattern of long-run costs.

Multiple Choice Questions

1. Which of the following statements about the isoquant diagram is *false*?
   A. Each isoquant shows the technologically efficient combinations of labor and capital that can produce a particular level of output.
   B. For a given labor/capital combination, the slope of the isoquant at that point is the $MRTS_{LK}$.
   C. An isoquant is downward sloping since points to the northeast would be technologically inefficient ways of producing that level of output.
   D. Isoquants are convex due to diminishing marginal returns.

2. Which of the following statements about the marginal rate of technical substitution of labor for capital is *false*?
   A. The $MRTS_{LK}$ gives the rate at which capital can be substituted for labor while keeping output constant.
   B. The $MRTS_{LK}$ is equal to the ratio of marginal products.
   C. The $MRTS_{LK}$ along an isoquant is increasing as more labor and less capital is used.
   D. All points on the expansion path have the same $MRTS_{LK}$.

3. The short-run production possibilities on the isoquant diagram show the combinations of labor and capital that
   A. are available to the firm in the short run.
   B. produce given levels of output at the least possible total cost.
   C. produce the most possible output for given levels of total cost.
   D. All of the above

4. Which of the following would cause the total product curve to shift upward?
   A. An increase in the amount of labor employed.
   B. An increase in the amount of capital employed.
   C. An increase in the wage rate.
   D. An increase in the rental rate.

5. In the short run, marginal cost becomes upward sloping due to
   A. rising input prices.
   B. decreasing marginal product of labor.
   C. decreasing returns to scale.
   D. Both A and B

6. If average cost is falling, then marginal cost
   A. must be above average cost.
   B. must be below average cost.
   C. must be equal to average cost.
   D. Any of the above are possible

7. Assume capital is fixed in the short run. If the rental rate of capital rises, which of the following short-run cost curves will shift upward?
   A. The marginal cost curve.
   B. The average cost curve.
   C. The average variable cost curve.
   D. Both A and B

8. A firm is currently producing 500 units of output using 100 man-hours of labor and 50 machine-hours of capital. For this production process, the marginal product of labor is 20 units of output per man-hour and the marginal product of capital is 10 units of output per machine-hour. The wage rate is $5/man-hour and the rental rate is $5/machine-hour. Which of the following statements is *true*?
   A. The firm's production process is cost-efficient.
   B. The firm can produce more output for the same total cost by using more labor and more capital.
   C. The firm can produce more output for the same total cost by using more labor and less capital.
   D. The firm can produce more output for the same total cost by using less labor and more capital.

9. The expansion path shows the combinations of labor and capital that
   A. the firm will choose to employ in the long run.
   B. produce given levels of output at the least possible total cost.
   C. produce the most possible output for given levels of total cost.
   D. All of the above

10. If the rental rate of capital rises, the expansion path will
   A. shift up.
   B. shift down.
   C. shift unpredictably.
   D. not change.

***Questions 11-13 refer to Figure 6b, where it is assumed that the wage rate is $20/man-hour and the rental rate is $10/machine-hour.

Figure 6b

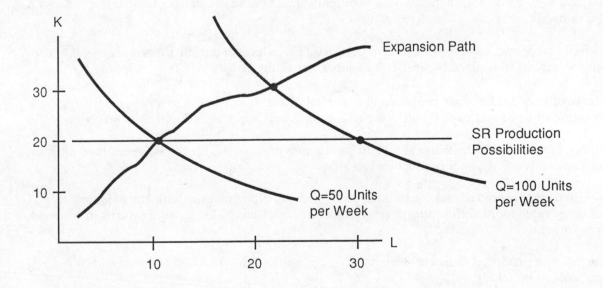

11. The short-run total cost of producing 100 units of output per week is
    A. $40.
    B. $70.
    C. $80.
    D.   Cannot be calculated from the given information

12. The long-run total cost of producing 100 units of output per week is
    A. $40.
    B. $70.
    C. $80.
    D.   Cannot be calculated from the given information

13. The short-run total cost curve must be tangent to the long-run total cost curve
    A.   at 50 units of output per week.
    B.   at 100 units of output per week.
    C.   between 50 and 100 units of output per week.
    D.   at some output level below 50 units per week.

14. Which of the following may explain how decreasing returns to scale could occur?
    A.   Diminishing marginal rate of technical substitution of labor for capital along an isoquant.
    B.   Increasing then diminishing marginal returns to labor.
    C.   Mass production techniques.
    D.   Firm bureaucracy.

15. When input prices are fixed, increasing returns to scale implies that long-run average cost is
    A.   downward sloping.
    B.   horizontal.
    C.   upward sloping.
    D.   U-shaped.

Solutions

1. D. Isoquants are convex since the $MRTS_{LK}$ is diminishing along an isoquant as more labor and less capital is used.

2. C. As more labor and less capital is used to produce a given level of output, it becomes easier to use additional capital to replace the last unit of labor, meaning that the $MRTS_{LK}$ is falling.

3. A. The firm may not have the proper level of capital in the short run to use a cost-efficient combination of labor and capital on the expansion path, making choices B and C incorrect.

4. B. With greater capital, the firm's short-run production possibilities on the isoquant map shift up, shifting up the resulting total product curve.

5. B. Marginal cost is upward sloping past the point of diminishing marginal returns to labor. A higher wage rate would shift up the entire marginal product curve. Decreasing returns to scale is a long run concept.

6. B. The last unit produced must cost less than average for it to pull the average down and cause average cost to be falling.

7. B. Since fixed costs have increased, so will total and average cost. Changes in fixed cost do not affect marginal cost.

8. C. MP_L/P_L equals 4 units of output per dollar spent on labor, and MP_K/P_K equals 2 units of output per dollar spent on capital. Labor is a better buy of output than capital. So to keep total cost fixed and get more output, the firm should use more labor and less capital.

9. D. The expansion path shows all points where $MP_L/P_L = MP_K/P_K$, which indicates that the firm's production process is cost-efficient.

10. B. When the rental rate rises, the isocosts become flatter. We then have a new set of isoquant/isocost tangencies that are further down the isoquants.

11. C. Using the firm's short-run production possibilities, the firm will use 30 man-hours of labor and 20 machine-hours of capital, costing $80.

12. B. Using the firm's expansion path, the firm will use 20 man-hours of labor and 30 machine-hours of capital, costing $70.

13. A. The firm will use 10 man-hours of labor and 20 machine-hours of capital to produce 50 units of output in both the short run and the long run since this input combination is on both the firm's short-run production possibilities and the expansion path. The short-run and long-run total cost of 50 units of output is $40.

14. D. Under decreasing returns to scale, a 1% increase in all factors result in an increase in output of less than 1%. This may happen when the scale of operations is so large that organizational and management problems like an inefficient firm bureaucracy occur.

15. A. Under increasing returns to scale, a 1% increase in all factors will increase output by more than 1%. So output must have increased by a greater percentage than the firm's total cost, hence long-run average cost must have fallen.

Questions for Review

1. What does an isoquant show? Why must isoquants be downward sloping? Why must isoquants be convex?

2. What does the marginal rate of technical substitution show? Why is it decreasing along an isoquant? Can you think of a case where the $MRTS_{LK}$ would be constant?

3. What pattern does a firm's short-run production exhibit? Explain why we should expect this pattern to occur.

4. Suppose a firm's short-run production is described by the formula $Q = \sqrt{L}$. The firm's fixed costs are $100, and the wage rate is $P_L = \$5/\text{man-hour}$. Find and simplify algebraic formulas expressing the firm's short-run total, average, and marginal cost as functions of output.

5. What is the significance of the points on the firm's expansion path? What equations characterize these labor/capital combinations?

6. What is the relation between the firm's short-run and long-run total costs? Explain why this relation holds.

7. How are marginal returns to labor and returns to scale similar? How are they different?

Solutions

1. An isoquant shows the technologically efficient combinations of labor and capital that can be used to produce a particular level of output. All labor/capital combinations to the northeast of any point on the isoquant are technologically inefficient (i.e., contain more inputs than are necessary to produce that output), so isoquants cannot slope in the northeast direction (i.e., slope upward). An isoquant must be convex because the $MRTS_{LK}$ is decreasing along the isoquant as more labor and less capital is used.

2. The $MRTS_{LK}$ shows the amount of capital that can be substituted for the last unit of labor used and still keep the same level of output. As we move down the isoquant using more labor and less capital, it becomes easier to substitute capital for the increasingly abundant labor, making the $MRTS_{LK}$ fall. The $MRTS_{LK}$ would be constant if two inputs are perfect substitutes in production; then the firm could always substitute one input for the other at the same rate. For example, when men and women can perform a job equally well, the MRTS of women for men would always equal 1 woman per man.

3. When there is a fixed factor, there tend to be increasing marginal returns to a variable factor at low levels of output followed by diminishing marginal returns. Suppose capital is the fixed factor and labor is the variable factor. At low levels of output, there is too little labor to efficiently work with the fixed capital. The last units of labor added yield increasing increments in output as the firm takes advantage of the benefits of specialization of labor. However, these advantages of specialization are eventually exhausted, and there becomes too little capital for the labor to use. As the fixed capital gets overused, the last units of labor add less and less additional output, which implies diminishing marginal returns to labor.

4. Notice that the short-run production function implies $L = Q^2$. So $VC = P_L \cdot L = 5Q^2$. Hence $TC = VC + FC = 5Q^2 + 100$ and $AC = TC/Q = (5Q^2 + 100)/Q = 5Q + (100/Q)$. Since fixed costs do not affect marginal costs, we may use either VC or TC to calculate the cost of the last unit. Using VC, we find $MC = 5Q^2 - 5(Q-1)^2 = 5Q^2 - (5Q^2 - 10Q + 5) = 10Q - 5$. (Note—If we make our units arbitrarily small, this formula simplifies to $MC = 10Q$.)

5. The expansion path illustrates the combinations of labor and capital that the firm will employ in the long run. Any one of these production processes will (1) produce the most output possible for a particular level of total cost, and (2) produce some given level of output at the least possible total cost. Combinations of labor and capital that have these properties are characterized by the equations $MRTS_{LK} = P_L/P_K$ and $MP_L/P_L = MP_K/P_K$.

6. The short-run total cost curve corresponding to each level of capital is above and tangent to the long-run total cost curve. When the firm makes its long-run choice from the expansion path, it is committed to that level of capital for the short run. As long as the firm stays on the expansion path, it will minimize the cost of producing its output for the short run. But should the firm make any short-run deviation from the long-run production choice, its costs will be higher than the minimum possible, since the firm cannot vary the level of its capital. Hence the firm's short-run total costs will be higher than the long-run total costs for levels of output different from its long-run choice.

7. Marginal returns to labor and returns to scale both describe how output changes as factor use changes. Marginal returns to labor look at the *addition* to output from the *last* unit of labor employed; returns to scale considers the percentage changes in the *total* output and factor levels. Marginal returns to labor is a short-run concept that assumes capital is fixed and explains why short-run marginal cost is U-shaped. Returns to scale is a long-run concept that assumes all factors are variable and explains why long-run average cost is U-shaped.

Problems for Analysis

1. (i) Assume that in food production, land and capital are fixed inputs and labor is a variable input. Furthermore, assume this production exhibits diminishing marginal returns to labor, with output increasing at a diminishing rate, at *all* levels of labor (i.e., there are never increasing marginal returns to labor in food production). On the axes below, draw total product and marginal product curves showing this assumption.

   (ii) Suppose food requirements for society increase at a constant rate as the population increases. On your diagrams from part (i), draw graphs illustrating society's total and marginal food requirements.

   (iii) On your graphs, show the population level where the society exceeds its food requirements by the greatest amount. On the total food production/requirements graph, show the population levels that you would expect famine to occur.

Total Food Output and
Total Food Requirements

Labor
(population)

105

Marginal Food Output and
Marginal Food Requirements

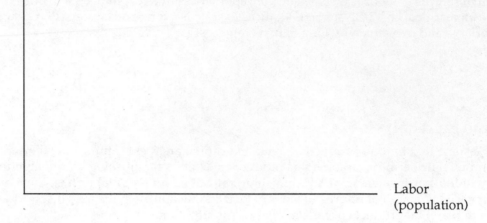

Labor
(population)

(iv)   In his book *Essay on the Principle of Population* (1798), the nineteenth-century British economist Thomas Malthus used the ideas in parts (i)-(iii) to predict that population growth would eventually cause widespread famine. Yet almost 200 years later, mankind has still not starved to death despite its incredible population growth.

Use the concept of diminishing marginal returns to explain why Malthus' prediction was wrong. In other words, why would it be wrong to use the graphs you've drawn to conclude that there will be eventual famine?

2. A firm is currently employing 100 man-hours of labor and 50 machine-hours of capital to produce 500 units of output. Labor costs $4 per hour and capital costs $8 per hour. For the quantities employed, the marginal product of labor is 1 unit of output per man-hour and the marginal product of capital is 4 units of output per machine-hour.

(i)   Give an isocost and an isoquant on the diagram below to illustrate this situation.

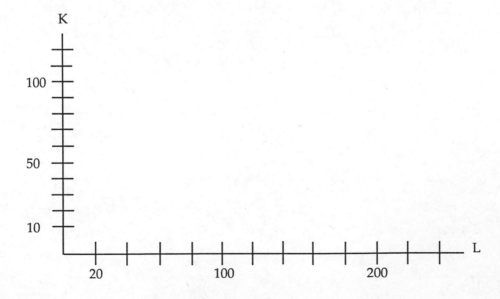

(ii) Carefully explain how the firm can produce more output at the same total cost. Illustrate this on the isoquant/isocost diagram above.

(iii) Carefully explain how the firm can produce the same output at a lower total cost. Illustrate this on the isoquant/isocost diagram above.

3. We have indicated that returns to scale are the major determinant of the shape of long-run average cost (LRAC). We showed that when output prices are fixed, LRAC is downward (upward) sloping when there are increasing (decreasing) returns to scale. In this problem, we investigate how constant returns to scale affects the shape of LRAC.

(i) Suppose the firm's technology is given by the production function

$$Q = \sqrt{K \cdot L} \ .$$

Graph the isoquants for the output levels $Q = 2,4,6$. (Hint—You need to find combinations of L and K that will give these values for Q in the formula of the production function. For example, both L=1, K=4 and L=2, K=2 yield Q=4 in the above formula, so both of these points are on the Q=4 isoquant.)

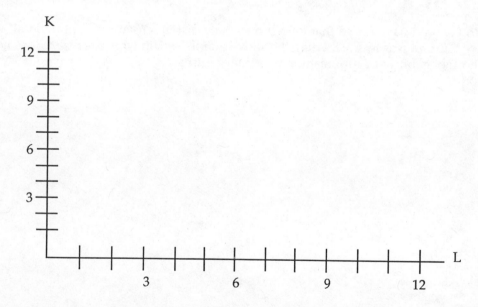

(ii) Suppose $P_L = \$3$/man-hour and $P_K = \$3$/machine-hour. On your isoquant map, graph the isocosts corresponding to TC = \$12, \$24, and \$36 to get three points on the expansion path. Sketch in the expansion path on your diagram.

(iii) Explain why this technology exhibits constant returns to scale.

(iv)   Using the three points found on the long-run expansion path, complete the table below and sketch the long-run average cost curve.

(v)   Using your isoquant map, find three of the firm's short-run production possibilities corresponding to the capital level K = 4. Complete the appropriate table below and sketch this SRAC curve on your graph from part (iv) to show its relationship to the LRAC curve.

L	K	LRTC	Q	LRAC

L	K	SRTC	Q	SRAC

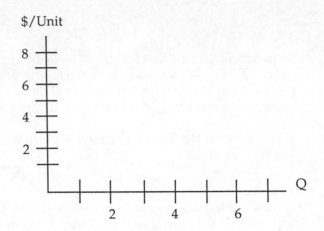

(vi)   You should have found that long-run average cost is constant (i.e., horizontal) when there are constant returns to scale. Using the above graph, explain why this result does not contradict the inevitability of diminishing marginal returns.

Solutions

1.(i)-(iii)

Figure 6c

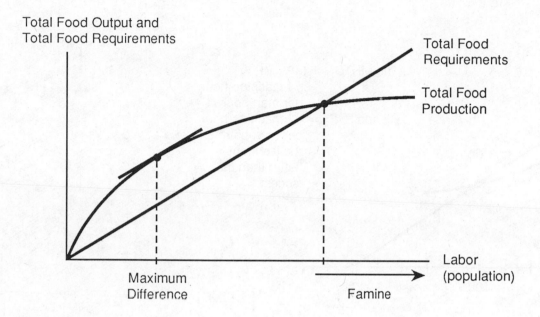

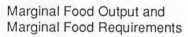

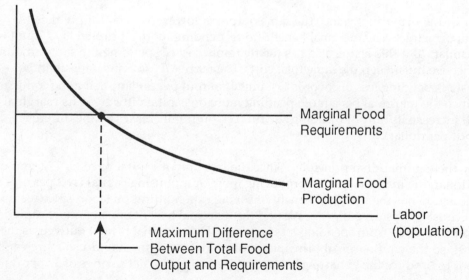

(iv) Malthus has confused the short run and the long run. Population growth is a long-run concept, but the pattern of diminishing marginal returns is only applicable to the short run when some inputs are fixed. Malthus has neglected increases in capital and increases in technology. Both of these would shift the total product curve upward, postponing the widespread famine.

2. (i)

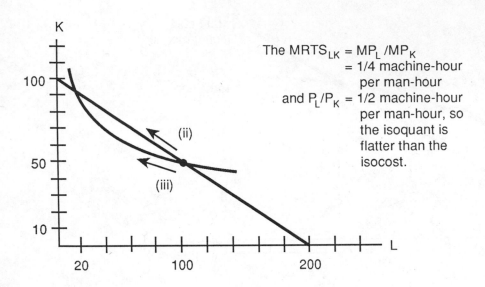

Figure 6d

The $MRTS_{LK} = MP_L/MP_K$
= 1/4 machine-hour per man-hour
and P_L/P_K = 1/2 machine-hour per man-hour, so the isoquant is flatter than the isocost.

(ii) First notice that MP_L/P_L = 1/4 unit of output per dollar and MP_K/P_K = 1/2 unit of output per dollar. This tells us capital is a better buy of output, so the firm should use more capital and less labor.

To see how the firm can produce the same output at lower total cost, apply the equimarginal principle. The marginal benefit from spending more on capital is 1/2 unit of output per dollar. But this action also has the marginal cost of spending the same amount less on labor, since we must keep the same total cost. The term MP_L/P_L indicates that the marginal cost of spending less on labor is 1/4 unit of output per dollar. Using the equimarginal principle, since the marginal benefit of spending more on capital outweighs its marginal cost, the firm will increase its output by doing so. (In fact, output increases by the difference, 1/4 unit of output per dollar).

(iii) Again apply the equimarginal principle. Since the last unit of capital gave us 1/2 unit of output per dollar, the marginal cost of producing more output using capital is $2 per unit of output. This action has the marginal benefit of saving expenditures on labor, since we must keep output constant. Using MP_L/P_L, we find the marginal benefit of using more capital is $4 per unit of output saved from spending less on labor. The marginal benefit outweighs the marginal cost, so the equimarginal principle implies that the firm should use more capital and less labor to produce the given level of output (resulting in a net savings of $2 per unit of output).

110

3. (i)-(ii)

Figure 6e

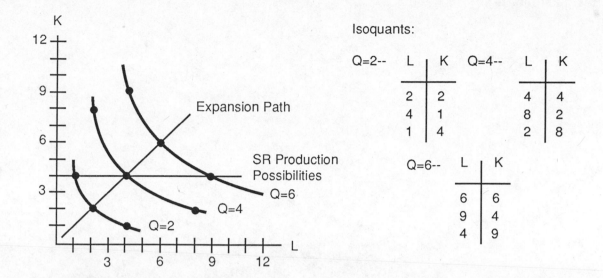

Isoquants:

Q=2--	L	K	Q=4--	L	K
	2	2		4	4
	4	1		8	2
	1	4		2	8

Q=6--	L	K
	6	6
	9	4
	4	9

(iii) Three points on the expansion path are (2,2), (4,4), and (6,6). Using the first two points, all inputs doubled and output also doubled from Q=2 to Q=4. Using the second two points, all factors increased by 50%, and output also increased by 50% from Q=4 to Q=6. By definition, this is constant returns to scale.

(iv)-(v)

Figure 6f

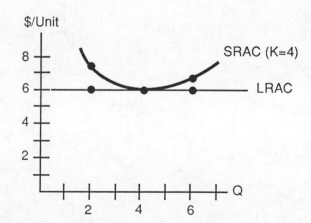

L	K	LRTC	Q	LRAC
2	2	12	2	6
4	4	24	4	6
6	6	36	6	6

L	K	SRTC	Q	SRAC
1	4	13	2	7.5
4	4	24	4	6
9	4	39	6	6.5

111

(vi) Diminishing marginal returns is a short-run concept; it only applies when there is at least one fixed input. The horizontal long-run average cost curve only reflects constant returns to scale, not marginal returns to labor. It does not contradict the inevitability of diminishing marginal returns or the shape of the short-run cost curves, as seen by the U-shaped short-run average cost curve. (If we had graphed marginal cost, it would be increasing, reflecting diminishing marginal returns.)

Solutions to Working Through the Graphs

Figure 6-1 From Production to Cost

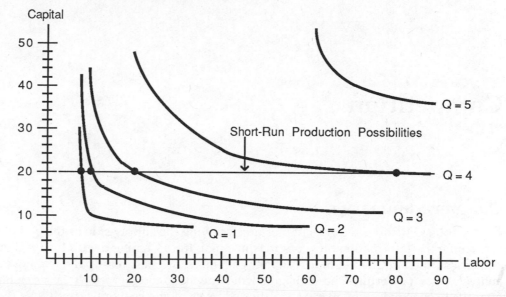

The Firm's Short-Run Production Choices (Capital fixed at K = 20)

Q	L	K
0	0 8	20
1	10	20
2	20	20
3	80	20
4		20

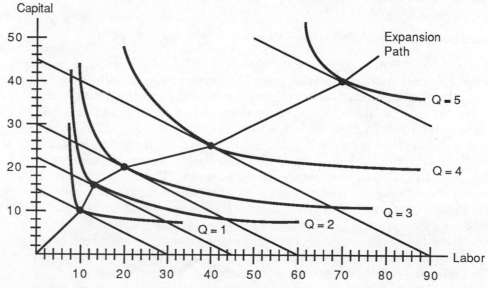

The Firm's Long-Run Production Choices (Wage = $1 per man-hour ; Rental = $2 per machine-hour)

Q	L	K
0	0	0
1	10	10
2	13	16
3	20	20
4	40	25
5	70	40

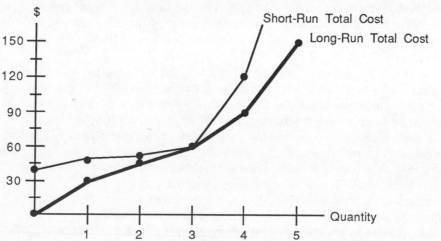

Short-Run and Long-Run Total Costs (Wage = $2 per man-hour; Rental = $1 per machine-hour)

Q	SRTC	LRTC
0	40	0
1	48	30
2	50	45
3	60	60
4	120	90
5		150

Chapter Seven

Competition

Chapter Summary

This chapter concludes a three-chapter unit studying the supply side of the goods market. By combining the information on profit maximization from Chapter 5 with the fundamentals of production and cost studied in Chapter 6, we can now gain more insights into supply, making our supply/demand analysis more powerful. These insights will allow us to more precisely describe how the price and quantity exchanged in the market are affected by changing economic conditions.

Section 7.1. The Competitive Firm

We say that a firm is *perfectly competitive* (or simply *competitive*) if the firm can sell any quantity of output at some particular market price. This typically occurs when the firm is so small in the market that it cannot appreciably affect the industry's total output and hence cannot influence the market price. So in effect, the competitive firm (like the competitive consumer) is a price taker; it simply chooses the quantity that will maximize its profits at that particular market price. Graphically, this assumption is shown by the demand for the firm's product being infinitely elastic (i.e., horizontal).

For a competitive firm, marginal revenue simply equals the market price. This is obvious from the definition of marginal revenue. Since the firm can sell any quantity desired at the market price, clearly the additional revenue brought in from selling the last unit must equal that market price. Recalling from Chapter 5 that any firm, if it chooses to produce any output at all, will maximize its profits by equating marginal cost and marginal revenue, we immediately conclude that the competitive firm would have maximum profits when marginal cost equals price.

This profit-maximizing condition is key to understanding the competitive firm's supply decision. We define the firm's *short-run supply curve (long-run supply curve)* as the set of price/quantity combinations that show the quantity supplied by the firm in the short run (long run) in response to any given price. But we have just seen that the competitive firm uses its marginal cost curve to determine what quantity to produce to maximize its profits. Combining these facts leads us to an important conclusion.

Recall that marginal cost shows the additional cost incurred from the last unit of production at any given quantity supplied, while supply shows the firm's quantity supplied at any given price. Since price equals marginal cost when the firm maximizes profits, these two curves must be the same. **Both marginal cost and supply represent the same set of price/quantity combinations. There is a duality between marginal cost and supply—they are different interpretations of the same curve.**

Our analysis of profit-maximizing behavior also indicates one important exception to this duality between supply and marginal cost—we must determine whether or not it is worthwhile for the firm to produce anything at all to properly describe the firm's supply.

For the case of short-run supply, recall that the firm's fixed costs are sunk and do not affect marginal cost or its short-run decision-making. Hence the firm should pursue production if its total revenues are at least as great as its variable costs. This occurs when price (which is the average revenue the firm receives from selling its product) is at least as great as average variable cost. When price falls below average variable cost, profits are insufficient at all levels of production and the firm should shut down. Combining this fact with the supply/marginal cost duality, we see that **the firm's short-run supply curve is the portion of the short-run marginal cost curve that lies above average variable cost.**

In the long run, there are no fixed costs, so production is worthwhile as long as the firm's total revenues are at least as great as its total costs. This implies that price must be at least as great as average cost for the firm to stay in the industry in the long run. Hence **the firm's long-run supply curve is the portion of the long-run marginal cost curve that lies above long-run average cost.**

Section 7.2. The Competitive Industry

In a *competitive industry*, (1) all firms are competitive and (2) any firm can freely enter or exit the industry in the long run. It is relatively straightforward to derive the short-run supply curve for the industry. For any given price, we must sum the quantities supplied by all firms in the industry. Graphically, this is shown by horizontally summing the firms' short-run supply curves.

There is one modification to this argument when the industry represents a substantial part of the demand for some factor of production. Suppose the industry increases its quantity supplied due to an increase in market price. There will then be higher demand for that factor of production, putting upward pressure on its price. This in turn raises the marginal costs of the firms in the industry. Using the supply/marginal cost duality, this implies lower supply for each firm in the industry, putting a downward pressure on quantity supplied. This situation is known as the *factor-price effect*—expansion in industry output forces up the price of a factor of production, raising marginal costs in the industry. Notice that the factor-price effect makes short-run industry supply less elastic, since the quantity supplied will increase by a lesser amount in response to a given increase in price.

Our analysis of the short-run supply in an industry shows us one of the advantages of using a competitive market system—**in a decentralized manner, the industry's short-run total cost of producing any level of output is minimized by the competitive market.**

To understand this, first notice what the equimarginal principle says about this cost-minimization problem. Making the short-run assumption that the number of firms is fixed, the industry's total cost of producing any given level of output will be the lowest when the marginal costs of firms are equalized. (For example, suppose the marginal cost at firm A were higher than the marginal cost in firm B. Then the marginal cost of increasing production at B would be exceeded by the marginal benefits from the savings achieved by producing the same amount less at firm A. So applying the equimarginal principle, total costs will be lowered if we move production from A to B.)

Now the individual firms aren't interested in the total costs in the industry; they only seek to maximize their profits. To do so, each equates its marginal cost to the market price. But since all firms in the industry are basing their decisions on the *same* market price, they end up equating all their marginal costs, which by the equimarginal principle indicates that the industry's total costs have been minimized. Without any intent or outside direction, profit-maximizing firms acting in their own self-interest produce the industry's output at the least possible total cost!

Section 7.3. The Competitive Industry in the Long Run

In a competitive industry in the long run, entry and exit of firms guarantee that profits will be driven to zero. Positive profits will attract new firms to the industry, putting upward pressure on quantity supplied and driving down price and profits. Negative profits will cause existing firms to exit the industry, lowering quantity supplied and putting upward pressure on price and profits.

Zero profits do not imply that more efficient firms do no better than less efficient firms. Suppose a firm's owner possesses an especially productive input, a better production process, or some other factor that gives his firm a comparative advantage not available to other firms. This firm will have lower *explicit* costs than other firms, but will have higher *opportunity* costs of using the factor in its own production instead of renting it out. The owner of the firm will benefit from earning economic *rent* (i.e., a payment to hire the factor), but when we measure cost correctly (as *opportunity cost*) the *profits* of the firm will still be zero.

So in the long run, all firms in the industry make zero economic profits (although the owners of some firms may be earning economic rent). When we consider the firm's long-run supply curve, we find there is only one place that corresponds to zero profits—the minimum of the long-run average cost curve. If we can discover how long-run average costs in an industry change as firms enter and exit in response to price changes, we will have discovered the pattern of long-run industry supply.

To do this analysis, we need one more definition. The *entry price* of a firm is that price at which a firm will be indifferent about entering an industry. Notice that more efficient firms (firms with a comparative advantage in an industry) will have lower entry prices than less efficient firms. With this concept, we can find four major cases that summarize the possibilities for an industry's long-run response to price changes.

Case 1—Identical Firms without any Factor-Price Effect. As firms enter and exit the industry, firms' long-run average costs and their entry prices are unaffected. As long as the market price equals the firms' entry price, the industry can support any number of firms to produce whatever quantity is desired. So long-run industry supply must be infinitely elastic (i.e., horizontal). Since the industry can produce any quantity at the same long-run average cost, we say this is a *constant cost industry*.

Case 2—Identical Firms with a Factor-Price Effect. As firms enter the industry, firms' long-run average costs will increase, forcing their entry price up. If market price increases above the entry price in the short run, firms will have the opportunity to make positive profits, and so will enter the industry in the long run. This will simultaneously put downward pressure on market price and upward pressure on firms' entry price. The industry will continue to expand until the market price again equals the (now higher) entry price and profits are returned to zero. So in this case, it takes a higher long-run price to get the industry to increase its output, and long-run industry supply must be upward sloping. Since higher quantities require higher long-run average costs in the industry, this is called an *increasing cost industry*.

Case 3—Non-Identical Firms. This time there are differing entry prices reflecting the difference in firms' efficiency. Again suppose that the market price rises above the entry price in the short run. This will encourage less efficient firms with higher entry prices to now enter this industry in the long run. As in Case 2, the industry expands until the market price equals the (now higher) entry price and profits are forced back to zero. Again the long-run industry supply curve is upward sloping. Also there are higher long-run average costs in the industry at higher output levels due to the entry of less efficient firms. This case gives another way that an *increasing cost industry* can occur.

Case 4—Cost Advantages Created by Entry. In this case, entry of firms causes new, more efficient sub-industries to be created, allowing firms to get a factor of production at lower cost, lowering average costs and entry prices. If the market price rises above the entry price in the short run, we will again have industry expansion as in the previous cases. Long-run equilibrium will be reached when the market price equals the (now lower) entry price, and the industry long-run supply curve will be downward sloping. This is called a *decreasing cost industry*, since higher output levels result in lower long-run average costs for the industry.

Working Through the Graphs—Constant Cost and Increasing Cost Industries

The long-run supply responses of an industry combine many of the ideas we have developed in previous chapters, so students frequently lose track of the various pieces of the puzzle. Complete the following steps to get a better idea of how to organize your thoughts when working out the long-run responses of an industry to changing economic conditions.

Figure 7-1.

Step 1. Suppose initially the industry is in the equilibrium where the market price and quantity are determined by the intersection of the demand curve D and the supply curve S. Verify that the entries in the accompanying table correctly describe this initial equilibrium shown by the graphs. Notice that since firms are making zero profits, this is indeed a long-run equilibrium.

Step 2. Now suppose that demand increases to D', creating a new short-run equilibrium. First locate the new equilibrium in the market, determine the new price and quantity, and place these two entries in the accompanying table.

Next, show how the firm reacts to this change in demand. To do this, in the second firm diagram draw the new marginal revenue curve, locate the new quantity supplied, and calculate the short-run profits of the firm. If you've done this correctly, you should find the firm produces 6 units at an average cost of \$2.50/unit and a price of \$4/unit. Summarize your short-run results in the table; notice that there is not sufficient time for entry and exit in the short run so the number of firms hasn't changed.

Step 3. Now consider the long run in which firms will enter the industry, attracted by the positive short-run profits. To find the new long-run price, there are two things to consider: how market supply changes and how firms' costs change. First notice that when firms enter, this will increase market supply, putting downward pressure on price. Second, in a constant cost industry, a firm's costs remain unaffected by the expansion in the industry, so the firm's cost curves do not change. The new long-run price will be where zero profits are reestablished; this must be at the minimum of average cost. So the new long-run price is again \$2/unit.

To diagram this, start with the market diagram and show supply increasing to a new supply curve S' (representing the entry of firms); make sure your new equilibrium shows the long-run equilibrium price of \$2/unit being reestablished. Next, complete the firm's diagram, showing the new marginal revenue curve and the corresponding quantity supplied. Verify that the firm's profits have indeed returned to zero. Finally summarize your results in the table; you should find that 140 firms are producing a total of 700 units in the new long-run equilibrium.

Step 4. In the market diagram, we now have two long-run equilibrium points. Since these each give the quantity that the industry is willing to supply in the long run at some price, they are both on the long-run supply curve. Connect these two points to get the long-run supply curve. You should find that long-run supply is horizontal for the competitive constant cost industry we have examined.

Figure 7-2.

Step 1. Again verify that the table's summary of the initial equilibrium determined by the demand curve D and the supply curve S is correct.

Figure 7-1 The Constant Cost Industry

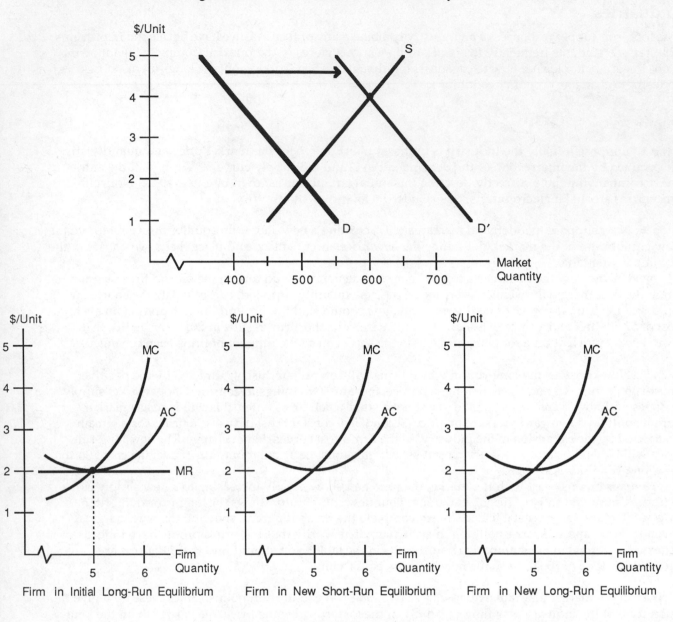

Firm in Initial Long-Run Equilibrium

Firm in New Short-Run Equilibrium

Firm in New Long-Run Equilibrium

	Market Price	Market Quantity	Firm Output	Firm Profits	Number of Firms
Initial Long-Run Equilibrium	$2/unit	500 units	5 units	$0	100 firms
New Short-Run Equilibrium					
New Long-Run Equilibrium					

Figure 7-2 The Increasing Cost Industry

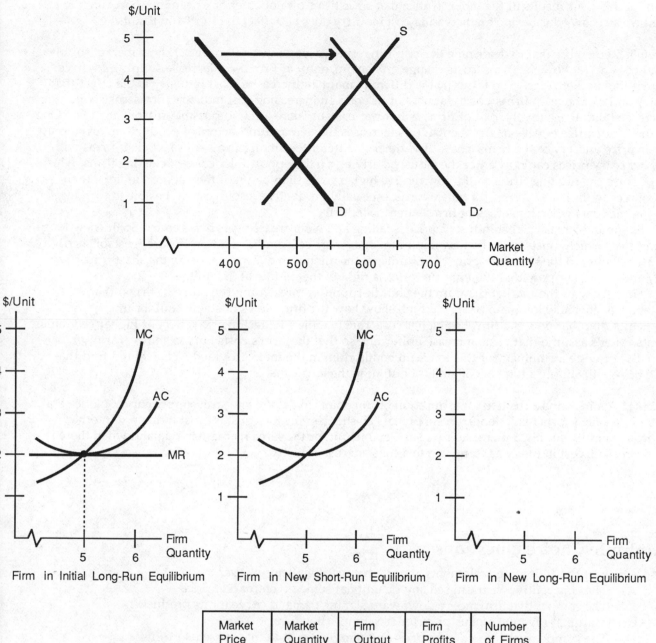

Firm in Initial Long-Run Equilibrium

Firm in New Short-Run Equilibrium

Firm in New Long-Run Equilibrium

	Market Price	Market Quantity	Firm Output	Firm Profits	Number of Firms
Initial Long-Run Equilibrium	$2/unit	500 units	5 units	$0	100 firms
New Short-Run Equilibrium					
New Long-Run Equilibrium					

Step 2. We again suppose that demand increases to D', creating a new short-run equilibrium. As before, find the new short-run market equilibrium, diagram the firm's viewpoint of this equilibrium, and summarize your results in the table. Notice that since firms do not enter or exit in the short run, the fact that we are now considering an increasing cost industry does not affect the short-run results.

Step 3. Remember that to determine the long-run response, you must determine (1) how market supply changes and (2) how the firms' costs change. As before, entry of firms will increase supply and drive down the market price. The thing that is different about an increasing cost industry is the effect that entry and exit have on firms' costs—as new firms enter an increasing cost industry, firms' costs will increase (and alternatively, exit of firms will lower costs). There are two possible reasons for this. One is the factor-price effect—as firms enter, this increases the demand for factors of production, driving up their price and hence the firms' costs. The other is differences among firms—less efficient firms with higher entry prices can now enter the industry, driving up the opportunity costs of existing firms. This is because the existing firms could now receive higher rents than before if they choose to lease their resources to these new firms. In other words, especially productive resources will be able to earn higher economic rents when less efficient firms enter the industry.

So for an increasing cost industry, price is falling and costs are rising as firms enter. So the new long-run price (which must equal the new minimum of average cost so that zero profits are reestablished) must be between the short-run price of $4/unit and the minimum of average cost in the short run of $2/unit. Let's suppose that the long-run price is right in the middle at $3/unit.

First show in the market diagram the shift in supply (representing the entry of firms) that establishes this new long-run price. Second, show how the firm views this new equilibrium, remembering that now the firm has higher costs due to either the factor-price effect or higher economic rents. (Let's assume that costs increase uniformly, so that the firm's costs curves shift vertically.) Finally, provide a summary of this long-run equilibrium in the table provided. You should find that 130 firms will supply a total of 650 units of output in the long run.

Step 4. Again connect the two long-run equilibrium points to get the long-run supply curve. Notice that the higher firm costs made long-run supply less elastic than for the constant cost industry. In other words, quantity supplied increases by a smaller amount for the same increase in demand when there is an increasing cost industry as compared to a constant cost industry.

Multiple Choice Questions

1. Which of the following statements about a competitive firm is *false*?
   A. The competitive firm can sell any quantity at some given market price.
   B. The competitive firm faces a downward sloping demand curve for its product.
   C. Marginal revenue equals price for the competitive firm.
   D. The competitive firm equates price and marginal cost to maximize its profits.

2. A competitive firm's marginal cost is U-shaped and equals marginal revenue at the quantities Q_1 and Q_2. The firm should
   A. always produce Q_1.
   B. always produce Q_2.
   C. produce Q_2 only if the losses on the first Q_1 units are outweighed by the profits gained on the units between Q_1 and Q_2.
   D. produce either Q_1 or Q_2, since both yield the same profits.

3. A competitive firm's supply curve also reflects
   A. the firm's marginal costs at various output levels.
   B. the firm's marginal costs at various price levels.
   C. the firm's marginal revenues at various output levels.
   D. the firm's marginal revenues at various price levels.

4. It is worthwhile for the competitive firm to produce in the short run as long as
   A. its total revenues exceed its total costs, since positive profits are then guaranteed.
   B. its total revenues exceed its fixed costs, since the variable costs are sunk.
   C. its total revenues exceed its variable costs, since the fixed costs are sunk.
   D. its marginal revenue exceeds its marginal cost.

5. In the short run a competitive firm will shut down if the market price is below _____, while in the long run the firm will exit the industry if the market price is below _____.
   A. average cost; long-run average cost
   B. average cost; long-run marginal cost
   C. average variable cost; long-run average cost
   D. average variable cost; long-run marginal cost

6. Which of the following statements about a competitive industry's short-run supply is *false?*
   A. The number of firms in the industry is variable, since we must account for entry and exit of firms.
   B. The individual firms' supply curves are horizontally summed.
   C. The quantities supplied by firms are summed at each and every price.
   D. The factor-price effect must be accounted for if the industry makes up a substantial part of the demand for some input.

7. The factor-price effect will make industry supply _____ elastic, since increased industry output will _____ marginal costs.
   A. more; increase
   B. more; decrease
   C. less; increase
   D. less; decrease

8. In short-run competitive equilibrium, the industry-wide costs of production by the fixed number of firms is minimized. This is because
   A. each firm applies the equimarginal principle to minimize the total costs incurred by the industry.
   B. each firm attempts to minimize costs, making marginal costs equal throughout the industry.
   C. each firm attempts to maximize profits, so all equate their marginal cost to the same market price.
   D. each firm attempts to maximize profits, and so must minimize its own total costs.

9. If there is an increase in fixed costs, the short-run industry supply curve will
   A. decrease in the short run, and decrease further in the long run.
   B. decrease in the short run, but not shift further in the long run.
   C. remain unchanged in the short run, but decrease in the long run.
   D. remain unchanged in both the short run and the long run.

10. If there is an increase in the price of raw materials, the short-run industry supply curve will
    A. decrease in the short run, and decrease further in the long run.
    B. decrease in the short run, but not shift further in the long run.
    C. remain unchanged in the short run, but decrease in the long run.
    D. remain unchanged in both the short run and the long run.

11. Which of the following statements on long-run competitive equilibrium is *false*?
    A. All firms make zero economic profits.
    B. All firms make zero economic rents.
    C. All firms produce where marginal revenue equals marginal cost.
    D. All firms produce where long-run average cost is minimized.

12. When will long-run industry supply be upward sloping?
    A. When long-run average costs in the industry increase as output is expanded.
    B. When firms are identical and there is a factor-price effect.
    C. When firms have different entry prices.
    D. All of the above

13. For a competitive constant cost industry,
    A. long-run supply is more elastic than short-run supply but is not perfectly elastic.
    B. long-run supply is less elastic than short-run supply but is not perfectly elastic.
    C. long-run supply is infinitely elastic.
    D. long-run supply is downward sloping.

14. What could cause a competitive industry to be a decreasing cost industry?
    A. The development of sub-industries as the industry expands.
    B. The factor-price effect.
    C. Increasing returns to scale in the firms' production processes.
    D. Differing quality of inputs across firms.

15. If an excise tax (i.e., a per unit tax) is imposed on firms in a competitive constant cost industry, _____ of the tax will be passed on to consumers in the short run and _____ of the tax will be passed on to consumers in the long run.
    A. none; none
    B. all; all
    C. part; all
    D. part; more but still not all

Solutions

1. B. The demand for a competitive firm's product is horizontal at the given market price.

2. C. Marginal cost exceeds marginal revenue before Q_1, so the firm has losses on these units. Between Q_1 and Q_2, marginal revenue exceeds marginal cost, so the firm gets profits on these units. These profits must exceed the losses on the first units for production to be worthwhile to the firm.

3. A. Supply and marginal cost are essentially different interpretations of the same curve. Supply uses price as the independent variable, while marginal cost treats quantity supplied as the independent variable.

4. C. The fixed costs are sunk, so only the variable costs affect the firm's economic decision-making in the short run.

5. C. In the short run, when price exceeds average variable cost, total revenues exceed variable costs and production is worthwhile (the fixed costs are irrelevant in the short run). In the long run, when price exceeds average cost, then total revenues exceed total costs and production is worthwhile (there are no fixed costs in the long run).

6. A. The number of firms is fixed in the short run. Entry and exit are treated as a long-run phenomenon.

7. C. As output expands, this puts upward pressure on the price of a resource. This raises firms' marginal costs and in part offsets the increase in output.

8. C. The equimarginal principle implies that firms' marginal costs should be equalized for the industry to have minimum costs. Competition achieves this in a decentralized way through the profit-maximizing behavior of firms.

9. C. Fixed costs do not affect firms' marginal costs, so their supply is unaffected in the short run. In the long run, some firms will leave the industry due to negative profits, causing supply to decrease.

10. A. The increase in the price of raw materials will increase firms' marginal costs, causing their supply to shift left. In the long run, some firms will leave the industry due to negative profits, causing supply to decrease.

11. B. More efficient firms with especially productive resources will have higher opportunity costs of using those resources in its production. These higher opportunity costs will cause more efficient firms to have zero profits like the less efficient firms, but the owners of the especially productive resources will be paid economic rent.

12. D. Since profits are zero in the long run, long-run industry supply follows the same pattern as the industry's long-run average costs. Factor-price effects and differing entry costs are two ways an increasing cost industry can occur.

13. C. For a competitive constant cost industry, the long-run average costs in the industry are unchanged as firms enter and exit. This allows any quantity to be supplied in the long run at the minimum of firms' long-run average costs which is their entry price.

14. A. For decreasing cost industries, long-run average costs in the industry are falling as industry output expands. One way this can happen is that the industry becomes large enough to support a sub-industry that can provide a factor of production at lower cost.

15. C. Marginal cost, average cost, short-run supply, and long-run supply all increase by the amount of the tax. The intersection of demand and short-run supply will be higher by an amount less than the tax. The intersection of demand and long-run supply will be higher by the full amount of the tax.

Questions for Review

1. Compare and contrast a competitive firm's marginal cost with the firm's supply curve.

2. In the short run, at what market prices will the competitive firm earn (a) positive profits, (b) zero profits, (c) economic losses (but still continues to produce goods), and (d) shut down production?

3. Explain why it might be better for the firm to produce and earn economic losses in the short run instead of simply shutting down.

4. Explain why a factor-price effect tends to make industry supply less elastic.

5. We would expect that a more efficient firm would be doing better than a less efficient firm, but both earn zero profits in the long run. Resolve this apparent contradiction.

6. What is the connection between the long-run average costs in an industry and the industry's long-run supply?

7. Describe situations in which the long-run average costs in an industry would (a) increase, (b) decrease, and (c) remain constant as firms enter the industry. What names do we give to these situations?

Solutions

1. Since competitive firms maximize profits at the quantity where price equals marginal cost, the price/quantity combinations on the supply curve are also on the marginal cost curve. However, supply treats price as the independent variable on this curve, while marginal cost treats quantity supplied as the independent variable. Supply must also consider whether or not it is worthwhile for the firm to produce output, so supply considers only those points above average variable cost in the short run and those points above long-run average cost in the long run.

2. Recall that price represent average or per unit revenue. So if price exceeds average cost, the firm earns positive profits. If price equals average cost, the per unit and total profits are zero. To see if production is worthwhile in the short run, fixed costs are unimportant. So the firm will produce with economic losses if price is below average cost and above average variable cost. The firm will shut down if price falls below average variable cost.

3. Since fixed costs are sunk, they are irrelevant to the firm's economic decision making. As long as the firm's total revenue exceeds its variable costs, the firm will be able to recover at least part of its fixed costs. Hence production will benefit the firm even if it does not recover all of its fixed costs and makes economic losses.

4. When an industry makes up a substantial proportion of demand for some factor of production, higher industry output will put upward pressure on the price of that factor. This will increase firms' marginal costs, putting downward pressure on the firms' output levels. Since a given price increase will result in a smaller quantity response by the industry when this occurs, supply will be less elastic when there is a factor-price effect.

5. The more efficient firm has access or ownership of some particularly productive input or technology. Although this firm may have lower explicit costs than the less efficient firm, it will have higher opportunity costs of using this resource or technology instead of renting it out. So both firms will earn zero profits, but the owner of the especially productive input or technology will be paid its higher opportunity cost, called economic rent.

6. Profits are zero in the long run for firms in a competitive industry, and this occurs precisely when price equals the minimum of firms' long-run average cost curves. So long-run price will be higher, lower, or constant as the industry expands its output depending on whether firms' long-run average costs are increasing, decreasing, or remaining constant as firms enter the industry.

7. Long-run average costs increase when differences among firms or factor-price effects cause firms' long-run average costs to increase as firms enter the industry; industries where these occur are called increasing cost industries. Long-run average costs will decrease when expansion of the industry permits the development of sub-industries that can provide factors of production at lower costs; industries of this type are called decreasing cost industries. If all firms are identical and there are no factor-price effects, the industry can produce any level of output at the same average cost simply by increasing or decreasing the number of firms; this is the case of the constant cost industry.

Problems for Analysis

1. Suppose a firm has two plants, one in Albany and one in Buffalo. Let MC_A and MC_B denote the marginal cost schedules at the Albany and Buffalo plants, respectively. The two marginal cost schedules are not necessarily identical.

   (i) Suppose the firm wants to produce a given level of output at the lowest possible cost. Use the equimarginal principle to explain why the firm should divide its production between the two plants so that the marginal costs of production are equated (i.e., so that $MC_A = MC_B$).

   (ii) Suppose the marginal cost schedules at the Albany and Buffalo plants are given by the formulas

   $$MC_A = 3q_A \text{ and } MC_B = 6q_B$$

   where q_A and q_B are the quantities produced at the Albany and Buffalo plants, respectively. Show that the firm will always produce 2/3 of its output at Albany and the other 1/3 of its output at Buffalo.

   (iii) Show that this firm's marginal cost schedule (which determines its supply schedule) is given by the formula

   $$MC = 2q$$

   where q is the total quantity produced by the firm.

   (iv) If these two plants were in actuality separate competitive firms, what could you predict about the quantities they would supply to the market? Explain.

125

2. (i) Consider a competitive constant cost industry initially in long-run equilibrium. For each of the following situations, use a supply/demand diagram to determine how market price and quantity will be affected in both the short run and long run.

a. A recession causes a decrease in demand.

$/Unit

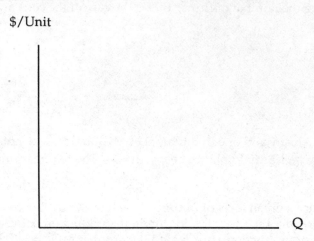

b. The government imposes an annual licensing fee on all firms in the industry.

$/Unit

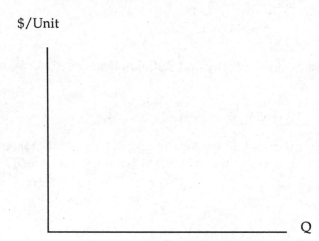

c. The government grants an excise subsidy to all firms in the industry.

$/Unit

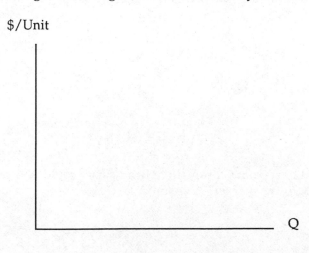

(ii) Repeat part (i) for a competitive increasing cost industry.

a. $/Unit

b. $/Unit

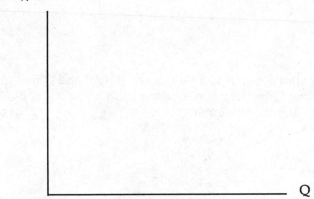

c. $/Unit

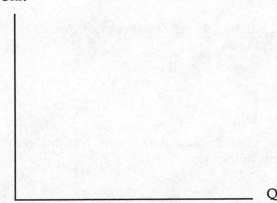

3. Consider a competitive constant cost industry in which all firms are identical. Each firm's marginal and average cost is given by

$$MC = 4q \text{ and } AC = 2q + (50/q)$$

where q is the firm's quantity supplied.

(i) Determine the market price and the quantity supplied by each firm in the long run.

(ii) Suppose the market demand for the good produced by this industry is given by

$$P = 320 - 2Q$$

where Q is the quantity exchanged in the market. Using your answer to part (i), find the quantity exchanged and the number of firms in the long run.

(iii) Ignoring the possibility of shut down, find a formula relating P and Q that gives the short-run market supply corresponding to the long-run equilibrium in part (ii). (Hint—Combine the equations $P = MC$ and $Q = $ (number of firms) $\cdot q$.)

(iv) Suppose market demand increases to

$$P = 480 - 2Q.$$

Using your answer to part (iii), find the new market price, quantity exchanged, and profits made by each firm in the short run.

(v) Using your answer to part (i), find the new market price, quantity exchanged, and the number of firms in the new long-run equilibrium.

Solutions

1. (i) Suppose that the firm divides its output so that MC_A is greater than MC_B. Since the Buffalo plant has the lower marginal cost, this indicates that the firm should move output away from the Albany plant to the Buffalo plant. The marginal benefit (in the form of reduced costs) of producing less in Albany is MC_A \$/unit; the marginal cost of producing the same amount more in Buffalo is MC_B \$/unit. Since the marginal benefit of switching output from Albany to Buffalo outweighs the marginal cost, the firm will improve its situation (i.e., will lower its total costs while producing the same level of output). A similar argument would apply if the firm divided its output so that MC_B were greater than MC_A. By the equimarginal principle, the cost-minimizing way for the firm to produce any level of output is to equate the marginal costs of the two firms.

    (ii) Let q denote the firm's total output, so that $q = q_A + q_B$, which can be rewritten as $q_B = q - q_A$. Since the firm will produce output so that $MC_A = MC_B$, using the given formulas for marginal cost we have $3q_A = 6q_B$. Substituting for q_B, we get $3q_A = 6(q - q_A)$. This simplifies to $3q_A = 6q - 6q_A$, which can be rewritten as $9q_A = 6q$. Dividing both sides by 9 yields $q_A = (2/3)q$. So the amount produced in Albany (q_A) is 2/3 the total amount produced (q). This leaves the other 1/3 to be produced in Buffalo.

    (iii) If the last unit is produced in the Albany plant, its marginal cost will be $MC_A = 3q_A = 3 \cdot (2/3)q = 2q$. If the last unit is produced in the Buffalo plant, its marginal cost will be $MC_B = 6q_B = 6 \cdot (1/3)q = 2q$. Since the firm equates marginal costs to minimize the total cost of producing its output q, it does not matter which plant we consider as having produced the last unit, and the marginal cost of production is $MC = 2q$.

    (iv) If the two plants were separate competitive firms, each would equate its marginal cost to the same market price, making their marginal costs equal to each other. So we would still expect he Albany plant to produce twice as much output as the Buffalo plant as in part (ii).

2. Long-run supply is horizontal for a competitive constant cost industry and is upward sloping for an increasing cost industry. The intersection of demand and short-run supply will indicate the effect on price and quantity in the short run. The intersection of demand and long-run supply will indicate the effect on price and quantity in the long run; notice that as firms enter or exit, the short-run supply curve will shift to this intersection.

Figure 7a

a.
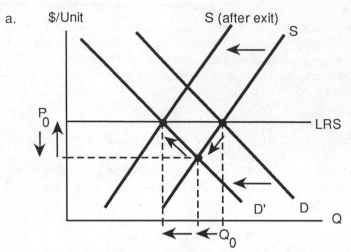

The decrease in demand will lower price and lower output in the short run. Due to negative profits, firms will exit the industry in the long run, forcing output down further and price back up to the original level.

b.
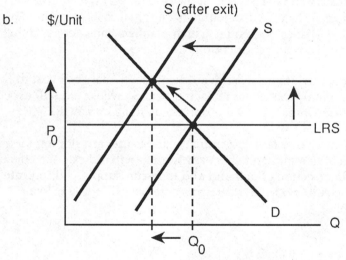

We treat the licensing fee as a new fixed cost. Since fixed costs do not affect marginal cost, supply and the market equilibrium do not change in the short run. However, the fee does raise firms' long-run average costs and their entry price, so long-run supply shifts up. Firms exit the industry in the long run, forcing price up and industry output down.

c.
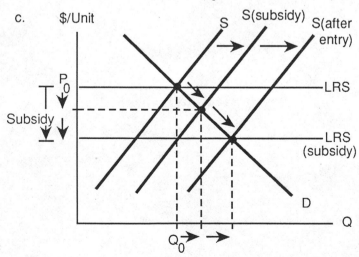

In this case, the firms' variable costs have fallen. This decreases marginal cost, causing an increase in short-run supply, which increases industry output, profits, and the net price producers receive (including the subsidy). Since the price plus subsidy has risen above firms' entry price, firms enter the industry, driving the price down. Notice that the entire subsidy has been passed on to consumers.

Figure 7b

a.

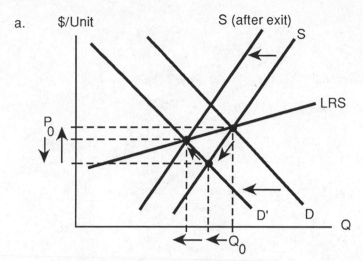

This is the same as in part (i), except that the price does not rise back fully to the original level. This is because the remaining firms either have lower entry prices or have lower average costs due to the factor-price effect.

b.

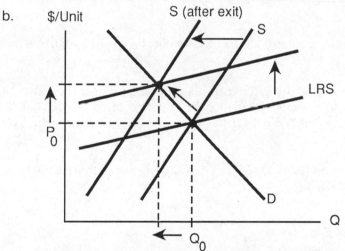

This is the same as in part (i), except that the price does not rise as much in the long run as in the constant cost industry. Again this is because the remaining firms either have lower entry prices or have lower average costs due to the factor-price effect.

c.

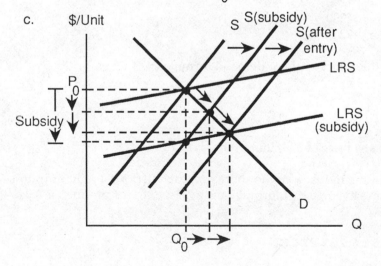

This is the same as in part (i), except that the subsidy is not fully passed on to consumers in the long run. This is because part of the subsidy is used to offset the higher costs of firms caused by the factor-price effect or by the entry of less efficient firms.

3. (i) In the long run, the firm will produce the quantity where average cost is a minimum, which is the only quantity where MC = AC. Using this formula, we have the following string of equations:

$$4q = 2q + (50/q)$$

(Multiplying by q) $\quad 4q^2 = 2q^2 + 50$

$$2q^2 = 50$$

(Dividing by 2) $\quad q^2 = 25$

(Taking square root) $\quad q = 5$.

Since in long run equilibrium P = MC = AC, substituting for q we get

$$P = AC = 2q + (50/q) = 2 \cdot 5 + (50/5) = 10 + 10 = 20$$
or $\quad P = MC = 4q = 4 \cdot 5 = 20$.

So the long-run price is \$20/unit and each firm produces 5 units.

(ii) Substituting the long-run price from part (i) into the demand curve, we get the following equations:

$$20 = 320 - 2Q$$
$$2Q = 300$$
$$Q = 150$$.

Since each firm produces 5 units in the long run for a total of 150 units, the number of firms must be 150/5 or 30 firms.

(iii) Since firms use P = MC to maximize profits, using the formula for marginal cost the individual firm's supply decision is given by the formula P = 4q. Since the number of firms is fixed at 30 in the short run, q = (1/30)Q. Substituting yields P = 4 · (1/30)Q or P = 2Q/15 as the industry's short-run supply.

(iv) We have supply (P = 2Q/15) and demand (P = 480 - 2Q). Equating these two to find the new short-run equilibrium, we get the following:

$$2Q/15 = 480 - 2Q$$

(Multiplying by 15) $\quad 2Q = 7200 - 30Q$

$$32Q = 7200$$

(Dividing by 32) $\quad Q = 225$.

To get the market price, now use either the supply or demand formulas,

$$P = 2 \cdot 225/15 = 450/15 = 30$$
or $\quad P = 480 - 2 \cdot 225 = 480 - 450 = 30$.

So the industry produces 225 units at a price of \$30/unit in the short run.

Since there are 30 identical firms in the industry in the short run, each firm's share in output is 225/30 or 7 1/2 units. Using the firm's average cost formula, the average cost of producing 7 1/2 units is

$$AC = 2 \cdot (7\ 1/2) + 50/(7\ 1/2) = 15 + 6\ 2/3 = 21\ 2/3.$$

132

So profits must equal

$$(P - AC) \cdot q = (30 - 21\ 2/3) \cdot 7\ 1/2$$
$$= 8\ 1/3 \cdot 7\ 1/2 = 62\ 1/2.$$

So the firm produces 7 1/2 units at a price of $30 per unit and an average cost of $21 2/3 per unit, resulting in total profits of $62 1/2.

(v)   For a competitive constant cost industry, the long-run price is constant at the minimum of firms' average cost. As shown in part (i), the long run price is $20/unit. Substituting this into the new demand curve, we get

$$20 = 480 - 2Q$$
$$2Q = 460$$
$$Q = 230.$$

As shown in part (i), each firm produces 5 units in the long run, so there must be 230/5 or 46 firms.

Solutions to Working Through the Graphs

Figure 7-1   The Constant Cost Industry

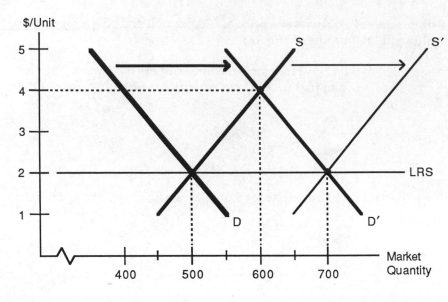

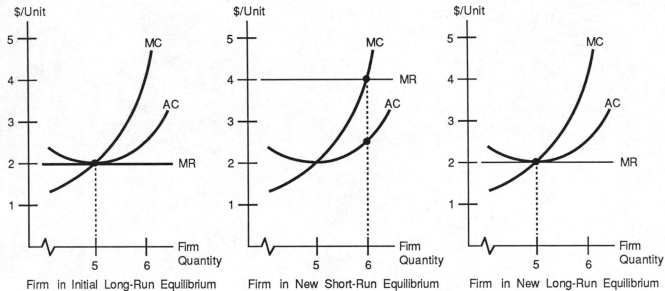

Firm in Initial Long-Run Equilibrium   Firm in New Short-Run Equilibrium   Firm in New Long-Run Equilibrium

	Market Price	Market Quantity	Firm Output	Firm Profits	Number of Firms
Initial Long-Run Equilibrium	$2/unit	500 units	5 units	$0	100 firms
New Short-Run Equilibrium	$4/unit	600 units	6 units	$9	100 firms
New Long-Run Equilibrium	$2/unit	700 units	5 units	$0	140 firms

Figure 7-2 The Increasing Cost Industry

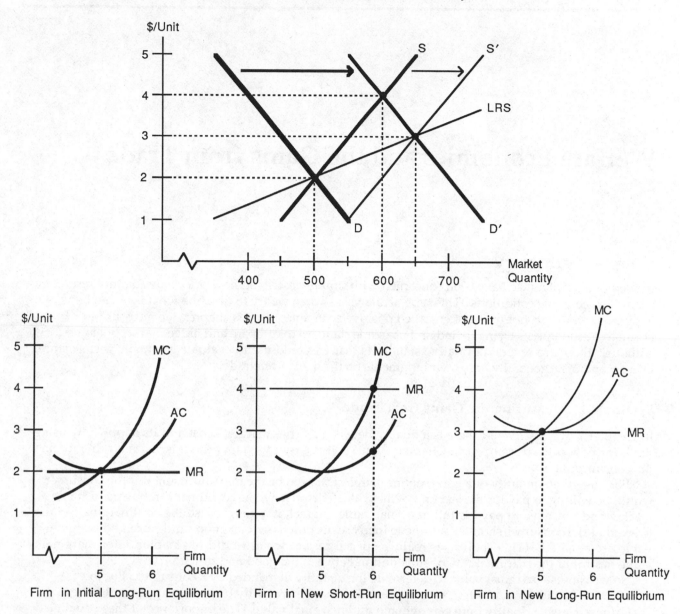

Firm in Initial Long-Run Equilibrium

Firm in New Short-Run Equilibrium

Firm in New Long-Run Equilibrium

	Market Price	Market Quantity	Firm Output	Firm Profits	Number of Firms
Initial Long-Run Equilibrium	$2/unit	500 units	5 units	$0	100 firms
New Short-Run Equilibrium	$4/unit	600 units	6 units	$9	100 firms
New Long-Run Equilibrium	$3/unit	650 units	5 units	$0	130 firms

Chapter Eight

Welfare Economics and the Gains from Trade

Chapter Summary

In previous chapters we have been concerned with simply describing how price and quantity respond to changing economic conditions. This type of analysis—when we try to describe what is or can be happening in the economy—is often called positive economics. In this chapter, we now turn to normative economics—trying to find and use some standard to compare and judge market outcomes. Although there are several normative standards that we could use to evaluate economic performance, microeconomists generally base their judgments on the gains from trade.

Section 8.1. Measuring the Gains from Trade

In Chapter 7, we discovered there is a duality between a firm's marginal cost and its supply. By using the information we developed in Chapters 3 and 4, it is easy to see that there is a similar duality on the consumption side.

For any given quantity of a good, define *marginal value* to be the maximum amount the consumer would be willing to pay for the last unit of the good. Fortunately, the consumer can buy goods in the market and not have to pay his full marginal value. In fact, it is easy to use the equimarginal principle to see that the consumer should continue to increase his purchases of a good until price and marginal value are equated. (This analysis is really a special case of what we did in Chapter 3, for marginal value is simply the marginal rate of substitution between the good and dollars.)

So we can use marginal value to determine the quantity demanded by a consumer. But this is precisely what the demand curve tells us! **Just like there is a duality between supply and marginal cost, there is also a duality between demand and marginal value.** The importance of these dualities should not be underestimated. One consequence of understanding the supply/marginal cost and demand/marginal value dualities is that they allow us to measure the gains from trade.

Consumers' surplus measures the consumers' gains from trade; it is their total net gain (measured in dollars) from purchasing and consuming a good rather than doing without. The net gain that consumers receive from each unit of the good is the difference between the marginal value the consumers place on that unit and the price they pay for it. By adding up all the net gains from all units purchased, we have a measure of the consumers' gains from trade or consumers' surplus. Using the duality between demand and marginal value, we see that geometrically consumers' surplus is the area under the demand curve down to the price paid and out to the quantity demanded.

Producers' surplus measures the producers' gains from trade; it is their total net gain (measured in dollars) from producing and selling a good rather than producing nothing. By comparing price and marginal cost we can measure the producers' net gain from each unit produced and sold, and by summing all of these net gains we can measure producers' surplus. As with the consumption side, the duality between supply and marginal cost allows us to have a visual representation of producer's surplus. It is the area above the supply curve up to the price received and out to the quantity supplied.

The sum of the consumers' and producers' surplus (along with any gains from trade received by any other market participants such as tax recipients) is called the *social gain* or *welfare gain* from the market. Social gain provides a convenient way of measuring the total gains from trade generated by the market system, telling us how much wealth or surplus value was created for society's members in the course of our trading.

Using these measurements of surplus value, we can derive two criteria for comparing different market outcomes under alternative policies. The first of these is the *Pareto criterion*, which says that one market outcome is better than another only if every individual agrees that it is preferable. When a situation is deemed better than another under the Pareto criterion, we say it is *Pareto-preferred;* when there is no situation that everyone can agree is better than the current one, we say that it is *Pareto-optimal*. For example, if you and I can find a mutually agreeable trade, the post-trade situation would be Pareto-preferred to the pre-trade situation. If we cannot find a mutually agreeable trade, then this would be Pareto-optimal since there is no situation that we can both agree is preferable to the current one. Furthermore, notice that there could easily be more than one Pareto-optimal situation.

The second welfare-based normative criterion is called the *efficiency criterion*. This says that one market outcome is "better" than another if it creates more social gain; we say the former situation is *more efficient* than the latter. When an economic policy makes the market less efficient, the reduction in social gain that results is called the *deadweight loss*.

Notice the difference between the efficiency and Pareto criteria—the former only looks at the total surplus value created while the latter considers each individual's. If a policy causes some people to gain and others to lose, it cannot be Pareto-preferred to the current situation, but there will be a more efficient result if the winners' gains outweigh the losers' losses. Since most economic policies create both winners and losers, you will find the efficiency criterion being applied more often than the Pareto criterion to choose between different policies.

Section 8.2. The Invisible Hand

We have all heard economists (among others) extol the virtues of competition. By using the two normative criteria we developed in the previous section, we can now make some judgments as to how well the competitive market works and see why economists so strongly promote free trade.

It should be easy to see that the supply/demand equilibrium gives the most efficient outcome possible. We cannot make the social gain—the sum of consumers' and producers' surplus—any larger. Producing more or less than the equilibrium output level would create a deadweight loss.

Furthermore, the competitive market equilibrium is also Pareto-optimal. (Notice that if it were not efficient, it could not be Pareto-optimal.) We cannot give more surplus value to consumers without taking it away from producers, and *vice versa*. Since we cannot redistribute the gains from trade in a way that everyone would agree to, we have a Pareto-optimal distribution.

So using either the efficiency or Pareto criteria, competition can't be beat. However, this analysis is limited because it is only partial equilibrium analysis—analysis that focuses on a single market and ignores the effects between this and other markets. If we analyze *all* markets simultaneously—a process called *general equilibrium analysis*—would the competitive outcome still be judged so highly?

The answer is yes—the competitive outcome is both efficient and Pareto-optimal, even when all markets are considered. This result is called the *First Fundamental Theorem of Welfare Economics* or the *Invisible Hand Theorem*, and it is truly beautiful and incredible. Without any outside guidance or intervention, individuals and firms acting in their own self-interests produce a result that is best (using the efficiency and Pareto criteria) for society as a whole.

Although it would take advanced mathematical techniques to prove the Invisible Hand Theorem, we can illustrate it for a simple economy using a tool known as the Edgeworth box. Suppose there are only two consumers and two goods. We will assume that the goods have already been produced, so we are considering only trading and not production in the Edgeworth box model. (Economists sometimes call this a "two-person exchange economy.")

To form the Edgeworth box, consider the indifference curve diagrams of the two consumers and the total amounts of the goods available. Take the diagram representing one of the consumers, rotate it 180°, and superimpose it on the other consumer's diagram so that the dimensions of the box formed are exactly the same as the total amounts of goods available. That's all there is to it.

Notice that each point in the Edgeworth box has four coordinates (two for each consumer), so each point represents some possible way of distributing the goods among the consumers. For example, the lower right-hand corner of the box represents the situation where each consumer has all of one good and none of the other. You will also find several points where the consumers' indifference curves are tangent—the set of all these points is called the *contract curve* and represents the various Pareto-optimal ways of distributing the goods (i.e., the situations where there are no mutually agreeable trades).

To use the Edgeworth box to study the competitive market system, we start off by giving the consumers some arbitrary distribution of the two goods. This starting point is called the *endowment point*. Notice that the two indifference curves through the endowment point form a lens-shaped area; this is called the *region of mutual advantage* because these are the distributions of the goods that are Pareto-preferred to the endowment point (i.e., that would make both consumers better off).

By drawing a budget line through the endowment point, the tangency between the indifference curves and the budget line will show us how much each consumer desires to trade. They may or may not want to trade the same amounts, but you will always be able to find *some* budget line where their desires coincide. When this happens, you have found a competitive equilibrium—the slope of this budget line represents the prices that will make quantity supplied equal to quantity demanded in both markets. Since the two indifference curves are tangent at this equilibrium, this shows us that the competitive outcome is Pareto-optimal, which is the claim of the Invisible Hand Theorem.

Section 8.3. Other Normative Criteria

There are of course other normative criteria that can and should be used to judge market outcomes. For example, suppose I have all the goods in the world and you have none. If I'm greedy and care nothing about your welfare, then this is Pareto-optimal since there will be no redistribution of goods we could both agree on. So our Pareto criterion implies nothing about fairness or equity.

Economists and others have developed several criteria to evaluate the fairness of the economy's outcome. One such criterion is to see if the resulting distribution of goods is *envy-free*. An envy-free distribution is one in which each consumer prefers his own bundle of goods to anyone else's. One interesting fact about competition is that when the endowment point gives everyone an equal share in all commodities, the consumers will then trade to an envy-free distribution of goods. So when we begin equally, competition will both fully exploit the gains from trade and treat consumers fairly.

Working Through the Graphs—Calculating Deadweight Loss

Exhibit 8-11 of the textbook gives a step-by-step procedure for analyzing the gains from trade change which result in a market. If you've achieved the objectives of previous chapters, this procedure should make it easy for you to use the efficiency criterion to judge the outcome of many economic policies. Figures 8-1 and 8-2, as completed by following the steps below, provide two examples of this analysis.

Figure 8-1.

Step 1. Always begin with a supply/demand diagram illustrating the policy you wish to analyze. For this example, we've chosen to study the effects of an excise tax imposed on producers. For convenience, there are two copies of this diagram to work with; the diagram on the left highlights the initial situation in the boldface, and the diagram on the right puts the after-tax situation in boldface. Verify that these diagrams correctly illustrate the effects of the excise tax, where P_0, Q_0 is the initial equilibrium, Q_{tax} is the after-tax quantity exchanged, P_D is the price paid by consumers after the tax is imposed, and P_S is the price producers get to keep after paying the tax.

Figure 8-1 Calculating Deadweight Loss for a Sales Tax

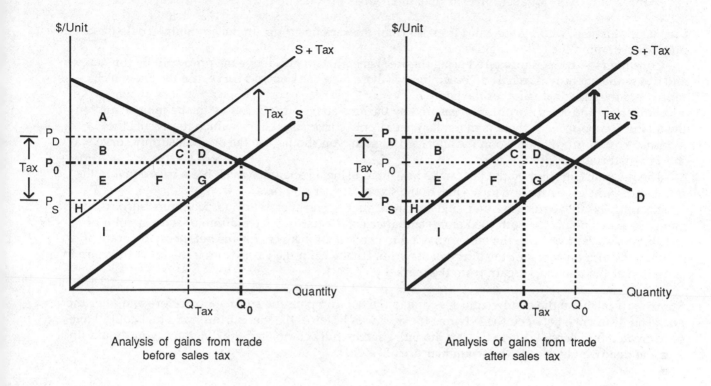

Analysis of gains from trade
before sales tax

Analysis of gains from trade
after sales tax

	Gains from Trade Before Tax	Gains from Trade After Tax	
Consumers' Surplus	A + B + C + D		
Producers' Surplus	E + F + G + H + I		
Tax Recipients			Deadweight Loss Due to Tax
Social Gain	A + B + C + D + E + F + G + H + I		

Notice how the equilibrium prices and quantities divide the diagram into several areas. The areas relevant to the analysis have been labelled with letters of the alphabet. There is no hard-and-fast rule for determining which areas are and are not relevant; this simply comes with practice and experience. However, it never hurts to label more areas than needed.

Step 2. In this step, we find the gains from trade for the various groups in the economy. To do this, you must keep in mind the following basics.

Consumers' surplus is measured using the area beneath demand, above the price paid by consumers, and out to the quantity purchased. When there is more than one demand curve, use the one which represents the marginal value of the good.

Similarly, producers' surplus is measured by the area above supply, below the price paid, and out to the quantity produced. If there is more than one supply curve, use the one which represents the marginal cost of production (so in the after-tax diagram, you should use the original supply curve S, not the tax-distorted supply S + tax).

The revenue collected by the tax can be measured using a rectangle which has a base equal to the number of units taxed and a width equal to the size of the per unit tax.

Keeping the above rules in mind, find and shade in the consumers' surplus, producers' surplus, and gains to tax recipients for both the before- and after-tax diagrams. Use a different style or color of shading for each area. Use the table provided to check your answers for the before-tax diagram and summarize your answers for the after-tax diagram. Finally, sum the gains from trade for each group in order to get the total social gain from the market.

Step 3. To calculate the deadweight loss due to the tax, compare the social gains before and after the tax. The difference between these two is the deadweight loss—the gains from trade that could have been created but weren't due to the tax. If you've successfully completed the diagrams, you should find that the deadweight loss is the triangular area D + G .

Figure 8-2.

Step 1. This time we analyze the effects of a price ceiling. Verify that the effects of this policy have been correctly illustrated in Figure 8-2, where P_0, Q_0 is the initial equilibrium, $Q_{ceiling}$ is the quantity exchanged under the price ceiling, $P_{ceiling}$ is the after-ceiling price received by producers, and $P_{ceiling}$ + searching costs is the after-ceiling net price paid by consumers.

To understand this latter price, notice that the price ceiling originally creates a shortage of $Q_{ceiling}$ - $Q_{demanded}$; this shortage will cause consumers to compete with one another to locate and purchase the scarce good. Using the demand curve, consumers will pay an additional premium (in the form of time and energy searching for the good and waiting in line) and raise the net price they pay to $P_{ceiling}$ + searching costs.

Finally, again notice how the equilibrium prices and quantities divide the diagram into several areas which have already been labelled.

Step 2. Using the rules stated in Step 2 for the previous diagram, find and shade in the consumers' and producers' surplus for both the before- and after-ceiling diagrams. Using these areas, then calculate the social gain generated by the market. Again use the table provided to check and summarize your answers.

Step 3. Calculate the deadweight loss by finding the difference in the social gains before and after the ceiling. If you've done the analysis correctly, you should find that the deadweight loss is the area B + C + D + E .

Figure 8-2 Calculating Deadweight Loss for a Price Ceiling

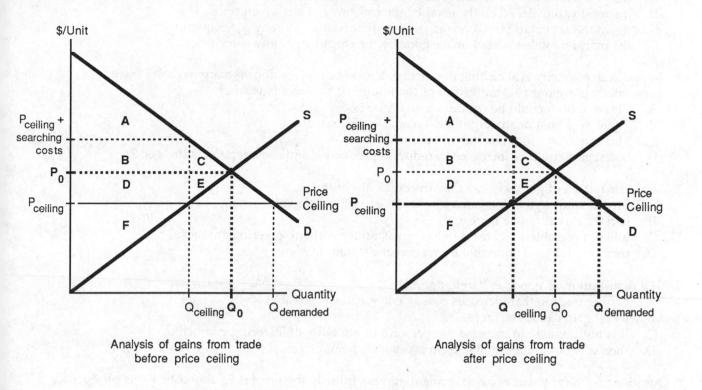

Analysis of gains from trade before price ceiling

Analysis of gains from trade after price ceiling

	Gains from Trade Before Ceiling	Gains from Trade After Ceiling	
Consumers' Surplus	A + B + C		
Producers' Surplus	D + E + F		Deadweight Loss Due to Ceiling
Social Gain	A + B + C + D + E + F		

141

Multiple Choice Questions

1. An individual's demand curve also shows
   A. the total value placed on the good by the consumer at any given quantity.
   B. the total value placed on the good by the consumer at any given price.
   C. the marginal value placed on the good by the consumer at any given quantity.
   D. the marginal value placed on the good by the consumer at any given price.

2. Suppose an economy is allocating resources to a good so that producers' marginal costs exceed consumers' marginal values. Which of the following statements is *false*?
   A. This situation could be created by an excise tax.
   B. There will be a deadweight loss created in this situation.
   C. This outcome cannot be Pareto-optimal.
   D. Social gain could be increased by reducing production and consumption of this good.

3. If a distribution of goods is "best" by the efficiency criterion,
   A. further trading that increases consumers' surplus is possible.
   B. social gain cannot be increased.
   C. it is not possible to increase one person's utility without lowering another's.
   D. then it is fair and equitable from everyone's point of view.

4. If a distribution of goods is Pareto-optimal,
   A. further trading that increases consumers' surplus is possible.
   B. social gain cannot be increased.
   C. it is not possible to increase one person's utility without lowering another's.
   D. then it is fair and equitable from everyone's point of view.

***Questions 5-7 refer to the accompanying diagram. Initially the price is P_0, domestic firms produce Q_0 units, and $Q_1 - Q_0$ units are imported from foreign firms. Then a tariff is imposed, raising price to $P_0 + t$.

Figure 8a

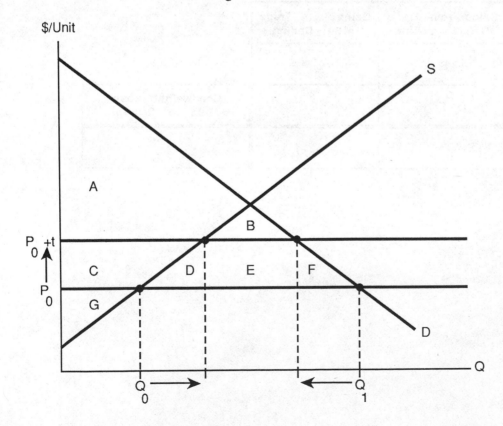

5. When the tariff is imposed, consumers' surplus
   A. falls from A + B + C + D + E + F to A + B.
   B. falls from A + B + C + D + E to A + B.
   C. falls from A + C + G to A + C.
   D. falls from A + C to A.

6. When the tariff is imposed, producers' surplus increases from G to
   A. C + G.
   B. C + G - B.
   C. C + G - D - E - F.
   D. C + D + E + F + G.

7. The result of the tariff is to
   A. collect tax revenue E and create a deadweight loss of B + D + F.
   B. collect tax revenue E and create a deadweight loss of D + F.
   C. collect tax revenue D + E + F and create a deadweight loss of B.
   D. collect tax revenue D + E + F without creating a deadweight loss.

***Questions 8-9 refer to the accompanying diagram which shows the effects of an excise subsidy given to firms. The initial price and quantity are P_0, Q_0. After the subsidy, quantity increases to Q_1, firms receive price P_S, and consumers pay price P_D.

Figure 8b

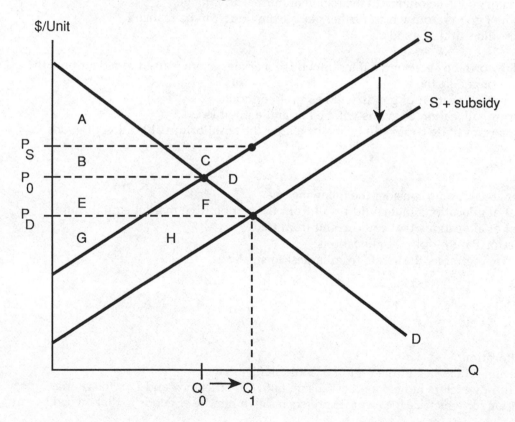

143

8. Before the subsidy, the social gain is
   A. A + B.
   B. A + B + E + F.
   C. A + B + E + G.
   D. E + G.

9. After the subsidy, the social gain is
   A. A + B + E + G.
   B. A + B + E + G - D.
   C. A + B + E + F + G + H.
   D. A + B + E + F + G + H - C - D.

10. Which of the following statements about value is *false*?
    A. If the total value of our consumption of water is high, we should not expect the price of water to also be high.
    B. If the marginal value of our consumption of water is low, then we should expect the price of water to also be low.
    C. The amount of labor used in the production of a good does not determine the value of that good.
    D. We should expect that professions which provide a large total value to society will also command high salaries.

11. In the Edgeworth box economy, an allocation of goods where the consumers' indifference curves are tangent represents
    A. a Pareto-optimal allocation of goods.
    B. an allocation of goods belonging to the region of mutual advantage.
    C. an allocation of goods from which further gains from trade can be realized.
    D. an envy-free allocation of goods.

12. Consider the Edgeworth box economy. If a competitive market system is used to redistribute the initial endowment of goods, then
    A. the equilibrium allocation of goods will be Pareto-optimal.
    B. the equilibrium allocation of goods will be fair and equitable.
    C. further gains from trade could still be realized after the equilibrium allocation of goods is achieved.
    D. Both A and B

13. For a given endowment point, consider the following sets:
    I.   the set of allocations that could result from the competitive market equilibrium,
    II. the set of allocations that could result from trade,
    III. the set of Pareto-optimal allocations.
    Which of the following ranks these sets from largest to smallest?
    A. I, II, III.
    B. II, III, I.
    C. III, I, II.
    D. III, II. I.

14. An envy-free allocation
    A. is an allocation which lies in the region of mutual advantage.
    B. is an allocation which is judged as "best" using both the efficiency and Pareto criteria.
    C. is an allocation for which each consumer prefers his own bundle of goods to that owned by any other consumer.
    D. is the allocation in which consumers own identical bundles of goods.

144

15. Suppose consumers have identical bundles of goods at the endowment point. Trading in the competitive market will result in an allocation of goods that is
    A. Pareto-optimal.
    B. envy-free.
    C. Both A and B
    D. Neither A nor B

Solutions

1. C. Demand and marginal value are different interpretations of the same curve. Price is the independent variable when we interpret it as a demand curve; quantity is the independent variable when we interpret it as a marginal value curve.

2. A. An excise tax would cause marginal value to exceed marginal cost, indicating that the social gain could be increased if society increased production and consumption of the good. Whenever marginal value is larger or smaller than marginal cost, there will be a deadweight loss and the situation is not Pareto-optimal.

3. B. The efficiency criterion looks at the total surplus value created, not the individual welfare of each consumer.

4. C. For a distribution to be Pareto-preferred, it must be preferred by everyone. If there is no alternative distribution that is preferred by all, as in choice C, then we have a Pareto-optimal distribution of goods. Notice that choice B must be true for a Pareto-optimal allocation, but does not fully describe such an allocation. Different market outcomes could be judged as being equally desirable by the efficiency criterion (choice B), but cannot be compared using the Pareto criterion (choice C).

5. A. Compare demand to the price paid by consumers to find the areas measuring consumers' surplus, except when demand no longer reflects marginal value.

6. A. Compare supply to the price received by producers to find the areas measuring producers' surplus, except when supply no longer reflects marginal cost.

7. B. To find an area representing the tax revenue, use the number of units taxed as the base and the per unit tax as the width of the area. This gives area E as the tax revenue. Using the answers to the previous two questions, social gain before the tariff is A + B + C + D + E + F + G. Similarly, after the tariff social gain is A + B + C + E + G, where the gain to tax recipients (area E) must be added to the consumers' and producers' surplus to get social gain. The difference between these two, D + F, is the deadweight loss.

8. C. The consumers' surplus is A + B and the producers' surplus is E + G, resulting in a total social gain of A + B + E + G.

9. B. Using demand and the consumers' new price P_D, consumers' surplus is now A + B + E + F. To get the producers' surplus, we must use the pre-subsidy supply curve (not the lower post-subsidy supply curve) because it is the one that represents the marginal cost of production. So comparing pre-subsidy supply with the producers' new price of P_S, producers' surplus is B + C + E + G under the subsidy. The number of units subsidized is Q_1 and the per unit subsidy is $P_S - P_D$, so the area B + C + D + E + F represents the amount paid by taxpayers to provide this subsidy. The social gain is the consumers' surplus plus the producers' surplus minus the amount paid to finance the subsidy.

This gives $(A + B + E + F) + (B + C + E + G) - (B + C + D + E + F)$, which equals $A + B + E + G - D$. Alternatively, you can directly compare marginal value (shown by demand) and marginal cost (shown by the pre-subsidy supply) through the subsidy quantity Q_1 to find the social gain under the subsidy.

10. D. Price reflects a good's marginal value, while consumers' surplus indicates the good's total value. We would expect a high salary for the profession only when it gives society a high *marginal* value (i.e., when the last member of the profession contributes high additional value to society).

11. A. When indifference curves are tangent, there is no alternative allocation of goods that both consumers would agree upon. Any change would give a lower level of utility to at least one consumer. Put another way, there are no mutually agreeable trades remaining. All of these statements describe a Pareto-optimal distribution of goods.

12. A. This is the claim of the Invisible Hand Theorem as applied to the Edgeworth box economy— trading in the competitive market will achieve a Pareto-optimal allocation of goods within the region of mutual advantage. The Invisible Hand Theorem implies nothing about equity or fairness.

13. D. The Pareto-optimal allocations are illustrated by the set of tangencies between indifference curves in the Edgeworth box. The possible results from trade are a subset of these possibilities; they are the Pareto-optimal allocations within the region of mutual advantage (the lens-shaped area formed by the indifference curves that pass through the endowment point). By the Invisible Hand Theorem, competitive equilibrium will result in a Pareto-optimal allocation in the region of mutual advantage. So III contains II contains I.

14. C. This is simply the definition of an envy-free allocation.

15. C. If everyone begins with identical endowments initially, each consumer will prefer what his post-trade bundle of goods to that attained by other consumers (which was essentially determined by what he traded away), making the result envy-free. The Invisible Hand Theorem guarantees that the result of competition will be Pareto-optimal.

Questions for Review

1. Compare and contrast the consumer's demand curve with his marginal value curve.

2. What are consumers' and producers' surplus and what do they attempt to measure? How and why can demand and supply curves be used to measure consumers' and producers' surplus respectively?

3. What is a deadweight loss? Using the concepts of marginal value and marginal cost, carefully explain why the deadweight loss represents unrealized gains from trade.

4. Name some situations which will create a deadweight loss. According to the Invisible Hand Theorem, when will a deadweight loss not be created?

5. What are the efficiency and Pareto criteria? Why do economists use these criteria? Within the framework of a single market (i.e., using a partial equilibrium framework), explain why a market outcome that is less efficient than competition cannot be Pareto-optimal.

6. Using an Edgeworth box diagram, how do we illustrate (a) a Pareto-optimal distribution of goods, (b) the region of mutual advantage, (c) the distribution of goods resulting from trade, and (d) a

competitive equilibrium? What does the Invisible Hand Theorem claim about the relationship between the allocation of goods resulting from a competitive equilibrium and those that result from trade?

7. Why are the efficiency and Pareto criteria at times inadequate for judging market outcomes? What is an envy-free allocation of goods and how does it differ from an efficient or Pareto-optimal allocation of goods? Can an allocation of goods simultaneously be Pareto-optimal and envy-free?

Solutions

1. There is a duality between demand and marginal value; they are the same curve read in different ways. Using this set of points as a demand curve, for any given price we can read off the quantity demanded. Using it as a marginal value curve, for any given quantity we can read off the additional value the consumer received from the last unit consumed. (Notice that since this curve represents the consumer's willingness to pay, it actually represents the *compensated* demand curve introduced in Chapter 4. This will coincide with the ordinary demand curve if there are no income effects.)

2. Consumers' and producers' surplus attempt to measure the gains from trade received by consumers and firms, respectively. Consumers' surplus shows the total net benefit consumers receive from purchasing and consuming the good rather than purchasing nothing. Producers' surplus shows the total net benefit firms receive from producing and selling the good rather than producing nothing.

   Since the demand curve also represents consumers' marginal value from the good, comparing demand against price at any quantity shows the additional net benefit the consumer receives from purchasing and consuming the last unit of the good. Adding up all of these net benefits will give consumers' surplus. So consumers' surplus is the area under demand, above price, out to the quantity consumed.

   Since there is a duality between supply and marginal cost, the difference between price and the supply curve at any quantity shows the additional net benefit from producing and selling the last unit of the good. Adding all of these net benefits gives producers' surplus, so the area above supply, below price, and out to the quantity supplied gives a geometric measure of producers' surplus.

3. A deadweight loss is any social gain (or gains from trade) that could have been generated by the market but for some reason (such as government intervention) was not achieved. If marginal value does not equal marginal cost, the equimarginal principle implies that there has been a deadweight loss.

   For example, if marginal value exceeds marginal cost, the last unit produced and consumed was worth more to society than what it cost. This indicates that the total social gain is continuing to increase as we dedicate further resources to this good. Since all the possible gains from trade were not realized, there has been a deadweight loss.

   Similarly, if marginal value is smaller than marginal cost, then the last unit created more additional costs than benefits. Applying the equimarginal principle, social gain would increase if production and consumption were reduced. Since social gain is not as large as it could be, this again implies that there is a deadweight loss.

4. When demonstrating how to calculate deadweight loss, the textbook gives several examples showing when a deadweight loss can be created. These situations include sales taxes and subsidies (which are equivalent to excise taxes and subsidies), price floors and ceilings, tariffs and quotas, and robbery. The Invisible Hand Theorem (when illustrated with a single competitive market) shows that competition makes the social gain will be as large as possible, so there is no deadweight loss created when the competitive market is in equilibrium.

5. The efficiency criterion ranks market outcomes depending on the total amount of social gain created. The Pareto criterion will rank one market outcome as better than another if all consumers prefer the former situation; notice that unlike the efficiency criterion, two market outcomes may not be comparable using the Pareto criterion. If a market outcome is less efficient than competition, then there are unrealized gains from trade (i.e., there is a deadweight loss). By changing the market outcome to generate these unrealized gains from trade, and then distributing this additional surplus value among the market participants, everyone is made better off. Hence the new situation is Pareto-preferred to the initial situation. This implies that the market outcome with the deadweight loss cannot be Pareto-optimal.

6. (a) In the Edgeworth box, Pareto-optimal allocations of goods occur where the consumers' indifference curves are tangent; any change from this situation would make at least one consumer worse off. (b) The region of mutual advantage is the set of distributions of goods that both consumers prefer to the endowment point. This is the lens-shaped area between the two indifference curves passing through the endowment point. (c) Trade between the two consumers will result in a Pareto-optimal distribution of goods within the region of mutual advantage. (d) A budget line drawn through the endowment point will represent the budgets faced by both consumers in a competitive market. If both indifference curves are tangent to the budget line at the same distribution of goods, then their desires to trade goods will coincide and there is a competitive equilibrium.

   The Invisible Hand Theorem claims that competition exploits all the possible gains from trade, so the competitive equilibrium will be one of those allocations that could result from trade. In other words, competition results in a Pareto-optimal allocation of goods within the region of mutual advantage.

7. The efficiency and Pareto criteria rank market outcomes solely on the basis of gains from trade; they ignore other factors that may be important such as fairness and equity. An envy-free allocation of goods is one in which each consumer prefers his own bundle of goods to that owned by any other consumer. Notice that this ignores possible unexploited gains from trade that would be important when applying the efficiency and Pareto criteria. It is possible for an allocation of goods to be both Pareto-optimal and envy-free. If all consumers begin with equal shares in the endowment point then competition will result in such a distribution of goods.

Problems for Analysis

1. Consider a competitive market described by the following equations, where P is the market price and Q is the market quantity.

   Demand/Marginal Value curve: $P = 300 - (1/6)Q$;
   Supply/Marginal Cost curve: $P = 240 + (1/3)Q$.

   (i) Calculate the equilibrium price, equilibrium quantity, consumers' surplus, and producers' surplus. Be sure to include appropriate units with your answers. (Hint—A sketch of the graph will help you determine the appropriate calculations.)

(ii) Suppose the government imposes a $12/unit excise tax on firms in this market. First find a formula for the after-tax supply curve. Then calculate the new equilibrium quantity, price paid by consumers, price received by producers, total tax revenue collected by government, and the resulting deadweight loss due to the tax. Include appropriate units with your solutions. (Hint—Again, a sketch will help you determine the appropriate calculations.)

(iii) How would the size of the deadweight loss change if the government imposed a price floor at $284/unit in place of the excise tax? Explain.

2. (i) Suppose the government imposes a sales tax on consumers. All other things being equal, determine how will the elasticity of supply affect the size of the resulting deadweight loss by completing the diagrams below. Assume that the initial equilibrium is P_0, Q_0. The following should be labelled:

     a.   an appropriate supply curve for each diagram,
     b.   the shift in demand due to the tax,
     c.   the new equilibrium quantity (Q_1), price paid by consumers (P_C), and price received by producers (P_S),
     d.   the consumers' and producers' surplus after the tax, and
     e.   the deadweight loss due to the sales tax.

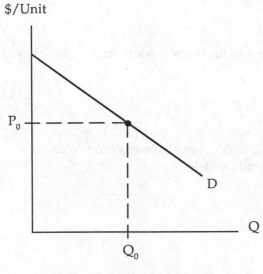

Sales tax imposed when supply is elastic

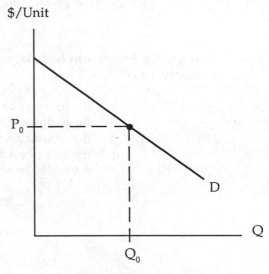

Sales tax imposed when supply is inelastic

(ii) Based on your answer to part (i), how will the deadweight loss due to a sales tax vary from the short run to the long run?

149

(iii) Considering your analysis from part (i), make a conjecture about how the price elasticity of demand will affect the size of the deadweight loss.

(iv) Using your answers to parts (i) and (iii), in what two situations will the deadweight loss from a sales tax be zero?

3. Suppose there are 16 units of food and 12 units of clothing to distribute between Alex and Betty. The endowment point of food and clothing is $(F_A, C_A; F_B, C_B) = (16, 6; 0, 6)$. At this allocation, the agents' marginal rates of substitution are

$$MRS^A_{PC} = 1/2 \text{ unit of clothing per unit of food and}$$

$$MRS^B_{PC} = 1/2 \text{ unit of clothing per unit of food and}$$

(i) Determine whether or not this distribution of goods is Pareto-optimal. Justify your answer by using the equimarginal principle to explain why there is or is not a mutually beneficial trade available.

(ii) Complete the Edgeworth box diagram below to illustrate this situation. The following should be clearly labelled:

    a. the dimensions of the Edgeworth box
    b. the endowment point,
    c. the consumers' MRSs, and
    d. the rate of exchange at which the consumers can trade (if a mutually beneficial trade exits).

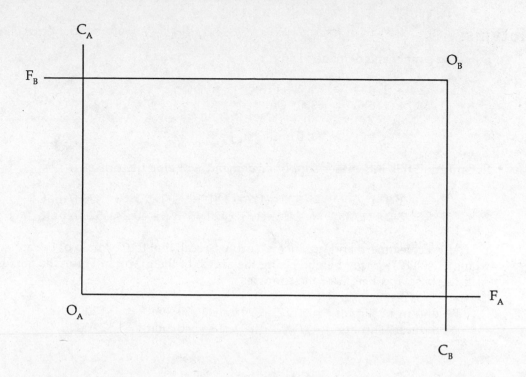

(iii) Repeat parts (i) and (ii) for the case where the endowment point
       is $(F_A, C_A; F_B, C_B) = (0, 6; 16, 6)$.

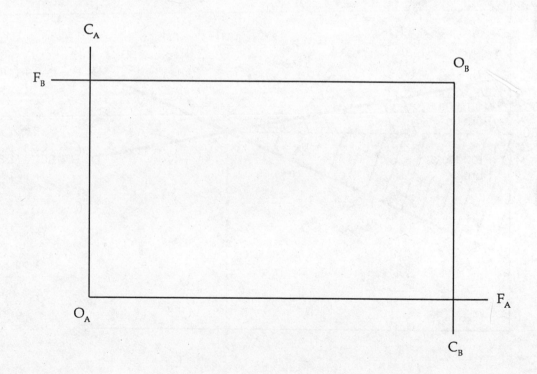

Solutions

1. (i) Equating supply and demand yields

$$240 + (1/3)Q = 300 - (1/6)Q$$
$$(1/3)Q + (1/6)Q = 300 - 240$$
$$(1/2)Q = 60$$
$$Q = 120 \text{ units.}$$

Substituting this into either supply or demand will give the price:

$$P = 300 - (1/6)Q = 300 - (1/6) \cdot 120 = 300 - 20 = \$280/\text{unit}$$
or $$P = 240 + (1/3)Q = 240 + (1/3) \cdot 120 = 240 + 40 = \$280/\text{unit.}$$

To find consumers' and producers' surplus, recall that the formula of the area of a triangle is $(1/2) \cdot$ base $\cdot$ height. Using the sketch of the graph in Figure 8c makes it easy to find the base and height of the triangles.

$$\text{Consumers' surplus} = (1/2) \cdot 120 \text{ units} \cdot \$20/\text{unit} = \$1200.$$
$$\text{Producers' surplus} = (1/2) \cdot 120 \text{ units} \cdot \$40/\text{unit} = \$2400.$$

Figure 8c

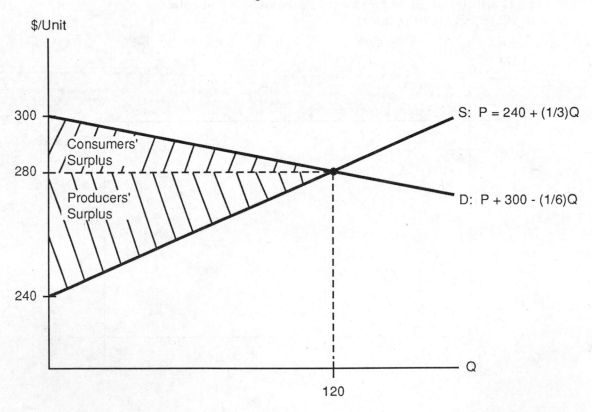

(ii) Since producers must receive $12/unit more to produce the same quantity, the new formula for the supply curve is

(the new supply price) = (the original formula) + (tax).
so   P   =   240 + (1/3)Q   +   12
which simplifies to P = 252 + (1/3)Q.

Equating supply and demand gives

$$
\begin{aligned}
252 + (1/3)Q &= 300 - (1/6)Q \\
(1/3)Q + (1/6)Q &= 300 - 252 \\
(1/2)Q &= 48 \\
Q &= 96 \text{ units.}
\end{aligned}
$$

Substituting this into the demand formula gives the price consumers pay:

P = 300 - (1/6)Q = 300 - (1/6) · 96 = 300 - 16 = $284/unit.

Producers must pay the tax, so the price they receive is $12/unit lower, so their price is $284/unit - $12/unit or $272/unit. Figure 8d is helpful in determining the various dimensions needed to calculate the areas measuring consumers' surplus, producers' surplus, tax revenue, and deadweight loss. When calculating producers' surplus, remember that the original supply curve is the one that represents marginal costs so it is the one that should be used.

Consumers' surplus   =   (1/2) · 96 units · $16/unit   = $768.
Producers' surplus   =   (1/2) · 96 units · $32/unit   = $1,536.
Tax revenue   =   (number of units taxed) · (tax per unit)
              =   96 units · $12/unit = $1,152.
Deadweight loss   =   (1/2) · base · height
                  =   (1/2) · 24 units · $12/unit = $144.

Figure 8d

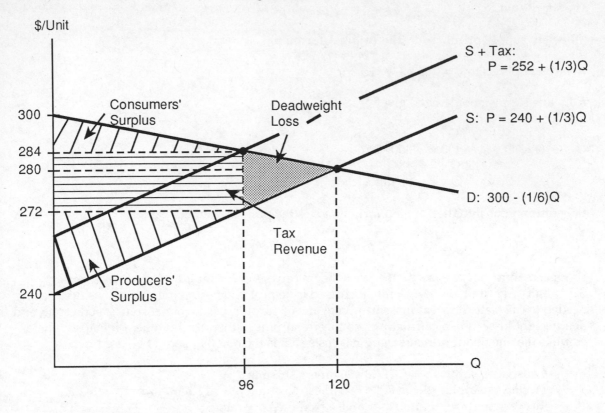

(iii) The tax revenue would become deadweight loss, so the new deadweight loss would be $1,296. This is because producers will compete with each other to try to satisfy the limited demand. Using the supply curve, this will drive the price producers receive from the floor price of $284/unit down to $272/unit.

154

2. (i) Using the diagrams in Figure 8e, we see that the deadweight loss becomes larger as supply becomes more elastic. When doing these diagrams, be sure to keep all other factors (like the size of the tax) the same.

Figure 8e

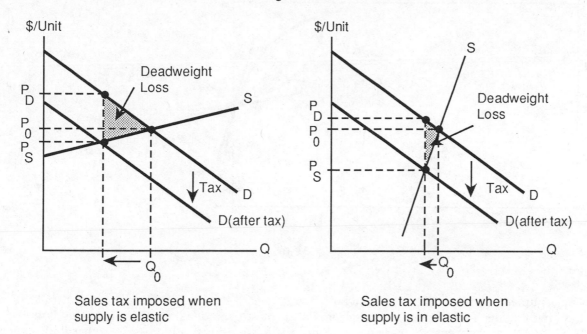

Sales tax imposed when supply is elastic

Sales tax imposed when supply is in elastic

(ii) From Chapter 7, we know that long-run supply is more elastic than short-run supply. So we would expect the deadweight loss due to a sales tax to increase as the industry has greater time to readjust its quantity supplied. Notice that the consumers' share in paying the tax becomes larger and the producers' share becomes smaller as this occurs.

(iii) Like supply, the more elastic demand becomes the greater will be the deadweight loss. This is because the tax will cause a greater reduction in the equilibrium quantity when demand is more elastic, causing a greater reduction in the amount of social gain.

(iv) When either supply or demand is infinitely inelastic (i.e., vertical), then the deadweight loss will be zero. This is because the equilibrium quantity will remain unaffected by the sales tax, and hence there will be no reduction in social gain.

3. (i) If mutually beneficial trade is available, it must be at a rate between the two MRSs. For convenience, let's consider a trade at the rate of 1 unit of clothing per unit of food.

Alex's marginal benefit from trading away 1 unit of food to Betty is 1 unit of clothing (using the rate of exchange). His marginal cost of trading away this unit of food to Betty is 1/2 unit of clothing (using his MRS). So by the equimarginal principle, this trade is beneficial to Alex.

Betty's marginal cost of accepting 1 unit of food from Alex is 1 unit of her clothing (using the rate of exchange). Her marginal benefit of receiving this unit of food from Alex is 1 1/2 units of clothing (using her MRS). Applying the equimarginal principle, this trade also benefits Betty.

Since there is a redistribution of goods that both will agree is better, the initial situation is not Pareto-optimal.

155

Figure 8f

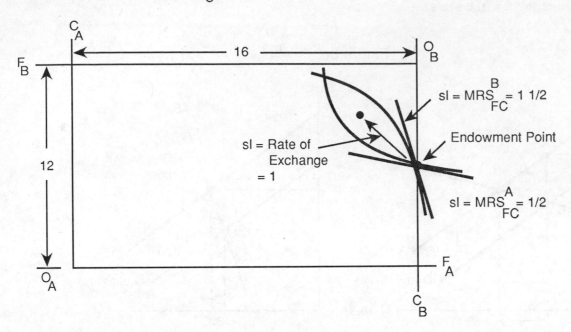

(iii) The argument from part (i) shows that both would benefit if Alex would trade away 1 unit of food in exchange for 1 unit of clothing from Betty. But this trade is not possible in this case because Alex has no food to trade away! Since there is no physically possible redistribution of goods that both can agree on, this situation is Pareto-optimal. In the diagram, notice that there is no region of mutual advantage within the Edgeworth box.

Figure 8g

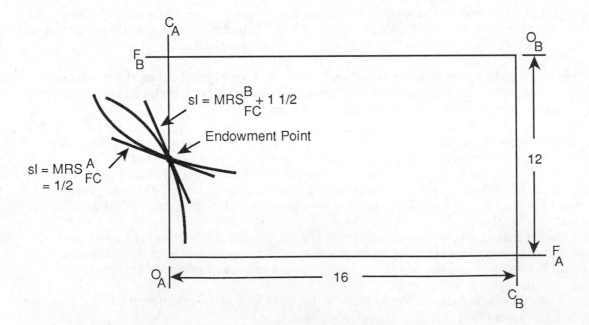

Solutions to Working Through the Graphs

Figure 8-1 Calculating Deadweight Loss for a Sales Tax

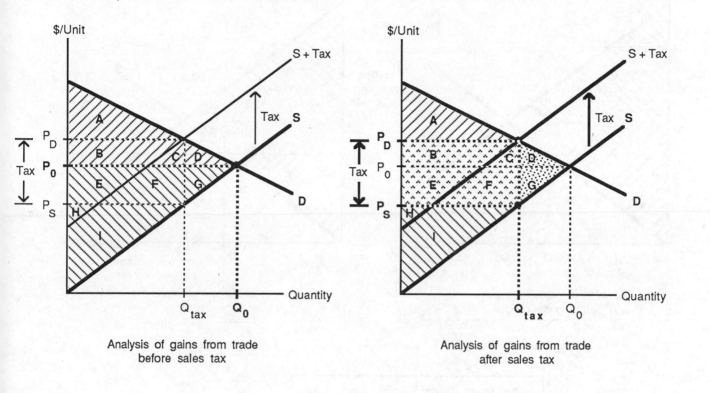

Analysis of gains from trade
before sales tax

Analysis of gains from trade
after sales tax

	Gains from Trade Before Tax	Gains from Trade After Tax	
Consumers' Surplus	A + B + C + D	A	
Producers' Surplus	E + F + G + H + I	H + I	
Tax Recipients		B + C + E + F	Deadweight Loss Due to Tax
Social Gain	A + B + C + D + E + F + G + H + I	A + B + C + E + F + H + I	D + G

Figure 8-2 Calculating Deadweight Loss for a Price Ceiling

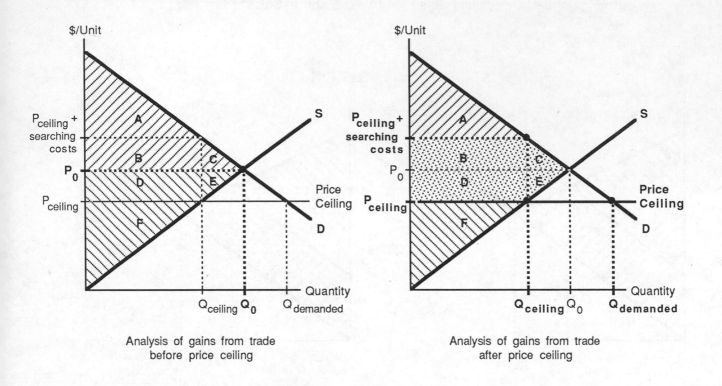

Analysis of gains from trade
before price ceiling

Analysis of gains from trade
after price ceiling

	Gains from Trade Before Ceiling	Gains from Trade After Ceiling	
Consumers' Surplus	A + B + C	A	
Producers' Surplus	D + E + F	F	Deadweight Loss Due to Ceiling
Social Gain	A + B + C + D + E + F	A + F	B + C + D + E

Chapter Nine

Knowledge in Society

Chapter Summary

In this chapter, we continue our study of the competitive market's ability to attain the most gains from trade possible for the economy. Economists find that using the price system to synthesize and communicate society's knowledge is far superior to anything a benevolent social planner could ever hope to achieve.

Section 9.1. The Informational Content of Prices

The equilibrium price of a competitive market summarizes vast amounts of knowledge—literally all the pertinent knowledge of everyone in the economy. This is because each individual's demand contributes to the market demand curve, and each firm's supply contributes to the market supply curve. Price is determined jointly by demand and supply and hence incorporates the unique knowledge possessed by each individual consumer and firm.

The supply/marginal cost and demand/marginal value dualities we developed in Chapters 7 and 8 provide further insight into the connection between prices and knowledge. The equilibrium market price jointly represents the marginal cost of production (from the supply curve) and the marginal value of consumption (from the demand curve). Furthermore, the price communicates this information to consumers and firms and provides incentives for them to apply their own unique knowledge and circumstances.

For example, suppose the price of a good rises to eliminate a shortage in the market. This *communicates* to firms that the marginal value of the good to consumers has risen. In response, firms—trying to maximize their profits—will have the *incentive* to increase their production as long as their marginal costs are smaller than the new higher price/marginal value. On the other hand, the higher market price *communicates* to consumers that the marginal cost of production has risen—that is, the opportunity cost of the resources needed to produce the last unit of the good has risen. This signals the reality of scarcity to consumers. In trying to maximize their utility, they have the *incentive* to reduce consumption as long as their marginal value is less than the now-higher price/marginal cost.

To summarize, the competitive equilibrium price acts through supply and demand to *synthesize* the knowledge of society's members, *communicate* this information back to consumers and firms, and *provide incentive* for them to use this information and act upon their own unique knowledge. The incredible fact is that this can be and is done without an omniscient presence sitting in an ivory tower. Instead it is the natural result of each consumer and firm acting in its own self-interest, working hand-in-Invisible Hand.

It should be apparent that a benevolent social planner could not achieve the gains from trade attained in a competitive market system. For example, let's consider an extremely clever social planner who has figured out the market supply and demand curves of a good. From this information, he can determine the quantity to produce and consume in the economy that would create the maximum gains from trade (i.e., that would create no deadweight loss). Applying the Invisible Hand Theorem, this quantity is of course the one determined by the intersection of supply and demand.

But now our kind social planner faces an unsolvable problem—how much of this quantity should *each* firm produce and how much should *each* individual consume? To maximize the gains from trade, each consecutive unit should be produced by the firm with the lowest marginal cost and consumed by the individual with the highest marginal value. Without access to the unique knowledge possessed by each firm and consumer, the odds that our social planner do this range from slim to none (with the latter heavily favored).

However when firms and consumers act in their own self-interest in a competitive market system, the market price coordinates their actions so that the good is produced by those with the lowest marginal costs and consumed by those with the highest marginal value. So by synthesizing and communicating society's knowledge via price, the competitive market can efficiently allocate production and consumption across individual firms and consumers—a task which is impossible for any social planner to perform.

Ignoring the ability of the price system to synthesize and communicate society's knowledge can create serious flaws in economic reasoning. Such was the case with the Fabian socialists' argument concerning rent.

As we mentioned in Chapter 7, factors of production that are fixed in supply earn economic rent. To be more precise, *rent* is the amount of payment in excess of the minimum amount needed to hire the factor. If a factor is fixed in supply, this would be shown graphically by supply becoming vertical at the limited quantity; rent refers to producers' surplus in this case of a vertical (or almost entirely vertical) supply curve.

The Fabian socialists argued that the payment of rent serves no economic purpose. Higher prices due to higher demand would simply increase the rent earned by the factor of production without generating any additional output; these rents simply enrich the owner of the resource without requiring any additional contribution to society. The Fabian socialists argued that the government should confiscate these unfair rents and pay the owner the minimum amount of income required for him to provide the resource. Since these rents did not contribute to additional output, their confiscation would not lower social welfare.

This argument is clearly wrong, because it ignores the informational aspects of price. For there to be no loss in social welfare, the resource must be provided to those individuals who would receive the highest marginal value. There would be no way for the owner of the resource to determine who these individuals are if the government confiscated rent and paid the owner of the resource directly. The Fabian scheme would lower social welfare by resulting in an inefficient allocation of the resource; only by communicating information through the price system can we guarantee that the owner will supply the resource to those with the highest marginal value.

Section 9.2. The Informational Content of Prices: Applications

The fact that prices communicate knowledge is one of the most important and pervasive ideas in economics. In this section, we consider only two of the many applications of this essential concept.

The opportunity to profit through investing in financial markets provides one interesting application. An *efficient market* is one in which the price fully reflects all available information. Of course it takes time for new information to become reflected in the price of a good, so we can only guarantee that competitive markets will be efficient in the "long run."

Many believe that they can use this "long-run" period to profit through investments in the stock market by using new information to predict whether the price of the stock will go up or down. However, economic studies have shown that financial securities markets like the stock market are incredibly efficient. The evidence is that the "long run"—the period of time needed for price to adjust and reflect new information—is under 30 seconds.

The informational aspects of price studied in this chapter reveal the futility of "technical analysis" (attempting to predict future stock prices based on the pattern of past prices) and other similar analysis of market conditions. It is mistaken to believe that past prices can provide additional information to an investor because the current price of a stock already reflects all available information.

A second application of the ability of prices to communicate information comes from macroeconomics, providing one possible reason why we often observe a tradeoff between inflation and unemployment.

We know from Chapter 2 that only relative prices are relevant to determining equilibrium quantities. If prices and wages increased by 10%, this would have no effect on the amount people choose to work since relative prices would be unchanged.

Suppose consumers base their decisions on the expectation that inflation will be 5% this year, and then are offered a 10% wage increase. Thinking that their wages have increased purchasing power, consumers will react by increasing the amount of labor they supply, which reduces unemployment. For example, discouraged workers without jobs may reenter the work force, and non-working spouses may now take a part-time jobs.

But now suppose that consumers' inflationary expectations were wrong—suppose inflation for the year is actually 10%. As people discover that prices have risen 10% instead of 5%, they find that the purchasing power of their wages did not increase. The unexpected inflation fooled people into increasing their labor supply; if they had realized that *both* wages and prices were increasing by 10%, they wouldn't have changed their employment status.

Notice the macroeconomic implication of our thought experiment—unexpected inflation caused a decrease in unemployment. Uncertainty about inflation dilutes the ability of prices to communicate information and gives us one reason why we often observe a tradeoff between inflation and unemployment.

Working Through the Graphs—A Social Planner versus a Competitive Market

Competitive prices allow the economy to generate the most gains from trade possible because they convey information and provide incentive to consumers and firms. In Figures 9-1 and 9-2, we compare a social planner's allocation of resources with that of a competitive market for a simple economy to see the power of the informational aspect of prices.

Figure 9-1.

Step 1. The top graph shows the supply and demand for a good. Since supply represents marginal cost and demand represents marginal benefit, the shaded areas represent the social gain that can be created by this market as we saw in Chapter 8. Determine the area of each rectangle and complete the table to find the maximum social gain possible. If you've done this correctly, you should find that $30 of surplus value can be created.

Step 2. Let's suppose that a social planner has access to the supply and demand curves in the top graph and knows that 6 units of output would create the maximum social gain. The first problem is to divide the production of these 6 units between firms A, B, and C.

We know supply comes from adding the individual firms' supply curves; the second diagram shows whether each unit on the supply curve came from firm A, firm B, or firm C's supply curve. Notice that firm A has the lowest marginal costs, followed by firm C, with firm B being the least efficient in producing this good.

Unfortunately, there is no way our social planner can have access to this specialized knowledge of the individual firms. Believing that everyone should be treated equally, our social planner divides the production equally among the three firms as summarized in the table accompanying the supply graph. Shade in the rectangles representing the costs incurred when each firm produces two units (use a different style or color of shading for each firm). Then complete the table to calculate the cost of producing 6 units of output under our social planner; if you've done this correctly, you should find that this way of dividing production costs $25.

Figure 9-1 A Social Planner's Allocation of Resources

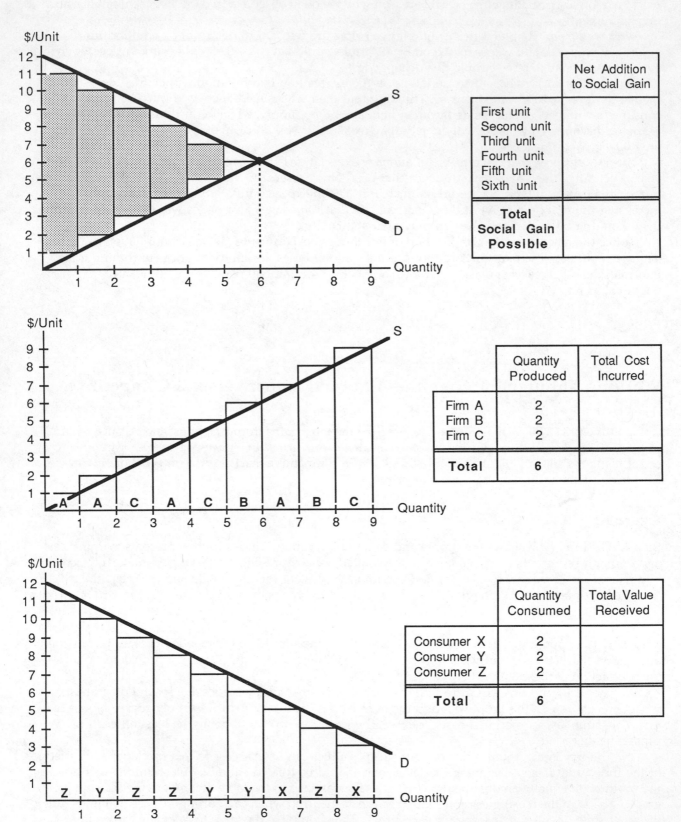

	Net Addition to Social Gain
First unit	
Second unit	
Third unit	
Fourth unit	
Fifth unit	
Sixth unit	
Total Social Gain Possible	

	Quantity Produced	Total Cost Incurred
Firm A	2	
Firm B	2	
Firm C	2	
Total	**6**	

	Quantity Consumed	Total Value Received
Consumer X	2	
Consumer Y	2	
Consumer Z	2	
Total	**6**	

Social Gain Created by Planner = _____

162

Step 3. In the third graph, we turn to the problem of determining how to divide the 6 units of output among consumers X, Y, and Z.

The demand curve comes from the sum of the individuals' demand curves; we've labelled the diagram to indicate whether each unit represents the contribution from X, Y, or Z's demand curve. Notice that consumer Z receives the highest marginal value from this good, followed by consumer Y, followed by consumer X.

Our social planner of course has no way of knowing the unique preferences of each consumer. Still thinking that everyone should be treated equally, he chooses to give the consumers 2 units each as summarized in the table. Shade in the rectangles representing the value each consumer receives from this distribution of goods. (Again use a different style or color of shading for each consumer.) Next summarize your results in the table and calculate the total value of consuming 6 units of output under our social planner. If you've done this correctly, you should find that this way of dividing consumption creates $45 of value.

Step 4. Compare the total value received by consumers with the total cost incurred by firms to find the amount of social gain created by our planner. Notice that social gain under the planner is only $20, as compared to the $30 we discovered was possible in the first graph. Without access to the specialized knowledge of each firm and consumer, the social planner created only 2/3 of the gains from trade possible!

Figure 9-2.

Step 1. The top graph summarizes the maximum social gain that we calculated in Figure 9-1. This time we will use a competitive market to allocate production and consumption. First, use the supply/demand graph to verify that a competitive market would establish a price of $6/unit for this good.

Step 2. Use the second graph to determine how the market will distribute the production among firms. Remembering that firms produce up to the point where marginal cost (shown by the supply curve) equals price, shade in the rectangles representing each firm's cost of production and complete the accompanying table to summarize your results. You should find that the competitive market allocates the production of 6 units of the good at a total cost of $21.

Step 3. Use the third graph to determine how the market will allocate the goods among the consumers. Remembering that consumers purchase a good up to the point where marginal value (shown by the demand curve) equals price, shade in the rectangles representing each consumer's value from consuming the good and complete the table to summarize your results. You should find that the market created $51 in value from the 6 units of the good. Notice that consumer X has zero units of the good; he would rather have his share of the economy's wealth in the form of other goods.

Step 4. Calculate the social gain created by the competitive market. You should discover that the market—by using price to convey information and provide incentives—generated all the possible gains from trade shown in the top graph. This of course should not be a surprise if you truly understand the Invisible Hand Theorem.

Figure 9-2 The Competitive Market's Allocation of Resources

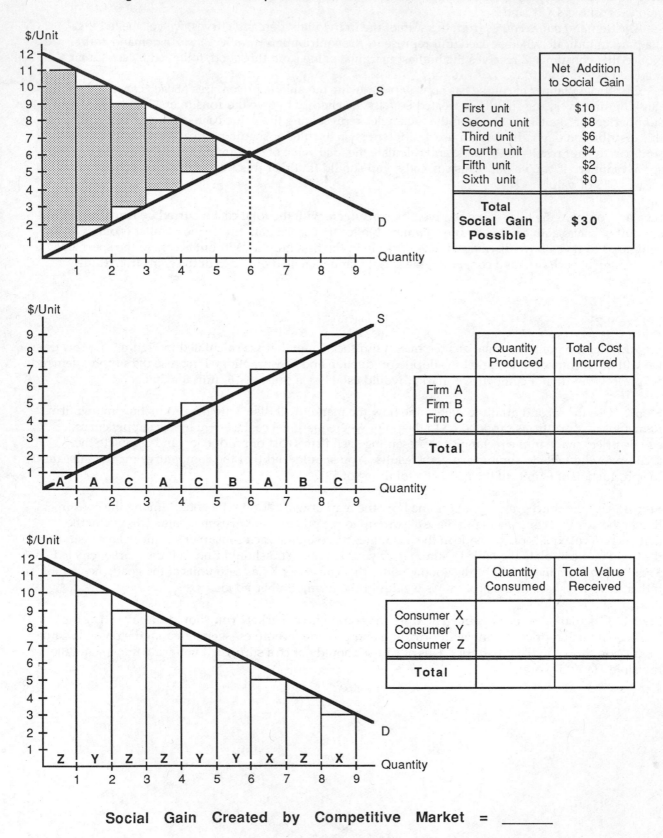

	Net Addition to Social Gain
First unit	$10
Second unit	$8
Third unit	$6
Fourth unit	$4
Fifth unit	$2
Sixth unit	$0
Total Social Gain Possible	**$30**

	Quantity Produced	Total Cost Incurred
Firm A		
Firm B		
Firm C		
Total		

	Quantity Consumed	Total Value Received
Consumer X		
Consumer Y		
Consumer Z		
Total		

Social Gain Created by Competitive Market = _____

Multiple Choice Questions

1. Which of the following statements on the function of competitive prices is *false?*
   A. Prices embody the knowledge of society's members.
   B. Prices convey information to society's members.
   C. Prices provide incentive for society's members to act upon their own unique knowledge.
   D. Prices work through supply and demand to guarantee that there is an equitable allocation of resources among society's members.

2. Producing and consuming the quantity where marginal cost equals marginal value does not guarantee the maximum gains from trade. We must also make sure that the good is produced by those with the _____ marginal cost and consumed by those with the _____ marginal value.
   A. lowest;   lowest
   B. lowest;   highest
   C. highest; lowest
   D. highest; highest

***Questions 3 and 4 refer to the accompanying table which shows three different consumers' marginal values from consuming a good.

Consumer X		Consumer Y		Consumer Z	
Quantity	MV	Quantity	MV	Quantity	MV
1	$ 3/unit	1	$ 7/unit	1	$ 6/unit
2	$ 2/unit	2	$ 5/unit	2	$ 3/unit
3	$ 1/unit	3	$ 3/unit	3	$ 2/unit

3. Suppose a social planner has 6 units of this good to allocate among the three consumers. To create the most social gain possible, how much should he give to consumers X, Y, and Z?
   A. 2 units to each consumer.
   B. 3, 0, and 3 units respectively.
   C. 1, 3, and 2 units respectively.
   D. 0, 3, and 3 units respectively.

4. The greatest total value that these three consumers can receive from 6 units of the good is
   A. $3.
   B. $18.
   C. $26.
   D. $27.

***Questions 5 and 6 refer to the accompanying table which shows three different firms' marginal costs of producing a good.

Firm A			Firm B			Firm C	
Quantity	MC		Quantity	MC		Quantity	MC
1	$ 3/unit		1	$ 1/unit		1	$ 1/unit
2	$ 5/unit		2	$ 3/unit		2	$ 2/unit
3	$ 7/unit		3	$ 5/unit		3	$ 3/unit

5. Suppose the equilibrium quantity in the competitive market for this good is 6 units. If the competitive price system is used to allocate production, these six units will be produced for a total cost of
   A. $3.
   B. $10.
   C. $13.
   D. $15.

6. Suppose a social planner allocates production of the 6 units by dividing it equally among the three firms. This will result in a social loss of
   A. $0 (i.e., there will be no social loss).
   B. $2.
   C. $3.
   D. $10.

***Questions 7 and 8 refer to Figure 9a which shows the supply and demand for military service.

Figure 9a

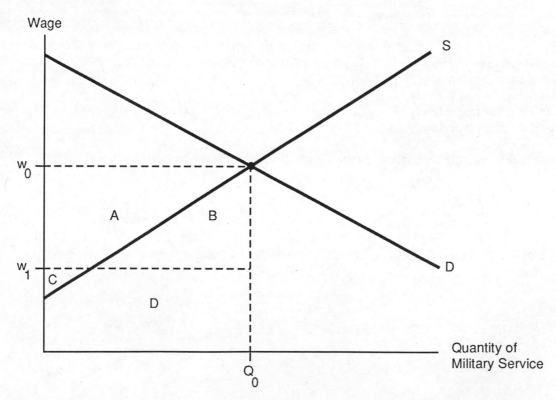

7. Suppose the government pays soldiers the wage w_0 and relies on a volunteer army of size Q_0. The cost to society of this army is
   A. the area A + C.
   B. the area A + B + C + D.
   C. the area B + D.
   D. impossible to determine from the given information.

8. Suppose the government switches from the volunteer army in Question 7 to a draft. The government drafts Q_0 persons into the army and pays them the wage w_1. Society's cost of having this army
   A. will remain unchanged.
   B. will be lowered to the area C + D.
   C. will be greater than the area B + D.
   D. None of the above

9. Economic rent
   A. is the amount earned in excess of the minimum amount necessary to hire a factor of production.
   B. is the same as social gain.
   C. provides incentives for owners of a resource to provide it to those with the lowest marginal value.
   D. provides no social gain and simply enriches owners of a resource.

***Questions 10-12 refer to Figure 9b, where the owner of a resource is receiving price P_0 and providing the quantity Q_0.

Figure 9b

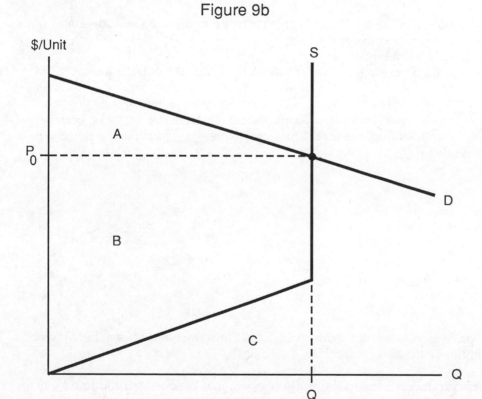

167

10. The revenue collected by the owner is measured by the area
    A. B.
    B. C.
    C. A + B.
    D. B + C.

11. Rent is measured by the area
    A. B.
    B. C.
    C. A + B.
    D. B + C.

12. Suppose the government confiscates the rents and pays the owner area C to supply Q_0 units of the resource. We can expect the result to be inefficient because
    A. the resulting total value of the resource to consumers will be smaller than the area A + B + C.
    B. the area B will become a deadweight loss.
    C. the resulting producers' surplus will be smaller than area B.
    D. All of the above

13. In an efficient market
    A. no economic rents will be created.
    B. the current price will fully reflect all available information.
    C. the pattern of past prices will provide useful information about future prices unavailable elsewhere.
    D. the informational content of prices is diluted by inflation.

14. Suppose prices and wages both increase by 5%. If people correctly anticipate this inflation,
    A. there will be no change in the unemployment rate.
    B. relative prices will remain unchanged.
    C. the ability of prices to communicate information will not be diluted by this inflation.
    D. All of the above

15. Suppose prices and wages both increase by 5%, but people base their decisions on the expectation that inflation is 8%. Then people will believe that their wages have _____ purchasing power, causing the unemployment rate to _____.
    A. higher; increase
    B. higher; decrease
    C. lower; increase
    D. lower; decrease

Solutions

1. D. Using a competitive pricing system will maximize the gains from trade but does not guarantee anything about equity in the distribution of income.

2. B. The area that measures producers' surplus implicitly assumes that the good is produced by firms with the lowest marginal cost. Similarly, the area that measures consumers' surplus implicitly assumes that the good is consumed by those with the highest marginal value. When this is not the case, these areas overstate the actual gains to society.

3. C. Each unit should be allocated to the consumer with the highest marginal value. So the first unit should be given to consumer Y, the second unit to consumer Z, the third unit to consumer Z. Each consumer should receive one of the last three units.

4. D. Using the marginal value schedules and the distribution of goods in Question 3, consumer X gets $3 in value from 1 unit of the good, consumer Y gets $15 in value from 3 units, and consumer Z gets $9 in value from 2 units. This gives a total value of $27.

5. C. In competition, the marginal costs of firms will be equated. When 6 units are produced, this occurs at a marginal cost of $3/unit. A will produce 1 unit for a cost of $3, B will produce 2 units for a cost of $4, and C will produce 3 units for a cost of $6. The total cost is then $13.

6. B. Using the marginal cost schedules, if firms A, B, and C each produce two units, their total costs will be $8, $4, and $3, respectively. The total cost will be $15, which is $2 greater than the total cost achieved by the competitive market.

7. C. The cost of the army is the opportunity cost of having men and women in military service instead of some other occupation. Using the supply/marginal cost duality, this is the area under the supply curve. The wage bill (area A + B + C + D) is merely a transfer of income from taxpayers to soldiers, so does not represent the cost to society.

8. C. If the government drafts men and women with high marginal costs instead of those with low marginal costs, area B + D will underestimate the actual cost of the army.

9. A. This is the definition of rent. The social role of rent is to provide owners incentive to locate those who would receive the highest marginal value from the resource.

10. D. The owner of the resource is paid a total of B + C, since this rectangle has the quantity supplied as the base and the price per unit as the width. Area A + B is the social gain.

11. A. Rent is simply another name for producers' surplus in this special case where supply is almost entirely vertical.

12. A. Although the confiscation of rents makes producers' surplus zero, the result could still be efficient if the resource is given to those consumers with the highest marginal value. But without the price system to give the owner incentive to find those consumers, the area under demand (area A + B + C) will overestimate the actual total value generated. Consequently, area A + B will overestimate the actual social gain (the total value to consumers minus the total cost of hiring the resource).

13. B. This is the definition of an efficient market.

14. D. Since the inflation is correctly anticipated, relative prices will be unchanged and people will continue to work the same amount.

15. C. Relative prices are in actuality unchanged, but people think prices are rising faster than wages. They are fooled into thinking that their wages are not keeping up with inflation, and so cut back on their labor supply, causing unemployment to increase. The unexpectedly low inflation has diluted the ability of price to convey information, creating a tradeoff between inflation and unemployment.

Questions for Review

1. How can the specialized knowledge of each individual and firm be fully incorporated into the decisions of resource allocation made in an economy?

2. Compare and contrast an economy that allocates resources through competitive prices with one where people are actively altruistic and cater to your every whim.

3. Consider an economy run by a benevolent dictator. Suppose that the quantity of a good produced and consumed in this economy is the same as what would result from using a competitive market. Would the social gain from this good be maximized? Explain.

4. What is the cost of maintaining an army? Why is this cost not affected by the wage paid to soldiers? Name two ways that an army could be unnecessarily costly.

5. What is rent? Since confiscation of rents won't affect the quantity supplied, how could this cause a loss in efficiency?

6. Given the obvious risks, why is insider trading of stocks so tempting?

7. Explain why unexpectedly low inflation may increase unemployment.

Solutions

1. Each individual's knowledge about the value of goods is reflected in his demand curve, which is a part of market demand. Each firm's knowledge about the production of goods is reflected in its supply curve, which is a part of market supply. So price, as determined by the demand and supply in the competitive market, embodies the specialized knowledge of all individuals and firms.

2. You would probably favor the world where people cater to your every whim on the basis of income distribution—your share of the pie will be very large in such a world. However, the pie will also be smaller, because lacking the specialized knowledge of others you will find it very difficult to communicate your desires. The economy with competitive prices will be much more efficient—that is, it will create a much larger pie. This is because prices are able to convey information and provide incentive to people to act on their own knowledge.

3. It is virtually impossible for the benevolent dictator to create the most social gain possible, even if the quantity produced and consumed is the competitive equilibrium quantity. This is because the goods must be produced by those with the lowest marginal cost and consumed by those with the highest marginal value to create the most social gain. Without the specialized knowledge of each individual and firm, efficient allocation of production across firms and consumption across individuals cannot be achieved by the benevolent dictator.

4. As discussed in the textbook, the cost of an army is the opportunity cost of not using its soldiers in other occupations. The wages paid are simply a transfer of income from taxpayers to soldiers and so do not affect this opportunity cost. An army could be unnecessarily costly if it is the wrong size (i.e., if the marginal value received from the last soldier is not equal to the marginal cost of not employing him elsewhere) or if it consists of the wrong people (i.e., if society drafts men and women with high opportunity costs instead of those with lower opportunity costs).

5. Rent is any payment for a resource in excess of the minimum amount necessary to call it into existence. The problem with confiscation of rents is that it may eliminate the price system. Without the incentives provided by price, the owners will be unable to identify those who would receive the largest marginal value from the resource. In that case, the resource will not create the maximum value possible for consumers, causing a loss in efficiency.

6. The stock market tends to be highly efficient—all available information is already reflected in the price of the stock. So only inside information may not yet be reflected in the price, making it much easier to predict how the price of a stock will change. Hence inside information provides a far greater opportunity to earn a profit than publicly known information.

7. If inflation is lower than what people expect, wages are rising by a smaller amount than the amount people think prices are rising by. This fools people into thinking that the purchasing power of their wages is falling, causing people to reduce the amount of labor they provide and increasing unemployment. If people had not been fooled by the lower-than-expected inflation and had correctly realized that prices and wages were rising by the same amount, they would have seen that relative prices were unchanged and would not have adjusted their work effort.

Problems for Analysis

1. Consider the owner of a firm who has superior managerial skills that make her firm more efficient than most others in the industry.
   (i) On the axes below, sketch the owner's marginal cost of providing managerial skills to her firm, assuming Q_{max} is the maximum number of hours she can supply weekly.

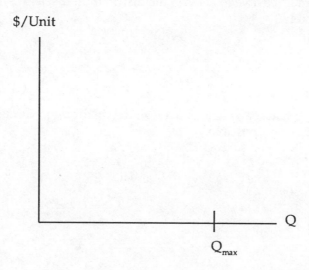

(ii) Suppose the price of the good produced by her firm increases, causing new, less efficient firms to enter the industry in the long run. What will happen to the opportunity cost of supplying Q_{max} hours of managerial services to her firm weekly? What will happen to her firm's profits? Using the marginal cost curve drawn in part (i), give a supply/demand diagram to justify your answer.

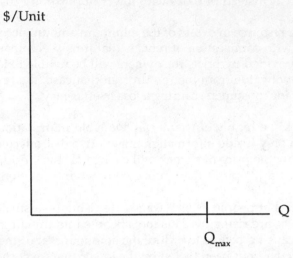

2. Consider an economy with only two consumers: Alex and Betty. Let MV_A and MV_B represent the marginal value that Alex and Betty, respectively, receive from consumption of a good. Their marginal value curves are not necessarily identical. Suppose there is a fixed quantity of the good to distribute between Alex and Betty.

(i) Use the equimarginal principle to explain why the distribution of the fixed quantity that equates their marginal values (i.e., that makes $MV_A = MV_B$) will make the total value received from this good as large as possible.

(ii) Would a social planner be able to achieve the distribution discussed in part (i)? Explain; be as detailed as possible.

(iii) Would a competitive market be able to achieve the distribution discussed in part (i)? Explain; be as detailed as possible.

3. A city council determines that the city's air pollution is caused by its two major firms (call them A and B). A regulatory body is charged with the duty of achieving a total reduction in air pollution emissions of 10 units. The marginal costs that each firm faces for reducing its emissions are given in the following tables.

Firm A		Firm B	
Reduction in air pollution (# of units)	MC of achieving this reduction ($/unit)	Reduction in air pollution (# of units)	MC of achieving this reduction ($/unit)
1	2	1	4
2	3	2	6
3	4	3	8
4	5	4	10
5	6	5	12
6	7	6	14
7	8	7	16
8	9	8	18
9	10	9	20
10	11	10	22

(i) Determine the least cost method of achieving the city council's goal.

(ii) Suppose the regulators decide to treat the two firms equally and establish a standard requiring each firm to reduce its emissions by 5 units. Calculate the total cost of achieving the city council's goal under this plan.

(iii) Suppose the regulatory body imposes a tax on these firms of $8 per unit of air pollution they emit. First use the equimarginal principle to describe how the firms will react to this tax. Then calculate the total cost of achieving the city council's goal under this plan.

(iv) Compare the efficiency of the standard and taxation approaches.

173

Solutions

1. (i) We should expect marginal cost (i.e., supply) to be upward sloping until Q_{max}, when it would become vertical.

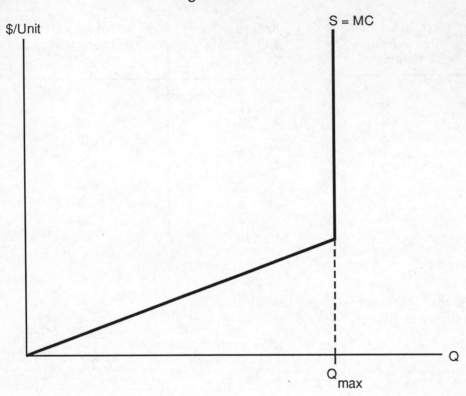

Figure 9c

(ii) The higher price for the product and the entry of less efficient firms will increase the demand for the owner's managerial skills. This will in turn increase the economic rent paid to hire those services, as shown in Figure 9d. The higher opportunity costs of using her managerial skills in her own firm instead of renting them out will drive up the costs of her firm. This (along with the lower price caused by entry of firms) will drive her firm's profits back to zero in the long run.

Figure 9d

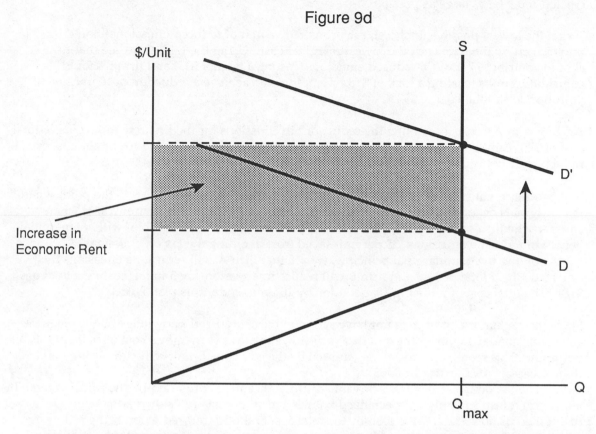

2. (i) Suppose we have distributed the goods so that Alex's marginal value (MV_A) is greater than Betty's (MV_B). This tells us that Alex places a higher value on the last unit of the good consumed than Betty does. In this case, we should give more of the good to Alex. The marginal benefit of giving more to Alex is MV_A dollars per unit; the marginal cost of this action (i.e., the loss in value from taking the same amount away from Betty) is MV_B dollars per unit. So the total value created will increase when we give more to Alex since the marginal benefit of doing so outweighs the marginal cost.

Similarly, if we distributed the goods so that Betty's marginal value were greater than Alex's, the marginal benefit of giving more to Betty would outweigh the marginal cost.

Using the equimarginal principle, we see that in order to create the most value possible the good should be distributed so that Alex's and Betty's marginal values are equated (i.e., so that $MV_A = MV_B$).

(ii) It would be unlikely that a social planner could achieve the distribution that gives the largest social gain. To equate Alex's and Betty's marginal value, the planner would have to know their preferences, and he is unlikely to be able to obtain this information.

(iii) A competitive market would achieve the distribution that gives the greatest social gain. When Alex purchases goods in the market, he will buy the good up to the point where his marginal value equals the price paid. Betty will also buy the quantity of the good where her marginal value equals the price paid. Since both are equating their marginal values to the same price (i.e., since $MV_A = P$ and $MV_B = P$), their independent actions have equated their marginal values (i.e., $MV_A = MV_B$). The equimarginal principle tells us that the total value created must be as large as possible.

3. (i) To get the lowest possible total cost, each consecutive unit of reduced emissions should be undertaken by the firm with the lowest marginal cost. Using the tables, we see that firm A should contribute 7 units in reduced emissions (costing a total of $35) and firm B should contribute 3 units (costing a total of $18). Hence we can achieve a reduction of 10 units of air pollution for a total cost of $53.

(ii) Adding firm A's costs of making the reductions in emissions for the first five units gives a total cost of $20. Similarly, the cost of firm B to reduce emissions by 5 units is $40. So the cost of reducing air pollution under the standard is $60.

(iii) The equimarginal principle says that the firm will reduce its emissions up to the point where the marginal cost of doing so equals the tax of $8 per unit. This result is immediate when we compare the firm's marginal cost of reducing emissions (given by the table) with its marginal benefit of reducing emissions ($8 per unit saved from avoiding the tax on emissions).

Applying the equimarginal principle, we see that firm A will reduce its emissions by 7 units (costing a total of $35) and firm B will reduce its emissions by 3 units (costing a total of $18). The total cost of reducing air pollution by 10 units under this plan is $53.

(iv) Since the regulatory body does not have access to the specialized knowledge about the firms' costs, the standard ignores the fact that firm A has the lowest marginal cost of reducing its air pollution. This results in a social loss, as seen by the cost of a 10-unit reduction being higher than necessary ($60 instead of $53).

The tax on emissions takes advantage of the incentives provided by the price system. It allows each firm to apply its specialized knowledge of its costs to its own advantage. As a result there is no social loss, as seen by the total cost of the 10-unit reduction being as low as possible. (Notice that the tax itself is a transfer of income from the firms to tax recipients.)

Solutions to Working Through the Graphs

Figure 9-1   A Social Planner's Allocation of Resources

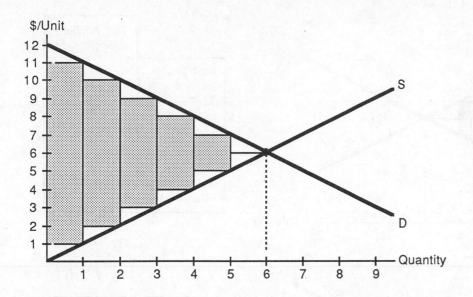

	Net Addition to Social Gain
First unit	$10
Second unit	$8
Third unit	$6
Fourth unit	$4
Fifth unit	$2
Sixth unit	$0
Total Social Gain Possible	**$30**

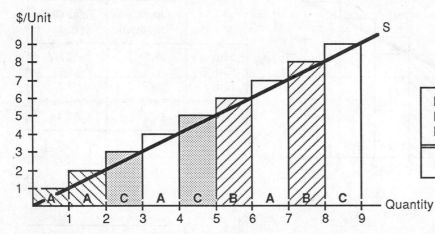

	Quantity Produced	Total Cost Incurred
Firm A	2	$3
Firm B	2	$14
Firm C	2	$8
Total	**6**	**$25**

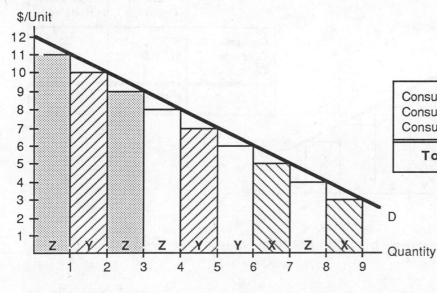

	Quantity Consumed	Total Value Received
Consumer X	2	$8
Consumer Y	2	$17
Consumer Z	2	$20
Total	**6**	**$45**

Social Gain Created by Planner = $20

177

Figure 9-2 The Competitive Market's Allocation of Resources

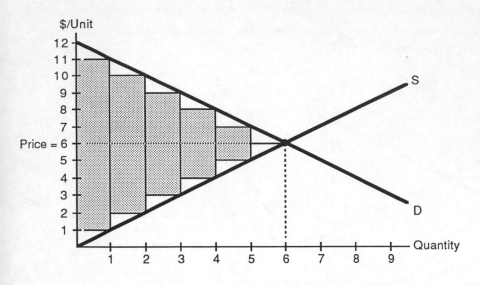

	Net Addition to Social Gain
First unit	$10
Second unit	$8
Third unit	$6
Fourth unit	$4
Fifth unit	$2
Sixth unit	$0
Total Social Gain Possible	**$30**

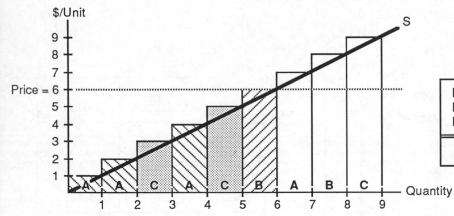

	Quantity Produced	Total Cost Incurred
Firm A	3	$7
Firm B	1	$6
Firm C	2	$8
Total	**6**	**$21**

	Quantity Consumed	Total Value Received
Consumer X	0	$0
Consumer Y	3	$23
Consumer Z	3	$28
Total	**6**	**$51**

Social Gain Created by Competitive Market = $30

Chapter Ten

Monopoly

Chapter Summary

At this point you should have a good understanding of how the market works under competition when no one firm's decisions can affect the price of its product. In this chapter we will study the other extreme—monopoly. Although many texts define monopoly as a single seller in the market, this begs the question of how to define the scope of the market. To avoid this problem, we will say that a firm has *monopoly power* whenever its actions can influence the market price. This implies that a firm with monopoly power, unlike a competitive firm, faces a downward sloping demand curve for its product.

Section 10.1. Price and Output under Monopoly

As with any firm, a monopoly will produce the quantity where marginal revenue equals marginal cost. The monopoly will then charge the price for that quantity as dictated by the demand for its product. In this case where demand is downward sloping, there are four basic facts to remember.

First notice that marginal revenue must be smaller than price; in other words the marginal revenue curve must be beneath the demand curve. This is immediate from the definition of marginal revenue. Since demand is downward sloping, the monopoly must offer a lower price to convince consumers to purchase a higher quantity, and this lower price applies to all units sold. So the revenue generated by the last unit sold (i.e., marginal revenue) is the price received for that unit minus the price reduction on the other items that are now sold at the new lower price.

The second basic fact about monopoly is the relationship between marginal revenue and the price elasticity of demand (which is denoted by the symbol μ). This relationship is summarized by the formula $MR = P \cdot (1 - 1/|\eta|)$. Applying this formula, we see that marginal revenue is positive when demand is elastic ($|\eta| > 1$) and negative when demand is inelastic ($|\eta| < 1$). Since the profit-maximization rule marginal revenue equals marginal cost can only be satisfied at a quantity where marginal revenue is positive, this tells us that a monopoly will only operate on the elastic portion of the demand curve.

The third fact to remember is that a monopoly has no supply curve because the concept of a supply curve is inapplicable to the monopoly's problem. A competitive firm reacts to a given market price by finding the quantity supplied that will maximize profits; the supply curve summarizes the firm's reactions to each possible going market price. But a monopoly does not react to a going market price; instead its actions determine the price charged. So a monopoly does not have a supply curve since the monopoly is a price maker, not a price taker.

The final basic monopoly result is that a monopoly will produce a smaller quantity than a competitive industry facing the same situation, resulting in a deadweight loss. Both monopolies and competitive firms produce to the point where marginal revenue equals marginal cost. But a competitive firm can sell any quantity at the going market price, so marginal revenue equals price (a.k.a., marginal value). We can conclude (as we did in Chapter 8) that marginal value equals marginal cost in competition, which indicates no deadweight loss. But since a monopoly must lower price to increase sales, marginal revenue is smaller than price (marginal value). Combining this with the profit-maximization rule, we find that marginal cost is smaller than marginal value under monopoly. This indicates there is a deadweight loss, since the last unit of the product is worth more to consumers than what it cost to produce.

Two public policies could be used to eliminate the deadweight loss caused by monopoly: a subsidy and a price ceiling. The subsidy would reduce the monopoly's marginal cost, stimulating its output. If the subsidy is properly chosen, consumers would receive the same consumers' surplus as in competition, the monopoly would receive the producer's surplus plus the subsidy, and taxpayers would lose the subsidy. The price ceiling works by affecting marginal revenue. Marginal revenue would now equal the ceiling price for those quantities where consumers are willing to pay a greater price and be unaffected for other quantities. If the price ceiling is set at the level where demand crosses marginal cost, then the consumers' and producer's surplus would be the same as in competition.

It would be mistaken to think that policy makers could eliminate the deadweight loss by forcing the monopoly to earn zero profits. It is true that efficiency and zero profits coexist in a competitive long-run equilibrium, but this is a consequence of price-taking behavior and entry and exit of firms. Unlike competition, average cost, marginal cost and demand will rarely coincide when a firm has monopoly power, so zero-profit regulation will almost never totally eliminate deadweight loss. In fact when the monopoly is required to produce the quantity where average cost crosses demand (forcing zero profits), this quantity may be above or below the efficient quantity where marginal value (demand) equals marginal cost.

Section 10.2. Sources of Monopoly Power

There are four major sources of monopoly power: natural monopolies, patents, resource monopolies, and legal barriers to entry.

A *natural monopoly* exists when the firm's average cost is still decreasing as it crosses the demand curve. One situation which can create a natural monopoly is when production exhibits high fixed costs and low marginal costs, such as in electric power generation. An industry which has this relation between demand and firms' average costs can only support a single seller and cannot support a competitive market.

For example, consider a hypothetical competitive industry in this situation. The competitive price (where the sum of marginal costs crosses demand) is beneath firms' average cost, guaranteeing losses under competition. Exit of firms would occur until only one firm is left in the market, since just one optimal-sized firm (i.e., one that has minimized long-run average cost) could more than satisfy the entire market demand. So competition would *naturally* result in a "single seller" monopoly. Our welfare comparison between monopoly and competition in the previous section is invalid for the natural monopoly case, since competition cannot survive when average cost is decreasing over the relevant market quantities.

Patents give producers a legally protected monopoly for 17 years after the development of a new invention. As with natural monopoly, the social loss due to monopoly created by patents is uncertain. Without patents new inventions could be copied and produced competitively, eliminating the deadweight loss due to monopoly shown in the previous section. On the other hand the incentive to pursue the research and development needed to create an invention would be greatly reduced without patents, having a negative effect on social welfare.

A third source of monopoly power occurs when a single firm gains control of a resource essential to producing the good. The prime example of this is Alcoa, which managed to continue its domination of the aluminum industry through its ownership of virtually all the available bauxite ore from which aluminum is derived.

Finally, the government sometimes legally grants firms monopoly power by guaranteeing that entry by other firms will be prohibited. One example of this is the right granted by state governments to operate restaurants and gas stations along toll highways. Our welfare analysis underestimates the social loss due to this type of monopoly since firms will spend resources lobbying legislators to gain this monopoly power and the associated profits.

Section 10.3. Price Discrimination

In Section 10.1, we only considered the situation where the monopoly charges a single per-unit price for the product. However there are several other pricing schemes a monopoly can pursue to further increase its profits. The variety of these pricing strategies shows how complicated it is for firms with monopoly power to choose the method that would work best for its product and consumers.

When a monopoly charges different prices for identical goods, we say that it practices *price discrimination*. In addition to having monopoly power, the firm must be able to prevent resale of its product and find some mechanism of discriminating against the appropriate groups of consumers for price discrimination to be successful.

First-degree price discrimination occurs when the monopoly charges each consumer the most he is willing to pay (as read from the demand curve) for each unit of the good. As long as consumers' marginal value exceeds the monopoly's marginal cost, there is the possibility for the monopoly to increase its profits using first-degree price discrimination. So the monopoly will produce up to the point where marginal value equals marginal cost and hence will produce the same quantity as a competitive industry. The monopoly will earn the entire social gain possible as producer's surplus, consumers will receive no surplus value, and there will be no deadweight loss.

Second-degree price discrimination occurs when customers are treated identically but the price charged varies with the quantity purchased. Quantity discounts are one common form of second-degree price discrimination. Like first-degree price discrimination, this scheme also increases the monopolist's output and hence increases social gain. Since the monopoly is not necessarily charging the highest price consumers are willing to pay, both consumers' and producer's surplus are higher in second-degree price discrimination than in simple profit-maximizing pricing behavior.

Third-degree price discrimination is a situation where the firm faces distinct groups of consumers with different demands. To maximize profits in this situation, the equimarginal principle implies that marginal revenues across groups must be equated. Graphically this is shown by horizontally summing the different marginal revenue curves; the result represents the firm's marginal revenue curve. The firm then chooses quantity so that marginal revenue equals marginal cost and divides this quantity among the various consumer groups so that their marginal revenues are also equated to marginal cost. The price charged depends on each group's demand curve; the more inelastic a group's demand is, the higher the price charged to that group.

Another pricing scheme available to a monopoly is the *two-part tariff*. Here the firm charges consumers an entry fee for the right to purchase its product. Club memberships provide a common example. In a perfect two-part tariff the firm should charge an entry fee equal to consumers' surplus, since this is the maximum amount that consumers will pay for the right to purchase the good. So to maximize profits the firm should maximize the sum of producer's and consumers' surplus. This implies that the monopoly produces the competitive quantity and appropriates all the social gain, resulting in no deadweight loss under the two-part tariff.

Working Through the Graphs—Eliminating the Deadweight Loss due to Monopoly

One problem with simple profit-maximizing monopoly is that it underproduces its product relative to the efficient level of output produced by a competitive industry, resulting in a deadweight loss. In Figures 10-1 and 10-2 we consider two public policies that can remedy this problem: a subsidy and a price ceiling.

Figure 10-1.

Step 1. The top diagram shows the typical monopoly situation, where Q_C is the competitive quantity, Q_M is the monopoly quantity, and P_M is the monopoly price. Locate and shade in the consumers' surplus, producer's surplus, and deadweight loss in the monopoly equilibrium; use a different color or style of shading for each area.

Step 2. To eliminate the deadweight loss, we want the monopoly to increase output to the competitive quantity Q_C. Since the monopoly quantity Q_M is determined by the intersection of marginal revenue and marginal cost, public policy can achieve our goal by properly altering either marginal revenue or marginal cost.

An excise subsidy uses the former strategy, lowering marginal cost and increasing the monopoly output. To eliminate the deadweight loss, we want to reduce marginal cost sufficiently so that the new intersection between marginal revenue and marginal cost is at the competitive quantity Q_C.

Use the lower graph of Figure 10-1 to diagram such a subsidy. Draw in the marginal cost under the subsidy, remembering that an excise subsidy results in a parallel shift downward in marginal cost. Be sure that you've chosen the size of the subsidy so that the monopoly will now produce the efficient quantity Q_C.

Step 3. Now do the welfare analysis of the post-subsidy monopoly equilibrium. First shade in the consumers' and producer's surplus; remember to use the original marginal cost curve for the producer's surplus since this is the one that represents the true marginal cost of production.

Next find the revenue paid out in the subsidy. To do this, remember that the vertical distance between the two marginal cost curves gives the subsidy paid on each unit; by summing all of these we get a parallelogram representing the total subsidy paid to the monopoly.

Finally calculate the social gain. You should find that it equals the sum of the consumers' and producer's surplus, resulting in no deadweight loss. The amount paid in the subsidy is a transfer of income from taxpayers to the monopoly, so it makes a net contribution of zero in the social gain calculation.

Figure 10-2.

Step 1. The top diagram summarizes the information about the monopoly equilibrium discovered in Step 1 of Figure 10-1. Verify that the information given in this diagram is correct.

Step 2. This time we will use a price ceiling to eliminate the deadweight loss, to be diagrammed in the lower graph. This uses the strategy of altering the monopoly's marginal revenue curve, making it more closely resemble the marginal revenue faced by a competitive firm.

For this strategy, we will set the price ceiling at the competitive price. First locate this price in the diagram.

Next we need to determine how the price ceiling changes the monopoly's marginal revenue curve. To do this, first notice that the price ceiling is above the price consumers are willing to pay for quantities larger than Q_C. Since the monopoly must charge a price lower than the ceiling for these quantities, the price ceiling will have no effect and so marginal revenue will be unchanged beyond Q_C.

On the other hand, notice that the price ceiling is below the price consumers are willing to pay for quantities smaller than Q_C, so the price ceiling does affect the price the monopoly can receive. The monopoly's demand is now made horizontal at the ceiling price just like a competitive firm's, so marginal revenue is equal to the ceiling price for the quantities below Q_C.

Figure 10-1   Using a Subsidy to Eliminate the Deadweight Loss
Due to Monopoly

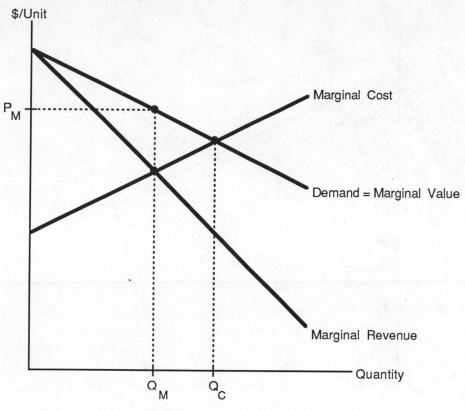

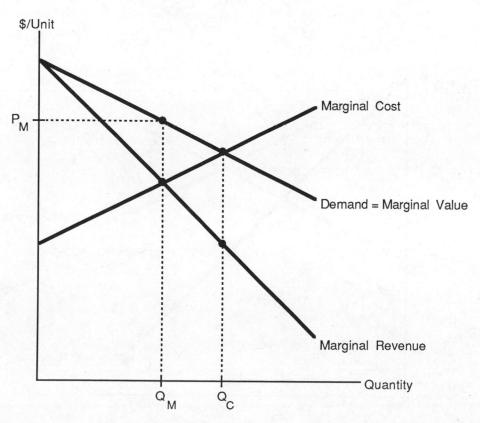

Figure 10-2 Using a Price Ceiling to Eliminate the Deadweight Loss
Due to Monopoly

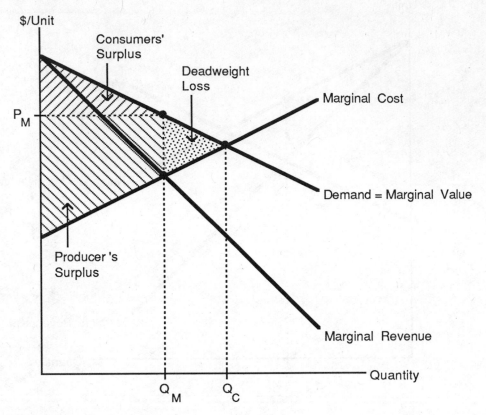

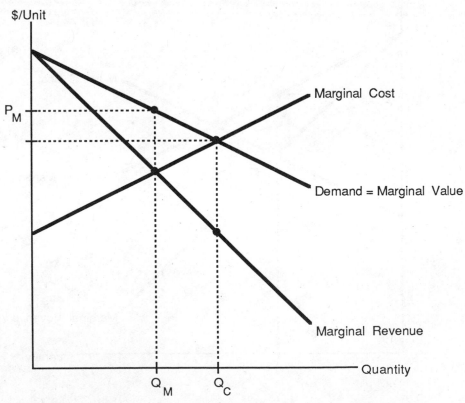

Keeping the above facts in mind, draw in the marginal revenue curve under the price ceiling and locate the new equilibrium price and quantity. Your marginal revenue curve should resemble the one in Exhibit 10-4 of the textbook.

Step 3. Complete your graph by performing the welfare analysis. Locate and shade in the consumers' and producer's surplus and verify that the price ceiling has eliminated the deadweight loss.

Multiple Choice Questions

1. Which of the following conditions holds for a competitive firm in long-run equilibrium?
   A. Marginal revenue equals marginal cost.
   B. Price equals marginal cost.
   C. Price equals average cost.
   D. All of the above

2. Which of the following conditions holds for a simple profit-maximizing monopoly in the long run?
   A. Marginal revenue equals marginal cost.
   B. Price equals marginal cost.
   C. Price equals average cost.
   D. All of the above

3. Consider two demand curves, D_1 and D_2, which are crossing at the point (Q_0, P_0). At this point, both are elastic, with D_1 being more elastic than D_2. At the quantity Q_0, the marginal revenue for D_1 is _____ than that for D_2, with both being _____.
   A. larger; positive
   B. larger; negative
   C. smaller; positive
   D. smaller; negative

4. The monopoly's supply curve
   A. is its marginal cost curve above average variable cost.
   B. is its marginal cost curve above average cost.
   C. does not exist where demand is inelastic, since marginal revenue is negative for these quantities.
   D. does not exist since there is no going market price.

5. An excise tax on a monopoly's output will _____ the monopoly's profits and _____ the deadweight loss.
   A. lower; increase
   B. lower; decrease
   C. not affect; increase
   D. not affect; decrease

6. Which of the following *cannot* eliminate the deadweight loss due to monopoly?
   A. An excise subsidy.
   B. A price ceiling set below the monopoly price.
   C. Zero-profit regulation.
   D. First-degree price discrimination.

7. A price ceiling will affect a monopoly's _____, causing the monopoly to _____ its output level.
   A. marginal revenue; increase
   B. marginal revenue; decrease
   C. marginal cost; increase
   D. marginal cost; decrease

8. Which of the following statements about natural monopoly is *false?*
   A. For a natural monopoly, average cost is decreasing where it crosses demand.
   B. A natural monopoly is likely to exist when production exhibits low fixed costs and high marginal costs.
   C. In the natural monopoly situation, no firm could earn positive economic profits at the competitive price.
   D. The welfare consequences of natural monopoly are uncertain since comparison with competition is invalid.

9. The welfare analysis comparing competition and monopoly shows that the latter creates a deadweight loss. This analysis underestimates the social loss due to monopoly power when it results from
   A. a natural monopoly.
   B. patents.
   C. ownership of an essential resource.
   D. a legal barrier to entry.

10. A store advertises its shirts at "$13 each, 3 for $25." This is an example of
    A. first-degree price discrimination.
    B. second-degree price discrimination.
    C. third-degree price discrimination.
    D. a two-part tariff.

11. Coupons allow manufacturers to offer lower prices to those who are willing to take the time and effort to redeem them. This is an example of
    A. first-degree price discrimination.
    B. second-degree price discrimination.
    C. third-degree price discrimination.
    D. a two-part tariff.

12. IBM was able to charge different prices to different consumers for computer services by requiring computer cards be purchased separately. Those who placed a higher marginal value on computer services ended up purchasing more cards and hence paying a higher price for computer services than other consumers. This is an example of
    A. first-degree price discrimination.
    B. second-degree price discrimination.
    C. third-degree price discrimination.
    D. a two-part tariff.

13. A country club charges a membership fee. Members pay standard prices for the club's recreation and restaurant services. This is an example of
    A. first-degree price discrimination.
    B. second-degree price discrimination.
    C. third-degree price discrimination.
    D. a two-part tariff.

14. Which of the following is *not* a good example of third-degree price discrimination?
    A. Free delivery available for pizzas.
    B. Senior citizen discounts for prescription drugs.
    C. Lower airline prices for staying over a Saturday night.
    D. Lower salad bar prices for those who purchase an entree.

15. Which of the following pricing practices will increase the social gain from simple monopoly profit-maximizing behavior?
    A. First-degree price discrimination.
    B. Second-degree price discrimination.
    C. A two-part tariff.
    D. All of the above

Solutions

1. D. For a competitive firm, marginal revenue equals price, so choices A and B both represent profit maximization. Choice C implies there are zero profits.

2. A. Marginal revenue is smaller than price for a monopoly, so only choice A and not choice B represents profit maximization. If the monopoly has a barrier to entry, it can keep price above average cost and preserve positive profits.

3. A. Recall that $MR = P \cdot (1 - 1/|\eta|)$ where η is the price elasticity of demand. The more elastic demand is, the larger $|\eta|$ and the larger marginal revenue are. Marginal revenue is positive when demand is elastic and negative when demand is inelastic.

4. D. A supply curve presumes that a firm determines its level of output based on a given market price. Since the monopoly's actions determine price, there is no going market price and the concept of a supply curve is meaningless for a monopoly.

5. A. A monopoly can pass on some but not all of an excise tax to consumers since marginal revenue is downward sloping. (It is straightforward to show this graphically.) Since the tax increases the monopoly's marginal cost, it decreases the quantity supplied under monopoly causing the deadweight loss to increase.

6. C. Almost never will the quantity where demand equals marginal cost (the efficient quantity) be the same as the quantity where demand equals average cost (the zero-profit quantity).

7. A. For quantities where consumers are willing to pay more than the price ceiling, marginal revenue will be horizontal at the ceiling price. This change in marginal revenue will cause the monopoly to increase its output.

8. B. Since $AC = FC/Q + MC$ and FC/Q is always decreasing, AC will likely be decreasing when it crosses demand when FC is large and MC is small. This is what happens in the natural monopoly of electric power generation.

9. D. Firms will spend resources lobbying legislators to obtain the legally-created monopolies, increasing the social loss.

10. B. In second-degree price discrimination, the firm attempts to increase producer's surplus by lowering price to sell further units without lowering the price on the previous units sold.

11. C. In third-degree price discrimination, producers attempt to divide the market into distinguishable groups with different demands. People who use their time to do "comparison shopping" and clip and collect coupons generally have more elastic (i.e., "price-sensitive") demand for these goods. Hence they are offered a lower price when third-degree price discrimination is practiced.

12. A. In first-degree price discrimination, the monopoly attempts to charge each consumer the maximum amount he is willing to pay. This is what IBM was attempting to do with its sale of computer services by requiring computer cards be purchased separately well above marginal cost.

13. D. In a two-part tariff, the monopoly tries to appropriate the consumers' surplus through the use of an "entry fee."

14. D. Since those people who order an entree will generally eat less from a salad bar than those who don't, a restaurant is not actually charging different prices for the same good. The lower price is best explained by the lower cost for the "salad bar with entree," which is really a different good from the higher cost "salad bar without entree."

15. D. All three pricing policies cause the monopoly to increase its output, reducing deadweight loss. When first-degree price discrimination and two-part tariffs are completely successful, there will in fact be no deadweight loss.

Questions for Review

1. Why is marginal revenue smaller than price for a monopoly? Why does this fact imply that there will be a deadweight loss when the monopoly practices simple profit-maximization?

2. Explain why a simple profit-maximizing monopoly will not produce and sell a quantity at which demand is inelastic.

3. Provide a sketch similar to Exhibit 10-5 of the textbook showing that it is possible that zero-profit regulation can eliminate deadweight loss. Explain why this is an extremely unlikely occurrence. What policies provide better approaches to eliminating deadweight loss?

4. List four sources of monopoly power. For each source, indicate how the basic analysis of deadweight loss under monopoly should be modified.

5. What is a natural monopoly? Why can't the market support a competitive industry under the conditions of natural monopoly?

6. What is price discrimination? When does price discrimination hurt the consumers? Does price discrimination ever benefit consumers? Does price discrimination ever increase social gain?

7. For each of the following pricing schemes, give a sketch showing the quantity produced, price(s) charged, consumers' surplus, producer's surplus, deadweight loss, and any other relevant factors.
   (a) Simple profit maximization.
   (b) First-degree price discrimination.
   (c) Second-degree price discrimination.
   (d) A two-part tariff.

Solutions

1. A monopoly's marginal revenue consists of two parts: the price received on the last unit sold (which increases total revenue) and the price reduction on all previous units to persuade consumers to increase their quantity demanded (which decreases total revenue). A competitive firm's marginal revenue consists of only the former, making its marginal revenue equal to price.

   Since the monopoly will produce where marginal revenue equals marginal cost, using the above we see that price (marginal value) must be larger than marginal cost in the monopoly equilibrium. Marginal value being larger than marginal cost indicates that there is a deadweight loss since consumers are willing to pay more for the last unit sold than what it cost to produce.

2. Marginal revenue is positive where demand is elastic and negative where demand is inelastic. Since the simple profit-maximizing monopoly will produce the quantity where marginal revenue equals marginal cost, and since the latter is always positive, the profit-maximizing quantity must be where marginal revenue is positive. This implies that demand must be elastic at the profit-maximizing quantity.

3.

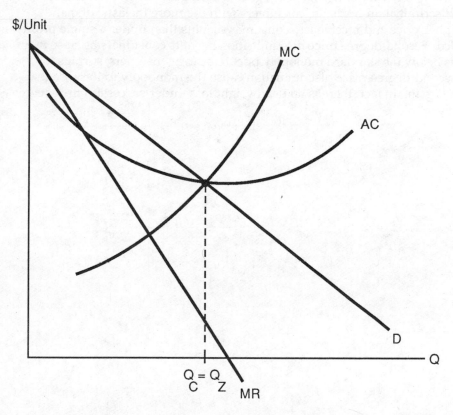

Figure 10a

For zero-profit regulation to eliminate deadweight loss, demand must intersect the cost curves where marginal cost equals average cost (i.e., at the minimum of average cost). However, the revenue and cost sides are distinct, so this intersection could only be a lucky coincidence. It is more likely that demand intersects average cost and marginal cost at different points, which implies that there will be a deadweight loss under zero-profit regulation as shown in Exhibit 10-5 of the textbook. A subsidy (by lowering the monopoly's marginal cost) or a price ceiling (by altering the monopoly's marginal revenue), when properly administered, would be more effective in eliminating the deadweight loss due to monopoly.

189

4. Four common sources of monopoly power are natural monopoly, patents, control of an essential resource, and legal barriers to entry. For natural monopoly, it is uncertain if the deadweight "loss" is truly a loss since competition cannot exist under the conditions of natural monopoly. Since the monopoly power granted by patents provides an incentive to firms to pursue the development of some inventions (but not others), the effect on the deadweight loss is also uncertain in this case. The textbook does not mention any serious alterations to the welfare analysis in the case of a resource monopoly. When legal barriers to entry are available, the basic welfare analysis underestimates the true social loss because firms will spend resources on lobbying efforts to gain the right to operate in the entry-restricted market and the resulting monopoly profits.

5. A natural monopoly exists when average cost is still decreasing as it crosses demand. This implies that marginal cost crosses demand at a lower price than where average cost crosses demand. So competitive pricing (i.e., when price equals firms' marginal costs) would always result in a price below firms' average costs. Hence competition would guarantee losses to all firms, and no firm would enter such a market.

6. Price discrimination occurs whenever a monopoly charges different prices for identical products. First-degree price discrimination hurts consumers because the monopoly charges each consumer the maximum amount he is willing to pay for each unit of the good, causing consumers' surplus to fall to zero. Third-degree price discrimination hurts the consumers with the more inelastic demand, because they will pay a higher price and receive less consumer surplus than under a single profit-maximizing monopoly price. Second-degree price discrimination benefits consumers because they are offered additional units below the standard monopoly price, causing consumers' surplus to increase. Both first- and second-degree price discrimination cause the monopoly to increase its output, increasing the social gain. In fact, there is no deadweight loss under successful first-degree price discrimination.

7. (a) In simple profit maximization, the monopoly produces the quantity where marginal revenue equals marginal cost.

Figure 10b

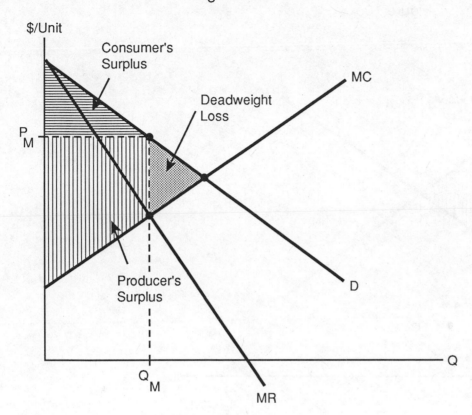

(b) In first-degree price discrimination, the monopoly charges the maximum price consumers are willing to pay for each unit of the product, receiving the entire social gain as producer's surplus.

Figure 10c

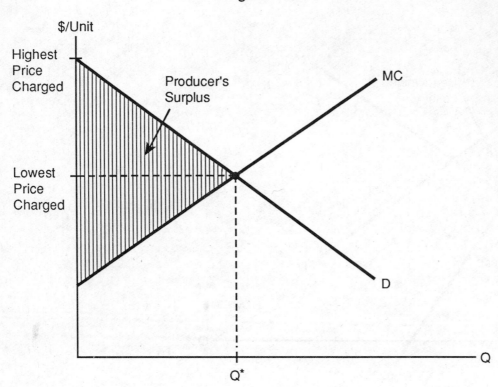

(c) In second-degree price discrimination, the monopoly lowers price to increase sales while keeping a higher price on previous units sold.

Figure 10d

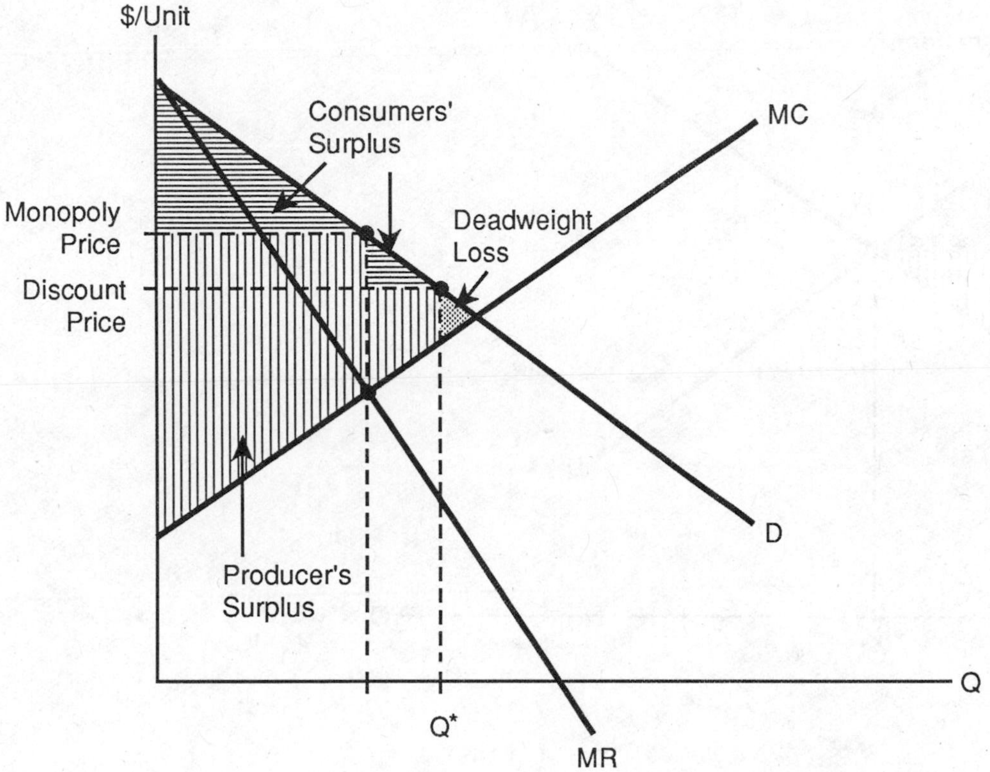

(d)   In a two-part tariff, the monopoly appropriates the consumers' surplus by charging an entry fee.

Figure 10e

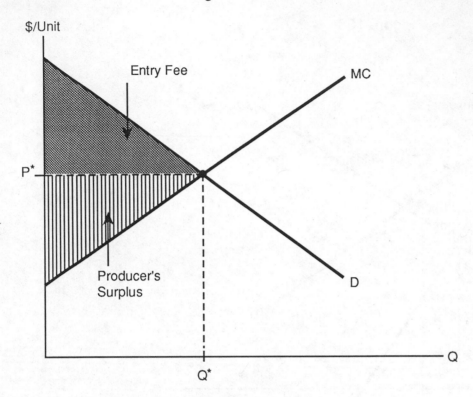

Problems for Analysis

1.   (i)   Consider two market structures: a competitive constant cost industry in the long run and a monopoly with constant long-run average and marginal costs. Suppose the government places an excise tax on the producers in these industries. Complete the diagrams below to show that deadweight loss is increased when these markets are taxed, assuming all factors are identical save for the market structure. The following should be labelled:

      a.   LRAC and LRMC for the monopoly and LRS for the competitive industry,
      b.   how equilibrium price and quantity change due to the tax,
      c.   consumers' surplus after the tax,
      d.   total revenue collected by the government,
      e.   the monopoly's after-tax profits, and
      f.   the increase in deadweight loss due to the tax.

194

Figure 10f

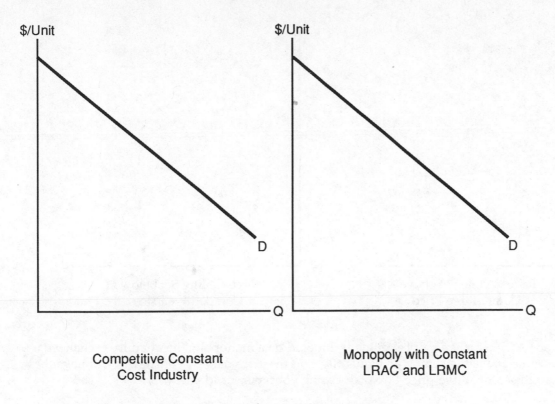

Competitive Constant Cost Industry

Monopoly with Constant LRAC and LRMC

(ii) To what degree did the competitive industry "pass on" the excise tax to consumers? The monopoly? Attempt to explain why we get this result.

(iii) Suppose the monopoly and competitive industry above experience the same increase in the cost of factors of production. Would you expect the monopoly or competitive industry to be more likely to pass on the increase in costs to consumers? Explain, using your answers to parts (i) and (ii).

2. (i) Complete the diagrams below to show (1) the effects of a price ceiling set above the competitive price but below the monopoly equilibrium price and (2) a price ceiling set below the competitive price. The following should be labelled:

a. the quantity produced under the price ceiling (Q*),
b. the price paid by consumers (P_C) and the ceiling price and
c. the deadweight loss.

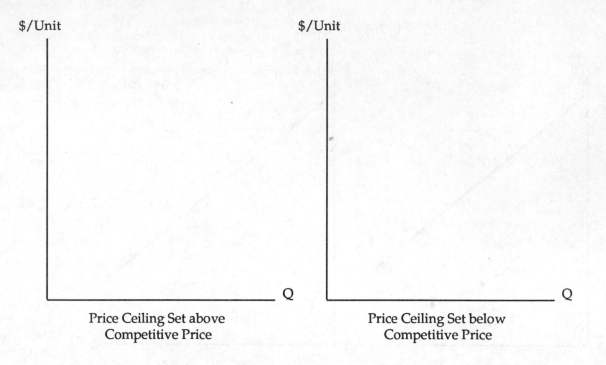

$/Unit	$/Unit
Q	Q
Price Ceiling Set above Competitive Price	Price Ceiling Set below Competitive Price

(ii)   TRUE or FALSE: "When a price ceiling is imposed on a monopoly, the quantity exchanged will never be above the competitive quantity, and the price paid by consumers will never be less than the competitive price." Explain, using your answer to part (i).

(iii) Suppose a monopoly can still make positive economic profits if it charges the competitive price. Can a price ceiling be used to achieve zero-profit regulation? Explain, using your answer to part (ii). (Hint—Consider the graph on the left in Exhibit 10-5 of the textbook.)

3. Suppose a monopoly practices third-degree price discrimination by separating the market into those consumers under 65 and senior citizens. Let

MR_1 = marginal revenue from consumers under 65,
MR_2 = marginal revenue from senior citizens, and
MR = marginal revenue for the monopolist.

(i)   For any given level of output produced by the monopoly, it should divide the output between the two markets so that $MR_1 = MR_2$. Explain why, using the equimarginal principle. (Notice that this implies that the monopoly's marginal revenue MR equals both MR_1 and MR_2.)

196

Now suppose the monopoly faces the following information:

Marginal cost is given by $MC = (4/9)Q$, where Q is the total output produced by the monopoly.

The demand and marginal revenue for consumers under 65 are given by $P = 240 - 2Q_1$ and $MR_1 = 240 - 4Q_1$ respectively, where Q_1 is the quantity demanded by consumers under 65.

The demand and marginal revenue for senior citizens are given by $P = 120 - Q_2$ and $MR_2 = 120 - 2Q_2$ respectively, where Q_2 is the quantity demanded by senior citizens.

(ii) Recall that the monopoly's marginal revenue curve is given by the horizontal sum of the marginal revenue curves of the two markets. Find a formula expressing the monopoly's marginal revenue in terms of its output level Q. (Hint—This isn't easy! First use the formulas $MR_1 = MR_2$ and $Q = Q_1 + Q_2$ to show that $Q_1 = (1/3)Q + 20$ and $Q_2 = (2/3)Q - 20$. Then use these formulas and the fact from part (i) that MR equals both MR_1 and MR_2 to get a formula for MR in terms of Q.)

(iii) Using your answer to part (ii), determine the monopoly's profit-maximizing output Q, the common value of marginal revenue (MR) and marginal cost (MC), the market price and quantity for consumers under 65 (P_1 and Q_1), and the market price and quantity for senior citizens (P_2 and Q_2).

Solutions

1. (i)

Figure 10g

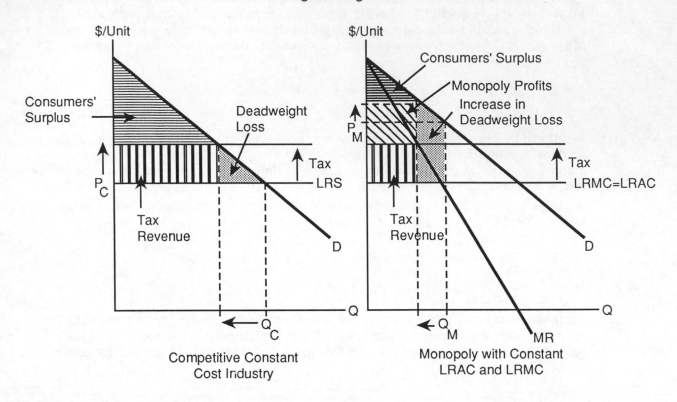

Competitive Constant Cost Industry

Monopoly with Constant LRAC and LRMC

(ii) The competitive industry passed on the entire tax to consumers, while the monopoly passed on only part of the tax. The competitive industry can pass on the tax to consumers by reducing the number of firms in the industry, while this option is not available to the monopoly. This reduction in the industry's output does not affect the competitive firms' profits, which return to zero in the long run. But reductions in output will affect the monopoly's profits, so it is better for the monopoly to absorb some of the tax instead of reducing output to the point of passing on the entire tax to the consumers.

(iii) Just like the excise tax, an increase in costs will raise the competitive industry's long-run supply curve and the monopoly's marginal cost curve. So we should expect the competitive constant cost industry to pass on the full cost increase, while the monopoly will only pass on part of the cost increase.

198

2. (i)

Figure 10h

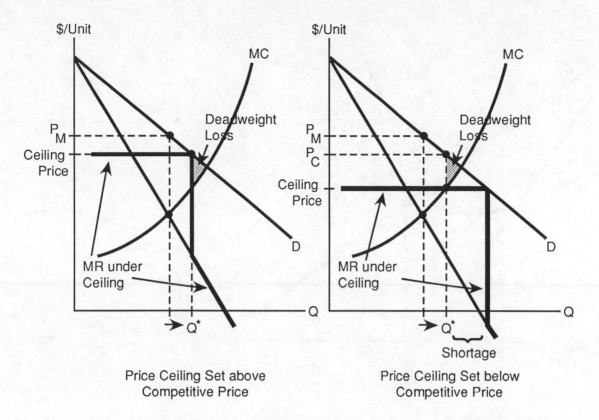

Price Ceiling Set above
Competitive Price

Price Ceiling Set below
Competitive Price

(ii) This statement is true. As shown by the diagram on the right, a shortage will be created if regulators attempt to set the price below the equilibrium price. The time and effort consumers spend competing to get the scarce good will add to the price they pay for the good, forcing it back above the competitive price.

(iii) No, a price ceiling cannot force the monopoly to earn zero profits in this case. Recall that the competitive price is where price equals marginal cost. If the monopoly is making positive profits in this situation, then this price must be above its average cost as in the left graph of Exhibit 10-5 of the textbook, reproduced below. Zero-profit regulation in this case requires the monopoly to produce more than the competitive quantity as shown. As we discovered in part (ii), a price ceiling cannot be used to get the monopolist to produce more than the competitive quantity.

Figure 10i

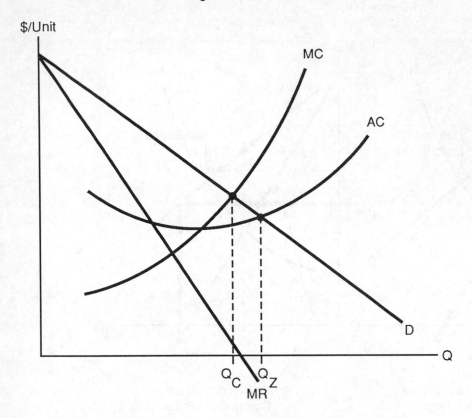

3. (i) Suppose the monopoly distributes its fixed output so that $MR_1 > MR_2$. This inequality tells us that the additional revenue generated by selling the last unit to consumers under 65 is greater than that received from selling the last unit to senior citizens. This tells us that the monopoly should consider selling more to consumers under 65. The marginal benefit of doing this is MR_1 dollars per unit of output, while the marginal cost of this action is MR_2 dollars per unit (since the amount sold to senior citizens must be decreased by the same amount, reducing the monopoly's revenue). Since the marginal benefit outweighs the marginal cost, the monopoly can increase its revenues by selling more to consumers under 65 and less to senior citizens in this case.

A similar argument shows that if the monopoly distributes the fixed output so that $MR_1 < MR_2$, then the monopoly can increase its revenues by increasing its sales to senior citizens and decreasing its sales to consumers under 65.

So using the equimarginal principle, we see that the monopoly creates the most revenue by equating MR_1 and MR_2.

(ii) From $MR_1 = MR_2$, we get $240 - 4Q_1 = 120 - 2Q_2$. Notice that the equation $Q = Q_1 + Q_2$ can be rewritten as either $Q_1 = Q - Q_2$ or $Q_2 = Q - Q_1$. Substituting these into the above equation, we get

$$
\begin{aligned}
240 - 4Q_1 &= 120 - 2Q_2 \quad \text{and} \\
240 - 4(Q - Q_2) &= 120 - 2Q_2 \\
240 - 4Q + 4Q_2 &= 120 - 2Q_2 \\
6Q_2 &= 4Q - 120 \\
Q_2 &= (2/3)Q - 20
\end{aligned}
\qquad
\begin{aligned}
240 - 4Q_1 &= 120 - 2Q_2 \\
240 - 4Q_1 &= 120 - 2(Q - Q_1) \\
240 - 4Q_1 &= 120 - 2Q + 2Q_1 \\
-6Q_1 &= -2Q - 120 \\
Q_1 &= (1/3)Q + 20
\end{aligned}
$$

200

which are the formulas given in the hint. Now use these to substitute into $MR = MR_1$ and $MR = MR_2$.

$$
\begin{array}{rclcrcl}
MR = MR_1 & = & 240 - 4Q_1 & \quad\text{and}\quad & MR = MR_2 & = & 120 - 2Q_2 \\
& = & 240 - 4((1/3)Q + 20) & & & = & 120 - 2((2/3)Q - 20) \\
& = & 240 - (4/3)Q - 80 & & & = & 120 - (4/3)Q + 40 \\
& = & 160 - (4/3)Q. & & & = & 160 - (4/3)Q.
\end{array}
$$

(Note—This formula assumes that the monopoly sells some output to each market.)

(iii) First use $MC = MR$ to find the monopoly's output level:

$$
\begin{array}{rcl}
(4/9)Q & = & 160 - (4/3)Q \\
(4/9)Q + (4/3)Q & = & 160 \\
(16/9)Q & = & 160 \\
Q & = & 90 \text{ units}.
\end{array}
$$

Substituting this into the formulas for MC and MR, we find that

$$MC = (4/9)Q = (4/9) \cdot 90 = 40 \text{ dollars per unit}$$

and

$$
\begin{array}{rcl}
MR & = & 160 - (4/3)Q = 160 - (4/3) \cdot 90 \\
& = & 160 - 120 = 40 \text{ dollars per unit}.
\end{array}
$$

Now use $MR = MR_1$ to get the quantities for each market (you can also use $MR = MR_2$):

$$
\begin{array}{rcl}
MR & = & MR_1 \\
40 & = & 240 - 4Q_1 \\
4Q_1 & = & 200 \\
Q_1 & = & 50 \text{ units, and } Q_2 = Q - Q_1 = 90 - 50 = 40 \text{ units}.
\end{array}
$$

Finally substitute these quantities into the demand curves to get the prices:

$$
\begin{array}{rclcrcl}
P_1 & = & 240 - 2Q_1 & \quad\text{and}\quad & P_2 & = & 120 - Q_2 \\
& = & 240 - 2 \cdot 50 & & & = & 120 - 40 \\
& = & 240 - 100 & & & = & 80 \text{ dollars per unit}. \\
& = & 140 \text{ dollars per unit}. & & & &
\end{array}
$$

Solutions to Working Through the Graphs

Figure 10-1   Using a Subsidy to Eliminate the Deadweight Loss
              Due to Monopoly

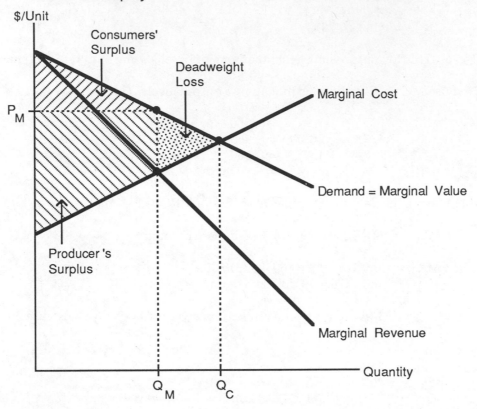

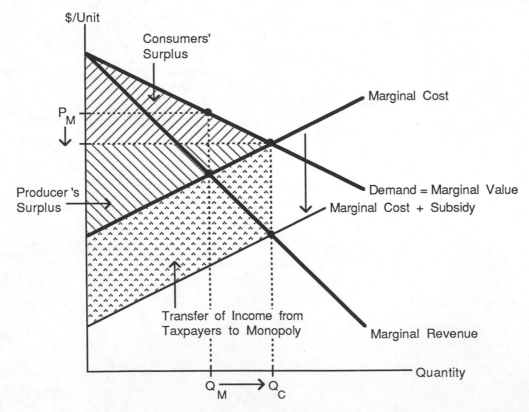

Figure 10-2   Using a Price Ceiling to Eliminate the Deadweight Loss
Due to Monopoly

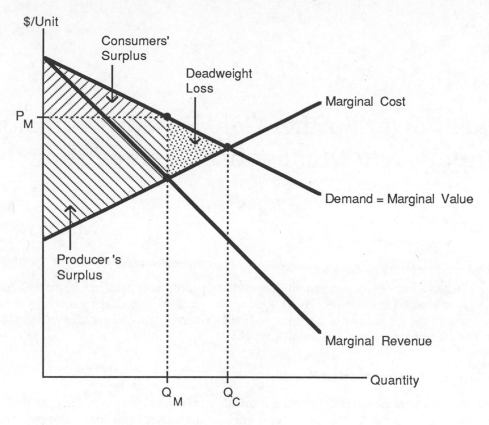

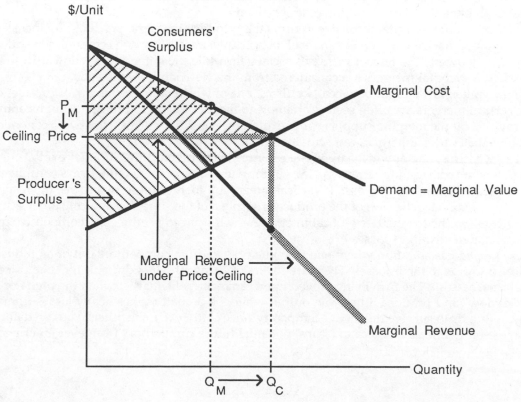

Market Power Further Considered: Collusion, Oligopoly, and Monopolistic Competition

Chapter Summary

Firms want to have monopoly power and the resulting profits as shown in Chapter 10, but the forces of competition we studied in Chapter 7 work against this desire. This chapter surveys several models and examples illustrating the problems encountered when firms attempt to acquire and exploit monopoly power in the face of actual and potential competition.

Section 11.1. Acquiring Market Power

Many firm practices are perceived by noneconomists as blatant attempts to acquire and exploit monopoly power, lowering social gain. But economic analysis reveals that these practices are often for reasons that both benefit the firm and increase social gain.

Horizontal integration is a merger between firms that produce the same product. By increasing the scale of operations, a horizontal merger can result in both lower costs through economies of scale and increased market power. The former increases social gain while the latter tends to lower it, so there is a tradeoff when horizontal mergers are considered from the viewpoint of efficiency.

Vertical integration is a merger between two firms, one of which supplies factors of production to the other. Vertical mergers are often seen as attempts to monopolize an industry (through control of the resource provided by the merging supplier) or to exploit the subsidiary firms. However economic analysis shows that vertical mergers can actually reduce monopoly power.

Consider two firms, one of which supplies a resource to the other. If the supplier exploits its monopoly power, it reduces output, raises price, appropriates some of the buying firm's consumer's surplus, and creates a deadweight loss. If vertical integration merges these two firms, the resulting firm will want to maximize the sum of the producer's surplus (of the supplier) and consumer's surplus (of the buying firm). So the firm under vertical integration will want to produce the competitive quantity and eliminate the deadweight loss.

Predatory pricing is a situation where one firm attempts to drive competitors out of an industry by setting price so low as to incur losses. There are several reasons why it is difficult for this "price war" strategy to be successful. The firm being preyed upon can reenter the market when the predator raises its prices, "lay low" and produce little or no output while the predator takes heavy losses from its price cuts, or borrow funds to survive during the temporary price cutting. On the other hand, predatory pricing may be profitable as a device to "scare" potential future competitors from ever entering the market.

In *resale price maintenance,* a monopoly supplier sets the retail price and forbids the retailers to undercut this price. To the layman this appears to be an attempt to keep high monopoly prices, but we know from Chapter 10 that it would be easier to do this by simply restricting output. One explanation of resale price maintenance is that it forces retailers to compete on the basis of customer service instead of price. This gives a guarantee to the monopoly supplier that these services to assist and promote the sales of its product are available to consumers.

Section 11.2. Collusion

Another way that firms attempt to achieve monopoly power is through *collusion*—firms acting together to set prices and output. We say that the colluding firms have formed a *cartel.* The cartel tries to restrict the industry's output to the monopoly level, allowing the firms in the cartel to charge a monopoly price and maximize the total producers' surplus.

Cartels require some form of enforcement because each firm has great incentive to cheat on the cartel agreement. By expanding its output beyond the agreed-upon level, a member will lower the price for the entire cartel. The cheating member gets all of the benefits from a higher sales volume but shares the losses caused by the falling price with the other cartel members. So the cheating firm gets larger profits at the cost of lower profits for other cartel members. But if all cartel members cheat, the monopoly profits would no longer be possible and all firms would be worse off than if they had all kept the cartel agreement. The Prisoner's Dilemma game provides a good illustration of this problem facing the cartel.

So for a cartel to be successful, it needs some form of enforcement to punish members that break the cartel agreement. As shown in the next section, government regulation is often used to provide this means of enforcement.

Section 11.3. Regulation

Government regulation of industries can have many intents, including the protection of consumers and the promotion of competition. However industries often find regulation desirable, because it often manages to keep output restricted and price high better than any private unenforced cartel agreement could.

The textbook gives several examples of how government regulation can act as the enforcement of a cartel agreement. The Interstate Commerce Commission (ICC) helps to restrict the production of trucking services by requiring ICC approval for all aspects of operation, including entry into the trucking industry and expansion of existing services. The Food and Drug Administration (FDA) enforces minimum quality standards on drug manufacturers. This has dramatically reduced and delayed the introduction of new drugs in the marketplace, keeping the price of existing drugs high by restricting the entry of new possible substitutes. Many of the professional licensing practices of the American Medical Association (AMA) appear to be designed to restrict entry into the medical profession. By prohibiting sales of certain goods on Sundays, "blue laws" seem little different than a cartel agreement to restrict production by limiting the times for business activity.

Just like the incentive to cheat on a cartel agreement, any individual firm has the incentive to avoid the effects of regulation. One way of doing this is called *creative response*—conforming to the letter of the law while finding ways to circumvent its intent. For example, when affirmative action laws were passed to eliminate the difference in wages paid to black workers and white workers, some firms complied by raising the wages of black workers (satisfying the law) and reducing their on-the-job training (violating the spirit of the law), keeping the total compensation to black employees unchanged.

Section 11.4. Oligopoly

An *oligopoly* is an industry in which each firm is able to affect market conditions. So an oligopoly generally consists of a few number of firms, each with some degree of monopoly power. A number of factors affect the behavior of firms in an oligopoly, including the threat of entry by other firms and the expectations about rival firms' behavior.

To show how the threat of entry affects the behavior of oligopoly firms, the contestable market model has recently been developed. A *contestable market* is one in which firms can enter and exit costlessly, so new firms will enter a contestable market whenever price rises above the minimum of average cost.

Consider a contestable market which is large enough to hold several firms (i.e., in which average cost curve is increasing when it crosses the industry demand curve). Also assume that all firms are identical, so that all firms have the same entry price. Market price in this contestable market cannot be higher than the minimum of firms' average costs, since any higher price would attract entry and drive the price back down. So in this type of oligopoly the threat of entry is sufficient to make firms behave competitively, even though each firm has some monopoly power. Each firm will produce the quantity at the minimum of its average cost curve, and price, average cost, and marginal cost will all be equal just like the long-run equilibrium for a competitive firm.

A contestable market will also affect the behavior of a natural monopoly. If this firm exploited its monopoly power, it would earn positive profits and attract new firms trying to steal its monopoly position. So the threat of entry forces the natural monopoly to produce the zero-profit quantity where average cost crosses demand. Although there will still be a deadweight loss, the contestable market situation increases the social gain attained under natural monopoly.

The *Cournot model* and *Bertrand model* of oligopoly show how minor differences in the way firms form their expectations about rivals' behavior can make major differences in the market outcome. Both models assume that the number of firms is fixed and that there is no collusion between firms. In the Cournot model each firm assumes that its rivals' *output* levels will remain unchanged. Under this assumption it can be shown mathematically that the industry will produce more than the monopoly output level but less than the competitive level, resulting in some deadweight loss. In the Bertrand model each firm assumes that its rivals' *price* levels will remain unchanged. In this model each firm will attempt to capture the entire market by undercutting other firms' prices, resulting in the competitive output and price and no deadweight loss in equilibrium. Although the Cournot and Bertrand models fail to make realistic assumptions about firms' expectations of rivals' behavior, their drastically different results show how important these expectations are to modelling oligopoly behavior.

Section 11.5. Monopolistic Competition and Product Differentiation

When a firm produces a good that is unique but has many close substitutes (such as its own brand of a common product), it is attempting to use *product differentiation* to gain monopoly power in a market that is essentially competitive. *Monopolistic competition* is a theory attempting to explain economic behavior in such markets with many similar but differentiated products.

Demand for a monopolistic competitor is drawn under the assumption that rivals do not change their price; this is reasonable when the firm is such a small part of the industry that its actions would not affect rivals' behavior. Demand is downward sloping (reflecting the monopoly power attained through product differentiation) but is much more elastic than demand faced by an ordinary monopoly (reflecting the fact that there are many close substitutes for the firm's product).

As with any firm, the monopolistic competitor will maximize profits and produce the quantity that equates marginal revenue and marginal cost. The monopolistic competitor may earn economic profits or losses in the short run, but entry and exit of firms will drive profits to zero in the long run. At the long-run equilibrium quantity, demand is tangent to the firm's average cost indicating zero profits. Since this tangency is not at the minimum of average cost, monopolistic competition does not minimize the industry's total costs of production like competition does. Also price remains above marginal cost in the long run indicating a deadweight loss. However these negative aspects must be weighed against the benefits of having the variety of choices offered by product differentiation when judging the welfare effects of monopolistic competition.

Working Through the Graphs—Welfare Analysis of Mergers

Mergers are frequently treated as attempts to gain monopoly power. Although this can be the case, there are also other economic reasons for firms to pursue mergers. As shown by Figures 11-1 and 11-2, mergers may not only increase firms' profits but also social gain.

Figure 11-1.

Step 1. Suppose the firm behaves competitively before a horizontal merger as highlighted in the top graph, producing output Q_C and charging price P_C. Locate and shade in the consumers' and producer's surplus to illustrate the social gain in this situation. Use a different color or style of shading for each area, and summarize your results in the accompanying table.

Step 2. The second graph in Figure 11-1 highlights the two effects that a horizontal merger can have. The resulting economies of scale can lower the firm's marginal costs (shown by the downward shift in the marginal cost curve), and the larger size can give the firm increased monopoly power (shown by the firm producing the monopoly output Q_M and charging the monopoly price P_M). Find and shade in the consumers' and producer's surplus after the merger and summarize the results in the second column of the table.

Step 3. Complete the table by calculating the difference in social welfare caused by the merger. If you've done everything correctly, you should find that the merger increased social gain by area F + G and lowered it by area E.

Notice that the merger was beneficial from the firm's viewpoint—producer's surplus increased due to the merger. However the horizontal merger has ambiguous results from a welfare perspective—the lower costs increase social gain but the increased monopoly power lowers social gain.

Figure 11-2.

Step 1. The top graph highlights the situation before a vertical merger, where one firm exploits its monopoly power when providing a resource to another firm, charging the price P_M and supplying Q_M. Perform the welfare analysis of this situation, shading in the consumer's and producer's surplus and summarizing your results in the table provided.

Step 2. The second graph highlights the situation after a vertical merger places these firms under the same management. This new management desires to maximize the sum of consumer's and producer's surplus in this market, since both contribute to the new management's profits. To do this the new management requires the competitive price and quantity in this market. As you did in Step 1, perform the welfare analysis of this situation in the second graph.

Step 3. Complete the table by calculating the increase in social gain in this market resulting from the vertical merger. If you've done everything correctly, you should find social gain increased by the area E + H.

Figure 11-1 Welfare Analysis of a Horizontal Merger

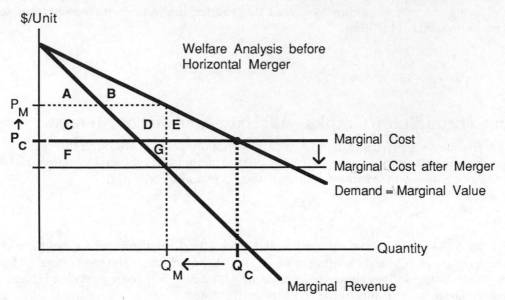

Welfare Analysis before Horizontal Merger

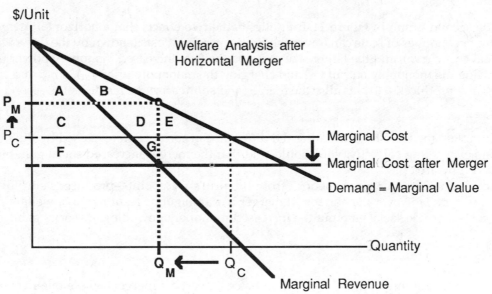

Welfare Analysis after Horizontal Merger

	Gains from Trade before Merger	Gains from Trade after Merger	
Consumers' Surplus			
Producers' Surplus			Change in Social Welfare Due to Merger
Social Gain			

Figure 11-2 Welfare Analysis of a Vertical Merger

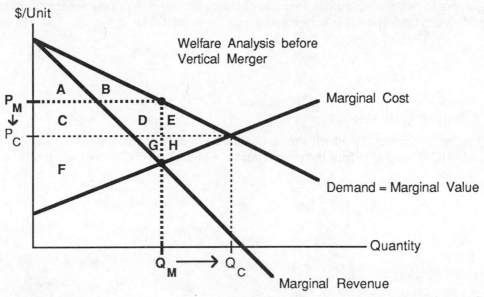

Welfare Analysis before Vertical Merger

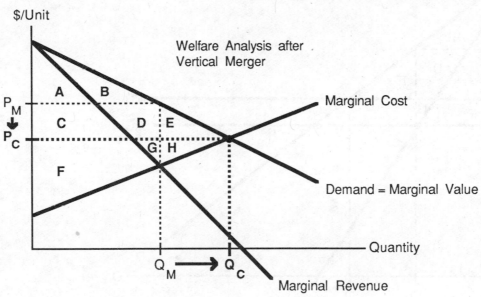

Welfare Analysis after Vertical Merger

	Gains from Trade before Merger	Gains from Trade after Merger	
Consumers' Surplus			
Producers' Surplus			**Increase in Social Welfare Due to Merger**
Social Gain			

Notice that before the vertical merger there was a deadweight loss representing the gains from trade between the two firms that were not attained. Being adversaries, they could not reach an enforceable agreement to exploit these potential gains from trade to the benefit of both. The role of the vertical merger was to provide an enforcement mechanism (through the new management) to guarantee that all the gains from trade possible between the two firms would be achieved.

Multiple Choice Questions

***Question 1 refers to Figure 11a which shows the effects of a horizontal merger. Marginal cost, price, and quantity are MC, P, and Q before the merger and are MC', P', and Q' after the merger.

Figure 11a

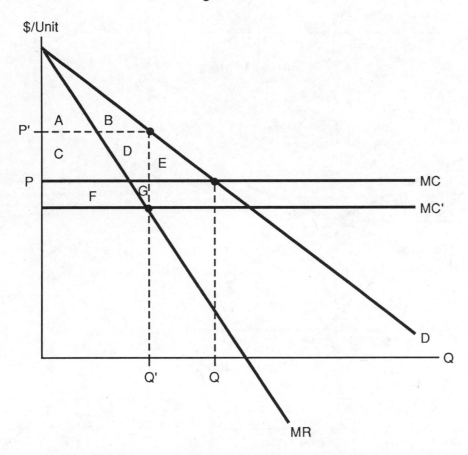

1. This horizontal merger will increase economic efficiency if
   A. area A + B outweighs area C + D + F + G.
   B. area C + D + F + G outweighs area A + B.
   C. area E outweighs area F + G.
   D. area F + G outweighs area E.

Figure 11b

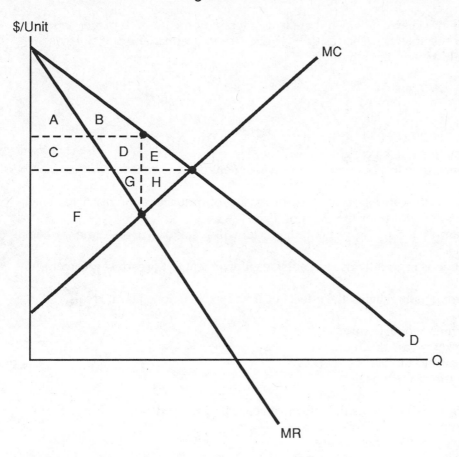

2. If there is a vertical merger,
    A.   social welfare will increase by the area E + H.
    B.   social welfare will decrease by the area E + H.
    C.   social welfare will remain unchanged.
    D.   the firm on the demand side will be further exploited by the supplier, making consumer's surplus smaller than area A + B.

3. Brown is a shoe manufacturer and Kinney both manufactures shoes and sells them in its retail outlets. A merger between Brown and Kinney would be
    A.   a horizontal merger.
    B.   a vertical merger.
    C.   a horizontal merger (since both manufacture shoes) and a vertical merger (since one can retail what the other manufactures).
    D.   a horizontal merger (since one can retail what the other manufactures) and a vertical merger (since both manufacture shoes).

4. Which of the following is *not* a difficulty in making predatory pricing a successful strategy?
    A.   Reemergence of rival firms when the predator restores the higher price.
    B.   Greater losses for the predator than for rival firms.
    C.   The possibility that rival firms may borrow funds to survive the period of price cutting.
    D.   The prevention of entry by potential rivals.

5. Why might a firm practice resale price maintenance?
   A. To guarantee high monopoly prices.
   B. To guarantee that retailers will supply customer services.
   C. To prevent retailers from appropriating part of the firm's monopoly profits.
   D. To force retailers to absorb the costs of selling the good.

6. Consider a Prisoner's Dilemma game in which there is no cooperation with each player acting competitively in his own self-interest. The result _____ be Pareto-optimal and the so Invisible Hand Theorem _____ hold true in this situation.
   A. will; does
   B. will; does not
   C. will not; does
   D. will not; does not

7. Which of the following statements on cartels is *false*?
   A. A member has the incentive to cheat on the cartel agreement only when it fears other members will also cheat.
   B. A member can cheat on the cartel agreement by increasing output above the restricted level, resulting in much higher profits for the cheating firm.
   C. If all members cheat on the cartel agreement, the cartel will break down, resulting in the competitive outcome.
   D. Government regulation is frequently used as outside enforcement to the cartel agreement.

8. Which of the following models highlights the effects of firm's expectations about rivals' behavior?
   A. The Prisoner's Dilemma model of cartels.
   B. The contestable market model of oligopoly.
   C. The Cournot and Bertrand models of oligopoly.
   D. The monopolistic competition model.

9. Which of the following models highlights the effects of costless entry and exit on firm behavior?
   A. The Prisoner's Dilemma model of cartels.
   B. The contestable market model of oligopoly.
   C. The Cournot and Bertrand models of oligopoly.
   D. The monopolistic competition model.

10. Which of the following models highlights the effects of product differentiation on the market outcome?
    A. The Prisoner's Dilemma model of cartels.
    B. The contestable market model of oligopoly.
    C. The Cournot and Bertrand models of oligopoly.
    D. The monopolistic competition model.

11. Consider an oligopoly in a contestable market. Suppose all firms are identical and their average cost curves are upward sloping at the point where they cross the industry demand curve. We can predict that
    A. price and quantity will be the same as if the market were competitive.
    B. price and quantity will be the same as if the market were a monopoly.
    C. the equilibrium quantity will be greater than the monopoly quantity but smaller than the competitive quantity.
    D. Any of the above are possible outcomes

12. In the Cournot oligopoly model, each firm treats its rivals' _____ as fixed. This results in an industry output _____ the competitive level.
    A. quantity; equal to
    B. quantity; below
    C. price; equal to
    D. price; below

13. In the Bertrand oligopoly model, each firm treats its rivals' _____ as fixed. This results in an industry output _____ the competitive level.
    A. quantity; equal to
    B. quantity; below
    C. price; equal to
    D. price; below

14. Which of the following best describes the firm's long-run equilibrium in monopolistic competition?
    A. Price equals average cost, but is greater than marginal cost.
    B. Price equals the minimum of average cost, but is greater than marginal cost.
    C. Price equals marginal cost, but is greater than average cost.
    D. Price equals both marginal cost and the minimum of average cost.

15. As compared to competition, monopolistic competition creates
    A. lower social welfare because it does not minimize the industry's total cost of production.
    B. lower social welfare because firms produce quantities where marginal value exceeds marginal cost.
    C. higher social welfare because it offers a variety of product options not offered by competition.
    D. All of the above

Solutions

1. D. Before the merger with competitive behavior but higher costs, social gain is A + B + C + D + E. After the merger with monopoly behavior and lower costs, social gain is A + B + C + D + F + G. The merger changes social gain by the difference F + G - E.

2. A. When the firms are separate the supplier acts like a monopoly to maximize its producer's surplus, resulting in a social gain of A + B + C + D + F + G. When the two are merged into one firm, the new firm wants to maximize the sum of consumer's and producer's surplus and produces the competitive output, resulting in a social gain of A + B + C + D + E + F + G + H. Social welfare has increased by the difference E + H.

3. C. This simply applies the definitions of horizontal and vertical integration.

4. D. The possibility of "scaring" potential competitors from entering the industry in the future is one possible benefit to a firm practicing predatory pricing.

5. B. Resale price maintenance forces retailers to compete on a non-price basis, such as through the quality of customer services offered.

6. D. Both parties would be made better off if they cooperated and chose the "not confess" or "not cheat" strategy. Competitive behavior results in both choosing the "confess" or "cheat" strategy, causing a non-Pareto-optimal result. Since competitive behavior does not create a Pareto-optimal outcome, the Invisible Hand Theorem is violated.

7. A. As shown by the Prisoner's Dilemma game, it is in each member's self-interest to cheat whether or not other cartel members cheat.

8. C. Comparing the Cournot and Bertrand models shows that the oligopoly market outcome is quite sensitive to the assumptions made about firm's expectations concerning rivals' behavior.

9. B. A contestable market is defined to be one with costless entry and exit.

10. D. Monopolistic competition considers markets in which there are many similar but differentiated products.

11. A. The importance of the contestable market model is that it shows that competitive results can be attained even when there is only a small number of firms.

12. B. After taking its rivals' output into account, each firm in the Cournot oligopoly model practices monopoly pricing on the remainder of the market. This results in an output level above the simple monopoly level but below the competitive level.

13. C. Thinking its rivals' price is fixed, each firm in the Bertrand oligopoly model undercuts its rivals' price to steal the market. This drives price down (and hence quantity up) to the competitive level.

14. A. The monopolistic competitor's downward-sloping demand curve is tangent to average cost in long-run equilibrium, so price equals average cost where average cost is downward sloping. Since marginal revenue equals marginal cost in equilibrium and marginal revenue lies beneath the demand curve, price remains above marginal cost.

15. D. These welfare implications result from product differentiation and interpretation of the long-run equilibrium position in monopolistic competition.

Questions for Review

1. What are horizontal and vertical integration? What economic reasons are there for firms to undertake such integration? What role have these economic reasons played in Supreme Court rulings on antitrust law?

2. What is resale price maintenance? How does it benefit the producer? How does it benefit consumers?

3. What problem facing cartels is illustrated by the Prisoner's Dilemma game? How can this problem be remedied?

4. List some of the specific ways that government regulation is used to direct the activities of firms, providing examples of each. How can such regulation serve to restrict output and keep prices high?

5. What is a contestable market? What is the significance of this contribution to the study of oligopoly?

6. Compare and contrast the Cournot and Bertrand models of oligopoly.

7. For each of the following conditions, (a) indicate whether it is true for competition or monopolistic competition in the long run, and (b) indicate what welfare consequences can be deduced from the condition.

   (i)   Price equal to marginal cost.
   (ii) Price above marginal cost.
   (iii) Price equal to the minimum of firms' average cost.
   (iv) Price equal to firms' average cost where average cost is decreasing.

Solutions

1. A horizontal merger between firms occurs when the firms produce the same commodity. A vertical merger between firms occurs when one firm supplies a factor of production to the other. Horizontal mergers give firms lower costs from economies of scale and monopoly power from larger size. Vertical mergers have the advantage of providing a central management to prohibit the monopoly behavior that may occur when the firms are independent. The Supreme Court has rejected welfare implications of antitrust law, claiming the law exists to protect the interests of smaller firms that could not compete with the larger more efficient firm that could result from a horizontal merger. With respect to vertical integration, the Court has erroneously used the argument that the larger firm would exploit its subsidiary.

2. Resale price maintenance occurs when a monopoly supplier sets the retail price for its product and forbids retailers to undercut this price. The producer benefits from guaranteeing that customer services are provided by retailers, which increases demand for the product and the resulting producer's surplus. By receiving services that are greater in value than the retailers' required markup over wholesale, consumers' surplus also increases under resale price maintenance.

3. Each member of the cartel has the incentive to cheat on the cartel agreement, regardless of the actions of other members. If all members cheat on the agreement, then the monopoly profits will no longer be attainable. If there is some way to enforce the cartel agreement and punish members in violation, then this problem of cartel breakdown can be greatly diminished.

4. Regulation can affect the specific production activities and expansion of firms (as with the ICC), establish minimum quality standards (as with the FDA and professional licensing), restrict advertising (as in the medical and legal professions), establish minimum prices (as with the minimum wage law), and dictate times of business (as with "blue laws"). These regulations can restrict output by limiting existing firms' production and the entry of new firms.

5. A contestable market is one in which there is costless entry and exit. Contestable markets show that potential entry can force firms to behave as competitors, even when there are few firms in the market. This result can occur when firms' average cost is still increasing as it crosses market demand.

6. The Cournot and Bertrand models of oligopoly emphasize firms' expectations about their rivals' behavior. In the Cournot model each firm assumes its rivals' quantity remains unchanged, while in the Bertrand model each firm assumes its rivals' price remains fixed. The two models result in different market outcomes, with industry output being at the competitive level in the Bertrand model and between the monopoly and competitive levels in the Cournot model.

7. (i) Price equals marginal cost in competition and indicates that social gain is as large as possible. (ii) Price above marginal cost occurs in monopolistic competition. It indicates a deadweight loss because consumers are still willing to pay more than the cost of production for the last unit of the

firm's commodity. (iii) In competition in the long run price equals the minimum of firms' average costs, so the total costs of production are minimized. (iv) Demand is tangent to average cost where average cost is still decreasing in monopolistic competition in the long run. The same level of output could be produced at a lower total cost by decreasing the number of firms and increasing the output of remaining firms.

Problems for Analysis

1. Suppose the demand and marginal revenue curves for a firm's product are given by $P = 20 - (1/2)Q$ and $MR = 20 - Q$, where Q is the quantity exchanged and P is the price charged. Also suppose this firm's marginal cost is constant at $MC = 10$.

   (i)   Find the quantity exchanged, price charged, the consumers' and producer's surplus, and the social gain if the firm charges the competitive price.

   (ii) Suppose this firm undertakes a horizontal merger that not only lowers its marginal cost, but also gives it sufficient market power that the firm begins to charge the monopoly price. If marginal cost falls by x percent, what will be the social gain under the horizontal merger?

   (iii) By what percentage must marginal cost fall for social gain to increase under this horizontal merger? (Note—This problem requires use of the quadratic formula, which says that the equation $ax^2 + bx + c = 0$ has solutions at $x = (-b \pm \sqrt{b^2 - 4ac})/2a$.)

2. This problem analyzes a producer's use of resale price maintenance.
   Let

   P_0 = price that the producer charges retailers,
   P_1 = price that retailers are required to charge under the resale price maintenance agreement,
   V = value per unit that retailers' services are worth to consumers,
   C = cost per unit incurred by retailers to provide services to consumers.

   (i)   Assuming that retailers have no other costs other than the purchase of the good from the producer and the services provided to consumers, explain why retailers will supply services that cost $P_1 - P_0$ (i.e., explain why $C = P_1 - P_0$).

(ii) Suppose the demand and marginal revenue for the producer's product in the absence of retailers' services are given by $P = 180 - Q$ and $MR = 180 - 2Q$. Also suppose the producers marginal cost is constant and given by $MC = 140$. Calculate the price charged, quantity produced, consumers' surplus, and producer's surplus if there is no resale price maintenance.

(iii) Using the above demand formula and the variables C and V, find new equations expressing the retailers' demand and the producer's demand when the producer undertakes resale price agreement.

(iv) Suppose C and V are related by the equation $V = 9C - C^2$. What value for C will the producer choose to make his demand as large as possible? (Note—Use the fact that the function $kC - C^2$ is maximized at $C = k/2$.)

(v) Using your answer to part (iv), find the price P_0 charged by the producer, the resulting consumers' and producer's surplus, and the price P_1 that the producer will require retailers to charge. (Note—Use the fact that when demand is given by the formula $P = K - Q$, then marginal revenue has the formula $MR = K - 2Q$.)

3. (i) Draw a diagram of a firm in monopolistic competition making positive economic profits.

$/Unit

Q

(ii) Suppose demand for this firm's product falls due to entry of new firms into the industry. Use your diagram above to show that the firm's profits can fall for three different reasons: lower quantity, lower price, and higher average cost.

(iii) Firms frequently practice brand proliferation, in which the firm offers increasing numbers of variations of its product. For example, over the past few years Coca-Cola has expanded its offerings to include Classic Coca-Cola, New Coke, Caffeine-Free Coca-Cola, Diet Coke, Caffeine-Free Diet Coke, Cherry Coke, and Diet Cherry Coke each in a variety of 1-liter bottles, 2-liter bottles, 6-pack cans, 12-pack cans, and returnable bottles. Using the results to part (ii), explain why firms may find brand proliferation to be profitable.

Solutions

1. (i) In competition price is equated to marginal cost. This gives the equations

$$
\begin{aligned}
P &= MC \\
20 - (1/2)Q &= 10 \\
10 &= (1/2)Q \\
Q &= 20 \text{ units.}
\end{aligned}
$$

To get price, substitute this into the demand curve:

$P = 20 - (1/2)Q = 20 - (1/2) \cdot 20 = 20 - 10 = 10$ dollars per unit.

Using the sketch of the graph in Figure 11c, we have:

$$
\begin{aligned}
\text{consumers' surplus} &= 1/2 \cdot \text{base} \cdot \text{height} \\
&= 1/2 \cdot 20 \text{ units} \cdot \$10/\text{unit} \\
&= \$100, \\
\text{producers' surplus} &= \$0, \text{ and social gain} = \$100.
\end{aligned}
$$

Figure 11c

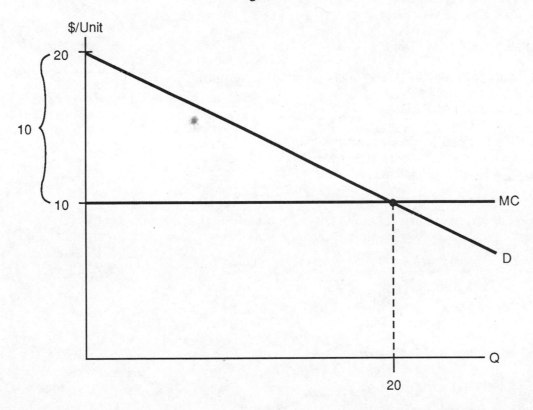

(ii)   Letting x equal the percentage by which marginal cost falls, the post-merger marginal cost is $(1 - x) \cdot 10$ or $10 - 10x$. Since the firm practices monopoly pricing, it equates marginal revenue and marginal cost. This gives the equations

$$
\begin{aligned}
MR &= MC \\
20 - Q &= 10 - 10x \\
10 + 10x &= Q \\
Q &= 10 + 10x \text{ units.}
\end{aligned}
$$

Substitute this into demand to find price:

$$
\begin{aligned}
P &= 20 - (1/2)Q = 20 - (1/2) \cdot (10 + 10x) = 20 \cdot (5 + 5x) \\
&= 20 - 5 - 5x = 15 - 5x \text{ dollars per unit.}
\end{aligned}
$$

Using the sketch of this information in Figure 11d, it is straightforward to calculate social gain:

consumers' surplus $= 1/2 \cdot$ base $\cdot$ height

$$
\begin{aligned}
&= 1/2 \cdot (10 + 10x \text{ units}) \cdot (20 - (15 - 5x) \text{ dollars per unit}) \\
&= 1/2 \cdot (10 + 10x) \cdot (5 + 5x) \\
&= 1/2 \cdot (50 + 100x + 50x^2) \\
&= 25 + 50x + 25x^2 \text{ dollars,}
\end{aligned}
$$

producer's surplus $=$ base $\cdot$ height

$$
\begin{aligned}
&= (10 + 10x \text{ units}) \cdot ((15 - 5x) - (10 \cdot 10x) \text{ dollars per unit}) \\
&= (10 + 10x) \cdot (5 + 5x) \\
&= 50 + 100x + 50x^2 \text{ dollars,}
\end{aligned}
$$

social gain $=$ consumers' surplus $+$ producer's surplus

$$
\begin{aligned}
&= (25 + 50x + 25x^2) + (50 + 100x + 50x^2) \\
&= 75 + 150x + 75x^2 \text{ dollars.}
\end{aligned}
$$

Figure 11d

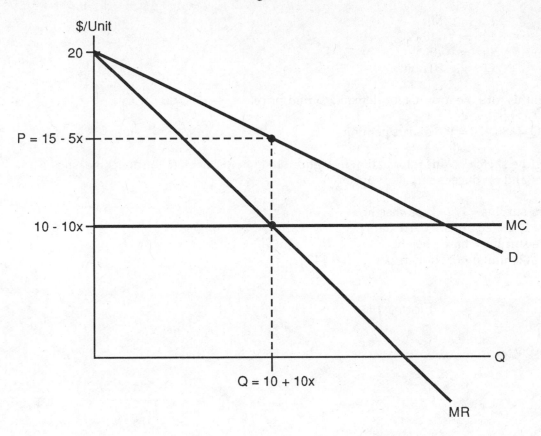

(iii) For social gain to have increased under the horizontal merger, the formula found in part (ii) must be larger than the $100 found in part (i). First find where the two social gains are equal by solving the equality

$$75 + 150x + 75x^2 = 100$$
$$75x^2 + 150x - 25 = 0$$
(Divide by 25) $$3x^2 + 6x - 1 = 0.$$

Using the quadratic equation, this has solutions at $-1 - 2\sqrt{3}/3$ and $-1 + 2\sqrt{3}/3$, which equal approximately -2.155 and 0.155. The negative solution is superfluous. Using the positive solution, the percentage decrease in marginal cost x must be larger than 0.155 or 15.5 percent for social gain to be larger after the merger.

2. (i) Since all retailers offer the same price P_1, consumers will purchase the good from the retailer who offers the most value in customer services. As long as $C < P_1 - P_0$, a retailer can increase his producer's surplus by increasing the value of services offered (V) with an increase in his costs (C). This will cause his quantity to increase greatly, while his marginal costs ($P_0 + C$) will still remain above his price (P_1). This competition for consumers will cause firms to drive C up until it finally equals $P_1 - P_0$.

221

(ii) Using marginal cost equals marginal revenue yields

$$
\begin{aligned}
MC &= MR \\
140 &= 180 - 2Q \\
2Q &= 40 \\
Q &= 20 \text{ units.}
\end{aligned}
$$

Substitute this into the formula for demand to find price:

$P = 180 - Q = 180 - 20 = 160$ dollars per unit.

Using the sketch of this information in Figure 11e to help calculate the areas measuring consumers' and producer's surplus, we get:

consumers' surplus = 1/2 · base · height
 = 1/2 · (20 units) · (20 dollars per unit) = $200 ,
producer's surplus = base · height
 = (20 units) · (20 dollars per unit) = $400 .

Figure 11e

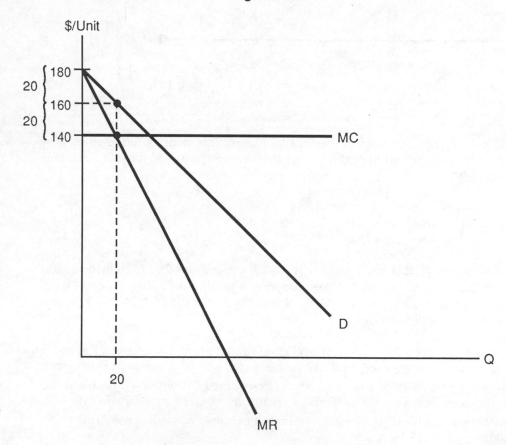

222

(iii) To get the retailers' demand, notice that

the price consumers are willing to pay retailers	=	the marginal value of the good to consumers	+	the value of services offered by retailers
so P	=	$180 - Q$	+	V .

For the producer's demand, notice that $C = P_1 - P_0$ can be rewritten as $P_0 = P_1 - C$. This says that

the price received by the producer	=	the price received by retailers	-	the per unit cost of services
so P	=	$180 - Q + V$	-	C .

To summarize, the retailers' demand is given by $P = 180 - Q + V$ and the producer's demand is given by $P = 180 - Q + V - C$.

(iv) Since the producer's demand is given by $P = 180 - Q + V - C$, to make demand as large as possible we must choose $V - C$ to be as large as possible. Using the given formula for V, we have $V - C = (9C - C^2) - C = 8C - C^2$. Using the information given in the note, this is maximized at $C = k/2 = 8/2 = 4$ and $V = 9C - C^2 = 9 \cdot 4 - 4^2 = 36 - 16 = 20$.

(v) Substituting the answers to part (iv) into the demand formula found in part (iii), the producer's demand is given by $P = 196 - Q$. Using the information given in the note, marginal revenue is given by $MR = 196 - 2Q$.

Use marginal cost equal marginal revenue to find the producer's profit-maximizing output level:

$$
\begin{aligned}
MC &= MR \\
140 &= 196 - 2Q \\
2Q &= 56 \\
Q &= 28 \text{ units.}
\end{aligned}
$$

Then substitute this into the formula for demand to find price:

$P_0 = 196 - Q = 196 - 28 = 168$ dollars per unit.

Using the sketch of this information in Figure 11f to help calculate the areas measuring consumers' and producer's surplus, we get:

consumers' surplus = 1/2 · base · height
   = 1/2 · (28 units) · (28 dollars per unit) = \$392 ,
producer's surplus = base · height
   = (28 units) · (28 dollars per unit) = \$784 .

Notice that both consumers' and producer's surplus have significantly increased due to resale price maintenance.

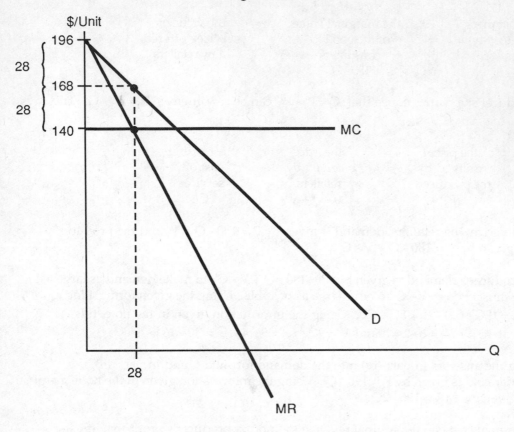

Figure 11f

To find P_1, use either the demand curve for retailers ($P = 180 - Q + V$) or the fact that $C = P_1 - P_0$; either gives $P_1 = 172$ dollars per unit.

3. (i),(ii)

Figure 11g

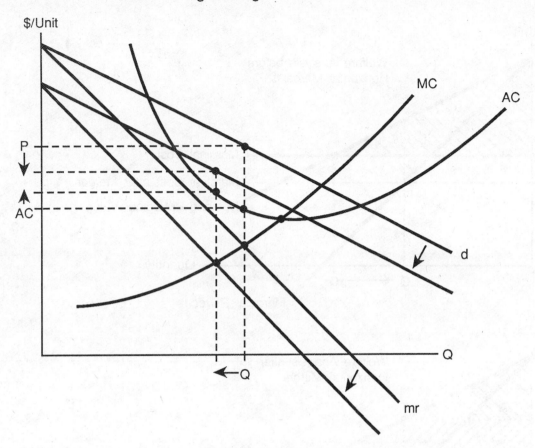

(iii)   Brand proliferation can make entry by new firms difficult, especially when retailers have limited shelf space for the various brands of a product it wishes to sell. If brand proliferation successfully prevents entry, this will keep demand high. So the benefits of using brand proliferation are to prevent the fall in price and quantity and the increase in average costs shown in part (ii). The cost of using brand proliferation is the increase in average cost required to offer the expanding number of varieties of the product. This cost is likely to be minor compared to the benefits of preventing entry and the accompanying fall in demand.

Solutions to Working Through the Graphs

Figure 11-1   Welfare Analysis of a Horizontal Merger

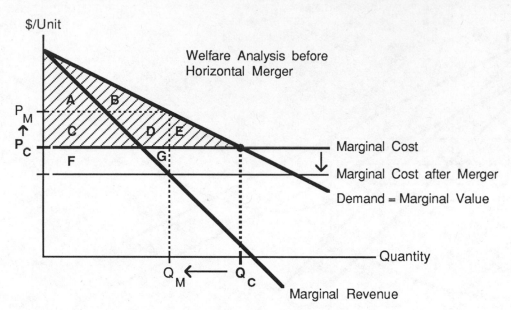

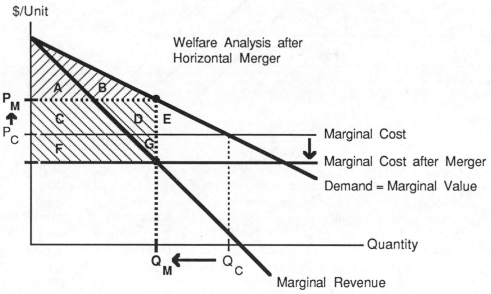

	Gains from Trade before Merger	Gains from Trade after Merger	
Consumers' Surplus	A + B + C + D + E	A + B	
Producers' Surplus	Zero	C + D + F + G	**Change in Social Welfare Due to Merger**
Social Gain	A + B + C + D + E	A + B + C + D + F + G	F + G - E

Figure 11-2 Welfare Analysis of a Vertical Merger

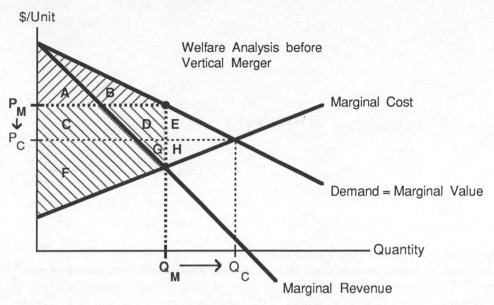

Welfare Analysis before Vertical Merger

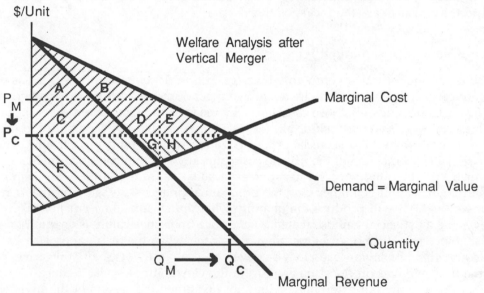

Welfare Analysis after Vertical Merger

	Gains from Trade before Merger	Gains from Trade after Merger	
Consumers' Surplus	A + B	A + B + C + D + E	
Producers' Surplus	C + D + F + G	F + G + H	**Increase in Social Welfare Due to Merger**
Social Gain	A + B + C + D + F + G	A + B + C + D + E + F + G + H	E + H

Chapter Twelve

External Costs and Benefits

Chapter Summary

Previous chapters have considered the consequences of buyers and sellers voluntarily participating in trade. However trade often imposes costs and benefits on other people involuntarily. When consumption or production activities impose costs (benefits) on others, we say there is a *negative (positive) externality*. Externalities—these costs and benefits which are external to the market—are the focus for this chapter.

Section 12.1. Costs Imposed on Others

When a firm's economic activity involuntarily imposes costs or benefits on others (such as when the firm's production creates pollution), there are two types of marginal costs to consider. The *private marginal costs* include only those costs borne by the firm and considered in its supply decision. The *social marginal costs* include all the costs borne by society as a whole. So the private marginal costs take the costs of labor, capital, and raw materials into account, while the social marginal costs include all the private costs plus any external costs or benefits.

When a firm's production imposes a negative externality (as from pollution, for example), the social marginal cost will be higher than the private marginal cost. Assuming the firm behaves competitively, it will produce the quantity where price equals its *private* marginal cost. However the most social gain is created where price (marginal value) is equated to *social* marginal cost. Since private and social marginal costs differ when the firm imposes an externality, competitive behavior leads to a deadweight loss. In this case of a negative externality the firm will overproduce the good from the viewpoint of social welfare.

Notice that this problem of externalities does not invalidate the results of the Invisible Hand Theorem, which claims that the competitive market system results in the maximum social gain. Externalities occur precisely when no market (let alone a competitive one) exists to allocate some disputed resource, for it is this situation that creates external costs and benefits not reflected in market prices. (For example, pollution creates a negative externality because there is no market to allocate the air being polluted. Pollution would be "paid for" if the air needed to pollute could be bought and sold.) So when externalities exist, the conditions of the Invisible Hand Theorem are not satisfied because some market is lacking.

If the external costs would be treated as private costs so that they would enter the decision-making process, then the deadweight loss from a firm's negative externality would be eliminated. When this happens we say that the externality has been *internalized*. The traditional method that economists have recommended to internalize a negative externality is taxation. If the firm is required to pay a per unit tax equal to the amount of the externality (called a *Pigou tax*), its private marginal costs will increase to agree with the social marginal costs. Then competitive behavior will lead to the maximum social gain, and the tax will have eliminated the deadweight loss.

A second method of internalizing an externality is to implement a law requiring the firm to pay compensation to those damaged by the externality—we say that the firm is made *liable* for its external costs. A third method is to grant the injured party the *property right* to the disputed resource causing the externality; this allows the firm to be charged for use of the resource. Both methods are equivalent to a Pigou tax where the proceeds go to the injured party—in each case there is a transfer of income from the firm to the injured party equal to the total amount of external costs. This payment forces the firm to internalize the external costs.

Section 12.2. The Coase Theorem

The costs of negotiating and enforcing a contract are called *transactions costs*. As shown by Ronald Coase in 1960, the above analysis of externalities is incomplete because it fails to account for transactions costs. As a result, the analysis of externalities is not as simple as the Pigovian approach of the previous section would lead one to believe.

This section and the next survey Coase's analysis of the externality problem. In this section we assume that there are no transactions costs; the next section considers the externality problem in the presence of transactions costs.

The *Strong Coase Theorem* states: **In the absence of transactions costs, the assignment of property rights has *no* effect on the allocation of resources.** The *Weak Coase Theorem* states: **In the absence of transactions costs, the assignment of property rights does not affect the *efficiency* of resource allocation.** Put another way, these theorems claim that the externality problem disappears because private bargaining guarantees that private and social costs will be equal when there are no transactions costs.

This result is due to the fact that the involved parties can make "side payments" or "bribes" to one another over the use of the disputed resource causing the externality. Each person, by using his own unique knowledge and considering all available options, can determine the value of the resource to him. In the absence of transactions costs, the involved parties can then use this information and bargain for the right to use the disputed resource. No matter who owns the property right to the resource, the party who values it most will purchase that property right leaving others to pursue their less-costly options. Private bargaining guarantees all available options will be explored and that the most efficient solution to the externality problem will be found.

The difference between the Weak and Strong Coase Theorems results from the fact that the assignment of property rights to the disputed resource *will* affect the resulting distribution of income. When one of the involved parties is granted the property right, he is made better off whether he keeps or sells this right. So the assignment of property rights creates a wealth effect which shifts the distribution of income. If this wealth effect causes no significant changes in market demands, then the Strong Coase Theorem holds as stated. But if the wealth effects are large enough to shift the market demand curves, then the resulting allocation of resources (but not its efficiency) will also be affected and only the Weak Coase Theorem holds.

Section 12.3. Transactions Costs

When transactions costs make private bargaining infeasible, we may be tempted to rely on the traditional methods of internalizing an externality (i.e., using a Pigou tax or an equivalent property right or liability assignment). But even in the presence of transactions costs, Coase shows that the traditional analysis of externalities is still incomplete and that these policies may not achieve efficiency.

If private bargaining is possible, all parties involved have incentive to find the least-cost method of dealing with the externality regardless of liability. But when transactions costs make private bargaining infeasible, the assignment of liability has an important effect on economic incentives—**those parties receiving liability payments have no incentive to pursue other possible ways of resolving the externality.** So a Pigou tax cannot guarantee an efficient outcome because an improper assignment of liability may destroy the incentive to find the efficient solution. This problem that a Pigou tax may not assign liability to the "right" party reemphasizes the fact that externalities are caused by disputes over the use of a resource—it is mistaken to think that one party should be assigned liability because it "causes" the externality.

It may be difficult to determine which party has access to the least-cost method of resolving the externality problem. This is because the desire to avoid liability provides an incentive for parties to hide this information. As a result it may be more efficient to try to reduce transactions costs so that private bargaining can attain efficiency.

Transactions costs can arise from unobservable behavior, incomplete property rights, or free riders. We consider each of these in turn.

When one person pays another in exchange for some particular action or behavior, the former party to the contract is called the *principle* and the latter is called the *agent*. A *principle-agent problem* occurs when the principle cannot observe whether or not the agent is abiding by the terms of the contract. The principle-agent problem makes it difficult to enforce contracts resulting from private bargaining and hence creates a transactions cost. In the absence of other transactions costs, liability should be assigned to agents to guarantee they have the incentive to resolve any externality; the Coase Theorem guarantees that the principle already has the appropriate incentives.

Incomplete property rights exist when the ownership of a resource is not clearly defined or does not exist. Obviously this makes it costlier to bargain for the right to use the resource, and hence creates a transactions cost. Liability rules frequently confer property rights on an industry instead of particular firms, resulting in incomplete property rights. This can cause inefficiency as the receipt or forfeiture of liability payments will affect the incentives of firms considering entry.

The *free rider* problem can create a transactions cost affecting the costs of negotiating a contract when large numbers of people are involved. If a group is trying to collect contributions for a "bribe" to internalize an externality, each member will have the incentive not to contribute. It is in the self-interest of each member to try to get a "free ride"—share in the benefits of the contract without contributing to the costs. This is just like the Prisoner's Dilemma problem—the rational behavior of individual members can prevent the optimal contract from being reached.

Section 12.4. The Law and Economics

Using Coase's insights we can see how *common law*—the system of legal precedents that has evolved from centuries of court decisions—can promote economic efficiency. It can (1) provide incentives for solving problems in the least expensive way and (2) reduce transactions costs so private bargaining may remedy the problem.

The common law concerning *torts*—actions which intentionally or unintentionally damage another party—provides some insights into this relation between law and economic efficiency. Under the law of torts, liability is assigned in different ways depending on the situation. Simple *negligence* holds you liable if the amount you could have spent to avoid the accident is less than the damages you caused times the probability of the accident's occurrence. To promote economic efficiency, this standard is often modified to take other, lower-cost preventions into account. The defense of *contributory negligence* does not allow the accident victim to collect for damages if he could have prevented the accident at a lower cost than the negligence standard above. If there is no reasonable cost at which the accident could have been prevented you may still have to pay for damages under *strict liability*; this standard provides incentive for you to find alternatives to the activity which caused the accident.

Judge Richard Posner argues that common law has been rather successful in promoting economic efficiency. One of his examples is the doctrine of *respondeat superior*, in which an employer is liable for torts committed by his employees save for those in which another employee is the accident victim. This doctrine promotes private bargaining to resolve problems between employees (where there are low transactions costs) and encourages low-cost prevention by the employer with regards to nonemployees (where high transactions costs prohibit private bargaining).

Professor Richard Epstein, among others, argues that goals other than economic efficiency should be given greater emphasis in tort law. He argues for a strict liability system, claiming it is both possible to identify the person that causes damages (contrary to Coase's argument that externalities are reciprocal) and desirable to assign liability accordingly (contrary to Posner's argument above). One of Epstein's examples is the *Good Samaritan Rule*, under which a bystander has no duty to rescue a stranger in trouble. This doctrine goes against economic efficiency (since the benefits of rescue outweigh the bystander's costs), and supports Epstein's position of strict liability (since the bystander is not the cause of the accident, he should have no liability).

Working Through the Graphs—The Coase Theorem

Figure 12-1 illustrates the story of Bridgman the confectioner and Sturges the doctor. Bridgman's production of candy causes noise which interferes with Sturges' work. By completing the following steps, we can find the implications and limitations of the Coase Theorem.

Step 1. Each graph in Figure 12-1 shows Bridgman's private marginal cost (MC_P) which represents Bridgman's supply. Also shown is the social marginal cost (MC_S) which includes the external costs imposed on Sturges. The equilibrium quantity in the absence of private bargaining is Q_E. The socially optimal quantity is Q_0, assuming there are no alternative solutions available which remove the externality at a sufficiently lower cost. Verify these facts.

Step 2. Using the first graph, perform the welfare analysis when Bridgman freely creates noise and there is no private bargaining between him and Sturges. First shade in the producer's surplus when Bridgman produces Q_E. Recalling that the vertical distance between the private and social marginal costs represents the external cost of each unit Bridgman produces ($2/unit), next shade in the total external costs (i.e., the uncompensated noise damage) borne by Sturges. Use a different color or style of shading for each area, and summarize your results in the accompanying table. If you've done this step correctly, you should find that the social gain is measured by area A - B.

Step 3. For the second graph, we assume that the property right to a noise-free work place has been given to Sturges. Bridgman must purchase the right to make noise from Sturges. We will assume that Sturges accepts the minimum compensation he requires for any noise damage ($2/unit). This increases Bridgman's marginal cost to MC_S. Again perform the welfare analysis by shading in Bridgman's gains and Sturges' losses and completing the table. You should find that the result is optimal, with a social gain of area A being created.

Step 4. For the final graph, we assume that the property right to make noise has been given to Bridgman. Sturges must purchase noise reduction from Bridgman. We will assume Sturges offers the maximum amount he is willing to pay for noise reduction ($2/unit). This has two effects. First, Bridgman can earn the entire value of the external costs (area B + C + D as you found in

Figure 12-1   The Coase Theorem

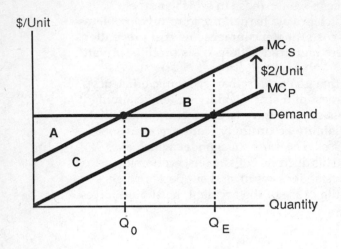

Welfare Analysis before Bargaining

Bridgman's Gains--	
Producers' Surplus =	_____
Transfer from Sturges =	Zero
Sturges' Losses--	
Uncompensated Noise Damage =	_____
Transfer to Bridgman =	Zero
Social Gain--	_____

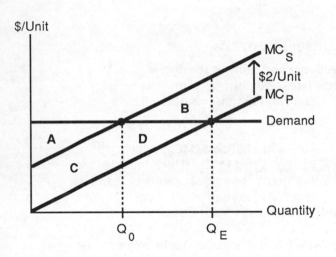

Welfare Analysis with Property Rights Assigned to Sturges

Bridgman's Gains--	
Producers' Surplus =	_____
Transfer from Sturges =	Zero
Sturges' Losses--	
Uncompensated Noise Damage =	_____
Transfer to Bridgman =	Zero
Social Gain--	_____

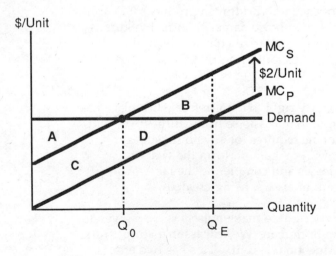

Welfare Analysis with Property Rights Assigned to Bridgman

Bridgman's Gains--	
Producers' Surplus =	_____
Transfer from Sturges =	_____
Sturges' Losses--	
Uncompensated Noise Damage =	_____
Transfer to Bridgman =	_____
Social Gain--	_____

Step 2) by producing nothing, so Sturges' offer has transferred this amount of wealth from Sturges to Bridgman. Second, Bridgman's marginal cost of production has risen to MC_S since he must now consider the opportunity cost of forgoing $2 from Sturges for every unit he produces. Using these two facts, perform the welfare analysis for this case. You should find that the result is again optimal, with area A created in social gain.

Step 5. Compare the three graphs. From an efficiency viewpoint, it did not matter whether we assigned the property rights to Sturges or Bridgman—the social optimum was achieved in both cases. This is the basic claim of the Coase Theorem.

Also notice that the distributions of income are very different under different property right assignments. Each person is made better off when he is awarded the property right over the noise problem. This shows the limitation of the Coase Theorem—it only guarantees an efficient outcome and makes no promises about the resulting distribution of income.

Multiple Choice Questions

1. The automobiles driven along a highway emit noxious fumes which damage neighboring farmlands. In this situation
   A. the social marginal value of driving is greater than the private marginal value.
   B. the private marginal value of driving is greater than the social marginal value.
   C. the private marginal cost of farming is greater than the social marginal cost.
   D. None of the above

***Questions 2-5 refer to Figure 12a, which shows the effects of a negative externality imposed by an industry's production activities.

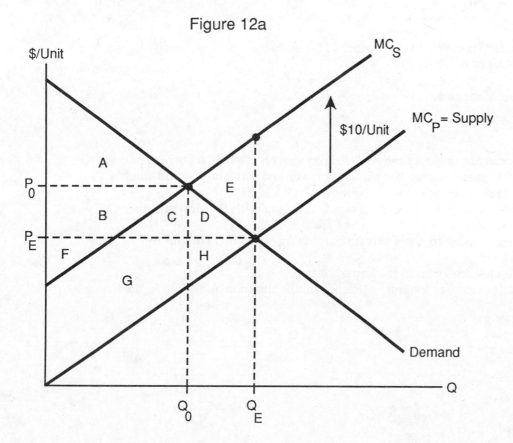

Figure 12a

233

2. When the industry behaves competitively, the total value of the external costs is measured by
   A. area A + B + F.
   B. area B + C.
   C. area C + G.
   D. area C + D + E + G + H.

3. Suppose a Pigou tax causes the industry to reduce production to Q_0. The traditional analysis of externalities states that this will eliminate the deadweight loss of _____ and increase social gain to _____.
   A. area C + D + E + G + H; area A + B + F
   B. area E; area A + B + F
   C. area E; area A + B + C + F + G
   D. area D + E + H; area A + B + C + F + G

4. Suppose there are no transactions costs and the externality is internalized by the damaged parties offering producers a bribe of $10/unit to reduce their production. The damaged parties will pay bribes totalling
   A. area C + D + E + G + H.
   B. area C + D + G + H.
   C. area D + E + H.
   D. area E.

5. Suppose transactions costs prohibit private bargaining. Also suppose that the externality can be removed by relocating those damaged by the firms' production. Assigning liability to firms would be inefficient if the cost of relocation is smaller than
   A. area D + E + H.
   B. area E.
   C. area C + D + G + H.
   D. area C + G.

6. According to the Coase Theorem, in the absence of transactions costs the reassignment of property rights will have no effect on
   A. efficiency.
   B. the distribution of income.
   C. Both A and B
   D. Neither A nor B

7. Suppose a firm's production imposes external costs on some households. There are no transactions costs to prevent private bargaining between the firm and the households. When could a Pigou tax lower economic efficiency?
   A. If tax recipients are unable to enter private bargaining with the firm and the households.
   B. If tax recipients are able to enter private bargaining with the firm and the households.
   C. When tax revenues are given to the households.
   D. A Pigou tax cannot lower economic efficiency in this situation according to the Coase Theorem.

8. Which of the following statements on the Coase Theorem is *false*?
   A. The Strong and Weak Coase Theorems both apply when transactions costs are present.
   B. The Weak Coase Theorem guarantees that efficiency will be unaffected by reassignment of property rights.
   C. The Strong Coase Theorem guarantees that the allocation of resources will be unaffected by reassignment of property rights.
   D. The Strong Coase Theorem is violated when reassignment of property right changes the distribution of income enough to affect market demands.

***Questions 9-11 refer to the following situation. A factory's production processes create smoke. This smoke makes it harder to clean clothes, increasing the costs of the neighboring dry cleaners by $500. The factory can install an air cleaning system for $250, and the dry cleaners can install a new ventilation system for $150. Both systems would remedy the smoke damage at the dry cleaners.

9. Suppose transactions costs are zero. If the factory is not liable and can continue to produce smoke,
   A. the factory will pay the cleaners $500 in smoke damages.
   B. the cleaners will bear the $500 cost of smoke damages.
   C. the factory will install the air cleaning system.
   D. the cleaners will install the ventilation system.

10. Again suppose transactions costs are zero. If the factory is assigned liability for the smoke damage,
   A. the factory will pay the cleaners $500 for smoke damages.
   B. the cleaners will bear the $500 cost of smoke damages.
   C. the factory will install the air cleaning system.
   D. the cleaners will install the ventilation system.

11. Now suppose transactions costs preclude the possibility of private bargaining between the factory and the dry cleaners. If a Pigou tax is levied on the factory with the proceeds given to the dry cleaners, then
   A. the factory will pay the cleaners $500 for smoke damages.
   B. the cleaners will bear the $500 cost of smoke damages.
   C. the factory will install the air cleaning system.
   D. the cleaners will install the ventilation system.

12. A firm uses a lake for cooling. This activity makes the lake warmer, damaging the quality of fishing at the lake. In resolving the dispute between the firm and the fishermen over use of the lake, the court assigns liability to the firm. The firm wishes to negotiate with the fishermen, but finds this difficult due to the continual entry of new fishermen at the lake. This is an example of
   A. the Coase Theorem.
   B. the principle-agent problem.
   C. incomplete property rights.
   D. the free rider problem.

13. Only about 10% of the viewers of public television contribute to help pay for the costs of operation. This is an example of
   A. the Coase Theorem.
   B. the principle-agent problem.
   C. incomplete property rights.
   D. the free rider problem.

14. Inspectors are hired to certify the quality of all welds in a nuclear power plant. The owners of the power plant have no way to guarantee that the inspectors have not simply randomly checked the welds. This is an example of
    A. the Coase Theorem.
    B. the principle-agent problem.
    C. incomplete property rights.
    D. the free rider problem.

15. What is the most efficient liability rule when transactions costs are imposed by a principle-agent problem?
    A. Making the agent liable for all damages resulting from the interaction of the principle and agent.
    B. Making the principle liable for all damages resulting from the interaction of the principle and agent.
    C. Making the principle and agent equally liable for all damages resulting from the interaction of the principle and agent.
    D. All of the above are equally efficient according to the Coase Theorem.

Solutions

1. B. The private marginal value of driving must be adjusted downward to account for the external costs it imposes through polluting the air and damaging farmlands.

2. D. The vertical distance between the private and social marginal costs represents the external cost from each unit produced. Summing all of these gives the total value of the external costs.

3. B. Comparing demand (social marginal value) and social marginal cost gives the social gain and any deadweight loss.

4. C. The damaged parties are willing to offer up to the total value of the external costs (area $C + D + E + G + H$) in bribes. The producers will forgo area $C + G$ in bribes, since the price of the good still exceeds their marginal cost for the first Q_0 units when the opportunity cost of forgoing the bribe is included. They will accept the difference, $D + E + H$, for reducing production from Q_E to Q_0 units.

5. C. If liability is assigned to the firms, social gain will be measured by area $A + B + F$. If damaged parties are relocated then the social marginal cost curve will be shifted down to agree with the private marginal cost curve. In this case, social gain will be area $A + B + C + D + F + G + H$ minus the costs of relocation. Comparing these two social gains, the latter will be the larger if $C + D + G + H$ outweighs the costs of relocation.

6. A. Reassignment of property rights will alter the distribution of income.

7. A. The firm would have a double incentive to reduce production—one incentive from households' bribes and another from the Pigou tax. This forces output below the efficient level. This case does not violate the Coase Theorem because transactions costs are not zero if tax recipients cannot enter the negotiations.

8. A. The Coase Theorem applies to the case where transactions costs are absent.

9. D. The cleaners will offer the factory up to $150 to eliminate the smoke. Since the factory cannot do so for less than this, the cleaners will install the ventilation system. Notice that this is the most efficient choice.

10. D. Since the factory is now liable, it will offer the cleaners up to $250 to put up with the smoke. Since the cleaners can deal with the problem for less than this figure, the two will strike a deal somewhere between $150 and $250 and the efficient choice will again be achieved. The difference between the situations in questions 9 and 10 is the distribution of income—the cleaners are better off when the factory has the liability for the smoke damage and *vice versa*.

11. C. The Pigou tax assigns liability to the factory, giving the cleaners no incentive to solve the smoke problem. In this case the Pigou tax does not reach the efficient solution due to its effects on incentives.

12. C. This liability rule did not give the property rights to specific fishermen, but to all fishermen in general. This creates a transactions cost for the firm wishing to negotiate.

13. D. Most viewers are attempting to take a "free ride" and enjoy the benefits without sharing in the costs.

14. B. The behavior of the inspectors is unobservable. If this were the optimal contract to resolve an externality between the power plant and neighboring residents, this principle-agent problem would constitute a transactions cost preventing its enforcement.

15. A. Since the agent's actions are unobservable, there is no incentive for him to prevent damages caused by his interaction with the principle. Applying the Coase Theorem, private negotiations between the agent and principle give the principle incentive to prevent these damages.

Questions for Review

1. What is an externality? Why can an externality be viewed as a dispute over the use of a resource?

2. What is a Pigou tax? According to the Strong and Weak Coase Theorems, in what sense is the imposition of a Pigou tax unnecessary?

3. A common Friday night activity in some towns is "cruising Main Street," during which teenagers drive their cars and socialize in the downtown area. The noise continues well past midnight, disturbing neighboring residents. Compare and contrast the results of assigning liability to one party versus the other, assuming there are no transactions costs.

4. When the presence of transactions costs prohibits private bargaining, how can the imposition of a Pigou tax lead to inefficiency? What other alternative could be used to internalize an externality in this case?

5. What is the principle-agent problem and why is it a source of transactions costs? What is the most efficient liability rule in the presence of a principle-agent problem? What are some other sources of transactions costs?

6. When does common law promote economic efficiency? Discuss Posner's and Epstein's stands on this relation between law and economics.

7. Discuss the implications of contributory negligence and strict liability for economic efficiency.

Solutions

1. An externality occurs when costs or benefits are involuntarily imposed on others. If markets exist for all resources, there would be no externalities since *all* costs and benefits would be considered in the marginal cost (supply) and marginal value (demand) for the resource and hence reflected in the market price. Participation in the market guarantees that all costs and benefits of the resource will be borne voluntarily. So externalities occur when there is no market to allocate the use of a resource—without the market to determine the most valuable use of the resource, different parties have conflicting uses of the resource, resulting in external costs and benefits.

2. A Pigou tax is a per unit tax imposed to internalize a negative externality. If the tax is set equal to the per unit value of the external cost, the tax will increase the private marginal costs so they equal the social marginal costs. The Weak Coase Theorem claims that the assignment of property rights (as is done through a Pigou tax) has no effect on the efficiency of resource allocation. The Strong Coase Theorem claims that the assignment of property rights will have no effect at all on the resulting allocation of resources; this result requires the additional assumption that changes in income distribution caused by reassignment of property rights are so small that they do not change the market demands for goods. Both theorems hold only in the case where there are no transactions costs. Also notice that the Coase Theorem shows that use of a Pigou tax is unnecessary with respect to efficiency goals, but not income distribution goals.

3. Applying the Strong Coase Theorem, the actual solution to the noise problem will be the same no matter who is assigned liability. Let's assume the teenagers can solve the noise problem at the lowest cost by relocating their cruising activity. If the teenagers are assigned liability for the noise, they will relocate to avoid the liability payments. If the neighborhood residents are liable, they will purchase the right to a noise-free downtown by bribing the teenagers to relocate. Contrasting these solutions, they result in different income distributions. The teenagers are better off when the residents have liability, and the residents are better off when the teenagers have liability.

4. The Pigou tax assigns liability to the party paying the tax, so only that party has the incentive to search for a lower-cost solution to the externality problem. If some other party has access to the low-cost solution, and transactions costs prohibit the liable party from purchasing this solution, the Pigou tax will result in inefficiency. Alternatively, we could attempt to reduce the transactions costs in this case, so that private bargaining could achieve the low-cost solution.

5. When the principle is unable to observe whether or not the agent is abiding by the terms of a contract, there is a principle-agent problem. This inability to enforce the contract can prevent the optimal contract resolving an externality problem to be achieved, and hence constitutes a transactions cost. Since the principle has the incentive to seek low-cost solutions to an externality problem from private negotiations with the agent and since the agent has no incentive to do the same due to his unobservable behavior, liability should be assigned to the agent. Other sources of transactions costs include incomplete property rights and the free rider problem.

6. Common law can promote economic efficiency by creating incentives to solve problems at the lowest cost and by reducing transactions costs to allow private bargaining to achieve a low-cost solution. Posner believes that the common law has been successful in providing doctrines that promote economic efficiency. Epstein believes that other goals should be given greater weight because he believes that the "cause" of an externality can be identified and should be used to assign liability.

7. Contributory negligence promotes economic efficiency because it gives the damaged party the incentive to avoid and prevent accidents. However this can create inefficiency since it provides no incentive for other involved parties to seek solutions that could have been avoided or prevented accidents at still lower costs. When an activity risks accidents that cannot be avoided under any reasonable costs, strict liability provides the incentive to search for other less-risky alternatives and so promotes economic efficiency.

Problems for Analysis

1. The demand for cigarettes is given by the formula $P = 5 - (1/100)Q$, and supply is given by $P = (1/400)Q$, where P is the price in dollars per pack and Q is the quantity of cigarettes in millions of packs. Smoking a pack of cigarettes results in external costs on others of $0.50 per pack.

   (i) Find a formula for the social marginal value of smoking cigarettes.

   (ii) Calculate the quantity, price, producers' and consumers' surplus, total external damages, and net social gain in this market. (Hint—Use a sketch of the graph to help you calculate the various areas.)

   (iii) Suppose the government imposes a Pigou tax of $0.50 per pack on cigarette smokers. Calculate the price received by producers, net price paid by smokers, producers' and consumers' surplus, total external costs, tax revenue collected, and net social gain in this market. Who truly paid the Pigou tax?

(iv) Suppose instead of a Pigou tax, nonsmokers offer smokers $0.50 per pack for every pack by which they reduce their consumption. Will this deal at all affect cigarette producers?

2. This problem reexamines the externality between Sturges the doctor and Bridgman the confectioner. The graph showing Bridgman's candy production is reproduced in Figure 12b.

Figure 12b

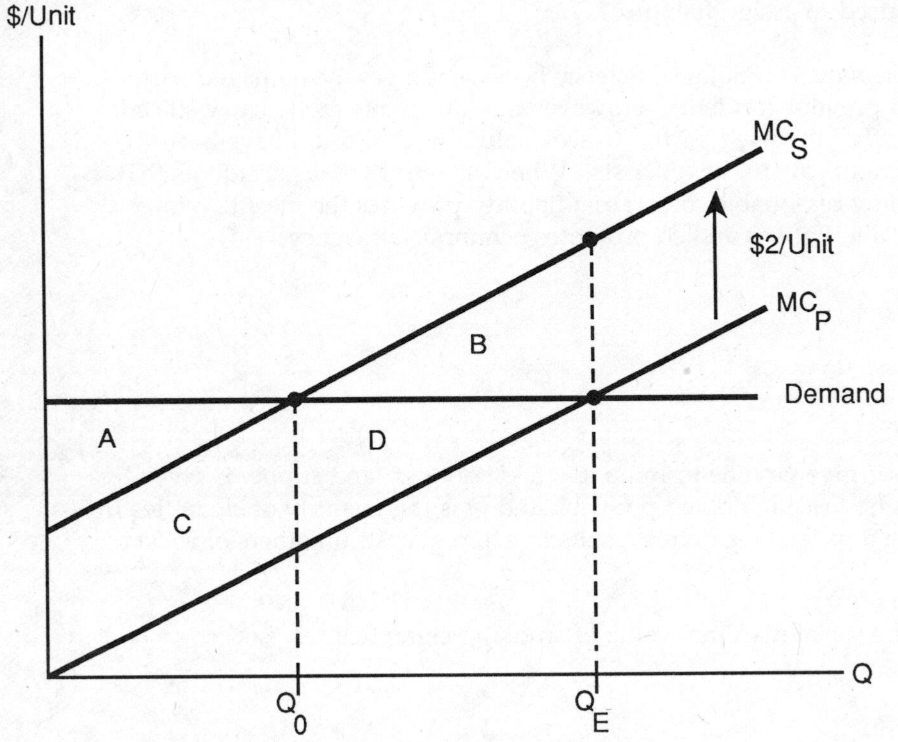

(i) Suppose Bridgman owns the property right to make noise. Sturges offers Bridgman a bribe totalling $\frac{1}{2}B + C + D$ minus $2 for every pound of candy Bridgman produces. Fully describe the gains from trade before and after the bribe. Show that this bribe will make both better off and calculate the net transfer payment from Sturges to Bridgman.

(ii) Suppose Bridgman reneges on the agreement, keeping the net transfer payment from Sturges without reducing the level of his candy production. Fully describe the gains from trade under this situation.

(iii) Suppose instead that Sturges reneges on the agreement, receiving the benefits of Bridgman reducing his candy production without paying the bribe. Describe the gains from trade under this situation.

(iv) Suppose the contract in part (i) is unenforceable and either can violate the contract without repercussions. Summarize Bridgman's gains and Sturges' losses in the table below and predict the result of this situation.

	Bridgman reneges on contract	Bridgman abides by contract
Sturges reneges on contract		
Sturges abides by contract		

(v) What limitation of the Coase Theorem is illustrated by the result in part (iv)?

3. So-called "976" telephone numbers which provide sexually-oriented messages have recently caused disputes. When these numbers are dialed, the telephone company automatically bills the charge to the telephone number from which the call is made. These numbers are openly advertised, generally but not exclusively in sexually-explicit magazines.

   The problem is that minors have been getting access to these numbers, leaving parents upset and with tremendous phone bills. In one case where a minor was sexually molested by another minor, 976 numbers are alleged to have played a role.

(i) What is the missing market causing this externality?

(ii) Discuss the possibilities in assigning liability to promote efficiency in this situation.

(iii) Suppose access to 976 numbers is restricted by providing a subscription service. Persons desiring the use of 976 services would be required to pay a membership fee; in return they would receive an exclusive authorization code that must be used to obtain the 976 services. Suppliers of 976 numbers would be required to restrict membership to those over 21 years of age. Discuss the principle-agent problems involved in such a scheme and the implications these problems have for assigning liability.

Solutions

1. (i) The private marginal value (demand) must be adjusted downward to account for the external costs. Since

the social value placed on the last pack	=	the value that smokers place on the last pack	-	the external cost of the last pack

we have

$$MV_S \quad = \quad 5 - (1/100)Q \quad - \quad 0.50$$

so $MV_S = 4.50 - (1/100)Q$.

(ii) First solve for quantity by equating supply and demand:

$$
\begin{aligned}
(1/400)Q &= 5 - (1/100)Q \\
(1/400)Q + (1/100)Q &= 5 \\
(5/400)Q &= 5 \\
(1/80)Q &= 5 \\
\text{(Multiply by 80)} \quad Q &= 400 \text{ million packs}.
\end{aligned}
$$

242

Substitute into either supply or demand to get price:

P = (1/400)Q = (1/400) • 400 = 1 dollar per pack or
P = 5 - (1/100)Q = 5 - (1/100) • 400 = 5 - 4 = 1 dollar per pack.

As always, summarizing the information in the sketch below helps to calculate the various areas:

consumers' surplus	=	1/2 • base • height
	=	1/2 • 400 • 4
	=	800 million dollars ,
producers' surplus	=	1/2 • base • height
	=	1/2 • 400 • 1
	=	200 million dollars ,
external damages	=	(external cost per pack) • (number of packs)
	=	0.50 • 400
	=	200 million dollars ,
net social gain	=	consumers' surplus + producers' surplus
		- external damages
	=	800 + 200 - 200
	=	800 million dollars .

Figure 12c

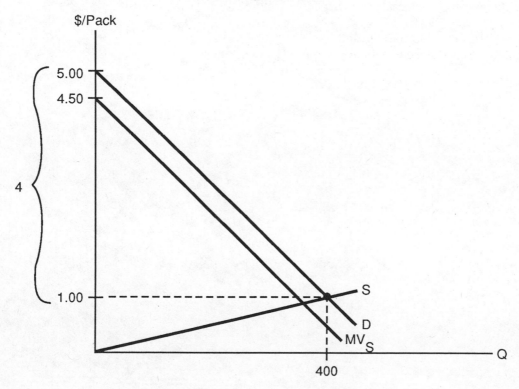

(iii)   The Pigou tax lowers demand to agree with the social marginal value. So supply is now equated to social marginal value:

$$
\begin{aligned}
(1/400)Q &= 4.50 - (1/100)Q \\
(1/400)Q + (1/100)Q &= 4.50 \\
(5/400)Q &= 4.50 \\
(1/80)Q &= 4.50 \\
\text{(Multiply by 80)} \quad Q &= 360 \text{ million packs .}
\end{aligned}
$$

Substitute into supply or demand to get the new price for cigarettes:

$$
P = (1/400)Q = (1/400) \cdot 360 = 0.90 \text{ dollars per pack or}
$$
$$
\begin{aligned}
P = 4.50 - (1/100)Q = 4.50 - (1/100) \cdot 360 &= 4.50 - 3.60 \\
&= 0.90 \text{ dollars per pack.}
\end{aligned}
$$

Finally, use Figure 12d to calculate the various areas:

$$
\begin{aligned}
\text{consumers' surplus} &= 1/2 \cdot \text{base} \cdot \text{height} \\
&= 1/2 \cdot 360 \cdot (4.50 - 0.90) \\
&= 1/2 \cdot 360 \cdot 3.60 \\
&= 648 \text{ million dollars,} \\
\text{producers' surplus} &= 1/2 \cdot \text{base} \cdot \text{height} \\
&= 1/2 \cdot 360 \cdot 0.90 \\
&= 162 \text{ million dollars ,} \\
\text{tax revenue} &= (\text{tax per pack}) \cdot (\text{number of packs}) \\
&= 0.50 \cdot 360 \\
&= 180 \text{ million dollars,} \\
\text{external damages} &= (\text{external cost per pack}) \cdot (\text{number of packs}) \\
&= 0.50 \cdot 360 \\
&= 180 \text{ million dollars ,} \\
\text{net social gain} &= \text{consumers' surplus + producers' surplus} \\
&\quad\quad + \text{tax revenue - external damages} \\
&= 648 + 162 + 180 - 180 \\
&= 810 \text{ million dollars .}
\end{aligned}
$$

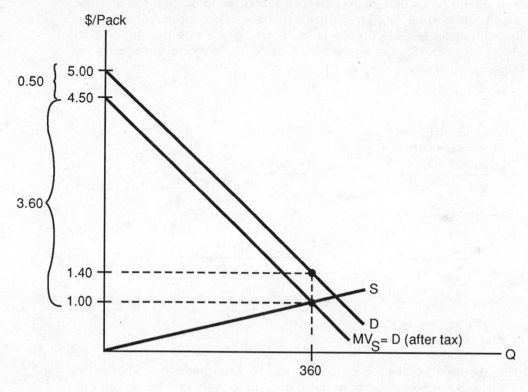

The original price was $1.00 per pack; after the tax producers receive $0.90 per pack and consumers pay a price of $1.40 per pack (including the tax). So consumers "passed back" some of the tax to producers, and both share in paying the Pigou tax.

(iv)   This will work just like a Pigou tax, lowering the marginal value of smoking by the amount of the forgone bribe. As with the tax, consumers will "pass back" to producers some of the higher costs of smoking caused by the forgone bribe.

2. (i)   Before the bribe, the gains to Bridgman are the producer's surplus and the losses to Sturges are the external costs due to noise damage.

Bridgman's gains—	
Producer's surplus	A + C + D
Transfer	—
Total	A + C + D
Sturges' losses—	
Noise damage	B + C + D
Transfer	—
Total	B + C + D

Social gain = Bridgman's gains - Sturges' losses = A - B .

The bribe is a transfer of wealth of area $\frac{1}{2}B + C + D$ from Sturges to Bridgman. This transfer of wealth raises Bridgman's marginal costs (due to the opportunity cost of forgoing a bribe) by \$2/unit. Bridgman's gains are the new producer's surplus (area A) plus the transfer (area $\frac{1}{2}B + C + D$), while Sturges' losses are simply the transfer area $\frac{1}{2}B + C + D$. (Sturges is now compensated for any noise damage from Bridgman forgoing the bribe.)

Bridgman's gains—	
Producer's surplus	A
Transfer	$\frac{1}{2}B + C + D$
Total	$A + \frac{1}{2}B + C + D$

Sturges' losses—	
Noise damage	—
Transfer	$\frac{1}{2}B + C + D$
Total	$\frac{1}{2}B + C + D$

Social gain = Bridgman's gains - Sturges' losses = A .

Comparing the situations before and after the bribe, Bridgman's gains have increased by $\frac{1}{2}B$ and Sturges' losses have fallen by $\frac{1}{2}B$, so both have benefitted from the bribe.

Since Bridgman is producing Q_0 after the bribe, he forgoes area C in bribe payments. This leaves $\frac{1}{2}B + D$ as the net transfer payment from Sturges to Bridgman.

(ii) Bridgman was to cut production and sacrifice area D in producer's surplus in exchange for the net transfer payment; Sturges gains from this exchange is a reduction in noise damage of area B + D. By reneging on the agreement, Bridgman increases his producer's surplus by area D and Sturges does not get the agreed-upon noise reduction of B + D. So now

Bridgman's gains—	
Producer's surplus	A + D
Transfer	$\frac{1}{2}B + C + D$
Total	$A + \frac{1}{2}B + C + D + D$

Sturges' losses—	
Noise damage	B + D
Transfer	$\frac{1}{2}B + C + D$
Total	$\frac{1}{2}B + B + C + D + D$

Social gain = Bridgman's gains - Sturges' losses = A - B .

(iii)   By reneging on the agreement, Sturges is no longer transferring wealth to Bridgman. Since Bridgman has reduced output he has sacrificed area D in producer's surplus, and Sturges benefits from this by receiving area B + D less noise damage.

Bridgman's gains—
Producer's surplus   A + C
Transfer   —
Total   A + C

Sturges' losses—
Noise damage   C
Transfer   —
Total   C

(iv)

	Bridgman reneges on contract	Bridgman abides by contract
Sturges reneges on contract	Bridgman gains A + C + D. Sturges loses B + C + D.	Bridgman gains A + C. Sturges loses C.
Sturges abides by contract	Bridgman gains A + 1/2B + C + D + D. Sturges loses 1/2B + B + C + D + D.	Bridgman gains A + 1/2B + C + D. Sturges loses 1/2B + C + D.

This situation is identical to the Prisoner's Dilemma game. It is in the self-interest of both parties to renege on the contract.

(v)   The Prisoner's Dilemma game shows that the Coase Theorem does not hold when transactions costs make the optimal contract unenforceable.

3. (i)   There is no market to allocate the access to the 976 numbers.

    (ii) Liability should be assigned depending on which group may have the low-cost solution to the problem. Parents could be assigned liability if tighter control over their children's behavior appears to be the optimal solution. The telephone company could be assigned liability if it could provide parents a service to block access of 976 numbers from their telephones at low cost. The owners of 976 numbers could be assigned liability if they could switch to a credit card or subscription service at low cost. If possible, transactions costs between these groups could be reduced to allow private bargaining to determine the lowest-cost solution.

    (iii) The owners of 976 services have contracted with parents not to allow those under 21 to subscribe. This behavior is largely unobservable to parents, so the owners should be held liable for any damages resulting from a minor subscribing to the 976 service. Subscribers to the service have contracted with the owners to not allow minors access to their authorization codes. This behavior is unobservable to the owners, so subscribers should be held liable for any damages that result when minors get access to authorization codes.

Solutions to Working Through the Graphs

Figure 12-1   The Coase Theorem

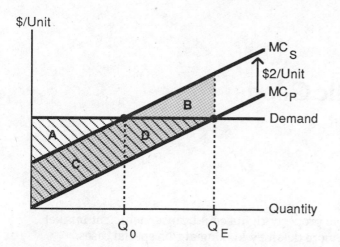

Welfare Analysis before Bargaining

Bridgman's Gains--	
Producers' Surplus =	A + C + D
Transfer from Sturges =	Zero

Sturges' Losses--	
Uncompensated Noise Damage =	B + C + D
Transfer to Bridgman =	Zero

Social Gain--	A - B

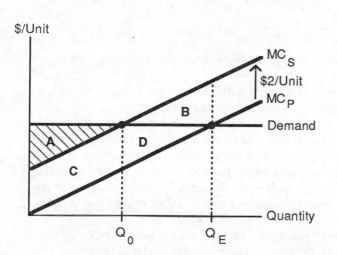

Welfare Analysis with Property Rights Assigned to Sturges

Bridgman's Gains--	
Producers' Surplus =	A
Transfer from Sturges =	Zero

Sturges' Losses--	
Uncompensated Noise Damage =	Zero
Transfer to Bridgman =	Zero

Social Gain--	A

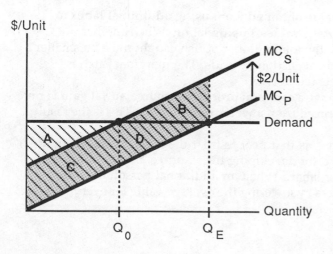

Welfare Analysis with Property Rights Assigned to Bridgman

Bridgman's Gains--	
Producers' Surplus =	A
Transfer from Sturges =	B + C + D

Sturges' Losses--	
Uncompensated Noise Damage =	Zero
Transfer to Bridgman =	B + C + D

Social Gain--	A

Chapter Thirteen

Common Property and Public Goods

Chapter Summary

In the previous chapter we discovered how incomplete property rights could cause inefficient market outcomes. In this chapter we discuss this problem in more detail by looking at two special cases: common property resources and public goods.

Section 13.1. The Tragedy of the Commons

A *common property* is one that is owned by no one; its use is open to all who choose to take advantage of the opportunity.

One problem with common property is that too many resources will be allocated to exploit the property. This problem is known as *dissipation of rents* or the *tragedy of the commons.*

To see this problem, consider a common property lake from which people can obtain fish. As more people fish at the lake, it is more and more difficult to catch fish due to the resulting congestion. So the average value per person received from the lake is falling as the number of people is increasing. As long as this average value exceeds the marginal cost of the last fisherman, people will continue to increase their use of the lake because their gain from entry outweighs their cost. **So a common property resource is used up to the point where the common property's** *average* **value per unit of labor equals the marginal cost of that labor.**

Let's compare this situation with the socially optimal solution. To find the amount of labor to use on the common property, simply apply the equimarginal principle. **To maximize social gain, a common property resource should be used up to the point where the common property's** *marginal* **value per unit of labor equals the marginal cost of that labor.**

The important thing to note is that **the marginal value obtained from using additional labor to develop the common property is smaller than the average value of using labor.** When another fisherman is added to the lake, the amount he adds to the total number of fish caught must be smaller than the previous average catch due to the additional congestion he adds. The marginal catch is smaller than the average catch, and this pulls the average down.

Combining these facts we conclude that **when we have a common property resource, social gain is not maximized and the common property resource is overused from a welfare viewpoint.** This is the result known as the "tragedy of the commons."

The reason that the tragedy of the commons occurs is that people treat the *average value* of their labor from using the resource as the price they are paid for developing the resource, but for efficiency they should be considering the *marginal value* of their labor. When an additional person uses the common property, he imposes an external cost on others by lowering the average value for everyone. Failure to consider this external cost causes the inefficiency.

One way to resolve the tragedy of the commons is to make the common property into a privately-owned resource. The owner would charge an entry fee to those who want to use the resource. If the owner behaves competitively, he will charge an entry fee equal to the difference between the average and marginal value at the efficient level of labor needed to develop the resource. Doing so will maximize the social gain from using labor to develop the resource.

One interesting special case is when the marginal cost of labor to develop the common property is constant. Then the marginal cost of labor equals its average cost. We conclude that the common property is used to the point where the average value of labor equals the average cost of labor, so there is a net gain of zero from using labor on the common property. When marginal cost is constant, the social gain (or *rent*) obtained from the common property is zero. This "dissipation of rents" totally eliminates any incentive to make improvements to the common property. On the other hand, a private owner of the common property would have an incentive to make improvements due to the additional rent (collected via entry fees) that could be earned.

Section 13.2. Public Goods

A *public good* is one where one person's consumption of that good automatically increases the amount available to everyone. Generally economists think of public goods as being *nonexcludable* (i.e., no one can be excluded from consumption of the good at any reasonable cost) and *nonrivalrous* (i.e., additional people can consume the good at no additional cost). The best example of a public good is national defense.

The provision of public goods is a special case of the positive externalities presented in the last chapter. One person's consumption of a public good creates external benefits since it automatically causes everyone else's consumption to also increase. So the social marginal value of a public good is far greater than any one person's private marginal value. As a result, the competitive market would allocate too few resources to the provision of a public good.

Generally government is relied on to provide public goods, but determining the most efficient level to supply is a difficult matter. Under some conditions voting can reveal the optimal level of provision, but voting fails to reveal the intensity of people's desire to have the public good. One possibility is that government could ask people how much they value having the public good, but then people would have the incentive to exaggerate their preferences to guarantee that the good is provided. Another possibility is that government could again ask people to reveal the degree to which they value the public good, and then make the person's tax share to finance the provision proportional to his revealed value. The problem with this scheme is that each person has the incentive to understate his preferences in an attempt to share in the benefits of the public good without sharing in the costs. This is the free rider problem that was discussed as a source of transactions costs in the previous chapter.

Economists have developed several mechanisms to elicit truthful responses from people so that the social marginal value of a public good can be discovered and the free rider problem can be overcome. We describe one such scheme for the simple case where the marginal cost of providing the public good is zero; keep in mind that the person may not want this public good and may place a negative value on it.

Suppose the government will pay each person the sum of the values reported by everyone else if the public good is provided. (If this sum is negative, the person would have to pay a tax in this amount.) Any given person would want to have the public good provided if this payment (or tax) plus the value he *actually* receives from the public good is positive; the government plans on providing the public good if this payment (or tax) plus the value he *reports* he receives from the public good is positive. On the other hand, a person does not want the public good provided if the sum of others' reported values plus the value he *actually* receives from the public good is negative, and the government plans not to provide the public good if this sum plus the value he *reports* is negative. Comparing the individual's incentives with the government's scheme, we see that the best strategy for the person to follow is to truthfully reveal his preferences for the public good. However one problem is that these payments to individuals (or taxes collected from them) must come from (or go to) an outside source; otherwise they would distort the incentives faced by the individuals.

Working Through the Graphs—The Tragedy of the Commons

The tragedy of the commons is a special case in the study of externalities. This problem is illustrated by Figure 13-1, which when completed will show how competitive behavior can cause a common property resource to be overused.

The graphs in Figure 13-1 show the three curves needed to study the tragedy of the commons. The marginal cost curve simply shows the opportunity cost that the last unit of labor incurs when it chooses to use the common property. The average and marginal value curves describe the value that labor receives from working on the common property. **The marginal value curve shows the addition that the last unit of labor contributes to the total value obtained from the common property** (e.g., the addition to the total catch resulting from the last fisherman or the addition to the total harvest resulting from the last laborer). **The average value curve shows the value per unit of labor obtained from the common property** (e.g., the average catch per fisherman or the average harvest per laborer). We can think of the average value as showing us the price that labor is paid for its work on the common property (e.g., the average catch is what the fisherman receives for his efforts or the average harvest is what the laborer receives from his work).

With these facts in hand, we can now complete Figure 13-1.

Step 1. In the top graph we consider what happens when there is uninhibited entry to the common property. Laborers will compare the price they receive from working on the common property (from the average value curve) against their marginal cost of entry. Laborers will continue to enter until these two quantities are equated, so Q_C units of labor will work on the common property receiving an average value of P_C for their work. Locate and shade in the producers' surplus generated in this situation; summarize your result in the appropriate column of the table.

Step 2. In the lower graph we consider what happens when labor is charged a competitive entry fee to work on the common property. The Invisible Hand Theorem guarantees that the result will maximize the social gain, and using the equimarginal principle we know this occurs where the marginal value is equated to the marginal cost. So we must find an entry fee that causes Q_0 units of labor to use the common property. Using the marginal cost curve, we see that a price of P_1 is needed to get Q_0 units of labor to enter. Using the average value curve, we see that laborers would actually receive a price of P_2 when there are only Q_0 units of labor. The difference between these two, $P_2 - P_1$, must be the competitive entry fee.

Use these facts to do the welfare analysis of this situation. First shade in the producers' surplus, keeping in mind that labor receives the price P_1 after paying the entry fee. Next find the total earnings generated by the entry fee. To do this remember that Q_0 units of labor are paying an entry fee of $P_2 - P_1$ each; these figures give you the dimensions of the rectangle that represents the total earnings.

Summarize your results in the table provided. If you've done everything correctly, you should find that the social gain is measured by area $C + D + F + G + I$. The Invisible Hand Theorem guarantees that this is the maximum social gain that can be created.

Step 3. Compare the two graphs. Notice from the top graph that uninhibited entry resulted in overuse of the resource since Q_C is larger than Q_0. This result is called the tragedy of the commons.

The bottom graph shows how the tragedy of the commons can be resolved. If the government or a private owner can restrict entry by charging a competitive entry fee, the social welfare obtained from the common property can be maximized.

252

Figure 13-1   The Tragedy of the Commons

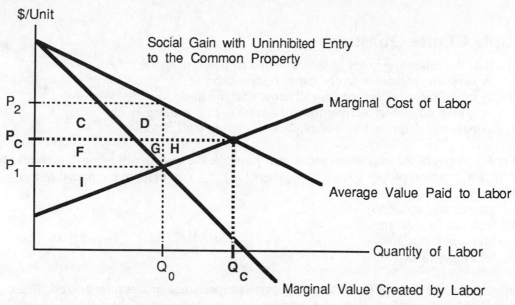

$/Unit

Social Gain with Uninhibited Entry
to the Common Property

Marginal Cost of Labor

P_2

C   D

P_C

F   G H

P_1

I

Average Value Paid to Labor

Quantity of Labor

Q_0 Q_C

Marginal Value Created by Labor

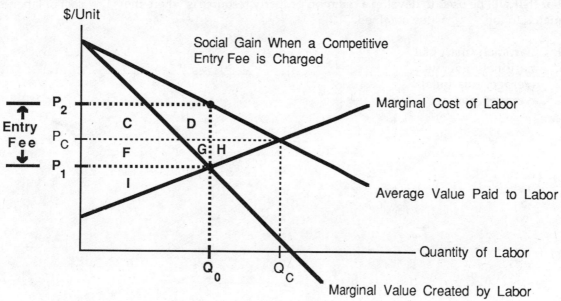

$/Unit

Social Gain When a Competitive
Entry Fee is Charged

Marginal Cost of Labor

P_2

Entry
Fee

C   D

P_C

F   G H

P_1

I

Average Value Paid to Labor

Quantity of Labor

Q_0 Q_C

Marginal Value Created by Labor

	Gains from Trade with Uninhibited Entry	Gains from Trade with Competitive Entry Fee
Producers' Surplus		
Earnings from Entry Fee	Zero	
Social Gain		

253

Multiple Choice Questions

1. Which of the following is *not* an example of a common property?
   A. A lake that residents freely use to obtain fish.
   B. A forest that is developed by all firms wishing to do so.
   C. A grasslands which all members of a tribe use for grazing.
   D. A national defense which is jointly consumed by all citizens.

2. In order to create the maximum social gain possible, the quantity of labor that should be used to develop a common property resource is where the _____ cost of labor is equated to the _____ value obtained.
   A. marginal; marginal
   B. marginal; average
   C. average; marginal
   D. average; average

3. Suppose the use of labor to develop a common property resource is unrestricted. The quantity of labor that will be used to develop a common property resource is where the _____ cost of labor is equated to the _____ value obtained.

   A. marginal; marginal
   B. marginal; average
   C. average; marginal
   D. average; average

Figure 13a

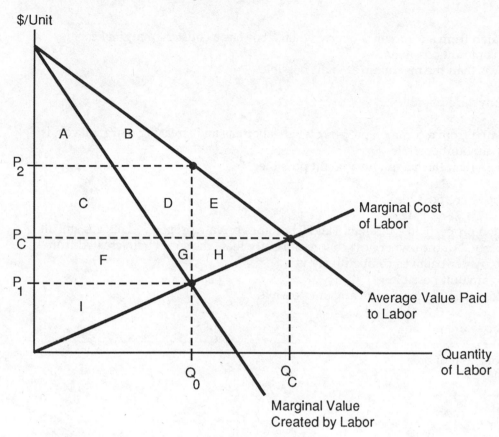

4. If access to the common property is uninhibited, the resulting social gain is measured by
    A.   area I.
    B.   area F + G + H + I.
    C.   area C + D + F + G + I.
    D.   area A + B + C + D + E + F + G + H + I.

5. The maximum social gain that can be obtained from using labor to exploit the common property is measured by
    A.   area I.
    B.   area F + G + H + I.
    C.   area C + D + F + G + I.
    D.   area A + B + C + D + E + F + G + H + I.

6. Suppose the common property becomes privately owned. The owner behaves competitively and establishes an entry fee for labor to enter and use the property. The amount earned by the owner is measured by
    A.   area I.
    B.   area F + G + H + I.
    C.   area C + D + F + G.
    D.   area A + B + C + D + E.

7. Again consider the situation in Question 6. The surplus value earned by labor from the use of the property is measured by
   A. area I.
   B. area F + G + H + I.
   C. area C + D + F + G.
   D. area A + B + C + D + E.

8. The social gain created from a common property when labor has a constant marginal cost is
   A. the maximum amount possible.
   B. positive but less than the maximum amount possible.
   C. zero.
   D. Any of the above are possible

9. The social gain created from a common property when labor has an increasing marginal cost is
   A. the maximum amount possible.
   B. positive but less than the maximum amount possible.
   C. zero.
   D. Any of the above are possible

10. Suppose the common property in Questions 8 and 9 becomes private property. Labor is still allowed to exploit the property, but the owner now charges an entry fee. The social gain created from the property when the owner behaves competitively is
    A. the maximum amount possible.
    B. positive but less than the maximum amount possible.
    C. zero.
    D. Any of the above are possible

11. The consumption of a loaf of bread is
    A. nonexcludable.
    B. nonrivalrous.
    C. Both A and B
    D. Neither A nor B

12. The consumption of a common property is
    A. nonexcludable.
    B. nonrivalrous.
    C. Both A and B
    D. Neither A nor B

13. A fireworks display for a community is worth $10 to each of 100 residents. The display costs $750. Which of the following statements is *false*?
    A. The social value of the fireworks display exceeds its cost.
    B. No one individual is willing to purchase the fireworks display.
    C. A private group could provide the fireworks display by asking each resident to contribute $7.50.
    D. By imposing a tax of $7.50 per person, the government could provide the fireworks display and increase social welfare.

14. The government faces a free rider problem when trying to determine if it is optimal to tax people and provide a public good. People have the incentive to _____ their preferences for the public good if the value they report to government is _____ to their tax share.
    A. understate; related
    B. understate; unrelated
    C. overstate; related
    D. overstate; unrelated

15. The marginal cost of providing a public good is zero. Overall, others do not want the public good, having reported that the good would make them $X worse off. You will be required to pay $X in taxes if the public good is provided. Then
   A. you want the public good provided if it is worth more than $X to you.
   B. the government will provide the public good if you report that it is worth more than $X to you.
   C. Both A and B
   D. Neither A nor B

Solutions

1. D. National defense does not have nonrivalrous consumption like a common property resource. Unlike a common property resource, the entry of an additional person to the national defense does not lower the value others get from the defense.

2. A. This is simply an application of the equimarginal principle.

3. B. Laborers will continue to use the common property as long as the average value they receive from the common property exceeds their marginal cost of entry.

4. B. Uninhibited entry will cause Q_C units of labor to be used. Comparing the "price" that the labor is paid (i.e., the average value that the labor receives) against its marginal cost measures the social gain.

5. C. The quantity Q_0 maximizes social gain since marginal value and marginal cost are equated. As in the previous question, we can compare the "price" labor is paid against the marginal cost to find the social gain.

6. C. The owner will charge an entry fee of $P_2 - P_1$. The area C + D + F + G measures the total amount earned since the amount of labor that enters is the base of this rectangle and the per unit entry fee is the width.

7. A. The "price" paid to labor is the average value minus the entry fee, which equals P_1. Comparing this price against the marginal cost of labor gives the surplus value. Notice that the owner's earnings in Question 6 plus the surplus value to labor in this question sum to the maximum social gain found in Question 5.

8. C. Uninhibited entry equates the average value obtained from the labor and the marginal cost of labor. Average cost equals marginal cost in this case, so the common property is used to the point where the average value obtained from the labor equals the average cost of labor. This implies that the total social gain is zero.

9. B. This result is immediate from comparing the answers to Questions 4 and 5.

10. A. As long as all agents are behaving competitively and there are well-defined property rights, the Invisible Hand Theorem guarantees that the result is efficient.

11. D. It is easy to exclude any given person from consuming the loaf of bread, so it cannot be nonexcludable. Furthermore, when one person consumes the loaf of bread it is extremely difficult (not to mention a bit disgusting) to permit another person to consume the same loaf of bread; hence bread consumption cannot be nonrivalrous.

12. A. Since anyone can use the common property, its use is nonexcludable. But since the entry of an additional person lowers the value that each person receives from the common property, it cannot be nonrivalrous.

13. C. Each person would have the incentive to take a "free ride" and attempt to enjoy the benefits of the fireworks display without sharing in the costs. This free rider problem constitutes a transactions costs that prevents the optimal contract from being reached through private bargaining.

14. A. When people realize that their tax payments are connected to the value they report that they receive, they will understate their preferences in an attempt to share in the benefits but not the costs of the public good. This is another example of the free rider problem.

15. C. Comparing these two statements, we see that this scheme provides the incentive for each individual to properly reveal his preferences. This scheme is one way that the free rider problem can be overcome.

Questions for Review

1. Explain why common property resources and public goods are both special cases of externalities.

2. Why does the average value of labor using a common property resource decrease as the number of laborers increases? Why is the marginal value of labor using a common property resource less than the average value?

3. Why does uninhibited entry to a common property resource lead to overuse of the resource?

4. Compare and contrast the effects of uninhibited entry to a common property resource when there is (a) constant marginal cost of using labor and (b) increasing marginal cost of using labor.

5. How can private ownership of a common property resource achieve efficiency? Can the result under private ownership ever be inefficient?

6. Explain why consumption of national defense is both nonexcludable and nonrivalrous.

7. How does the free rider problem affect the government's provision of public goods? How can the free rider problem be overcome?

Solutions

1. When an additional person chooses to use a common property resource, the resulting congestion lowers the average value each receives from the labor he applies to the resource. This constitutes an external cost that the entrant imposes on others. A fishery is an excellent example of this.

When one person chooses to consume more of a public good, everyone receives benefits (or possibly costs) from that additional consumption. So one person's consumption imposes external benefits (or costs) on others. This is because consumption of a public good is nonexcludable and nonrivalrous.

2. Consumption of a common property is rivalrous; the average value each laborer receives from working on the common property falls because of the resulting congestion. For example, the entry of an additional fisherman lowers the average catch for everyone.

    Consider the increase the total value received from the common property when the last laborer is added; this amount (the marginal value) must be lower than the average value for it to cause the average to be decreasing. Your grade point average provides a simple example; if the grade you get in this course (the marginal grade) is lower than your current grade point average (the average grade) then your grade point average will fall.

3. Consider the situation faced by the typical laborer. If he uses one additional hour of labor, he receives the average value of labor from using the common property. (For example, the fisherman will receive the average catch from an additional hour of using the fishery.) He will pursue this activity if it exceeds his marginal cost of entry. So common property resources are used to the point where the marginal cost of labor is equated to the average value that labor receives from using the common property. But the equimarginal principle tells us that efficient use will occur where the marginal cost of labor equals the marginal value it receives. Since the marginal value is smaller than the average value received by labor, this implies that the common property is overused relative to the efficient level.

4. In both situations the surplus value created from labor using the common property is smaller than the maximum amount possible. When the marginal cost of labor is increasing the rent from the common property is positive. But when the marginal cost of labor is constant, uninhibited entry drives the social gain to zero and the rents are fully dissipated. In this case no improvements to the common property are worthwhile—the social value of such improvements will be zero (since entry will again drive the social gain to zero) and will be outweighed by their social cost.

5. A private owner can impose an entry fee to reduce the amount of labor working on the property to the optimal level. Assuming that the owner behaves competitively, the Invisible Hand Theorem guarantees that the entry fee achieving the maximum social welfare will be charged. The result can be inefficient if the owner behaves as a monopoly. The entry fee charged will be above the competitively established one, and so the common property will be underused with respect to the social optimum.

6. It would be virtually impossible to deny any one citizen the right to consume of the national defense, so consumption is nonexcludable. The additional cost of allowing an additional citizen to consume the national defense is zero (as proved by the births of thousands every day), so consumption is nonrivalrous.

7. The government must both determine the value of the public good to citizens (to determine the optimal provision) and raise revenues to finance its provision. If citizens realize that their stated preferences for the public good are related to the tax share they pay, this will create a free rider problem. They will have an incentive to understate their preferences to attempt to share in the benefits of the public good (which cannot be denied since consumption is nonexcludable) without sharing in the costs.

    By changing incentives so that the person's tax share is unrelated to the value reported, the free rider problem can be overcome. For the case of zero cost, when each person is promised to be paid the amount reported by others if the public good is provided (and required to pay a tax if this amount is negative), then each person has the incentive to correctly reveal his preferences.

Problems for Analysis

1. This question reconsiders the problem of the giant and the dwarves discussed in the textbook. Exhibit 13-2 from the text illustrates this situation and is reproduced below.

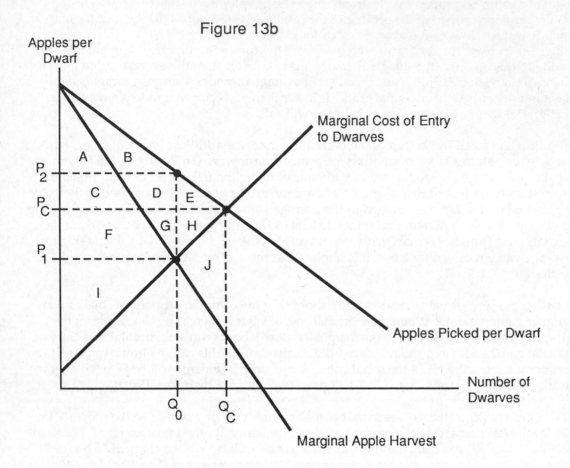

Figure 13b

(i) The text shows that area $F + G + H + I$ measures the social gain when dwarves are allowed uninhibited access to the forest. Show that this area is equal to area $A + C + F + I - J$. (Hint—Use the fact that the marginal value curve is exactly twice as steep as the average value curve.)

Now suppose that the giant has claimed the forest. However instead of charging dwarves an entry fee, the giant has decided to hire dwarves to pick the apples for himself.

(ii) Assume that both the giant and the dwarves behave competitively. In the above figure, label the giant's demand and dwarves' supply of labor to pick apples. Find the price that the giant will pay the dwarves, the consumer's surplus the giant receives from the dwarves' labor, the producer's surplus the dwarves receive, and the resulting social gain.

(iii) Show that the giant's consumer's surplus is equal to the amount he would earn if he charged a competitive entry fee. Use this fact to show that the system where the giant charges an entry fee results in the same social gain as the situation where the giant hires dwarves to pick apples.

(iv) Use the Invisible Hand Theorem to explain why the result in part (iii) is not surprising.

2. (i) We have shown that common property resources are a special case of externalities. Could the Coase Theorem be applied to resolve the common property problem? If "yes," describe the possible results of private bargaining. If "no," describe the transactions costs that prevent private bargaining from being effective.

(ii) Repeat part (i) for public goods.

3. (i) Show that the externality created by one person's consumption of a public good can be measured by the vertical sum of everyone else's demands.

(ii) Prove that the vertical sum of all individuals' demands shows the social marginal value of the public good at each and every quantity provided.

Solutions

1. (i) Since the marginal value curve is twice as steep as the average value curve, the triangles A + C and G + H + J must have the same dimensions. So area A + C = area G + H + J which implies area A + C - J = area G + H . Since the social gain equals area F + G + H + I, substituting the above we find that it must also equal area F + (A + C - J) + I, or area A + C + F + I - J .

261

This result should be no surprise because this area is obtained by comparing marginal value and marginal cost out to the quantity Q_C, which is how we usually find the social gain in a market.

(ii)   Using the results from Chapters 7 and 8, the giant's demand is given by the marginal value curve and the dwarves' supply is given by the marginal cost curve. Treating this like any other competitive market, the dwarves will be paid the price P_1, the consumer's surplus for the giant will be area $A + C + F$, the producers' surplus for the dwarves will be area I, and the social gain will be area $A + C + F + I$ (which is the maximum amount possible).

(iii)   As shown in the textbook, the competitive entry fee charged by the giant is area $C + D + F + G$. Since marginal value is twice as steep as average value, triangles A and $D + G$ must have the same area. So the entry fee area $C + D + F + G$ must equal the area $A + C + F$ which is the consumer's surplus. So the giant receives the same amount in the two situations. Notice that the dwarves receive a price of P_1 and producers' surplus area I whether they pay an entry fee or are hired by the giant. So the social gain in both situations is area $A + C + F + I$ (which equals area $C + D + F + G + I$).

(iv)   The Invisible Hand Theorem guarantees that the results of competition will create the most social gain possible, so it is no surprise that the maximum social gain from the common property is created whether the giant competitively hires the dwarves or charges them a competitive entry fee.

2. (i)   It may be possible for private bargaining to resolve the tragedy of the commons, but it will be difficult to overcome the transactions costs of negotiating and enforcing the optimal contract. First, there must be a sufficiently small number of agents involved so that the proper tax, entry fee, or quota for use of the common property can be negotiated. Second, the transactions cost of enforcing the optimal contract must be overcome. Since each agent will have the incentive to violate the agreement on the use of the common property, there must be a way of prohibiting unauthorized use of the common property. The transactions cost of enforcement would be prohibitive if agents' use of the common property is largely unobservable. (For example, it may be too costly to count each hunter's kills or every fisherman's catch.)

(ii)   It would also be difficult for private bargaining to obtain the optimal provision of a public good due to the transactions costs of negotiations. Public goods often involve large numbers of people (like with the national defense). Furthermore, the free rider problem constitutes a transactions cost of negotiation which must be overcome.

3. (i)   When any one person chooses to consume a public good, that amount is also consumed by everyone else since consumption is nonexcludable and nonrivalrous. To find the external benefits they receive from this consumption, recall from Chapter 8 that a person's demand curve also shows the marginal value (using the vertical coordinate) that he receives from the good at any given quantity. Since the vertical coordinates of everyone else's demands show the marginal values they receive from the public good, the vertical sum of their demands must show the total external benefits that one person's additional consumption creates for others.

(ii)   From Chapter 12 we know that a person's private marginal value (demand) must be adjusted upwards to get the social marginal value when there is a positive externality. From part (i) we know that this external benefit is measured by the vertical sum of everyone else's demands. Combining these two facts, the vertical sum of all individuals' demand curves gives the social marginal benefit of the public good.

Solutions to Working Through the Graphs

Figure 13-1   The Tragedy of the Commons

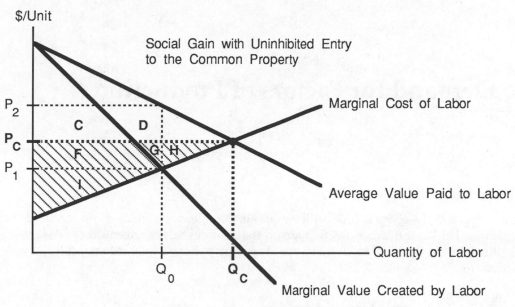

Social Gain with Uninhibited Entry to the Common Property

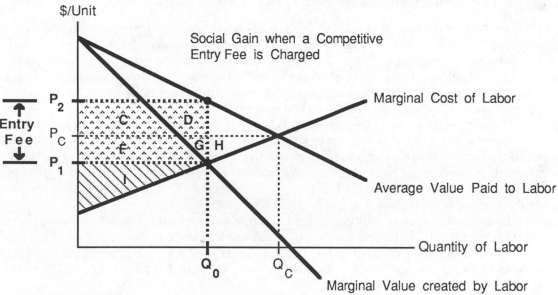

Social Gain when a Competitive Entry Fee is Charged

	Gains from Trade with Uninhibited Entry	Gains from Trade with Competitive Entry Fee
Producers' Surplus	F + G + H + I	I
Earnings from Entry Fee	Zero	C + D + F + G
Social Gain	F + G + H + I	C + D + F + G + I (maximum)

Chapter Fourteen

The Demand for Factors of Production

Chapter Summary

We now begin a three-chapter unit on the markets that allocate factors of production. This chapter focuses on the behavior of the firms that are on the demand side of this market. For concreteness we discuss the demand for labor below, but the ideas are applicable to the demand for any factor of production.

Section 14.1. The Firm's Demand for Factors in the Short Run

The *marginal revenue product of labor* (MRP_L) is the additional revenue generated from the additional output produced by the last unit of labor. MRP_L is calculated by multiplying the firm's marginal revenue by its marginal product of labor. If the firm is competitive then marginal revenue equals the price of output, so MRP_L is simply the price of output times the marginal product of labor. Applying the equimarginal principle, an immediate result is that **the firm's short-run demand for labor coincides with the downward-sloping portion of its marginal revenue product curve.**

Be sure to notice the difference between the effects of a change in the wage and a change in the price of output. If there is a rise in the wage, this raises the firm's marginal cost of production and causes the firm to produce less output. To produce less output in the short run (assuming capital is fixed), the firm must use less labor. Since there has been no change in either marginal revenue or the marginal product of labor, the marginal revenue product of labor curve is unaffected. This decrease in labor use due to the increase in the price of labor is shown as a movement along the MRP_L curve.

A fall in the price of output will cause the firm to move down its marginal cost (i.e., supply) curve and reduce its output level. As before, the firm will now use less labor in the short run. Since marginal revenue (i.e., the competitive firm's price) has fallen, the marginal revenue product curve has changed. The decrease in labor use caused by the fall in the price of output is diagrammed as a shift to the left in the MRP_L curve.

Since the amount of capital available in the short run will affect the productivity of labor, a change in capital will also shift the MRP_L curve. Since an increase in capital use can either increase or decrease the marginal product of labor, the short run demand for labor (shown by the MRP_L curve) can either increase or decrease in this situation. When capital and labor are *complements in production*, additional capital increases the marginal product of labor and hence increases the short-run demand for labor. On the other hand, when additional capital lowers the marginal product of labor causing a decrease in the short-run demand for labor, we say that capital and labor are *substitutes in production*.

Section 14.2. The Firm's Demand for Factors in the Long Run

To derive the firm's long-run demand for labor, we assume that the firm's technology, the price of output, and the price of capital are fixed. We need to find the amount of labor demanded in the long run at any given wage. Starting with a given wage, we can find the firm's isocosts and expansion path as shown in Chapter 6. Using the expansion path and the prices of labor and capital, we can calculate the firm's long-run marginal cost (LRMC). By comparing LRMC against marginal revenue, the firm's output level is determined. Using the isoquant map, this output level determines the amount of labor used in the long run corresponding to the wage that we started with. By repeating this process for several different wage rates, we can derive the long-run demand for labor.

Notice that the firm's labor decision depends on the situation in the output market. Should the marginal revenue in the output market change, then the entire long-run demand for labor will be different. We say that the demand for labor is a *derived demand* since it is partly derived from information in an additional market external to the labor market.

The derivation of the long-run demand for labor also shows that a change in the wage will affect the amount of labor hired for two different reasons. These are called the *substitution effect* and the *scale effect*. In the substitution effect when there is an increase in the wage, the firm will use more capital and less labor to produce any given level of output. This is shown by the firm moving up along the isoquant when the isocosts become steeper due to the higher wage. The scale effect results from the fact that the increase in wage will change the firm's costs and its level of output. The different level of output will also change the amount of labor used by the firm. This is shown by the firm moving to a different isoquant when the wage changes. To summarize, the substitution effect shows that the firm will substitute capital for labor to produce any given amount of output when the wage increases, and the scale effect shows that the increase in the wage will affect the firm's output decision and hence the amount of labor needed.

The substitution effect will always support the law of demand for factors of production. When the wage goes up and the isocosts become steeper, the firm will always use less labor and more capital to produce a particular level of output since the isoquants are convex. The scale effect may or may not support the law of demand. If the increase in wage also causes long-run marginal cost to increase, then this will lower the amount of output produced and hence lower the amount of labor needed. In this case, the scale effect will reinforce the substitution effect. On the other hand, the increase in wage could lower the firm's long-run marginal cost and increase the firm's output. Then the scale effect causes the firm to use more labor when the wage increases and so works against the law of demand. In this case, labor is called a *regressive factor*. It can be shown mathematically that the scale effect will not outweigh the substitution effect when labor is a regressive factor, so the long-run demand for labor will always be downward sloping.

Section 14.3. The Industry's Demand Curve for Factors of Production

For the case where the scale effect reinforces the substitution effect, the industry's demand for labor is less elastic than the sum of the individual firms' demands. This is because the scale effect will be in part offset by the effects of changes in the price of output. When the wage rate increases, the scale effect shows that the firm's output will be lowered, causing the quantity demanded of labor to fall. But the higher wage also increases all firms' marginal costs, in turn decreasing supply and increasing the price of output. The higher price of output will encourage firms to increase their output level and their use of labor, in opposition to the scale effect. Hence each firm's quantity demanded for labor will not fall by as much in reaction to a rise in the wage, and so the industry demand is less elastic than the sum of individual firm's demands.

265

The above analysis has assumed that the labor market is competitive. However, a firm hiring labor can also face an upward sloping supply curve instead of one horizontal at the market wage. Such a firm is called a *monopsonist,* and the analysis of this situation parallels that for a monopoly. The marginal cost of hiring labor will lie above the supply curve, since to hire the last unit of labor the firm must not only pay the wage to that unit but also bid up the wages of other workers. Profits are maximized where the marginal revenue product of labor equals the marginal cost of labor; the wage paid is determined by the supply curve. The monopsony hires less labor and pays a lower wage than if the labor market were competitive.

Section 14.4. The Distribution of Income

The supply and demand of a factor can be used to illustrate the distribution of income. The area under the firm's demand curve (i.e., the marginal revenue product curve) out to the quantity hired represents the firm's total revenues. Using the factor price paid, this can be divided into two areas: the rectangular area below the factor price represents the total income earned by the resource and the triangular area above the factor price is the amount paid to other factors and profits. The part of the resource's total income above the supply curve is the producer's surplus or rent received for supplying the resource. Rent is an important concept because it shows the payments the factor receives above and beyond the opportunity costs incurred for supplying that factor.

The difference between the producer's surplus received by the firm and the rents paid to all the factors of production is the firm's profits. (Notice that this difference can be positive or negative.) In long-run equilibrium a competitive firm's profits are zero, so the producer's surplus earned by the firm are fully distributed to the various factors of production.

It is the elasticity of the supply of a factor, not the size of the factor price, which shows the degree to which it benefits or loses from changing conditions in an industry. Notice that the more inelastic a factor's supply is, the greater proportion of its total income is rent. So factors with very inelastic supply have more to gain or lose from changes in the demand for the industry's output than other factors with less inelastic supply.

Since some factors are fixed in the short run but variable in the long run, an increase in the price of output would benefit these factors more in the short run than in the long run. These temporary short-run rents are sometimes called *quasi-rents.*

Working Through the Graphs—Derivation of the Firm's Long-Run Demand for Labor

Since the long-run demand for labor is a derived demand, its derivation is somewhat complicated. Figure 14-1 shows the various stages of the process.

Step 1. We assume that the firm's technology (shown by the isoquants), the price of capital ($P_K = \$2$ per machine-hour), and the price of output ($10 per unit) are all fixed. Figure 14-1 shows how to get the point on the long-run labor demand curve corresponding to the wage rate of $P_L = \$1$ per man-hour.

Follow the panels clockwise to see the four steps in deriving a point on the long-run demand for labor. (a) For the chosen wage and the given price of capital, plot the isocosts to find the firm's expansion path. (b) Use the points on the expansion path to calculate the firm's long-run marginal cost (LRMC). (c) Compare LRMC against the marginal revenue faced by the firm to find the level of output that the firm will choose to produce. (d) Use the isoquant map to find the amount of labor needed to produce this level of output in the long run. By plotting this amount of labor (on the horizontal axis) against the chosen wage rate that we started with (on the vertical axis), we have one point on the firm's long-run demand curve for labor.

Verify that these four steps have been done correctly for the wage of $1 per man-hour in Figure 14-1.

Figure 14-1   Derivation of the Firm's Long-run Demand for Labor

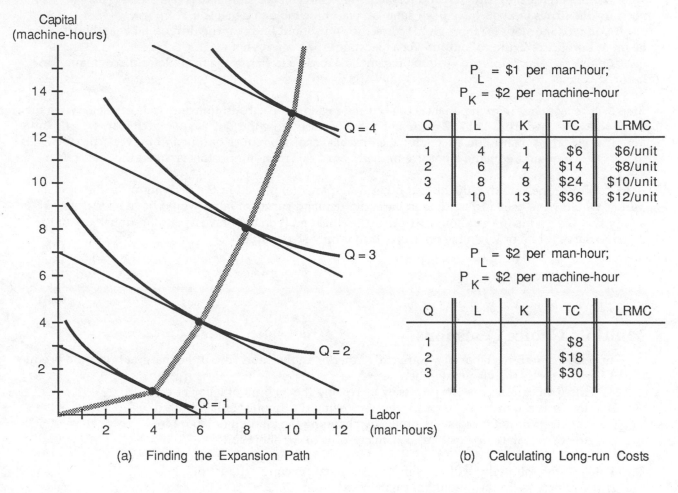

Capital (machine-hours)

Q = 4
Q = 3
Q = 2
Q = 1

Labor (man-hours)

P_L = \$1 per man-hour;
P_K = \$2 per machine-hour

Q	L	K	TC	LRMC
1	4	1	\$6	\$6/unit
2	6	4	\$14	\$8/unit
3	8	8	\$24	\$10/unit
4	10	13	\$36	\$12/unit

P_L = \$2 per man-hour;
P_K = \$2 per machine-hour

Q	L	K	TC	LRMC
1			\$8	
2			\$18	
3			\$30	

(a)   Finding the Expansion Path

(b)   Calculating Long-run Costs

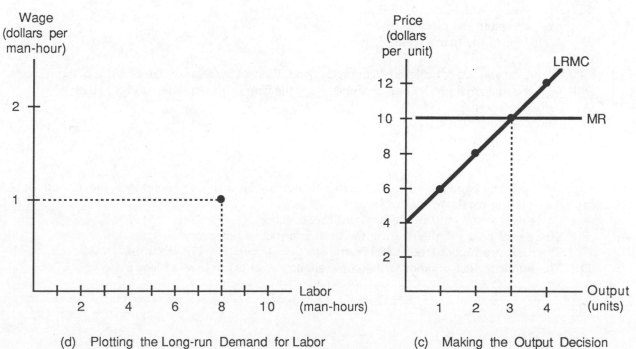

Wage (dollars per man-hour)

Labor (man-hours)

Price (dollars per unit)

LRMC
MR

Output (units)

(d)   Plotting the Long-run Demand for Labor

(c)   Making the Output Decision

Step 2. Now consider the wage rate of $2 per man-hour. Repeat steps (a) through (d) above to get a second point on the long-run demand for labor. For convenience, the three levels of total cost you will need for the firm's isocosts have been summarized in the table in panel (b).

If you've done steps (a) through (d) correctly, you should find that the firm uses 2 man-hours of labor and produces 2 units of output when the wage is $2 per man-hour.

Connect the two points we've found in panel (d) to get a sketch of the firm's long-run demand for labor.

Step 3. The isoquant map in panel (a) can be used to show the substitution and scale effects. When the wage rate increased from $1 to $2 per man-hour, labor use along the Q=3 isoquant fell from 8 to 4 man-hours; this is the substitution effect. But the firm also chose to reduce output and moved from the Q=3 to the Q=2 isoquant, reducing labor use further from 4 to 2 man-hours; this is called the scale effect.

Step 4. Notice the role that the output decision in panel (c) played in the derivation. If the price of output would have been different, then the entire demand curve for labor would have been different. Verify that the points (6 man-hours, $1 per man-hour) and (1 man-hour, $2 per man-hour) are on the demand curve for labor when the price of output is only $8 per unit.

Multiple Choice Questions

1. Suppose a firm hires labor in a competitive market in the short run. If the marginal revenue product of labor exceeds the wage rate, then
   A. the firm can increase its profits by increasing the amount of labor hired.
   B. the firm can increase its profits by decreasing the amount of labor hired.
   C. the firm cannot increase its profits by changing the amount of labor hired.
   D. the firm is making positive economic profits in the short run.

2. Which of the following will *not* shift the marginal revenue product of labor?
   A. An increase in the amount of capital used.
   B. An increase in the price of output.
   C. An increase in the price of labor.
   D. A change in the firm's technology.

3. If labor and capital are complements in production, then an increase in the amount of capital will _____ the marginal product of labor and _____ the firm's short-run demand for labor.
   A. increase; increase
   B. increase; decrease
   C. decrease; increase
   D. decrease; decrease

4. Suppose labor and capital are substitutes in production. How will an increase in the amount of capital affect the total product of labor?
   A. There will be no shift in the total product of labor.
   B. There will be a parallel shift in the total product of labor.
   C. The total product of labor will become steeper at every level of labor use.
   D. The total product of labor will become shallower at every level of labor use.

5. Which of the following is *not* fixed along the firm's long-run demand for labor?
   A. The technology available to the firm.
   B. The rental rate on capital.
   C. The amount of capital employed.
   D. The market price of output.

***Question 6 refers to Figure 14a which shows that a firm's long-run use of labor increases from L_0 to L_1 in response to a fall in the wage rate.

Figure 14a

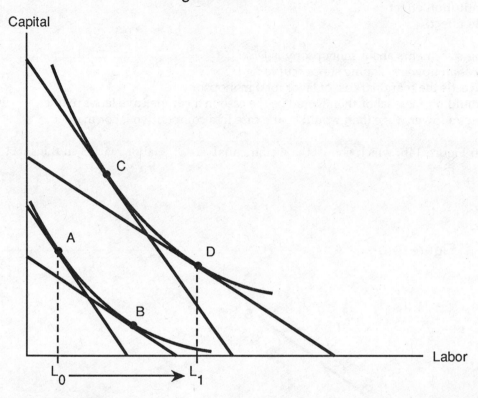

6. The substitution effect is shown by the movement from _____, and the scale effect is shown by the movement from _____.
   A. A to B; B to D
   B. A to B; C to D
   C. A to C; B to D
   D. A to C; C to D

7. If the substitution and scale effects are in opposite directions, then
   A. labor is a regressive factor.
   B. labor is not a regressive factor.
   C. labor and capital are complements in production.
   D. labor and capital are substitutes in production.

8. If labor is a regressive factor, an increase in the wage rate will
   A. increase the marginal product of labor.
   B. decrease the marginal product of labor.
   C. increase the firm's long-run marginal cost of production.
   D. decrease the firm's long-run marginal cost of production.

9. Assume labor is not a regressive factor. The industry's demand for labor is _____ than the sum of individual firms' demands. This is because a higher wage will increase the price of output and stimulate firms' production, in part offsetting the _____.
   A. more elastic; substitution effect
   B. more elastic; scale effect
   C. less elastic; substitution effect
   D. less elastic; scale effect

10. Which of the following statements about monopsony is *false*?
    A. A monopsony faces an upward-sloping supply curve for labor.
    B. The wage rate exceeds the marginal cost of labor for a monopsony.
    C. A monopsony would hire less labor than would be the case in a competitive labor market.
    D. A monopsony pays a lower wage than would be the case in a competitive labor market.

***Questions 11-13 refer to Figure 14b, which shows the welfare analysis of a labor market in the short run.

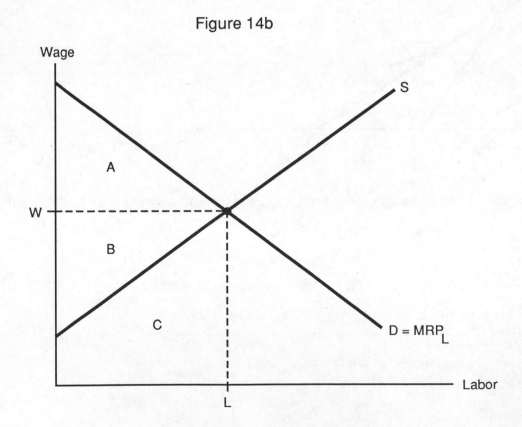

Figure 14b

270

11. The total revenue earned by the firms in the industry equals
    A. area A + B + C.
    B. area A + B.
    C. area B + C.
    D. area A.

12. The income earned by laborers is given by
    A. area A + B.
    B. area B + C.
    C. area B.
    D. area C.

13. The rent earned by laborers is given by
    A. area A + B.
    B. area B + C.
    C. area B.
    D. area C.

14. In the long run, the producers' surplus created in the goods market represents
    A. the firms' profits.
    B. total payments made to owners of the factors of production.
    C. rents to owners of the factors of production.
    D. quasi-rents paid to owners of the factors of production.

15. Suppose there is a fall in demand for a good. The factors of production that will lose the most from this change are those factors which have _____ supply, because these are the factors which earn the highest _____.
    A. inelastic; wages.
    B. inelastic; rents.
    C. elastic; wages.
    D. elastic; rents.

Solutions

1. A. The last unit of labor hired generates more revenue for the firm than what it costs to hire, so the firm should continue to hire more labor until the marginal revenue product is equated to the wage.

2. C. The marginal revenue product of labor will shift whenever the firm's marginal revenue or the marginal product of labor changes. A change in the price of labor will cause the firm to move along the marginal revenue product curve.

3. A. When capital and labor are complements in production, increased use of capital will make labor more productive at the margin. This in turn will increase the marginal revenue product of labor and hence increase the short-run demand for labor.

4. D. When capital and labor are substitutes in production, increased use of capital will lower the marginal product of labor. MP_L is shown geometrically as the slope of the total product curve of labor, so total product must become shallower at every level of labor.

5. C. In the long run, both labor and capital are variable factors. When the price of labor changes, this will change the amounts of both labor and capital used as the firm moves to a different expansion path and a different isoquant.

6. A. The lower wage causes the firm to substitute labor for capital to produce any given level of output, shown by the movement from A to B along the isoquant. The lower wage also changes the firm's long-run marginal costs and the profit-maximizing level of output, causing the firm to move to a new isoquant as shown by the movement from B to D.

7. A. When labor is a regressive factor, an increase in the wage will lower the firm's long-run marginal cost. This causes the firm to increase its output level. So the scale effect puts upward pressure on labor use contrary to the substitution effect.

8. D. This is simply the definition of a regressive factor.

9. D. In the typical case, the scale effect puts downward pressure on output and labor use when the wage increases. But when the price of output rises, this puts upward pressure on output and labor use in opposition to the scale effect. This makes labor demand less sensitive (i.e., less elastic) to changes in the wage than when the price of output is held constant as in the individual firms' demands.

10. B. To hire the last unit of labor, the monopsony must not only pay the wage to that unit but also bid up the wages of the previous units of labor hired. This implies that the marginal cost of labor is higher than the wage rate for a monopsony.

11. A. The marginal revenue product curve tells us the amount of revenue generated for the firm by each unit of labor hired. Adding all of these amounts (i.e., the individual rectangles underneath MRP_L) gives the firm's total revenue.

12. B. This rectangle has the number of hours worked as the base and the wage received as the width. The area of this rectangle is the product of these two, which equals the total wage bill.

13. C. Rent, or producers' surplus, is the net gain of the laborers after their opportunity costs of supplying labor have been taken into account. These opportunity costs are the area under the supply curve out to the quantity supplied (area C). Since their total income is area B + C, this leaves area B as rent to the laborers.

14. C. Any remaining producers' surplus (either positive or negative) after paying rents to owners of the factors of production are profits for the firm. In the long run profits are zero, so all producers' surplus is fully distributed to owners of the factors of production in the form of rents. (Alternatively we can say the total revenues received by the firm are fully distributed in the total payments made to the owners of factors in the long run.)

15. B. The more inelastic a factor's supply is, the greater proportion of its income is in the form of rent. It is rent, not wages, that tells us how a factor benefits since rent takes the opportunity cost of supplying the factor into account.

Questions for Review

1. Explain why the firm's short-run demand for labor coincides with the downward-sloping portion of its marginal revenue product curve for labor.

2. How will the firm's short-run demand for labor be affected by (a) an increase in the price of output, (b) an increase in the price of labor, and (c) an increase in the use of capital?

3. When are labor and capital considered to be complements in production? When are they substitutes in production? Which is the most common case?

4. How is the long-run demand for labor derived from the isoquant/isocost map?

5. Define substitution and scale effects. What roles do these effects play in determining the slope of the long-run demand for labor?

6. Assuming labor is not a regressive factor, explain why the industry demand curve for labor is less elastic than the sum of individual firms' demands.

7. How does the elasticity of factor supply affect the rents earned by a factor of production? How are these rents related to the producers' surplus earned by firms?

Solutions

1. If the given market wage is smaller than labor's marginal revenue product, then the revenue the last unit of labor generates for the firm outweighs the costs incurred from hiring that unit. Hence the firm benefits from increasing the amount of labor hired. If the wage exceeds the marginal revenue product, then the last unit of labor cost more than what it was worth to the firm and the firm would increase its profits by hiring less labor. Applying the equimarginal principle, the firm will hire labor so that the wage and the marginal revenue product are equated. This implies that the demand curve for labor coincides with the marginal revenue product curve. This is only the short-run demand for labor since we have implicitly held the capital level constant.

2. (a) When output can be sold at a higher price, this increases labor's marginal revenue product and hence increases the short-run demand for labor. (b) There is no change in the demand for labor. An increase in the wage causes the firm to move up along the marginal revenue product curve. (c) If labor and capital are complements in production, then an increase in capital will increase the marginal productivity of labor and hence will increase the demand for labor. If labor and capital are substitutes in production, increases in capital lower labor's marginal product and decrease the demand for labor.

3. If increased capital shifts up the total product so that it becomes steeper at every level of labor usage, then the marginal product of labor has risen and the two factors are complements. If extra capital shifts up the total product curve so that it becomes shallower at every level of labor, then the marginal product of labor falls and the two factors are substitutes. Capital and labor are generally found to be complements in production.

4. The technology, price of capital, and price of output are assumed to be given and fixed. Then any chosen wage rate determines the slope of the isocosts and the firm's expansion path. From the expansion path, the firm's long-run marginal costs can be determined using the prices of factors. Comparing the marginal cost against the price of output determines the level of output the firm will produce, and the corresponding isoquant gives the amount of labor (and capital) used. This amount of labor is plotted against the wage that began the process to get one point on the long-run demand for labor.

5. When the price of labor rises, the firm changes its labor usage for two reasons. The substitution effect shows that the firm will substitute capital for labor to produce any given level of output. The scale effect shows that the firm will change its labor usage because its marginal costs and the profit-maximizing level of output have changed. The substitution effect always causes the firm to reduce labor usage when the wage rises, and so always supports the law of demand. Usually the

higher wage also increases the firm's long-run marginal cost causing output and labor use to fall, and so the scale effect also supports the law of demand. However labor can be a regressive factor, meaning that the higher wage lowers the firm's long-run marginal cost causing output and labor use to rise. In this case the scale effect works against the law of demand, but it can be shown mathematically that the scale effect cannot outweigh the substitution effect. So the law of demand always holds in the labor market.

6. Suppose the wage increases. Then both the substitution and scale effects put downward pressure on labor usage. But the higher wage increases all firms' marginal costs, and so this decreases market supply and increases market price. The increase in market price puts an upward pressure on firms' output and labor usage, in part offsetting the scale effect. So as compared to the case where only a single firm is considered, labor usage is less sensitive to a percentage increase in the wage when the entire industry is affected. This says that the industry demand is less elastic than the sum of individual firms' demands.

7. Rent is simply the producer's surplus earned by the factor; it is the difference between the factor's total income earned and its opportunity costs of supplying the factor. The more inelastic the factor's supply is, the greater the percentage of its income is in the form of rent. The producers' surplus earned by firms is paid out to the factors of production in the form of rent with any remaining amount (positive or negative) kept by the firm as profits. In the long run when profits are zero, the producers' surplus earned by firms is completely exhausted by the rent payments to the factors of production.

Problems for Analysis

1. In this problem, you will mathematically derive the demand curve for labor. Remember that the firm's technology, the rental rate of capital (R), and the price of output (P) are considered fixed; and the wage rate (W), amount of labor (L), and amount of capital (K) are variables.

   (i) Suppose that the firm's isoquants are given by the formula $Q^4 = L \cdot K$ (so the underlying production function is given by $Q = L^{1/4} \cdot K^{1/4}$). Using calculus, it can be shown that the slope of an isoquant is given by $-K/L$. Show that the expansion path is a straight line with slope W/R.

   (ii) Use the formula for the expansion path in part (i) to show that the firm's total cost is given by the formula $TC = 2\sqrt{RW} \cdot Q^2$. Using calculus, we can then show that this formula implies that the firm's long-run marginal cost is given by $MC = 4\sqrt{R/W} \cdot Q$. (Hint—You will need to use the expansion path formula and the production function to show that $L = \sqrt{R/W} \cdot Q^2$.)

(iii)   Show that the firm will choose to produce $P/4\sqrt{RW}$ units of output when it behaves competitively.

(iv)   Combine the answer to part (iii) with the hint to part (ii) to show that the firm's demand for labor is given by $L = (P^2/16\sqrt{R}) \cdot 1/W\sqrt{W}$.

(v)   Verify that the firm's demand for labor is downward sloping.

2. Suppose that a firm's isoquants are right-angled as shown in Figure 14c.

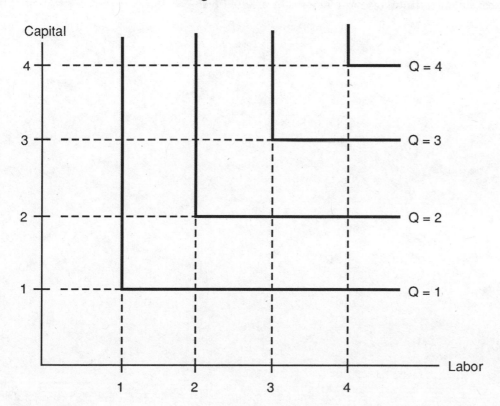

Figure 14c

275

(i)   Describe the expansion path for the firm. How does the expansion path change if the wage rate or rental rate changes?

(ii) Show that the firm's long-run marginal cost for any wage W and rental R is given by LRMC = W + R .

(iii) Use your answer to part (ii) to determine whether labor is or is not a regressive factor.

(iv) Describe the substitution and scale effects that would be caused by a wage increase.

(v)   Are labor and capital substitutes or complements in production?

3. Figure 14d shows the demand and supply curves for labor in the United States. Suppose a group of immigrants enters the U.S. The immigrants have perfectly inelastic supply of labor, causing a parallel shift in the supply curve as shown on the graph. Furthermore, suppose the immigrants own no nonlabor factors of production.

Figure 14d

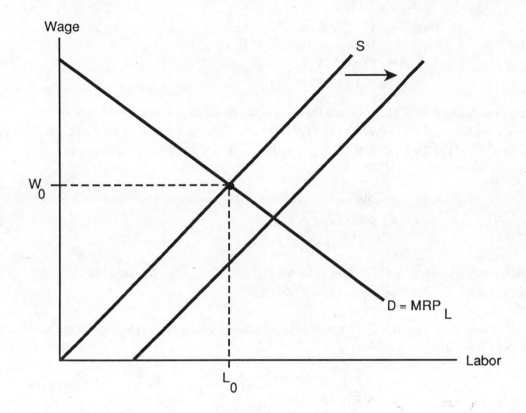

(i) On Figure 14d show how immigration affects the wage and the employment level in the U.S.

(ii) Suppose the two equilibrium points shown in Figure 14d are long-run equilibria in which firms are making zero profits. Label areas on the diagram to show the rent earned by American laborers, the rent earned by immigrants, and the payments made to owners of other factors of production.

(iii) Did the immigration hurt or benefit Americans? Explain, using your answer to part (ii).

Solutions

1. (i) Along the expansion path, the slope of the isoquants equals the slope of the isocosts. So $-K/L = -W/R$, which implies $K = (W/R) \cdot L$. This is the formula for a straight line from the origin with slope W/R.

   (ii) The amount spent on labor is $W \cdot L$, and the amount spent on capital is $R \cdot K$. So using the result from part (i),

$$
\begin{aligned}
TC &= W \cdot L + R \cdot K \\
&= W \cdot L + R \cdot [(W/R) \cdot L] \\
&= W \cdot L + W \cdot L \\
&= 2W \cdot L.
\end{aligned}
$$

We now need to substitute for L to get Q into the equation. To do this, since $Q^4 = L \cdot K$ and $K = (W/R) \cdot L$, we have $Q^4 = L \cdot (W/R) \cdot L = (W/R) \cdot L^2$. Taking the square root of both sides, we have $Q^2 = \sqrt{W/R} \cdot L$, which can be rewritten as $L = \sqrt{R/W} \cdot Q^2$. Using this formula, we now have

$$
\begin{aligned}
TC &= 2W \cdot L \\
&= 2W \cdot (\sqrt{R/W} \cdot Q^2) \\
&= 2\sqrt{RW} \cdot Q^2.
\end{aligned}
$$

   (iii) The firm will choose its output level so that price and marginal cost are equated. So $P = 4\sqrt{RW} \cdot Q$, which can be rewritten as $Q = P/4\sqrt{RW}$.

   (iv) We have shown that $L = \sqrt{R/W} \cdot Q^2$ in part (ii) and that $Q = P/4\sqrt{RW}$ in part (iii). Combining these two equations, we have

$$
\begin{aligned}
L &= \sqrt{RW} \cdot (P/4\sqrt{RW})^2 \\
&= \sqrt{RW} \cdot P^2/16RW \\
&= (P^2/16\sqrt{R}) \cdot 1/W\sqrt{W}.
\end{aligned}
$$

This last equation, $L = (P^2/16\sqrt{R}) \cdot 1/W\sqrt{W}$, gives the firm's demand for labor.

   (v) If W increases, then $W\sqrt{W}$ also increases. This means that $1/W\sqrt{W}$ decreases and hence L falls, so the law of demand holds.

2. (i) The "tangencies" between the isocosts and the isoquants will be at the corners of the isoquants. So the expansion path will be a 45° line from the origin. These "tangencies" will not change as the slope of the isocosts change, so the expansion path will remain unchanged if the wage or rental rates change.

   (ii) Using the expansion path, we see that the last unit of output requires 1 man-hour of labor and 1 machine-hour of capital no matter what the wage and rental are. So long-run marginal cost—the cost of the last unit of output in the long run—is $W + R$ dollars per unit of output.

278

(iii)   If the wage rises, then long-run marginal cost (which equals W + R) also increases. So labor is not a regressive factor.

(iv)   An increase in the wage causes a zero substitution effect, since the firm will use the same combination of labor and capital to produce any given level of output. (In other words, there is no movement along the isoquant when the wage increases.) Since the increase in the wage rate will increase long-run marginal cost, the firm will reduce its output level. So the firm moves to a lower isoquant and the scale effect reduces the amount of labor (and capital) employed.

(v)   Labor and capital are complements in production. For example when there are only 2 machine-hours of capital, the marginal product of the third man-hour of labor will be zero (since that man-hour will create no additional output). The addition of a third machine-hour of capital will increase the marginal product of that third man-hour of labor to 1 unit of output per man-hour (since the third man-hour will combine with the third machine-hour to produce another unit of output). Since an increase in capital raises the marginal productivity of labor, labor and capital are complements in production.

3. (i),(ii)

Figure 14e

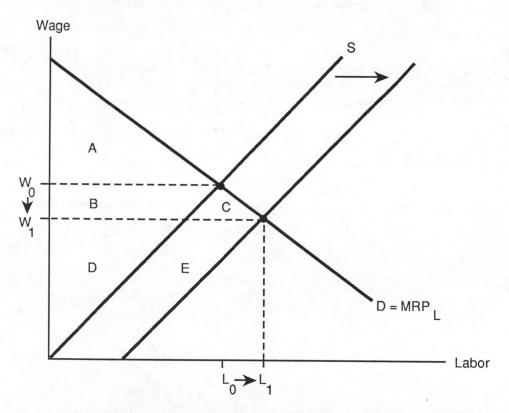

The rent paid to American workers falls from area B + D to area D. Immigrants are paid income of area E; since their supply of labor is perfectly inelastic this also equals the rent they are paid. The payments to other factors increase from area A to area A + B + C.

(iii)   Since Americans are the only owners of nonlabor factors of production, we see that immigration has made Americans better off. Before immigration, rents to labor plus nonlabor factor payments equalled area A + B + D. After immigration, rents to labor plus nonlabor factor payments for Americans equals area A + B + C + D. So the gains to American owners of nonlabor factors of production will outweigh the losses to American suppliers of labor. The net gain is that portion of area C that owners of nonlabor factors receive as rent.

Solutions to Working Through the Graphs

Figure 14-1   Derivation of the Firm's Long-run Demand for Labor

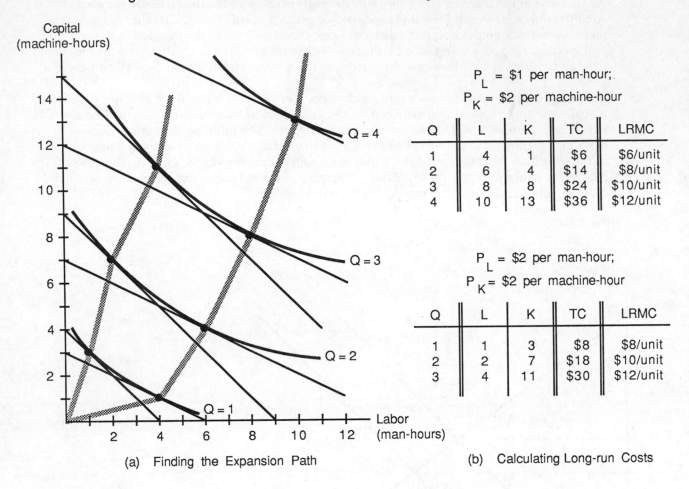

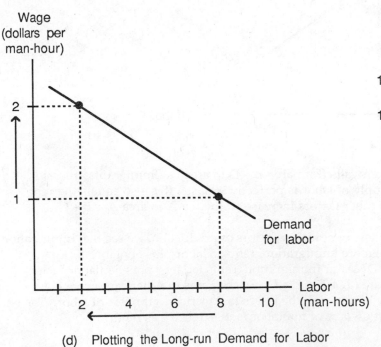

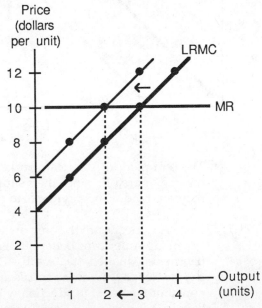

(a)   Finding the Expansion Path

(b)   Calculating Long-run Costs

P_L = \$1 per man-hour;
P_K = \$2 per machine-hour

Q	L	K	TC	LRMC
1	4	1	\$6	\$6/unit
2	6	4	\$14	\$8/unit
3	8	8	\$24	\$10/unit
4	10	13	\$36	\$12/unit

P_L = \$2 per man-hour;
P_K = \$2 per machine-hour

Q	L	K	TC	LRMC
1	1	3	\$8	\$8/unit
2	2	7	\$18	\$10/unit
3	4	11	\$30	\$12/unit

(d)   Plotting the Long-run Demand for Labor

(c)   Making the Output Decision

280

Chapter Fifteen

The Market for Labor

Chapter Summary

This chapter discusses the economic behavior of the individuals who are on the supply side of the markets for factors of production. We will first show how individuals' preferences determine labor supply, and then use this information to study labor supply for the entire economy. Combining this analysis with that of the previous chapter, we can then determine the equilibrium in the labor market and predict how that equilibrium changes when market conditions change. The chapter concludes by discussing the reasons wages differ across individuals.

Section 15.1. Individual Labor Supply

To model the consumer's labor supply decision, we consider two goods: *leisure* (time spent on all activities other than labor supplied to the market) and *consumption* (representing all goods that can be purchased, measured in terms of the worker's output). Consumption is placed on the vertical axis, and leisure is placed on the horizontal axis. However, we flip the leisure axis so it reads right to left—this allows us to interpret the horizontal coordinate as labor supplied. The indifference curves between leisure and consumption must also then be flipped, so we draw these indifference curves upward sloping and convex. We assume that both leisure and consumption are normal goods.

The budget line has two important features—its slope is the worker's wage rate (measured in terms of output per man-hour) and its vertical intercept represents *nonlabor income* (income from other sources than wages). As usual equilibrium occurs where an indifference curve is tangent to the budget line; at this point the marginal value of leisure is equated to the wage rate.

An increase in nonlabor income will cause a parallel shift in the budget line. Since both goods are normal, this will cause the worker to choose more consumption and more leisure. More leisure implies less labor supplied, so we conclude that an increase in nonlabor income unambiguously causes a decrease in labor supplied.

The individual's labor supply curve is derived by seeing how the equilibrium changes as the wage rate changes. When the wage goes up, leisure becomes more expensive, so the substitution effect causes the worker to substitute consumption for leisure. Since this substitution causes labor supplied to increase, the substitution effect supports the law of supply for labor. The increase in the wage also causes an income effect which increases the quantities of both consumption and leisure, causing the worker to reduce labor supplied and working against the substitution effect.

We cannot guarantee that the individual's labor supply curve is upward sloping since the substitution and income effects on leisure are in opposite directions. Typically the income effect will be small when wages and labor income are low, so in this case the substitution effect will dominate and supply will be upward sloping. When wages and labor income are high, the income effect will be large and can dominate the substitution effect. This shows that an individual's demand curve can be "backward bending"—labor supply begins upwards sloping at low wages but "bends backward" if the income effect outweighs the substitution effect at higher wages.

Section 15.2. Labor Supply to the Entire Economy

To derive the economy-wide labor supply curve, we must consider two distinct income effects: the *labor income effect* and the *nonlabor income effect.* A change in the wage rate will alter the worker's real income by affecting both labor and nonlabor income. The labor income effect measures how much better or worse off the worker is due to the effects of the wage change on labor income. The nonlabor income effect is the income effect of a wage change due to the change in the value of the nonlabor productive assets owned by the worker. For the economy as a whole, the labor and nonlabor income effects will exactly offset each other. This is because a wage increase which makes workers better off (as measured by the labor income effect) will also make those people who hire that labor worse off (as measured by the nonlabor income effect).

We can extend our consumption/leisure model to include changes in the value of productive assets so that the nonlabor income effect can be represented. A total product curve showing the consumption that the worker can obtain from his productive assets is added to the consumption/leisure graph. The worker's budget line will now be tangent to both the total product curve and an indifference curve. The tangency to the total product curve gives the amount of labor the worker wants to hire to work on his productive assets, while the vertical intercept of the budget line measures the nonlabor income received from the productive asset. Notice that an increase in the wage will reduce the value of the productive asset. As in the previous section, the tangency to the indifference curve shows the labor supply decision. The distance between the vertical intercept of the budget line and the final consumption level gives the worker's labor income.

The indifference curve and the total product curve do not have to be tangent to the budget line at the same place. If the indifference curve is tangent to the left of where the total product curve is, the worker supplies less labor than he demands for use on his productive assets—we say that the worker is a *net demander of labor.* On the other hand the indifference curve can be tangent to the right of the tangency with the total product curve. In this case the worker supplies more labor than he demands, and the worker is a *net supplier of labor.* By allowing the wage rate to vary, we can derive the individual's supply of labor as in the previous section while this time taking changes of the value of his productive assets (i.e., the nonlabor income effect) into account.

To determine the shape of the economy-wide labor supply curve, we consider a fictional character called the *representative agent* whose tastes and assets are representative of the entire economy. Since the quantity of labor demanded equals the quantity of labor supplied in the economy, the representative agent cannot be either a net demander or a net supplier of labor. His indifference curve must be tangent to the budget line at the same place as his total product curve. Furthermore, the representative agent will experience no income effect due to a wage change. If the wage increases, the representative agent gains as a supplier of labor but loses the same amount as a demander of labor. Since the labor and nonlabor income effects offset each other, the representative agent's supply of labor is determined only by a substitution effect. This eliminates the possibility of the "backward bending" supply curve of the previous section. The representative agent's supply curve, and hence that for the entire economy, must obey the law of supply.

Section 15.3. Equilibrium in the Labor Market

The ideas of the previous two sections, combined with the concepts developed in the previous chapter, can be used to analyze how changing market conditions affect wages and employment. As with any market, you need to determine how demand and/or supply are affected by a given event. Demand for labor is based on its marginal revenue product (or simply its marginal product when we measure the wage in terms of output per man-hour), so for example technological change would shift the demand for labor. Supply of labor is based on preferences and nonlabor income, so increases in wealth and changes in working conditions can shift the supply of labor.

The results obtained from the analysis of the labor market can be verified using the representative agent model. The total product curve (its slope, to be specific) represents the demand side of the labor market, and the indifference curves and nonlabor income represent the supply side of the market. Where the two curves are tangent, the slope gives the equilibrium wage and the horizontal coordinate gives the employment level.

For example, an exogenous increase in wealth (that is, "manna from heaven") would cause a parallel shift in total product (so this represents no change in labor demand since there is no change in the slope of total product). The new tangency moves to the left (showing lower employment) and has a steeper slope (showing a higher wage). This analysis of the representative agent agrees with that obtained from using the labor market, where the exogenous increase in wealth causes a decrease in labor supply.

It should be noted that the labor market is drawn under the assumption that there is a fixed time period under consideration. Wages in other time periods can affect market demand, since workers may choose to work more on one day in exchange for working less on another. This phenomenon is known as *intertemporal substitution*.

To see how intertemporal substitution can affect our analysis of the labor market, suppose that there is a recession during which firms decrease their demand for labor. Since consumers would have lower nonlabor incomes, we would expect an increase in the supply for labor. But if workers perceive this recession as temporary instead of permanent, this income effect and the resulting increase in supply is likely to be small. Furthermore workers will engage in intertemporal substitution and lower their labor supply during the recession, planning on working more in the future when wages recover. So intertemporal substitution could cause labor supply to decrease along with labor demand, causing employment to fall by a much greater degree than wages (which in fact is the pattern observed during recessions).

Section 15.4. Differences in Wages

How can there be differences in wages when market forces tend to determine a single wage? This section discusses four possible explanations: human capital, access to capital, compensating differentials, and signaling.

Human capital refers to the skills that a worker has developed from prior investments like education and training. Since human capital is a fixed factor of production, payments to human capital are a form of rent. The payments to a worker (commonly called wages) include the rent to human capital, and differences in these rents can cause apparent differences in the total "wages" received by different workers.

Since the worker's wage depends in part on labor's marginal product and the available capital affects this marginal product, we might think that the differences in workers' access to capital could cause differences in productivity and hence wages. But since mobility of capital and labor would tend to equalize marginal products and wages, there must be something preventing this from occurring if this explanation is to be plausible. One suggestion is that the human capital of workers generates a positive externality, and so capital and workers become centralized in order to exploit these external benefits, preventing the mobility of factors that would tend to equalize wages.

Market forces guarantee that workers will be indifferent among different occupations, assuming there is a large group of equally talented workers available for those occupations. In order to bring about this equilibrium situation, *compensating differentials* adjust wages to compensate workers for especially pleasant or unpleasant aspects of these occupations and can cause differences in wages.

Various intrinsic skills are valuable to employers but difficult to identify in employees. So employees use *signals*—activities that convey information about these skills but do not directly contribute to production—to permit employers to identify these skills. A college education and proper dressing for interviews are examples of signaling. Employers pay higher wages to those that give the signal, and employees will purchase the signal in order to get the higher wage if it will benefit them overall. Employees without the talents desired by employers will find it too costly to obtain the signal (like a college education) and will accept the lower wage. Those that possess the desired talents will have lower opportunity costs in obtaining the signal; they will purchase the signal and the higher wage will more than compensate them for its cost. This gives a *signaling equilibrium*, in which employers and employees use the signal to identify who possesses the desired skills.

Section 15.5. Discrimination

There are substantial wage differentials between the average black person and the average white person, and between the average man and the average woman. It is a difficult problem to determine whether or not these wage differentials are the result of discrimination.

Statistical tests face the difficulty of identifying and measuring all the relevant market characteristics that could account for differences in wages. Theoretical models encounter the problem that discrimination is costly and runs counter to the profit-maximizing behavior of firms. Worker preferences, such as the desire to keep the family together, can cause women to voluntarily accept lower wages than have been offered in other locales. Past discrimination against blacks may have caused differences in the amounts of human capital that have been inherited; this makes it difficult to determine if the blacks' lower wage is due to past discrimination, present discrimination, both, or neither. The bottom line is that economists do not know the degree to which discrimination creates the observed wage differentials between blacks and whites, and women and men.

Working Through the Graphs—Derivation of Labor Supply

The worker's choice between leisure and consumption can be combined with a total product curve showing the value of the worker's productive assets to get a powerful model of labor supply. This model is illustrated in Figure 15-1. Remember that we choose to measure the wage in terms of units of output per man-hour (not dollars per man-hour) for this model.

Step 1. Figure 15-1 shows the worker's budget line when the wage rate is 1 unit of output per man-hour. This wage rate is reflected in the slope of the budget line. There are two tangencies to consider. The budget line is tangent to the total product curve, showing the amount of labor demanded by the worker to develop his productive assets like his house and land. The budget line is also tangent to an indifference curve, showing the worker's final consumption of output and leisure.

The information in the accompanying table can be read off the diagram. The tangency to the total product curve tells us how much labor the worker chooses to employ and how much output is produced using his assets. The vertical intercept of the budget line divides this output into two parts: the nonlabor income received by the worker (i.e., the value of his productive assets) and the wages paid for labor. The tangency to the indifference curve gives the labor supply decision (the horizontal coordinate) and the worker's total income and consumption (the vertical coordinate). The vertical intercept of the budget line divides this income into two parts: the nonlabor income and the labor income received by the worker.

Using the above information, verify the entries in the table for the wage of 1 unit of output per man-hour. Notice that this information includes one point on the worker's supply of labor in the lower graph—the worker provides 2 man-hours of labor when the wage is 1 unit of output per man-hour.

Step 2. Suppose the wage increases to 3 units of output per man-hour. First find the new budget line— the tangency to the total product curve (8 units of output for 2 man-hours of labor) has already been marked. Then use the information summarized in the previous step to complete the table. Finally, find a second point on the worker's labor supply to plot in the lower graph and sketch the labor supply curve.

If you've done this step correctly, you should find that the worker supplies 10 man-hours of labor at the wage of 3 units of output per man-hour, earning 30 units of output in labor income and 2 units of output in nonlabor income.

Figure 15-1 Derivation of Labor Supply

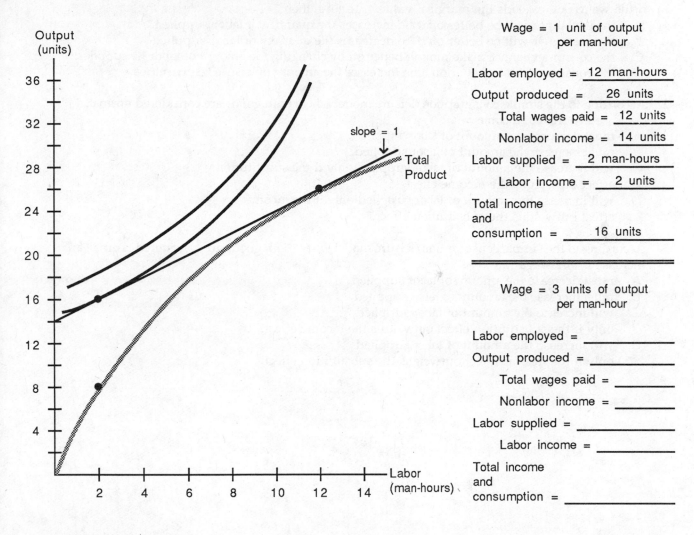

Wage = 1 unit of output
per man-hour

Labor employed = ___12___ man-hours

Output produced = ___26___ units

Total wages paid = ___12___ units

Nonlabor income = ___14___ units

Labor supplied = ___2___ man-hours

Labor income = ___2___ units

Total income
and
consumption = ___16___ units

Wage = 3 units of output
per man-hour

Labor employed = _____

Output produced = _____

Total wages paid = _____

Nonlabor income = _____

Labor supplied = _____

Labor income = _____

Total income
and
consumption = _____

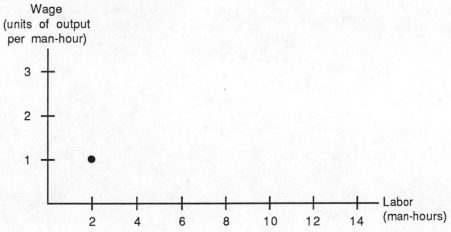

Multiple Choice Questions

1. If the wage rate exceeds the marginal value of leisure, then
   A. the consumer will be better off if he increases the quantity of labor supplied.
   B. the consumer will be better off if he decreases the quantity of labor supplied.
   C. the consumer cannot make himself better off by changing the amount of labor he supplies.
   D. the consumer will be better off if he increases the amount of leisure he consumes.

2. According to the simple consumption/leisure model where both goods are considered normal, a decrease in nonlabor income
   A. must decrease the amount of labor supplied.
   B. must increase the amount of labor supplied.
   C. will increase the amount of labor supplied only if the substitution effect outweighs the income effect.
   D. will increase the amount of labor supplied only if the income effect outweighs the substitution effect.

3. According to the simple consumption/leisure model where both goods are considered normal, an increase in the wage rate
   A. must decrease the amount of labor supplied.
   B. must increase the amount of labor supplied.
   C. will increase the amount of labor supplied only if the substitution effect outweighs the income effect.
   D. will increase the amount of labor supplied only if the income effect outweighs the substitution effect.

***Questions 4-7 refer to Figure 15a, which shows a worker's labor supply decision when he owns a productive asset.

Figure 15a

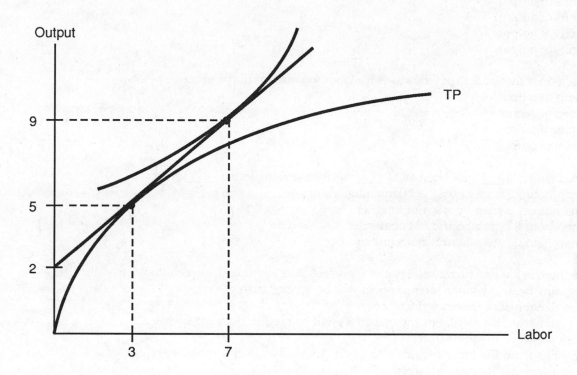

4. How much does the worker earn in nonlabor income?
   A. 2 units of output.
   B. 3 units of output.
   C. 5 units of output.
   D. 7 units of output.

5. How much does the worker earn in labor income?
   A. 2 units of output.
   B. 3 units of output.
   C. 5 units of output.
   D. 7 units of output.

6. How much does the worker pay in wages for labor to work on his productive assets?
   A. 2 units of output.
   B. 3 units of output.
   C. 5 units of output.
   D. 7 units of output.

7. The worker supplies _____ and demands _____ of labor, making him a _____ of labor.
   A. 7 man-hours, 3 man-hours; net demander
   B. 7 man-hours, 3 man-hours; net supplier
   C. 3 man-hours, 7 man-hours; net demander
   D. 3 man-hours, 7 man-hours; net supplier

8. Suppose there is a wage increase. For the representative agent and the economy overall,
   A. the gains from the labor income effect will be greater than the losses
      from the nonlabor income effect.
   B. the gains from the nonlabor income effect will be greater than the losses
      from the labor income effect.
   C. the gains from the labor income effect will be exactly offset by the losses
      from the nonlabor income effect.
   D. the gains from the nonlabor income effect will be exactly offset by the losses
      from the labor income effect.

9. Which of the following statements correctly describes the slope of labor supply?
   A. Labor supply for both individuals and the economy can be
      backward bending due to income effects.
   B. Labor supply for both individuals and the economy can be
      backward bending due to substitution effects.
   C. Labor supply can be backward bending for individuals due to income effects, but must be
      upward-sloping for the economy since the net income effect for the economy is zero.
   D. Labor supply can be backward bending for individuals due to substitution effects, but must be
      upward-sloping for the economy since the net substitution effect for the economy is zero.

***Question 10 refers to Figure 15b, which shows the effect of a change in market conditions on the representative agent.

Figure 15b

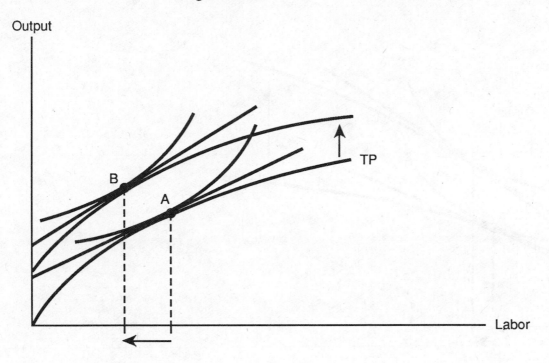

10. Which of the following could have caused the effect on the representative agent shown?
    A. An exogenous increase in wealth.
    B. An increase in labor productivity where the income effect is negligible.
    C. An increase in labor productivity where the income effect is substantial.
    D. A decrease in labor productivity.

***Question 11 refers to Figure 15c, which shows the effect of a change in market conditions on the representative agent.

Figure 15c

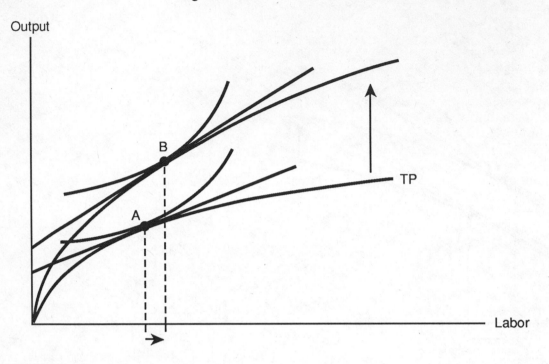

11. Which of the following could have caused the effect on the representative agent shown?
    A. An exogenous increase in wealth.
    B. An increase in labor productivity where the income effect is negligible.
    C. An increase in labor productivity where the income effect is substantial.
    D. A decrease in labor productivity.

12. Suppose workers perceive a technological improvement as temporary and engage in intertemporal substitution. How will the supply of labor be affected?
    A. The increase in wealth from the technological improvement tends to decrease supply, but intertemporal substitution tends to increase supply.
    B. The increase in wealth from the technological improvement tends to increase supply, but the intertemporal substitution tends to decrease supply.
    C. Both the increase in wealth from the technological improvement and the intertemporal substitution tend to increase supply.
    D. Both the increase in wealth from the technological improvement and the intertemporal substitution tend to decrease supply.

13. Employees are paid rent for the specialized skills and talents resulting from earlier investments in their lives, and this rent is included in the employees' wages. The reason for the resulting differences in employees' wages is
    A. human capital.
    B. access to capital.
    C. compensating differentials.
    D. signaling.

14. Employers use certain nonproductive activities pursued by potential employees to identify those who have desired skills and then pay these employees higher wages. The reason for the resulting differences in employees' wages is
    A. human capital.
    B. access to capital.
    C. compensating differentials.
    D. signaling.

15. Suppose employers are indifferent between hiring whites and blacks, but discriminate against blacks because their white employees have a distaste for associating with blacks. A theory of discrimination based on this premise would predict
    A. wage differentials between whites and blacks.
    B. a heavily segregated work force.
    C. Both A and B
    D. Neither A nor B

Solutions

1. A. The consumer can sell the last hour of leisure consumed for more than he thinks it is worth, so the consumer will benefit from decreasing his leisure and increasing his labor supplied.

2. B. A decrease in nonlabor income is pure income effect; there will be no substitution effect. With lower income, the consumer will desire less leisure and hence increase his labor supplied.

3. C. When the wage rises, the consumer wishes to substitute consumption for leisure, causing labor supplied to increase. The higher wage also means that the consumer has a higher real income, which causes the consumer to want more leisure and hence lowers labor supplied. Only when the substitution effect is the larger will the net effect be to increase labor supplied.

4. A. Nonlabor income is given by the vertical intercept of the budget line.

5. D. Using the tangency between the budget line and the indifference curve, the worker chooses 9 units of consumption. Since 2 units are earned in nonlabor income, the remaining 7 units of consumption are earned by supplying labor.

6. B. Using the tangency between the budget line and the total product curve, the worker's productive assets produce 5 units of output at the given wage. Since the worker keeps 2 units in nonlabor income, the remaining 3 units of output are paid in wages.

7. B. The tangency to the indifference curve shows the worker supplies 7 man-hours of labor, and the tangency to the total product curve shows the worker demands 3 man-hours of labor. Since more hours are supplied than demanded, the worker is a net supplier of labor.

8. C. Suppliers of labor will benefit from the wage increase through the labor income effect, and demanders of labor will be hurt by the wage increase through the nonlabor income effect. The representative agent is neither a net demander nor a net supplier of labor, so the two effects exactly offset each other. Similarly, the overall income effect for the economy must be zero.

9. C. Substitution effects support the law of supply for labor, and income effects work against the law of supply. Income effects may be substantial for any given individual when wages are high, so an individual's labor supply may become backward bending. Income effects for the entire economy are zero, so the economy's labor supply must obey the law of supply since only substitution effects are relevant.

10. A. The parallel shift in total product shows that there is no change in labor demand. The higher vertical intercept of the budget line shows the increase in wealth and represents a decrease in labor supply. The net effect is to lower the equilibrium employment (shown by the horizontal coordinate of the equilibrium point moving to the left) and to increase the equilibrium wage (shown by the slope at the tangency becoming steeper).

11. B. The total product curve has become steeper showing the increase in labor productivity, which implies an increase in the demand for labor. This has increased the representative agent's wealth, decreasing labor supply as shown by the higher vertical intercept of the budget line. The former effect puts upward pressure on employment, and the latter effect puts downward pressure on employment. Since the graph shows an increase in employment, the change in labor demand must outweigh the income effect that shifted labor supply.

12. A. Since workers perceive a temporary increase in wages, they will increase supply in the current period planning on reducing supply in the future. This will be in opposition to the increase in wealth which puts downward pressure on labor supply.

13. A. This simply applies the definition of human capital.

14. D. The nonproductive activities (such as college education and dressing for interviews) act as signals to employees that the desired skills are possessed.

15. B. Some employers would attempt to have lower costs by hiring all-black work forces to pay the lower black wage without having to deal with the effect on white employees. Employers competing for the all-black work forces would bid up the wages of blacks and remove the wage differential.

Questions for Review

1. Why do the substitution and income effects on leisure due to a wage increase work in opposite directions? When will the substitution effect be dominant and when might the income effect be dominant?

2. Distinguish between the labor and nonlabor income effects. Why is this distinction important for the analysis of labor supply?

3. Compare and contrast the economy's supply curve of labor with an individual's supply curve of labor.

4. Explain how the supply/demand analysis of the labor market and the indifference curve/total product curve analysis of the representative agent are related.

5. Compare and contrast the effects of a permanent and a temporary increase in the marginal productivity of labor.

6. Briefly summarize four reasons why wages differ among different workers.

7. Why is it difficult to find a theory of discrimination that is consistent with sustained wage differentials? What other problems are there in determining if discrimination is responsible for wage differentials?

Solutions

1. When the wage increases, this has two effects on the worker's labor supply decision. First, since the price of consuming leisure has increased, the worker substitutes consumption for leisure implying that labor supplied increases. Second, since the higher wage increases the worker's real income, he chooses to have more of consumption and leisure implying that labor supplied decreases. If the wage is low, then this income effect is likely to be small and the substitution effect will be dominant. If the wage is high, both the income and substitution effects can be substantial, so either can dominate. This implies that the worker's labor supply curve will either be upward sloping or backward bending.

2. When the wage rate increases, it changes the worker's real income in two ways. He benefits from an increase in his labor income (the amount of this benefit is measured by the labor income effect) and he loses since the value of his productive assets falls (the size of this loss is measured by the nonlabor income effect). Put another way, the worker gains as a supplier of labor and loses as a demander of labor. Since every hour of labor supplied is also an hour of labor demanded, the gains from a wage increase (the labor income effect) are offset by the losses (the nonlabor income effect) when the economy as a whole is considered. The distinction between labor and nonlabor income effects is important since it shows us that the market labor supply must be upward sloping. Since the two income effects net out to zero, and since it is only the income effect that can make labor supply be backward bending, we are guaranteed that the law of supply holds in the labor market.

3. The individual's supply curve of labor contains an income effect that works against the law of supply. The income effect will be small for low wages, so the law of supply will hold at low wages. However the income effect will be large at high wages, so the individual's supply may begin to bend backwards. However the overall income effect for the entire economy is zero, so the backward bending supply curve is not a possibility for the market supply. So the law of supply must hold in the labor market, although it may be violated at high wages for any given individual.

4. Like the entire economy, the representative agent can be neither a net demander nor a net supplier of labor. The demand for labor is reflected in the slope of the total product curve; an increase in the demand for labor is shown by the total product curve getting steeper. The supply of labor is reflected by the worker's preferences (the indifference curves) and his nonlabor income (the vertical intercept of the budget line). A decrease in the supply of labor caused by an increase in wealth would be shown by a higher vertical intercept of the budget line. The equilibrium in the labor market is shown by the tangency between the indifference curve and total product curve, with the employment level given by the horizontal coordinate and the wage given by the slope of the curves at the tangency.

5. Both the permanent and temporary increases in labor productivity cause an increase in the demand for labor. Both also increase the worker's wealth, putting downward pressure on the supply of labor. However this wealth effect will be small when the increase in productivity is only

temporary. Also workers will feel the higher wage due to the better productivity is temporary and engage in intertemporal substitution, putting upward pressure on the supply of labor. So labor supply can actually increase if the change in productivity is temporary, and hence employment will rise more substantially than wages. If the change is permanent, the wage will rise and the effect on employment is ambiguous.

6. Workers may receive different rents for their skills due to differences in human capital. If the positive externalities generated by employees' human capital prevents some mobility of capital, differing access to capital can cause wage differences among workers. Compensating differentials may be necessary to compensate workers for especially pleasant or unpleasant aspects of their occupations. Finally when desirable skills are unobservable, wage differentials may result due to signaling behavior.

7. If discrimination causes one group to have lower wages than another, profit-maximizing behavior would cause firms to seek out these employees and bid up their wages, eliminating the wage differential. In addition to finding an acceptable theory, (1) statistical problems in measuring and isolating factors relevant to the labor decision, (2) voluntary choices by workers that can cause wage differences, and (3) the difficulty of separating the effects of past discrimination from current discrimination all make it hard to determine when discrimination is responsible for differences in wages.

Problems for Analysis

1. As shown in Figure 15d, a worker has no nonlabor income and can earn a wage of $10 per man-hour.

Figure 15d

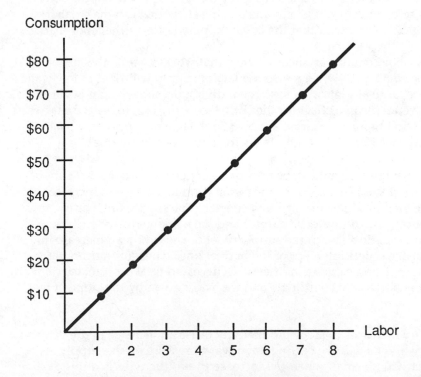

(i) Suppose the government implements a 50% tax on wages, but gives all workers a $20 rebate. In Figure 15d, show how this policy affects the worker's budget line.

(ii) Using Figure 15d, explain why this policy will make anyone who originally made less than $40 better off.

(iii) Use income and substitution effects to explain why this policy may either increase or decrease the quantity of labor supplied.

(iv) As shown in part (ii), this policy is designed to improve the welfare of the poor. Using your answer to part (iii), what effect do you think this policy will have on the amount of labor supplied by the poor? Explain.

2. This problem reconsiders the problem of immigration discussed in problem 3 of Chapter 14. In that problem, we assumed a group of immigrants with perfectly inelastic labor supply and no nonlabor assets entered the American labor market.

(i) Consider an American who was initially neither a net demander or a net supplied of labor. On the axes below, show how the immigration affects this worker. Is the worker made better or worse off by immigration? Does the worker's labor income increase or decrease? Does the worker's nonlabor income increase or decrease? Does the worker become a net demander or a net supplier of labor? Verify that these results agree with the welfare analysis performed in problem 3 of Chapter 14.

(ii) Complete the axes below to perform the representative agent analysis of the changes in the economy's labor market due to immigration. Provide an interpretation of your diagram.

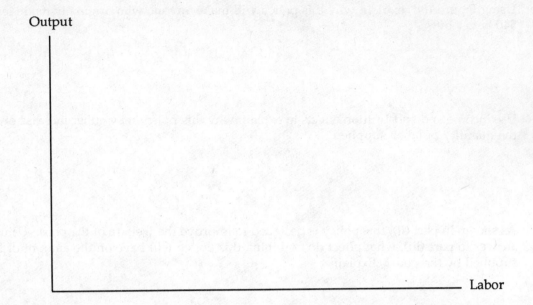

3. This problem develops a model of wage discrimination. The supply of labor for men and for women in a given industry is shown in Figure 15e. Labor supplied by both men and women in this industry provides the same marginal revenue product, assumed constant for convenience.

Figure 15e

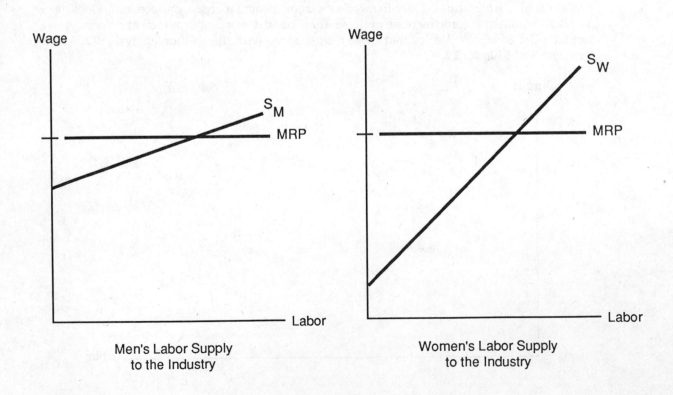

(i)   Discrimination against women restricts the number of occupations they are allowed to enter. Explain why this would make the supply of labor for women more inelastic than the supply of labor for men as shown in Figure 15e.

(ii) Suppose the industry graphed above hires labor competitively. In Figure 15e, label the wage (W_C) and amounts of labor hired (L_C). Does this profit-maximizing behavior result in any wage differences between men and women?

(iii) Now suppose the industry uses monopsony pricing when hiring labor. In Figure 15e, label the wage (W_M) and amounts of labor hired (W_M). Does this profit-maximizing behavior result in any wage differences between men and women?

(iv) Critique the model of discrimination described in parts (i) through (iii).

Solutions

1. (i)

Figure 15f

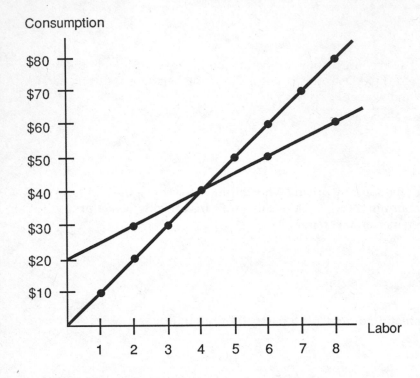

(ii) If the worker had earned $40 or less prior to the policy, his initial equilibrium point is below the new budget line. This implies that he will move to a higher indifference curve when moving to the new budget line.

(iii) The policy both lowers the effective wage and increases nonlabor income. The lower effective wage has a substitution effect which puts downward pressure on labor supplied and an income effect which puts upward pressure on labor supplied. The $20 rebate adds an additional income effect which puts downward pressure on labor supplied. Hence the net effect is ambiguous. If the income effect due to the wage change is not very substantial, we can expect that labor supplied will decrease. However, labor supplied can increase if the income effect due to the wage change outweighs the substitution effect and the income effect of the rebate.

(iv) The poor can be expected to reduce their labor supplied under this policy. When income is low, the income effect due to a wage change will be relatively small. As shown in our analysis of the backward bending supply curve, we can expect the substitution effect to outweigh the income effect in this situation. When the income effect due to the $20 rebate reinforces the substitution effect, this further strengthens the conclusion that labor supplied will fall when the worker has a low income.

2. (i)

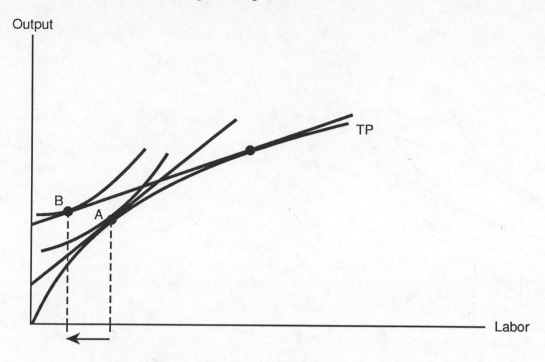

The worker is better off since he moves to a higher indifference curve (from point A to point B above). Since the vertical intercept of the budget line shifts up, nonlabor income must increase. The vertical distance between the budget line's intercept and the final consumption point has been reduced, so labor income has fallen. Since the worker now demands more hours of labor than he supplies, the worker has become a net demander of labor. This analysis agrees with our results in problem 3 of Chapter 14, where we saw that immigration caused the rent paid to American laborers to fall, payments to nonlabor factors of production to rise, and the overall social gain to Americans to increase.

Figure 15h

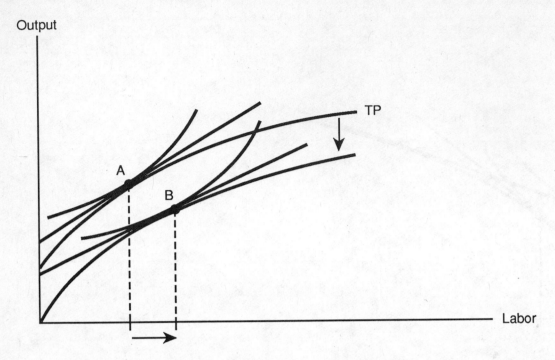

Output

A

B

TP

Labor

Since the immigrants own no nonlabor factors of production, the average person in the economy (i.e., the representative agent) now owns fewer productive assets. This is shown by the parallel shift down in the total product curve—the shift must be parallel since there has been no change in the marginal product of labor. Since the vertical intercept of the budget line has fallen, we can conclude that the representative agent has less nonlabor income and increases his labor supply. The tangency moves to the left, showing that overall employment increases. The budget line has gotten flatter, showing that the equilibrium wage has fallen.

3. (i) As a worker has more options for his occupation, there are more alternative uses for his labor that may be of comparable value and so his labor supply would be made more elastic. When discrimination limits the number of occupational opportunities of women, they have relatively fewer alternative uses for their labor available. This would make women's labor supply more inelastic than that for men.

Figure 15i

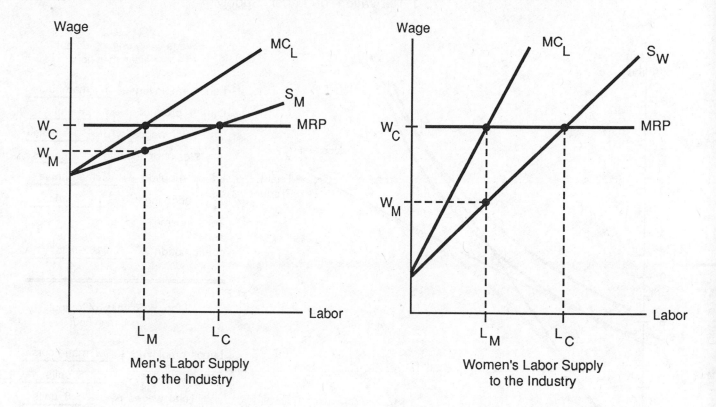

Men's Labor Supply
to the Industry

Women's Labor Supply
to the Industry

When the industry behaves competitively, the wage is equal to the marginal revenue product and so there would be no difference between men's and women's wages. When the industry behaves as a monopsony, it equates the marginal cost of labor with the marginal revenue product of labor. This implies that women, with the more inelastic supply, will receive a lower wage than men as shown above.

(iv) Although this model predicts sustained wage differentials under discrimination, it fails on two important accounts. First, if it is found that women's supply of labor is indeed more inelastic than men's, it would be difficult to test if this is indeed the result of discrimination. It is possible that women may be "clumped" into a small number of occupations by choice instead of by discrimination.

More importantly, the model depends on an industry successfully practicing monopsony pricing. As shown by part (ii), competitive pricing would fail to create any wage differential. But as discussed in Chapter 14, monopsony power is an elusive goal for firms. Firms within the industry would have incentive to compete for workers and hence bid up the wage. Furthermore, this industry must compete with other industries to hire this labor which would also destroy the monopsony power.

These two flaws cause us to reject the ability of the model to explain how wage differentials due to discrimination can occur in spite of profit-maximizing behavior of firms.

Solutions to Working Through the Graphs

Figure 15-1 Derivation of Labor Supply

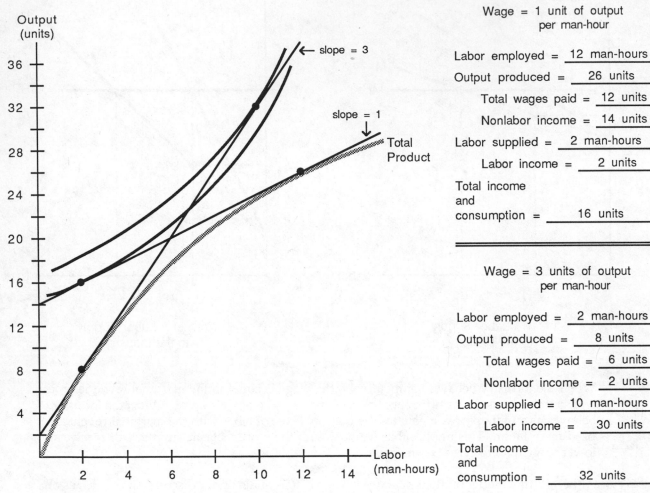

Wage = 1 unit of output
per man-hour

Labor employed = __12 man-hours__

Output produced = __26 units__

Total wages paid = __12 units__

Nonlabor income = __14 units__

Labor supplied = __2 man-hours__

Labor income = __2 units__

Total income
and
consumption = __16 units__

Wage = 3 units of output
per man-hour

Labor employed = __2 man-hours__

Output produced = __8 units__

Total wages paid = __6 units__

Nonlabor income = __2 units__

Labor supplied = __10 man-hours__

Labor income = __30 units__

Total income
and
consumption = __32 units__

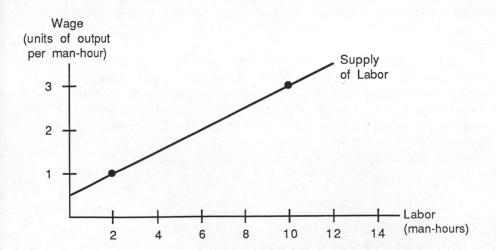

Chapter Sixteen

Allocating Goods over Time

Chapter Summary

In addition to allowing us to trade one good for another, markets also allow us to trade current goods for future goods and *vice versa* by using an interest rate to establish appropriate prices. This chapter studies the demand and supply of the market which determines the interest rate and allocates goods over time.

Section 16.1. Interest Rates

It is straightforward to generalize the basic consumer choice model of Chapters 3 and 4 to handle the allocation of goods over time. We assume there is a single good (for example, apples or the composite-good) that can be consumed in two different time periods (for example, today and tomorrow or this year and next year). Consumption in the current time period is placed on the horizontal axis, and consumption in the next time period is placed on the vertical axis. The consumer's indifference curves between these two goods have the standard properties.

We give a special name to the marginal rate of substitution in this case—the *discount rate* is the marginal rate of substitution minus one. When the consumer sacrifices a unit of current consumption in exchange for a unit of future consumption, the discount rate is the additional payment the consumer requires to remain indifferent. We assume that the consumer's discount rate is positive when his *endowment* (i.e., the basket of goods he starts with prior to trading) contains equal amounts of goods in the two time periods. This assumption implies that the consumer with this endowment must receive more than one unit of future consumption to be willing to trade away a unit of current consumption. It also implies that the indifference curves have slope with magnitude larger than one along the 45° line.

By finding all the trades available to the consumer, we see that the budget line must pass through the endowment point and has slope with magnitude of one plus the interest rate. The optimum occurs at the tangency between the budget line and an indifference curve, where the interest rate and the discount rate are equated. If the optimum is to the right of the endowment, the consumer demands more current consumption than he supplies and so is a *borrower*. The consumer is a *lender* when he supplies more current consumption than he demands; this occurs when the optimum falls to the left of the endowment. As has been our standard procedure, by letting the relative price of current consumption (which equals one plus the interest rate) vary and seeing how the consumer's optimum changes, we can derive the demand curve for current consumption.

The supply of current consumption will be fixed if (1) it is determined solely by people's endowments and cannot be changed and (2) consumption cannot be "stored" and vanishes if it is not consumed in the time period when it is available. We can then use either the supply/demand diagram or the representative agent diagram to see how the interest rate changes when market conditions change. (Recall from Chapter 15 that the *representative agent* is a fictional consumer whose tastes and assets are representative of the entire economy. In this model, the representative agent—like the economy as a whole—cannot be either a borrower or a lender, so the representative agent's optimum occurs at his endowment.)

The model can be extended by introducing *capital*—goods used to produce future consumption. When consumption goods themselves are used as capital, we say the goods have been *invested*. The *gross marginal product of capital (GMPK)* is the amount of additional future consumption generated by the last unit of capital, and the *net marginal product of capital (MPK)* is the additional future consumption created by the last unit of capital after replacing the investment. So the (net) marginal product of capital exceeds the gross marginal product of capital by one.

We usually express the marginal product of capital in percentage terms and graph it with the amount of current consumption remaining after investment (i.e., the endowment minus the amount of capital invested) on the horizontal axis. Since the marginal cost of current consumption is determined by the sacrificed investment, we can conclude that the supply of current consumption is given by the upward sloping GMPK curve. From the supply/demand diagram, we can conclude that **in equilibrium the interest rate, individuals' discount rates, and the marginal product of capital are all equated.** Also notice this information on investment combined with the basic information on resource markets in Chapter 14 shows us that **the rental rate on capital equals the interest rate.**

Standard supply/demand analysis can now be used to determine how changing market conditions affect the interest rate. For example, an increase in future productivity would raise the gross marginal product of capital and cause a decrease in supply of current consumption (since the quantity of goods invested increases). Since people are wealthier, the demand for current consumption also increases. Combining these shifts, we see that the increase in future productivity will increase the interest rate but have an ambiguous effect on current consumption.

Notice that this supply/demand model determines the *real rate of interest*—the rate of return to a lender in terms of consumption goods. When loans are made in currency, we must adjust the interest payment for inflation. This *nominal rate of interest* is equal to the real interest rate plus the inflation rate.

Section 16.2. Present Values

The interest rate also allows us to calculate the value of future consumption in terms of present consumption. This is called the *present value* of the future consumption. If the interest rate is constant at r, then the present value of a unit of consumption 1 time period into the future is $1/(1 + r)$ units of current consumption, the present value of a unit of consumption 2 time periods into the future is $1/(1 + r)^2$ units of current consumption, the present value of a unit of consumption 3 time periods into the future is $1/(1 + r)^3$ units of current consumption, and so forth.

These discounting formulas can be used to show the relationship between the prices and returns on bonds. A *bond* is simply a promise to pay a given amount (called the *face value* of the bond) at some specified time in the future. The buyer of a bond is a lender, and the seller of a bond is a borrower. The bond is said to *mature* at the future date when the obligation to pay is met. Since present consumption is valued more highly than future consumption, a bond will of course not sell for its face value—it must be discounted to account for the accumulation of interest. We say that the bond sells at a *discount;* the discount equals the face value of the bond minus the current price. The above discounting formulas show how the current price of a bond and the interest rate are related. For example, a bond with a $10,000 face value that matures in 1 year during which the nominal interest rate is 10% has a price of $10,000 \cdot 1/(1 + .10)$ or $9,090.91.

A *coupon bond* is a bond which promises a series of different payments on different dates. To calculate the present value of a coupon bond, we can simply calculate the present value of each of the payments and then sum these present values.

The present value of a durable good can be calculated in the same manner. A durable good gives a consumer a stream of benefits—or *dividends*—and the present value of these dividends can be used to find the highest price the consumer is willing to pay for a durable good.

A *perpetuity* is a bond that pays a fixed amount in every time period forever. It can be shown that a perpetuity paying $1 every time period when the interest rate is r has a present value equal to $(1/r)$.

The price of a bond may have to be adjusted to reflect the possibility that the issuer may not meet his obligations. This possibility is known as *default risk,* and the borrower may have to pay additional interest known as a *risk premium* to compensate the lender for this risk.

Section 16.3. Government Policy

There has been significant discussion as to whether government deficits have any significant effect on the economy and in particular on interest rates. The *Ricardian Equivalence Theorem* uses the ideas developed in this chapter to show that government borrowing does not influence the demand for current consumption and hence cannot affect interest rates.

The argument behind the Ricardian Equivalence Theorem is very simple. We assume that the level of government spending has already been chosen; only the method of financing this spending is left to be determined. The government (1) may tax you today to pay for its spending, (2) may borrow the money it needs and tax you in the future to pay off the debt and the interest accumulated, or (3) may borrow the money it needs and never pay it back, taxing you forever to pay the interest every year. A moment's reflection should convince you that the present value of your taxes is the same under the three financing schemes. You will have a different endowment point under each of the schemes, but these endowment points all lie on the same budget line. All three schemes leave you with the same budget line, so your final consumption is not affected by the government's choice of how to finance its spending.

It is uncertain whether the Ricardian Equivalence Theorem gives a good description of the situation in our economy. Default risk and misperceptions are two factors in the economy through which government borrowing can cause the demand for current consumption (and hence interest rates) to rise.

If a consumer must pay a risk premium when borrowing (but not lending) money to cover default risk, then the budget line will be "kinked" at the endowment point. The slope to the left of the endowment is determined by the interest rate paid when the consumer lends money, and the slope to the right of the endowment is determined by the higher interest the consumer must pay if he borrows. If government borrowing decreases the consumer's current tax burden and increases his future tax burden, then the consumer's endowment point and budget line will change. The consumption choices of the consumer will expand, and the consumer's demand for current consumption will increase.

The consumer may also have misperceptions about the effects of government borrowing. He may correctly see that his present tax burden is reduced but fail to realize that his future tax burden is increased. Then the consumer mistakenly perceives that his endowment point has shifted to the right, causing a parallel shift in the budget line and increasing the demand for current consumption.

It is uncertain whether either of these possibilities is sufficiently prevalent in our economy for government borrowing to actually cause increases in the market demand for current consumption and subsequent increases in the interest rate.

Section 16.4. Some Applications

This section develops four applications of the above material: planned obsolescence, artists' royalties, taxes on land, and the pricing of exhaustible resources.

Many people believe that firms practice "planned obsolescence" and knowingly produce goods that wear out quickly in order to keep sales high. But as we've shown, if goods are made more durable this will increase their present value to consumers. As long as the cost of the improvement in quality is less than the additional present value it creates for consumers, firms will find it beneficial to improve the quality of their products.

Should artists receive royalties on future resale of their works? To the average artist it doesn't matter, for this will reduce the present value of artistic works by precisely the present value of the expected future royalty payments. The artist gets a lower price today and more royalty payments in the future, giving him the same present value. If an artist becomes successful and his works become more valuable than expected, then his future royalty payments will be unexpectedly large and more than offset the lower price. So the successful artist will be made better off under this plan. If an artist is unsuccessful, just the opposite would happen. We can conclude that requiring royalties on future resales of artists' works will transfer wealth from unsuccessful to successful artists.

Suppose the government imposes an annual tax on land to be paid in all future years. Only the current landowners will bear the burden of this tax; future landowners will be unaffected. The value of the land will fall by the present value of the perpetuity represented by the tax; the tax on future landowners will be offset by a lower price of land.

An exhaustible resource (e.g., oil) is one for which one unit of consumption today implies a one-unit sacrifice in future consumption. If there are no marginal costs to extract an exhaustible resource, and if producers behave competitively, then the price of the exhaustible resource will grow at exactly the rate of interest. If the price were growing faster than the rate of interest, then the resource would be a good investment. Producers would extract less to make this investment, forcing up today's price and lowering the future price. This adjustment to prices would continue until the future price is precisely $(1 + r)$ times the current price.

Working Through the Graphs—Analysis of Interest Rates Using a Representative Agent

There are two ways that we can analyze how the interest rate is affected by changing market conditions: using a supply/demand diagram and using a representative agent diagram. These two approaches are illustrated in Figures 16-1 and 16-2. For convenience we will assume the supply of current consumption is fixed; problem 2 in this chapter shows how the analysis can be generalized to handle the case where supply is upward sloping.

Figure 16-1.

Step 1. The lower diagram of Figure 16-1 shows the supply and demand for current consumption, where an equilibrium interest rate of 33 1/3 percent has been established. The upper diagram shows the same equilibrium using a representative agent or "average consumer." Since the amount borrowed equals the amount lent in the economy, the representative agent cannot be a borrower or a lender—the representative agent's optimum must be at the endowment point. Recalling that the magnitude of the budget line's slope equals one plus the interest rate, verify that the representative agent diagram correctly illustrates the market shown in the lower diagram.

Step 2. Suppose that next year's productivity is expected to be higher, moving the representative agent's endowment to point B. Draw the new budget line that the representative agent faces, and calculate the new interest rate from the slope of this budget line. (The intercepts of the new budget line have been marked for convenience.) If you've calculated the new interest rate correctly, you should find that it increases to 50%.

Step 3. Show how the increase in future productivity affects the market for current consumption. To do this, notice there is no change in supply since there is no change in this year's endowment. However there will be an increase in demand since the representative agent's wealth has increased. Be sure that the new equilibrium agrees with the interest rate shown in the representative agent diagram. If you've completed the diagram correctly, it should resemble Exhibit 16-5 of the textbook.

Notice that either the representative agent diagram or the supply/demand diagram can be used to show that an increase in future productivity will increase interest rates.

Figure 16-1 Analysis of Interest Rates Using a Representative Agent--
An Increase in Future Productivity

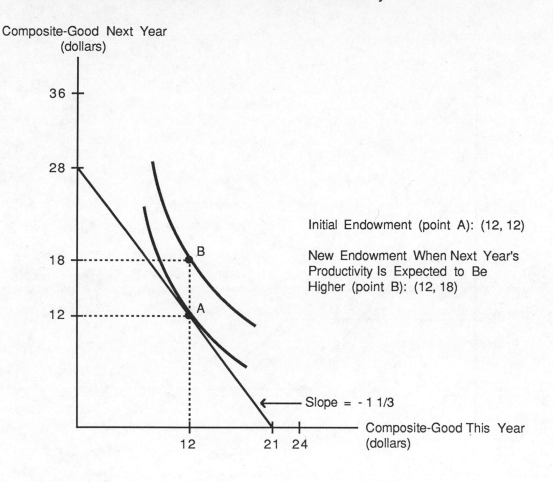

Composite-Good Next Year
(dollars)

Initial Endowment (point A): (12, 12)

New Endowment When Next Year's
Productivity Is Expected to Be
Higher (point B): (12, 18)

Slope = - 1 1/3

Composite-Good This Year
(dollars)

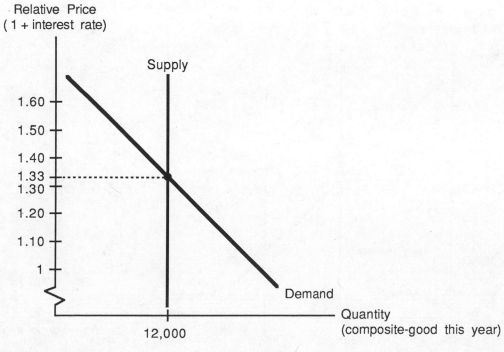

Relative Price
(1 + interest rate)

Supply

Demand

Quantity
(composite-good this year)

Figure 16-2 Analysis of Interest Rates Using a Representative Agent-- An Increase in Current Output

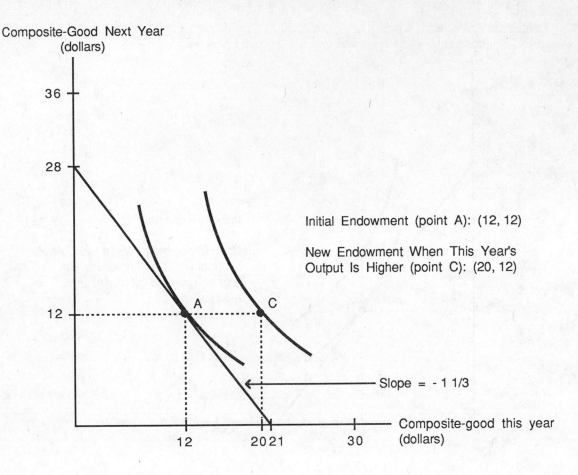

Composite-Good Next Year (dollars)

Initial Endowment (point A): (12, 12)

New Endowment When This Year's Output Is Higher (point C): (20, 12)

Slope = - 1 1/3

Composite-good this year (dollars)

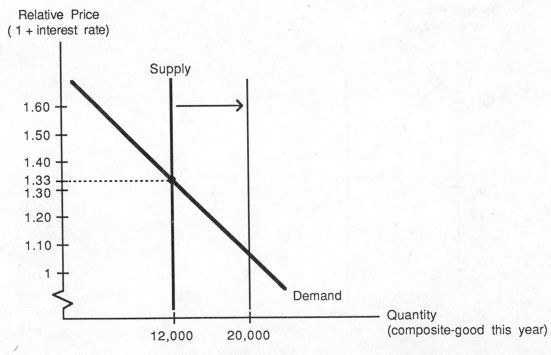

Relative Price (1 + interest rate)

Supply

Demand

Quantity (composite-good this year)

Figure 16-2.

Step 1. We start with the same initial equilibrium; this time we will use the two approaches to find the effect that an increase in current output will have on the interest rate. The increase in current output causes a shift to the right in the representative agent's endowment, moving it to point C. As before, draw in the new budget line and calculate the new interest rate. You should find that the interest rate falls from 33 1/3 percent to 20 percent.

Step 2. Now use the supply/demand diagram to show how the increase in current output affects the interest rate. Notice that there are two shifts in this case: the supply of current consumption increases (since this year's endowment has increased) and the demand for current consumption increases (since the representative agent is now wealthier). The latter shift is the smaller since the increase in current output will also increase the demand for future consumption. Be sure that the equilibrium in your supply/demand diagram agrees with that shown in the representative agent diagram. If you've completed this graph correctly, it should resemble Exhibit 16-6 of the textbook.

Multiple Choice Questions

1. Suppose the consumer is at his endowment point. If the consumer's discount rate is larger than the interest rate that prevails in the market, then
   A. the consumer is at his optimum.
   B. the consumer will be better off if he decreases his current consumption and increases his future consumption through lending.
   C. the consumer will be better off if he increases his current consumption and decreases his future consumption through borrowing.
   D. his discount rate must be negative.

***Questions 2 and 3 refer to Figure 16a which shows a consumer's choice between current and future consumption.

Figure 16a

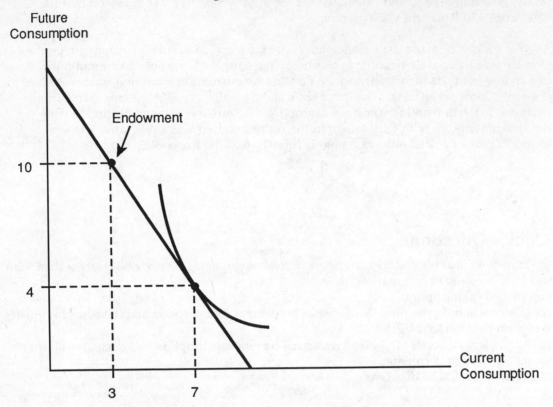

2. The interest rate is
   A. 1/2 of 1 percent.
   B. 1 1/2 percent.
   C. 50 percent.
   D. 150 percent.

3. The consumer is a _____, and his quantity demanded is _____.
   A. borrower; 4 units
   B. borrower; 7 units
   C. lender; 4 units
   D. lender; 7 units

***Question 4 refers to Figure 16b which shows the effect of a change in the endowment point on the representative agent. The old endowment is at point A, and the new endowment is at point B. We are assuming that the supply of current consumption is determined by people's endowments and investment is impossible.

Figure 16b

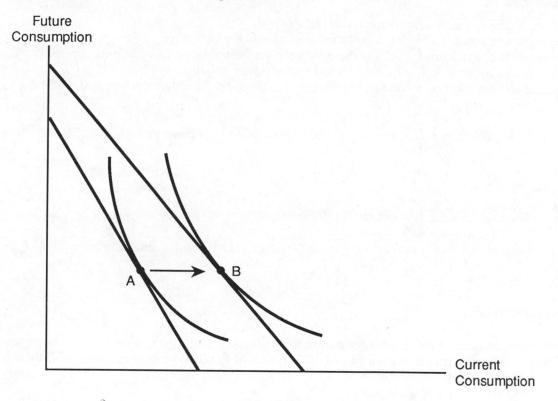

4. Which of the following gives the best interpretation of the representative agent diagram in Figure 16b?
   A. An increase in the supply of current consumption will cause a rise in the interest rate.
   B. An increase in the supply of current consumption will cause a fall in the interest rate.
   C. An increase in the supply of future consumption will cause a rise in the interest rate.
   D. An increase in the supply of future consumption will cause a fall in the interest rate.

5. In the supply/demand model showing the determination of the interest rate, the supply of current consumption is determined by
   A. the gross marginal product of capital.
   B. the net marginal product of capital.
   C. the discount rate of consumers.
   D. the interest rate.

6. Which of the following is *not* equated to the interest rate in equilibrium?
   A. All consumers' discount rates.
   B. The gross marginal product of capital.
   C. The net marginal product of capital.
   D. The rental rate of capital.

7. In the supply/demand model showing the determination of interest rates, suppose investment opportunities cause the supply of current consumption to be upward sloping. An expected increase in future productivity will cause
   A. the interest rate to fall and current consumption to rise.
   B. both the interest rate and current consumption to rise.
   C. the interest rate to rise and current consumption to fall.
   D. the interest rate to rise and have an ambiguous effect on current consumption.

8. Which of the following statements on bonds is *false*?
   A. The buyer of a bond is a lender, and the seller of a bond is a borrower.
   B. A bond sells at a discount, which is the difference between its face value and its current price.
   C. The value of a bond will fall if the market rate of interest falls.
   D. A size of the discount on a bond denominated in dollars should reflect the nominal, not the real, interest rate.

9. A bond with a $10,000 face value sells at a $2,000 discount one year prior to maturity. The effective return on the bond is
   A. 5 percent.
   B. 20 percent.
   C. 25 percent.
   D. impossible to determine without more information.

10. What is the present value of a perpetuity paying $100 per year when the interest rate is 5%?
   A. $500.
   B. $1,000.
   C. $2,000.
   D. None of the above

11. Suppose the government spends $3,000 per person this year. Assuming the market for borrowing and lending is competitive with an interest rate of 10%, which of the following plans to pay off this government debt is the best for consumers?
   A. A tax of $3,000 per person this year.
   B. A tax of $3,300 per person next year.
   C. An annual tax of $300 per person forever.
   D. All of the above have the same effect on consumers.

***Questions 12 and 13 refer to Figure 16c, which shows two potential endowments (at points A and B) and budget lines for a consumer.

Figure 16c

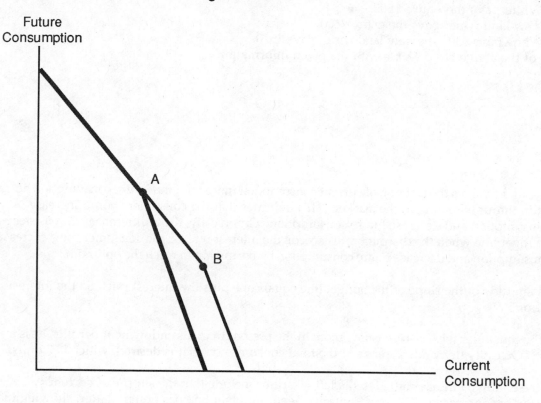

12. The consumer must borrow at a _____ rate of interest than he can lend due to the problem of _____.
    A. higher; default risk
    B. higher; misperceptions
    C. lower; default risk
    D. lower; misperceptions

13. Suppose the level of government spending that the consumer's taxes must finance has already been determined. Also suppose the government chooses to borrow money to pay for its spending instead of taxing the consumer immediately. This moves the consumer's endowment from _____ and causes the demand for current consumption to _____.
    A. point A to point B; increase
    B. point A to point B; decrease
    C. point B to point A; increase
    D. point B to point A; decrease

14. The market rate of interest is 20%. A producer can make a quality improvement in his product that will increase its value to consumers by $36 per year for three years. The producer
    A. should not make the quality improvement because it will have a negative influence on sales.
    B. should make the quality improvement only if its cost is less than $36.
    C. should make the quality improvement only if its cost is less than $91.
    D. should make the quality improvement only is its cost is less than $180.

313

15. Suppose the interest rate is 5%. The government imposes a tax of $30 per acre on farmland, so the tax has a present value of $600 per acre. The supply of farmland is fixed, and the market for farmland is competitive. The year after the tax is imposed, Dr. White sells the land on which he grew tobacco. How is the economic burden of the tax divided between Dr. White and the new landowner?
   A. Dr. White pays the entire $600.
   B. The new landowner pays the entire $600.
   C. Dr. White pays $30; the new landowner pays $570.
   D. Any of the above are possible with the given information.

Solutions

1. C. The consumer values the last unit of current consumption more than the future consumption he could obtain through loaning in the market. This indicates that the consumer should increase current consumption and decrease future consumption. Graphically, the indifference curve is steeper than the budget line when the discount rate exceeds the interest rate, so the consumer must increase current consumption and decrease future consumption by borrowing to reach the optimum.

2. C. The magnitude of the slope of the budget line equals one plus the interest rate. So the interest rate is 1/2 or 50%.

3. B. Since the consumer wishes to consume more in the present than his endowment permits, he is a borrower. "Quantity demanded" refers to the total consumption that is desired, which is 7 units.

4. B. Since the endowment has shifted to the left, we can conclude that the supply of current consumption has increased. The representative agent's budget line has gotten flatter, showing that the interest rate has fallen.

5. A. The opportunity cost of current consumption is the sacrifice in future consumption entailed. This would equal the original investment plus any return, which is the gross marginal product of capital.

6. B. The market for current consumption (where the price is given in terms of future consumption) shows that (1) the price of current consumption equates the gross marginal product of capital and consumers' marginal rates of substitution, and (2) the interest rate (which equals the rental rate on capital) equates the (net) marginal product of capital and consumers' discount rates.

7. D. The demand for current consumption will increase because the improved productivity will increase consumers' wealth. The supply of current consumption will decrease because the improved productivity provides a new incentive for investment. The combination of these two shifts will cause the price of current consumption (which equals one plus the interest rate) to increase and have an ambiguous effect on the quantity of current consumption.

8. C. The present value of the face value of the bond will increase when the interest rate falls. In other words, the bond can be sold at a lower discount when the interest rate falls.

9. C. The bond must have a present value of $8,000 (the difference between the face value and the discount). Using the discounting formula, the bond's present value is $10,000 \cdot 1/(1+r)$. This equals $8,000 when the interest rate is 1/4 or 25%.

10. C. The present value of a $100 perpetuity is given by the formula $100 \cdot (1/r)$. Since the interest rate equals 5% or 1/20, the latter factor equals 20 and the perpetuity is worth $2,000.

11. D. The present value of all three tax schemes is $3,000. This comparison of present values provides the reasoning that supports the Ricardian Equivalence Theorem.

12. A. The slope of the budget line is steeper to the right of the endowment, showing that the interest rate is higher when the consumer borrows to increase his current consumption. This is to compensate the lender for the risk that the consumer may not repay the loan.

13. A. Since the government has postponed the tax payment required to finance its spending, this increases the current consumption and decreases the future consumption available in the consumer's endowment. As shown in Figure 16c, this moves the endowment from A to B and increases the budget options available. This will increase the consumer's demand for current consumption. If a large enough number of consumers are affected in this way, government borrowing will put upward pressure on the interest rate.

14. C. The producer can profit if the cost of the quality improvement is less than its value to consumers. Using the discounting formula, the present value of the improvement is $36 + $36 \cdot 1/1.20 + $36 \cdot 1/1.20^2$ which equals $36 + $30 + $25 or $91.

15. A. The demand for farmland will shift down by the present value of the tax, which is $600 per acre. Since the supply of farmland is vertical, the price of land will fall by precisely $600 per acre and the entire burden of the tax will fall on the present landowners.

Questions for Review

1. How can the basic consumer choice model of Chapter 3 be modified to show how a consumer allocates goods over time?

2. What is the price of current consumption? How is the demand for current consumption derived? How is the supply of current consumption derived?

3. What do the discount rate and the marginal product of capital represent? Explain why competitive behavior causes these to be equated to the interest rate.

4. Use the supply/demand model to show how the interest rate and current consumption are affected by (a) a one-shot increase in current productivity and (b) an expected increase in future productivity.

5. What is a bond? What is a perpetuity? How are the prices of bonds and perpetuities related to the interest rate?

6. What does the Ricardian Equivalence Theorem claim? How can this claim be justified?

7. Under what conditions could government deficits increase interest rates?

Solutions

1. For the two goods in the consumer choice model, we use current consumption (on the horizontal axis) and future consumption (on the vertical axis). We assume the consumer has an initial endowment of current and future consumption; the interest rate establishes the rate at which the consumer can trade this endowment for other combinations of current and future consumption. This establishes a budget line through the endowment point with the magnitude of the slope equalling one plus the interest rate. At the optimum the slope of the budget line equals the slope of the indifference curve. This implies that the discount rate (the amount by which the MRS exceeds one) equals the interest rate.

2. One unit of current consumption can be exchanged for one unit of future consumption plus interest. So the price of current consumption is $(1 + r)$ units of future consumption per unit of current consumption, where r is the interest rate. The demand for current consumption is derived using the consumer choice model described in question 1. We vary the price of current consumption (shown by rotating the budget line) and see how the consumer's optimum level of current consumption changes. The supply of current consumption is determined by the gross marginal product of capital. The marginal cost of the last unit of current consumption is the sacrificed future consumption that could have been obtained from investing that unit—this opportunity cost is precisely what the gross marginal product of capital defines. Notice that this is the same way any other demand and supply curves are derived—we look at marginal value (defined by the indifference curves in the consumer choice model) to find demand and at marginal cost to find supply.

3. The discount rate is the additional payment that a consumer must receive to stay indifferent when making a one-to-one trade of current consumption in exchange for future consumption. The marginal product of capital is the additional amount of future consumption earned from the last unit of capital invested (after "getting back" that last unit of capital). Both the discount rate and the marginal product of capital are generally expressed in percentage terms. The discount rate reflects the marginal value of current consumption, while the marginal product of capital reflects the marginal cost of current consumption. The interest rate determines the price of current consumption, so in equilibrium the discount rate and the marginal product of capital are equated as shown in Figure 16d.

Figure 16d

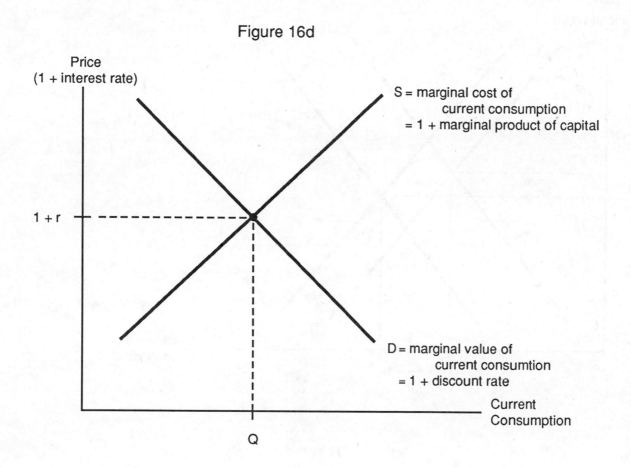

4. (a) The one-time increase in current productivity causes a windfall which increases the
         supply of current consumption. This windfall also increases consumers' wealth,
         increasing the demand for both current and future consumption (since consumers' wealth
         has increased). We may conclude that the shift in supply is larger than the shift in
         demand, so current consumption increases and interest rates fall as shown in Figure 16e.

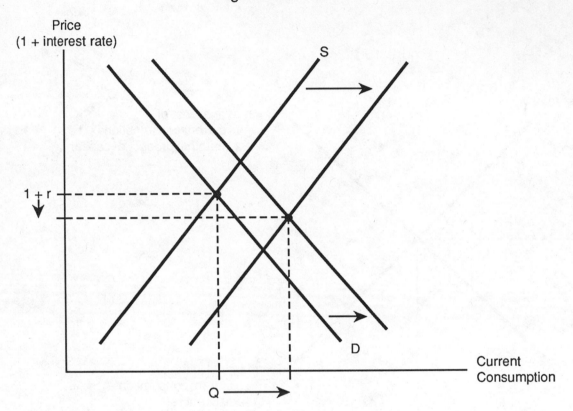

Figure 16e

(b)   The expected increase in future productivity will increase the demand for current consumption since this increases consumers' wealth. The supply of current consumption will fall since more goods will be invested and fewer goods will be available for consumption. This will increase the interest rate but have an ambiguous effect on current consumption as shown in Figure 16f.

Figure 16f

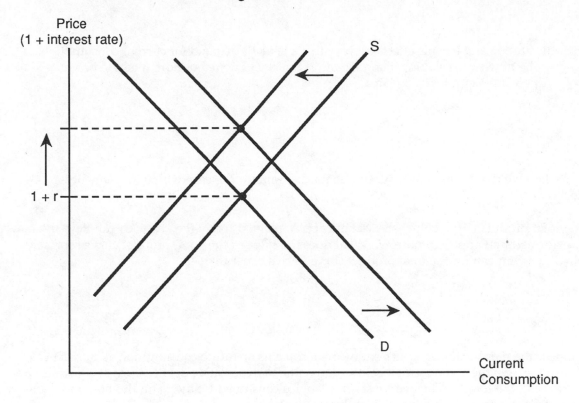

5.   A bond is a promise to pay a specified amount at some specified future date; the present value of a bond with a face value of $X to be paid n years in the future is $X \cdot 1/(1 + r)^n$ where r is the annual interest rate. A perpetuity is a promise to pay some fixed amount periodically forever; the present value of a perpetuity paying $X every year is $X \cdot 1/r$.

6.   The Ricardian Equivalence Theorem claims that government borrowing cannot effect the demand for current consumption and hence cannot affect interest rates. To finance its spending, the government can (1) tax you this year to pay for its spending, (2) borrow money to pay for its spending and tax you in the future to pay off its loan, or (3) borrow money to pay for its spending and never pay off its loan, taxing you annually to make its interest payments. The present value of your taxes are identical under these three plans. Since your wealth is the same in the three cases, your budget and hence your demand for current consumption are unaffected by government's decision to borrow money.

7.   Government borrowing to finance deficits could increase the demand for current consumption and hence interest rates (contrary to the claim of the Ricardian Equivalence Theorem) if either default risk or misperceptions are common in the economy. Under default risk consumers must borrow at higher interest rates than they can lend at; government borrowing lowers consumers' current tax burden, giving them an endowment outside their initial budget and increasing their available budget opportunities. Under misperceptions, consumers believe their available budget opportunities have increased because they do not realize that their future tax burden will be higher due to the government's borrowing. In either case, the increased opportunities will increase the demand for current consumption and put upward pressure on the interest rate.

319

Problems for Analysis

1. (i) Use substitution and income effects to explain why a borrower's demand for current consumption must be downward sloping.

   (ii) Use substitution and income effects to show that a lender's demand for current consumption may not be downward sloping. For a lender, is the law of demand more likely to be violated at low or high interest rates? Explain.

2. In this problem we derive the representative agent diagram for the case where investment is possible.

   (i) The total product curve below shows how apples planted today (i.e., capital) can be transformed into apples tomorrow. What does the slope of this total product curve represent? What does it mean for the total product curve to be steeper than 45°?

   (ii) Suppose the representative agent's endowment contains no future consumption as shown in Figure 16g. On the second graph below, derive the representative agent's budget constraint by regraphing the total product curve so that "apples consumed today" is on the horizontal axis. (Hint—Compare with Exhibit 16-7 of the textbook.)

   (iii) Complete your diagram to show the representative agent for the economy. The following should be labelled:

           a. the optimum point,
           b. current consumption at the optimum (Q^*),
           c. the equilibrium interest rate (r^*),
           d. the discount rate (p^*), and
           e. the marginal product of capital (MPK^*).

   (Hint—Like the economy as a whole, the representative agent cannot be a borrower or a lender. So the optimum must lie on the budget constraint.)

320

Figure 16g

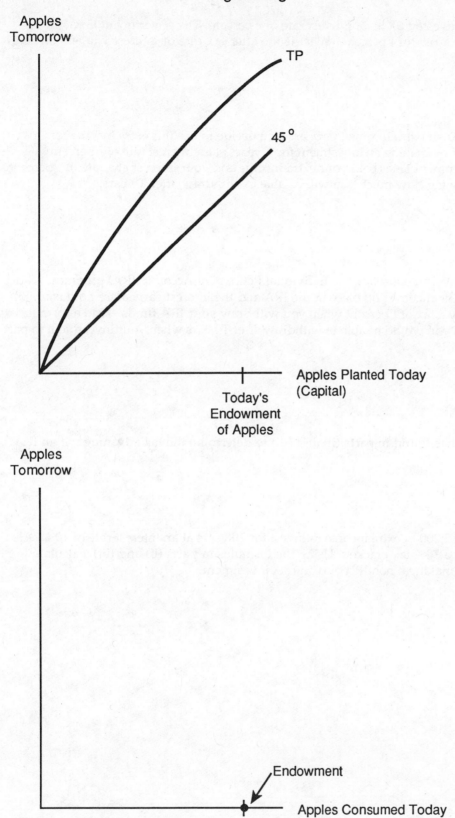

3. This problem explores the tax advantages of Individual Retirement Accounts (IRAs).

  (i)   Suppose you have invested $X at an interest rate of r percent. The government taxes the interest you earn at a rate of t percent. What is the after-tax rate of interest you are earning?

  (ii) Suppose you have $X of extra income this year. You decide to use this extra income for retirement purposes by making an investment for T years at an interest rate of r percent. However, the government taxes both your extra income and your interest at a rate of t percent. Find a formula showing how much you will be able to withdraw after T years.

  (iii) Now suppose the government sets up an Individual Retirement Account (IRA) program. Under certain conditions, the income you place in the IRA and the interest earned are not taxed. But you will have to pay a tax of t percent when you withdraw your IRA funds. Find a formula showing how much you would be able to withdraw after T years when your investment in part (ii) is placed in an IRA.

  (iv) Compare the formulas found in parts (ii) and (iii) to determine the tax advantage of an IRA.

  (v)   Suppose you have $2,000 in extra income to invest for 20 years at an interest rate of 10%. Also suppose you are in a 30% tax bracket. Using the formulas in parts (ii) and (iii), calculate the difference between making a non-IRA and an IRA investment.

Solutions

1. (i) Suppose the interest rate increases; we want to show that the borrower's current consumption falls. When the interest rate increases, this makes the budget line steeper and rotates it inward away from the original optimum. The price of current consumption relative to future consumption is now higher, so the substitution effect causes the consumer to choose less current consumption and more future consumption. Furthermore, the consumer's real income has fallen since he can no longer purchase the original optimum. So the income effect puts downward pressure on both current and future consumption. We find that both the substitution and income effects support the law of demand, so the borrower's demand for current consumption must be downward sloping.

   (ii) Again suppose the interest rate rises. As with the borrower, since current consumption is now relatively more expensive than future consumption, the lender will substitute away from current goods and purchase more future goods. So the substitution effect again supports the law of demand. But for a lender, an increase in the interest rate increases the budget opportunities available. The lender's real income has risen since he can purchase baskets on higher indifference curves than his original optimum. So the income effect puts upward pressure on both current and future consumption. This time the substitution and income effects are in opposite directions, so we cannot guarantee that the lender's demand for current consumption will be downward sloping. The law of demand is more likely to be violated when the interest rate is high, because then the lender's interest income will be substantial. In this case the income effect may be large enough to outweigh the substitution effect.

2. (i) The slope of the total product curve represents the gross marginal product of capital—the additional apples generated by the last apple invested. When the total product curve is steeper than 45°, it shows that the gross marginal product of capital is larger than one. This implies that the net marginal product of capital is positive.

   (ii) Since "apples consumed today" equals the endowment minus the number of apples invested as capital, the budget constraint is simply the mirror image of the total product curve.

Figure 16h

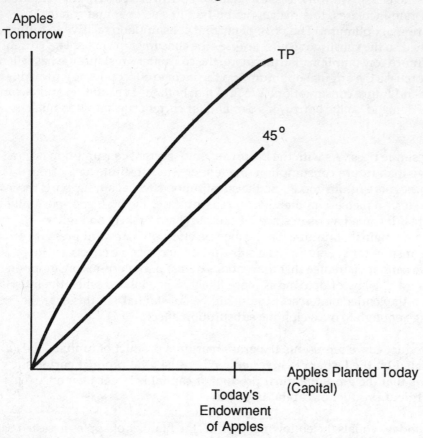

Apples
Tomorrow

TP

45°

Apples Planted Today
(Capital)

Today's
Endowment
of Apples

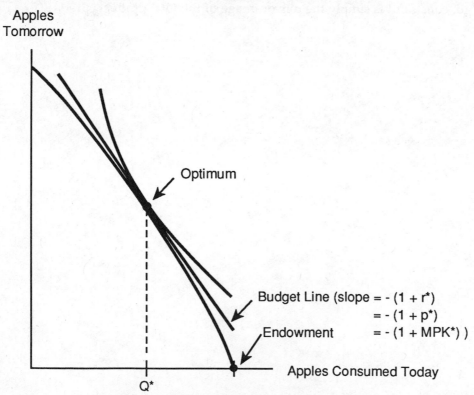

Apples
Tomorrow

Optimum

Budget Line (slope = - (1 + r*)
= - (1 + p*)

Endowment = - (1 + MPK*))

Apples Consumed Today

Q*

3. (i) You earn \$rX in interest. The government collects t percent of this amount, which equals \$trX. This leaves you \$rX - \$trX = \$(1 - t)rX in interest income to keep. So your \$X investment earned an after-tax rate of (1 - t)r percent.

(ii) Of your \$X in income, the government takes \$tX. This leaves \$X - \$tX = \$(1 - t)X to invest. Since your interest is taxed, it earns an interest rate of (1 - t)r percent. Letting this investment compound for T years, you will withdraw $\$(1 - t)X \cdot (1 + (1 - t)r)^T$.

(iii) Under the IRA, you can invest the full \$X at an interest rate of r percent. Letting this compound for T years, you will withdraw $\$X \cdot (1 + r)^T$. The government takes t percent of this amount, leaving you $\$(1 - t)X \cdot (1 + r)^T$.

(iv) Comparing the two formulas, the IRA offers the advantage of tax-free interest. With the IRA you earn r percent in interest; without the IRA you only earn (1 - t)r percent.

(v) Without the IRA, your \$2,000 investment will earn

$\$(1 - t)X \cdot (1 + (1 - t)r)^T$
$= \$1,400 \cdot (1.07)^{20} = \$1,400 \cdot 3.87 = \$5,418.$

With the IRA, your \$2,000 investment will earn

$\$(1 - t)X \cdot (1 + r)^T$
$= \$1,400 \cdot (1.10)^{20} = \$1,400 \cdot 6.73 = \$9,422.$

Clearly, the tax-free interest the IRA offers can make a substantial difference.

Solutions to Working Through the Graphs

Figure 16-1   Analysis of Interest Rates Using a Representative Agent--
An Increase in Future Productivity

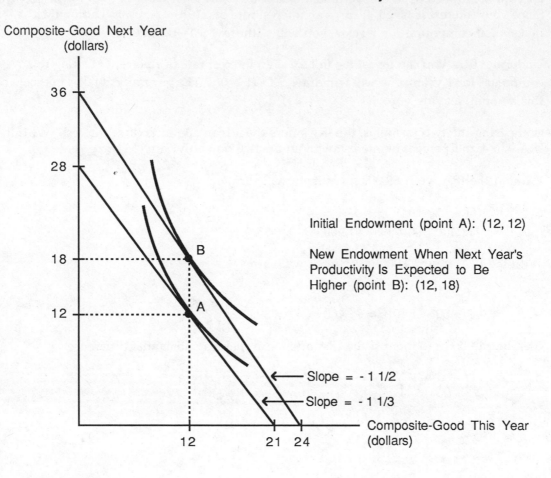

Composite-Good Next Year
(dollars)

Initial Endowment (point A): (12, 12)

New Endowment When Next Year's
Productivity Is Expected to Be
Higher (point B): (12, 18)

Slope = - 1 1/2

Slope = - 1 1/3

Composite-Good This Year
(dollars)

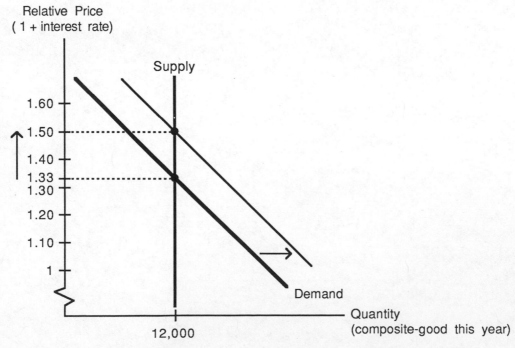

Relative Price
(1 + interest rate)

Supply

Demand

Quantity
(composite-good this year)

Figure 16-2 Analysis of Interest Rates Using a Representative Agent--
An Increase in Current Output

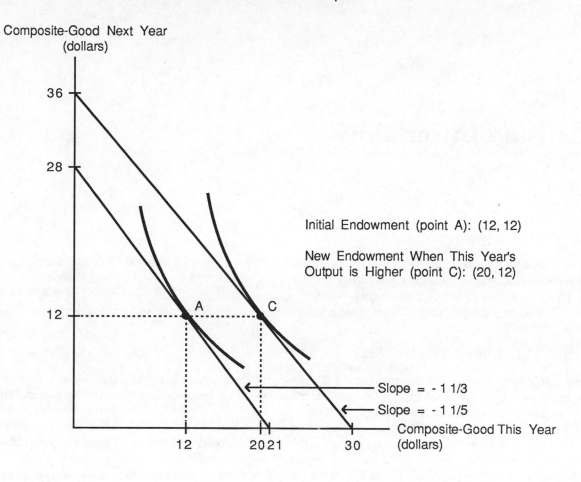

Composite-Good Next Year
(dollars)

Initial Endowment (point A): (12, 12)

New Endowment When This Year's
Output is Higher (point C): (20, 12)

Slope = - 1 1/3

Slope = - 1 1/5

Composite-Good This Year
(dollars)

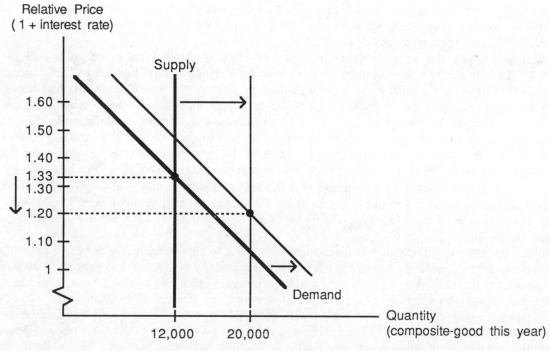

Relative Price
(1 + interest rate)

Supply

Demand

Quantity
(composite-good this year)

327

Chapter Seventeen

Risk and Uncertainty

Chapter Summary

In the models studied so far, we have assumed that economic agents have a wealth of information known with certainty. However the future is always unknown, and individuals and firms must somehow deal with the risk and uncertainty they face. This chapter surveys several of the models and ideas that have been developed to explore economic behavior under risk and uncertainty.

Section 17.1. Attitudes toward Risk

A consumer's future wealth is uncertain. It depends on the *state of the world*—the actual set of conditions which occurs. To model the consumer's behavior under uncertainty, we will assume there are only two possible states of the world (e.g., "fire" and "no fire," or "drought" and "no drought"). We plot the consumer's income in one state of the world on the horizontal axis and his income in the other state of the world on the vertical axis. Any point on this graph represents a basket of possible outcomes. We can draw a consumer's indifference curves between these two situations, realizing there is a major difference in our interpretation of these preferences. These are *ex ante* preferences—preferences before the state of the world is known—and they depend on the probabilities at which the various states of the world can occur. Previously we have been dealing with *ex post* preferences for which the state of the world is already known to the consumer.

Any basket of possible outcomes is characterized by two features: its expected value and its riskiness. The *expected value* of a basket is calculated by averaging together the possible income levels for each state of the world with each being weighted by its probability. A mathematical result known as the *law of large numbers* shows that if a gamble is repeated many times, the average outcome will be the expected value of the gamble. The *riskiness* of a basket is the amount of variation in the possible outcomes. For example, baskets on the 45° line are *risk-free*—the outcome will be the same no matter what the state of the world is, so there is no variation in the possible outcomes. In general if two baskets have the same expected value, the one further away from the 45° line will be the riskier.

Let P_1 and P_2 represent the probabilities that the first and second states of the world will occur; these two states are assumed to be represented on the horizontal and vertical axes, respectively. Baskets with the same expected value will lie on a line with slope $-P_1/P_2$. Such a line is called an iso-expected value line.

We can use the expected value and riskiness of baskets to show that there are three possible types of preferences a consumer may have. First, a consumer may only care about the expected value of a basket and have no interest in its riskiness. Such a consumer is said to be *risk-neutral,* and his indifference curves—like the iso-expected value lines—will be straight lines with slope $-P_1/P_2$. Second, when a consumer prefers the basket with the least risk among those with the same expected value, he is said to be *risk-adverse*. The indifference curves of a risk-adverse consumer are downward-sloping and convex, with slope equal to $-P_1/P_2$ at risk-free baskets (i.e., along the 45° line). Finally, a consumer is *risk-preferring* when he prefers the most risky basket among those with the same expected value. A risk-preferring consumer has downward-sloping, concave indifference curves, again with slope equal to the ratio of probabilities along the 45° line.

The consumer has the opportunity to change his basket of outcomes and his level of welfare when he is offered a gamble. The slope of the resulting budget line will be determined by the odds offered. If the odds offered reflect the true probabilities of the states of the world, then the budget line corresponds to an iso-expected value line.

We can now use an indifference curve/budget line diagram to show how a consumer will react to a given gamble. For example, a risk-neutral individual will be indifferent as to how much he bets when offered fair odds because his indifference curve will lie directly on top of his budget line—this is because he can *diversify* or reduce his risk in the long run by playing often enough to guarantee he earns the expected value of the gamble. On the other hand, a risk-neutral person will wager everything on one outcome or the other if offered unfair odds; his optimum will be a corner equilibrium in this case. Turning to the risk-adverse individual, he will always consume a risk-free bundle when offered a gamble at fair odds (i.e., the optimum will lie on the 45° line). When offered favorable odds, the risk-adverse person will accept a small gamble but will reject one that is too large.

Section 17.2. The Market for Insurance

Insurance is simply another kind of gamble. If you are insured against having an automobile accident, you have accepted a gamble where your wealth is lowered if the state of the world is "no accident occurs" and your wealth is increased if the state of the world is "accident occurs." Because insurance companies are diversified (i.e., since they reduce their risk by "betting" many times over), one might expect them to be able to offer consumers fair odds. This section examines three reasons—moral hazard, adverse selection, and uninsurable risks—that explain why this is generally not the case.

The problem of *moral hazard* occurs because insurance companies are unable to monitor the behavior of the parties they insure. For example, suppose an individual is offered fair odds when being insured against fire. The optimum point lies on the 45° line, so the individual has the same wealth whether or not a fire happens. The insurance makes the consumer indifferent as to whether or not a fire occurs, and this may change his behavior. He may become more careless and take fewer precautions, changing the odds that a fire will occur and making the odds unfavorable for the insurance company. To resolve this problem of moral hazard, the insurance company may require some form of observable behavior like the installation of smoke alarms. More likely, the insurance company will offer the consumer less than fair odds. Then the risk-adverse person will still purchase some insurance but not be fully insured.

Consumers often have access to information about their own risk that is unavailable to insurers, and as a result the insurer may not be able to offer fair odds to all insured parties. This is the problem of *adverse selection*. For example health insurers know far less about the odds that a consumer will become ill than the consumer himself—the consumer has access to the early warning signals of illness like pain and weakness that the insurer cannot know. This lack of information makes it impossible for the insurer to offer fair odds to everyone.

To resolve this problem of adverse selection, insurers can limit the amount of insurance available at the most favorable odds (which would be fair odds for the healthiest consumers in our example). Insurance at less favorable odds (which would be fair odds for the sickliest consumers in our example) is available at unlimited amounts. The amount of insurance available at favorable odds is sufficiently limited so that only those customers with the lowest risks find it optimum to purchase insurance at these odds, even though the limit means that they will not be fully insured. People with higher risks find themselves better off if they fully insure themselves at the less favorable odds. So by appropriately limiting the amount of insurance available at the most favorable odds, the insurer can cause consumers to voluntarily select the policy that offers fair odds.

An *uninsurable risk* is one that cannot be diversified. Insurance companies diversify—reduce their risk—by "betting" on many different insured parties. By repeating their gamble over and over, an insurance company, like the risk-neutral gambler, can be guaranteed to receive the expected value of their bets on insured parties. But some risks cannot be diversified in this way because they affect everyone in the same manner. For example a nuclear war would affect everyone, and hence the gamble of insuring a person against nuclear war cannot be repeated over and over. The insurer would have to pay off in either all or no cases, not just a fraction of the cases, and so cannot be guaranteed to receive the expected value of the gamble. Thus when risk cannot be diversified, the insurance company cannot remain risk-neutral and cannot offer fair odds.

Section 17.3. Future Markets

Futures markets, like markets for insurance, allow risk to be transferred from one party to another. A *futures contract* is an agreement to deliver a specified amount of a good at a specified future date for some specified price. Futures contracts can be traded like any other good, and the *futures market* is a market established for this trading. Of course there are also markets for the good which require immediate (instead of future) delivery, and this kind of market is called the *spot market* in order to distinguish it from the futures markets. The price in the spot market is called the *spot price* of the good. To summarize, trading in spot markets promises immediate delivery of the good while trading in futures markets promises delivery at some given date in the future.

Money can be made and lost in the futures markets, because the current futures price may be different than the spot price when delivery is required. For example, suppose the futures price of September wheat is $3.00 per bushel in July, and then in September the spot price is $3.50 per bushel. If you sold a futures contract in July, you will lose money because the wheat you deliver in September can be sold for more than the $3.00 per bushel you are receiving. You will make a hefty profit if you bought a futures contract in July because you can take the wheat you paid $3.00 per bushel for and immediately resell it for $3.50 per bushel in September. A *speculator* is a person who tries to predict where the spot price will be in the future (by trying to predict future changes in supply and demand) in order to make profits from trading in the futures markets.

In the absence of speculators, suppliers will adjust their provision of goods so that the current spot price is equal to the spot price they expect in the future (assuming that the complications of storage and discounting are negligible). If speculators feel that suppliers' expectations about future demand and the spot price in the future are incorrect, they will trade in the futures market to take advantage of this situation. This will affect the futures price of the good, and in turn affect suppliers' expectations about the spot price in the future. Suppliers will react by adjusting their provision of the good accordingly. If the speculators are correct in their guess about future demand, then the resulting adjustment in the provision of the good will increase social gain. But if the speculators are incorrect about their expectations of future demand, the adjustment in supplies caused by the speculators' actions will lower social gain.

Section 17.4. Markets for Risky Assets

People who choose to buy risky assets like corporate stocks in order to increase their wealth are commonly but misleadingly called *investors.* Stocks offer various gains to the owner, such as dividends and increased value over time, called *returns.* The actual returns from a stock are uncertain, and the expected present value of these returns is known as the *expected return* of the stock. Generally investors do not own a single stock, but instead investors choose *portfolios* which combine several risky assets. This section introduces the *capital asset pricing model,* which models how an investor chooses his portfolio and is used to study markets for risky assets.

In the capital asset pricing model, we assume that investors are concerned with only two characteristics of their stocks and portfolios: the expected return and the riskiness. The riskiness of a stock or portfolio is measured by a mathematical concept known as the *standard deviation.* You would learn the exact formula for the standard deviation in a statistics or econometrics course. For our purposes it suffices to know that the standard deviation measures the "spread" between the possible outcomes and is expressed as the percentage of the risky asset's current value. The greater the variation in the risky asset's possible returns, the higher the standard deviation; an asset that offers a certain return has a standard deviation of zero.

By putting the standard deviation of a stock or portfolio on the horizontal axis and its expected return on the vertical axis, we can graphically show the choices available to an investor. Each stock or portfolio will be represented as a single point on this graph. When stocks are combined, the resulting portfolio's expected return will be the average of the stocks' expected returns. Furthermore, the resulting portfolio's standard deviation will be less than or equal to the average of the stocks' standard deviations. These two facts imply that the set of all portfolios will be an area with an upward-sloping, concave boundary. This boundary shows the portfolios that give the lowest level of risk for any desired expected return. Since these are the only portfolios a risk-adverse investor would choose, the portfolios on the boundary are called *efficient portfolios* and the entire boundary is called the *efficient set*.

Since expected return is a "good" and standard deviation is a "bad" for the risk-adverse investor, the investor's indifference curves will be upward-sloping and convex. The investor's optimum portfolio will be where an indifference curve is tangent to the efficient set. So this model is yet another variation of the basic consumer choice model first introduced in Chapter 3.

The model can be extended to include the possibility of owning a risk-free asset such as a government bond. A risk-free asset has a zero standard deviation, so is graphically represented as a point on the vertical axis in our model. The line connecting this point with any portfolio (called the *market line*) represents the expected returns and standard deviations that the investor can achieve when he combines the risk-free asset and the portfolio. A risk-adverse investor will choose the portfolio where the market line is just tangent to the efficient set; this preferred portfolio is called the *market portfolio*. It can be shown that a portfolio consisting of all the economy's risky assets held in proportion of their existing quantities must be a market portfolio. The point where the investor's indifference curve is tangent to the market line shows the precise combination of the market portfolio and the risk-free asset that will be chosen.

Section 17.5. Rational Expectations

Consumers and firms often lack definite information on which to base their economic decisions and instead must rely on their expectations. If market participants have expectations that lead to systematic errors, rational behavior would lead them to revise those predictions. On the other hand, when their expectations are on average fulfilled, then they should continue using those expectations. We summarize this argument by saying that the market participants have *rational expectations*.

The use of rational expectations by consumers and firms can easily lead economists to make errors when making predictions. By looking at past trends, economists and econometricians formulate some hypotheses (generally expressed through equations in an economic model) about an economic situation and determine policies to address the situation. However, these policies often change the circumstances faced by consumers and firms. Applying rational expectations, this change will cause these agents to modify their behavior and invalidate the model and equations on which the economists' predictions were based. As a result, the model which made accurate predictions in the past now proves to be terribly wrong following the recommended policy change.

Working Through the Graphs—Moral Hazard

One reason that insurance companies cannot offer customers fair odds is the problem of moral hazard. Figure 17-1 shows how the model of consumer choice under risk and uncertainty can be used to analyze this situation.

Step 1. We will consider two states of the world: "fire" (with probability 1/3) and "no fire" (with probability 2/3). Two identical pictures of an individual's preferences are shown in Figure 17-1. The individual without insurance is at point A. His income will be $1,100 if a fire does not occur, but his income will be lowered to $200 if a fire destroys most of his productive assets. Verify that the indifference curves are correctly drawn to represent a risk-adverse individual—be sure to check both the shape of the indifference curves and their slope at the risk-free baskets on the 45° line.

Figure 17-1 Moral Hazard

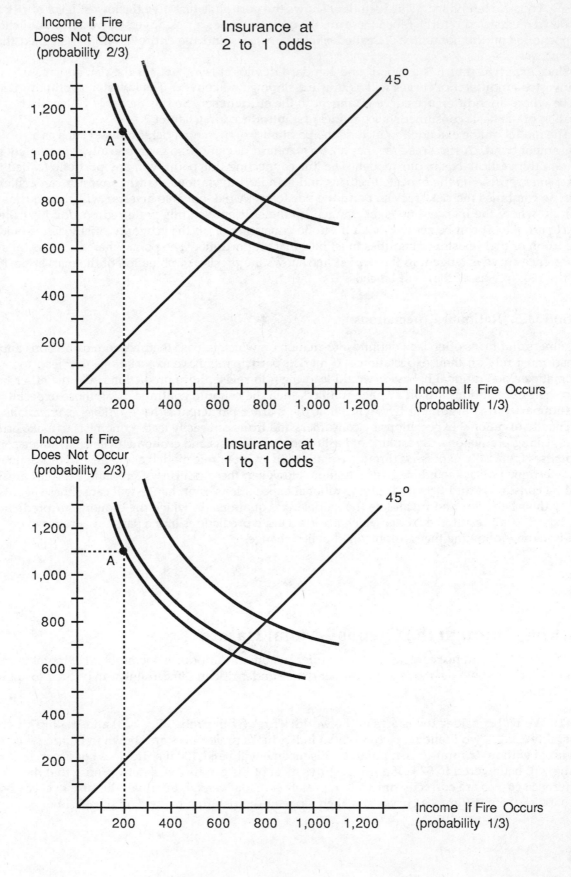

332

Step 2. In the top diagram, show what happens when the insurance company offers fair odds. To do this, recall that the slope of the budget line (1) passes through the initial point A and (2) has a slope of $-P_1/P_2$ where P_1 is the probability that a fire occurs and P_2 is the probability that a fire does not occur. Draw in the budget line and label the new optimum "B." You should find that the individual purchases $300 of fire insurance, and the insurance company will pay $600 if there is a fire.

Notice that the risk-adverse individual elects to be fully insured when offered fair odds, choosing a risk-free income of $800. This situation, combined with the possibility of unobservable behavior, creates the problem of moral hazard. Since he is fully insured, the individual is indifferent as to whether or not a fire occurs. As a result, he may change his behavior in ways unobservable to the insurance company and become less careful. This increases the odds that a fire will occur, and so the original 2 to 1 odds will now be unfavorable for the insurance company. Such unfavorable odds would guarantee losses for the insurance company in the long run (i.e., the expected value of its insurance policies would be negative) and prevent the insurance company from offering fair odds.

Step 3. Use the second diagram of Figure 17-1 to show a possible solution to the moral hazard problem. The insurance company must estimate what will be fair odds after insurance affects the individual's behavior. Let's suppose that for an insured individual the estimate is that a fire will occur with 1 to 1 odds. Draw in the budget line and find the optimum (label it "C") when the insurance company offers these odds. Then determine how much insurance the consumer will purchase and how much the insurance company pays if there is a fire. If you've done this correctly, you should find that the individual now purchases $200 of insurance.

Step 4. Compare the optimum points B and C in the two situations. Use the diagrams to verify that (1) the consumer chooses not to be fully insured when the insurance company adjusts its odds to deal with moral hazard and (2) the consumer would be better off if the insurance company could observe his behavior to circumvent the problem of moral hazard.

Multiple Choice Questions

1. Which of the following statements about a consumer's preferences under uncertainty is *false*?
    A. The indifference curves show the consumer's preferences between income levels obtained in two possible states of the world.
    B. The consumer's preferences in this model are *ex ante* instead of *ex post* preferences and depend on the probabilities at which the states of the world will occur.
    C. At risk-free baskets, the slope of the indifference curves equals the ratio of the probabilities of the states of the world.
    D. The consumer's indifference curves are convex as in the standard consumer choice model.

2. When an individual is offered fair odds, all baskets on his budget line
    A. have the same expected value.
    B. have the same degree of risk.
    C. have the same expected value and the same degree of risk.
    D. are equally desirable.

3. Suppose that an individual who is offered a gamble at fair odds is indifferent as to how much he bets. Then the individual is
    A. risk-neutral.
    B. risk-adverse.
    C. risk-preferring.
    D. either risk-neutral or risk-adverse.

4. Suppose that an individual who is offered a gamble at fair odds chooses a risk-free basket of outcomes. Then the individual is
   A. risk-neutral.
   B. risk-adverse.
   C. risk-preferring.
   D. either risk-neutral or risk-adverse.

5. Suppose a risk-adverse individual is offered the opportunity to place a bet at favorable odds. Then he will
   A. always accept the bet.
   B. always decline the bet.
   C. accept the bet if it is sufficiently small and decline the bet if it is too large.
   D. accept the bet if it is sufficiently large and decline the bet if it is too small.

6. Suppose some consumers conceal information about their risks, and insurance companies are unable to learn this information. Then the insurance companies cannot offer fair odds to all consumers due to the problem of
   A. moral hazard.
   B. adverse selection.
   C. uninsurable risk.
   D. risk-preferring behavior.

7. Suppose that a risk cannot be diversified because a large number of people would be adversely affected by the event. Then the insurance companies cannot offer fair odds to all consumers due to the problem of
   A. moral hazard.
   B. adverse selection.
   C. uninsurable risk.
   D. risk-preferring behavior.

8. Suppose the purchase of insurance to achieve a risk-free basket of outcomes causes consumers to change their behavior in ways that are unobservable to insurance companies. Then the insurance companies cannot offer fair odds to all consumers due to the problem of
   A. moral hazard.
   B. adverse selection.
   C. uninsurable risk.
   D. risk-preferring behavior.

9. Suppose speculators believe demand for a good will be lower in the future than what suppliers in the market currently expect. Which of the following statements is *false?*
   A. Speculators will purchase futures contracts.
   B. The spot price suppliers expect to see in the future will be bid down.
   C. Suppliers will adjust by increasing current supplies and decreasing future supplies.
   D. Speculators will increase social gain if they are correct in their expectations.

10. Suppose a stock currently sells for $50. The stock returns either -$10 or $20 with equal probability. The expected return of the stock is
    A. 10 percent.
    B. 20 percent.
    C. 30 percent.
    D. 40 percent.

11. The stock in question 10 has a standard deviation of
    A. 10 percent.
    B. 20 percent.
    C. 30 percent.
    D. 40 percent.

12. The expected return of a portfolio is _____ the average of the expected returns of the individual stocks, and the standard deviation of a portfolio is _____ the average of the standard deviations of the individual stocks.
    A. equal to; equal to
    B. equal to; less than or equal to
    C. less than or equal to; equal to
    D. less than or equal to; less than or equal to

13. Which of the following statements about the investor's choice of portfolios is *false?*
    A. The risk-adverse investor views a portfolio's expected return as a "good" and its standard deviation as a "bad."
    B. The investor may not be indifferent between two portfolios with the same expected return and standard deviation.
    C. The market line shows the various expected returns and standard deviations the investor can achieve from portfolios combining a risk-free asset and the market portfolio.
    D. A portfolio containing all of the economy's risky assets in proportion to their existing quantities is a market portfolio.

***Questions 14 and 15 refer to the following tables which show the supply and demand curves for a market. Demand is uncertain, with D_1 and D_2 each occurring 50% of the time. Suppliers must base their decisions on the expected price and must sell all goods they bring to the market at the going market price.

D_1: P	Q	D_2: P	Q	S: P	Q
$1.00	30	$1.00	50	$1.00	10
$1.50	25	$1.50	45	$1.50	15
$2.00	20	$2.00	40	$2.00	20
$2.50	15	$2.50	35	$2.50	25
$3.00	10	$3.00	30	$3.00	30
$3.50	5	$3.50	25	$3.50	35

14. Suppose suppliers are expecting a price of $3.00 per unit. How will suppliers revise their expectations about price?
    A. Suppliers will revise their price expectations downward because they are receiving less than $3.00 per unit on average.
    B. Suppliers will revise their price expectations upward because they are receiving more than $3.00 per unit on average.
    C. Suppliers will not revise their price expectations because they are receiving $3.00 per unit on average.
    D. Suppliers will not revise their price expectations because their expectations are correct 50% of the time.

15. If suppliers have rational expectations, what will be the equilibrium price in this market?
    A. $2.00 per unit.
    B. $2.50 per unit.
    C. $3.00 per unit.
    D. $3.50 per unit.

335

Solutions

1. D. Only risk-adverse consumers have convex indifference curves. The indifference curves are linear if the consumer is risk-neutral and are concave if the consumer is risk-preferring.

2. A. When offered fair odds, the budget line coincides with an iso-expected value line.

3. A. When there are fair odds, all points on the budget line have the same expected value but different levels of risk. If the individual is indifferent among these points, he must be indifferent about risk. This is the case of a risk-neutral individual.

4. B. As in question 3, all points on the budget line have the same expected value but different levels of risk. Since the individual chooses the basket with the least level of risk, he must be risk-adverse.

5. C. A small movement along the budget line will move the risk-adverse individual to a higher indifference curve, so he is willing to accept a small bet. However, a bet that is too large is too risky and would put the risk-adverse individual on a lower indifference curve. This is illustrated by Exhibit 17-8 of the textbook.

6. B. The problem of adverse selection results when insurance companies know less about the odds than their customers do. This forces insurance companies to limit the amount of insurance available at favorable odds so that those with unfavorable odds will voluntarily select insurance at fair odds.

7. C. This is the definition of uninsurable risk. The insurance companies cannot be risk-neutral and cannot offer fair odds because there is no opportunity for diversification.

8. A. If insurance were offered at fair odds, the risk-adverse consumer would choose to be fully insured and would no longer have the incentive to avoid risky behavior. This is the problem of moral hazard.

9. A. Speculators will sell futures contracts since they believe that the spot price will be lower than expected in the future. They are planning to purchase the good at a low price in the future and resell it at the higher price they have "locked in" with the futures contract.

10. A. To calculate expected value, the possible outcomes are averaged together with each outcome being weighted by its probability. So the expected return is $1/2 \cdot -10 + 1/2 \cdot 20 = -5 + 10 = 5$ dollars. Since the stock sells for $50 dollars, this is a return of 10%.

11. C. To find standard deviation in this case, we take the spread in the outcomes and express it as a percentage. The spread between -$10 and $20 is $15. (In other words, the outcome is $5 \pm $15.) Since the stock sells for $50, this $15 spread is 30% of the current value.

12. B. The standard deviation of the portfolio can be less than the average of the standard deviations of the individual stocks because the portfolio is more diversified than the individual stocks.

13. B. If two portfolios have the same expected return and the same standard deviation, then they occupy the same point on the graph of the capital asset pricing model. Hence this model must assume that the investor cares only about expected return and standard deviation.

14. A. Suppliers will bring 30 units of output to the market. When demand is D_1 they will get a price of $1.00 per unit, and when demand is D_2 they will get a price of $3.00 per unit. So on average suppliers get a price of $2.00 per unit when they expect a price of $3.00 per unit. This will cause suppliers to revise their expectations about price downward.

15. B. By averaging together the quantities demanded at each possible price, the average demand is given by the accompanying table.

Average Demand :	P	Q
	$1.00	40
	$1.50	35
	$2.00	30
	$2.50	25
	$3.00	20
	$3.50	15

Comparing this table with the supply schedule, we find that quantity supplied equals the average quantity demanded at a price of $2.50 per unit.

Questions for Review

1. Contrast the indifference curves used to model the consumer's behavior under risk and uncertainty with the indifference curves used in the standard consumer choice model.

2. Define the terms *risk-neutral* and *risk-adverse.* When are we likely to observe risk-neutral preferences?

3. Briefly describe three reasons why an insurance company may not offer customers fair odds despite the fact that it is highly diversified.

4. How can insurers resolve the problems of moral hazard and adverse selection?

5. How can speculation in futures markets improve social welfare?

6. What is the market portfolio and why is it significant? How can an investor construct a market portfolio?

7. What are rational expectations? How will suppliers with rational expectations behave when facing uncertain demand?

Solutions

1. The standard consumer choice model uses *ex post* preferences which assume complete knowledge of relevant information. Also, the indifference curves in the standard model must be convex. When we model the consumer's attitudes towards risk and certainty, we use *ex ante* preferences—preferences which assume the state of the world is unknown. These preferences depend on the probabilities at which the various states of the world can occur. Furthermore, the indifference curves for these preferences can be convex, linear, or concave depending on whether the consumer is risk-adverse, risk-neutral, or risk-preferring.

2. An individual is risk-neutral when he is indifferent between two baskets with the same expected value regardless of risk. An individual is risk-adverse when among baskets with the same expected value he prefers the basket with the least amount of risk. When a gamble can be repeated sufficiently often in the long run, the law of large numbers guarantees that the gambler will earn the expected value of the gamble. We say that the risk has been diversified, and in this case preferences are likely to be risk-adverse since only expected value matters in the long run.

3. (i) In the problem of moral hazard, unobservable behavior by consumers prevents insurance companies from offering fair odds. Risk-adverse individuals would choose to be fully insured when offered fair odds. Individuals would then be indifferent as to which state of the world occurs and be more likely to engage in risky behavior; then the odds offered by the insurance companies would no longer be fair. (ii) In the problem of adverse selection, consumers know more about the odds than insurance companies do. Insurance companies cannot distinguish between those who have more favorable odds and those with less favorable odds, and this prevents them from offering unlimited amounts of insurance at favorable odds. (iii) In the problem of uninsurable risks, the insurance company cannot offer fair odds because it is unable to diversify its risks. This happens when the event insured against would affect a large number of people in the same way.

4. (i) With moral hazard, insurers can offer customers the less favorable odds which would be fair if they engage in unobservable risky behavior. Risk-adverse individuals then would purchase some insurance but not be fully insured, leaving them incentive to avoid risky behavior. (ii) With adverse selection, insurers can limit the amount of insurance available at the more favorable odds while offering an unlimited amount of insurance at the less favorable odds. The limit is set sufficiently low so that individuals with less favorable odds prefer the latter policy option. Under this scheme individuals voluntarily select the policy that offers them fair odds, but those individuals with the most favorable odds are unable to be fully insured.

5. Speculators will buy and sell futures contracts based on their beliefs about future demand, and this will bid up or down the price of futures contracts. This in turn will affect the suppliers' expectations about the price in the future, and the suppliers will readjust supplies accordingly. When speculators are correct about their expectations, their behavior alerts suppliers to changes in the marginal value of the commodity, and the resulting adjustments in supply will increase social gain.

6. The market portfolio is that portfolio which in combination with a risk-free asset offers the investor the highest expected return at any given level of risk (i.e., any given standard deviation). It is significant because the market portfolio is the only portfolio that a rational risk-adverse investor would choose to own. A market portfolio can be constructed by combining all the risky assets in the economy in proportion to their existing quantities.

7. When the expectations of market participants eventually lead to a situation where those expectations are on average correct, we say there are rational expectations. When demand fluctuates from day to day, rational expectations cause suppliers to adjust their quantity supplied until the corresponding price from the supply curve equals the price they receive on average. This equilibrium occurs where the supply curve crosses the average demand curve.

Problems for Analysis

1. Many states run lotteries to raise revenues to finance state spending. Usually the revenues from lottery ticket sales are over twice as large as the prize money paid out.

(i)   Suppose a $1 state lottery ticket offers a 1/1,000 chance of winning $500. How much prize money does the state pay out when it earns $1 million in lottery ticket revenues? What is the expected value of a lottery ticket? Is the state offering fair, favorable, or unfavorable odds in its lottery?

(ii)   Will a risk-adverse person purchase a lottery ticket? Explain. (Hint—How much risk is there when a person does *not* buy a lottery ticket?)

(iii)   On the axes below, give a sketch justifying your answer to part (ii).

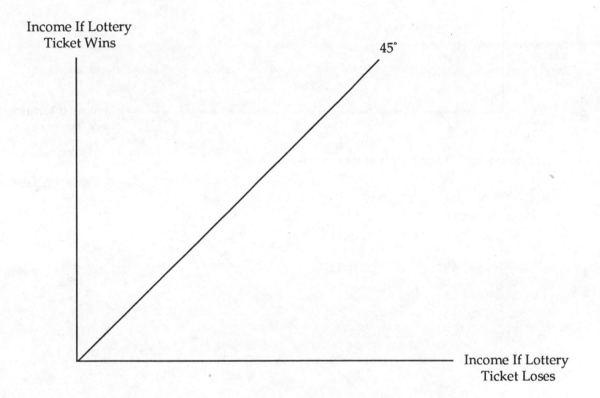

(iv)   Based on the analysis in parts (ii) and (iii), we would conclude that risk-adverse persons never purchase lottery tickets. Yet we observe that lotteries are very popular. Can you think of a reason why risk-adverse individuals may purchase lottery tickets?

2.   Suppose a tennis professional is about to play in the finals of a major championship. The winner of the tournament will receive $100,000, and the runner-up will receive $40,000. Before the match, her opponent offers to "split the pot" and agree that both will get ($100,000 + $40,000)/2 or $70,000 each no matter what the outcome of the final match.

(i)   Will the tennis professional agree to split the pot if she is risk preferring and believes she has a 50-50 chance of winning? On the axes below, give a diagram to justify your answer.

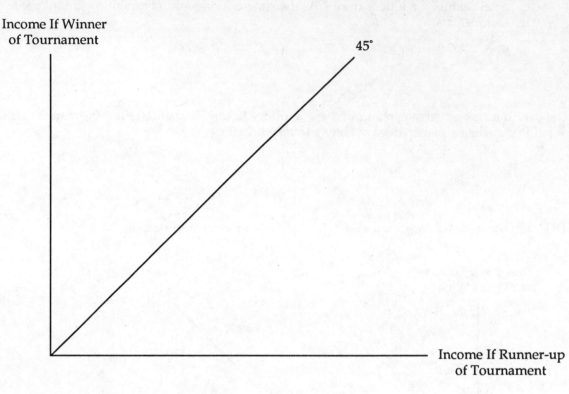

(ii) Repeat part (i) if the tennis player is risk-adverse.

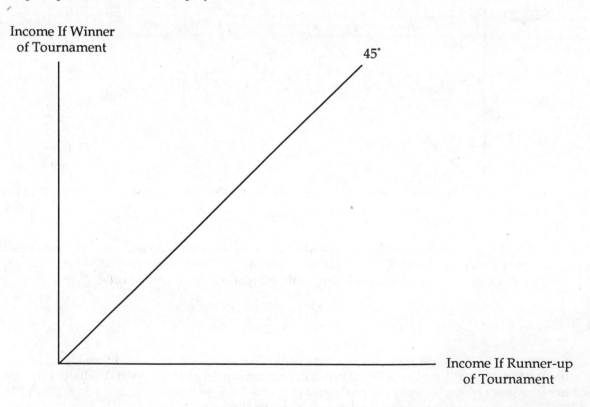

(iii) Prove that a risk-adverse player will choose not to split the pot if she believes she has a sufficiently large chance of winning the final match.

3. Consider the capital asset pricing model and suppose there is an increase in the return of the risk-free asset. How will this change affect (a) the expected return and the standard deviation of the market portfolio, (b) the expected return and the standard deviation of the typical consumer's portfolio? On the axes below, give a diagram to justify your answer.

Expected
Return

Standard
Deviation

Solutions

1. (i) The state will pay on 1/1,000 of the 1 million entries, so the state pays $1/1{,}000 \cdot 1{,}000{,}000 = 1{,}000$ winners. Each winner receives $500, so the state pays a total of $1{,}000 \cdot \$500 = \$500{,}000$. This is only half of the $1 million the state receives from selling lottery tickets.

   The lottery ticket pays $0 in 999 out of 1,000 cases and pays $500 in 1 out of every 1,000 cases. So the ticket's expected value is $\$0 \cdot 999/1{,}000 + \$500 \cdot 1/1{,}000 = \$0 + \$0.50 = \$0.50$. Since the $1.00 lottery ticket offers an expected value of only $0.50, the state is offering unfavorable odds in its lottery.

   (ii) If a risk-adverse person does not purchase a lottery ticket, he is in a risk-free situation—his income is the same whether or not the lottery ticket he can buy is a winner. Recall that a risk-adverse person will choose a risk-free basket of outcomes when offered fair odds. So if the lottery offered fair odds, the individual would not purchase a lottery ticket since he is already in a risk-free situation. Hence the risk-adverse person would certainly not purchase a lottery ticket when there are unfavorable odds.

   (iii)

Figure 17a

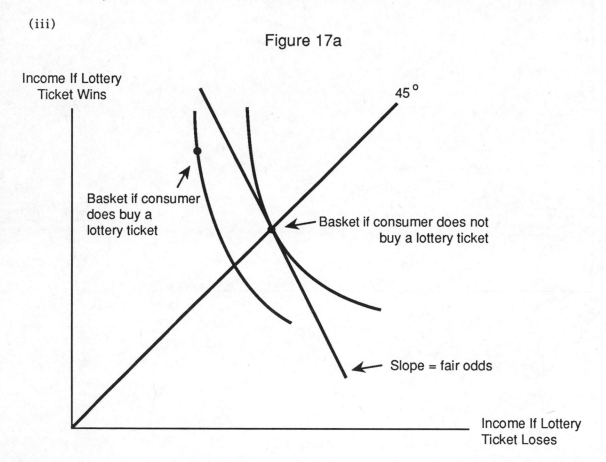

   (iv) One possibility is that people incorrectly perceive their chances in the lottery, thinking that the lottery offers a small bet at favorable odds. A more plausible explanation is that lotteries are often sold in the form of games, such as choosing lotto numbers or rubbing off lottery game may be enough to compensate him for bearing the minor risk he takes in the lottery.

2. (i) The tennis player has the same expected value whether or not she chooses to split the pot. Furthermore, splitting the pot is risk-free. If the tennis player is risk-preferring, she chooses the option that has the highest level of risk among options which have the same expected value. So she turns down the offer to split the pot.

Figure 17b

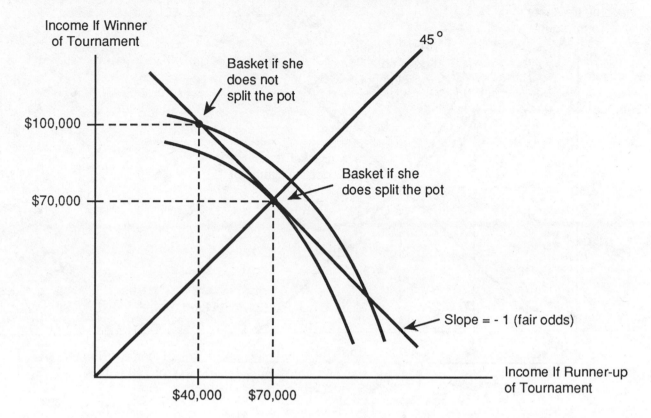

(ii) The risk-adverse tennis player will choose the option with the least amount of risk when faced with options which have the same expected value. In this case, the tennis player will choose the risk-free option of splitting the pot.

Figure 17c

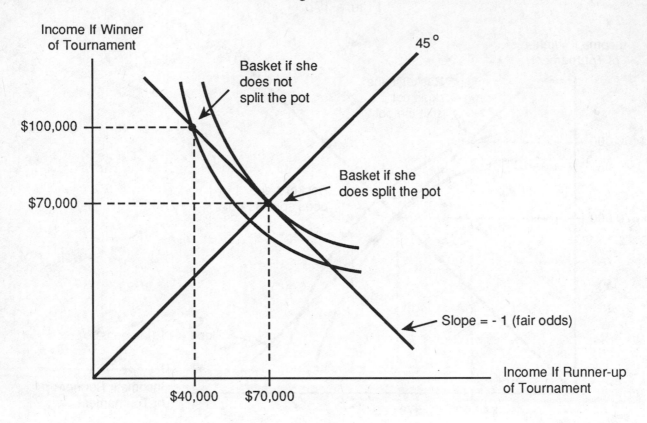

(iii) If the tennis player believes she has a better than 50-50 chance of winning the match, then the offer to split the pot is at less than fair odds. If she believes that she has a sufficiently good chance of winning the match, the tennis player would rather bear the risk of the final match than accept the unfavorable odds. This is illustrated by the diagram below.

Figure 17d

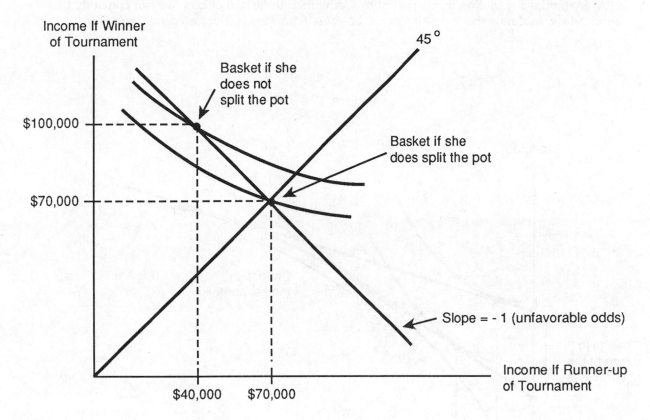

3. The market line will become flatter, so the market portfolio moves to the right on the efficient set. So the market portfolio has both a higher amount of risk and a higher expected return. To determine the effect on the typical investor's portfolio, consider the substitution and income effects. The substitution effect will cause the investor to accept a lower expected return in exchange for a lower amount of risk. Furthermore, the increase in the risk-free asset's return will increase the investor's real income. So the income effect causes the investor to desire a higher expected value at a lower standard deviation in his portfolio. Combining these two effects, we can conclude that the standard deviation of the investor's portfolio must fall. This is illustrated in Figure 17e.

Figure 17e

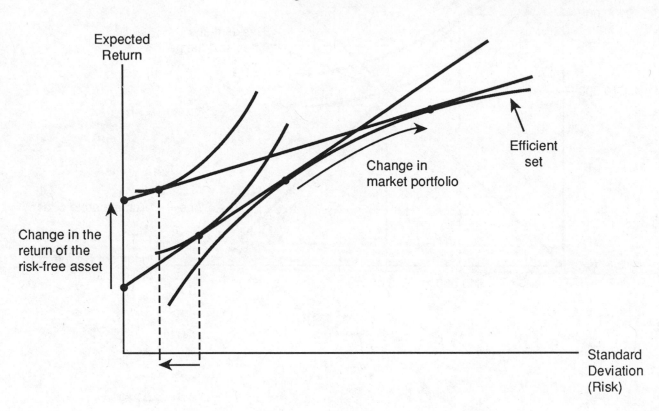

346

Solutions to Working Through the Graphs

Figure 17-1   Moral Hazard

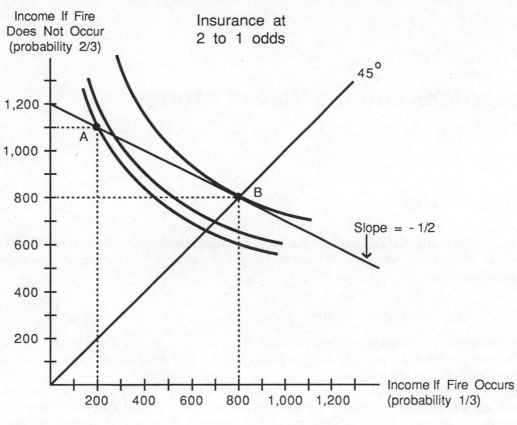

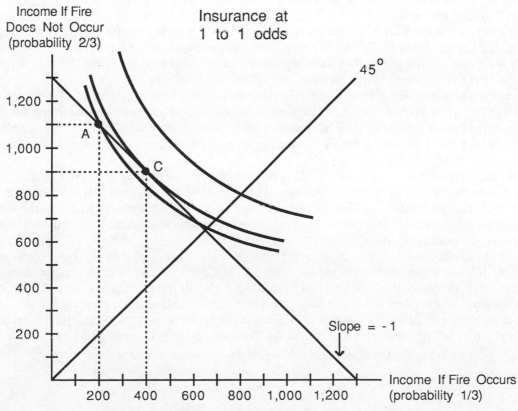

Chapter Eighteen

Transactions and the Role of Money

Chapter Summary

When we choose to hold money, we receive a valuable service—money makes it convenient for us to make transactions in the marketplace. As with any other good or service, there must then be a demand for money. In this chapter, we derive the demand for money and analyze the welfare consequences of inflation and deflation.

Section 18.1. The Demand for Money

Money is simply one way that we can choose to store our wealth—we can also choose to store wealth in homes, antiques, art, and a multitude of other goods. Hence the demand for money, like the demand for any other commodity, is not infinite.

To discuss the costs of holding money, we must first establish a *price level* which measures the price of goods in terms of money. In Chapter 3 we learned about some of the problems encountered when measuring the price level. To avoid these difficulties, we will assume there is a single good which has a price of P dollars per unit.

A person's *real balances* are the value of his money holdings in terms of goods. Suppose a person is holding $M of his wealth in the form of money. Since $1 can purchase 1/P units of the good, his $M can purchase M/P units of the good. This latter figure represents the consumer's real balances—the amount of the good that the consumer can purchase with his money holdings.

In general, the prefix *real* refers to something measured in terms of goods, and the prefix *nominal* refers to something measured in terms of money. For example, *real income* refers to the amount of goods that the consumer can purchase with his income, while *nominal income* (or *money income*) refers to the amount of money the consumer receives in earnings. We can always convert nominal quantities into real quantities by dividing by the price level.

One of the problems we face when deciding how to model the demand for money is choosing the best way to measure the price and quantity of money. For our model we will focus on the consumer's real balances. To measure the quantity of real balances, we define a unit of real balances as the amount of money required to purchase one unit of the good. This is convenient because it fixes the price of a unit of real balances at 1 unit of the good.

For example, suppose the price of the good is $5 per unit. Then a unit of real balances is represented by a $5 bill. If the consumer chooses to hold onto a $5 bill, then he sacrifices the opportunity to have 1 unit of the good. So the cost of holding real balances is 1 unit of the good per $5 bill. On the other hand, suppose the price of the good is 10¢ per unit. Then one unit of real balances is represented by a dime. The cost of holding real balances is now 1 unit of the good per dime, since the consumer sacrifices 1 unit of the good when he chooses to hold onto a dime. By appropriately choosing the way we measure real balances, we have fixed the price of real balances at 1.

Holding money is convenient—it's nice to be able to carry some of our wealth with us in an easily tradable form. This convenience, like any other good or service, provides value. The demand for real balances, like the demand for any other good or service, is determined by the consumer's marginal value. The marginal value of holding real balances follows the standard pattern, falling as the quantity of real balances increases. Since the price of real balances is fixed at 1, the consumer will choose to hold the quantity of real balances where his marginal value of holding real balances equals 1.

Changes in the demand for real balances will affect the price level. For example, consider the effect of a decrease in the demand for real balances. This of course lowers the equilibrium holdings of real balances. Since the level of real balances equals M/P as shown above, and since the total number of dollars M is fixed, the price level P must increase. People attempt to reduce their money holdings by increasing their spending, but on average cannot succeed since the total number of dollars is fixed. This results in the price level being bid up.

It is easy to see that the social gain in the market for real balances is not maximized. Since holding real balances does not affect the quantity of goods produced, the social marginal cost of holding real balances is zero. However, consumers base their holdings of real balances on a private marginal cost of one as shown above. Consumers therefore hold a suboptimal quantity of real balances.

Section 18.2. The Supply of Money and Equilibrium in the Money Market

The above model can be used to show the effects of changing the money supply. We will consider two possible actions by monetary authorities: a helicopter drop and seigniorage.

In a helicopter drop, monetary authorities print additional money and give it away to the populace. Suppose that there are M_0 dollars initially in circulation and the price level is initially at P_0. So the level of real balances is initially M_0/P_0. Now suppose a helicopter drop increases the amount of currency to M_1. Notice that the demand for real balances is unchanged by this action, so the equilibrium level of real balances is also unchanged. This implies that $M_0/P_0 = M_1/P_1$, where P_1 represents the price level after the helicopter drop. This equation can be rewritten as $P_1/P_0 = M_1/M_0$. The left-hand side represents the percentage increase in the price level, and the right-hand side represents the percentage increase in the amount of currency. We can conclude that **a helicopter drop which increases the supply of money will also increase the price level by the same percentage**.

Usually monetary authorities do not simply give away the money they print, but instead use it to purchase goods. Clearly monetary authorities gain from this process since they receive goods in exchange for formerly worthless pieces of paper. This gain is called *seigniorage*, and we can extend the above ideas to measure the amount the monetary authorities earn in seigniorage.

Return to our example of the helicopter drop and now suppose that the monetary authorities purchase goods with the new money instead of giving it away. As with the helicopter drop, we will find the price level increases by the same percentage as the money supply. Since the monetary authorities have printed $M_1 - M_0$ new dollars and are purchasing goods with these dollars at the new price level P_1, the gain to monetary authorities is $(M_1 - M_0)/P_1$ units of the good. If monetary authorities gain, who loses? Anyone that held money lost because the price level increased. People could originally purchase M_0/P_0 units of the good; the people holding those M_0 dollars could now only purchase M_0/P_1 units after the monetary authorities' actions. People who held money had a net loss of $M_0/P_0 - M_0/P_1 = M_1/P_1 - M_0/P_1 = (M_1 - M_0)/P_1$ units of the good, which is the same amount as the monetary authorities gain. So in addition to raising the price level, seigniorage also transfers wealth away from those who hold money to the monetary authorities.

Section 18.3. Inflation

Inflation is a continuous rise in the price level. The analysis of the helicopter drop suggests that if monetary authorities continually increase the money supply at some fixed percentage, then prices would continuously rise at that same percentage. However, we will see that this is not the full story because inflation also changes the price of holding real balances.

To see this, suppose you want to hold and maintain 1 unit of real balances—in other words, you want to hold enough money to be able to purchase 1 unit of the good at any point in time. In addition to the money you hold in the first year, you must increase your money holdings every year due to the inflation. Let's suppose that inflation is 5%. Then your real balances are eroding by 5% annually, so you must sacrifice an additional .05 units of consumption annually to hold enough money to maintain your unit of real balances. This additional maintenance payment is a perpetuity of .05 units of consumption. From Chapter 16, we know that the value of this perpetuity is $.05/r$, where r is the real interest rate. So the price of holding a unit of real balances has risen from 1 unit of the good to $1 + .05/r$ units. In general, if **inflation is x percent and the real interest rate is r percent, then the price of holding and maintaining a unit of real balances increases to $1 + x/r$.**

We see that inflation raises the price of real balances. One consequence of this is a phenomenon known as overshooting. Suppose the money supply and the price level are growing at 5 percent, then monetary authorities announce that they will increase money supply growth to 10 percent. As we've already seen, inflation must also be 10 percent to keep the level of real balances at equilibrium. But the higher inflation also raises the price of holding real balances from $1 + .05/r$ to $1 + .10/r$. This reduces the equilibrium level of real balances, so initially prices must increase by more than 10 percent to attain this lower equilibrium level. Hence there must be a period of overshooting—a period where inflation is higher than the rate of money growth—before the new equilibrium is reached.

Another consequence of the effect that inflation has on the price of real balances is that inflation lowers social gain. Recall that the social marginal cost of holding real balances is zero, while the private marginal cost when prices are constant equals one. Inflation pushes a person's marginal cost of holding real balances above one, causing people to hold still lower amounts of real balances. This in turn further reduces the social gain received from the convenience of holding real balances. So inflation acts like a tax on real balances and creates a deadweight loss.

To get the maximum social gain from holding real balances, we would like to lower the private marginal cost to the social marginal cost of zero. This could occur in a deflationary world. When prices fall by x percent annually, the price of holding real balances falls to $1 - x/r$. This would be zero if the rate of deflation equals the real interest rate. So the optimal rate of deflation—the rate that gives us the most social gain in the money market—is equal to the real rate of interest.

Working Through the Graphs—Social Welfare Under Inflation and Deflation

Inflation and deflation can affect the price of holding real balances and hence can affect social welfare. Use Figure 18-1 to show how social gain changes when there is inflation or deflation; your final results should resemble Exhibits 18-2, 18-5, and 18-6 of the textbook.

Step 1. When there is no inflation or deflation, the price of holding real balances is simply 1. This is because you are sacrificing the opportunity to have 1 unit of the good when you choose to carry a unit of real balances. In panel A, find and shade in the social gain in this case. Notice that there are two parts to this social gain: (1) the triangle above the price representing the consumer's surplus from holding real balances, and (2) the rectangle below the price showing the positive externality created by holding money.

Also notice that this is not the maximum social gain possible. Since the marginal value of holding money still exceeds the social marginal cost of zero, social gain could be increased. In panel A, also shade in the additional social gain that could be obtained.

Step 2. Recall that when there is inflation, the price of real balances rises to $1 + x/r$, where x is the inflation rate and r is the real rate of interest. Suppose inflation is 10 percent and the real interest rate is also 10 percent. First calculate the new price of holding real balances. Then on panel B, find and shade in the social gain we receive from holding real balances and the additional social gain that

Figure 18-1   Social Welfare Under Inflation and Deflation

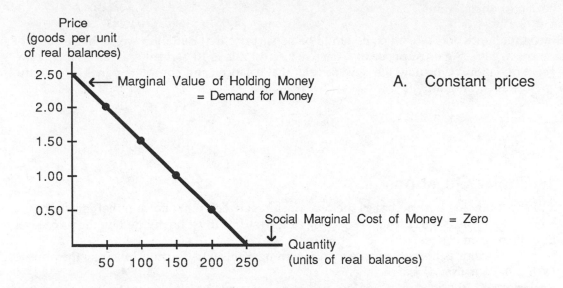

A.   Constant prices

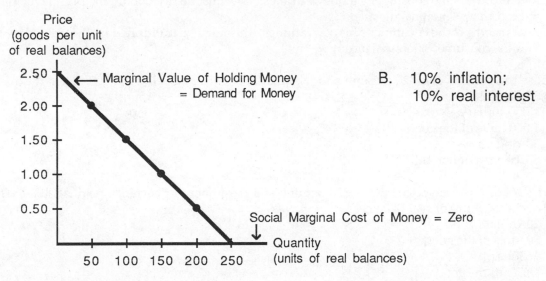

B.   10% inflation;
     10% real interest

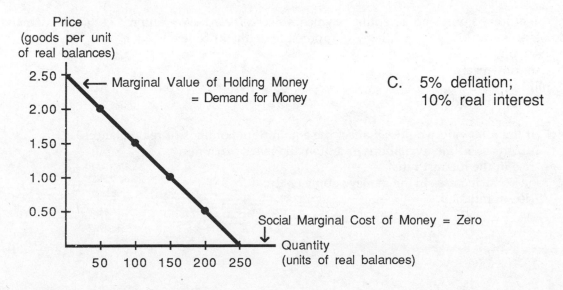

C.   5% deflation;
     10% real interest

could have been obtained. You should find that inflation created a deadweight loss; the social gain received in panel B should be significantly smaller than that in panel C. Like a tax, inflation adversely affected social gain

Step 3. Since inflation works like a tax, it should be no surprise that deflation works like a subsidy and can increase social gain. Again suppose that the real interest rate is 10 percent, but now suppose we have 5 percent deflation. Calculate the new price of real balances and complete panel C to verify that deflation increases social gain.

Multiple Choice Questions

1. Which of the following best describes the relationship between real and nominal income?
   A. Nominal income is the consumer's money earnings; this must be divided by the price level to find the consumer's real income.
   B. Nominal income is the consumer's money earnings; this must be multiplied by the price level to find the consumer's real income.
   C. Real income is the consumer's money earnings; this must be divided by the price level to find the consumer's nominal income.
   D. Real income is the consumer's money earnings; this must be multiplied by the price level to find the consumer's nominal income.

2. Suppose the price level is $20 per unit and the amount of currency held is $1,000. Then the quantity of real balances is
   A. 1,000 dollars.
   B. 1,000 units of the good.
   C. 50 dollars.
   D. 50 twenty-dollar bills.

3. Again suppose that the price level is $20 per unit and the amount of currency held is $1,000. Then the price of one unit of real balances is
   A. 20 dollars.
   B. 50 units of the good.
   C. 1 dollar.
   D. 1 unit of the good.

4. Suppose grocery stores start accepting payments by credit card. We can predict that the demand for real balances would _____, putting _____ pressure on the price level.
   A. rise; upward
   B. rise; downward
   C. fall; upward
   D. fall; downward

5. Which of the following would *not* affect the equilibrium holdings of real balances?
   A. An increase in the availability of automatic teller machines.
   B. A rise in the interest rate.
   C. A one-time increase in the money supply.
   D. A rise in inflation.

6. Suppose the inflation rate has held steady at 5 percent for several years. Which of the following could have caused this situation?
   A. A helicopter drop that increased the money supply by 5 percent.
   B. A one-time 5 percent increase in the money supply with seigniorage.
   C. Steady 5 percent annual growth in the money supply.
   D. An increase in the growth of the money supply from 2 to 5 percent.

7. Suppose we observe a single 5 percent rise in the price level that has no effect on people's real incomes. Which of the following could have caused this situation?
   A. A helicopter drop that increased the money supply by 5 percent.
   B. A one-time 5 percent increase in the money supply with seigniorage.
   C. Steady 5 percent annual growth in the money supply.
   D. An increase in the growth of the money supply from 2 to 5 percent.

8. Suppose we observe inflation first rising above 5 percent temporarily and then settling down to the 5 percent level. Which of the following could have caused this situation?
   A. A helicopter drop that increased the money supply by 5 percent.
   B. A one-time 5 percent increase in the money supply with seigniorage.
   C. Steady 5 percent annual growth in the money supply.
   D. An increase in the growth of the money supply from 2 to 5 percent.

9. Suppose we observe a single 5 percent rise in the price level which lowers the average consumer's real income. Which of the following could have caused this situation?
   A. A helicopter drop that increased the money supply by 5 percent.
   B. A one-time 5 percent increase in the money supply with seigniorage.
   C. Steady 5 percent annual growth in the money supply.
   D. An increase in the growth of the money supply from 2 to 5 percent.

10. Suppose the real rate of interest is 5 percent. If inflation rises from 10 to 15 percent, what will happen to the price of holding real balances?
    A. It will also increase from 10 to 15 percent.
    B. It will increase from 2 to 3 units of the good.
    C. It will increase from 3 to 4 units of the good.
    D. It will not change since the demand for real balances is not affected.

Figure 18a

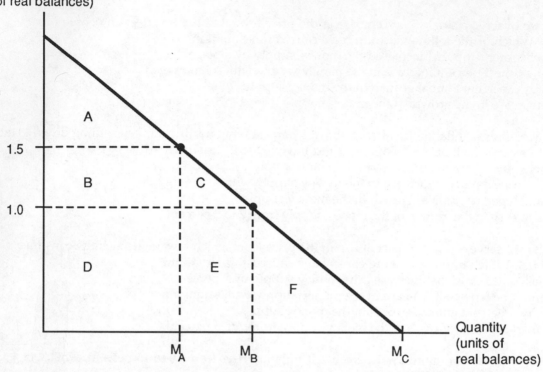

Price
(goods per unit
of real balances)

11. Assuming there is no inflation or deflation, what quantity of real balances will the consumer choose to hold?
    A. M_A.
    B. M_B.
    C. M_C.
    D. Some quantity between M_B and M_C.

12. In question 11, consumer's surplus is measured by
    A. area A.
    B. area A + B + C.
    C. area A + B + C + D + E.
    D. area A + B + C + D + E + F.

13. In question 11, the social gain attained is measured by
    A. area A.
    B. area A + B + C.
    C. area A + B + C + D + E.
    D. area A + B + C + D + E + F.

14. If the real interest rate is 10 percent, when will the consumer choose to hold M_A units of real balances?
    A. When inflation is 0 percent.
    B. When inflation is 5 percent.
    C. When inflation is also 10 percent.
    D. When deflation is 5 percent.

15. If the real interest rate is 10 percent, when will the social gain from holding money be maximized?
    A. When inflation is 0 percent.
    B. When inflation is also 10 percent.
    C. When deflation is 5 percent.
    D. When deflation is also 10 percent.

Solutions

1. A. The prefix "nominal" means "measured in terms of money," and the prefix "real" means "measured in terms of goods." To convert from nominal to real, we divide by the price level.

2. D. We use the formula M/P to calculate real balances, where M is the amount of money holdings and P is the price level. We define one unit of real balances to be the amount of currency required to purchase one unit of the good, which in this case is a twenty-dollar bill.

3. D. Our definition of a unit of real balances is chosen to guarantee that the price of holding real balances always equals one unit of the good when there is no inflation or deflation. In this example, when the consumer chooses to hold a twenty-dollar bill (i.e., a unit of real balances), he sacrifices the opportunity to purchase one unit of the good.

4. C. Consumers now get less convenience from holding money since they can make more purchases by credit card. This lowers the demand for real balances and lowers the equilibrium level of real balances M/P. Since the number of dollars M has not changed, the price level P must rise for real balances to fall to the new equilibrium level.

5. C. Increased availability of automatic tellers and an increase in the interest rate both lower the demand for real balances and hence lower the equilibrium quantity of real balances. A rise in inflation increases the price of holding money, causing us to move up the demand curve to a new lower level of real balances. A one-time increase in the money supply does not affect demand or the equilibrium level of real balances; instead the price level will rise to keep real balances at the desired level.

6. C. 5 percent growth in the money supply must be accompanied by 5 percent growth in the price level to maintain the equilibrium level of real balances. As long as this inflation is steady, the price of real balances will not change and will not affect this equilibrium quantity of real balances.

7. A. A helicopter drop does not affect the demand or price of real balances. The only effect of a helicopter drop is to increase the money supply and the price level by the same percentage.

8. D. Overshooting occurs when there in an increase in the growth of the money supply. The new higher level of inflation raises the price of holding real balances; this implies that people desire to hold a lower level of real balances. Inflation must temporarily rise above the new equilibrium rate for real balances to be lowered to the desired level.

9. B. As with a helicopter drop, the money supply and the price level must increase by the same percentage to maintain the equilibrium level of real balances. When monetary authorities choose to purchase goods with the newly printed money, income is transferred from people who were holding money to the monetary authorities.

10. C. The price of holding real balances equals $1 + x/r$ where x is the inflation rate and r is the real interest rate. Since r is 5 percent, the price of a unit of real balances is $1 + 10/5 = 1 + 2 = 3$ units of the good when inflation is 10 percent. Similarly, one unit of real balances costs $1 + 15/5 = 1 + 3 = 4$ units of the good when inflation is 15 percent.

11. B. When there is no inflation or deflation, the cost of holding one unit of real balances equals 1 unit of the good. Consumers will choose to hold the quantity of real balances where their marginal value equals 1.

12. B. Consumer's surplus is measured by the area beneath the demand curve above the price paid and out to the quantity of real balances held.

13. C. The social gain attained equals the consumer's surplus plus the value of the positive externality generated. Consumer's surplus is measured by area A + B + C. The positive externality created from holding real balances is area D + E—the difference between the private marginal cost of 1 and the social marginal cost of 0 out to the quantity of real balances held.

14. B. When the inflation rate is x percent and the real interest rate is 10 percent, the price of holding real balances will be $1 + x/10$. This equals 1.5 when the inflation rate is 5 percent.

15. D. The optimal rate of deflation is equal to the real interest rate, for then the price of holding real balances will fall to zero.

Questions for Review

1. How are the quantity and price of real balances measured? Why is this a convenient way of looking at the market for money?

2. What is the demand for real balances and why is it downward sloping?

3. Why does the holding of real balances create a positive externality? What should the price of real balances be if we want the maximum social gain possible?

4. Compare and contrast the effects of a helicopter drop and a one-shot increase in the money supply with seigniorage.

5. Explain how inflation increases the price of holding real balances.

6. Compare and contrast the effects of (a) a one-shot increase in the money supply and (b) an increase in the rate of growth of the money supply.

7. In what way is inflation like a tax? In what way is deflation like a subsidy? What is the optimal rate of deflation?

Solutions

1. One unit of real balances is defined to be the amount of currency required to purchase one unit of the good. The price of real balances is the amount of the good the consumer sacrifices when he chooses to hold a unit of real balances. This is convenient because the price of real balances will equal one when there is no inflation or deflation. For example, if the price of the good is $100 per unit, then the quantity of real balances is measured in $100 bills. Since the consumer sacrifices 1 unit of the good to hold onto a $100 bill, the price of a unit of real balances (i.e., the price of a $100 bill) must equal 1 unit of the good.

2. The demand for real balances is determined by the marginal value the consumer receives from the convenience of holding real balances. As with any other good or service, the marginal value of this convenience falls as the quantity of real balances held increases, making the demand curve downward sloping.

3. When a person chooses to hold real balances, he sacrifices the opportunity to purchase goods. This creates a positive externality by putting downward pressure on the demand for goods and the price level, which in turn puts upward pressure on others' holdings of real balances. (For this latter fact, recall that real balances are calculated by the formula M/P.) The positive externality can also be seen by noting that the private marginal cost of holding real balances equals 1 unit of the good, but the social marginal cost is zero since holding real balances does not affect the quantity of goods available in the economy. For the maximum social gain possible, we want to lower the price of holding real balances (i.e., the private marginal cost) to the social marginal cost of zero.

4. The increase in the money supply in both cases will not affect the demand for real balances and hence not affect the equilibrium quantity of real balances. Since real balances are calculated by the formula M/P, the price level P must increase by the same percentage as the increase in M caused by the monetary authorities.

    The only difference between the two cases is that there will also be a transfer of income under seigniorage. By purchasing goods with the newly printed money, the monetary authorities gain. Since purchasing power will be eroded by the higher price level resulting from the increase in the money supply, those holding money at the time of the monetary authorities' actions will lose. $(M_1 - M_0)/P_1$ units of the good will be transferred from people holding money to the monetary authorities.

5. Inflation will erode the purchasing power of real balances held. To keep enough real balances to purchase one unit of the good, this erosion of purchasing power must be replaced annually. If the rate of inflation is x percent, then the consumer must sacrifice an additional $x/100$ units of the good annually to continue holding one unit of real balances. So inflation forces the consumer to pay a perpetuity in order to maintain his unit of real balances. The size of this perpetuity is given by x/r where r is the real interest rate, and so inflation increases the price of holding a unit of real balances to $1 + x/r$ units of the good.

6. (a) As shown in question 4 above, a one-shot increase in the money supply will increase the price level by the same percentage. For example, a 10% increase in the money supply will increase the price level by 10%. There will be no overshooting in this case since there has been no change in the inflation rate and hence no change in the price or equilibrium level of real balances. (b) Like the previous case, an increase in the growth rate of the money supply will cause an identical increase in the inflation rate. For example, if the growth in the money supply is increased from 5 to 10 percent, then inflation will also increase from 5 to 10 percent. However overshooting will occur in this case

since higher inflation has increased the price of real balances and lowered the equilibrium quantity of real balances. In our example, if the price level only increased by 10 percent then the quantity of real balances would remain unchanged. So the price level must temporarily increase by more than 10 percent to drive down the quantity of real balances to the new equilibrium level.

7. Like a tax, inflation increases the price of real balances and so creates a deadweight loss. Furthermore, inflation also transfers income away from people holding money to the monetary authorities if there is seigniorage. Deflation, like a subsidy, will lower the price of real balances. As we showed in question 3 above, to maximize social gain we want to lower the price of holding real balances to zero. The price of real balances under deflation equals $1 - x/r$, where x is the rate of deflation and r is the real rate of interest. This price equals zero when $x = r$, so the optimal rate of deflation (i.e., the one that maximizes social gain in the money market) equals the real interest rate.

Problems for Analysis

1. In this problem, consider a world in which apples are the only commodity.

   (i)   In previous chapters, we measured the social gain obtained in the market for a good in terms of "dollars." What are the appropriate units of measurement for the social gain obtained in the market for real balances?

   (ii) Suppose the price level increases from $10 per unit to $20 per unit due to a one-time increase in the money supply. How does this affect (a) the demand for real balances and (b) the social gain obtained from holding real balances?

2. Suppose checking account balances are the only form of money held in the economy. Furthermore assume that checking account balances earn R percent interest. (Note—This rate may or may not equal the real interest rate of r percent.)

   (i)   What is the price of holding a unit of real balances when the inflation rate is x percent?

   (ii) When would a zero rate of inflation be optimal?

3. Many verses in the Old Testament of the Bible preach against the charging of interest (or "usury" as the Bible calls it). For example Exodus 22:25 says, "If thou lend money to any of my people that is poor by thee, thou shalt not be to him as an usurer, neither shalt thou lay upon him usury." Also Leviticus 25:35-37 says, "And if thy brother be waxen poor, and fallen in decay with thee; then thou shalt relieve him: yea, though he be a stranger, or a sojourner... Take thou no usury of him, or increase: but fear thy God... Thou shalt not give him thy money upon usury...."

Suppose we take these verses literally and require that all loans be made at a nominal interest rate of zero. Would this be beneficial for the economy in any way? (Hint—According to Chapter 16, how are the real and nominal interest rates related?)

Solutions

1. (i) The social gain in the market for real balances is measured in terms of apples. The marginal value of holding a unit of real balances is the number of apples the consumer would be willing to sacrifice for the convenience of keeping some of his wealth in the form of money. Similarly, the marginal cost is the number of apples sacrificed when the consumer chooses to hold and maintain a unit of real balances. Since the social gain is the difference between marginal value and marginal cost out to the amount of real balances held, this social gain must be measured in terms of apples. (In other words, each rectangle in the area that makes up the social gain represents some number of apples.)

   (ii) Neither the demand for real balances nor the social gain changes since an increase in the price level does not affect the marginal value of holding real balances. The only change in the graph showing the market for real balances is the way we measure real balances. When the price is $10 per apple, a unit of real balances is a $10 bill. When the price rises to $20 per unit, a unit of real balances is now a $20 bill. Notice that a unit of real balances can purchase one apple in both cases. So the marginal value of holding a unit of real balances (i.e., the number of apples in convenience the consumer receives from carrying enough additional real balances to buy an apple) must be the same in both cases.

2. (i) We need to calculate the cost of holding and maintaining a unit of real balances. Inflation will erode x percent of your real balances annually, but the interest on your checking account balances will boost your real balances by R percent annually. The net effect is that your real balances are eroding at $(x - R)$ percent annually. Like in the standard case, to maintain a unit of real balances you must pay a perpetuity valued at $(x - R)/r$ units of the good. So the total cost of a unit of real balances is $1 + (x - R)/r$ units of the good.

   (ii) For a zero percent inflation rate to be optimal, the price of a unit of real balances must equal zero when $x = 0$. Using the answer from part (i), this gives us the following series of equations—

$$
\begin{aligned}
1 + (0 - R)/r &= 0 \\
1 - R/r &= 0 \\
1 &= R/r \\
r &= R .
\end{aligned}
$$

So if the inflation rate is zero and if checking accounts earn the market rate of interest (i.e., if $x = 0$ and $r = R$), then the cost of holding real balances will be zero and the social gain will be maximized.

3. Again suppose the real interest rate is r percent and the deflation rate is x percent. Recall from Chapter 16 that the nominal interest rate equals the real interest rate plus the inflation rate. Alternatively we would say that the nominal interest rate equals the real interest rate minus the deflation rate. But if the deflation rate is optimal, then it equals the real interest rate (i.e., $x = r$). This would make the nominal interest rate (which equals $r - x$) equal to zero. So if the monetary authorities continually reduce the money supply to attain the optimal rate of deflation, then the nominal interest rate on loans would be 0 percent as the Bible suggests.

Solutions to Working Through the Graphs

Figure 18-1 Social Welfare Under Inflation and Deflation

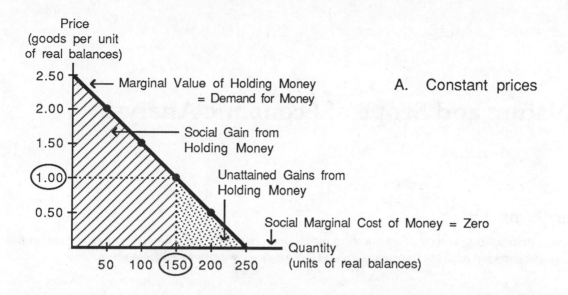

A. Constant prices

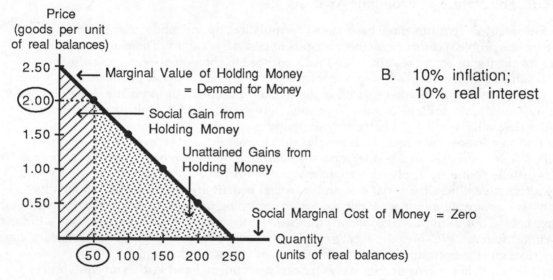

B. 10% inflation;
   10% real interest

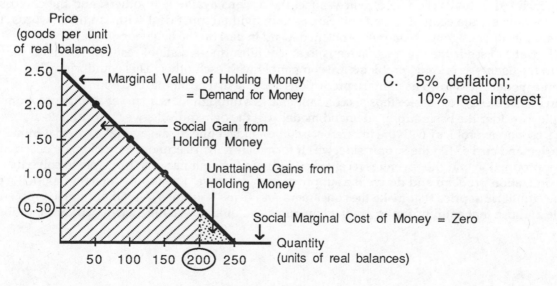

C. 5% deflation;
   10% real interest

Chapter Nineteen

The Nature and Scope of Economic Analysis

Chapter Summary

This chapter concludes our survey of microeconomic theory. To finish our course of study, we reexamine the types of problems we address in economics and the methods we use to address them.

Section 19.1. The Nature of Economic Analysis

Most economic analysis requires three basic steps: formulation, optimization, and equilibrium.

Any economic problem is driven by the trade-offs imposed by scarcity. There are competing alternatives for the use of scarce resources, and we are forced to choose between these alternatives. To model an economic problem, the first step is to formulate or describe this war between scarcity and desire. We must (1) show the trade-off faced in the economic problem by explicitly describing the costs—the forgone opportunities—of the competing alternatives, and (2) explicitly describe the benefits—the desirability—of the competing alternatives.

The second step in economic analysis is to solve each agent's economic problem. We assume that agents will optimize and choose the alternative for which the benefits most outweigh the costs. This optimum is usually found by applying the equimarginal principle, which states that the agent will choose the alternative where marginal cost and marginal benefit are equated. The rationality assumption—the assumption that economic agents act according to the equimarginal principle—is the driving force behind our solutions to economic problems. Furthermore, we do not restrict our solution to one set of circumstances. We solve the agent's economic problem under many hypothetical situations so we can describe how the optimum changes when the agent's constraints change.

The final step is to show how agents' economic decisions interact and lead to an equilibrium situation. Each individual's economic choices affect the options available to others, and the choices made by others affect the economic trade-off that each individual must deal with. In other words, the actual constraints in one agent's economic problem depend in part on the behavior of other economic agents. We want to see if this interaction leads to an equilibrium—a state of rest—in which all the solutions to the agents' economic problems are compatible with each other. This equilibrium "solves" the economic model and allows us to make predictions about actual economic behavior.

We have seen these three basic steps of economic analysis throughout our survey of microeconomics. For example, consider the basic supply/demand model. On the demand side, we (1) formulate a consumer's economic problem with the indifference curve/budget line model and (2) solve that model to derive the demand curve. On the supply side, we (1) formulate a firm's economic problem by describing the costs of production and the revenues received and (2) use the equimarginal principle to solve the profit-maximization problem and derive the supply curve. To "solve" the supply/demand model, we (3) find the equilibrium price that make the consumers' and firms' solutions to their economic problems compatible and use that equilibrium to predict how price and quantity change when market conditions change.

The economic models which result from the procedure outlined above are likely to be abstract and can never capture the full complexities of actual situations. Why then are these models of any interest? They allow us to develop a "feel" for how the economy works. They help us develop a sense of which factors really matter in the economy and which factors are truly unimportant. Economic models are a means of developing our intuition for the cause-and-effect relationships that hold in the actual economy.

Section 19.2. The Rationality Assumption

One of the most difficult problems faced by the student of economics is learning how to make the right simplifying assumptions in economic models. When being introduced to a new economic model, students are frequently disturbed by its assumptions. However there is no way to avoid making assumptions, even assumptions that are blatantly false. The economy is simply too complex to describe fully and accurately. On one hand we need to make simplifying assumptions to make our economic models tractable, yet on the other hand we want assumptions that do not affect our results in a crucial way. It is difficult to learn how to deal with this trade-off between simplicity and robustness. This is only learned by experience—by studying the models which economists have found successful in the past and working on economic problems on your own.

For example, consider the rationality assumption that underlies all of economic analysis. People in everyday life are clearly not always rational; people do not carry little calculators in their heads to measure and compare their marginal costs and marginal benefits. So why do economists persist in using the rationality assumption in their models of behavior? Such models have proven their value by allowing us to make accurate predictions about actual economic behavior in actual economic situations. This is because people in our world are often rational enough so that there are no unexploited profit opportunities; economic behavior in this situation closely resembles that in the imaginary world of our models where people are fully rational. The resulting bottom line is that the rationality assumption simplifies our models but leaves them robust.

Section 19.3. What Is an Economic Explanation?

Economists, like other social scientists, attempt to explain and predict human behavior. An economic explanation is distinguished from those offered by other disciplines by the economist's emphasis on rational decision making under the constraints imposed by scarcity.

Phenomena are frequently explained away by claims that people are tricked or fooled into their actions. Selling a good at $0.99 instead of an even $1.00 is dismissed as "a sales gimmick." Firms use expensive celebrity endorsements to fool people into thinking that the endorsement guarantees a higher quality. "Free" offers lure people into buying goods that they normally wouldn't. These types of explanations openly contradict the economists' assumption of rational behavior. Whether or not there are grains of truth in such explanations is irrelevant—they are not economic explanations.

Other explanations of phenomena are based on tradition or changes in people's tastes. Firms use celebrity endorsements and brand names because people prefer these to generic goods. Bars offer "happy hours" because it has become traditional to do so. People contribute to charitable organizations and political campaigns because they want to. These could be called "wimpy" economic explanations. Such explanations take the easy way out and avoid looking for deeper, more satisfying, and more testable explanations of the economic behavior.

Economic explanations rely on rationality, showing that economic behavior is the natural result of comparing benefits and costs. A firm uses celebrity endorsements to communicate the information to consumers that it is not a fly-by-night firm. Stockholders choose to pay corporate executives high salaries to give them the incentive to take more risks. A person dresses well for interviews to provide a signal to employers that he has other unobservable skills. Economists realize that a proper understanding of incentives and rational behavior can go far in explaining human behavior.

Section 19.4. The Scope of Economic Analysis

Traditionally economists restricted their study to the production, exchange, and consumption of marketable commodities. But in the past 30 years, economists have shown that their ideas can be successfully applied to a much wider variety of problems. The economic approach has been used to study love and marriage, the decision to have children, criminal behavior, legal institutions, and even medieval agriculture. Economic ideas appear to apply to all humans—past and present—and even to animals. Economics—our study of scarcity and choice, incentives and rational behavior—surrounds us every day.

Questions for Review

A specific list of review questions is unnecessary at this stage of the game. We hope that our survey of microeconomic theory has sharpened your economic intuition and given you a better understanding of the basic tools of our discipline. Reflect on the economic models we have introduced throughout the text—notice the basic steps of formulation, optimization, and equilibrium in these models. Reconsider the many examples in the text—notice the roles of incentives and rational behavior in the explanations offered for the phenomena. Finally, search out your own economic problems and try to offer your own economic explanations—the final problem set of the textbook gives some suggestions. Even though economics preaches some very simple ideas, it is difficult to become a good economist. Practice and experience are the best teachers.

The Use of Knowledge in Society[*]

F. A. Hayek

I

What is the problem we wish to solve when we try to construct a rational economic order?

On certain familiar assumptions the answer is simple enough. *If* we possess all the relevant information, *if* we can start out from a given system of preferences and *if* we command complete knowledge of available means, the problem which remains is purely one of logic. That is, the answer to the question of what is the best use of the available means is implicit in our assumptions. The conditions which the solution of this optimum problem must satisfy have been fully worked out and can be stated best in mathematical form: put at their briefest, they are that the marginal rates of substitution between any two commodities or factors must be the same in all their different uses.

This, however, is emphatically *not* the economic problem which society faces. And the economic calculus which we have developed to solve this logical problem, though an important step toward the solution of the economic problem of society, does not yet provide an answer to it. The reason for this is that the "data" from which the economic calculus starts are never for the whole society "given" to a single mind which could work out the implications, and can never be so given.

The peculiar character of the problem of a rational economic order is determined precisely by the fact that the knowledge of the circumstances of which we must make use never exists in concentrated or integrated form, but solely as the dispersed bits of incomplete and frequently contradictory knowledge which all the separate individuals possess. The economic problem of society is thus not merely a problem of how to allocate "given" resources—if "given" is taken to mean given to a single mind which deliberately solves the problem set by these "data." It is rather a problem of how to secure the best use of resources known to any of the members of society, for ends whose relative importance only these individuals know. Or, to put it briefly, it is a problem of the utilization of knowledge not given to anyone in its totality.

This character of the fundamental problem has, I am afraid been rather obscured than illuminated by many of the recent refinements of economic theory, particularly by many of the uses made of mathematics. Though the problem with which I want primarily to deal in this paper is the problem of a rational economic organization, I shall in its course be led again and again to point to its close connections with certain methodological questions. Many of the points I wish to make are indeed conclusions toward which diverse paths of reasoning have unexpectedly converged. But as I now see these problems, this is no accident. It seems to me that many of the current disputes with regard to both economic theory and economic policy have their common origin in a misconception about the nature of the economic problem of society. This misconception in turn is due to an erroneous transfer to social phenomena of the habits of thought we have developed in dealing with the phenomena of nature.

[*]Reprinted by permission of the American Economic Association from *American Economic Review*, September 1945.

II

In ordinary language we describe by the word "planning" the complex of interrelated decisions about the allocation of our available resources. All economic activity is in this sense planning; and in any society in which many people collaborate, this planning, whoever does it, will in some measure have to be based on knowledge which, in the first instance, is not given to the planner but to somebody else, which somehow will have to be conveyed to the planner. The various ways in which the knowledge on which people base their plans is communicated to them is the crucial problem for any theory explaining the economic process. And the problem of what is the best way of utilizing knowledge initially dispersed among all the people is at least one of the main problems of economic policy—or of designing an efficient economic system.

The answer to this question is closely connected with that other question which arises here, that of *who* is to do the planning. It is about this question that all the dispute about "economic planning" centers. This is not a dispute about whether planning is to be done or not. It is a dispute as to whether planning is to be done centrally, by one authority for the whole economic system, or is to be divided among many individuals. Planning in the specific sense in which the term is used in contemporary controversy necessarily means central planning—direction of the whole economic system according to one unified plan. Competition, on the other hand, means decentralized planning by many separate persons. The half-way house between the two, about which many people talk but which few like when they see it, is the delegation of planning to organized industries, or, in other words, monopoly.

Which of these systems is likely to be more efficient depends mainly on the question under which of them we can expect that fuller use will be made of the existing knowledge. And this, in turn, depends on whether we are more likely to succeed in putting at the disposal of a single central authority all the knowledge which ought to be used but which is initially dispersed among many different individuals, or in conveying to the individuals such additional knowledge as they need in order to enable them to fit their plans in with those of others.

III

It will at once be evident that on this point the position will be different with respect to different kinds of knowledge; and the answer to our question will therefore largely turn on the relative importance of the different kinds of knowledge; those more likely to be at the disposal of particular individuals and those which we should with greater confidence expect to find in the possession of an authority made up of suitably chosen experts. If it is today so widely assumed that the latter will be in a better position, this is because one kind of knowledge, namely, scientific knowledge, occupies now so prominent a place in public imagination that we tend to forget that it is not the only kind that is relevant. It may be admitted that, so far as scientific knowledge is concerned, a body of suitably chosen experts may be in the best position to command all the best knowledge available—though this is of course merely shifting the difficulty to the problem of selecting the experts. What I wish to point out is that, even assuming that this problem can be readily solved, it is only a small part of the wider problem.

Today it is almost heresy to suggest that scientific knowledge is not the sum of all knowledge. But a little reflection will show that there is beyond question a body of very important but unorganized knowledge which cannot possibly be called scientific in the sense of knowledge of general rules: the knowledge of the particular circumstances of time and place. It is with respect to this that practically every individual has some advantage over all others in that he possesses unique information of which beneficial use might be made, but of which use can be made only if the decisions depending on it are left to him or are made with his active cooperation. We need to remember only how much we have to learn in any occupation after we have completed our theoretical training, how big a part of our working life we spend learning particular jobs, and how valuable an asset in all walks of life is knowledge of people, of local conditions, and special circumstances. To know of and put to use a machine not fully employed, or somebody's skill which could be better utilized, or to be aware of a surplus stock which can be drawn upon during an interruption of supplies, is socially quite as useful as the knowledge of better alternative techniques. And the shipper who earns his living from using otherwise empty or half-filled journeys of tramp-steamers, or the estate agent whose whole knowledge is almost exclusively one of temporary opportunities, or the *arbitrageur* who gains from local differences of commodity prices, are all performing eminently useful functions based on special knowledge of circumstances of the fleeting moment not known to others.

It is a curious fact that this sort of knowledge should today be generally regarded with a kind of contempt, and that anyone who by such knowledge gains an advantage over somebody better equipped with theoretical or technical knowledge is thought to have acted almost disreputably. To gain an advantage from better knowledge of facilities of communication or transport is sometimes regarded as almost dishonest, although it is quite as important that society make use of the best opportunities in this respect as in using the latest scientific discoveries. This prejudice has in a considerable measure affected the attitude toward commerce in general compared with that toward production. Even economists who regard themselves as definitely above the crude materialist fallacies of the past constantly commit the same mistake where activities directed toward the acquisition of such practical knowledge are concerned—apparently because in their scheme of things all such knowledge is supposed to be "given." The common idea now seems to be that all such knowledge should as a matter of course be readily at the command of everybody, and the reproach of irrationality leveled against the existing economic order is frequently based on the fact that it is not so available. This view disregards the fact that the method by which such knowledge can be made as widely available as possible is precisely the problem to which we have to find an answer.

IV

If it is fashionable today to minimize the importance of the knowledge of the particular circumstances of time and place, this is closely connected with the smaller importance which is now attached to change as such. Indeed, there are few points on which the assumptions made (usually only implicitly) by the "planners" differ from those of their opponents as much as with regard to the significance and frequency of changes which will make substantial alterations of production plans necessary. Of course, if detailed economic plans could be laid down for fairly long periods in advance and then closely adhered to, so that no further economic decisions of importance would be required, the task of drawing up a comprehensive plan governing all economic activity would appear much less formidable.

It is, perhaps, worth stressing that economic problems arise always and only in consequence of change. So long as things continue as before, or at least as they were expected to, there arise no new problems requiring a decision, no need to form a new plan. The belief that changes, or at least day-to-day adjustments, have become less important in modern times implies the contention that economic problems also have become less important. This belief in the decreasing importance of change is, for that reason, usually held by the same people who argue that the importance of economic considerations has been driven into the background by the growing importance of technological knowledge.

Is it true that, with the elaborate apparatus of modern production, economic decisions are required only at long intervals, as when a new factory is to be erected or a new process to be introduced? Is it true that, once a plant has been built, the rest is all more or less mechanical, determined by the character of the plant, and leaving little to be changed in adapting to the ever-changing circumstances of the moment?

The fairly widespread belief in the affirmative is not, so far as I can ascertain, borne out by the practical experience of the business man. In a competitive industry at any rate—and such an industry alone can serve as a test—the task of keeping cost from rising requires constant struggle, absorbing a great part of the energy of the manager. How easy it is for an inefficient manager to dissipate the differentials on which profitability rests, and that it is possible, with the same technical facilities, to produce with a great variety of costs, are among the commonplaces of business experience which do not seem to be equally familiar in the study of the economist. The very strength of the desire, constantly voiced by producers and engineers, to be able to proceed untrammeled by considerations of money costs, is eloquent testimony to the extent to which these factors enter into their daily work.

One reason why economists are increasingly apt to forget about the constant small changes which make up the whole economic picture is probably their growing preoccupation with statistical aggregates, which show a very much greater stability than the movements of the detail. The comparative stability of the aggregates cannot, however, be accounted for—as the statisticians seem occasionally to be inclined to do—by the "law of large numbers" or the mutual compensation of random changes. The number of elements with which we have to deal is not large enough for such accidental forces to produce stability.

The continuous flow of goods and services is maintained by constant deliberate adjustments, by new dispositions made every day in the light of circumstances not known the day before, by B stepping in at once when A fails to deliver. Even the large and highly mechanized plant keeps going largely because of an environment upon which it can draw for all sorts of unexpected needs; tiles for its roof, stationery for its forms, and all the thousand and one kinds of equipment in which it cannot be self-contained and which the plans for the operation of the plant require to be readily available in the market.

This is, perhaps, also the point where I should briefly mention the fact that the sort of knowledge with which I have been concerned is knowledge of the kind which by its nature cannot enter into statistics and therefore cannot be conveyed to any central authority in statistical form. The statistics which such a central authority would have to use would have to be arrived at precisely by abstracting from minor differences between the things, by lumping together, as resources of one kind, items which differ as regards location, quality, and other particulars, in a way which may be very significant for the specific decision. It follows from this that central planning based on statistical information by its nature cannot take direct account of these circumstances of time and place, and that the central planner will have to find some way or other in which the decisions depending on them can be left to the "man on the spot."

V

If we can agree that the economic problem of society is mainly one of rapid adaptation to changes in the particular circumstances of time and place, it would seem to follow that the ultimate decisions must be left to the people who are familiar with these circumstances, who know directly of the relevant changes and of the resources immediately available to meet them. We cannot expect that this problem will be solved by first communicating all this knowledge to a central board which, after integrating *all* knowledge, issues its orders. We must solve it by some form of decentralization. But this answers only part of our problem. We need decentralization because only thus can we ensure that the knowledge of the particular circumstances of time and place will be promptly used. But the "man on the spot" cannot decide solely on the basis of his limited but intimate knowledge of the facts of his immediate surroundings. There still remains the problem of communicating to him such further information as he needs to fit his decisions into the whole pattern of changes of the larger economic system.
How much knowledge does he need to do so successfully? Which of the events which happen beyond the horizon of his immediate knowledge are of relevance to his immediate decision, and how much of them need he know?

There is hardly anything that happens anywhere in the world that *might* not have an effect on the decision he ought to make. But he need not know of these events as such, nor of *all* their effects. It does not matter for him *why* at the particular moment more screws of one size than of another are wanted, *why* paper bags are more readily available than canvas bags, or *why* skilled labor, or particular machine tools, have for the moment become more difficult to acquire. All that is significant for him is *how much more or less* difficult to procure they have become compared with other things with which he is also concerned, or how much more or less urgently wanted are the alternative things he produces or uses. It is always a question of the relative importance of the particular things with which he is concerned, and the causes which alter their relative importance are of no interest to him beyond the effect on those concrete things of his own environment.

It is in this connection that what I have called the economic calculus proper helps us, at least by analogy, to see how this problem can be solved, and in fact is being solved, by the price system. Even the single controlling mind, in possession of all the data for some small, self-contained economic system, would not—every time some small adjustment in the allocation of resources had to be made—go explicitly through all the relations between ends and means which might possibly be affected. It is indeed the great contribution of the pure logic of choice that it has demonstrated conclusively that even such a single mind could solve this kind of problem only by constructing and constantly using rates of equivalence (or "values," or "marginal rates of substitution"), *i.e.*, by attaching to each kind of scarce resource a numerical index which cannot be derived from any property possessed by that particular thing, but which reflects, or in which is condensed, its significance in view of the whole means-end structure. In any small change he will have to consider only these quantitative indices (or "values") in which all the relevant information is concentrated; and by adjusting the quantities one by one, he can appropriately rearrange his dispositions without having to solve the whole puzzle *ab initio*, or without needing at any stage to survey it at once in all its ramifications.

Fundamentally, in a system where the knowledge of the relevant facts is dispersed among many people, prices can act to coordinate the separate actions of different people in the same way as subjective values help the individual to coordinate the parts of his plan. It is worth contemplating for a moment a very simple and commonplace instance of the action of the price system to see what precisely it accomplishes. Assume that somewhere in the world a new opportunity for the use of some raw material, say tin, has arisen, or that one of the sources of supply of tin has been eliminated. It does not matter for our purpose—and it is very significant that it does not matter—which of these two causes has made tin more scarce. All that the users of tin need to know is that some of the tin they used to consume is now more profitably employed elsewhere, and that in consequence they must economize tin. There is no need for the great majority of them even to know where the more urgent need has arisen, or in favor of what other needs they ought to husband the supply. If only some of them know directly of the new demand, and switch resources over to it, and if the people who are aware of the new gap thus created in turn fill it from still other sources, the effect will rapidly spread throughout the whole economic system and influence not only all the uses of tin, but also those of its substitutes and the substitutes of these substitutes, the supply of all the things made of tin, and their substitutes, and so on; and all this without the great majority of those instrumental in bringing about these substitutions knowing anything at all about the original cause of these changes. The whole acts as one market, not because any of its members survey the whole field, but because their limited individual fields of vision sufficiently overlap so that through many intermediaries the relevant information is communicated to all. The mere fact that there is one price for any commodity—or rather that local prices are connected in a manner determined by the cost of transport, etc.—brings about the solution which (it is just conceptually possible) might have been arrived at by one single mind possessing all the information which is in fact dispersed among all the people involved in the process.

VI

We must look at the price system as such a mechanism for communicating information if we want to understand its real function—a function which, of course, it fulfills less perfectly as prices grow more rigid. (Even when quoted prices have become quite rigid, however, the forces which would operate through changes in price still operate to a considerable extent through changes in the other terms of the contract.) The most significant fact about this system is the economy of knowledge with which it operates, or how little the individual participants need to know in order to be able to take the right action. In abbreviated form, by a kind of symbol, only the most essential information is passed on, and passed on only to those concerned. It is more than a metaphor to describe the price system as a kind of machinery for registering change, or a system of telecommunications which enables individual producers to watch merely the movement of a few pointers, as an engineer might watch the hands of a few dials, in order to adjust their activities to changes of which they may never know more than is reflected in the price movement.

Of course, these adjustments are probably never "perfect" in the sense in which the economist conceives of them in his equilibrium analysis. But I fear that our theoretical habits of approaching the problem with the assumption of more or less perfect knowledge on the part of almost everyone has made us somewhat blind to the true function of the price mechanism and led us to apply rather misleading standards in judging its efficiency. The marvel is that in a case like that of a scarcity of one raw material, without an order being issued, without more than perhaps a handful of people knowing the cause, tens of thousands of people whose identity could not be ascertained by months of investigation, are made to use the material or its products more sparingly; *i.e.*, they move in the right direction. This is enough of a marvel even if, in a constantly changing world, not all will hit it off so perfectly that their profit rates will always be maintained at the same constant or "normal" level.

I have deliberately used the word "marvel" to shock the reader out of the complacency with which we often take the working of this mechanism for granted. I am convinced that if it were the result of deliberate human design, and if the people guided by the price changes understood that their decisions have significance far beyond their immediate aim, this mechanism would have been acclaimed as one of the greatest triumphs of the human mind. Its misfortune is the double one that it is not the product of human design and that the people guided by it usually do not know why they are made to do what they do. But those who clamor for "conscious direction"—and who cannot believe that anything which has evolved without design (and even without our understanding it) should solve problems which we should not be able to solve consciously—should remember this: The problem is precisely how to extend the span of our utilization of resources beyond the span of the control of any one mind; and, therefore, how to dispense with the need of conscious control and how to provide inducements which will make the individuals do the desirable things without anyone having to tell them what to do.

The problem which we meet here is by no means peculiar to economics but arises in connection with nearly all truly social phenomena, with language and most of our cultural inheritance, and constitutes really the central theoretical problem of all social science. As Alfred Whitehead has said in another connection, "It is a profoundly erroneous truism, repeated by all copy-books and by eminent people when they are making speeches, that we should cultivate the habit of thinking what we are doing. The precise opposite is the case. Civilization advances by extending the number of important operations which we can perform without thinking about them." This is of profound significance in the social field. We make constant use of formulas, symbols, and rules whose meaning we do not understand and through the use of which we avail ourselves of the assistance of knowledge which individually we do not possess. We have developed these practices and institutions by building upon habits and institutions which have proved successful in their own sphere and which have in turn become the foundation of the civilization we have built up.

The price system is just one of those formations which man has learned to use (though he is still very far from having learned to make the best use of it) after he had stumbled upon it without understanding it. Through it not only a division of labor but also a coordinated utilization of resources based on an equally divided knowledge has become possible. The people who like to deride any suggestion that this may be so usually distort the argument by insinuating that it asserts that by some miracle just that sort of system has spontaneously grown up which is best suited to modern civilization. It is the other way round: man has been able to develop that division of labor on which our civilization is based because he happened to stumble upon a method which made it possible. Had he not done so he might still have developed some other, altogether different, type of civilization, something like the "state" of the termite ants, or some other altogether unimaginable type. All that we can say is that nobody has yet succeeded in designing an alternative system in which certain features of the existing one can be preserved which are dear even to those who most violently assail it—such as particularly the extent to which the individual can choose his pursuits and consequently freely use his own knowledge and skill.

VII

It is in many ways fortunate that the dispute about the indispensability of the price system for any rational calculation in a complex society is now no longer conducted entirely between camps holding different political views. The thesis that without the price system we could not preserve a society based on such extensive division of labor as ours was greeted with a howl of derision when it was first advanced by von Mises twenty-five years ago. Today the difficulties which some still find in accepting it are no longer mainly political, and this makes for an atmosphere much more conducive to reasonable discussion. When we find Leon Trotsky arguing that "economic accounting is unthinkable without market relations"; when Professor Oscar Lange promises Professor von Mises a statue in the marble halls of the future Central Planning Board; when Professor Abba P. Lerner rediscovers Adam Smith and emphasizes that the essential utility of the price system consists in inducing the individual, while seeking his own interest, to do what is in the general interest, the differences can indeed no longer be ascribed to political prejudice. The remaining dissent seems clearly to be due to purely intellectual, and more particularly methodological, differences.

A recent statement by Professor Joseph Schumpeter in his *Capitalism, Socialism and Democracy* provides a clear illustration of one of the methodological differences which I have in mind. Its author is preeminent among those economists who approach economic phenomena in the light of a certain branch of positivism. To him these phenomena accordingly appear as objectively given quantities of commodities impinging directly upon each other, almost, it would seem, without any intervention of human minds. Only against this background can I account for the following (to me startling) pronouncement. Professor Schumpeter argues that the possibility of a rational calculation in the absence of markets for the factors of production follows for the theorist "from the elementary proposition that consumers in evaluating ('demanding') consumers' goods *ipso facto* also evaluate the means of production which enter into the production of these goods."[1]

Taken literally, this statement is simply untrue. The consumers do nothing of the kind. What Professor Schumpeter's *"ipso facto"* presumably means is that the valuation of the factors of production is implied in, or follows necessarily from, the valuation of consumers' goods. But this, too, is not correct. Implication is a logical relationship which can be meaningfully asserted only of propositions simultaneously present to one and the same mind. It is evident, however, that the values of the factors of production do not depend solely on the valuation of the consumers' goods but also on the conditions of supply of the various factors of production. Only to a mind to which all these facts were simultaneously known would the answer necessarily follow from the facts given to it. The practical problem, however, arises precisely because these facts are never so given to a single mind, and because, in consequence, it is necessary that in the solution of the problem knowledge should be used that is dispersed among many people.

The problem is thus in no way solved if we can show that all the facts, *if* they were known to a single mind (as we hypothetically assume them to be given to the observing economist), would uniquely determine the solution; instead we must show how a solution is produced by the interactions of people each of whom possesses only partial knowledge. To assume all the knowledge to be given to a single mind in the same manner in which we assume it to be given to us as the explaining economists is to assume the problem away and to disregard everything that is important and significant in the real world.

That an economist of Professor Schumpeter's standing should thus have fallen into a trap which the ambiguity of the term "datum" sets to the unwary can hardly be explained as a simple error. It suggests rather that there is something fundamentally wrong with an approach which habitually disregards an essential part of the phenomena with which we have to deal: the unavoidable imperfection of man's knowledge and the consequent need for a process by which knowledge is constantly communicated and acquired. Any approach, such as that of much of mathematical economics with its simultaneous equations, which in effect starts from the assumption that people's *knowledge* corresponds with the objective *facts* of the situation, systematically leaves out what is our main task to explain. I am far from denying that in our system equilibrium analysis has a useful function to perform. But when it comes to the point where it misleads some of our leading thinkers into believing that the situation which it describes has direct relevance to the solution of practical problems, it is time that we remember that it does not deal with the social process at all and that it is no more than a useful preliminary to the study of the main problem.

---

[1] J. Schumpeter, *Capitalism, Socialism, and Democracy* (New York, Harper, 1942), p. 175. Professor Schumpeter is, I believe, also the original author of the myth that Pareto and Barone have "solved" the problem of socialist calculation. What they, and many others, did was merely to state the conditions which a rational allocation of resources would have to satisfy, and to point out that these were essentially the same as the conditions of equilibrium of a competitive market. This is something altogether different from showing how the allocation of resources satisfying these conditions can be found in practice. Pareto himself (from whom Barone has taken practically everything he has to say), far from claiming to have solved the practical problem, in fact explicitly denies that it can be solved without the help of the market. See his *Manuel d'économie pure* (2nd ed., 1927), pp. 233-34. The relevant passage is quoted in an English translation at the beginning of my article on "Socialist Calculation: The Competitive 'Solution,'" in *Economica*, New Series, Vol. VIII, No. 26 (May, 1940), p. 125.

The Distinction Between Private and Social Benefits and Costs

The Problem of Social Cost[*]

Ronald Coase[1]

Born in London, Ronald H. Coase (B.Com., London, 1932; D.Sc., 1951) is now a professor at the University of Chicago and Editor of the *Journal of Law and Economics*. Before assuming his post at Chicago in 1964, he was on the faculties of the London School of Economics, the University of Buffalo, and the University of Virginia. Coase, whose research interests are in price theory, the history of economic thought, and the economics of public utilities and industrial organization, is one of the most careful and rigorous scholars in the profession. "The Nature of the Firm" and "The Marginal Cost Controversy," two of his most famous articles, both of which were originally published in *Economica*, have become acknowledged classics in the field.

I. The Problem to Be Examined

This paper is concerned with those actions of business firms which have harmful effects on others. The standard example is that of a factory the smoke from which has harmful effects on those occupying neighbouring properties. The economic analysis of such a situation has usually proceeded in terms of a divergence between the private and social product of the factory, in which economists have largely followed the treatment of Pigou in *The Economics of Welfare*. The conclusions to which this kind of analysis seems to have led most economists are that it would be desirable to make the owner of the factory liable for the damage caused to those injured by the smoke, or alternatively, to place a tax on the factory owner varying with the amount of smoke produced and equivalent in money terms to the damage it would cause, or finally, to exclude the factory from residential districts (and presumably from other areas in which the emission of smoke would have harmful effects on others). It is my contention that the suggested courses of action are inappropriate, in that they lead to results which are not necessarily, or even usually, desirable.

---

[*]Reprinted from the *Journal of Law and Economics* (October 1960) by permission of The University of Chicago Press, pp. 1-44.

[1]This article, although concerned with a technical problem of economic analysis, arose out of the study of the Political Economy of Broadcasting which I am now conducting. The argument of the present article was implicit in a previous article dealing with the problem of allocating radio and television frequencies ("The Federal Communications Commission," 2 *J. Law & Econ.* [1959]) but comments which I have received seemed to suggest that it would be desirable to deal with the question in a more explicit way and without reference to the original problem for the solution of which the analysis was developed.

II. The Reciprocal Nature of the Problem

The traditional approach has tended to obscure the nature of the choice that has to be made. The question is commonly thought of as one in which A inflicts harm on B and what has to be decided is: how should we restrain A? But this is wrong. We are dealing with a problem of a reciprocal nature. To avoid the harm to B would inflict harm on A. The real question that has to be decided is: should A be allowed to harm B or should B be allowed to harm A? The problem is to avoid the more serious harm. I instanced in my previous article[2] the case of a confectioner the noise and vibrations from whose machinery disturbed a doctor in his work. To avoid harming the doctor would inflict harm on the confectioner. The problem posed by this case was essentially whether it was worth while, as a result of restricting the methods of production which could be used by the confectioner, to secure more doctoring at the cost of a reduced supply of confectionery products. Another example is afforded by the problem of straying cattle which destroy crops on neighbouring land. If it is inevitable that some cattle will stray, an increase in the supply of meat can only be obtained at the expense of a decrease in the supply of crops. The nature of the choice is clear: meat or crops. What answer should be given is, of course, not clear unless we know the value of what is obtained as well as the value of what is sacrificed to obtain it. To give another example, Professor George J. Stigler instances the contamination of a stream.[3] If we assume that the harmful effect of the pollution is that it kills the fish, the question to be decided is: is the value of the fish lost greater or less than the value of the product which the contamination of the stream makes possible. It goes almost without saying that this problem has to be looked at in total *and* at the margin.

III. The Pricing System with Liability for Damage

I propose to start my analysis by examining a case in which most economists would presumably agree that the problem would be solved in a completely satisfactory manner: when the damaging business has to pay for all damage caused *and* the pricing system works smoothly (strictly this means that the operation of a pricing system is without cost).

A good example of the problem under discussion is afforded by the case of straying cattle which destroy crops growing on neighbouring land. Let us suppose that a farmer and cattle-raiser are operating on neighbouring properties. Let us further suppose that, without any fencing between the properties, an increase in the size of the cattle-raiser's herd increases the total damage to the farmer's crops. What happens to the marginal damage as the size of the herd increases is another matter. This depends on whether the cattle tend to follow one another or to roam side by side, on whether they tend to be more or less restless as the size of the herd increases and on other similar factors. For my immediate purpose, it is immaterial what assumption is made about marginal damage as the size of the herd increases.

To simplify the argument, I propose to use an arithmetical example. I shall assume that the annual cost of fencing the farmer's property is $9 and that the price of the crop is $1 per ton. Also, I assume that the relation between the number of cattle in the herd and the annual crop loss is as follows:

Number in herd (steers)	Annual crop loss (tons)	Crop loss per additional steer (tons)
1	1	1
2	3	2
3	6	3
4	10	4

Given that the cattle-raiser is liable for the damage caused, the additional annual cost imposed on the cattle-raiser if he increased his herd from, say, 2 to 3 steers is $3 and in deciding on the size of the herd,

---

[2]Coase, "The Federal Communications Commission," 2 *J. Law & Econ.* 26-27 (1959).

[3]G. J. Stigler, *The Theory of Price*, 105 (1952).

he will take this into account along with his other costs. That is, he will not increase the size of the herd unless the value of the additional meat produced (assuming that the cattle-raiser slaughters the cattle) is greater than the additional costs that this will entail, including the value of the additional crops destroyed. Of course, if, by the employment of dogs, herdsmen, aeroplanes, mobile radio and other means, the amount of damage can be reduced, these means will be adopted when their cost is less than the value of the crop which they prevent being lost. Given that the annual cost of fencing is $9, the cattle-raiser who wished to have a herd with 4 steers or more would pay for fencing to be erected and maintained, assuming that other means of attaining the same end would not do so more cheaply. When the fence is erected, the marginal cost due to the liability for damage becomes zero, except to the extent that an increase in the size of the herd necessitates a stronger and therefore more expensive fence because more steers are liable to lean against it at the same time. But, of course, it may be cheaper for the cattle-raiser not to fence and to pay for the damaged crops, as in my arithmetical example, with 3 or fewer steers.

It might be thought that the fact that the cattle-raiser would pay for all crops damaged would lead the farmer to increase his planting if a cattle-raiser came to occupy the neighbouring property. But this is not so. If the crop was previously sold in conditions of perfect competition, marginal cost was equal to price for the amount of planting undertaken and any expansion would have reduced the profits of the farmer. In the new situation, the existence of crop damage would mean that the farmer would sell less on the open market but his receipts for a given production would remain the same, since the cattle-raiser would pay the market price for any crop damaged. Of course, if cattle-raising commonly involved the destruction of crops, the coming into existence of a cattle-raising industry might raise the price of the crops involved and farmers would then extend their planting. But I wish to confine my attention to the individual farmer.

I have said that the occupation of a neighbouring property by a cattle-raiser would not cause the amount of production, or perhaps more exactly the amount of planting, by the farmer to increase. In fact, if the cattle-raising has any effect, it will be to decrease the amount of planting. The reason for this is that, for any given tract of land, if the value of the crop damaged is so great that the receipts from the sale of the undamaged crop are less than the total costs of cultivating that tract of land, it will be profitable for the farmer and the cattle-raiser to make a bargain whereby that tract of land is left uncultivated. This can be made clear by means of an arithmetical example. Assume initially that the value of the crop obtained from cultivating a given tract of land is $12 and that the cost incurred in cultivating this tract of land is $10, the net gain from cultivating the land being $2. I assume for purposes of simplicity that the farmer owns the land. Now assume that the cattle-raiser starts operations on the neighbouring property and that the value of the crops damaged is $1. In this case $11 is obtained by the farmer from sale on the market and $1 is obtained from the cattle-raiser for damage suffered and the net gain remains $2. Now suppose that the cattle-raiser finds it profitable to increase the size of his herd, even though the amount of damage rises to $3; which means that the value of the additional meat production is greater than the additional costs, including the additional $2 payment for damage. But the total payment for damage is now $3. The net gain to the farmer from cultivating the land is still $2. The cattle-raiser would be better off if the farmer would agree not to cultivate his land for any payment less than $3. The farmer would be agreeable to not cultivating the land for any payment greater than $2. There is clearly room for a mutually satisfactory bargain which would lead to the abandonment of cultivation.[4] But the same argument applies not only to the whole tract cultivated by the farmer but also to any subdivision of it. Suppose, for example, that the cattle have a well-defined route, say, to a brook or to a shady area. In these circumstances, the amount of damage to the crop along the route may well

---

[4]The argument in the text has proceeded on the assumption that the alternative to cultivation of the crop is abandonment of cultivation altogether. But this need not be so. There may be crops which are less liable to damage by cattle but which would not be as profitable as the crop grown in the absence of damage. Thus, if the cultivation of a new crop would yield a return to the farmer of $1 instead of $2, and the size of the herd which would cause $3 damage with the old crop would cause $1 damage with the new crop, it would be profitable to the cattle-raiser to pay any sum less than $2 to induce the farmer to change his crop (since this would reduce damage liability from $3 to $1) and it would be profitable for the farmer to do so if the amount received was more than $1 (the reduction in his return caused by switching crops). In fact, there would be room for a mutually satisfactory bargain in all cases in which a change of crop would reduce the amount of damage by more than it reduces the value of the crop (excluding damage)—in all cases, that is, in which a change in the crop cultivated would lead to an increase in the value of production.

be great and if so, it could be that the farmer and the cattle-raiser would find it profitable to make a bargain whereby the farmer would agree not to cultivate this strip of land.

But this raises a further possibility. Suppose that there is such a well-defined route. Suppose further that the value of the crop that would be obtained by cultivating this strip of land is $10 but that the cost of cultivation is $11. In the absence of the cattle-raiser, the land would not be cultivated. However, given the presence of the cattle-raiser, it could well be that if the strip was cultivated, the whole crop would be destroyed by the cattle. In which case, the cattle-raiser would be forced to pay $10 to the farmer. It is true that the farmer would lose $1. But the cattle-raiser would lose $10. Clearly this is a situation which is not likely to last indefinitely since neither party would want this to happen. The aim of the farmer would be to induce the cattle-raiser to make a payment in return for an agreement to leave this land uncultivated. The farmer would not be able to obtain a payment greater than the cost of fencing off this piece of land nor so high as to lead the cattle-raiser to abandon the use of the neighbouring property. What payment would in fact be made would depend on the shrewdness of the farmer and the cattle-raiser as bargainers. But as the payment would not be so high as to cause the cattle-raiser to abandon this location and as it would not vary with the size of the herd, such an agreement would not affect the allocation of resources but would merely alter the distribution of income and wealth as between the cattle-raiser and the farmer.

I think it is clear that if the cattle-raiser is liable for damage caused and the pricing system works smoothly, the reduction in the value of production elsewhere will be taken into account in computing the additional cost involved in increasing the size of the herd. This cost will be weighed against the value of the additional meat production and, given perfect competition in the cattle industry, the allocation of resources in cattle-raising will be optimal. What needs to be emphasized is that the fall in the value of production elsewhere which would be taken into account in the costs of the cattle-raiser may well be less than the damage which the cattle would cause to the crops in the ordinary course of events. This is because it is possible, as a result of market transactions, to discontinue cultivation of the land. This is desirable in all cases in which the damage that the cattle would cause, and for which the cattle-raiser would be willing to pay, exceeds the amount which the farmer would pay for the use of the land. In conditions of perfect competition, the amount which the farmer would pay for the use of the land is equal to the difference between the value of the total production when the factors are employed on this land and the value of the additional product yielded in their next best use (which would be what the farmer would have to pay for the factors). If damage exceeds the amount the farmer would pay for the use of the land, the value of the additional product of the factors employed elsewhere would exceed the value of the total product in this use after damage is taken into account. It follows that it would be desirable to abandon cultivation of the land and to release the factors employed for production elsewhere. A procedure which merely provided for payment for damage to the crop caused by the cattle but which did not allow for the possibility of cultivation being discontinued would result in too small an employment of factors of production in cattle-raising and too large an employment of factors in cultivation of the crop. But given the possibility of market transactions, a situation in which damage to crops exceeded the rent of the land would not endure. Whether the cattle-raiser pays the farmer to leave the land uncultivated or himself rents the land by paying the land-owner an amount slightly greater than the farmer would pay (if the farmer was himself renting the land), the final result would be the same and would maximise the value of production. Even when the farmer is induced to plant crops which it would not be profitable to cultivate for sale on the market, this will be a purely short-term phenomenon and may be expected to lead to an agreement under which the planting will cease. The cattle-raiser will remain in that location and the marginal cost of meat production will be the same as before, thus having no long-run effect on the allocation of resources.

IV. The Pricing System with No Liability for Damage

I now turn to the case in which, although the pricing system is assumed to work smoothly (that is, costlessly), the damaging business is not liable for any of the damage which it causes. This business does not have to make a payment to those damaged by its actions. I propose to show that the allocation of resources will be the same in this case as it was when the damaging business was liable for damage caused. As I showed in the previous case that the allocation of resources was optimal, it will not be necessary to repeat this part of the argument.

I return to the case of the farmer and the cattle-raiser. The farmer would suffer increased damage to his crop as the size of the herd increased. Suppose that the size of the cattle-raiser's herd is 3 steers (and that this is the size of the herd that would be maintained if crop damage was not taken into account). Then the farmer would be willing to pay up to $3 if the cattle-raiser would reduce his herd to 2 steers, up to $5 if the herd were reduced to 1 steer and would pay up to $6 if cattle-raising was abandoned. The cattle-raiser would therefore receive $3 from the farmer if he kept 2 steers instead of 3. This $3 foregone is therefore part of the cost incurred in keeping the third steer. Whether the $3 is a payment which the cattle-raiser has to make if he adds the third steer to his herd (which it would be if the cattle-raiser was liable to the farmer for damage caused to the crop) or whether it is a sum of money which he would have received if he did not keep a third steer (which it would be if the cattle-raiser was not liable to the farmer for damage caused to the crop) does not affect the final result. In both cases $3 is part of the cost of adding a third steer, to be included along with the other costs. If the increase in the value of production in cattle-raising through increasing the size of the herd from 2 to 3 is greater than the additional costs that have to be incurred (including the $3 damage to crops), the size of the herd will be increased. Otherwise, it will not. The size of the herd will be the same whether the cattle-raiser is liable for damage caused to the crop or not.

It may be argued that the assumed starting point—a herd of 3 steers—was arbitrary. And this is true. But the farmer would not wish to pay to avoid crop damage which the cattle-raiser would not be able to cause. For example, the maximum annual payment which the farmer could be induced to pay could not exceed $9, the annual cost of fencing. And the farmer would only be willing to pay this sum if it did not reduce his earnings to a level that would cause him to abandon cultivation of this particular tract of land. Furthermore, the farmer would only be willing to pay this amount if he believed that, in the absence of any payment by him, the size of the herd maintained by the cattle-raiser would be 4 or more steers. Let us assume that this is the case. Then the farmer would be willing to pay up to $3 if the cattle-raiser would reduce his herd to 3 steers, up to $6 if the herd were reduced to 2 steers, up to $8 if one steer only were kept and up to $9 if cattle-raising were abandoned. It will be noticed that the change in the starting point has not altered the amount which would accrue to the cattle-raiser if he reduced the size of his herd by any given amount. It is still true that the cattle-raiser could receive an additional $3 from the farmer if he agreed to reduce his herd from 3 steers to 2 and that the $3 represents the value of the crop that would be destroyed by adding the third steer to the herd. Although a different belief on the part of the farmer (whether justified or not) about the size of the herd that the cattle-raiser would maintain in the absence of payments from him may affect the total payment he can be induced to pay, it is not true that this different belief would have any effect on the size of the herd that the cattle-raiser will actually keep. This will be the same as it would be if the cattle-raiser had to pay for damage caused by his cattle, since a receipt foregone of a given amount is the equivalent of a payment of the same amount.

It might be thought that it would pay the cattle-raiser to increase his herd above the size that he would wish to maintain once a bargain had been made, in order to induce the farmer to make a larger total payment. And this may be true. It is similar in nature to the action of the farmer (when the cattle-raiser was liable for damage) in cultivating land on which, as a result of an agreement with the cattle-raiser, planting would subsequently be abandoned (including land which would not be cultivated at all in the absence of cattle-raising). But such manoeuvres are preliminaries to an agreement and do not affect the long-run equilibrium position, which is the same whether or not the cattle-raiser is held responsible for the crop damage brought about by his cattle.

It is necessary to know whether the damaging business is liable or not for damage caused since without the establishment of this initial delimitation of rights there can be no market transactions to transfer and recombine them. But the ultimate result (which maximises the value of production) is independent of the legal position if the pricing system is assumed to work without cost.

V. The Problem Illustrated Anew

The harmful effects of the activities of a business can assume a wide variety of forms. An early English case concerned a building which, by obstructing currents of air, hindered the operation of a windmill.[5] A

---

[5]See Gale on *Easements* 237-39 (13th ed. M. Bowles 1959).

recent case in Florida concerned a building which cast a shadow on the cabana, swimming pool and sunbathing areas of a neighbouring hotel.[6] The problem of straying cattle and the damaging of crops which was the subject of detailed examination in the two preceding sections, although it may have appeared to be rather a special case, is in fact but one example of a problem which arises in many different guises. To clarify the nature of my argument and to demonstrate its general applicability, I propose to illustrate it anew by reference to four actual cases.

Let us first reconsider the case of *Sturges v. Bridgman*[7] which I used as an illustration of the general problem in my article on "The Federal Communications Commission." In this case, a confectioner (in Wigmore Street) used two mortars and pestles in connection with his business (one had been in operation in the same position for more than 60 years and the other for more than 26 years). A doctor then came to occupy neighbouring premises (in Wimpole Street). The confectioner's machinery caused the doctor no harm until, eight years after he had first occupied the premises, he built a consulting room at the end of his garden right against the confectioner's kitchen. It was then found that the noise and vibration caused by the confectioner's machinery made it difficult for the doctor to use his new consulting room. "In particular . . . the noise prevented him from examining his patients by auscultation[8] for diseases of the chest. He also found it impossible to engage with effect in any occupation which required thought and attention." The doctor therefore brought a legal action to force the confectioner to stop using his machinery. The courts had little difficulty in granting the doctor the injunction he sought. "Individual cases of hardship may occur in the strict carrying out of the principle upon which we found our judgment, but the negation of the principle would lead even more to individual hardship, and would at the same time produce a prejudicial effect upon the development of land for residential purposes."

The court's decision established that the doctor had the right to prevent the confectioner from using his machinery. But, of course, it would have been possible to modify the arrangements envisaged in the legal ruling by means of a bargain between the parties. The doctor would have been willing to waive his right and allow the machinery to continue in operation if the confectioner would have paid him a sum of money which was greater than the loss of income which he would suffer from having to move to a more costly or less convenient location or from having to curtail his activities at this location or, as was suggested as a possibility, from having to build a separate wall which would deaden the noise and vibration. The confectioner would have been willing to do this if the amount he would have to pay the doctor was less than the fall in income he would suffer if he had to change his mode of operation at this location, abandon his operation or move his confectionery business to some other location. The solution of the problem depends essentially on whether the continued use of the machinery adds more to the confectioner's income than it subtracts from the doctor's.[9] But now consider the situation if the confectioner had won the case. The confectioner would then have had the right to continue operating his noise and vibration-generating machinery without having to pay anything to the doctor. The boot would have been on the other foot: the doctor would have had to pay the confectioner to induce him to stop using the machinery. If the doctor's income would have fallen more through continuance of the use of this machinery than it added to the income of the confectioner, there would clearly be room for a bargain whereby the doctor paid the confectioner to stop using the machinery. That is to say, the circumstances in which it would not pay the confectioner to continue to use the machinery and to compensate the doctor for the losses that this would bring (if the doctor had the right to prevent the confectioner's using his machinery) would be those in which it would be in the interest of the doctor to make a payment to the confectioner which would induce him to discontinue the use of the machinery (if the confectioner had the right to operate the machinery). The basic conditions are exactly the same in this case as they were in the example of the cattle which destroyed crops. With costless market transactions, the decision of the courts concerning liability for damage would be without effect on the allocation of resources. It was of course the view of the judges that they were affecting the working of

[6]See *Fontainebleu Hotel Corp. v. Forty-Five Twenty-Five, Inc.*, 114 So. 2d 357 (1959).

[7]11 Ch. D. 852 (1879).

[8]Auscultation is the act of listening by ear or stethoscope in order to judge by sound the condition of the body.

[9]Note that what is taken into account is the change in income after allowing for alterations in methods of production, location, character of product, etc.

the economic system—and in a desirable direction. Any other decision would have had "a prejudicial effect upon the development of land for residential purposes," an argument which was elaborated by examining the example of a forge operating on a barren moor, which was later developed for residual purposes. The judges' view that they were settling how the land was to be used would be true only in the case in which the costs of carrying out the necessary market transactions exceeded the gain which might be achieved by any rearrangement of rights. And it would be desirable to preserve the areas (Wimpole Street or the moor) for residential or professional use (by giving non-industrial users the right to stop the noise, vibration, smoke, etc., by injunction) only if the value of the additional residential facilities obtained was greater than the value of cakes or iron lost. But of this the judges seem to have been unaware.

Another example of the same problem is furnished by the case of *Cooke v. Forbes*.[10] One process in the weaving of cocoa-nut fibre matting was to immerse it in bleaching liquids after which it was hung out to dry. Fumes from a manufacturer of sulphate of ammonia had the effect of turning the matting from a bright to a dull and blackish color. The reason for this was that the bleaching liquid contained chloride of tin, which, when affected by sulphuretted hydrogen, is turned to a darker colour. An injunction was sought to stop the manufacturer from emitting the fumes. The lawyers for the defendant argued that if the plaintiff "were not to use . . . a particular bleaching liquid, their fibre would not be affected; that their process is unusual, not according to the custom of the trade, and even damaging to their own fabrics." The judge commented: ". . . it appears to me quite plain that a person has a right to carry on upon his own property a manufacturing process in which he uses chloride of tin, or any sort of metallic dye, and that his neighbour is not at liberty to pour in gas which will interfere with his manufacture. If it can be traced to the neighbour, then, I apprehend, clearly he will have a right to come here and ask for relief." But in view of the fact that the damage was accidental and occasional, that careful precautions were taken and that there was no exceptional risk, an injunction was refused, leaving the plaintiff to bring an action for damages if he wished. What the subsequent developments were I do not know. But it is clear that the situation is essentially the same as that found in *Sturges v. Bridgman*, except that the cocoa-nut fibre matting manufacturer could not secure an injunction but would have to seek damages from the sulphate of ammonia manufacturer. The economic analysis of the situation is exactly the same as with the cattle which destroyed crops. To avoid the damage, the sulphate of ammonia manufacturer could increase his precautions or move to another location. Either course would presumably increase his costs. Alternatively he could pay for the damage. This he would do if the payments for damage were less than the additional costs that would have to be incurred to avoid the damage. The payments for damage would then become part of the cost of production of sulphate of ammonia. Of course, if, as was suggested in the legal proceedings, the amount of damage could be eliminated by changing the bleaching agent (which would presumably increase the costs of the matting manufacturer) and if the additional cost was less than the damage that would otherwise occur, it should be possible for the two manufacturers to make a mutually satisfactory bargain whereby the new bleaching agent was used. Had the court decided against the matting manufacturer, as a consequence of which he would have had to suffer the damage without compensation, the allocation of resources would not have been affected. It would pay the matting manufacturer to change his bleaching agent if the additional cost involved was less than the reduction in damage. And since the matting manufacturer would be willing to pay the sulphate of ammonia manufacturer an amount up to his loss of income (the increase in costs or the damage suffered) if he would cease his activities, this loss of income would remain a cost of production for the manufacturer of sulphate of ammonia. This case is indeed analytically exactly the same as the cattle example.

Bryant v. Lefever[11] raised the problem of the smoke nuisance in a novel form. The plaintiff and the defendants were occupiers of adjoining houses, which were of about the same height.

---

[10]L. R. 5 Eq. 166 (1867-1868).

[11]4 C.P.D. 172 (1878-1879).

Before 1876 the plaintiff was able to light a fire in any room of his house without the chimneys smoking; the two houses had remained in the same condition some thirty or forty years. In 1876 the defendants took down their house, and began to rebuild it. They carried up a wall by the side of the plaintiff's chimneys much beyond its original height, and stacked timber on the roof of their house, and thereby caused the plaintiff's chimneys to smoke whenever he lighted fires.

The reason, of course, why the chimneys smoked was that the erection of the wall and the stacking of the timber prevented the free circulation of air. In a trial before a jury, the plaintiff was awarded damages of £40. The case then went to the Court of Appeals where the judgment was reversed. Bramwell, L.J., argued:

> ... it is said, and the jury have found, that the defendants have done that which caused a nuisance to the plaintiff's house. We think there is no evidence of this. No doubt there is a nuisance, but it is not of the defendant's causing. They have done nothing in causing the nuisance. Their house and their timber are harmless enough. It is the plaintiff who causes the nuisance by lighting a coal fire in a place the chimney of which is placed so near the defendants' wall, that the smoke does not escape, but comes into the house. Let the plaintiff cease to light his fire, let him move his chimney, let him carry it higher, and there would be no nuisance. Who then, causes it? It would be very clear that the plaintiff did, if he had built his house or chimney after the defendants had put up the timber on theirs, and it is really the same though he did so before the timber was there. But (what is in truth the same answer), if the defendants cause the nuisance, they have a right to do so. If the plaintiff has not the right to the passage of air, except subject to the defendants' right to build or put timber on their house, then his right is subject to their right, and though a nuisance follows from the exercise of their right, they are not liable.

And Cotton, L.J., said:

> Here it is found that the erection of the defendants' wall has sensibly and materially interfered with the comfort of human existence in the plaintiff's house, and it is said this is a nuisance for which the defendants are liable. Ordinarily this is so, but the defendants have done so, not by sending on to the plaintiff's property any smoke or noxious vapour, but by interrupting the egress of smoke from the plaintiff's house in a way to which ... the plaintiff has no legal right. The plaintiff creates the smoke, which interferes with his comfort. Unless he has ... a right to get rid of this in a particular way which has been interfered with by the defendants, he cannot sue the defendants, because the smoke made by himself, for which he has not provided any effectual means of escape, causes him annoyance. It is as if a man tried to get rid of liquid filth arising on his own land by a drain into his neighbour's land. Until a right had been acquired by user, the neighbour might stop the drain without incurring liability by so doing. No doubt great inconvenience would be caused to the owner of the property on which the liquid filth arises. But the act of his neighbour would be a lawful act, and he would not be liable for the consequences attributable to the fact that the man had accumulated filth without providing any effectual means of getting rid of it.

I do not propose to show that any subsequent modification of the situation, as a result of bargains between the parties (conditioned by the cost of stacking the timber elsewhere, the cost of extending the chimney higher, etc.), would have exactly the same result whatever decision the courts had come to since this point has already been adequately dealt with in the discussion of the cattle example and the two previous cases. What I shall discuss is the argument of the judges in the Court of Appeals that the smoke nuisance was not caused by the man who erected the wall but by the man who lit the fires. The novelty of the situation is that the smoke nuisance was suffered by the man who lit the fires and not by some third person. The question is not a trivial one since it lies at the heart of the problem under discussion. Who caused the smoke nuisance? The answer seems fairly clear. The smoke nuisance was caused both by the man who built the wall *and* by the man who lit the fires. Given the fires, there would have been no smoke nuisance without the wall; given the wall, there would have been no smoke nuisance without the fires. Eliminate the wall *or* the fires and the smoke nuisance would disappear. On the marginal principle it is clear that *both* were responsible and *both* should be forced to include the loss of amenity due to the smoke as a cost in deciding whether to continue the activity which gives rise to the smoke. And given the possibility of market transactions, this is what would in fact happen. Although the wall-builder was not liable legally for the nuisance, as the man with the smoking chimneys would presumably be willing to pay a sum equal to the monetary worth to him of eliminating the smoke, this sum would therefore become for the wall-builder a cost of continuing to have the high wall with the timber stacked on the roof.

The judges' contention that it was the man who lit the fires who alone caused the smoke nuisance is true only if we assume that the wall is the given factor. This is what the judges did by deciding that the man who erected the higher wall had a legal right to do so. The case would have been even more interesting if the smoke from the chimneys had injured the timber. Then it would have been the wall-builder who suffered the damage. The case would then have closely paralleled *Sturges v. Bridgman* and there can be little doubt that the man who lit the fires would have been liable for the ensuing damage to the timber, in spite of the fact that no damage had occurred until the high wall was built by the man who owned the timber.

Judges have to decide on legal liability but this should not confuse economists about the nature of the economic problem involved. In the case of the cattle and the crops, it is true that there would be no crop damage without the cattle. It is equally true that there would be no crop damage without the crops. The doctor's work would not have been disturbed if the confectioner had not worked his machinery; but the machinery would have disturbed no one if the doctor had not set up his consulting room in that particular place. The matting was blackened by the fumes from the sulphate of ammonia manufacturer; but no damage would have occurred if the matting manufacturer had not chosen to hang out his matting in a particular place and to use a particular bleaching agent. If we are to discuss the problem in terms of causation, both parties cause the damage. If we are to attain an optimum allocation of resources, it is therefore desirable that both parties should take the harmful effect (the nuisance) into account in deciding on their course of action. It is one of the beauties of a smoothly operating pricing system that, as has already been explained, the fall in the value of production due to the harmful effect would be a cost for both parties.

Bass v. Gregory[12] will serve as an excellent final illustration of the problem. The plaintiffs were the owners and tenant of a public house called the Jolly Anglers. The defendant was the owner of some cottages and a yard adjoining the Jolly Anglers. Under the public house was a cellar excavated in the rock. From the cellar, a hole or shaft had been cut into an old well situated in the defendant's yard. The well therefore became the ventilating shaft for the cellar. The cellar "had been used for a particular purpose in the process of brewing, which, without ventilation, could not be carried on." The cause of the action was that the defendant removed a grating from the mouth of the well, "so as to stop or prevent the free passage of air from [the] cellar upwards through the well. . . ." What caused the defendant to take this step is not clear from the report of the case. Perhaps "the air . . . impregnated by the brewing operations" which "passed up the well and out into the open air" was offensive to him. At any rate, he preferred to have the well in his yard stopped up. The court had first to determine whether the owners of the public house could have a legal right to a current of air. If they were to have such a right, this case would have to be distinguished from *Bryant v. Lefever* (already considered). This, however, presented no difficulty. In this case, the current of air was confined to "a strictly defined channel." In the case of *Bryant v. Lefever*, what was involved was "the general current of air common to all mankind." The judge therefore held that the owners of the public house could have the right to a current of air whereas the owner of the private house in *Bryant v. Lefever* could not. An economist might be tempted to add "but the air moved all the same." However, all that had been decided at this stage of the argument was that there could be a legal right, not that the owners of the public house possessed it. But evidence showed that the shaft from the cellar to the well had existed for over forty years and that the use of the well as a ventilating shaft must have been known to the owners of the yard since the air, when it emerged, smelt of the brewing operations. The judge therefore held that the public house had such a right by the "doctrine of lost grant." This doctrine states "that if a legal right is proved to have existed and been

---

[12] 25 Q.B.D. 481 (1890).

exercised for a number of years the law ought to presume that it had a legal origin."[13] So the owner of the cottages and yard had to unstop the well and endure the smell.

The reasoning employed by the courts in determining legal rights will often seem strange to an economist because many of the factors on which the decision turns are, to an economist, irrelevant. Because of this, situations which are, from an economic point of view, identical will be treated quite differently by the courts. The economic problem in all cases of harmful effects is how to maximise the value of production. In the case of *Bass v. Gregory* fresh air was drawn in through the well which facilitated the production of beer but foul air was expelled through the well which made life in the adjoining houses less pleasant. The economic problem was to decide which to choose: a lower cost of beer and worsened amenities in adjoining houses or a higher cost of beer and improved amenities. In deciding this question, the "doctrine of lost grant" is about as relevant as the colour of the judge's eyes. But it has to be remembered that the immediate question faced by the courts is *not* what shall be done by whom *but* who has the legal right to do what. It is always possible to modify by transactions on the market the initial legal delimitation of rights. And, of course, if such market transactions are costless, such a rearrangement of rights will always take place if it would lead to an increase in the value of production.

VI. The Cost of Market Transactions Taken into Account

The argument has proceeded up to this point on the assumption (explicit in Sections III and IV and tacit in Section V) that there were no costs involved in carrying out market transactions. This is, of course, a very unrealistic assumption. In order to carry out a market transaction it is necessary to discover who it is that one wishes to deal with, to inform people that one wishes to deal and on what terms, to conduct negotiations leading up to a bargain, to draw up the contract, to undertake the inspection needed to make sure that the terms of the contract are being observed, and so on. These operations are often extremely costly, sufficiently costly at any rate to prevent many transactions that would be carried out in a world in which the pricing system worked without cost.

In earlier sections, when dealing with the problem of the rearrangement of legal rights through the market, it was argued that such a rearrangement would be made through the market whenever this would lead to an increase in the value of production. But this assumed costless market transactions. Once the costs of carrying out market transactions are taken into account it is clear that such a rearrangement of rights will only be undertaken when the increase in the value of the production consequent upon the rearrangement is greater than the costs which would be involved in bringing it about. When it is less, the granting of an injunction (or the knowledge that it would be granted) or the liability to pay damages may result in an activity being discontinued (or may prevent its being started) which would be undertaken if market transactions were costless. In these conditions the initial delimitation of legal rights does have an effect on the efficiency with which the economic system operates. One arrangement of rights may bring about a greater value of production than any other. But unless this is the arrangement of rights established by the legal system, the costs of reaching the same result by altering and combining rights through the market may be so great that this optimal arrangement of rights, and the greater value of production which it would bring, may never be achieved. The part played by economic considerations in the process of delimiting legal rights will be discussed in the next section. I will take the initial delimitation of rights and the costs of carrying out market transactions as given.

It is clear that an alternative form of economic organisation which could achieve the same result at less cost than would be incurred by using the market would enable the value of production to be raised. As I explained many years ago, the firm represents such an alternative to organising production through

---

[13]It may be asked why a lost grant could not also be presumed in the case of the confectioner who had operated one mortar for more than 60 years. The answer is that until the doctor built the consulting room at the end of his garden there was no nuisance. So the nuisance had not continued for many years. It is true that the confectioner in his affidavit referred to "an invalid lady who occupied the house upon one occasion, about thirty years before" who "requested him if possible to discontinue the use of the mortars before eight o'clock in the morning" and that there was some evidence that the garden wall had been subjected to vibration. But the court had little difficulty in disposing of this line of argument: "... this vibration, even if it existed at all, was so slight, and the complaint, if it can be called a complaint, of the invalid lady ... was of so trifling a character, that ... the Defendant's acts would not have given rise to any proceeding either at law or in equity" (11 Ch.D. 863). That is, the confectioner had not committed a nuisance until the doctor built his consulting room.

market transactions.[14] Within the firm individual bargains between the various cooperating factors of production are eliminated and for a market transaction is substituted an administrative decision. The rearrangement of production then takes place without the need for bargains between the owners of the factors of production. A landowner who has control of a large tract of land may devote his land to various uses taking into account the effect that the interrelations of the various activities will have on the net return of the land, thus rendering unnecessary bargains between those undertaking the various activities. Owners of a large building or of several adjoining properties in a given area may act in much the same way. In effect, using our earlier terminology, the firm would acquire the legal rights of all the parties and the rearrangement of activities would not follow on a rearrangement of rights by contract, but as a result of an administrative decision as to how the rights should be used.

It does not, of course, follow that the administrative costs of organising a transaction through a firm are inevitably less than the costs of the market transactions which are superseded. But where contracts are peculiarly difficult to draw up and an attempt to describe what the parties have agreed to do or not to do (e.g. the amount and kind of a smell or noise that they may make or will not make) would necessitate a lengthy and highly involved document and, where, as is probable, a long-term contract would be desirable;[15] it would be hardly surprising if the emergence of a firm or the extension of the activities of an existing firm was not the solution adopted on many occasions to deal with the problem of harmful effects. This solution would be adopted whenever the administrative costs of the firm were less than the costs of the market transactions that it supersedes and the gains which would result from the rearrangement of activities greater than the firm's costs of organising them. I do not need to examine in great detail the character of this solution since I have explained what is involved in my earlier article.

But the firm is not the only possible answer to this problem. The administrative costs of organising transactions within the firm may also be high, and particularly so when many diverse activities are brought within the control of a single organisation. In the standard case of a smoke nuisance, which may affect a vast number of people engaged in a wide variety of activities, the administrative costs might well be so high as to make any attempt to deal with the problem within the confines of a single firm impossible. An alternative solution is direct government regulation. Instead of instituting a legal system of rights which can be modified by transactions on the market, the government may impose regulations which state what people must or must not do and which have to be obeyed. Thus, the government (by statute or perhaps more likely through an administrative agency) may, to deal with the problem of smoke nuisance, decree that certain methods of production should or should not be used (e.g. that smoke preventing devices should be installed or that coal or oil should not be burned) or may confine certain types of business to certain districts (zoning regulations).

The government is, in a sense, a superfirm (but of a very special kind) since it is able to influence the use of factors of production by administrative decision. But the ordinary firm is subject to checks in its operations because of the competition of other firms, which might administer the same activities at lower cost and also because there is always the alternative of market transactions as against organisation within the firm if the administrative costs become too great. The government is able, if it wishes, to avoid the market altogether, which a firm can never do. The firm has to make market agreements with the owners of the factors of production that it uses. Just as the government can conscript or seize property, so it can decree that factors of production should only be used in such-and-such a way. Such authoritarian methods save a lot of trouble (for those doing the organising). Furthermore, the government has at its disposal the police and the other law enforcement agencies to make sure that its regulations are carried out.

It is clear that the government has powers which might enable it to get some things done at a lower cost than could a private organisation (or at any rate one without special governmental powers). But the governmental administrative machine is not itself costless. It can, in fact, on occasion be extremely costly. Furthermore, there is no reason to suppose that the restrictive and zoning regulations, made by a fallible administration subject to political pressures and operating without any competitive check, will necessarily always be those which increase the efficiency with which the economic system operates. Furthermore, such general regulations which must apply to a wide variety of cases will be enforced in

---

[14]See Coase, "The Nature of the Firm," 4 *Economica*, New Series, 386 (1937). Reprinted in *Readings in Price Theory*, 331 (1952).

[15]For reasons explained in my earlier article, see *Readings in Price Theory*, n. 14 at 337.

some cases in which they are clearly inappropriate. From these considerations it follows that direct governmental regulation will not necessarily give better results than leaving the problem to be solved by the market or the firm. But equally there is no reason why, on occasion, such governmental administrative regulation should not lead to an improvement in economic efficiency. This would seem particularly likely when, as is normally the case with the smoke nuisance, a large number of people are involved and in which therefore the costs of handling the problem through the market or the firm may be high.

There is, of course, a further alternative, which is to do nothing about the problem at all. And given that the costs involved in solving the problem by regulations issued by the governmental administrative machine will often be heavy (particularly if the costs are interpreted to include all the consequences which follow from the Government engaging in this kind of activity), it will no doubt be commonly the case that the gain which would come from regulating the actions which give rise to the harmful effects will be less than the costs involved in Government regulation.

The discussion of the problem of harmful effects in this section (when the costs of market transactions are taken into account) is extremely inadequate. But at least it has made clear that the problem is one of choosing the appropriate social arrangement for dealing with the harmful effects. All solutions have costs and there is no reason to suppose that government regulation is called for simply because the problem is not well handled by the market or the firm. Satisfactory views on policy can only come from a patient study of how, in practice, the market, firms and governments can handle the problem of harmful effects. Economists need to study the work of the broker in bringing parties together, the effectiveness of restrictive covenants, the problems of the large-scale real-estate development company, the operation of Government zoning and other regulating activities. It is my belief that economists, and policy-makers generally, have tended to over-estimate the advantages which come from governmental regulation. But this belief, even if justified, does not do more than suggest that government regulation should be curtailed. It does not tell us where the boundary line should be drawn. This, it seems to me, has to come from a detailed investigation of the actual results of handling the problem in different ways. But it would be unfortunate if this investigation were undertaken with the aid of a faulty economic analysis. The aim of this article is to indicate what the economic approach to the problem should be.

VII. The Legal Delimitation of Rights and the Economic Problem

The discussion in Section V not only served to illustrate the argument but also afforded a glimpse at the legal approach to the problem of harmful effects. The cases considered were all English but a similar selection of American cases could easily be made and the character of the reasoning would have been the same. Of course, if market transactions were costless, all that matters (questions of equity apart) is that the rights of the various parties should be well-defined and the results of legal actions easy to forecast. But as we have seen, the situation is quite different when market transactions are so costly as to make it difficult to change the arrangement of rights established by the law. In such cases, the courts directly influence economic activity. It would therefore seem desirable that the courts should understand the economic consequences of their decisions and should, insofar as this is possible without creating too much uncertainty about the legal position itself, take these consequences into account when making their decisions. Even when it is possible to change the legal delimitation of rights through market transactions, it is obviously desirable to reduce the need for such transactions and thus reduce the employment of resources in carrying them out.

A thorough examination of the presuppositions of the courts in trying such cases would be of great interest but I have not been able to attempt it. Nevertheless it is clear from a cursory study that the courts have often recognized the economic implications of their decisions and are aware (as many economists are not) of the reciprocal nature of the problem. Furthermore, from time to time, they take these economic implications into account, along with other factors, in arriving at their decisions. The American writers on this subject refer to the question in a more explicit fashion than do the British. Thus, to quote Prosser on Torts, a person may

> make use of his own property or . . . conduct his own affairs at the expense of some harm to his neighbors. He may operate a factory whose noise and smoke cause some discomfort to others, so long as he keeps within reasonable bounds. It is only when his conduct is unreasonable, *in the light of its utility and the harm*

which results [italics added], that it becomes a nuisance. . . . As it was said in an ancient case in regard to candle-making in a town, "Le utility del chose excusera le noisomeness del stink."

The world must have factories, smelters, oil refineries, noisy machinery and blasting, even at the expense of some inconvenience to those in the vicinity and the plaintiff may be required to accept some not unreasonable discomfort for the general good.[16]

The standard British writers do not state as explicitly as this that a comparison between the utility and harm produced is an element in deciding whether a harmful effect should be considered a nuisance. But similar views, if less strongly expressed, are to be found.[17] The doctrine that the harmful effect must be substantial before the court will act is, no doubt, in part a reflection of the fact that there will almost always be some gain to offset the harm. And in the reports of individual cases, it is clear that the judges have had in mind what would be lost as well as what would be gained in deciding whether to grant an injunction or award damages. Thus, in refusing to prevent the destruction of a prospect by a new building, the judge stated:

I know no general rule of common law, which . . . says, that building so as to stop another's prospect is a nuisance. Was that the case, there could be no great towns; and I must grant injunctions to all the new buildings in this town. . . .[18]

In *Webb v. Bird*[19] it was decided that it was not a nuisance to build a schoolhouse so near a windmill as to obstruct currents of air and hinder the working of the mill. An early case seems to have been decided in an opposite direction. Gale commented:

In old maps of London a row of windmills appears on the heights to the north of London. Probably in the time of King James it was thought an alarming circumstance, as affecting the supply of food to the city, that anyone should build so near them as to take the wind out from their sails.[20]

In one of the cases discussed in Section V, *Sturges v. Bridgman*, it seems clear that the judges were thinking of the economic consequences of alternative decisions. To the argument that if the principle that they seemed to be following:

were carried out to its logical consequences, it would result in the most serious practical inconveniences, for a man might go—say into the midst of the tanneries of *Bermondsey*, or into any other locality devoted to any particular trade or manufacture of a noisy or unsavoury character, and by building a private residence upon a vacant piece of land put a stop to such trade or manufacture altogether,

the judges answered that

whether anything is a nuisance or not is a question to be determined, not merely by an abstract consideration of the thing itself, but in reference to its circumstances; What would be a nuisance in *Belgrave Square* would not necessarily be so in *Bermondsey*; and where a locality is devoted to a particular trade or manufacture carried on by the traders or manufacturers in a particular and established manner not

---

[16]See W. L. Prosser, *The Law of Torts* 398-99, 412 (2d ed. 1955). The quotation about the ancient case concerning candle-making is taken from Sir James Fitzjames Stephen, *A General View of the Criminal Law of England* 106 (1890). Sir James Stephen gives no reference. He perhaps had in mind *Rex. v. Ronkett*, included in Seavey, Keeton and Thurston, *Cases on Torts* 604 (1950). A similar view to that expressed by Prosser is to be found in F. V. Harper and F. James, *The Law of Torts* 67-74 (1956); *Restatement, Torts* §§ 826, 827 and 828.

[17]See Winfield on *Torts* 541-48 (6th ed. T. E. Lewis 1954); Salmond on the *Law of Torts* 181-90 (12th ed. R.F.V. Heuston 1957); H. Street, *The Law of Torts* 221-29 (1959).

[18]*Attorney General v. Doughty*, 2 Ves. Sen. 453, 28 Eng. Rep. 290 (Ch. 1752). Compare in this connection the statement of an American judge, quoted in Prosser, *op. cit. supra* n. 16 at 413 n. 54: "Without smoke, Pittsburgh would have remained a very pretty village," Musmanno, J., in *Versailles Borough v. McKeesport Coal & Coke Co.*, 1935, 83 Pitts. Leg. J. 379, 385.

[19]10 C.B. (N.S.) 268, 142 Eng. Rep. 445 (1861); 13 C.B. (N.S.) 841, 143 Eng. Rep. 332 (1863).

[20]See Gale on *Easements* 238, n. 6 (13th ed. M. Bowles 1959).

constituting a public nuisance, Judges and juries would be justified in finding, and may be trusted to find, that the trade or manufacture so carried on in that locality is not a private or actionable wrong.[21]

That the character of the neighbourhood is relevant in deciding whether something is, or is not, a nuisance, is definitely established.

> He who dislikes the noise of traffic must not set up his abode in the heart of a great city. He who loves peace and quiet must not live in a locality devoted to the business of making boilers or steamships.[22]

What has emerged has been described as "planning and zoning by the judiciary."[23] Of course there are sometimes considerable difficulties in applying the criteria.[24]

An interesting example of the problem is found in *Adams v. Ursell*[25] in which a fried fish shop in a predominantly working-class district was set up near houses of a "much better character." England without fish-and-chips is a contradiction in terms and the case was clearly one of high importance. The judge commented:

> It was urged that an injunction would cause great hardship to the defendant and to the poor people who get food at his shop. The answer to that is that it does not follow that the defendant cannot carry on his business in another more suitable place somewhere in the neighbourhood. It by no means follows that because a fried fish shop is a nuisance in one place it is a nuisance in another.

In fact, the injunction which restrained Mr. Ursell from running his shop did not even extend to the whole street. So he was presumably able to move to other premises near houses of "a much worse character," the inhabitants of which would no doubt consider the availability of fish-and-chips to outweigh the pervading odour and "fog or mist" so graphically described by the plaintiff. Had there been no other "more suitable place in the neighbourhood," the case would have been more difficult and the decision might have been different. What would "the poor people" have had for food? No English judge would have said: "Let them eat cake."

The courts do not always refer very clearly to the economic problem posed by the cases brought before them but it seems probable that in the interpretation of words and phrases like "reasonable" or "common or ordinary use" there is some recognition, perhaps largely unconscious and certainly not very explicit, of the economic aspects of the questions at issue. A good example of this would seem to be the judgment in the Court of Appeals in *Andreae v. Selfridge and Company Ltd.*[26] In this case, a hotel (in Wigmore Street) was situated on part of an island site. The remainder of the site was acquired by Selfridges which demolished the existing buildings in order to erect another in their place. The hotel suffered a loss of custom in consequence of the noise and dust caused by the demolition. The owner of the hotel brought an action against Selfridges for damages. In the lower court, the hotel was awarded £4,500 damages. The case was then taken on appeal.

The judge who had found for the hotel proprietor in the lower court said:

> I cannot regard what the defendants did on the site of the first operation as having been commonly done in the ordinary use and occupation of land or houses. It is neither usual nor common, in this country, for people to excavate a site to a depth of 60 feet and then to erect upon that site a steel framework and fasten the steel frames together with rivets. . . . Nor is it, I think, a common or ordinary use of land, in this country, to act as the defendants did when they were dealing with the site of their second operation—

---

[21]11 Ch.D. 865 (1879).

[22]Salmond on the *Law of Torts* 182 (12th ed. R.F.V. Heuston 1957).

[23]C. M. Haar, *Land-Use Planning, A Casebook on the Use, Misuse, and Re-use of Urban Land* 95 (1959).

[24]See, for example, *Rushmer V. Polsue and Alfieri, Ltd.* [1906] 1 Ch. 234, which deals with the case of a house in a quiet situation in a noisy district.

[25][1913] 1 Ch. 269.

[26][1938] 1 Ch. 1.

namely, to demolish all the houses that they had to demolish, five or six of them I think, if not more, and to use for the purpose of demolishing them pneumatic hammers.

Sir Wilfred Greene, M.R., speaking for the Court of Appeals, first noted

that when one is dealing with temporary operations, such as demolition and re-building, everybody has to put up with a certain amount of discomfort, because operations of that kind cannot be carried on at all without a certain amount of noise and a certain amount of dust. Therefore, the rule with regard to interference must be read subject to this qualification. . . .

He then referred to the previous judgment:

With great respect to the learned judge, I take the view that he has not approached this matter from the correct angle. It seems to me that it is not possible to say . . . that the type of demolition, excavation and construction in which the defendant company was engaged in the course of these operations was of such an abnormal and unusual nature as to prevent the qualification to which I have referred coming into operation. It seems to me that, when the rule speaks of the common or ordinary use of land, it does not mean that the methods of using land and building on it are in some way to be stabilised for ever. As time goes on new inventions or new methods enable land to be more profitably used, either by digging down into the earth or by mounting up into the skies. Whether, from other points of view, that is a matter which is desirable for humanity is neither here not there; but it is part of the normal use of land, to make use upon your land, in the matter of construction, of what particular type and what particular depth of foundations and particular height of building may be reasonable, in the circumstances, and in view of the developments of the day. . . . Guests at hotels are very easily upset. People coming to this hotel, who were accustomed to a quiet outlook at the back, coming back and finding demolition and building going on, may very well have taken the view that the particular merit of this hotel no longer existed. That would be a misfortune for the plaintiff; but assuming that there was nothing wrong in the defendant company's works, assuming the defendant company was carrying on the demolition and its building, productive of noise though it might be, with all reasonable skill, and taking all reasonable precautions not to cause annoyance to its neighbors, then the plaintiff might lose all her clients in the hotel because they have lost the amenities of an open and quiet place behind, but she would have no cause of complaint. . . . [But those] who say that their interference with the comfort of their neighbors is justified because their operations are normal and usual and conducted with proper care and skill are under a specific duty . . . to use that reasonable and proper care and skill. It is not a correct attitude to take to say: 'We will go on and do what we like until somebody complains!' . . . Their duty is to take proper precautions and to see that the nuisance is reduced to a minimum. It is no answer for them to say: 'But this would mean that we should have to do the work more slowly than we would like to do it, or it would involve putting us to some extra expense.' All these questions are matters of common sense and degree, and quite clearly it would be unreasonable to expect people to conduct their work so slowly or so expensively, for the purpose of preventing a transient inconvenience, that the cost and trouble would be prohibitive. . . . In this case, the defendant company's attitude seems to have been to go on until somebody complained, and further, that its desire to hurry its work and conduct it according to its own ideas and its own convenience was to prevail if there was a real conflict between it and the comfort of its neighbors. That . . . is not carrying out the obligation of using reasonable care and skill. . . . The effect comes to this . . . the plaintiff suffered an actionable nuisance; . . . she is entitled, not to a nominal sum, but to a substantial sum, based upon those principles . . . but in arriving at the sum . . . I have discounted any loss of custom . . . which might be due to the general loss of amenities owing to what was going on at the back. . . .

The upshot was that the damages awarded were reduced from £4,500 to £1,000.

The discussion in this section has, up to this point, been concerned with court decisions arising out of the common law relating to nuisance. Delimitation of rights in this area also comes about because of statutory enactments. Most economists would appear to assume that the aim of governmental action in this field is to extend the scope of the law of nuisance by designating as nuisances activities which would not be recognized as such by the common law. And there can be no doubt that some statutes, for example, the Public Health Acts, have had this effect. But not all Governmental enactments are of this kind. The effect of much of the legislation in this area is to protect businesses from the claims of those they have harmed by their actions. There is a long list of legalized nuisances.

The position has been summarized in *Halsbury's Laws of England* as follows:

Where the legislature directs that a thing shall in all events be done or authorises certain works at a particular place for a specific purpose or grants powers with the intention that they shall be exercised, although leaving some discretion as to the mode of exercise, no action will lie at common law for nuisance or damage which is the inevitable result of carrying out the statutory powers so conferred. This is so whether the act causing the damage is authorised for public purposes or private profit. Acts done under powers granted by persons to whom Parliament has delegated authority to grant such powers, for example, under provisional orders of the Board of Trade, are regarded as having been done under statutory authority. In the absence of negligence it seems that a body exercising statutory powers will not be liable to an action merely because it might, by acting in a different way, have minimised an injury.

Instances are next given of freedom from liability for acts authorised:

An action has been held not to be against a body exercising its statutory powers without negligence in respect of the flooding of land by water escaping from watercourses, from water pipes, from drains, or from a canal; the escape of fumes from sewers; the escape of sewage: the subsidence of a road over a sewer; vibration or noise caused by a railway; fires caused by authorised acts; the pollution of a stream where statutory requirements to use the best known method of purifying before discharging the effluent have been satisfied; interference with a telephone or telegraph system by an electric tramway; the insertion of poles for tramways in the subsoil; annoyance caused by things reasonably necessary for the excavation of authorised works; accidental damage caused by the placing of a grating in a roadway; the escape of tar acid; or interference with the access of a frontager by a street shelter or safety railings on the edge of a pavement.[27]

The legal position in the United States would seem to be essentially the same as in England, except that the power of the legislatures to authorise what would otherwise be nuisances under the common law, at least without giving compensation to the person harmed, is somewhat more limited, as it is subject to constitutional restrictions.[28] Nonetheless, the power is there and cases more or less identical with the English cases can be found. The question has arisen in an acute form in connection with airports and the operation of aeroplanes. The case of *Delta Air Corporation v. Kersey, Kersey v. City of Atlanta*[29] is a good example. Mr. Kersey bought land and built a house on it. Some years later the City of Atlanta constructed an airport on land immediately adjoining that of Mr. Kersey. It was explained that his property was "a quiet, peaceful and proper location for a home before the airport was built, but dust, noises and low flying of airplanes caused by the operation of the airport have rendered his property unsuitable as a home," a state of affairs which was described in the report of the case with a wealth of distressing detail. The judge first referred to an earlier case, *Thrasher v. City of Atlanta*[30] in which it was noted that the City of Atlanta had been expressly authorised to operate an airport.

By this franchise aviation was recognised as a lawful business and also as an enterprise affected with a public interest . . . all persons using [the airport] in the manner contemplated by law are within the protection and immunity of the franchise granted by the municipality. An airport is not a nuisance per se, although it might become such from the manner of its construction or operation.

Since aviation was a lawful business affected with a public interest and the construction of the airport was authorised by statute, the judge next referred to *Georgia Railroad and Banking Co. v. Maddox*[31] in which it was said:

Where a railroad terminal yard is located and its construction authorized, under statutory powers, if it be constructed and operated in a proper manner, it cannot be adjudged a nuisance. Accordingly, injuries

---

[27]See 30 Halsbury, *Law of England* 690-91 (3d ed. 1960), Article on Public Authorities and Public Officers.

[28]See Prosser, *op. cit. supra* n. 16 at 421; Harper and James, *op. cit. supra* n. 16 at 86-87.

[29]Supreme Court of Georgia 193 Ga. 862, 20 S.E. 2d 245 (1942).

[30]178 Ga. 514, 173 S.E. 817 (1934).

[31]116 Ga. 64, 42 S.E. 315 (1902).

and inconveniences to persons residing near such a yard, from noises of locomotives, rumbling of cars, vibrations produced thereby, and smoke, cinders, soot and the like, which result from the ordinary and necessary, therefore proper, use and operation of such a yard, are not nuisances, but are the necessary concomitants of the franchise granted.

In view of this, the judge decided that the noise and dust complained of by Mr. Kersey "may be deemed to be incidental to the proper operation of an airport, and as such they cannot be said to constitute a nuisance." But the complaint against low flying was different:

> . . . can it be said that flights . . . at such a low height [25 to 50 feet above Mr. Kersey's house] as to be imminently dangerous to . . . life and health . . . are a necessary concomitant of an airport? We do not think this question can be answered in the affirmative. No reason appears why the city could not obtain lands of an area [sufficiently large] . . . as not to require such low flights. . . . For the sake of public convenience adjoining-property owners must suffer such inconvenience from noise and dust as result from the usual and proper operation of an airport, but their private rights are entitled to preference in the eyes of the law where the inconvenience is not one demanded by a properly constructed and operated airport.

Of course this assumed that the City of Atlanta could prevent the low flying and continue to operate the airport. The judge therefore added:

> From all that appears, the conditions causing the low flying may be remedied; but if on the trial it should appear that it is indispensable to the public interest that the airport should continue to be operated in its present condition, it may be said that the petitioner should be denied injunctive relief.

In the course of another aviation case, *Smith v. New England Aircraft Co.*,[32] the court surveyed the law in the United States regarding the legalizing of nuisances and it is apparent that, in the broad, it is very similar to that found in England:

> It is the proper function of the legislative department of government in the exercise of the police power to consider the problems and risks that arise from the use of new inventions and endeavor to adjust private rights and harmonize conflicting interests by comprehensive statutes for the public welfare. . . . There are . . . analogies where the invasion of the airspace over underlying land by noise, smoke, vibration, dust and disagreeable odors, having been authorized by the legislative department of government and not being in effect a condemnation of the property although in some measure depreciating its market value, must be borne by the landowner without compensation or remedy. Legislative sanction makes that lawful which otherwise might be a nuisance. Examples of this are damages to adjacent land arising from smoke, vibration and noise in the operation of a railroad . . . ; the noise of ringing factory bells . . . ; the abatement of nuisances . . . ; the erection of steam engines and furnaces . . . ; unpleasant odors connected with sewers, oil refining and storage of naphtha. . . .

Most economists seem to be unaware of all this. When they are prevented from sleeping at night by the roar of jet planes overhead (publicly authorised and perhaps publicly operated), are unable to think (or rest) in the day because of the noise and vibration from passing trains (publicly authorised and perhaps publicly operated), find it difficult to breathe because of the odour from a local sewage farm (publicly authorised and perhaps publicly operated) and are unable to escape because their driveways are blocked by a road obstruction (without any doubt, publicly devised), their nerves frayed and mental balance disturbed, they proceed to declaim about the disadvantages of private enterprise and the need for Government regulation.

While most economists seem to be under a misapprehension concerning the character of the situation with which they are dealing, it is also the case that the activities which they would like to see stopped or curtailed may well be socially justified. It is all a question of weighing up the gains that would accrue from eliminating these harmful effects against the gains that accrue from allowing them to continue. Of course, it is likely that an extension of Government economic activity will often lead to this protection against action for nuisance being pushed further than is desirable. For one thing, the Government is likely to look with a benevolent eye on enterprises which it is itself promoting. For another, it is possible

---

[32]270 Mass. 511, 523, 170 N.E. 385, 390 (1930).

to describe the committing of a nuisance by public enterprise in a much more pleasant way than when the same thing is done by private enterprise. In the words of Lord Justice Sir Alfred Denning:

> ... the significance of the social revolution of today is that, whereas in the past the balance was much too heavily in favor of the rights of property and freedom of contract, Parliament has repeatedly intervened so as to give the public good its proper place.[33]

There can be little doubt that the Welfare State is likely to bring an extension of that immunity from liability for damage, which economists have been in the habit of condemning (although they have tended to assume that this immunity was a sign of too little Government intervention in the economic system). For example, in Britain, the powers of local authorities are regarded as being either absolute or conditional. In the first category, the local authority has no discretion in exercising the power conferred on it. "The absolute power may be said to cover all the necessary consequences of its direct operation even if such consequences amount to nuisance." On the other hand, a conditional power may only be exercised in such a way that the consequences do not constitute a nuisance.

> It is the intention of the legislature which determines whether a power is absolute or conditional. ... [As] there is the possibility that the social policy of the legislature may change from time to time, a power which in one era would be construed as being conditional, might in another era be interpreted as being absolute in order to further the policy of the Welfare State. This point is one which should be borne in mind when considering some of the older cases upon this aspect of the law of nuisance.[34]

It would seem desirable to summarize the burden of this long section. The problem which we face in dealing with actions which have harmful effects is not simply one of restraining those responsible for them. What has to be decided is whether the gain from preventing the harm is greater than the loss which would be suffered elsewhere as a result of stopping the action which produces the harm. In a world in which there are costs of rearranging the rights established by the legal system, the courts, in cases relating to nuisance, are, in effect, making a decision on the economic problem and determining how resources are to be employed. It was argued that the courts are conscious of this and that they often make, although not always in a very explicit fashion, a comparison between what would be gained and what lost by preventing actions which have harmful effects. But the delimitation of rights is also the result of statutory enactments. Here we also find evidence of an appreciation of the reciprocal nature of the problem. While statutory enactments add to the list of nuisances, action is also taken to legalize what would otherwise be nuisances under the common law. The kind of situation which economists are prone to consider as requiring corrective Government action is, in fact, often the result of Government action. Such action is not necessarily unwise. But there is a real danger that extensive Government intervention in the economic system may lead to the protection of those responsible for harmful effects being carried too far.

VIII. Pigou's Treatment in "The Economics of Welfare"

The fountainhead for the modern economic analysis of the problem discussed in this article is Pigou's *Economics of Welfare* and, in particular, that section of Part II which deals with divergences between social and private net products which come about because

> one person A, in the course of rendering some service, for which payment is made, to a second person B, incidentally also renders services or disservices to other persons (not producers of like services), of such a sort that payment cannot be exacted from the benefited parties or compensation enforced on behalf of the injured parties.[35]

---

[33]See Sir Alfred Denning, *Freedom Under the Law* 71 (1949).

[34]M. B. Cairns, *The Law of Tort in Local Government* 28-32 (1954).

[35]A. C. Pigou, *The Economics of Welfare* 183 (4th ed. 1932). My references will all be to the fourth edition but the argument and examples examined in this article remained substantially unchanged from the first edition in 1920 to the fourth in 1932. A large part (but not all) of this analysis had appeared previously in *Wealth and Welfare* (1912).

Pigou tells us that his aim in Part II of *The Economics of Welfare* is

> to ascertain how far the free play of self-interest, acting under the existing legal system, tends to distribute the country's resources in the way most favorable to the production of a large national dividend, and how far it is feasible for State action to improve upon 'natural' tendencies.[36]

To judge from the first part of this statement, Pigou's purpose is to discover whether any improvements could be made in the existing arrangements which determine the use of resources. Since Pigou's conclusion is that improvements could be made, one might have expected him to continue by saying that he proposed to set out the changes required to bring them about. Instead, Pigou adds a phrase which contrasts "natural" tendencies with State action, which seems in some sense to equate the present arrangements with "natural" tendencies and to imply that what is required to bring about these improvements is State action (if feasible). That this is more or less Pigou's position is evident from Chapter I of Part II.[37] Pigou starts by referring to "optimistic followers of the classical economists"[38] who have argued that the value of production would be maximised if the Government refrained from any interference in the economic system and the economic arrangements were those which come about "naturally." Pigou goes on to say that if self-interest does promote economic welfare, it is because human institutions have been devised to make it so. (This part of Pigou's argument, which he develops with the aid of a quotation from Cannan, seems to me to be essentially correct.) Pigou concludes:

> But even in the most advanced States there are failures and imperfections. . . . there are many obstacles that prevent a community's resources from being distributed . . . in the most efficient way. The study of these constitutes our present problem. . . . its purposes is essentially practical. It seeks to bring into clearer light some of the ways in which it now is, or eventually may become, feasible for governments to control the play of economic forces in such wise as to promote the economic welfare, and through that, the total welfare, of their citizens as a whole.[39]

Pigou's underlying thought would appear to be: Some have argued that no State action is needed. But the system has performed as well as it has because of State action. Nonetheless, there are still imperfections. What additional State action is required?

If this is a correct summary of Pigou's position, its inadequacy can be demonstrated by examining the first example he gives of a divergence between private and social products.

> It might happen . . . that costs are thrown upon people not directly concerned, through, say, uncompensated damage done to surrounding woods by sparks from railway engines. All such effects must be included—some of them will be positive, others negative elements—in reckoning up the social net product of the marginal increment of any volume of resources turned into any use or place.[40]

The example used by Pigou refers to a real situation. In Britain, a railway does not normally have to compensate those who suffer damage by fire caused by sparks from an engine. Taken in conjunction with what he says in Chapter 9 of Part II, I take Pigou's policy recommendations to be, first, that there should be State action to correct this "natural" situation and, second, that the railways should be forced to compensate those whose woods are burnt. If this is a correct interpretation of Pigou's position, I would argue that the first recommendation is based on a misapprehension of the facts and that the second is not necessarily desirable.

---

[36]*Id.* at xii.

[37]*Id.* at 127-30.

[38]In *Wealth and Welfare*, Pigou attributes the "optimism" to Adam Smith himself and not to his followers. He there refers to the "highly optimistic theory of Adam Smith that the national dividend, in given circumstances of demand and supply, tends 'naturally' to a maximum" (p. 104).

[39]Pigou, *op. cit. supra* n. 35 at 129-30.

[40]*Id.* at 134.

Let us consider the legal position. Under the heading "Sparks from engines," we find the following in Halsbury's Laws of England:

> If railway undertakers use steam engines on their railway without express statutory authority to do so, they are liable, irrespective of any negligence on their part, for fires caused by sparks from engines. Railway undertakers are, however, generally given statutory authority to use steam engines on their railway; accordingly, if an engine is constructed with the precautions which science suggests against fire and is used without negligence, they are not responsible at common law for any damage which may be done by sparks. . . . In the construction of an engine the undertaker is bound to use all the discoveries which science has put within its reach in order to avoid doing harm, provided they are such as it is reasonable to require the company to adopt, having proper regard to the likelihood of the damage and to the cost and convenience of the remedy; but it is not negligence on the part of an undertaker if it refuses to use an apparatus the efficiency of which is open to bona fide doubt.

To this general rule, there is a statutory exception arising from the Railway (Fires) Act, 1905, as amended in 1923. This concerns agricultural land or agricultural crops.

> In such a case the fact that the engine was used under statutory powers does not affect the liability of the company in an action for the damage. . . . These provisions, however, only apply where the claim for damage . . . does not exceed £200, [£100 in the 1905 Act] and where written notice of the occurrence of the fire and the intention to claim has been sent to the company within seven days of the occurrence of the damage and particulars of the damage in writing showing the amount of the claim in money not exceeding £200 have been sent to the company within twenty-one days.

Agricultural land does not include moorland or buildings and agricultural crops do not include those led away or stacked.[41] I have not made a close study of the parliamentary history of this statutory exception, but to judge from debates in the House of Commons in 1922 and 1923, this exception was probably designed to help the smallholder.[42]

Let us return to Pigou's example of uncompensated damage to surrounding woods caused by sparks from railway engines. This is presumably intended to show how it is possible "for State action to improve on 'natural' tendencies." If we treat Pigou's example as referring to the position before 1905, or as being an arbitrary example (in that he might just as well have written "surrounding buildings" instead of "surrounding woods"), then it is clear that the reason why compensation was not paid must have been that the railway had statutory authority to run steam engines (which relieved it of liability for fires caused by sparks). That this was the legal position was established in 1860, in a case, oddly enough, which concerned the burning of surrounding woods by a railway,[43] and the law on this point has not been changed (apart from the one exception) by a century of railway legislation, including nationalisation. If we treat Pigou's example of "uncompensated damage done to surrounding woods by sparks from railway engines" literally, and assume that it refers to the period after 1905, then it is clear that the reason why compensation was not paid must have been that the damage was more than £100 (in the first edition of *The Economics of Welfare*) or more than £200 (in later editions) or that the owner of the wood failed to notify the railway in writing within seven days of the fire or did not send particulars of the damage, in writing, within twenty-one days. In the real world, Pigou's example could only exist as a result of a deliberate choice of the legislature. It is not, of course, easy to imagine the construction of a railway in a state of nature. The nearest one can get to this is presumably a railway which uses steam engines "without express statutory authority." However, in this case the railway would be obliged to compensate those whose woods it burnt down. That is to say, compensation would be paid in the absence of Government action. The only circumstances in which compensation would not be paid would be those in which there had been Government action. It is strange that Pigou, who clearly

---

[41]See 31 Halsbury, *Laws of England* 474-75 (3d ed. 1960), Article on Railways and Canals, from which this summary of the legal position, and all quotations, are taken.

[42]See 152 H.C. Deb. 2622-63 (1922); 161 H.C. Deb. 2935-55 (1923).

[43]*Vaughan v. Taff Vale Railway Co.*, 3 H. and N. 743 (Ex. 1858) and 5 H. and N. 679 (Ex. 1860).

thought it desirable that compensation should be paid, should have chosen this particular example to demonstrate how it is possible "for State action to improve on 'natural' tendencies."

Pigou seems to have had a faulty view of the facts of the situation. But it also seems likely that he was mistaken in his economic analysis. It is not necessarily desirable that the railway should be required to compensate those who suffer damage by fires caused by railway engines. I need not show here that, if the railway could make a bargain with everyone having property adjoining the railway line and there were no costs involved in making such bargains, it would not matter whether the railway was liable for damage caused by fires or not. This question has been treated at length in earlier sections. The problem is whether it would be desirable to make the railway liable in conditions in which it is too expensive for such bargains to be made. Pigou clearly thought it was desirable to force the railway to pay compensation and it is easy to see the kind of argument that would have led him to this conclusion. Suppose a railway is considering whether to run an additional train or to increase the speed of an existing train or to install spark-preventing devices on its engines. If the railway were not liable for fire damage, then, when making these decisions, it would not take into account as a cost the increase in damage resulting from the additional train or the faster train or the failure to install spark-preventing devices. This is the source of the divergence between private and social net products. It results in the railway performing acts which will lower the value of total production—and which it would not do if it were liable for the damage. This can be shown by means of an arithmetical example.

Consider a railway, which is *not* liable for damage by fires caused by sparks from its engines, which runs two trains per day on a certain line. Suppose that running one train per day would enable the railway to perform services worth $150 per annum and running two trains a day would enable the railway to perform services worth $250 per annum. Suppose further that the cost of running one train is $50 per annum and two trains $100 per annum. Assuming perfect competition, the cost equals the fall in the value of production elsewhere due to the employment of additional factors of production by the railway. Clearly the railway would find it profitable to run two trains per day. But suppose that running one train per day would destroy by fire crops worth (on an average over the year) $60 and two trains a day would result in the destruction of crops worth $120. In these circumstances running one train per day would raise the value of total production but the running of a second train would reduce the value of total production. The second train would enable additional railway services worth $100 per annum to be performed. But the fall in the value of production elsewhere would be $110 per annum; $50 as a result of the employment of additional factors of production and $60 as a result of the destruction of crops. Since it would be better if the second train were not run and since it would not run if the railway were liable for damage caused to crops, the conclusion that the railway should be made liable for the damage seem irresistible. Undoubtedly it is this kind of reasoning which underlies the Pigovian position.

The conclusion that it would be better if the second train did not run is correct. The conclusion that it is desirable that the railway should be made liable for the damage it causes is wrong. Let us change our assumption concerning the rule of liability. Suppose that the railway is liable for damage from fires caused by sparks from the engine. A farmer on lands adjoining the railway is then in the position that, if his crop is destroyed by fires caused by the railway, he will receive the market price from the railway; but if his crop is not damaged, he will receive the market price by sale. It therefore becomes a matter of indifference to him whether his crop is damaged by fire or not. The position is very different when the railway is *not* liable. Any crop destruction through railway-caused fires would then reduce the receipts of the farmer. He would therefore take out of cultivation any land for which the damage is likely to be greater than the net return of the land (for reasons explained at length in Section III). A change from a regime in which the railway is *not* liable for damage to one in which it *is* liable is likely therefore to lead to an increase in the amount of cultivation on lands adjoining the railway. It will also, of course, lead to an increase in the amount of crop destruction due to railway-caused fires.

Let us return to our arithmetical example. Assume that, with the changed rule of liability, there is a doubling in the amount of crop destruction due to railway-caused fires. With one train per day, crops worth $120 would be destroyed each year and two trains per day would lead to the destruction of crops worth $240. We saw previously that it would not be profitable to run the second train if the railway had to pay $60 per annum as compensation for damage. With damage at $120 per annum the loss from running the second train would be $60 greater. But now let us consider the first train. The value of the transport services furnished by the first train is $150. The cost of running the train is $50. The amount

393

that the railway would have to pay out as compensation for damage is $120. It follows that it would not be profitable to run any trains. With the figures in our example we reach the following result: if the railway is not liable for fire-damage, two trains per day would be run; if the railway is liable for fire-damage, it would cease operations altogether. Does this mean that it is better that there should be no railway? This question can be resolved by considering what would happen to the value of total production if it were decided to exempt the railway from liability for fire-damage, thus bringing it into operation (with two trains per day).

The operation of the railway would enable transport services worth $250 to be performed. It would also mean the employment of factors of production which would reduce the value of production elsewhere by $100. Furthermore it would mean the destruction of crops worth $120. The coming of the railway will also have led to the abandonment of cultivation of some land. Since we know that, had this land been cultivated, the value of the crops destroyed by fire would have been $120, and since it is unlikely that the total crop on this land would have been destroyed, it seems reasonable to suppose that the value of the crop yield on this land would have been higher than this. Assume it would have been $160. But the abandonment of cultivation would have released factors of production for employment elsewhere. All we know is that the amount by which the value of production elsewhere will increase will be less than $160. Suppose that it is $150. Then the gain from operating the railway would be $250 (the value of the transport services) minus $100 (the cost of the factors of production) minus $120 (the value of crops destroyed by fire) minus $160 (the fall in the value of crop production due to the abandonment of cultivation) plus $150 (the value of production elsewhere of the released factors of production). Overall, operating the railway will increase the value of total production by $20. With these figures it is clear that it is better that the railway should not be liable for the damage it causes, thus enabling it to operate profitably. Of course, by altering the figures, it could be shown that there are other cases in which it would be desirable that the railway should be liable for the damage it causes. It is enough for my purpose to show that, from an economic point of view, a situation in which there is "uncompensated damage done to surrounding woods by sparks from railway engines" is not necessarily undesirable. Whether it is desirable or not depends on the particular circumstances.

How is it that the Pigovian analysis seems to give the wrong answer? The reason is that Pigou does not seem to have noticed that his analysis is dealing with an entirely different question. The analysis as such is correct. But it is quite illegitimate for Pigou to draw the particular conclusion he does. The question at issue is not whether it is desirable to run an additional train or a faster train or to install smoke-preventing devices; the question at issue is whether it is desirable to have a system in which the railway has to compensate those who suffer damage from the fires which it causes or one in which the railway does not have to compensate them. When an economist is comparing alternative social arrangements, the proper procedure is to compare the total social product yielded by these different arrangements. The comparison of private and social products is neither here nor there. A simple example will demonstrate this. Imagine a town in which there are traffic lights. A motorist approaches an intersection and stops because the light is red. There are no cars approaching the intersection on the other street. If the motorist ignored the red signal, no accident would occur and the total product would increase because the motorist would arrive earlier at his destination. Why does he not do this? The reason is that if he ignored the light he would be fined. The private product from crossing the street is less than the social product. Should we conclude from this that the total product would be greater if there were no fines for failing to obey traffic signals? The Pigovian analysis shows us that it is possible to conceive of better worlds than the one in which we live. But the problem is to devise practical arrangements which will correct defects in one part of the system without causing more serious harm in other parts.

I have examined in considerable detail one example of a divergence between private and social products and I do not propose to make any further examination of Pigou's analytical system. But the main discussion of the problem considered in this article is to be found in that part of Chapter 9 in Part II which deals with Pigou's second class of divergence and it is of interest to see how Pigou develops his argument. Pigou's own description of this second class of divergence was quoted at the beginning of this section. Pigou distinguishes between the case in which a person renders services for which he receives no payment and the case in which a person renders disservices and compensation is not given to the injured parties. Our main attention has, of course, centred on this second case. It is therefore rather astonishing to find, as was pointed out to me by Professor Francesco Forte, that the problem of the smoking chimney—the "stock instance"[44] or "classroom example"[45] of the second case—is used by Pigou as an example of the first case (services rendered without payment) and is never mentioned, at any rate explicitly, in connection with the second case.[46] Pigou points out that factory owners who devote resources to preventing their chimneys from smoking render services for which they receive no payment. The implication, in the light of Pigou's discussion later in the chapter, is that a factory owner with a smoking chimney should be given a bounty to induce him to install smoke-preventing devices. Most modern economists would suggest that the owner of the factory with the smokey chimney should be taxed. It seems a pity that economists (apart from Professor Forte) do not seem to have noticed this feature of Pigou's treatment since a realisation that the problem could be tackled in either of these two ways would probably have led to an explicit recognition of its reciprocal nature.

In discussing the second case (disservices without compensation to those damaged), Pigou says that they are rendered "when the owner of a site in a residential quarter of a city builds a factory there and so destroys a great part of the amenities of neighbouring sites; or, in a less degree, when he uses his site in such a way as to spoil the lighting of the house opposite; or when he invests resources in erecting buildings in a crowded centre, which by contracting the air-space and the playing room of the neighbourhood, tend to injure the health and efficiency of the families living there."[47] Pigou is, of course, quite right to describe such actions as "uncharged disservices." But he is wrong when he describes these actions as "anti-social."[48] They may or may not be. It is necessary to weigh the harm against the good that will result. Nothing could be more "anti-social" than to oppose any action which causes any harm to anyone.

The example with which Pigou opens his discussion of "uncharged disservices" is not, as I have indicated, the case of the smokey chimney but the case of the overrunning rabbits: ". . . incidental uncharged disservices are rendered to third parties when the game-preserving activities of one occupier involve the overrunning of a neighboring occupier's land by rabbits. . . ." This example is of extraordinary interest, not so much because the economic analysis of the case is essentially any different from that of the other examples, but because of the peculiarities of the legal position and the light it throws on the part which economics can play in what is apparently the purely legal question of the delimitation of rights.

The problem of legal liability for the actions of rabbits is part of the general subject of liability for animals.[49] I will, although with reluctance, confine my discussion to rabbits. The early cases relating to rabbits concerned the relations between the lord of the manor and commoners, since, from the thirteenth century on, it became usual for the lord of the manor to stock the commons with conies (rabbits), both for the sake of the meat and the fur. But in 1597, in *Boulston*'s case, an action was brought by one landowner against a neighbouring landowner, alleging that the defendant had made coney-burrows and that the conies had increased and had destroyed the plaintiff's corn. The action failed for the reason that

---

[44]Sir Dennis Robertson, I *Lectures on Economic Principles* 162 (1957).

[45]E. J. Mishan, "The Meaning of Efficiency in Economics," 189, *The Banker's Magazine* 482 (June 1960).

[46]Pigou, *op. cit. supra* n. 35 at 184.

[47]*Id.* at 185-86.

[48]*Id.* at 186 n.1. For similar unqualified statements see Pigou's lecture "Some Aspects of the Housing Problem" in B. S. Rowntree and A. C. Pigou, "Lectures on Housing," in 18 *Manchester Univ. Lectures* (1914).

[49]See G. L. Williams, *Liability for Animals—An Account of the Development and Present Law of Tortious Liability for Animals. Distress Damage Feasant and the Duty to Fence, in Great Britain, Northern Ireland and the Common Law Dominions* (1939). Part Four, "The Action of Nuisance, in Relation to Liability for Animals," 236-62, is especially relevant to our discussion. The problem of liability for rabbits is discussed in this part, 238-47. I do not know how far the common law in the United States regarding liability for animals has diverged from that in Britain. In some Western States of the United States, the English common law regarding the duty to fence has not been followed, in part because "the considerable amount of open, uncleared land made it a matter of public policy to allow cattle to run at large" (Williams, *op. cit. supra* 227). This affords a good example of how a different set of circumstances may make it economically desirable to change the legal rule regarding the delimitation of rights.

. . . so soon as the coneys come on his neighbor's land he may kill them, for they are ferae naturae, and he who makes the coney-boroughs has no property in them, and he shall not be punished for the damage which the coneys do in which he has no property, and which the other may lawfully kill.[50]

As *Boulston*'s case has been treated as binding—Bray, J., in 1919, said that he was not aware that *Boulston*'s case has ever been overruled or questioned[51]—Pigou's rabbit example undoubtedly represented the legal position at the time *The Economics of Welfare* was written.[52] And in this case, it is not far from the truth to say that the state of affairs which Pigou describes came about because of an absence of Government action (at any rate in the form of statutory enactments) and was the result of "natural" tendencies.

Nonetheless, *Boulston*'s case is something of a legal curiosity and Professor Williams makes no secret of his distaste for this decision:

> The conception of liability in nuisance as being based upon ownership is the result, apparently, of a confusion with the action of cattle-trespass, and runs counter both the principle and to the medieval authorities on the escape of water, smoke, and filth. . . . The prerequisite of any satisfactory treatment of the subject is the final abandonment of the pernicious doctrine in *Boulston*'s case. . . . Once *Boulston*'s case disappears, the way will be clear for a rational restatement of the whole subject, on lines that will harmonize with the principles prevailing in the rest of the law of nuisance.[53]

The judges in *Boulston*'s case were, of course, aware that their view of the matter depended on distinguishing this case from one involving nuisance:

> This cause is not like to the cases put, on the other side, of erecting a lime-kiln, dyehouse, or the like; for there the annoyance is by the act of the parties who make them; but it is not so here, for the conies of themselves went into the plaintiff's land, and he might take them when they came upon his land, and make profit of them.[54]

Professor Williams comments:

> Once more the atavistic idea is emerging that the animals are guilty and not the landowner. It is not, of course, a satisfactory principle to introduce into a modern law of nuisance. If A. erects a house or plants a tree so that the rain runs or drips from it onto B.'s land, this is A.'s act for which he is liable; but if A. introduces rabbits into his land so that they escape from it into B.'s, this is the act of the rabbits for which A. is not liable—such is the specious distinction resulting from *Boulston*'s case.[55]

It has to be admitted that the decision in *Boulston*'s case seems a little odd. A man may be liable for damage caused by smoke or unpleasant smells, without it being necessary to determine whether he owns the smoke or the smell. And the rule in *Boulston*'s case has not always been followed in cases dealing with other animals. For example, in *Bland v. Yates*,[56] it was decided that an injunction could be granted to prevent someone from keeping an *unusual and excessive* collection of manure in which flies bred and which infested a neighbour's house. The question of who owned the flies was not raised. An economist would not wish to object because legal reasoning sometimes appears a little odd. But there is a sound economic reason for supporting Professor Williams' view that the problem of liability for animals (and particularly rabbits) should be brought within the ordinary law of nuisance. The reason is not that the man who harbours rabbits is solely responsible for the damage; the man whose crops are

---

[50]5 Coke (Vol. 3) 104 b. 77 Eng. Rep., 216, 217.

[51]See *Stearn v. Prentice Bros. Ltd.* (1919), 1 K.B., 395, 397.

[52]I have not looked into recent cases. The legal position has also been modified by statutory enactments.

[53]Williams, *op. cit. supra* n. 49 at 242, 258.

[54]*Boulston v. Hardy*, Cro. Eliz., 547, 548, 77 Eng. Rep. 216.

[55]Williams, *op. cit. supra* n. 49 at 243.

[56]58 Sol.J. 612 (1913-1914).

eaten is equally responsible. And given that the costs of market transactions make a rearrangement of rights impossible, unless we know the particular circumstances, we cannot say whether it is desirable or not to make the man who harbours rabbits responsible for the damage committed by the rabbits on neighbouring properties. The objection to the rule in *Boulston*'s case is that, under it, the harbourer of rabbits can *never* be liable. It fixes the rule of liability at one pole: and this is as undesirable, from an economic point of view, as fixing the rule at the other pole and making the harbourer of rabbits always liable. But, as we saw in Section VII, the law of nuisance, as it is in fact handled by the courts, is flexible and allows for a comparison of the utility of an act with the harm it produces. As Professor Williams says: "The whole law of nuisance is an attempt to reconcile and compromise between conflicting interests. . . ."[57] To bring the problem of rabbits within the ordinary law of nuisance would not mean *inevitably* making the harbourer of rabbits liable for damage committed by the rabbits. This is not to say that the sole task of the courts in such cases is to make a comparison between the harm and the utility of an act. Nor is it to be expected that the courts will always decide correctly after making such a comparison. But unless the courts act very foolishly, the ordinary law of nuisance would seem likely to give economically more satisfactory results than adopting a rigid rule. Pigou's case of the overrunning rabbits affords an excellent example of how problems of law and economics are interrelated, even though the correct policy to follow would seem to be different from that envisioned by Pigou.

Pigou allows one exception to his conclusion that there is a divergence between private and social products in the rabbit example. He adds: ". . . unless . . . the two occupiers stand in the relation of landlord and tenant, so that compensation is given in an adjustment of the rent."[58] This qualification is rather surprising since Pigou's first class of divergence is largely concerned with the difficulties of drawing up satisfactory contracts between landlords and tenants. In fact, all the recent cases on the problem of rabbits cited by Professor Williams involved disputes between landlords and tenants concerning sporting rights.[59] Pigou seems to make a distinction between the case in which no contract is possible (the second class) and that in which the contract is unsatisfactory (the first class). Thus he says that the second class of divergences between private and social net product

> cannot, like divergences due to tenancy laws, be mitigated by a modification of the contractual relation between any two contracting parties, because the divergence arises out of a service or disservice rendered to persons other than the contracting parties.[60]

But the reason why some activities are not the subject of contracts is exactly the same as the reason why some contracts are commonly unsatisfactory—it would cost too much to put the matter right. Indeed, the two cases are really the same since the contracts are unsatisfactory because they do not cover certain activities. The exact bearing of the discussion of the first class of divergence on Pigou's main argument is difficult to discover. He shows that in some circumstances contractual relations between landlord and tenant may result in a divergence between private and social products.[61] But he also goes on to show that Government-enforced compensation schemes and rent-controls will also produce divergences.[62] Furthermore, he shows that, when the Government is in a similar position to a private landlord, e.g. when granting a franchise to a public utility, exactly the same difficulties arise as when private individuals are involved.[63] The discussion is interesting but I have been unable to discover what general conclusions about economic policy, if any, Pigou expects us to draw from it.

Indeed, Pigou's treatment of the problems considered in this article is extremely elusive and the discussion of his views raises almost insuperable difficulties of interpretation. Consequently it is impossible to be sure that one has understood what Pigou really meant. Nevertheless, it is difficult to

---

[57]Williams, *op. cit. supra* n. 49 at 259.

[58]Pigou, *op. cit. supra* n. 35 at 185.

[59]Williams, *op. cit. supra* n. 49 at 244-47.

[60]Pigou, *op. cit. supra* n. 35 at 192.

[61]*Id.* 174-75.

[62]*Id.* 177-83.

[63]*Id.* 175-77.

resist the conclusion, extraordinary though this may be in an economist of Pigou's stature, that the main source of this obscurity is that Pigou had not thought his position through.

IX. The Pigovian Tradition

It is strange that a doctrine as faulty as that developed by Pigou should have been so influential, although part of its success has probably been due to the lack of clarity in the exposition. Not being clear, it was never clearly wrong. Curiously enough, this obscurity in the source has not prevented the emergence of a fairly well-defined oral tradition. What economists think they learn from Pigou, and what they tell their students, which I term the Pigovian tradition, is reasonably clear. I propose to show the inadequacy of this Pigovian tradition by demonstrating that both the analysis and the policy conclusions which it supports are incorrect.

I do not propose to justify my view as to the prevailing opinion by copious references to the literature. I do this partly because the treatment in the literature is usually so fragmentary, often involving little more than a reference to Pigou plus some explanatory comment, that detailed examination would be inappropriate. But the main reason for this lack of reference is that the doctrine, although based on Pigou, must have been largely the product of an oral tradition. Certainly economists with whom I have discussed these problems have shown a unanimity of opinion which is quite remarkable considering the meagre treatment accorded this subject in the literature. No doubt there are some economists who do not share the usual view but they must represent a small minority of the profession.

The approach to the problems under discussion is through an examination of the value of physical production. The private product is the value of the additional product resulting from a particular activity of a business. The social product equals the private product minus the fall in the value of production elsewhere for which no compensation is paid by the business. Thus, if 10 units of a factor (and no other factors) are used by a business to make a certain product with a value of $105; and the owner of this factor is not compensated for their use, which he is unable to prevent; and these 10 units of the factor would yield products in their best alternative use worth $100; then, the social product is $105 minus $100 or $5. If the business now pays for one unit of the factor and its price equals the value of its marginal product, then the social product rises to $15. If two units are paid for, the social product rises to $25 and so on until it reaches $105 when all units of the factor are paid for. It is not difficult to see why economists have so readily accepted this rather odd procedure. The analysis focusses on the individual business decision and since the use of certain resources is not allowed for in costs, receipts are reduced by the same amount. But, of course, this means that the value of the social product has no social significance whatsoever. It seems to me preferable to use the opportunity cost concept and to approach these problems by comparing the value of the product yielded by factors in alternative uses or by alternative arrangements. The main advantage of a pricing system is that it leads to the employment of factors in places where the value of the product yielded is greatest and does so at less cost than alternative systems (I leave aside that a pricing system also eases the problem of the redistribution of income). But if through some God-given natural harmony factors flowed to the places where the value of the product yielded was greatest without any use of the pricing system and consequently there was no compensation, I would find it a source of surprise rather than a cause for dismay.

The definition of the social product is queer but this does not mean that the conclusions for policy drawn from the analysis are necessarily wrong. However, there are bound to be dangers in an approach which diverts attention from the basic issues and there can be little doubt that it has been responsible for some of the errors in current doctrine. The belief that it is desirable that the business which causes harmful effects should be forced to compensate those who suffer damage (which was exhaustively discussed in Section VIII in connection with Pigou's railway sparks example) is undoubtedly the result of not comparing the total product obtainable with alternative social arrangements.

The same fault is to be found in proposals for solving the problem of harmful effects by the use of taxes or bounties. Pigou lays considerable stress on this solution although he is, as usual, lacking in detail and qualified in his support.[64] Modern economists tend to think exclusively in terms of taxes and in a very precise way. The tax should be equal to the damage done and should therefore vary with the

---

[64]*Id.* 192-4, 381 and *Public Finance* 94-100 (3d ed. 1947).

amount of the harmful effect. As it is not proposed that the proceeds of the tax should be paid to those suffering the damage, this solution is not the same as that which would force a business to pay compensation to those damaged by its actions, although economists generally do not seem to have noticed this and tend to treat the two solutions as being identical.

Assume that a factory which emits smoke is set up in a district previously free from smoke pollution, causing damage valued at $100 per annum. Assume that the taxation solution is adopted and that the factory owner is taxed $100 per annum as long as the factory emits the smoke. Assume further that a smoke-preventing device costing $90 per annum to run is available. In these circumstances, the smoke-preventing device would be installed. Damage of $100 would have been avoided at an expenditure of $90 and the factory owner would be better off by $10 per annum. Yet the position achieved may not be optimal. Suppose that those who suffer the damage could avoid it by moving to other locations or by taking various precautions which would cost them, or be equivalent to a loss in income of, $40 per annum. Then there would be a gain in the value of production of $50 if the factory continued to emit its smoke and those now in the district moved elsewhere or made other adjustments to avoid the damage. If the factory owner is to be made to pay a tax equal to the damage caused, it would clearly be desirable to institute a double tax system and to make residents of the district pay an amount equal to the additional cost incurred by the factory owner (or the consumers of his products) in order to avoid the damage. In these conditions, people would not stay in the district or would take other measures to prevent the damage from occurring, when the costs of doing so were less than the costs that would be incurred by the producer to reduce the damage (the producer's object, of course, being no so much to reduce the damage as to reduce the tax payments). A tax system which was confined to a tax on the producer for damage caused would tend to lead to unduly high costs being incurred for the prevention of damage. Of course this could be avoided if it were possible to base the tax, not on the damage caused, but on the fall in the value of production (in its widest sense) resulting from the emission of smoke. But to do so would require a detailed knowledge of individual preferences and I am unable to imagine how the data needed for such a taxation system could be assembled. Indeed, the proposal to solve the smoke-pollution and similar problems by the use of taxes bristles with difficulties: the problem of calculation, the difference between average and marginal damage, the interrelations between the damage suffered on different properties, etc. But it is unnecessary to examine these problems here. It is enough for my purpose to show that, even if the tax is exactly adjusted to equal the damage that would be done to neighbouring properties as a result of the emission of each additional puff of smoke, the tax would not necessarily bring about optimal conditions. An increase in the number of people living or of business operating in the vicinity of the smoke-emitting factory will increase the amount of harm produced by a given emission of smoke. The tax that would be imposed would therefore increase with an increase in the number of those in the vicinity. This will tend to lead to a decrease in the value of production of the factors employed by the factory, either because a reduction in production due to the tax will result in factors being used elsewhere in ways which are less valuable, or because factors will be diverted to produce means for reducing the amount of smoke emitted. But people deciding to establish themselves in the vicinity of the factory will not take into account this fall in the value of production which results from their presence. This failure to take into account costs imposed on others is comparable to the action of a factory owner in not taking into account the harm resulting from his emission of smoke. Without the tax, there may be too much smoke and too few people in the vicinity of the factory; but with the tax there may be too little smoke and too many people in the vicinity of the factory. There is no reason to suppose that one of these results is necessarily preferable.

I need not devote much space to discussing the similar error involved in the suggestion that smoke producing factories should, by means of zoning regulations, be removed from the districts in which the smoke causes harmful effects. When the change in the location of the factory results in a reduction in production, this obviously needs to be taken into account and weighed against the harm which would result from the factory remaining in that location. The aim of such regulation should not be to eliminate smoke pollution but rather to secure the optimum amount of smoke pollution, this being the amount which will maximise the value of production.

X. A Change of Approach

It is my belief that the failure of economists to reach correct conclusions about the treatment of harmful effects cannot be ascribed simply to a few slips in analysis. It stems from basic defects in the current approach to problems of welfare economics. What is needed in a change of approach.

Analysis in terms of divergencies between private and social products concentrates attention on particular deficiencies in the system and tends to nourish the belief that any measure which will remove the deficiency is necessarily desirable. It diverts attention from those other changes in the system which are inevitably associated with the corrective measure, changes which may well produce more harm than the original deficiency. In the preceding sections of this article, we have seen many examples of this. But it is not necessary to approach the problem in this way. Economists who study problems of the firm habitually use an opportunity cost approach and compare the receipts obtained from a given combination of factors with alternative business arrangements. It would seem desirable to use a similar approach when dealing with questions of economic policy and to compare the total product yielded by alternative social arrangements. In this article, the analysis has been confined, as is usual in this part of economics, to comparisons of the value of production, as measured by the market. But it is, of course, desirable that the choice between different social arrangements for the solution of economic problems should be carried out in broader terms than this and that the total effect of these arrangements in all spheres of life should be taken into account. As Frank H. Knight has so often emphasized, problems of welfare economics must ultimately dissolve into a study of aesthetics and morale.

A second feature of the usual treatment of the problems discussed in this article is that the analysis proceeds in terms of a comparison between a state of laissez faire and some kind of ideal world. This approach inevitably leads to a looseness of thought since the nature of the alternatives being compared is never clear. In a state of laissez faire, is there a monetary, a legal or a political system and if so, what are they? In an ideal world, would there be a monetary, a legal or a political system and if so, what would they be? The answers to all these questions are shrouded in mystery and every man is free to draw whatever conclusions he likes. Actually very little analysis is required to show that an ideal world is better than a state of laissez faire, unless the definitions of a state of laissez faire and an ideal world happen to be the same. But the whole discussion is largely irrelevant for questions of economic policy since whatever we may have in mind as our ideal world, it is clear that we have not yet discovered how to get to it from where we are. A better approach would seem to be to start our analysis with a situation approximating that which actually exists, to examine the effects of a proposed policy change and to attempt to decide whether the new situation would be, in total, better or worse than the original one. In this way, conclusions for policy would have some relevance to the actual situation.

A final reason for the failure to develop a theory adequate to handle the problem of harmful effects stems from a faulty concept of a factor of production. This is usually thought of as a physical entity which the businessman acquires and uses (an acre of land, a ton of fertiliser) instead of as a right to perform certain (physical) actions. We may speak of a person owning land and using it as a factor of production but what the land-owner in fact possesses is the right to carry out a circumscribed list of actions. The rights of a land-owner are not unlimited. It is not even always possible for him to remove the land to another place, for instance, by quarrying it. And although it may be possible for him to exclude some people from using "his" land, this may not be true of others. For example, some people may have the right to cross the land. Furthermore, it may or may not be possible to erect certain types of buildings or to grow certain crops or to use particular drainage systems on the land. This does not come about simply because of Government regulation. It would be equally true under the common law. In fact it would be true under any system of law. A system in which the rights of individuals were unlimited would be one in which there were no rights to acquire.

If factors of production are thought of as rights, it becomes easier to understand that the right to do something which has a harmful effect (such as the creation of smoke, noise, smells, etc.) is also a factor of production. Just as we may use a piece of land in such a way as to prevent someone else from crossing it, or parking his car, or building his house upon it, so we may use it in such a way as to deny him a view or quiet or unpolluted air. The cost of exercising a right (of using a factor of production) is always the loss which is suffered elsewhere in consequence of the exercise of that right—the inability to cross land, to park a car, to build a house, to enjoy a view, to have peace and quiet or to breathe clean air.

It would clearly be desirable if the only actions performed were those in which what was gained was worth more than what was lost. But in choosing between social arrangements within the context of which individual decisions are made, we have to bear in mind that a change in the existing system which will lead to an improvement in some decisions may well lead to a worsening of others. Furthermore we have to take into account the costs involved in operating the various social arrangements (whether it be the working of a market or of a government department), as well as the costs involved in moving to a new system. In devising and choosing between social arrangements we should have regard for the total effect. This, above all, is the change in approach which I am advocating.

GRAPHPAC

Exhibit 1–2 Shifting the Demand Curve

Table A. Your Original Demand for Coffee

Price	Quantity
20¢/cup	5 cups/day
30¢	4
40¢	2
50¢	1

Table B. Your New Demand for Coffee after Medical Advice to Cut Back

Price	Quantity
20¢/cup	3 cups/day
30¢	2
40¢	1
50¢	0

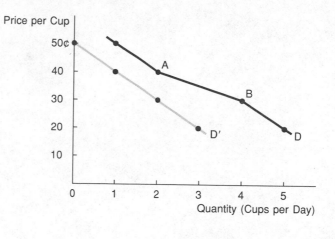

Your original demand curve for coffee is the curve labeled D. A change in price, say from 30¢ per cup to 40¢ per cup, would cause a movement along the curve from point A to point B. A change in something other than price, such as a doctor's suggestion that caffeine is bad for your health, can lead to a change in demand, represented by a shift to an entirely new demand curve. In this case the doctor's advice leads to a fall in demand, which is represented by a leftward shift of the curve.

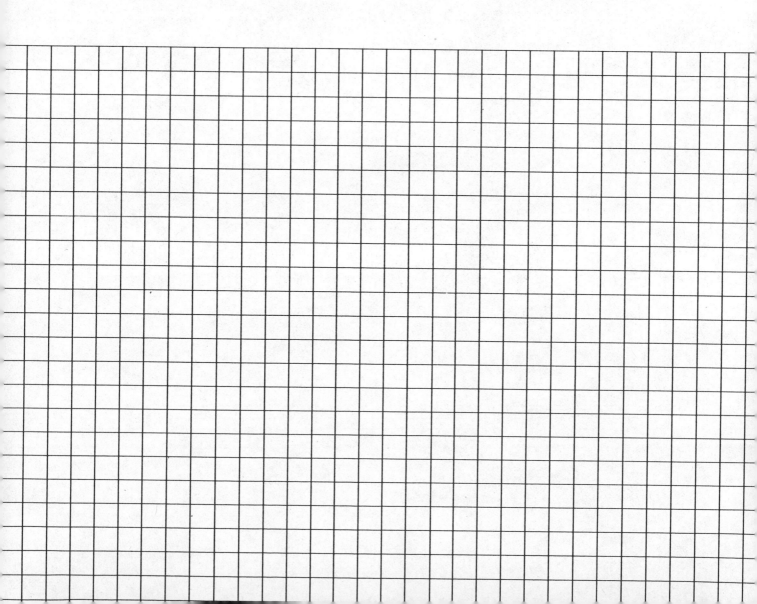

Exhibit 1–3   The Effect of a Sales Tax on Demand

Table A. Demand for
Coffee without Tax

Price	Quantity
20¢/cup	5 cups/day
30¢	4
40¢	2
50¢	1

Table B. Demand for
Coffee with Sales Tax of
10¢ per Cup

Price	Quantity
10¢/cup	5 cups/day
20¢	4
30¢	2
40¢	1

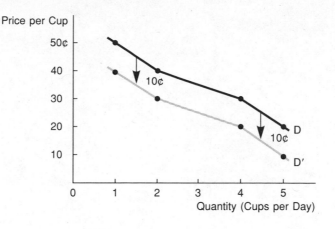

If the price of coffee is 10¢ per cup and there is a sales tax of 10¢, then it will actually cost you 20¢ to acquire a cup of coffee. Table A shows that under these circumstances you would purchase 5 cups per day. This is recorded in the first row of Table B. The other rows in that table are generated in a similar manner.

The rows of Table B contain the same quantities as the rows of Table A, but the corresponding prices are all 10¢ lower. Another way to say this is that each point on the new demand curve lies exactly 10¢ below a corresponding point on the original demand curve. Therefore the new demand curve lies exactly 10¢ below the original demand curve in vertical distance. The sales tax causes the demand curve to shift downward parallel to itself by the amount of the tax.

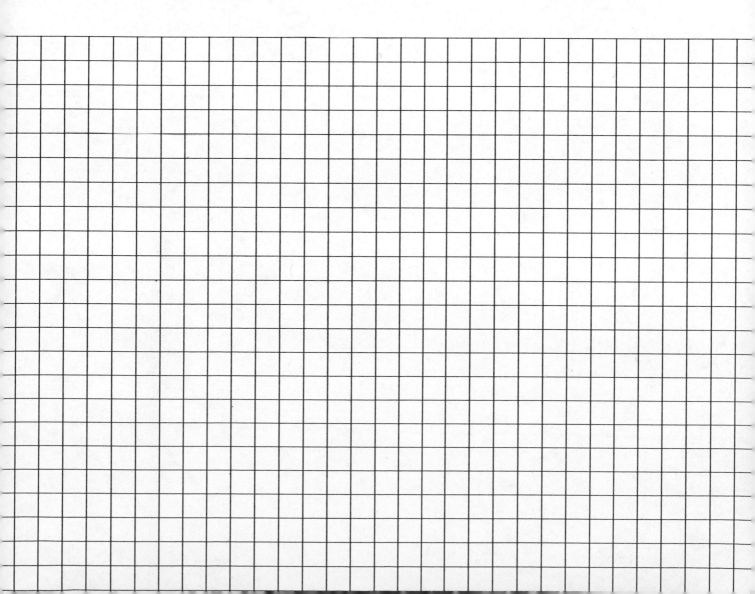

Exhibit 1–4 The Shape of the Demand Curve

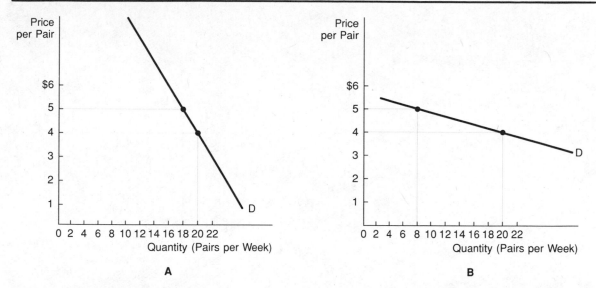

The two panels depict two possible demand curves for shoes. In panel A a given change in price (say from $4 per pair to $5 per pair) leads to a small change in quantity demanded (from 20 pairs of shoes per week to 18 pairs per week). In panel B the same change in price leads to a large change in quantity demanded (from 20 pairs per week to 8 pairs per week).

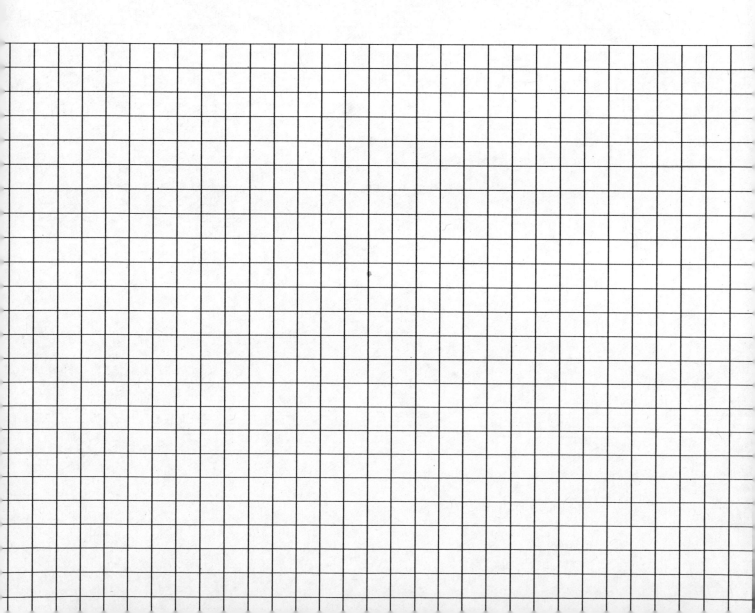

Exhibit 1–5   Slopes versus Elasticities

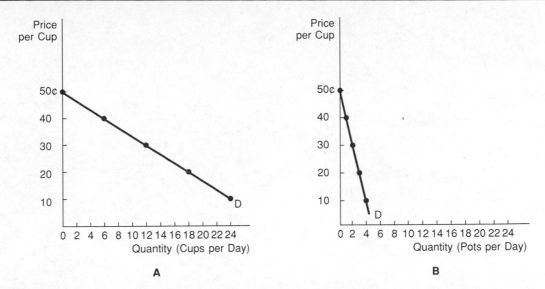

A

B

The two demand curves have different slopes even though they each represent the same demand for coffee. The different slopes result from the different choices of units on the quantity axis. However, both curves have the same elasticity. Elasticity is unaffected by the choice of units.

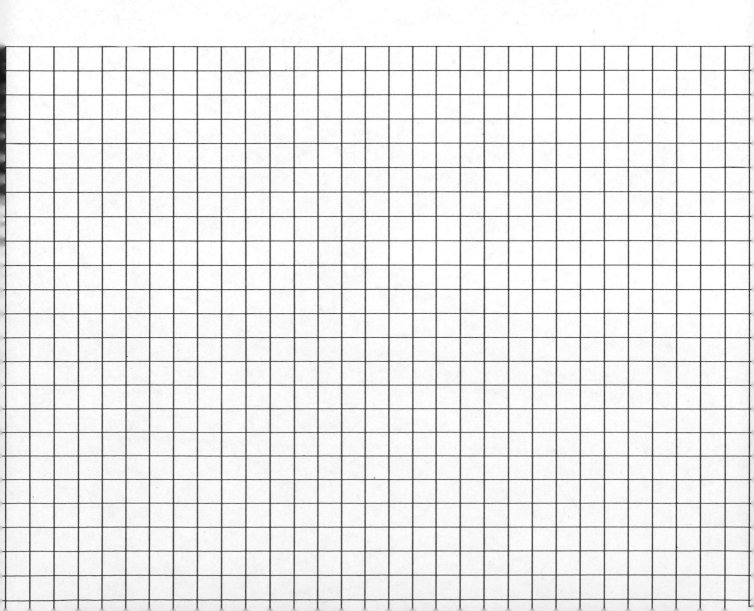

Exhibit 1–6   The Supply of Coffee

Table A. Supply of Coffee
to Your City

Price	Quantity
20¢/cup	100 cups/day
30¢	300
40¢	400
50¢	500

Table B. Supply of Coffee to
Your City Following the
Development of Better
Farming Methods

Price	Quantity
20¢/cup	200 cups/day
30¢	400
40¢	600
50¢	700

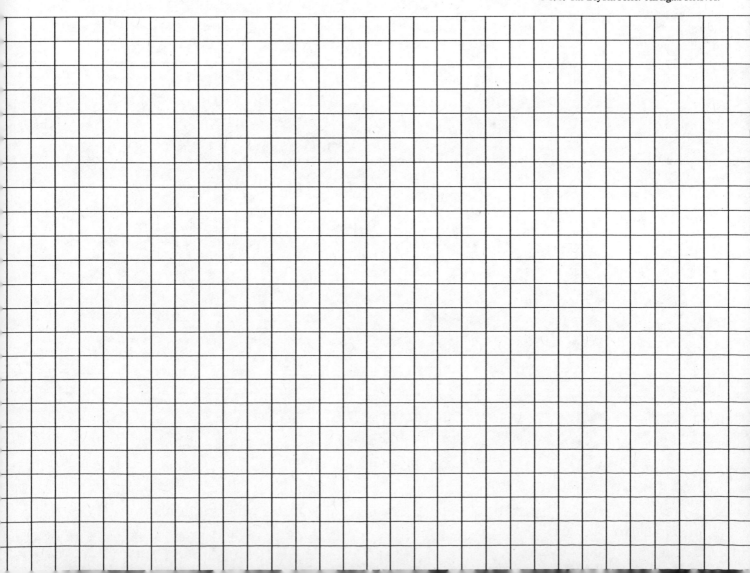

Table A shows, for each price, how much coffee would be supplied to your city. The same information is illustrated by the points in the graph. The curve labeled S is the corresponding supply curve. It conveys more information than the table by displaying the quantities supplied at intermediate prices. The law of supply is illustrated by the upward slope of the supply curve.

The invention of a cheaper way to produce coffee increases the willingness of suppliers to provide coffee at any given price. The new supply is shown in Table B and is illustrated by the curve S'. Although a change in price leads to a movement along the supply curve, a change in something other than price causes the entire curve to shift.

The curve S' lies to the right of S, indicating that the supply has increased.

Exhibit 1–7   Effect of an Excise Tax

Table A. Supply of Coffee
without Tax

Price	Quantity
20¢/cup	100 cups/day
30¢	300
40¢	400
50¢	500

Table B. Supply of Coffee
with Excise Tax of 10¢ Per
Cup

Price	Quantity
30¢/cup	100 cups/day
40¢	300
50¢	400
60¢	500

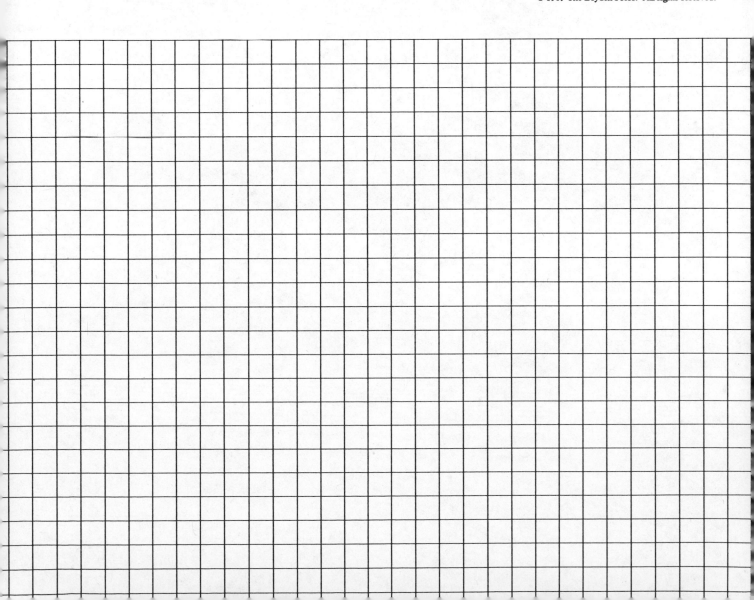

If the price of coffee is 30¢ per cup and there is an excise tax of 10¢, then a seller of coffee will actually get to keep 20¢ per cup sold. The original supply schedule (Table A) shows that under these circumstances suppliers would provide 100 cups per day. This is recorded in the first row of Table B. The other rows in that table are generated in a similar manner.

The rows of Table B contain the same quantities as the rows of Table A, but the corresponding prices are all 10¢ higher. Thus each point on the new supply curve S′ lies exactly 10¢ above a corresponding point on the old supply curve S. Therefore S′ lies exactly 10¢ above S in vertical distance. The excise tax causes the supply curve to shift upward parallel to itself a distance 10¢.

Exhibit 1–8   Equilibrium in the Market for Floppy Disks

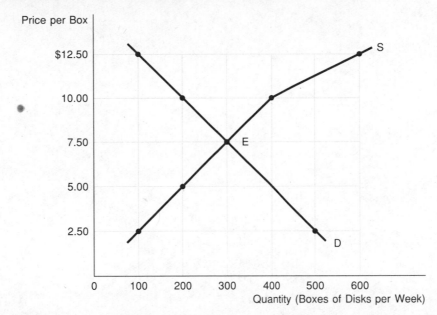

The graph shows the supply and demand curves for floppy computer disks. The equilibrium point, E, is located at the intersection of the two curves. The equilibrium price, $7.50 per box, is the only price at which quantity supplied and quantity demanded are equal.

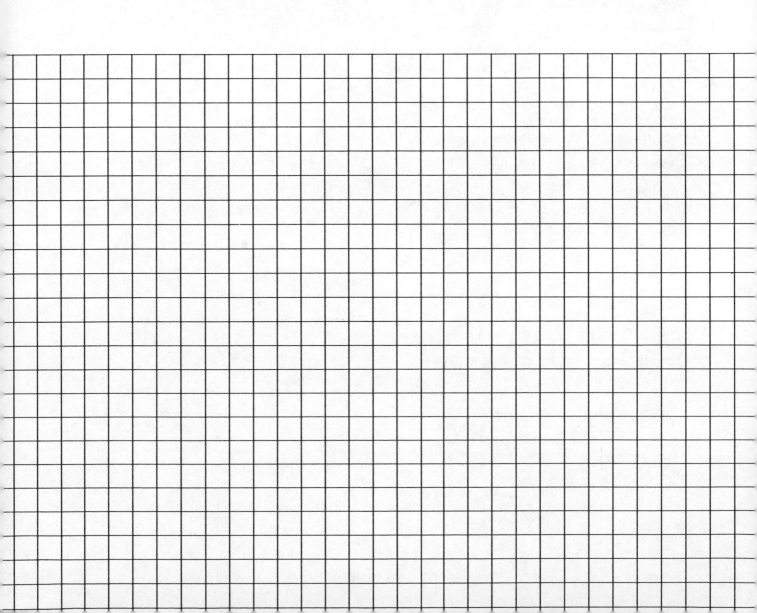

Exhibit 1–9   **The Effects of Supply and Demand Shifts**

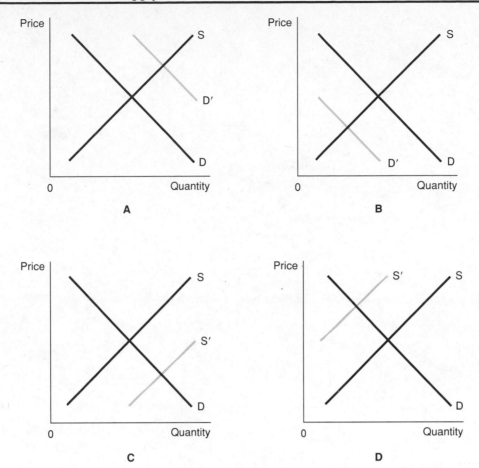

The graphs show the effects of various shifts in demand and supply. For example, in panel A we see that a rise in demand leads to a rise in price and a rise in quantity.

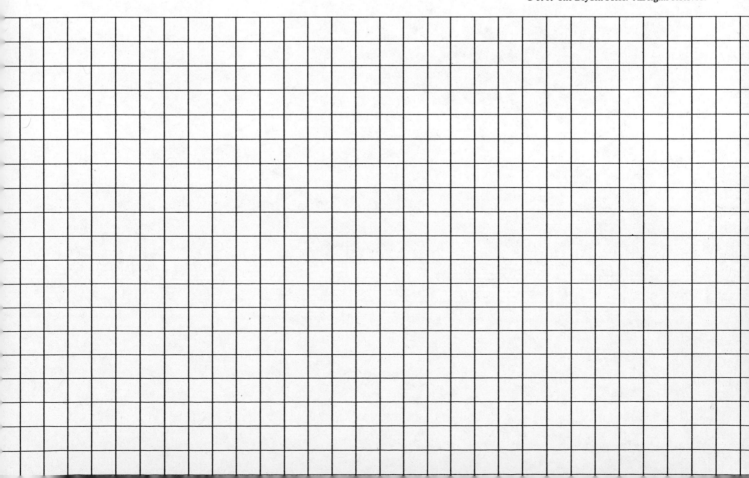

Exhibit 1–11   A Sales Tax versus an Excise Tax

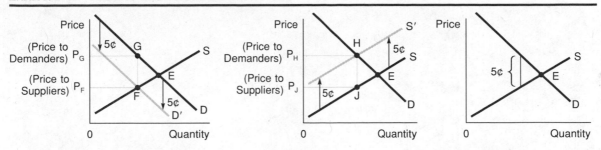

A. Effect of a Sales Tax   **B. Effect of an Excise Tax**   **C. Equilibrium without Any Tax**

Panel A is a reproduction of the graph from Exhibit 1–10, illustrating the effect of a 5¢ sales tax. Panel B illustrates the effect of a 5¢ excise tax: The supply curve shifts upward a vertical distance 5¢, leading to a new market equilibrium at point H. The corresponding price, P_H, is what demanders must pay for a head of lettuce. But suppliers keep less than P_H when a head of lettuce is sold—they keep P_H minus 5¢ tax. Thus the price to suppliers is 5¢ below P_H. To find the corresponding point, begin at H and move down a distance 5¢ to J. Since H is on the curve S', J must be on the curve S. The price to suppliers is P_J.

To compare the effects of the two taxes, we must compare the points G and F in panel A with the points H and J in panel B. In each case there is one point on the curve D and one point on the curve S, and in each case the two points are a distance 5¢ apart. There is only one possible location for such points, as shown in panel C. It follows that points G and F are identical to points H and J. In other words, the sales tax and the excise tax have exactly the same effects on both suppliers and demanders.

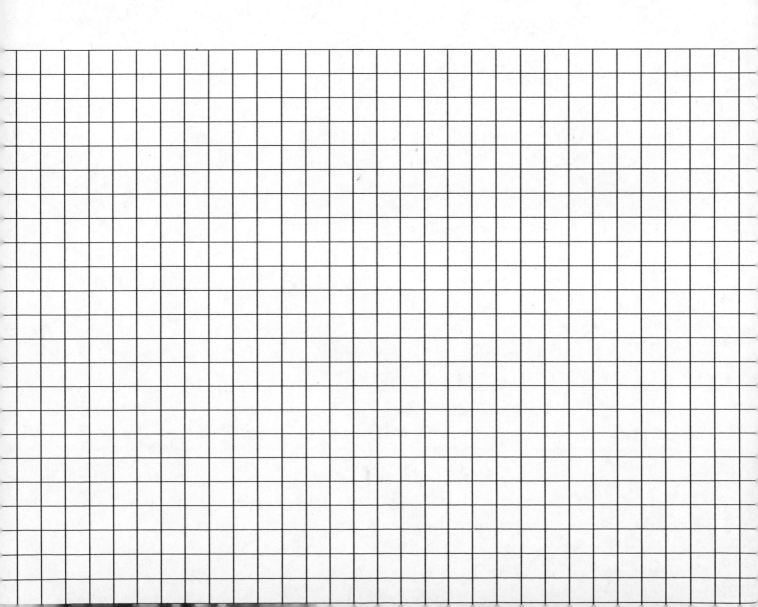

Exhibit 3–3 Indifference Curves Never Cross

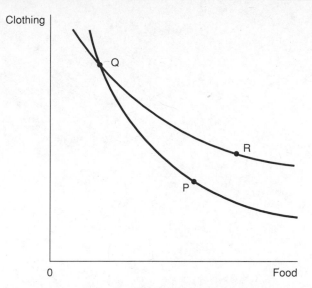

Crossing indifference curves, such as those shown in the graph, cannot occur. The consumer likes P and Q equally well because they are both on the same (black) indifference curve. He also likes R and Q equally well because they are both on the same (colored) indifference curve. We may infer that he likes P and R equally well, which we know to be false (in fact R is preferred to P). Thus the graph cannot be correct.

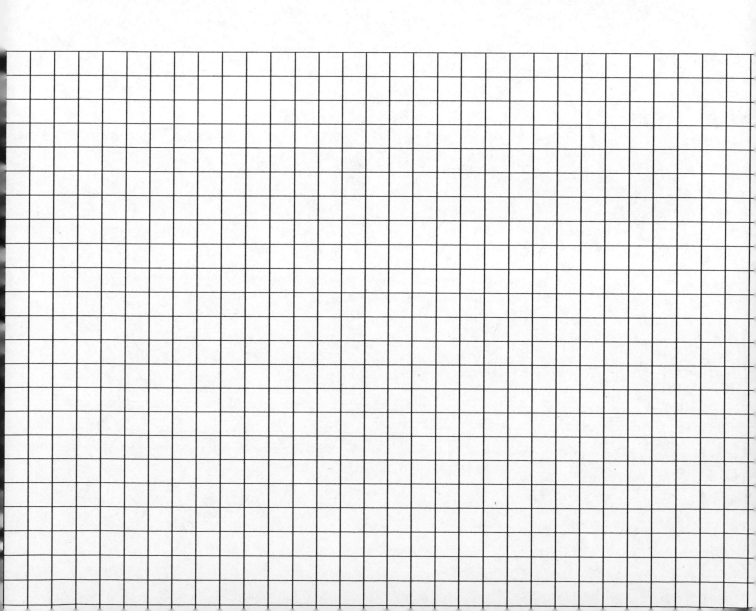

Exhibit 3–6   The Marginal Rate of Substitution as the Slope of the Tangent Line

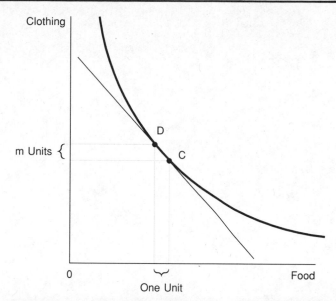

For a consumer starting with basket C, the marginal rate of substitution between food and clothing is given by the vertical distance m. This distance is also equal to the slope of the line through points C and D. When units are chosen very small, D is very close to C and the line through these points is essentially tangent to the curve. Therefore the marginal rate of substitution is equal to the slope of the tangent line to the indifference curve at C.

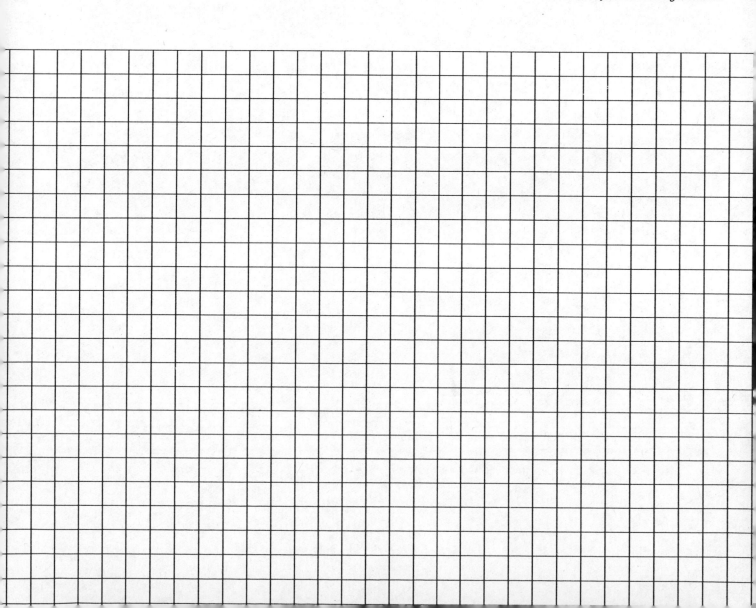

Exhibit 3–7 The Curvature of Indifference Curves

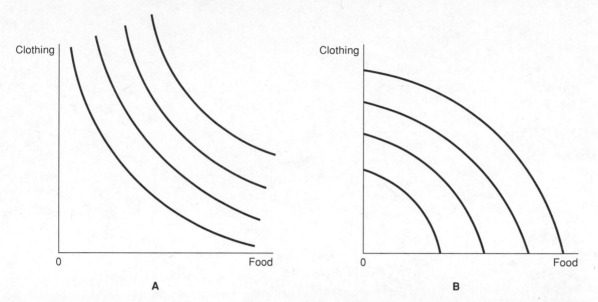

The indifference curves in panel A are convex (bowed in toward the origin), indicating that when the consumer is starving and well-dressed (in the "northwest" part of the diagram), his marginal rate of substitution between food and clothing is high—he would require many units of clothing to compensate him for the loss of one unit of food. We assume that indifference curves have this shape, rather than the alternative shape illustrated in panel B.

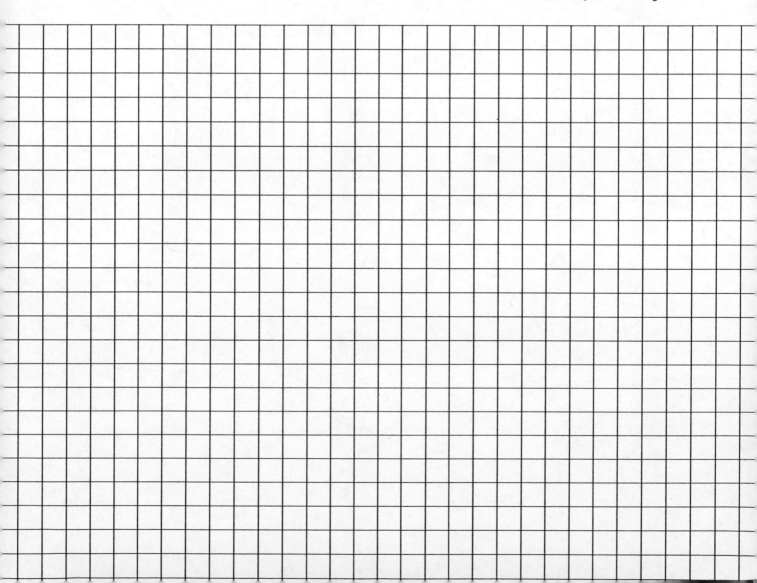

Exhibit 3–9 **The Consumer's Optimum**

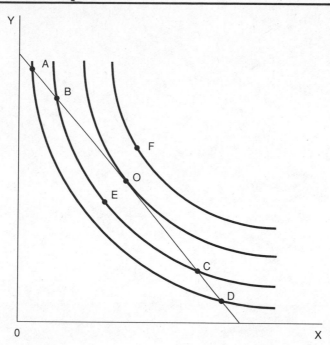

The consumer must choose one of the baskets that is on his budget line, such as A, B, O, C, or D. Of these, he will choose the one that is on the highest indifference curve, namely O. Thus the consumer is led to choose the basket at the point where his budget line is tangent to an indifference curve. This point is called the consumer's optimum.

At the consumer's optimum, the relative price of X in terms of Y (given by the slope of the budget line) and the marginal rate of substitution between X and Y (given by the slope of the tangent line to the indifference curve) are equal. The geometric reason for this is that the budget line is the tangent line to the indifference curve. The economic reason for it is that whenever the relative price is different from the MRS, the consumer will continue to make exchanges until the two become equal.

Exhibit 3–11 The Consumer's Choice with Nonconvex Indifference Curves

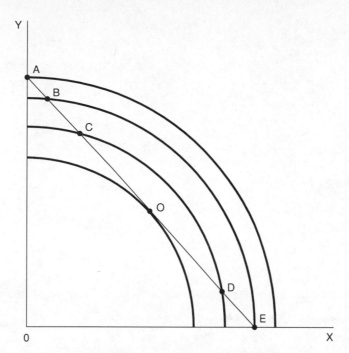

Nonconvex indifference curves always lead to a corner solution. The consumer pictured here will choose point A, which is on the highest possible indifference curve.

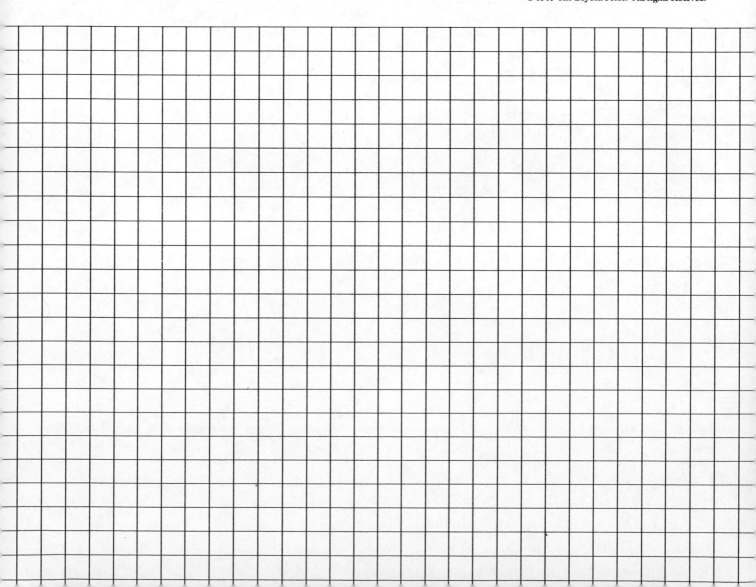

Exhibit 3–12 Your Original and New Budget Lines

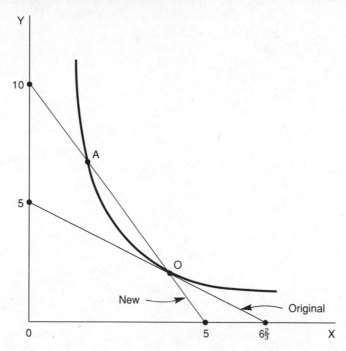

The graph shows the *original* and *new* budget lines that are specified in the problem. We know that an indifference curve is tangent to the *original* line at the point O. We can calculate that the *new* budget line passes through the point O.

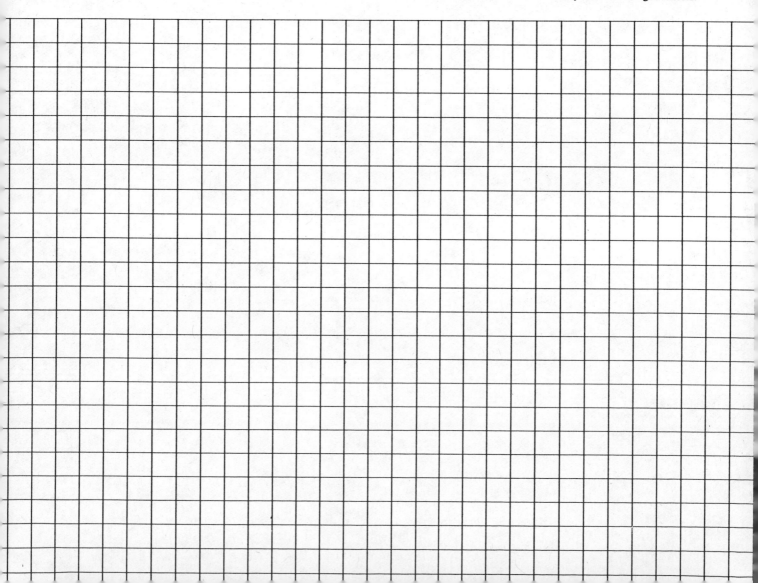

Exhibit 3–13 Finding the New Optimum

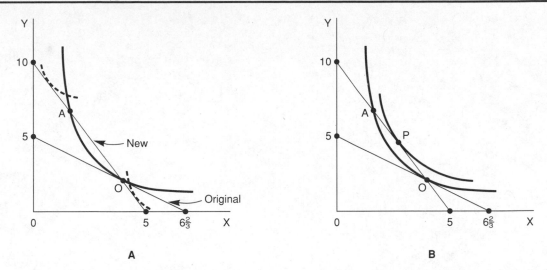

A

B

The dashed indifference curves in panel A cannot be correct, since they cross the indifference curve through O. The only correct way to draw an indifference curve tangent to the *new* budget line is with the tangency between A and O, at a point like P as in panel B. The new indifference curve is then necessarily higher than the old one, so you are better off at the new optimum.

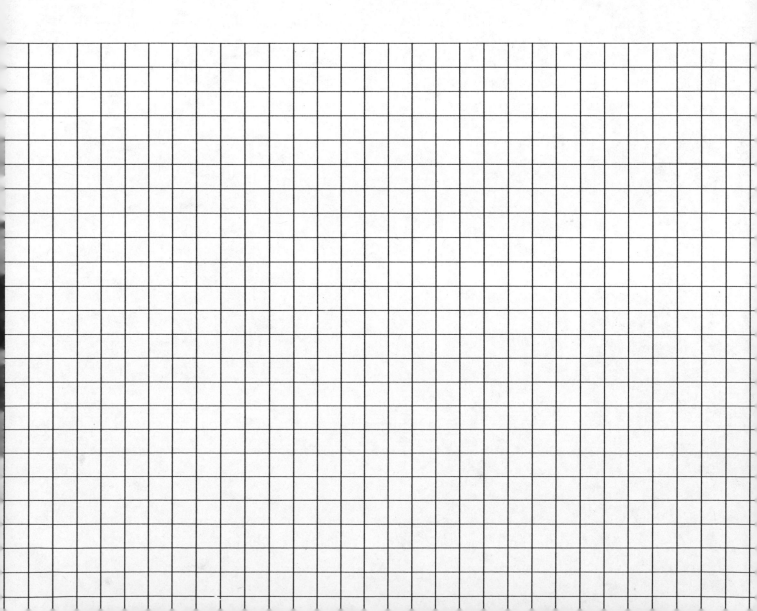

Exhibit 3–15 The Befuddled Former Peanut Farmer and the Aging Retired Movie Actor

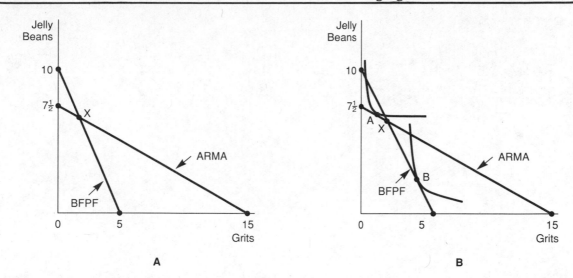

Panel A shows the budget lines of the BFPF and the ARMA. Panel B also shows their optima. The ARMA's optimum is at A and the BFPF's optimum is at B. The ARMA's black indifference curve and the BFPF's colored indifference curve must therefore cross and thus cannot be part of the same family of indifference curves. It follows that the ARMA and the BFPF have different tastes.

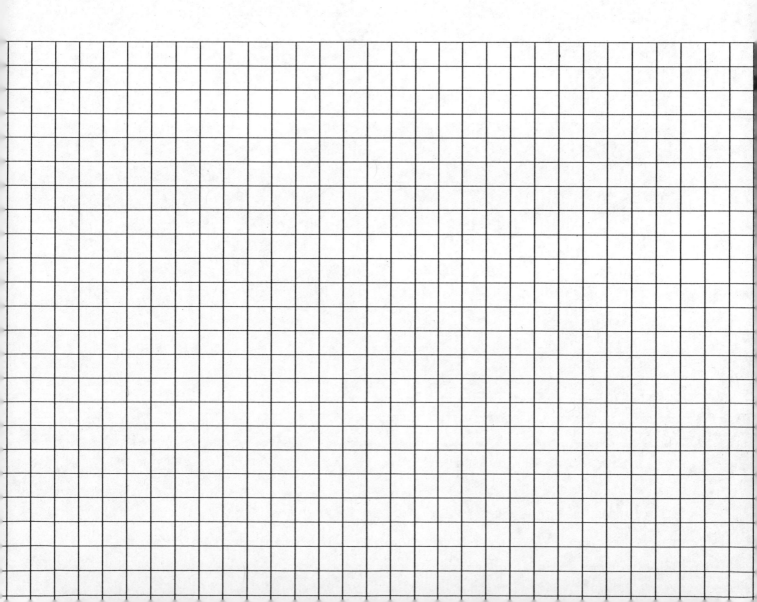

Exhibit 3–16   An Income Tax versus a Head Tax

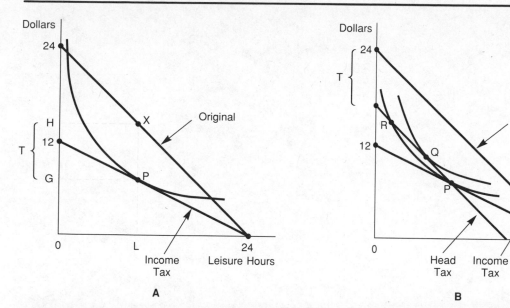

Panel A shows your *original* (untaxed) budget line and your *income tax* budget line. The optimum on the *income tax* line is at P. Your after-tax income is $G. Your before-tax income is equal to what you would earn if you were on your *original* budget line and working L hours, that is, $H. Your tax bill is the difference, or $T.

Panel B shows the *head tax* budget line, which lies a vertical distance $T below the *original* budget line and consequently passes through point P. The optimum on the *head tax* line must be at a point like Q between P and R, and it is consequently on a higher indifference curve. The head tax is thus preferable to the income tax.

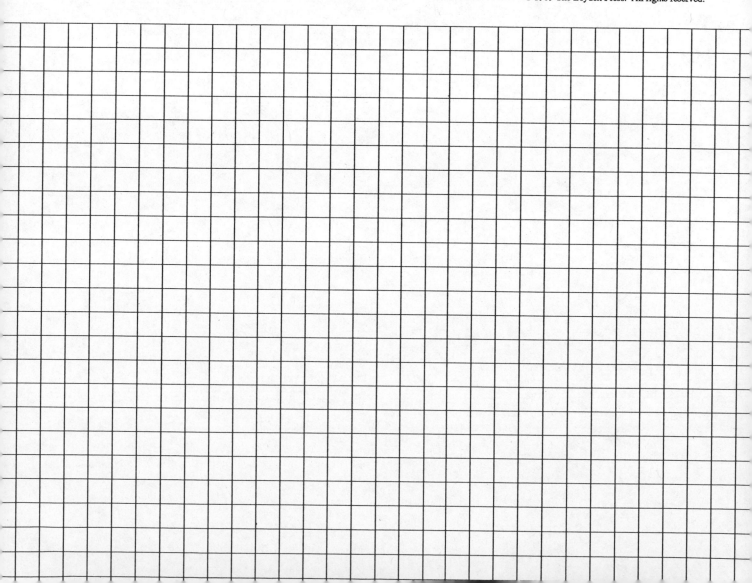

Exhibit 4–2 Income Changes and the Engel Curve

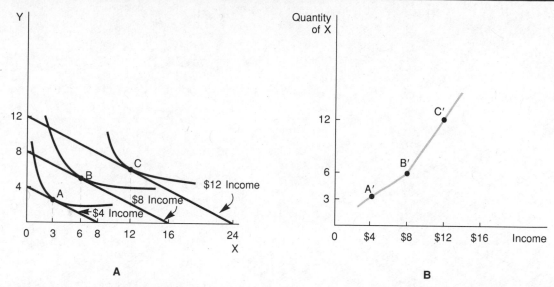

A

B

Points A, B, and C in panel A show the consumer's optima with a variety of incomes. (The prices of X and Y are held fixed at 50¢ per unit and $1 per unit throughout the discussion.) Points A, B, and C correspond to points A′, B′, and C′ in panel B, showing how much X is consumed for each level of income. The curve through the points in panel B is the Engel curve.

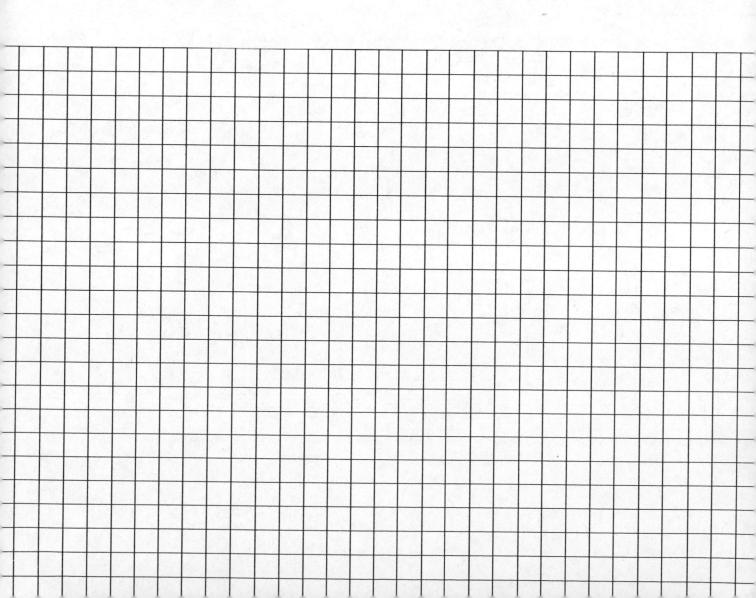

Exhibit 4–3 Income Changes and the Engel Curve: The Case of an Inferior Good

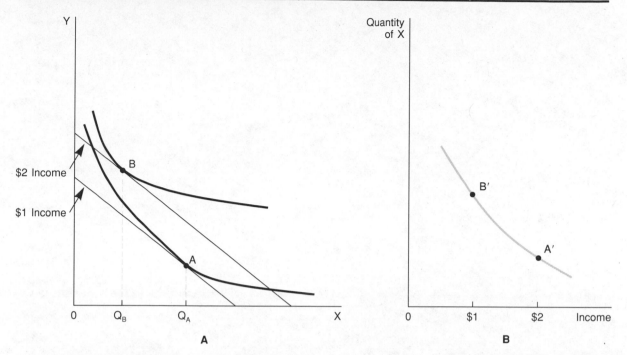

Points A and B in panel A show the optima with incomes of $1 and $2. Points A and B give rise to points A′ and B′ on the Engel curve in panel B. Because Q_B is less than Q_A, we can say that a rise in income leads to a fall in consumption of Hamburger Helper, or, in other words, that the Engel curve slopes downward. The downward slope is a result of the consumer's particular configuration of indifference curves. Any good for which the Engel curve slopes downward is referred to as an inferior good.

Exhibit 4–5   Price Changes and the Demand Curve

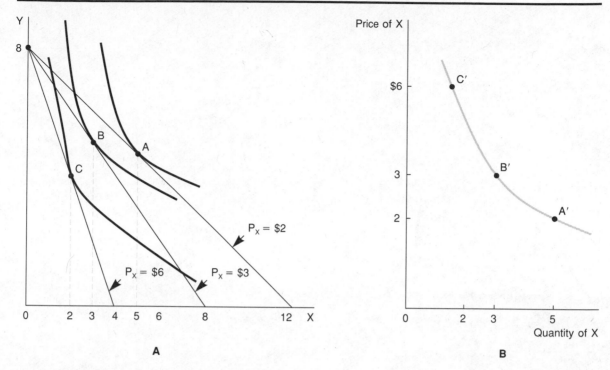

A

B

When the price of X is $2 per unit, you choose basket A containing 5 units of X. This information is recorded by point A' in panel B. Points B' and C' are generated similarly. The curve through these points is your demand curve for X.

Exhibit 4–8 The Income and Substitution Effects of a Price Increase

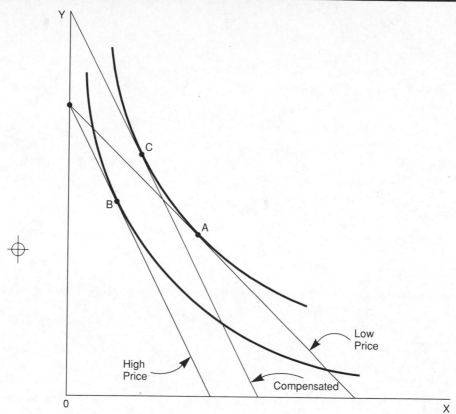

The graph shows the effect of a price increase from a *low price* to a *high price*. When the price goes up, the consumer moves from point A to point B and feels poorer. We imagine that he is compensated for this rise in price by an increase in income just sufficient to enable him to reach his original indifference curve. This causes the *high price* budget line to shift outward parallel to itself until it is just tangent to the original curve at point C. Point C is the consumer's optimum in the (imaginary) situation where the income effect is eliminated by the compensation scheme. Therefore the movement from A to C illustrates the pure substitution effect. Now we imagine the compensation being removed, so that the consumer returns from the *compensated* budget line to the *high price* budget line. This parallel shift, causing the consumer to move from C to B, represents a pure income effect.

Exhibit 4–9   The Compensated and Uncompensated Demand Curves

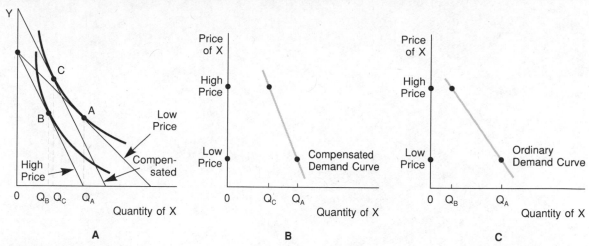

A	B	C

Suppose that X originally sells for a *low price*. The consumer chooses basket A, containing Q_A units of X. Therefore the quantity corresponding to *low price* is Q_A on both the compensated and the uncompensated demand curves.

Now suppose that the price of X rises to *high price*. At this price the consumer chooses basket B, containing Q_B units of X. Therefore the quantity corresponding to *high price* on the ordinary demand curve is Q_B.

We imagine the experiment in which the consumer is income-compensated for the price rise. In that case he would choose basket C, containing Q_C units of X. Therefore the quantity corresponding to *high price* on the compensated demand curve is Q_C.

Points on the compensated demand curve show how much X the consumer would buy at each given price, provided that he was always income-compensated for every price change. Points on the ordinary demand curve show how much X the consumer buys at each given price under the more realistic assumption that he is not income-compensated for price changes.

Exhibit 4–10   Income and Substitution Effects: The Case of an Inferior Good

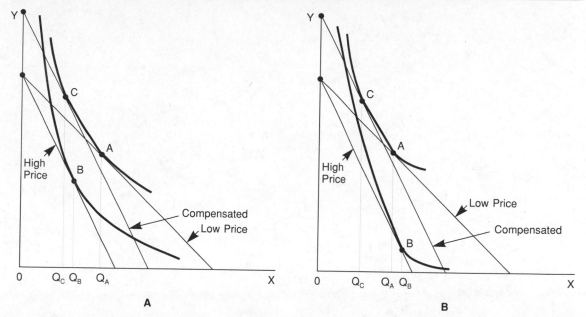

The graphs show two possible consequences of a rise in the price of an inferior good. In each case the substitution effect leads to a fall in quantity demanded (from Q_A to Q_C), and the income effect leads to a rise in quantity demanded (from Q_C to Q_B). In panel A the substitution effect is greater, so that the quantity demanded goes down and the demand curve for X slopes downward. In panel B the income effect is greater, so that the quantity demanded goes up and the demand curve for X slopes upward. In the latter case X is called a *Giffen good.*

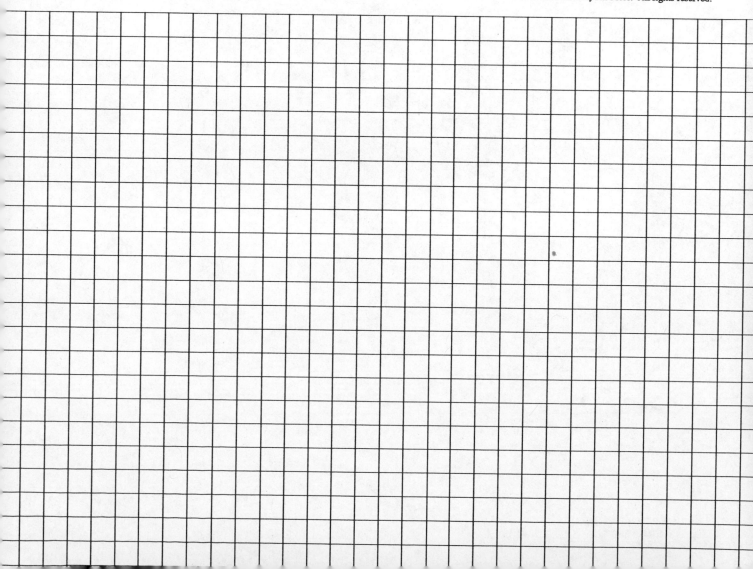

Exhibit 5–1   Maximizing Net Gain

No. of Acres Sprayed	Total Benefit	Marginal Benefit	Total Cost	Marginal Cost	Net Gain
0	$ 0		$ 0		$ 0
1	7	$7/acre	5	$5/acre	2
2	13	6	10	5	3
3	18	5	15	5	3
4	22	4	20	5	2
5	25	3	25	5	0
6	27	2	30	5	−3

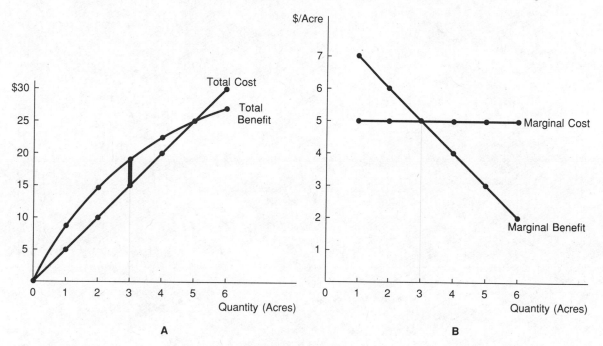

A

B

The graphs display the information in the table. Because Net gain = Total benefit − Total cost, the net gain is equal to the distance between the total cost and total benefit curves in panel A. For example, the heavy vertical line has length $3, representing the net gain of $3 when 3 acres are sprayed. Because the heavy line is the longest of the vertical lines, the farmer will maximize his net gain by spraying 3 acres. An alternative way to reach the same conclusion is to continue spraying as long as marginal benefit exceeds marginal cost and to stop when they become equal, at 3 acres.

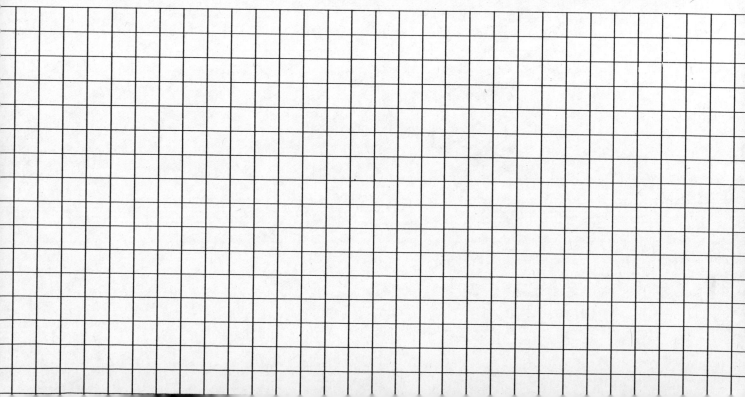

Exhibit 5–2 Maximizing Net Gain

No. of Acres Sprayed	Total Benefit	Marginal Benefit	Total Cost	Marginal Cost	Net Gain
1	$ 7	$7/acre	6	$5/acre	$ 1
2	13	6	11	5	2
3	18	5	16	5	2
4	22	4	21	5	1
5	25	3	26	5	− 1
6	27	2	31	5	− 4

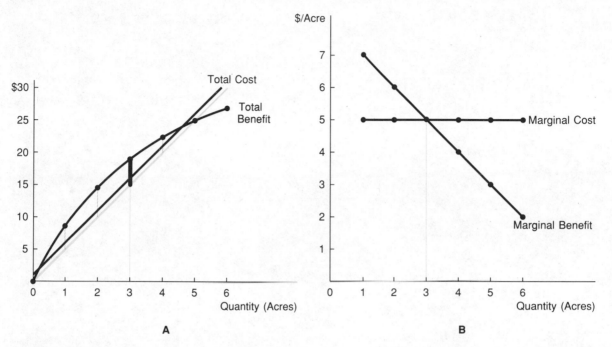

A

B

The table describes the situation after the crop duster institutes a $1 flat fee for coming out to the farm. The data from the table are displayed in the graphs. The light-colored curve in panel A is the old Total Cost curve from Exhibit 5–1 and is reproduced here for comparison. The marginal curves are the same as those in Exhibit 5–1. Therefore the optimal number of acres to spray, which is determined by the intersection of the marginal cost and the marginal benefit curves, is unchanged.

Exhibit 5–4 Total and Marginal Costs at the Tailor Dress Company

Quantity of Dresses	Total Cost	Marginal Cost
1	$ 6	$ 4/dress
2	11	5
3	17	6
4	24	7
5	32	8
6	41	9
7	51	10
8	62	11

A

B

The table and the graphs assume fixed costs of $2 at the Tailor Dress Company. This assumption has no effect on marginal costs, so the marginal cost curve is identical to that of Exhibit 5–3. The new $2 fixed cost does cause the total cost curve to shift upward a distance $2. Since the vertical shift is the same everywhere, the shape of the total cost curve remains unchanged. Another way to see that the slope remains unchanged is to recall that marginal cost is the slope of total cost, and this slope has not changed.

Exhibit 5–6 The Effect of a Rent Increase

Quantity of Dresses	Price	Total Revenue	Marginal Revenue	Total Cost	Marginal Cost	Profit
1	$10/dress	$10	$10/dress	$ 9	$ 4/dress	$ 1
2	9	18	8	14	5	4
3	8	24	6	20	6	4
4	7	28	4	27	7	1
5	6	30	2	35	8	−5
6	5	30	0	44	9	−14
7	4	28	−2	54	10	−26
8	3	24	−4	65	11	−41

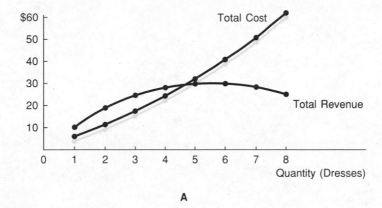

A

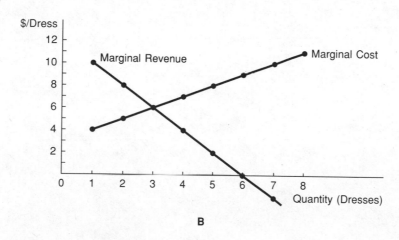

B

The table is derived from the table in Exhibit 5–5 by incorporating a $3 increase in rent. This increases total cost by $3 everywhere, but does not affect marginal cost. Therefore the point of maximum profit is unaffected. The light-colored curve in panel A is the old total cost curve, from Exhibit 5–5. Although the distance between total cost and total revenue has decreased, the point of maximum distance is still at a quantity of 3.

Exhibit 5–7   An Increase in the Price of Fabric

Quantity of Dresses	Price	Total Revenue	Marginal Revenue	Total Cost	Marginal Cost	Profit
1	$10/dress	$10	$10/dress	$ 9	$ 7/dress	$ 1
2	9	18	8	17	8	1
3	8	24	6	26	9	−2
4	7	28	4	36	10	−8
5	6	30	2	47	11	−17
6	5	30	0	59	12	−29
7	4	28	−2	72	13	−44
8	3	24	−4	86	14	−62

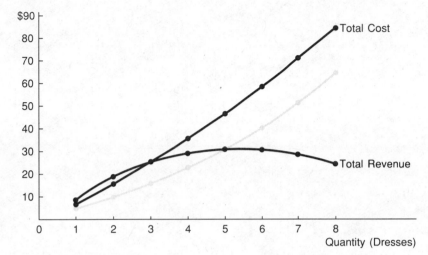

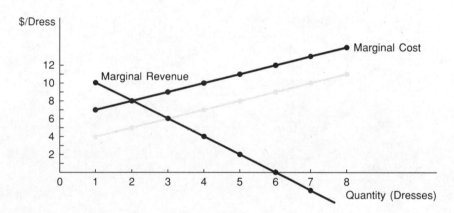

When the price of fabric increases by $3 per square yard, marginal costs increase at the Tailor Dress Company. The new cost curves can be compared with the original (light-colored) curves reproduced from Exhibit 5–5. The shift in total cost is no longer parallel, so the point of maximum distance between it and total revenue is able to shift. The new point of maximum profit occurs at a quantity of 2 and a price of $9.

Exhibit 6–2   **The Marginal Rate of Technical Substitution**

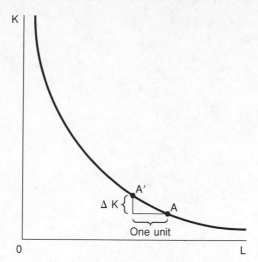

The firm produces one unit of X per day using basket A of inputs. When labor input is reduced by one unit, capital input must be increased by ΔK units in order for the firm to remain on the isoquant and maintain its level of output. The number ΔK is the marginal rate of technical substitution of labor for capital.

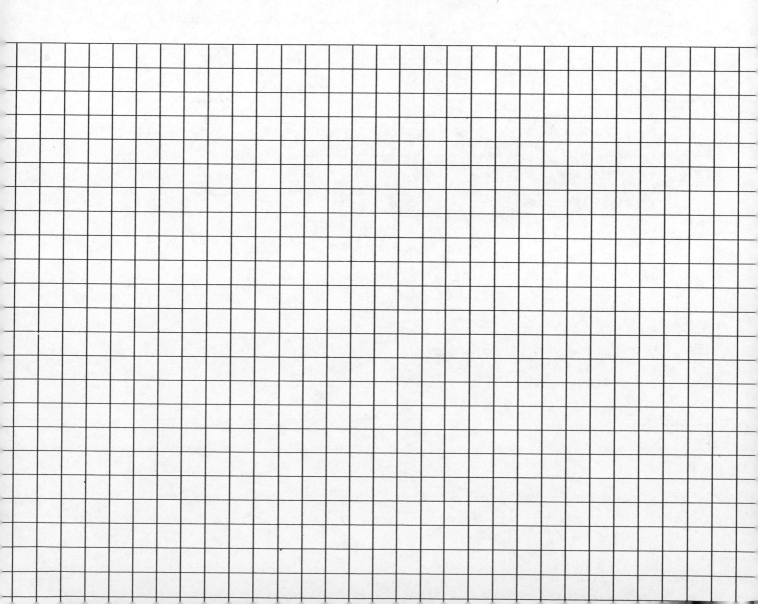

Exhibit 6–4　The Firm's Short-Run Production Possibilities

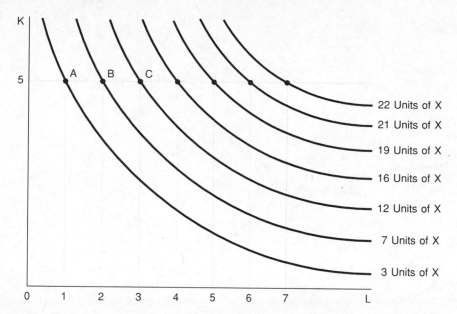

22 Units of X
21 Units of X
19 Units of X
16 Units of X
12 Units of X
7 Units of X
3 Units of X

If the firm employs 5 units of capital and cannot vary this in the short run, then the only possibilities available to it are those on the horizontal line. If it wants to produce 16 units of output, the only way it can do so is by employing 5 units of capital and 4 units of labor.

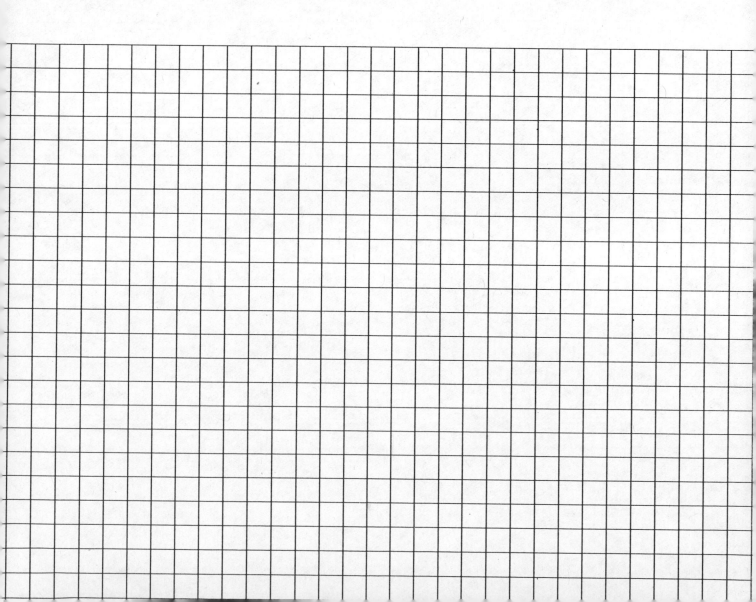

Exhibit 6–5   Total and Marginal Products

Quantity of Labor	Total Product	Marginal Product of Labor
1	3	3
2	7	4
3	12	5
4	16	4
5	19	3
6	21	2
7	22	1

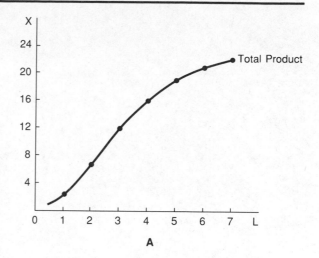

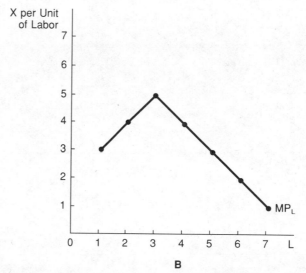

The total products in the table are taken from the graph in Exhibit 6–4. For example, the first row records the information from point A in Exhibit 6–4. The marginal product of labor (MP_L) is the additional output due to the last unit of labor employed. The MP_L is the slope of the total product curve.

Exhibit 6–6   The Variable Cost Curve

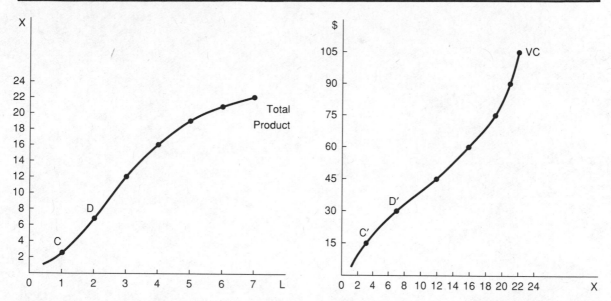

The total product curve is reproduced from Exhibit 6–5. The variable cost (VC) curve can be derived from the total product curve. For example, point C reveals that 3 units of X can be produced with 1 unit of labor, so the variable cost of producing 3 units of X is the cost of hiring 1 unit of labor. Assuming $P_L = \$15$, this gives point C'.

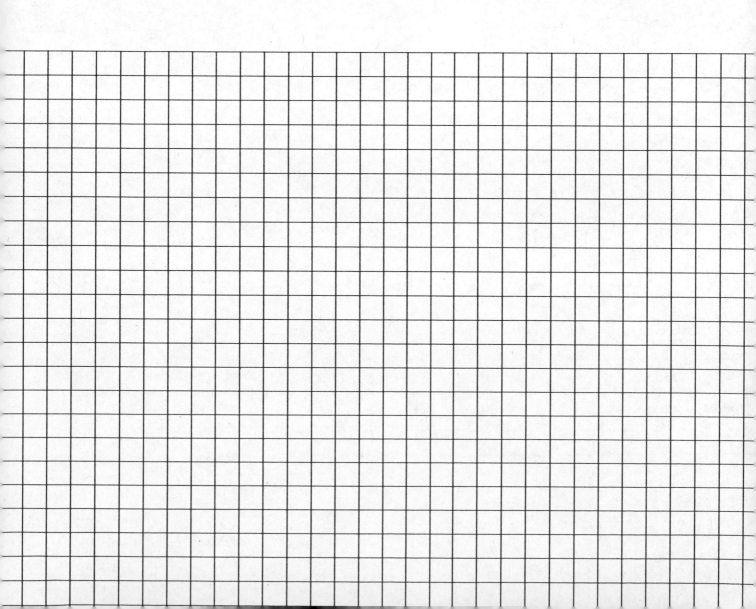

Exhibit 6–7   The Total Cost Curve

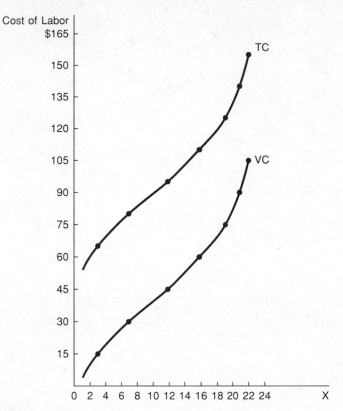

The variable cost (VC) curve is reproduced from Exhibit 6–6. The total cost (TC) curve is obtained by adding the fixed cost (in this example $50) to the VC curve. Thus the TC curve is always a parallel upward shift of the VC curve.

Exhibit 6–8 The Firm's Short-Run Cost Curves

Quantity	Variable Cost	Fixed Cost	Total Cost	Average Variable Cost	Average Cost	Marginal Cost
1	$ 5.58	$50	$ 55.58	$5.58	$55.58	$ 5.58
2	10.52	50	60.52	5.26	30.26	4.94
3	15	50	65	5.00	21.67	4.48
4	19.12	50	69.12	4.78	17.28	4.12
5	22.97	50	72.97	4.59	14.59	3.85
6	26.58	50	76.58	4.43	12.76	3.61
7	30	50	80	4.29	11.43	3.42
8	33.25	50	83.25	4.16	10.41	3.25
9	36.37	50	86.37	4.04	9.60	3.12
10	39.35	50	89.35	3.94	8.94	2.98
11	42.23	50	92.23	3.84	8.38	2.88
12	45	50	95	3.75	7.92	2.77
13	48.42	50	98.42	3.72	7.57	3.42
14	52.03	50	102.03	3.72	7.29	3.61
15	55.88	50	105.88	3.73	7.06	3.85
16	60	50	110	3.75	6.88	4.12
17	64.48	50	114.48	3.79	6.73	4.48
18	69.42	50	119.42	3.86	6.63	4.94
19	75	50	125	3.95	6.58	5.58
20	81.58	50	131.58	4.08	6.58	6.58
21	90	50	140	4.29	6.67	8.42
22	105	50	150	4.77	7.05	15.00

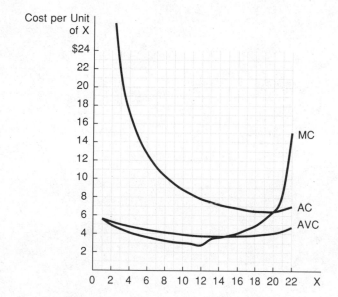

The table and the graph show the firm's average cost, average variable cost, and marginal cost at each level of output. All of this information can be calculated on the basis of knowing the firm's fixed and variable costs. The variable costs are displayed in Exhibit 6–6. The highlighted rows correspond to the darkened points in Exhibit 6–6, which come from the table in Exhibit 6–5.

Exhibit 6–9   Maximizing Output for a Given Expenditure

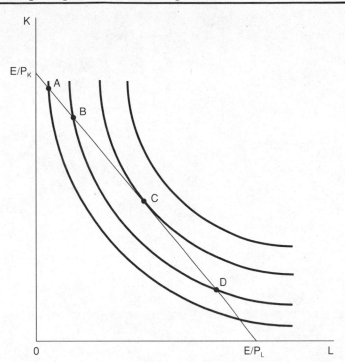

If the firm spends the amount E to hire inputs, it can choose any production process along the isocost line, such as A, B, C, or D. Of these it will choose the one that yields the greatest output, which is the point of tangency C.

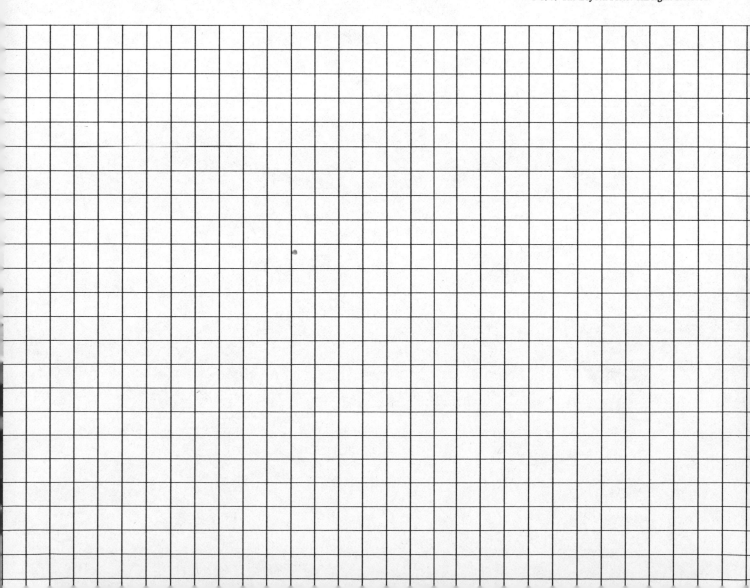

Exhibit 6–10   **The Expansion Path**

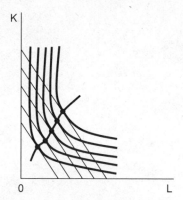

Unlike the consumer, who is constrained to his budget line, the firm can choose any level of expenditure on inputs. That is, it can choose to be on any isocost. It will always want to be at a point where the isocost is tangent to an isoquant. Thus the firm might choose any of the darkened points in the diagram. The curve through these points is the firm's expansion path. In order to determine which of the points on the expansion path the firm will choose, it is necessary to take account of the firm's marginal revenue curve. This requires additional information that is not shown in this diagram.

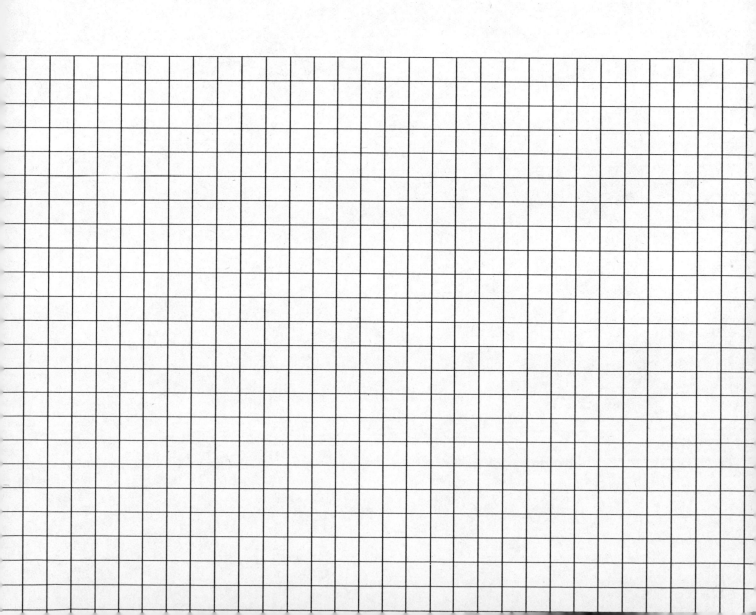

Exhibit 6–12   Short-Run versus Long-Run Production

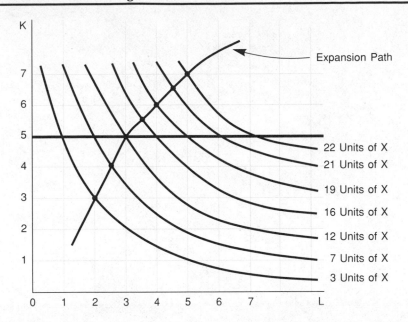

In the short run, the firm is committed to using 5 units of capital. Therefore if it wants to produce 19 units of output, it must select the production process where the 19-unit isoquant meets the horizontal line K = 5. There it employs 5 units of labor and 5 units of capital. In the long run, the firm can adjust its capital usage and can pick the least expensive production process on the isoquant, which occurs on the expansion path at (4,6). In the long run, the firm employs 4 units of labor and 6 units of capital.

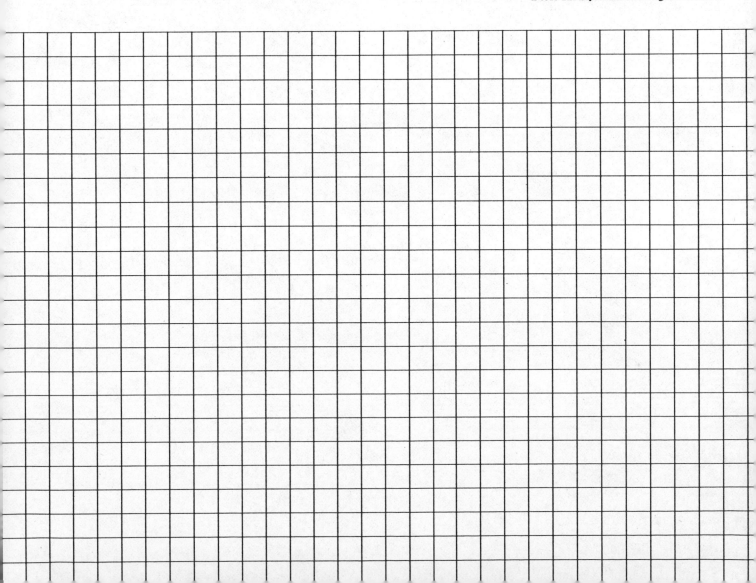

Exhibit 6–13   Short-Run and Long-Run Total Cost Curves

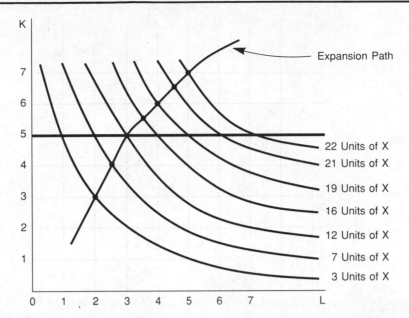

	Short Run					Long Run				
Quantity of Output	Factors Employed		Cost of Factors		Total Cost	Factors Employed		Cost of Factors		Total Cost
	K	L	K	L		K	L	K	L	
3	5	1	$50	$ 15	$ 65	3	2	$30	$30	$ 60
7	5	2	50	30	80	4	2.5	40	37.50	77.50
12	5	3	50	45	95	5	3	50	45	95
16	5	4	50	60	110	5.5	3.5	55	52.50	107.50
19	5	5	50	75	125	6	4	60	60	120
21	5	6	50	90	140	6.5	4.5	65	67.50	132.50
22	5	7	50	105	155	7	5	70	75	145

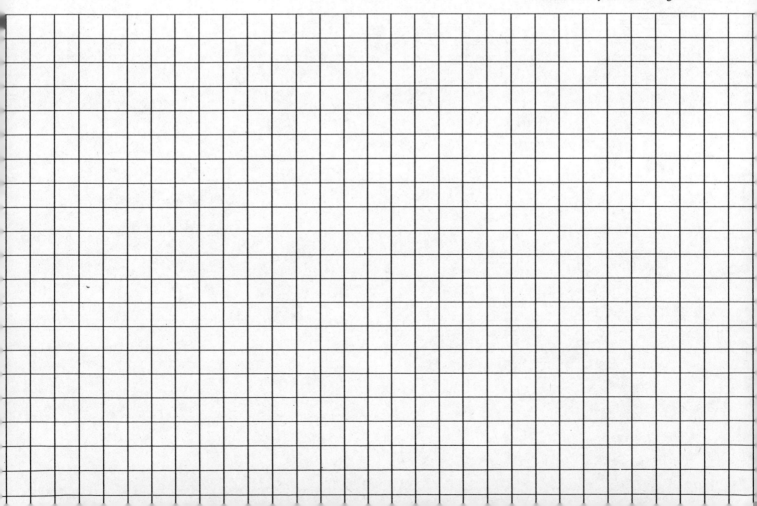

Exhibit 6A–2   Robinson Crusoe's Optimum

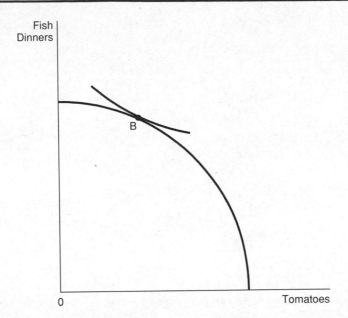

From the points on his production possibility curve, Robinson chooses point B, where he is on the highest possible indifference curve. At such a tangency the slopes of the production possibility curve and of the indifference curve are equal. That is, the relative price of tomatoes in terms of fish dinners is equal to Robinson's marginal rate of substitution between tomatoes and fish dinners.

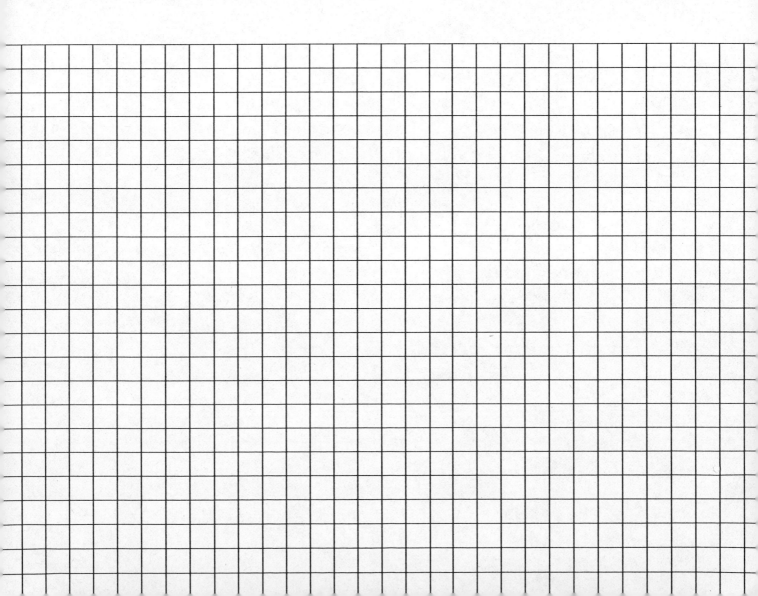

Exhibit 6A-3 Production and Consumption with Foreign Trade

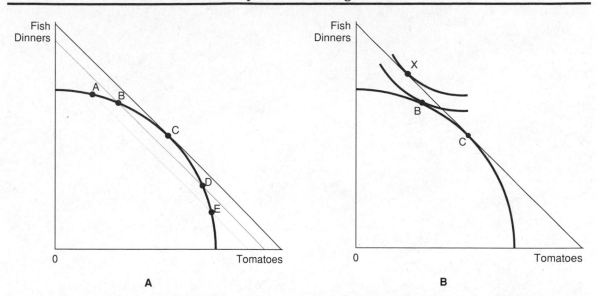

A

B

When Robinson can trade with his neighbors at a relative price of P fish dinners per tomato, he faces a budget line of absolute slope P. All of the lines in panel A have that slope. By choosing a basket to produce, Robinson can choose his budget line from among the lines pictured. If he produces basket A or basket E, he has the light budget line; if he produces basket B or basket D, he has the middle budget line; if he produces basket C, he has the dark budget line. The dark budget line is the best one to have, so Robinson produces basket C. He then trades along the budget line to his optimal basket X, shown in panel B. Without trade, Robinson would choose basket B. Since basket X is preferred to basket B, Robinson gains from trade.

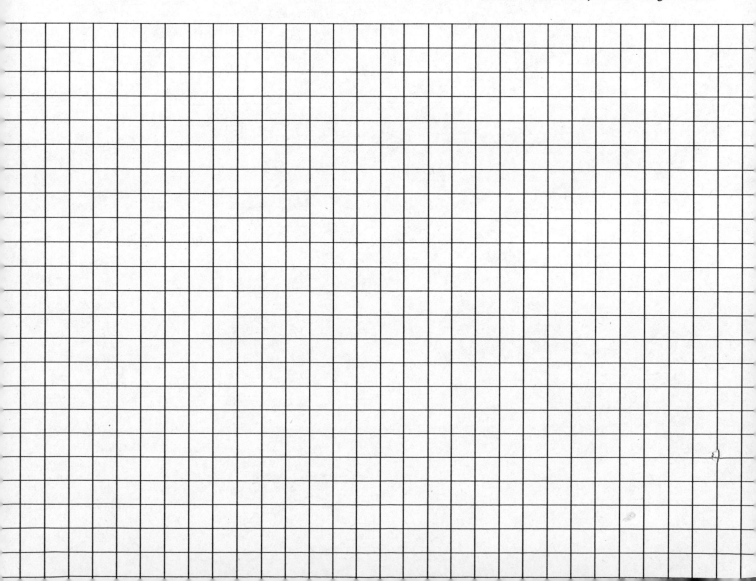

Exhibit 6A–4   Autarkic versus World Relative Prices

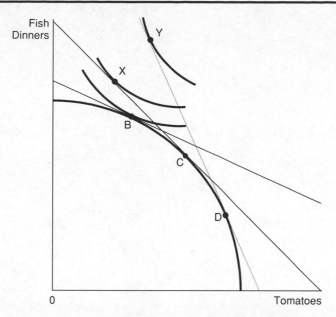

The slope of the blue line represents the autarkic relative price on Robinson's island. If the world relative price is the same as the autarkic relative price, then Robinson both produces and consumes basket B, just as he would with no opportunity to trade.

If, instead, the world relative price is given by the slope of the black line, then Robinson produces basket C and consumes basket X, which is an improvement over basket B. If the world relative price goes up to the slope of the gray line, then Robinson produces basket D and consumes basket Y, which is a further improvement.

The more the world relative price differs from the autarkic relative price, the more Robinson can gain from trade.

Exhibit 7–1   The Demand Curve for Wheat

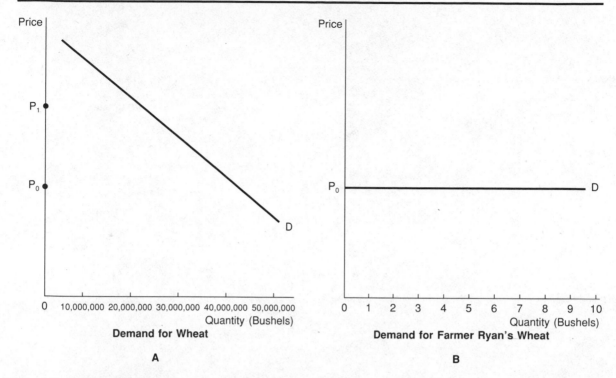

Panel A shows the downward-sloping demand curve for wheat. Panel B shows the horizontal demand curve for Farmer Ryan's wheat. If the price of all wheat goes up from P_0 to P_1, consumers will buy less wheat. If the price of just Farmer Ryan's wheat goes up from the market price of P_0 to P_1, consumers will buy none of it at all; they will shop elsewhere.

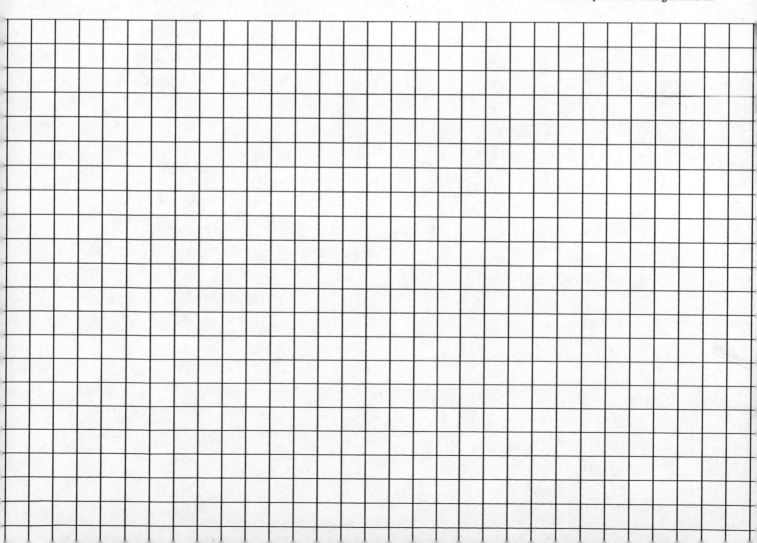

Exhibit 7–3 **The Optimum of the Competitive Firm**

Quantity	Marginal Cost	Marginal Revenue
1	$2/item	$5/item
2	3	5
3	4	5
4	5	5
5	6	5
6	7	5

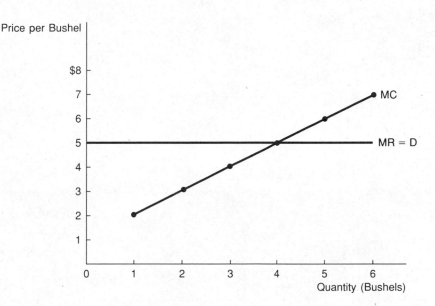

Farmer Ryan, like any profit-maximizing producer (competitive or not) produces at the point where marginal cost equals marginal revenue. Because he is a competitive producer, Farmer Ryan's marginal revenue curve is a horizontal line at the going market price. Thus it is equally correct to say that he operates where marginal cost equals price. In this case he produces 4 bushels of wheat at the market price of $5 per bushel.

Exhibit 7-4   **Marginal Cost and Supply**

Table A			Table B	
Quantity	**Marginal Cost**		**Price**	**Quantity**
1	$2/item		$2/item	1
2	3		3	2
3	4		4	3
4	5		5	4
5	6		6	5
6	7		7	6

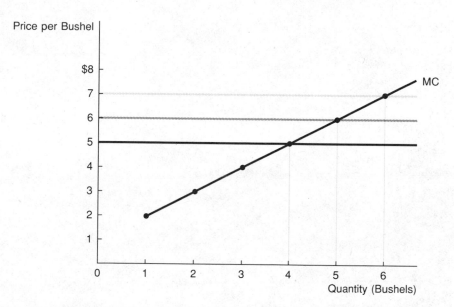

Table A is Farmer Ryan's marginal cost schedule; the graph shows his marginal cost curve.

Table B shows the quantity Farmer Ryan would supply at each price. Each entry is obtained by reading the marginal cost curve backward—we imagine a price, look for that price in the right-hand column of Table A (or on the vertical axis of the graph), and observe that the corresponding quantity is what Farmer Ryan would produce at that price.

The horizontal lines in the graph represent hypothetical market prices of $5, $6, and $7. At these prices the quantities supplied, read off the marginal cost curve, are 4, 5, and 6. These are entered as the last three rows of Table B.

If we plot a graph of Farmer Ryan's supply curve using the data points from Table B, it will look exactly like his marginal cost curve, because all of the numbers in Table B are the same as those in Table A.

Exhibit 7–8 The Competitive Firm's Short-Run Supply Curve

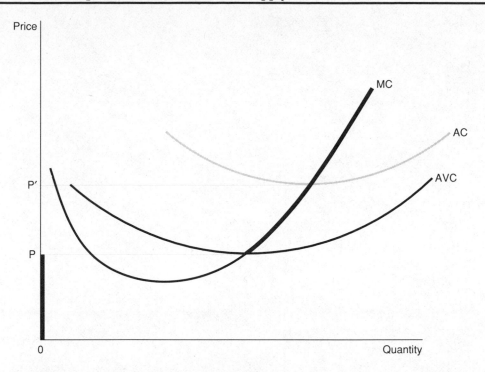

At prices below the shutdown price P, the firm cannot cover its variable costs and shuts down, producing zero output. At prices above P, it produces the quantity that equates price with marginal cost; this quantity can be read off the marginal cost curve. Thus the two heavy segments constitute the firm's short-run supply curve. At prices above P', the price of an item exceeds the average cost of production, so the firm earns positive profits. At prices below P', profits are negative.

Exhibit 7–9   The Competitive Firm's Long-Run Supply Curve

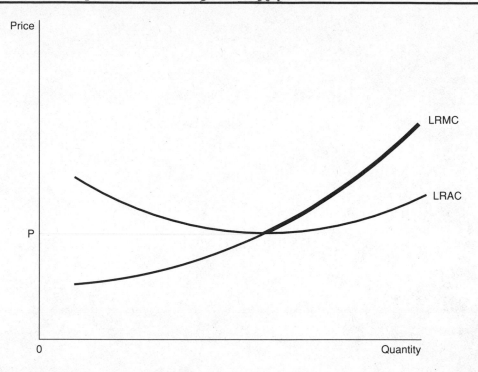

Unless the price is high enough to cover all of its costs, the firm will leave the industry in the long run. Therefore the long-run supply curve is that portion of the long-run marginal cost curve that lies above the long-run average cost curve. At prices below P, the firm leaves the industry and produces zero.

Exhibit 7–10 Long-Run and Short-Run Supply Responses

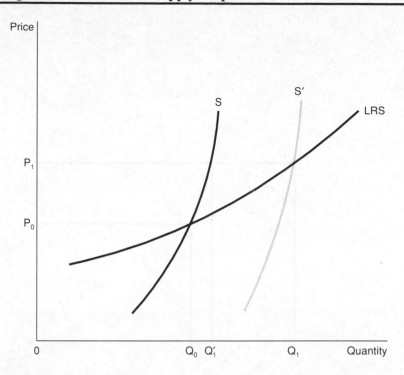

In long-run equilibrium at P_0, the firm is both on its long-run and short-run supply curves. A change in price, to P_1, has the immediate effect of causing the firm to move along its short-run supply curve S to the quantity Q_1'. In the long run, the firm can vary its plant capacity (for example, a hamburger stand can install more grills) and move along its long-run supply curve LRS to Q_1. With the new plant capacity, the firm has a new short-run supply curve S'. In the new equilibrium at price P_1 and quantity Q_1, the firm is again on both its long-run and short-run supply curves.

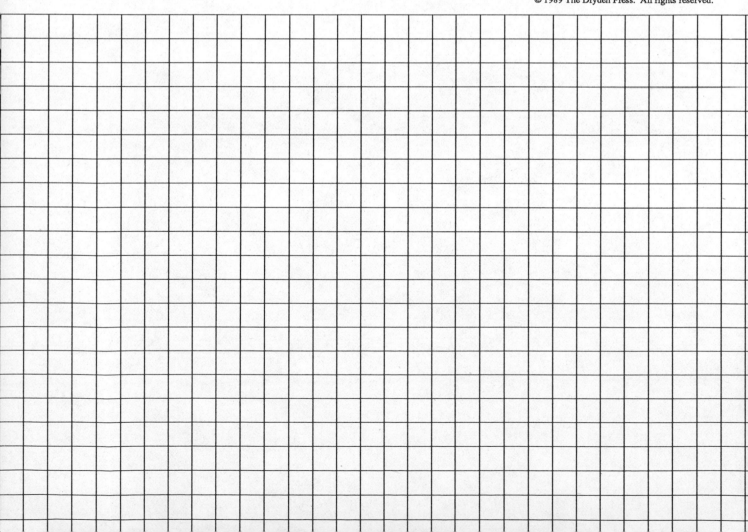

Exhibit 7–11 The Industry Supply Curve

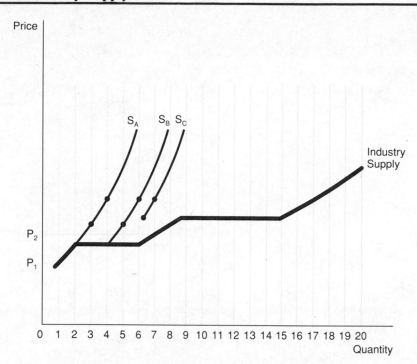

As the price goes up, two things happen. First, each firm that is producing increases its output. Second, firms that were not previously producing start up their operations. As a result, industry output increases more rapidly than that of any given firm, so the industry supply curve is more elastic than that of any given firm.

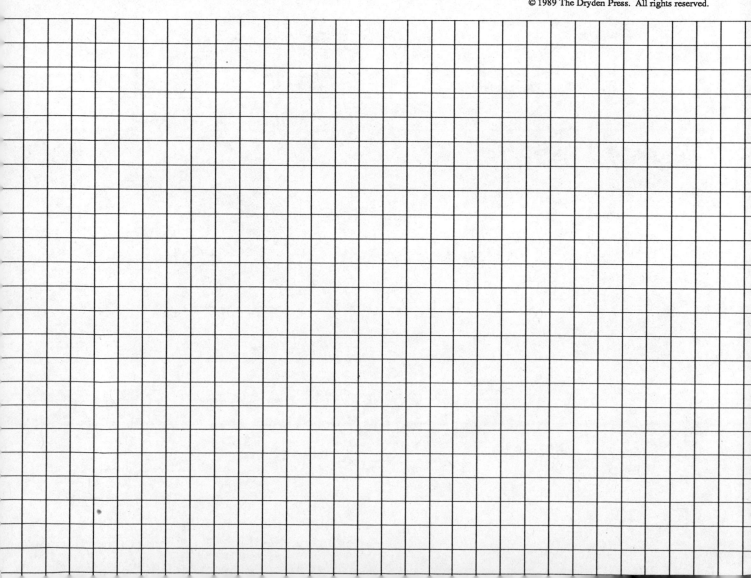

Exhibit 7–13   The Competitive Industry and the Competitive Firm

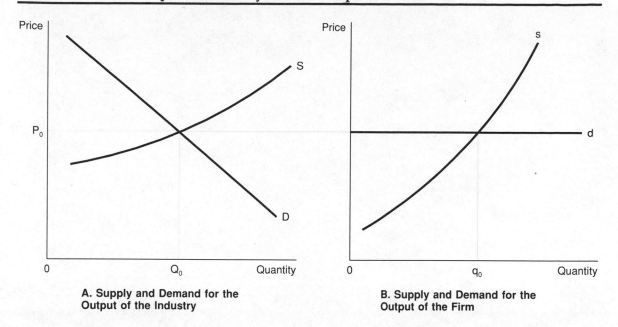

A. Supply and Demand for the Output of the Industry

B. Supply and Demand for the Output of the Firm

The equilibrium price P_0 is determined by the intersection of the industry's supply curve with the downward-sloping demand curve for the industry's product. The firm faces a horizontal demand curve at this going market price and chooses the quantity q_0 accordingly. The industry-wide quantity Q_0 is the sum of the quantities supplied by all of the firms in the industry.

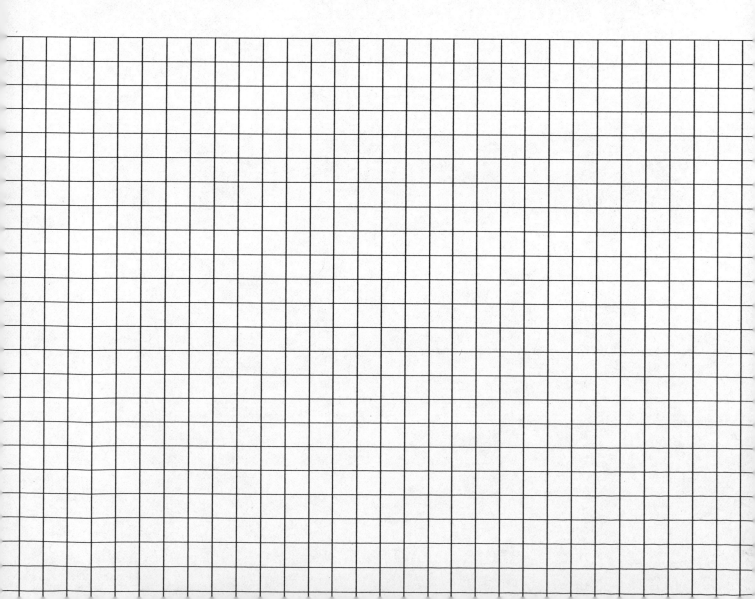

Exhibit 7–14 A Rise in Fixed Costs

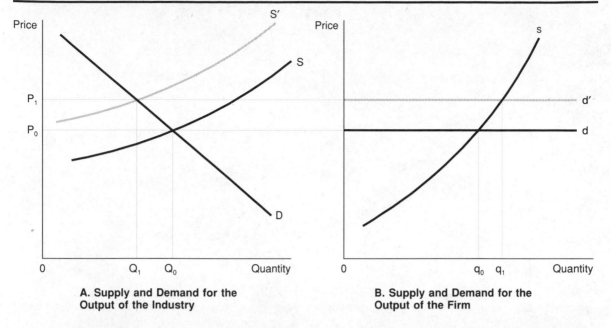

A. Supply and Demand for the Output of the Industry

B. Supply and Demand for the Output of the Firm

A rise in fixed costs leaves the firm's marginal costs, and hence its supply curve, unchanged. Thus the industry supply curve is unchanged, and both price and quantity are unchanged in the short run. Eventually, however, some firms will be driven from the industry by the increase in costs. The industry supply curve will now be the sum of fewer individual firm supply curves than before, so it shifts back to S'. The firm now faces a going market price of P_1 instead of P_0 and increases its quantity to q_1 from q_0.

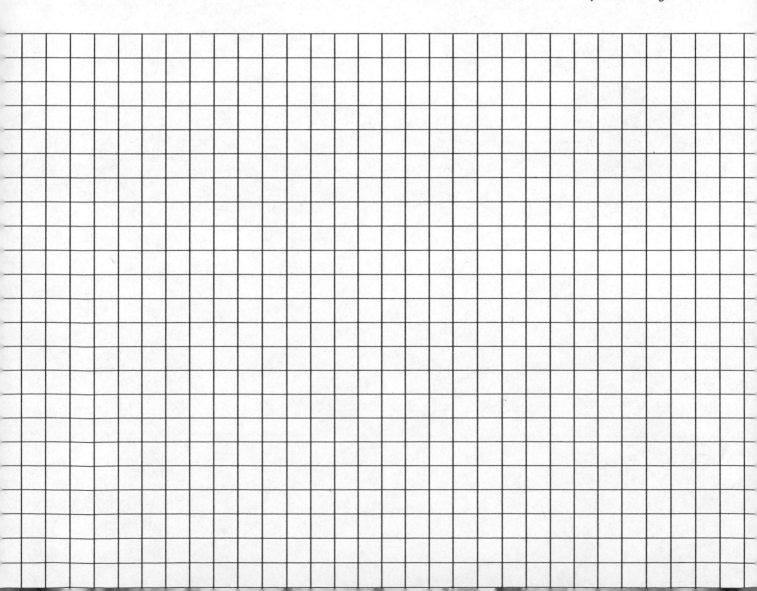

Exhibit 7–15   A Rise in Marginal Costs

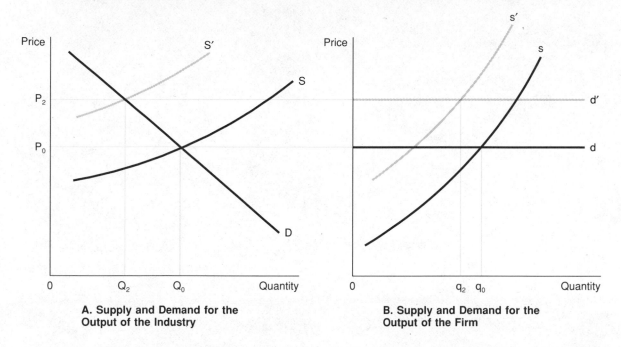

A. Supply and Demand for the Output of the Industry

B. Supply and Demand for the Output of the Firm

A rise in marginal costs causes the firm's supply curve to shift left from s to s' in panel B. The industry supply curve shifts left from S to S' in panel A, both because each firm's supply curve does and because some firms may shut down. The new market price is P_2. The firm operates at the intersection of s' with its new horizontal demand curve at P_2. Depending on how the curves are drawn, the firm could end up producing either more or less than it did before the rise in costs. (That is, q_2 could be either to the left or to the right of q_0.)

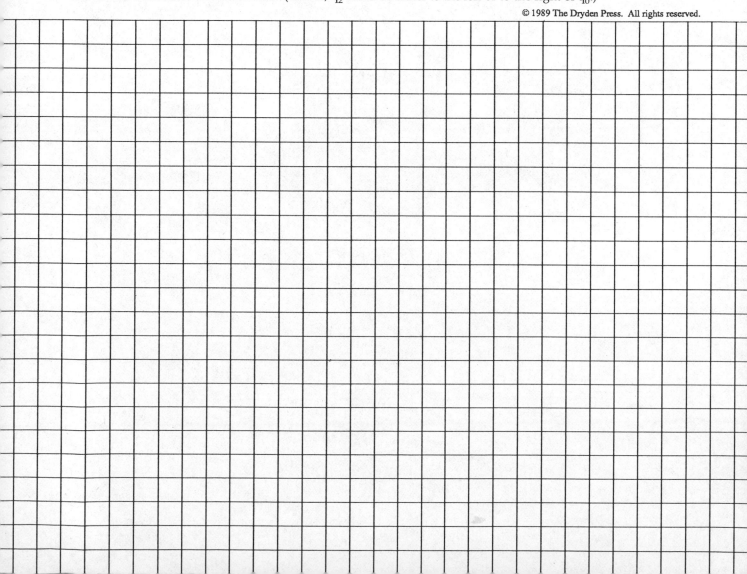

Exhibit 7–16   A Change in Demand

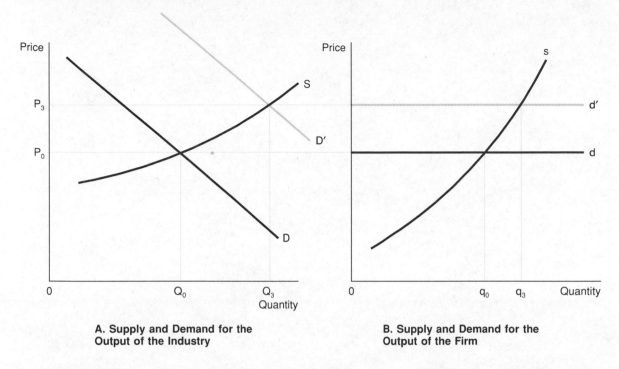

A. Supply and Demand for the Output of the Industry

B. Supply and Demand for the Output of the Firm

An increase in the demand for the industry's output raises the equilibrium price to P_3 and the firm's output to q_3.

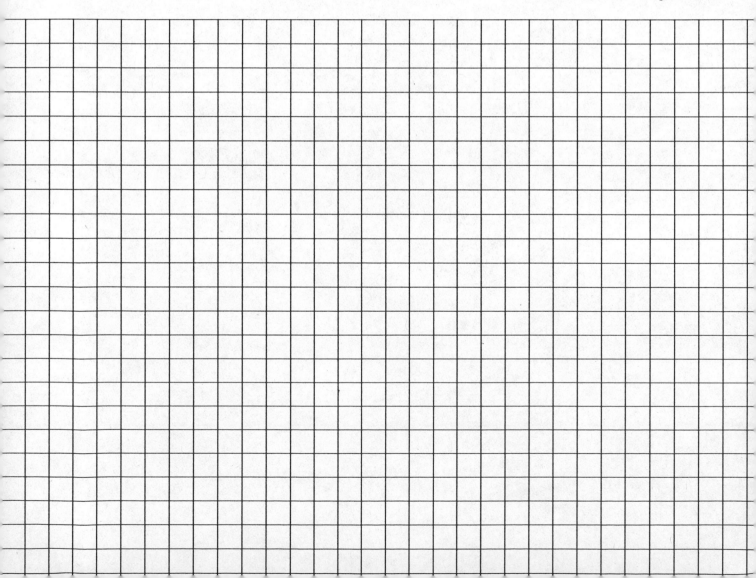

Exhibit 7–17 Long-Run Zero-Profit Equilibrium

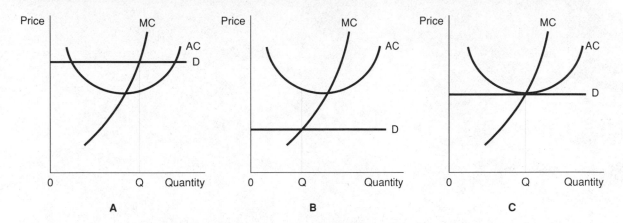

In each panel the firm produces quantity Q, where marginal cost equals price, so that profits are maximized. (Q is different in each panel.) In panel A price exceeds average cost at Q, so that the firm earns positive profits. This will attract entry, driving down the price. In panel B average cost exceeds price at Q, so that the firm earns negative profits. This leads to exit, driving up the price. In panel C price equals average cost, so that profits are zero. Panel C is the only correct depiction of a long-run zero-profits equilibrium.

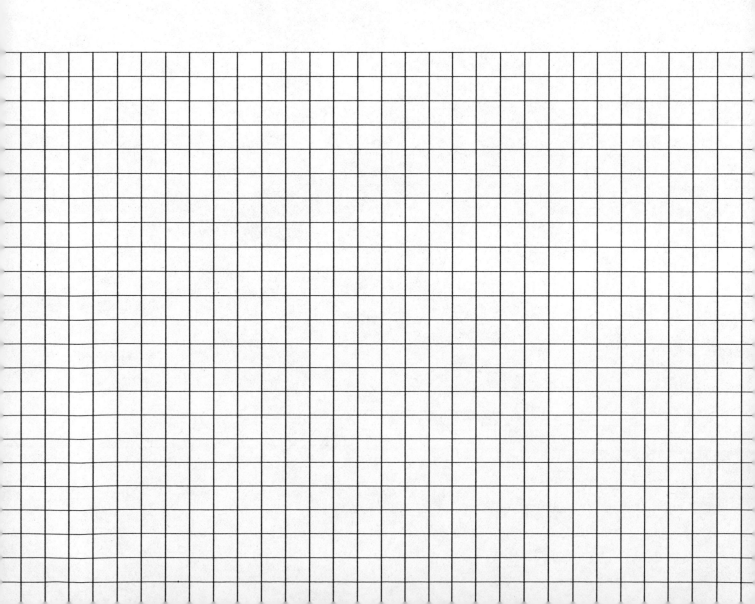

Exhibit 7–21   A Rise in Fixed Costs

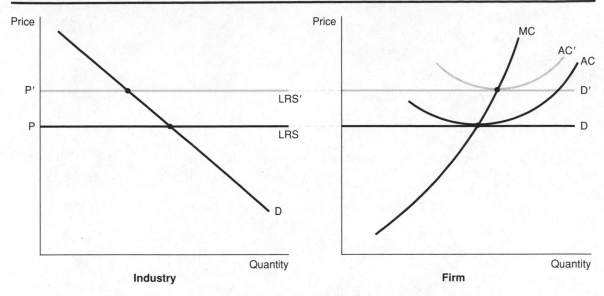

A. Constant Cost Industry

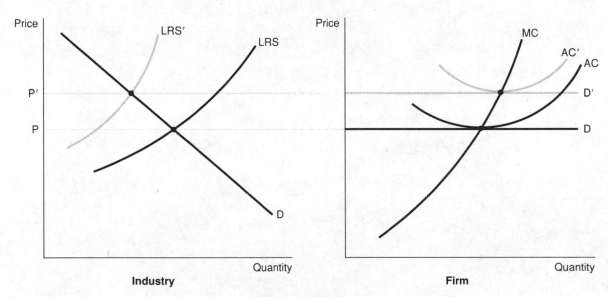

B. Increasing Cost Industry

Suppose that there is an increase in some cost that is a fixed cost for firms even in the long run. The top graphs show the effect on long-run competitive equilibrium in a constant cost industry and the bottom graphs show the effect on long-run competitive equilibrium in an increasing cost industry. In each case, the firm's average cost curve rises from AC to AC′, without any change in marginal cost. Now existing firms earn negative profits, so long-run industry supply shifts from LRS to LRS′, which is just far enough so that at the new equilibrium price P′ firms can earn zero profits again.

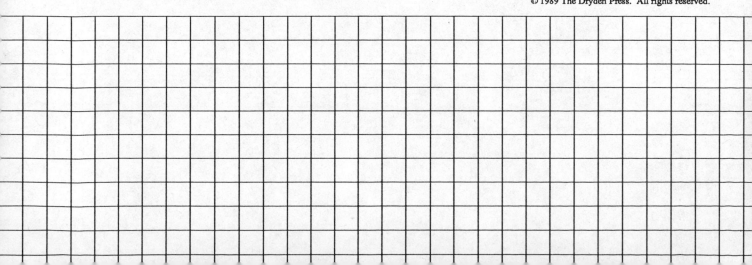

Exhibit 7–22　A Change in Marginal Cost

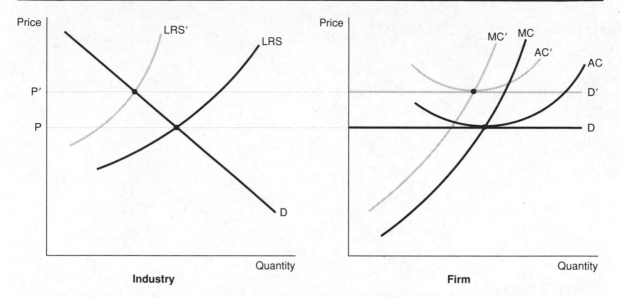

An increase in marginal cost raises the firm's marginal and average cost curves to MC' and AC'. Industry supply moves back to LRS', so that price rises to P' where firms can once again earn zero profits.

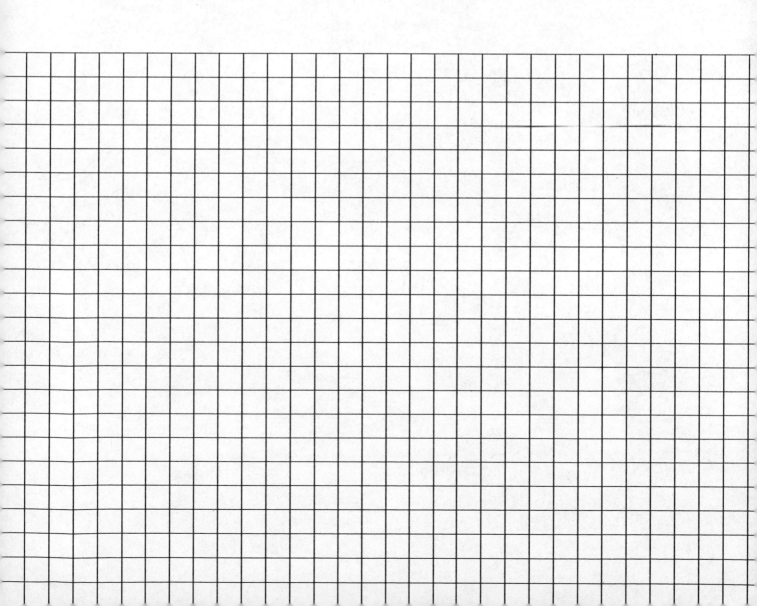

Exhibit 7–23 Constant Cost, Increasing Cost, and Decreasing Cost Industries

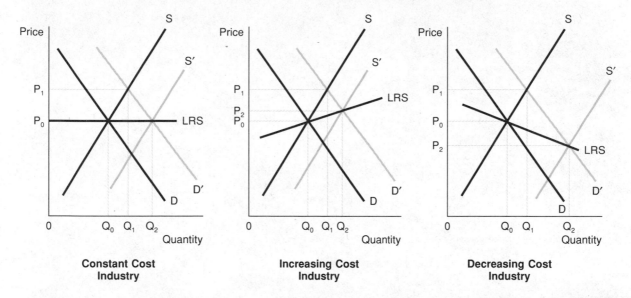

Constant Cost Industry   **Increasing Cost Industry**   **Decreasing Cost Industry**

The graphs show the long-run effects of a rise in demand in three kinds of industries.

In the constant cost case, the industry is initially in long-run equilibrium at a price of P_0. An increase in demand has the immediate effect of bidding up price to P_1 and output to Q_1 as the industry moves along its short-run supply curve S. At the new price of P_1, firms earn positive profits, so there is entry until the price is driven back down to P_0. The industry now produces Q_2 on its new short-run supply curve S′.

In the increasing cost case, the industry is initially in long-run equilibrium at a price of P_0. An increase in demand has the immediate effect of bidding up price to P_1 and quantity to Q_1 as the industry moves along its short-run supply curve S. At the new price of P_1, firms earn positive profits, so there is entry. Price is driven back down, but costs are driven up, either because the new firms are less efficient than the old ones or because of the factor-price effect. Therefore profits are driven to zero at a price higher than the original price P_0. That price is P_2, and industry output is Q_2 on its new short-run supply curve S′.

In the decreasing cost case, the industry is initially in long-run equilibrium at a price of P_0. An increase in demand has the immediate effect of bidding up price to P_1 and quantity to Q_1 as the industry moves along its short-run supply curve S. At the new price of P_1, firms earn positive profits, so there is entry. This entry reduces costs at the existing firms (as in the example of the printing industry described in the text). As the existing firms' marginal cost curves fall, a new short-run industry supply curve is established at S′ and the price drops to P_2, with industry output at Q_2.

Exhibit 7–24 A Tax on Motel Rooms near a Highway

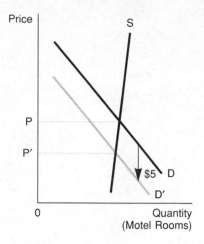

A. The Short Run

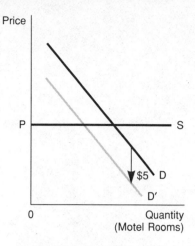

B. The Long Run If Motels Use a Small Percentage of the Land near the Highway

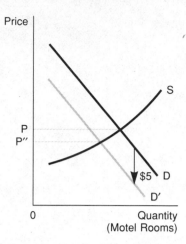

C. The Long Run If Motels Use a Large Percentage of the Land near the Highway

In the short run the number of motel rooms is nearly fixed. (It is not entirely fixed, because the number of rooms available on a given night can be stretched by the use of additional maintenance staff or other means.) As a result, the short-run supply curve is nearly vertical, so a sales tax lowers the price of rooms by almost the full amount of the tax, from P to P' in panel A. The tax burden falls almost entirely on suppliers.

In the long run the lowered price leads to exit from the industry, causing prices to rise until profits are zero again. If the marginal cost of building motels is constant, then price must be bid up to its original level P, as in panel B. Now demanders pay the full burden of the tax.

If, on the other hand, motels use a significant proportion of the land near the highway, then exit will drive down land prices and so drive down the cost of owning a motel. As a result, the new zero profits price will be lower than the original price, at P'' in panel C, though the price does not fall by as much as in the short run.

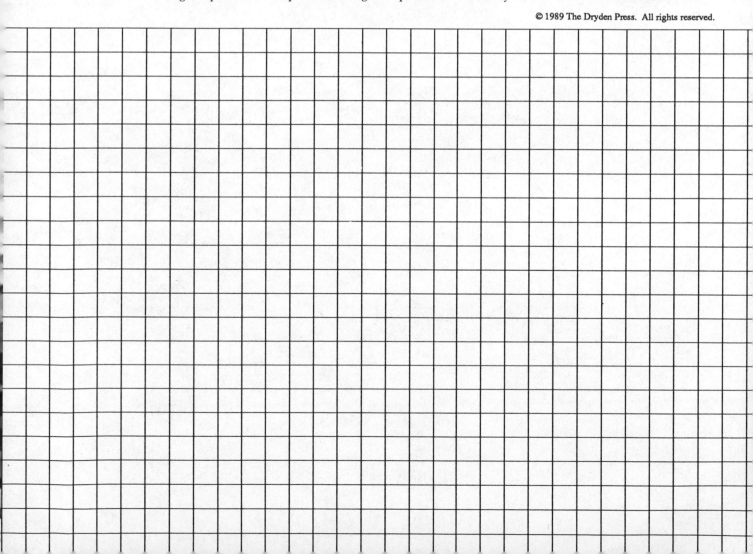

Exhibit 7–25 Tipping the Busboy

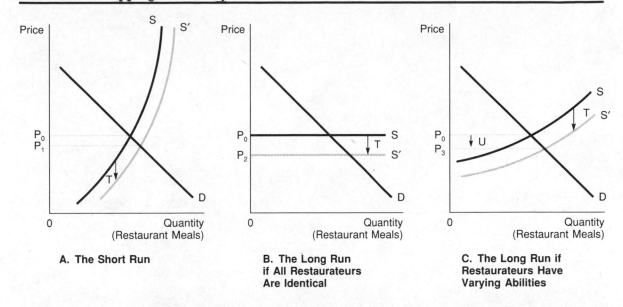

A. The Short Run

B. The Long Run if All Restaurateurs Are Identical

C. The Long Run if Restaurateurs Have Varying Abilities

Suppose that people decide to start tipping busboys. Because bussing services are provided at constant cost (there are many essentially identical busboys), the total compensation of busboys cannot change. Therefore wages are reduced by the amount of the tip, T. The marginal cost of serving meals falls by this amount.

In the short run (panel A), price falls, but by less than T. Part of the tip is returned to the customer through the lower price, and the rest goes to the restaurant owner.

In the long run, if all restauranteurs are identical (panel B), entry bids profits back down to zero only when the price of meals falls by the full amount T. We can see this geometrically: The horizontal supply curve falls by T, and the price falls by this full amount.

If not all restauranteurs are identical, then entry by less efficient firms can drive profits to zero even though the price is reduced by less than the full amount of the tip. This is shown in panel C, where the upward-sloping long-run supply curve drops by the amount T, but the price of meals falls by something less, which we label U. Those restauranteurs who were in the industry originally gain rents equal to $T - U$ per meal served (their marginal costs fall by T but their price falls by U, so they gain the difference), while customers get back U in the form of a lower price. The tip is split between the restauranteur and the customer; the busboy gets nothing.

Exhibit 8–1 Demand and Marginal Value

Table A: Total and Marginal Value

Quantity	Total Value	Marginal Value
1	$15	$15/egg
2	28	13
3	38	10
4	45	7
5	50	5
6	52	2

Table B: Demand

Price	Quantity
$15/egg	1
13	2
10	3
7	4
5	5
2	6

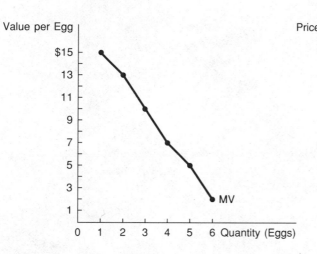

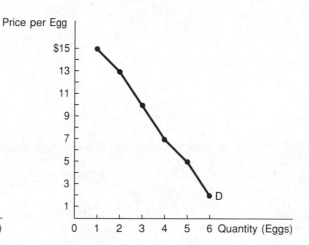

At a given market price the consumer will choose a quantity that equates price with marginal value. As a result, his demand curve for eggs is identical with his marginal value curve.

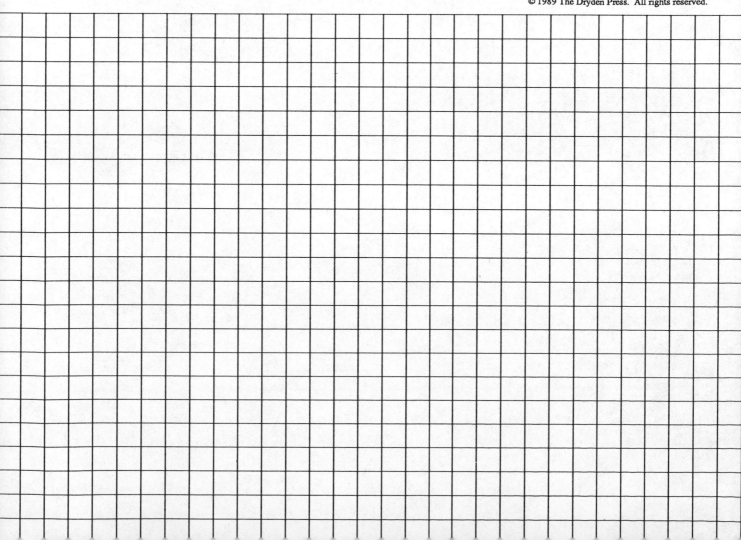

Exhibit 8–2   Total Value

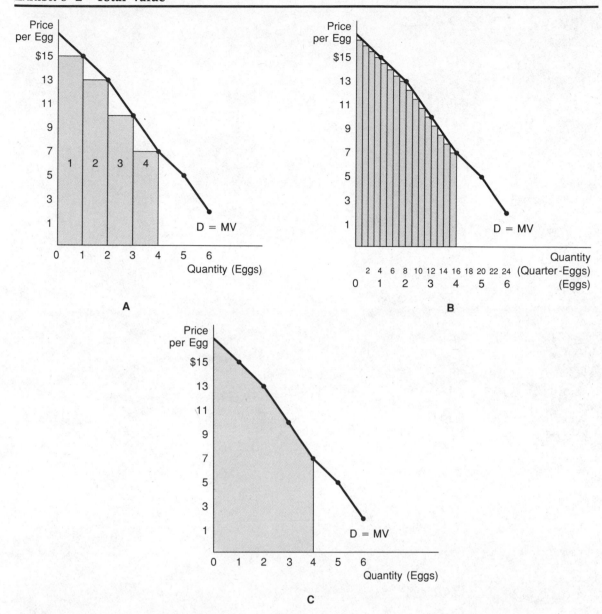

A

B

C

When the consumer buys 4 eggs, their marginal values ($15, $13, $10, and $7) can be read off the demand curve. Their values are represented by the areas of rectangles 1 through 4 in panel A. Therefore their total value is the sum of the areas of the rectangles.

We can get a more accurate estimate of total value if we measure eggs in smaller units. Panel B shows the calculation of total value when we measure by the quarter-egg instead of by the whole egg. As we take smaller and smaller units, we approach the shaded area in panel C, which is the exact measure of total value when the consumer buys 4 eggs.

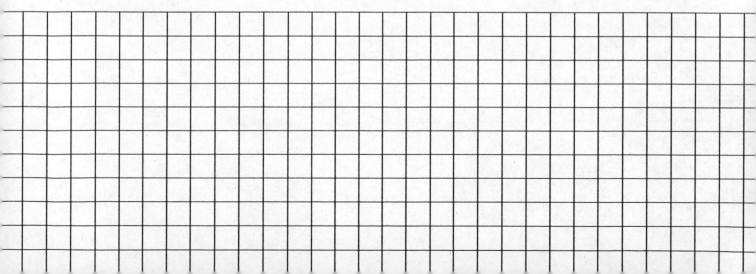

Exhibit 8–3   The Consumer's Surplus

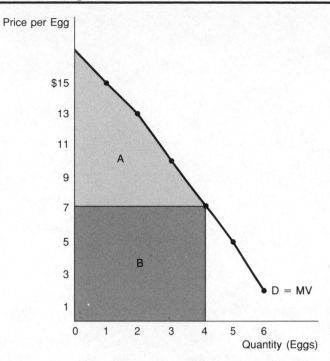

In order to acquire 4 eggs, the consumer would be willing to pay up to the entire shaded area, A + B. At a price of $7 per egg, his actual expenditure for 4 eggs is $28, which is area B. The difference, area A, is his consumer's surplus.

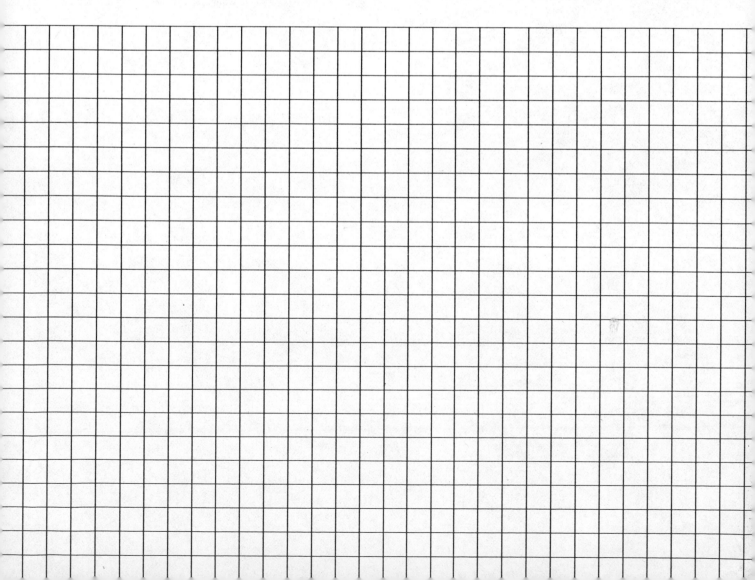

Exhibit 8–4   The Producer's Surplus

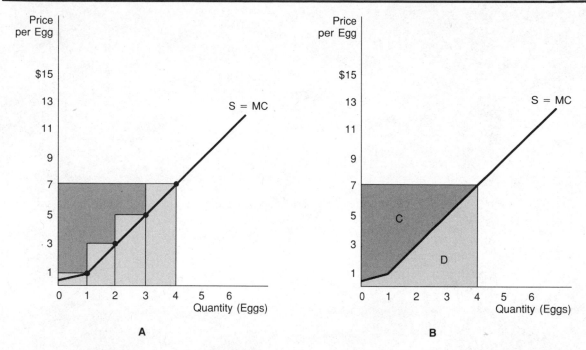

If the producer supplies 4 eggs, his cost is the sum of the 4 marginal costs, which are represented by the rectangles in panel A. If we measure eggs in very small units, we find that an exact measure of his cost is area D in panel B. At a market price of $7, his revenue is $7 × 4 = $28, which is the area of rectangle C + D. Thus his producer's surplus is area C.

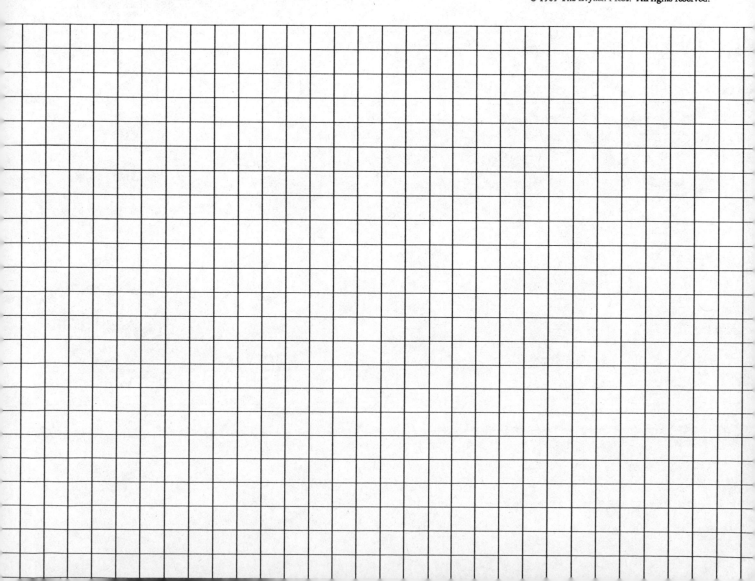

Exhibit 8–5 **Welfare Gains**

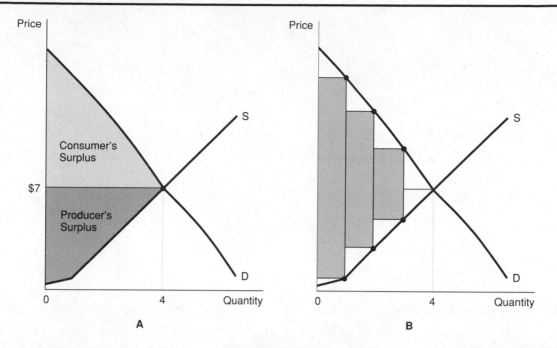

Panel A shows the consumer's surplus and the producer's surplus when 4 eggs are sold at a price of $7. The sum of these areas is the total welfare gain. The second panel shows another way to calculate the welfare gain. The first egg creates a gain equal to the area of the first rectangle, the second creates a gain equal to the area of the second rectangle, and so on. When units are taken to be small, the sum of these areas is the shaded region, which is the sum of the consumer's and producer's surpluses.

Exhibit 8-9　Deadweight Loss

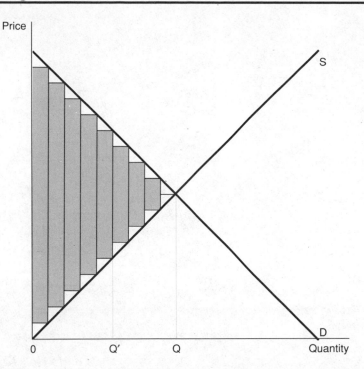

If the market operates at the equilibrium quantity Q, all of the rectangles are included in the social gain. If for any reason the market operates at the quantity Q' (for example, because of a tax), then only the blue rectangles are included. The units of output that could create the gray rectangles are never produced, and those rectangles of gain are never created. The gray rectangles, representing gains that could have been created but weren't, constitute the deadweight loss.

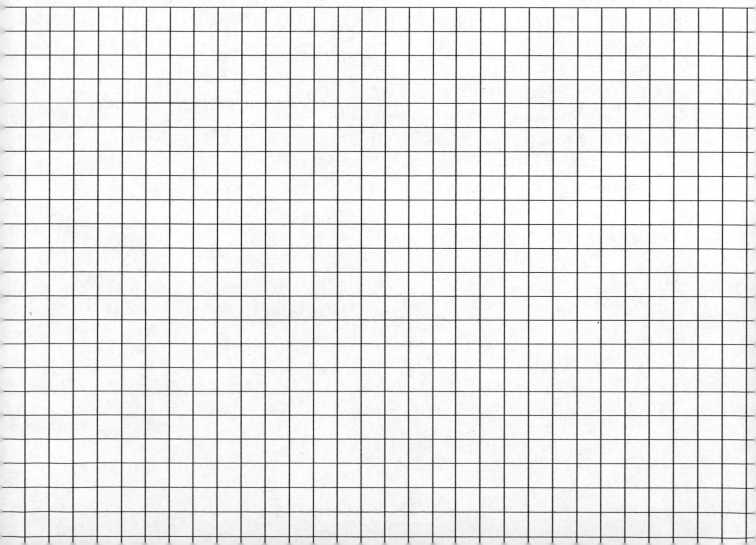

Exhibit 8–10 The Tax Collector versus Robin Hood

	Before Taxation	With Sales Tax	With Robin Hood Policy
Consumers' Surplus	A+B+C+D+E	A+B	A+B+½E
Producers' Surplus	F+G+H+I	I	½H+I
Tax Revenue	—	C+D+F+G	C+D+½E+F+G+½H
Social Gain	A+B+C+D+E+F+G+H+I	A+B+C+D+F+G+I	A+B+C+D+E+F+G+H+I
Deadweight Loss		E+H	

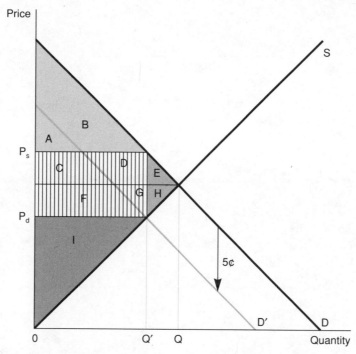

The table shows the effects of three different policies. In the first column there is no tax, in the second column there is a sales tax, and in the third column there is a Robin Hood policy whereby the tax collector unexpectedly takes C + D + ½E from the consumers, takes F + G + ½H from the producers, and gives all of the proceeds to the same group that gets the revenue from the sales tax.

Every member of society prefers the Robin Hood policy to the sales tax. Because the Robin Hood policy creates no deadweight loss, it makes it possible to give everyone a bigger share of the social pie.

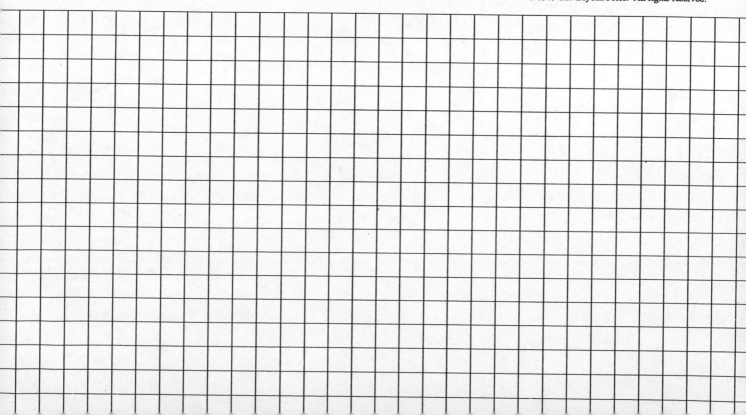

Exhibit 8–12   **The Effect of a Subsidy**

	Before Subsidy	After Subsidy
Consumers' Surplus	A + C	A + C + F + G
Producers' Surplus	F + H	C + D + F + H
Cost to Taxpayers	—	C + D + E + F + G
Social Gain	A + C + F + H	A + C + F + H − E
Deadweight Loss		E

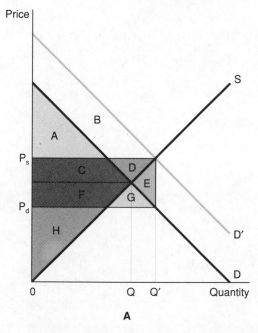

A

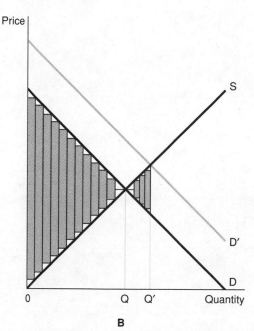

B

The table shows the gains to consumers and producers before and after the institution of a $50-per-unit government subsidy to home insulation. With the subsidy in effect, there is a cost to taxpayers that must be *subtracted* when we calculate the social gain. We find that the social gain with the subsidy is lower by E than the social gain without the subsidy. E is the deadweight loss.

To check our work, we can consider the social gain created by each individual unit of insulation, shown in panel B. Each unit up to the equilibrium quantity Q creates a rectangle of social gain. After Q units have been produced, we enter a region where marginal cost exceeds marginal value. Each unit produced in this region creates a social *loss* equal to the excess of marginal cost over marginal value; these losses are represented by the gray rectangles, which stop at the quantity Q′ that is actually produced. The social gain is equal to the sum of the blue rectangles minus the sum of the gray ones. Since the social gain without the subsidy is just the sum of the blue rectangles, the gray rectangles represent the deadweight loss.

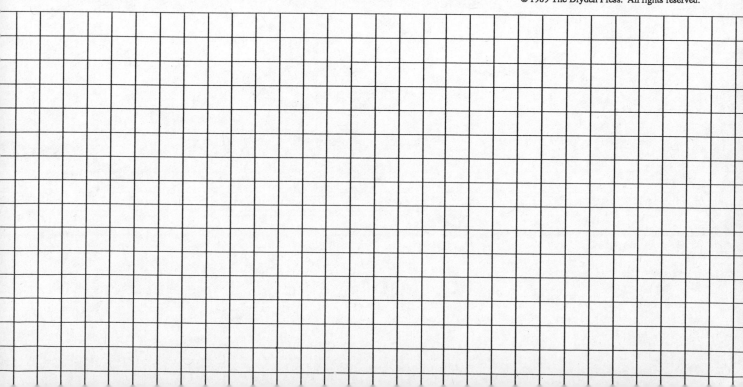

Exhibit 8–14 A Price Ceiling

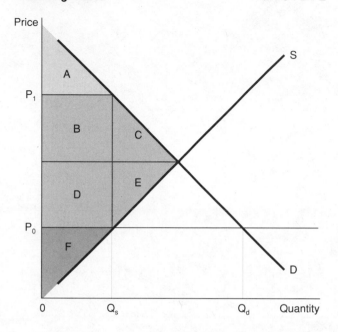

	Before Ceiling	After Ceiling
Consumers' Surplus	A + B + C	A
Producers' Surplus	D + E + F	F
Social Gain	A + B + C + D + E + F	A + F
Deadweight Loss		B + C + D + E

At a maximum legal price of P_0, demanders want to buy more than suppliers want to sell. Therefore they compete against each other for the available supply, by waiting in line, advertising, and so forth. This increases the actual price to consumers. The full price to consumers must be bid all the way up to P_1, since at any lower price the quantity demanded still exceeds the quantity supplied, leading to increases in the lengths of waiting lines.

The deadweight loss comes about for two reasons. First, there is the reduction in quantity from equilibrium to Q_s. This loss is the area C + E. Second, there is the value of the consumers' time spent waiting in line. This is equal to $P_1 - P_0$ times the quantity of items purchased, which is the rectangle B + D.

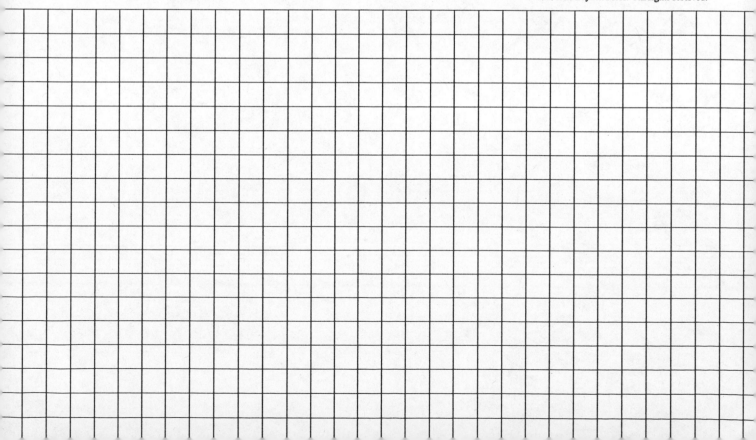

Exhibit 8–15   A Tax on Imported Cameras

	Before Tariff	After Tariff
Consumers' Surplus	A+B+C+D	A
Tariff Revenue	—	B+C+E+F
Social Gain	A+B+C+D	A+B+C+E+F

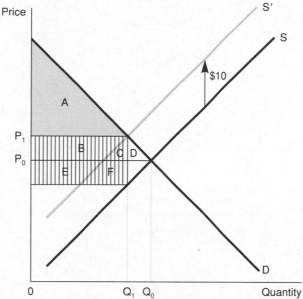

If cameras are supplied by foreigners and purchased by Americans, then a tariff affects Americans through the consumers' surplus and through the tax revenue that it generates.

Exhibit 8–16   A Tariff on Imported Cameras That Are Elastically Supplied

	Before Tariff	After Tariff
Consumers' Surplus	A + B + C	A
Tariff Revenue	—	B
Social Gain	A + B + C	A + B
Deadweight Loss		C

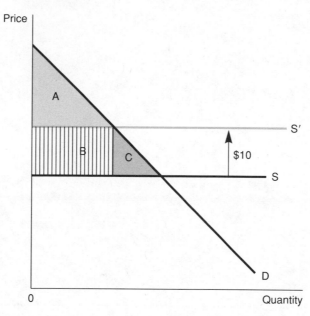

If the United States is a small part of the market to which the Japanese sell cameras, then Americans will face a flat supply curve. In this case a tariff always reduces the welfare of Americans.

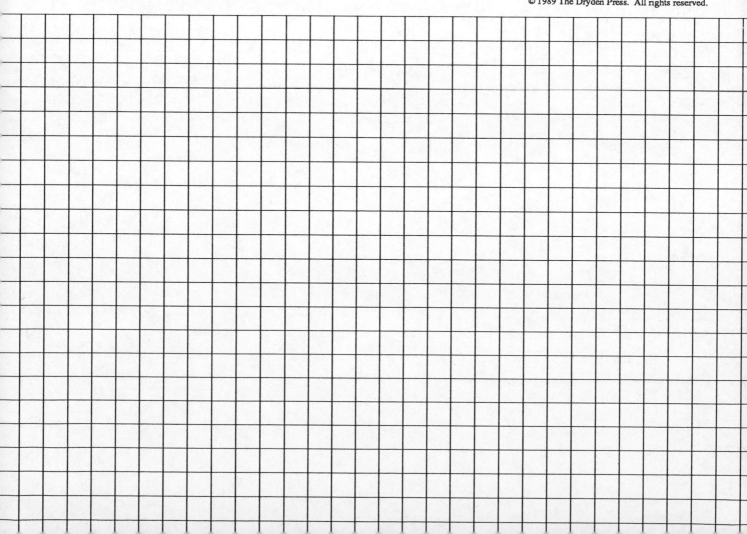

Exhibit 8–17 A Tariff When There Is a Domestic Industry

Table A

Consumers' Surplus	A + B
Producers' Surplus	C
Social Gain	A + B + C

Table B

	Before Tariff	After Tariff
Consumers' Surplus	E + F + G + H + I + J	E + F
Producers' Surplus	K	G + K
Tax Revenue	—	I
Social Gain	E + F + G + H + I + J + K	E + F + G + K + I
Deadweight Loss		H + J

A

B

We assume that Americans can buy any number of cars from Japan at the price P_0. The supply curve S shows how many cars American manufacturers will provide at each price. At the price P_0, American producers supply Q_0 cars and American consumers purchase Q_1 cars. The difference, $Q_1 - Q_0$, is the number of cars imported. Table A shows the gains to Americans.

In panel B we see the effect of a $500 tariff on imported cars. The price of a foreign car rises to $P_0 + \$500$, and the number of imports falls to $Q'_1 - Q'_0$. Table B compares gains before and after the tariff. Note that the first column of Table B is identical to Table A except that it uses the labels from panel B rather than panel A. The tariff revenue is computed by observing that the area of rectangle I is $(Q'_1 - Q'_0) \times \$500$.

Exhibit 8–21 **Trade in an Edgeworth Box Economy**

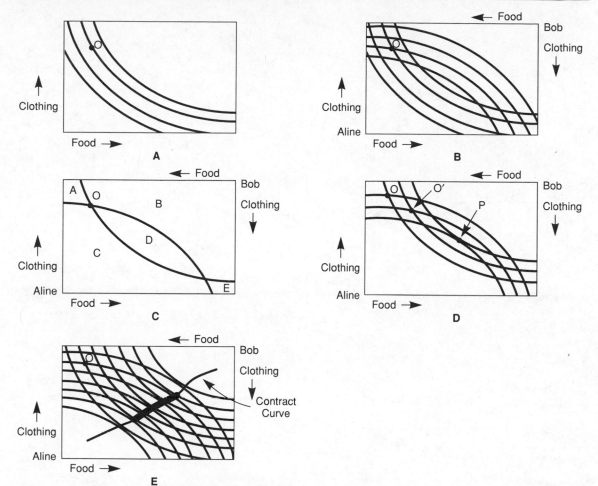

Panel A shows Aline's indifference curves and her endowment point O. Panel B adds Bob's (black) indifference curves, using the northeast corner of the box as origin. Measuring along Bob's axes, his endowment point is also O.

Panel C shows only those indifference curves that pass through the endowment point. Movements into the region of mutual advantage, D, benefit both parties. Moves into any other region will be vetoed by one or both of the parties.

Panel D shows the situation after Aline and Bob make the mutually beneficial trade to point O′. The shaded region is the new region of mutual advantage. Trade will continue until they reach a point like P in panel D, where there is no region of mutual advantage. Such points are on the contract curve, consisting of the tangencies between Aline's and Bob's indifference curves. The points on the contract curve are precisely those that are Pareto-optimal.

In panel E the shaded region is the original region of mutual advantage. Trade leads to the choice of a point on the contract curve in this region. The darker segment of the contract curve is the set of possible outcomes.

Exhibit 8–22   Competitive Equilibrium in an Edgeworth Box Economy

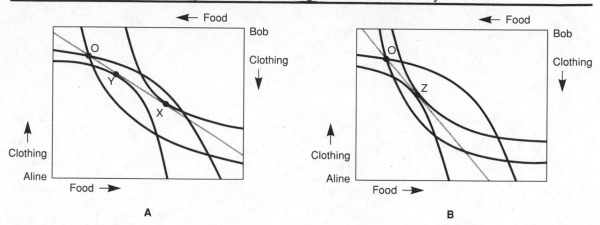

A

B

In panel A a relative price has been suggested that leads to the budget line pictured. (This is Aline's budget line from her perspective and Bob's budget line from his.) Aline chooses point X and Bob chooses point Y. But these points are not the same; the quantities that Aline wants to buy and sell are not the same quantities that Bob wants to sell and buy.

In panel B a different relative price has been suggested. At this price Aline's desires are compatible with Bob's. Point Z is a competitive equilibrium.

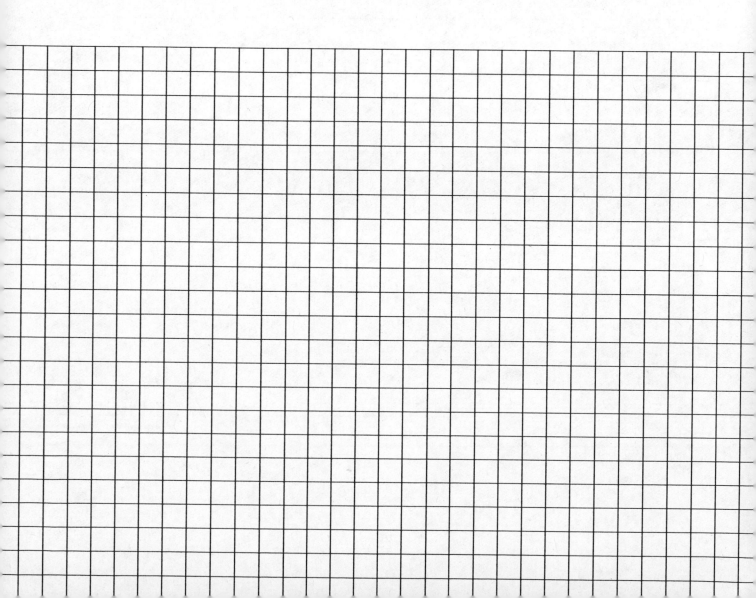

Exhibit 9–2   **The Costs of Misallocation**

Larry		Moe		Curly	
Quantity	**Marginal Value**	**Quantity**	**Marginal Value**	**Quantity**	**Marginal Value**
1	$15/egg	1	$13/egg	1	$7/egg
2	8	2	11	2	3

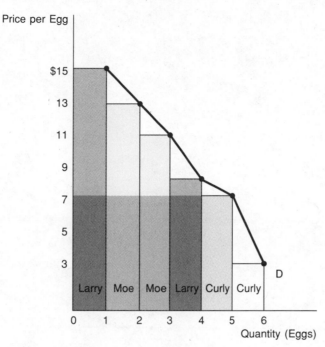

When the market price is $7 per egg, 5 eggs are sold (2 to Larry, 2 to Moe, and 1 to Curly) and their total value (the sum of the shaded rectangles) is $54. If the same 5 eggs were distributed by a mechanism other than the market, the total value might be less. For example, if a social planner gave 2 eggs to Larry, 1 to Moe, and 2 to Curly, the total value would be only $46. In this case, therefore, the usual measures of social gain would overstate the true social gain by $8.

Exhibit 9–3 Planning versus Markets

Firm A		Firm B		Firm C	
Quantity	Marginal Cost	Quantity	Marginal Cost	Quantity	Marginal Cost
1	$1	1	$ 5	1	$6
2	3	2	11	2	7

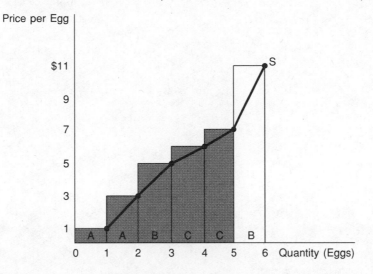

At a market price of $7, 5 eggs are produced in the least costly way possible. If a social planner orders 5 eggs to be produced and fails to realize that the low-cost producer is Firm A, then the total cost of production will be higher than necessary.

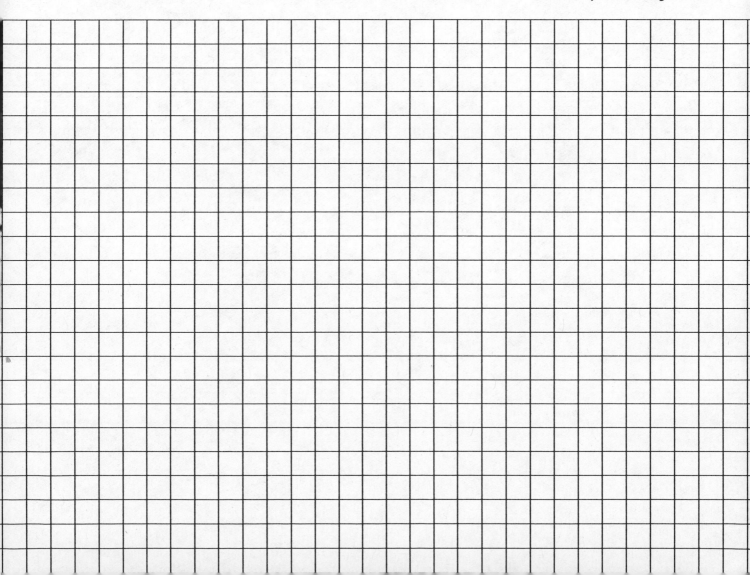

Exhibit 9–4　A Military Draft

	Volunteer Army	Draft	Limited Draft
Consumers' Surplus	A	A+B+C+D	A+B+C
Producers' Surplus	B+F	F−C−D−E	F−C
Social Gain	A+B+F	A+B+F−E	A+B+F
Deadweight Loss		E	

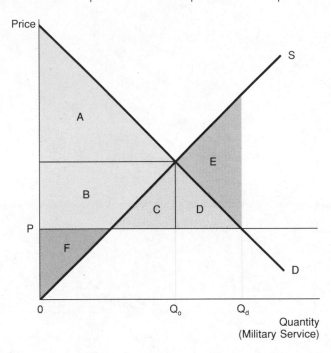

Military services are supplied by Young Men and demanded by society through the armed forces. The first column shows the gains at equilibrium, with a volunteer army. We assume that the wage rate is set at P, so that more Young Men are demanded than will volunteer. If the army can draft as many Young Men as it wants to at the price P, it will choose the quantity Q_d and social gains will be as depicted in the second column. If, on the other hand, the army is permitted to hire only Q_0 Young Men, social gains will be as in the third column, seemingly eliminating the deadweight loss. This leads to the apparent conclusion that the limited draft is as efficient as the volunteer army. As explained in the text, however, this conclusion is misleading.

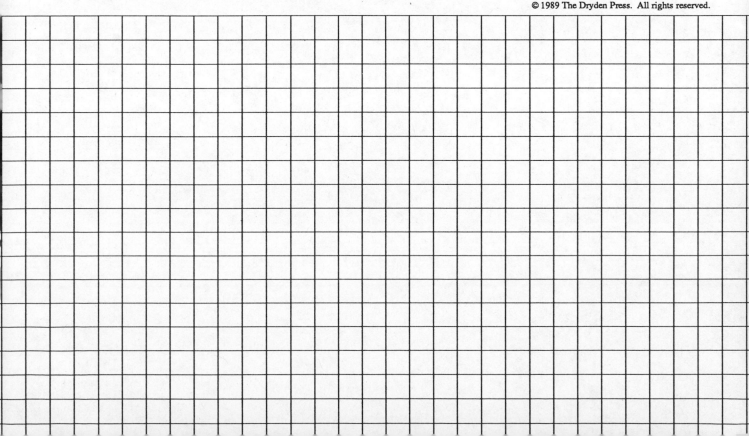

Exhibit 9–5 Computing Producers' Surplus with a Draft

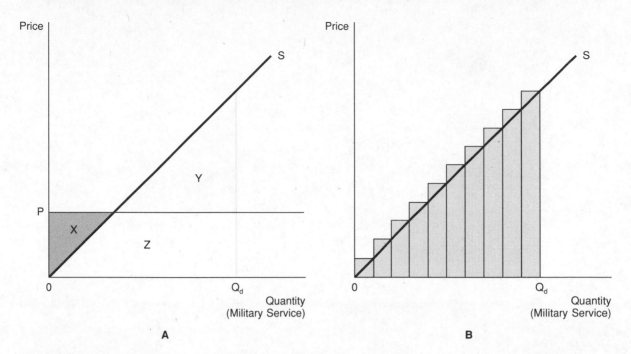

If the army forcibly hires Q_d soldiers at the price P, then soldiers will earn $P \times Q_d = X + Z$ in wages. Their opportunity cost of being in the army is the sum of all the rectangles in panel B, which is the same as area $Y + Z$ in panel A. This leaves a producers' surplus of $(X + Z) - (Y + Z) = X - Y$.

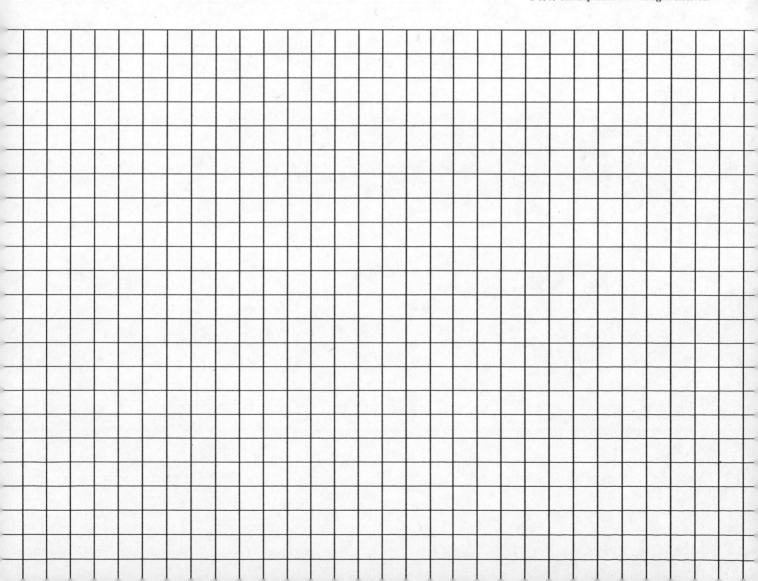

Exhibit 10–2 Monopoly versus Competition

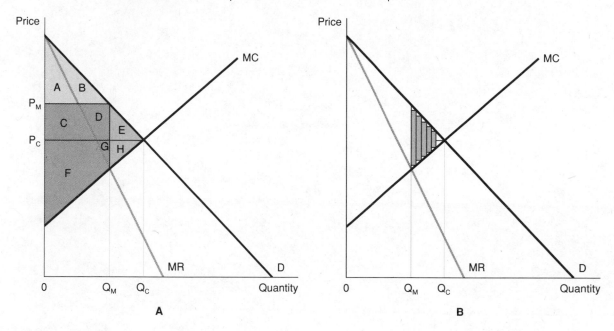

	Competition	Monopoly
Consumers' Surplus	A + B + C + D + E	A + B
Producers' Surplus	F + G + H	C + D + F + G
Social Gain	A + B + C + D + E + F + G + H	A + B + C + D + F + G
Deadweight Loss		E + H

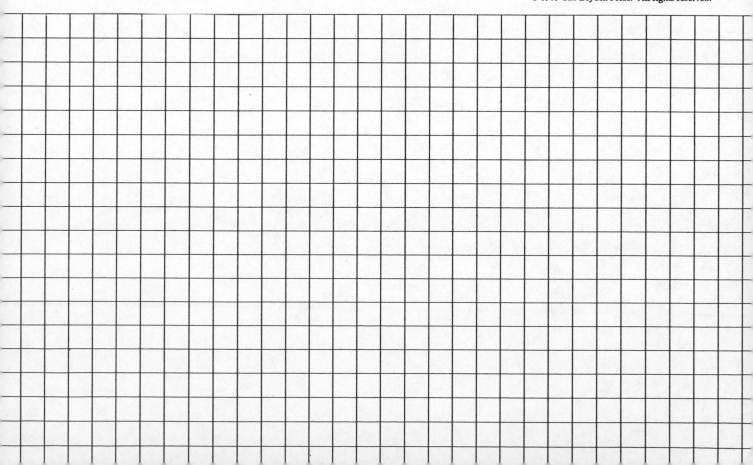

The table assumes that a monopoly and a competitive industry would have the same marginal cost curve. The competitive industry produces the equilibrium quantity Q_C and the monopolist produces its profit-maximizing quantity Q_M. Since marginal value still exceeds marginal cost at Q_M, it would be efficient for additional units to be produced. The social gains from additional units after Q_M are represented by the rectangles in panel B. Since the monopolist does not produce those units, those social gains are sacrificed, giving a deadweight loss of E + H.

Exhibit 10–3   A Subsidized Monopolist

	Competition	Unsubsidized Monopoly	Subsidized Monopoly
Consumers' Surplus	A+B+C+D+E	A+B	A+B+C+D+E
Producers' Surplus	F+G+H	C+D+F+G	F+G+H+I+J+K
Cost to Taxpayers			I+J+K
Social Gain	A+B+C+D+E+F+G+H	A+B+C+D+F+G	A+B+C+D+E+F+G+H

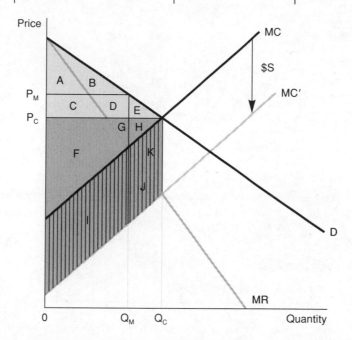

An unsubsidized monopolist produces the quantity Q_M. The subsidy of \$S per unit of output, which lowers the marginal cost curve to MC′, is chosen to be of just the right size so that the monopolist will now produce the competitive quantity Q_C. Since the competitive quantity maximizes social gain, the deadweight loss is eliminated.

The table confirms that social gain is the same as it would be under competition.

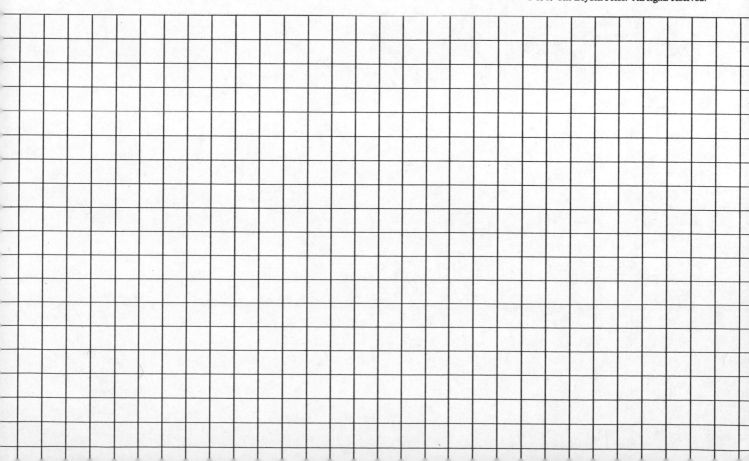

Exhibit 10–4   **A Price Ceiling**

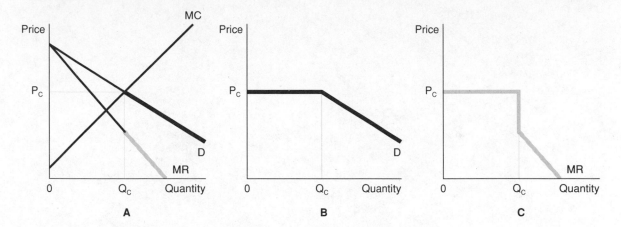

If a monopolist is required by law to charge no more than the competitive price P_C, then he effectively faces the demand and marginal revenue curves shown in panels B and C. He produces at the point Q_C, where marginal cost and marginal revenue are equal.

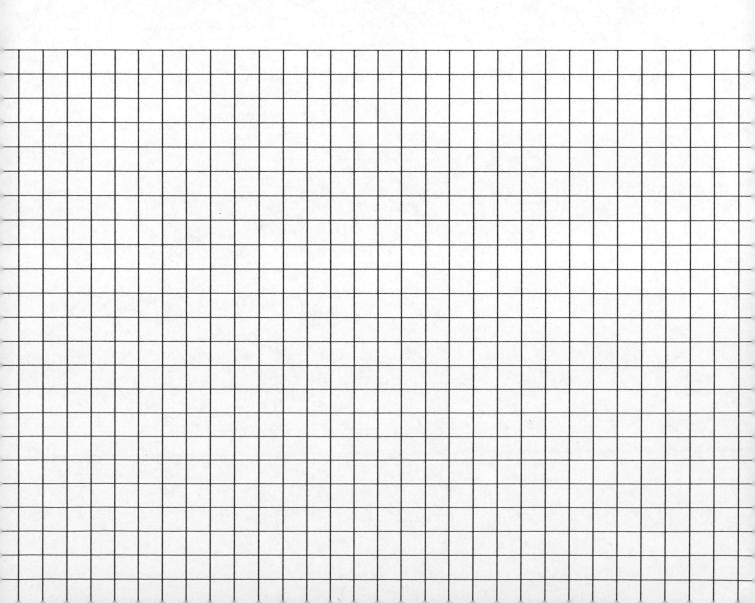

Exhibit 10–5 Zero Profits Regulation of Monopoly

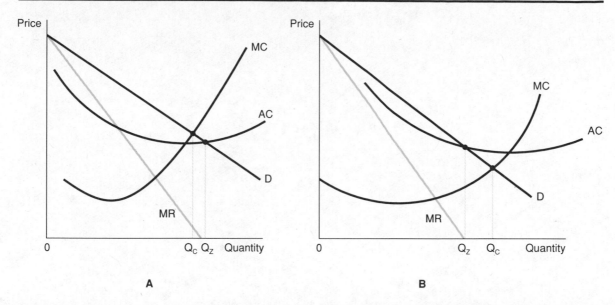

The two panels show two possible configurations of demand, marginal revenue, marginal cost, and average cost curves for a monopolist. If the monopolist is required by law to earn zero profits, he will produce that quantity Q_Z at which the demand price is equal to average cost. The efficient level of output is Q_C, where marginal cost equals demand. As the two panels show, Q_Z could be either greater or less than Q_C.

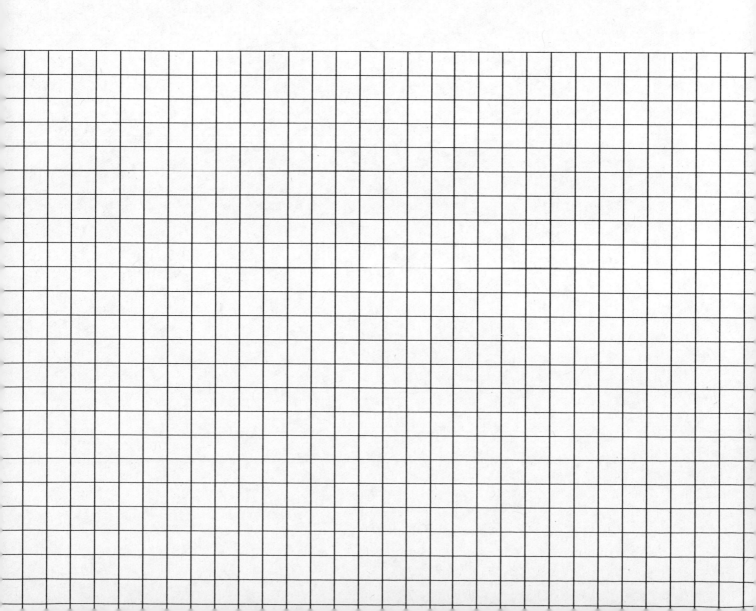

Exhibit 10–6 **Natural Monopoly**

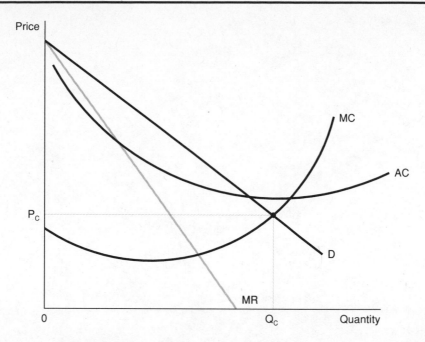

A natural monopoly occurs when each firm's average cost curve is downward sloping at the point where it crosses industry demand. Since marginal cost crosses average cost at the bottom of the U, marginal cost must cross demand at a point where price is below average cost. Thus if the firm priced competitively, it would earn negative profits.

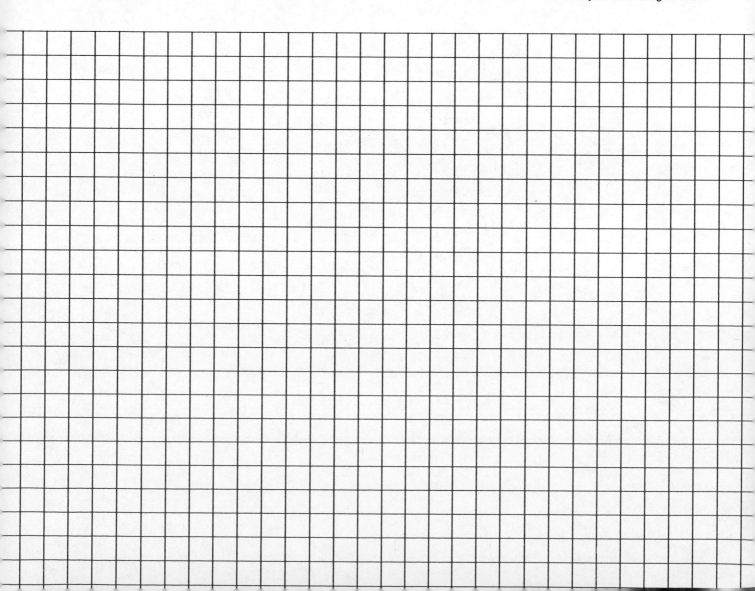

Exhibit 10–8 Mrs. Lovett's Pies

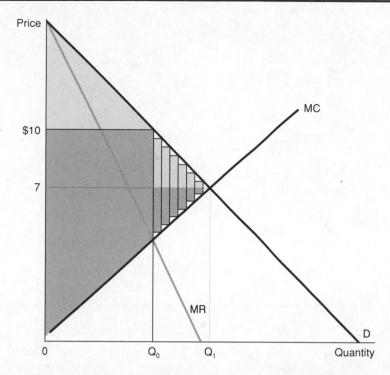

Mrs. Lovett, as a monopolist, produces Q_0 pies and sells them at a price of $10. Once she has done so, she can still sell additional pies at prices that exceed her marginal cost. For example, at the competitive price of $7, she could sell an additional $Q_1 - Q_0$ pies, creating additional social gains represented by the rectangles. The upper portions of the rectangles represent additions to consumers' surplus, and the lower portions represent additions to Mrs. Lovett's producer's surplus.

Exhibit 10-9 First-Degree Price Discrimination

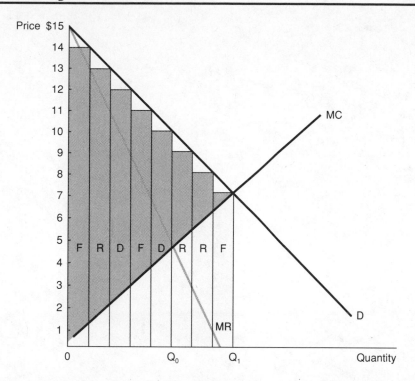

The rectangles show the marginal values of pies to Mrs. Lovett's customers, with each labeled by the initial of the corresponding customer. If she charges each customer the maximum amount that she is willing to pay for a pie, Flicka will have to pay $14 for her first pie, Ricka will pay $13 for her first pie, and so on. Since each consumer pays her marginal value for each pie, there is no consumers' surplus. All of the surplus is earned by Mrs. Lovett, who gains the entire shaded area.

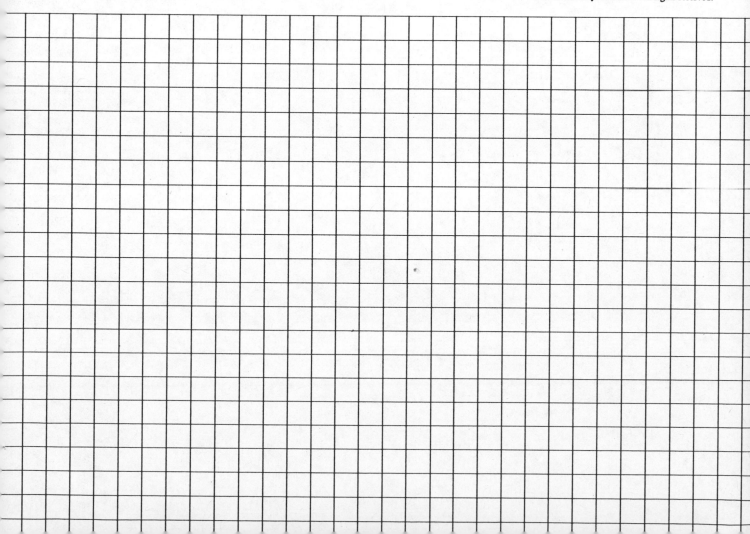

Exhibit 10–10 **Third-Degree Price Discrimination with Monopoly in One Market and Competition in the Other**

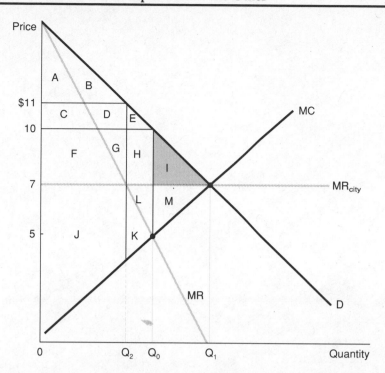

The demand and marginal revenue curves are from Mrs. Lovett's hometown market. In the distant city she can sell all of the pies she wants to at the competitive price of $7. In that case she will sell only Q_2 pies at home, as opposed to the ordinary monopoly quantity Q_0. The reason is that she can always earn $7 marginal revenue by selling pies in the city, so that she will not sell pies at home when her marginal revenue there falls below $7. When she sells Q_2 pies at home, she sets a price of $11, higher than the ordinary monopoly price of $10. The table shows what social gains would be if the pie industry were competitive, if Mrs. Lovett were an ordinary monopolist, and when Mrs. Lovett is able to sell pies in both markets at different prices.

In each case the consumers' surplus comes entirely from the local market. There is no consumers' surplus in the city market, because the demand curve there for Mrs. Lovett's pies is flat.

	Competition	Ordinary Monopoly	Price-Discriminating Monopoly
Consumers' Surplus	A+B+C+D+E+F+G+H+I	A+B+C+D+E	A+B
Producer's Surplus (Local)	J+K+L+M	F+G+H+J+K+L	C+D+F+G+J
Producer's Surplus (City)			K+L+M
Social Gain	A+B+C+D+E+F+G+H +I+J+K+L+M	A+B+C+D+E+F +G+H+J+K+L	A+B+C+D+F+G+J +K+L+M
Deadweight Loss		I+M	E+H+I

Exhibit 10–11   Third-Degree Price Discrimination by a Monopolist in Two Markets

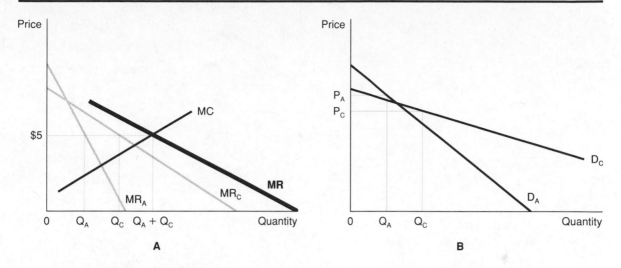

Benjamin Barker sells haircuts to adults and to children. The two groups have different marginal revenue curves, labeled MR_A and MR_C in panel A. The heavier curve **MR** is obtained by horizontally summing the curves MR_A and MR_C. Benjamin produces the quantity $Q_A + Q_C$ where MC crosses **MR**, selling Q_A haircuts to adults and Q_C to children. He chooses the corresponding prices of the adults' and children's demand curves, which are shown in panel B.

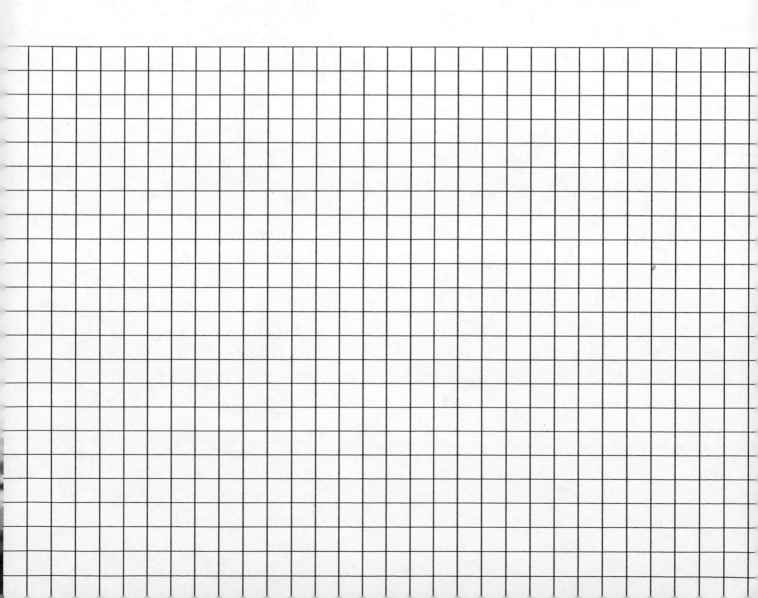

Exhibit 11–1   A Horizontal Merger

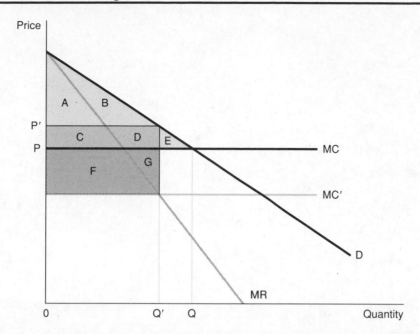

Initially, the industry's marginal cost (= supply) curve is MC. If the industry is competitive, it produces the equilibrium output Q at the price P. Because the MC curve is horizontal, there is no producers' surplus.

Following a merger, marginal cost is reduced to MC', but the newly created firm has monopoly power and so produces the quantity Q', where MC' crosses the marginal revenue curve MR. The monopoly price is P'. The table below computes welfare before and after the merger:

	Before Merger	After Merger
Consumers' Surplus	A+B+C+D+E	A+B
Producers' Surplus	—	C+D+F+G
Social Gain	A+B+C+D+E	A+B+C+D+F+G

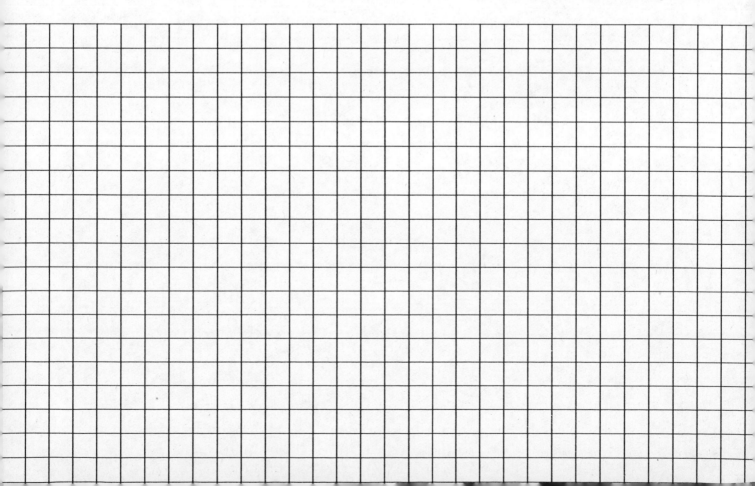

Exhibit 11–2   A Horizontal Merger Leading to a Large Cost Reduction

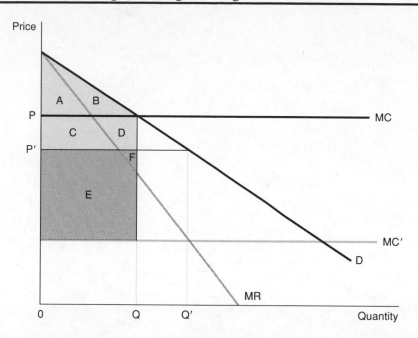

If the competitive industry's marginal cost curve is MC, and if a merger converts the industry into a monopoly with the much lower marginal cost curve MC', then price will fall from P to P', benefiting both consumers and producers.

	Before Merger	After Merger
Consumers' Surplus	A+B	A+B+C+D
Producers' Surplus	—	E+F
Social Gain	A+B	A+B+C+D+E+F

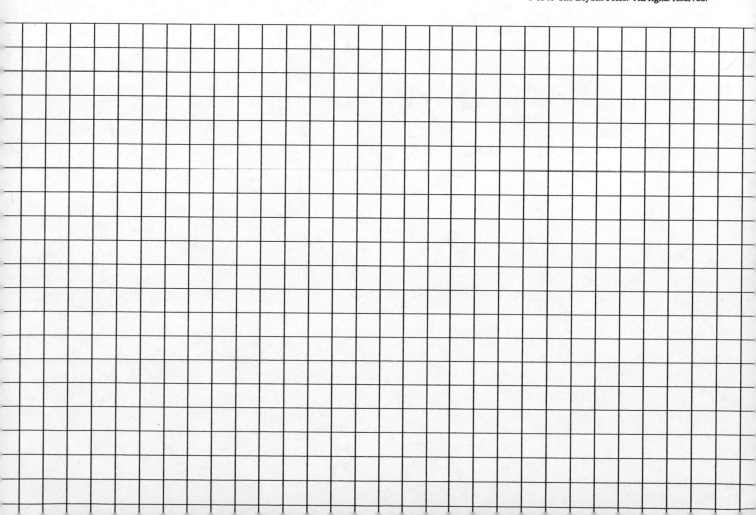

Exhibit 11–3 Vertical Integration

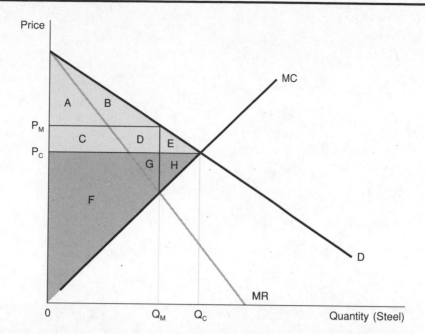

The monopolist Flemington Steel produces Q_M units of steel for sale to a monopoly automaker. This maximizes producer's surplus at C + D + F + G while restricting consumers' surplus to A + B.

If Flemington acquires ownership of the automaker, it will earn both the producer's and the consumers' surpluses and will therefore want to maximize the sum of the two. This is accomplished by producing the quantity Q_C of steel, creating a gain equal to the sum of all the lettered areas. Social gain is increased by E + H. More steel is produced, more cars are produced, and the price of cars to consumers goes down.

Exhibit 11–4 Resale Price Maintenance

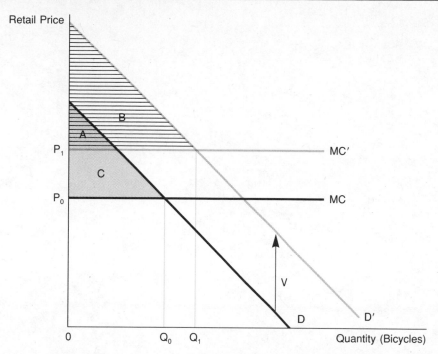

Suppose that Schwinn provides bicycles at a wholesale price of P_0 and that this is the only cost that retailers have. If the demand curve is D, then under competition the quantity sold is Q_0 and consumers' surplus is $A + C$.

If Schwinn maintains a retail price of P_1, dealers compete with each other by offering services that cost $P_1 - P_0$ per bicycle to provide. The value of these services to consumers is some amount V, so that the demand curve moves vertically upward a distance V to D'. The new quantity sold is Q_1.

Since Schwinn chooses to engage in the practice, we can assume that $Q_1 > Q_0$. Elementary geometry now reveals that $V > P_1 - P_0$ (the value of the dealer services exceeds the cost of producing them) and $A + B > A + C$ (consumers' surplus is increased).

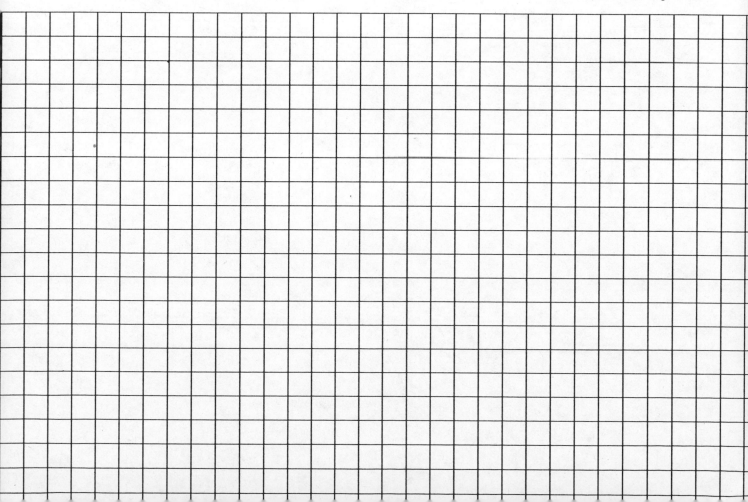

Exhibit 11–7   A Contestable Market

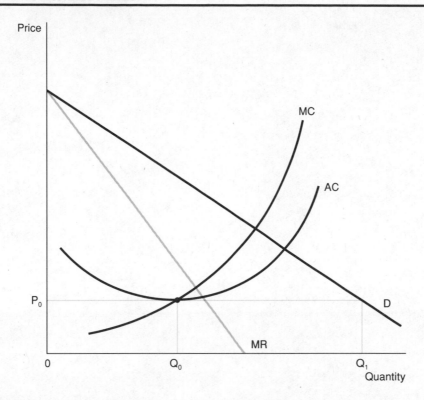

If the market is contestable, firms will enter at any price above P_0. Therefore the market price cannot be higher than P_0, because any higher price would attract entry. At this price the firm supplies Q_0 units of output and the market demands Q_1. Thus there is room in the industry for Q_1/Q_0 firms.

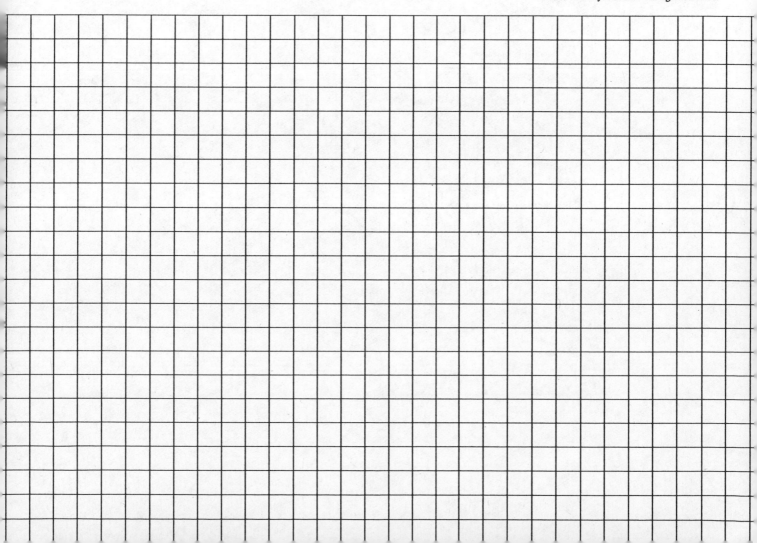

Exhibit 11–9   **The Cournot Model of Oligopoly**

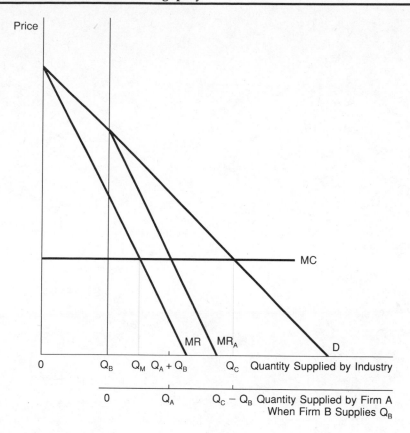

We assume that two identical firms have the flat marginal cost curve MC and face a market demand curve D. A competitive industry would produce the quantity Q_C. A monopolist would produce the quantity $Q_M = \frac{1}{2}Q_C$, where MC crosses the marginal revenue curve MR.

If Firm A assumes that Firm B will always produce quantity Q_B, then Firm A views itself as a monopolist in the market for the remaining quantity. The demand curve in that market is the blue part of the market demand curve, measured along the blue axis. The marginal revenue curve is the blue curve MR_A. Firm A produces the monopoly quantity Q_A, which is half the competitive quantity ($Q_C - Q_B$). Combining this fact with the equation $Q_A = Q_B$ (which follows from the fact that the firms are identical), we compute that $Q_A = Q_B = \frac{1}{3}Q_C$. Thus the industry output is $\frac{2}{3}Q_C$, less than the competitive output but more than the monopoly output.

Exhibit 11–10   Monopolistic Competition

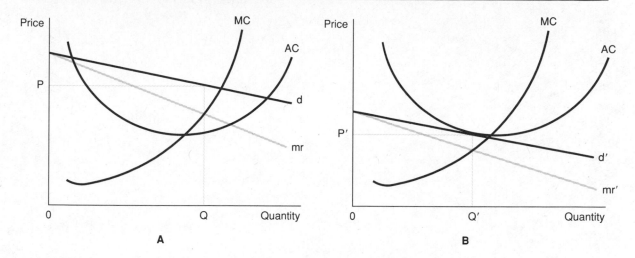

Panel A shows a short-run equilibrium in which the firm sells quantity Q at price P. Here price exceeds average cost, so the firm earns positive profits. In the long run entry drives the demand curve facing this firm down to d′ in panel B, where the firm is just able to earn zero profits by selling quantity Q′ at price P′.

Exhibit 12–1   **Private Costs versus Social Costs**

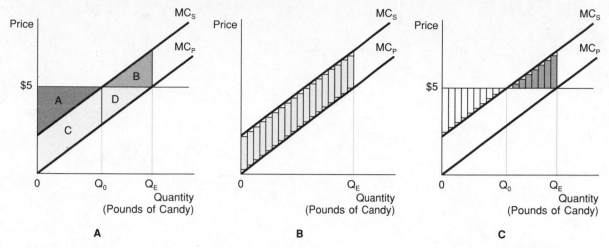

Bridgman, a confectioner, has the marginal cost curve MC_P. When he produces chocolate, he also imposes external costs on Sturges. The cost to society of producing candy is the sum of Bridgman's private cost MC_P and the external costs borne by Sturges. The curve MC_S shows this full social cost.

At a market price of $5, Bridgman produces Q_E pounds of candy. Each pound produced imposes on Sturges a marginal external cost represented by one of the rectangles in panel B. The total external cost is the sum of these rectangles, which is area B + C + D in panel A.

Bridgman earns a producer's surplus equal to A + C + D. Subtracting the externality imposed on Sturges, we find a net social gain of A − B. The reason for this result is demonstrated in panel C. Each pound of candy up to Q_0 creates a social gain equal to one of the unshaded rectangles. Each pound of candy after Q_0 creates a social loss equal to one of the shaded rectangles. The net social gain is the sum of the unshaded rectangles minus the sum of the shaded ones, or A − B.

Exhibit 12–3 Side Payments Cause Externalities to Be Internalized

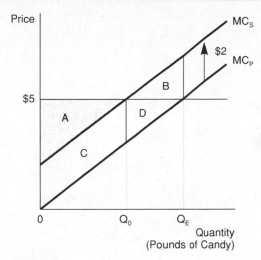

The graph is as in Exhibit 12–1. Each time Bridgman produces a pound of candy, he also imposes a $2 externality on Sturges. In the absence of transactions costs, Sturges will offer to pay Bridgman up to $2 for each pound of candy that he does *not* produce.

If Bridgman ceases production altogether, he can collect $2 \times Q_E = B + C + D$. This amount is a pure transfer of wealth from Sturges to Bridgman. Now for each pound of candy that Bridgman produces, he must return $2 to Sturges (that is, he must forgo the opportunity to collect the $2 in the first place). This forgone opportunity is exactly equivalent to a Pigou tax on Bridgman, with the proceeds assigned to Sturges. Thus Bridgman's private marginal cost curve rises to MC_S and he produces the quantity Q_0. Gains are shown in the table below.

	Original	With Pigou Tax (Proceeds to Sturges)	With Sturges Bribing Bridgman
Bridgman's Gains:			
Producer's Surplus	A + C + D	A	A
Transfer	—	—	B + C + D
Sturges's Gains:			
Tax Revenue		C	
Sturges's Losses:			
Noise Damage	B + C + D	C	—
Transfer	—	—	B + C + D
Social Gain	A – B	A	A

Exhibit 12–7 Sparks from Railroads

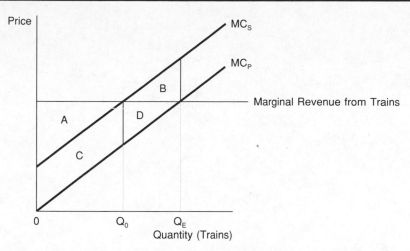

Because railway engines emit sparks that sometimes set fire to crops, the social marginal cost of running trains exceeds the private marginal cost. If the railroad is not liable, it runs Q_E trains and social gain is A − B. If the railroad is made liable, it takes account of all costs and runs Q_0 trains, for a social gain of A. Thus the standard Pigovian analysis suggests that the railroad should be liable.

But this analysis overlooks other possibilities. Suppose that the railroad is not liable and that as a result the farmers decide to move their crops away from the tracks. Then the externality is eliminated. Q_E trains are run (which is now the social optimum) and social gain is A + C + D minus the cost of moving the crops. This gain could be more or less than the gain of A that comes about when the railroad is liable. Thus the graph does not reveal the efficient solution.

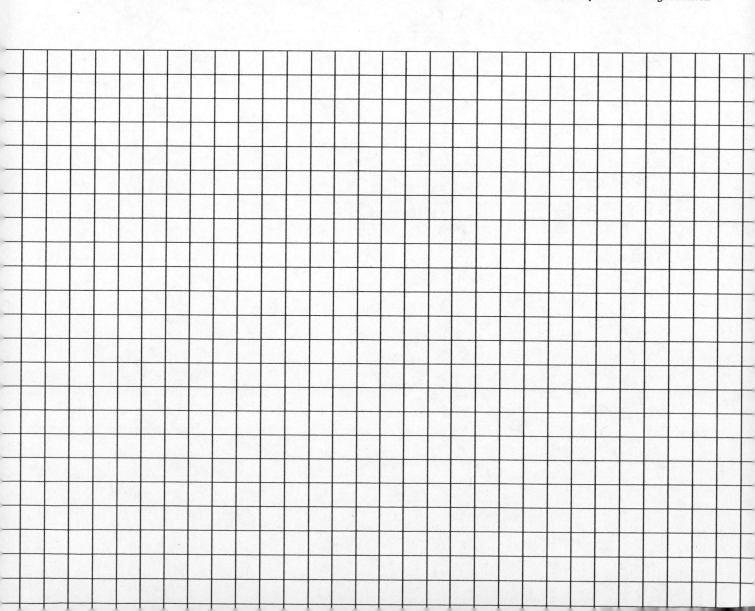

Exhibit 13–1   The Dissipation of Rents

Number of Dwarfs	Apples per Dwarf	Total Apple Harvest	Marginal Apple Harvest
1	10/day	10/day	10/day
2	9	18	8
3	8	24	6
4	7	28	4
5	6	30	2
6	5	30	0
7	4	28	−2
8	3	24	−4
9	2	18	−6
10	1	10	−8

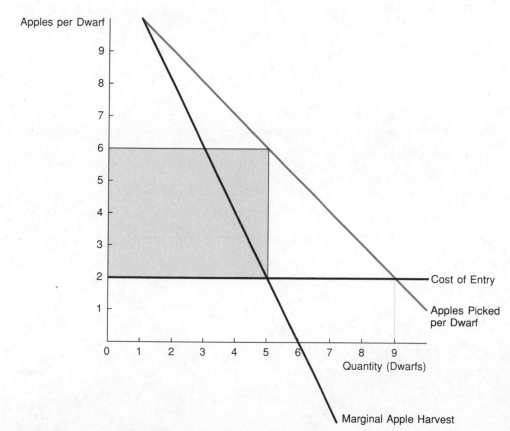

Each time a dwarf enters the forest, he reduces the number of apples picked by all of the other dwarfs. If the cost of entering is 2 apples per day per dwarf, dwarfs will continue to enter until no dwarf can pick more than 2 apples per day. This happens when 9 dwarfs have entered. At this point the rents are completely dissipated and the dwarfs get no benefit at all from the existence of the forest.

If only 5 dwarfs entered, each would gain 4 apples from the existence of the forest, making the total social gain equal to 20 apples, as illustrated by the shaded area.

Exhibit 13–2   Gains from the Forest When Dwarfs Are Not Identical

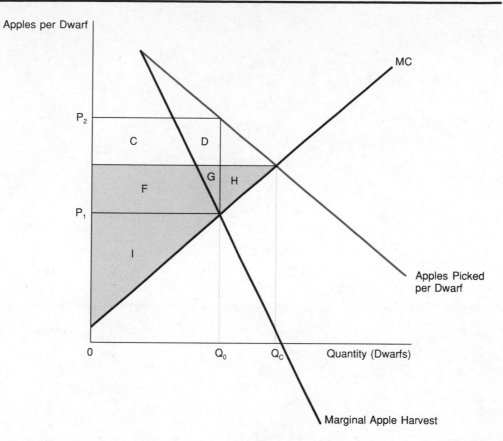

The MC curve shows the cost of adding additional dwarfs to the forest. Dwarfs will continue to enter until the last dwarf has an opportunity cost equal to the number of apples he can pick. This occurs at Q_C, and the dwarfs earn a surplus of $F + G + H + I$. If it were possible to control entry, the optimal number of dwarfs is Q_0, yielding the maximal possible surplus $C + D + F + G + I$.

Exhibit 14–1   The Total, Marginal, and Marginal Revenue Products of Labor

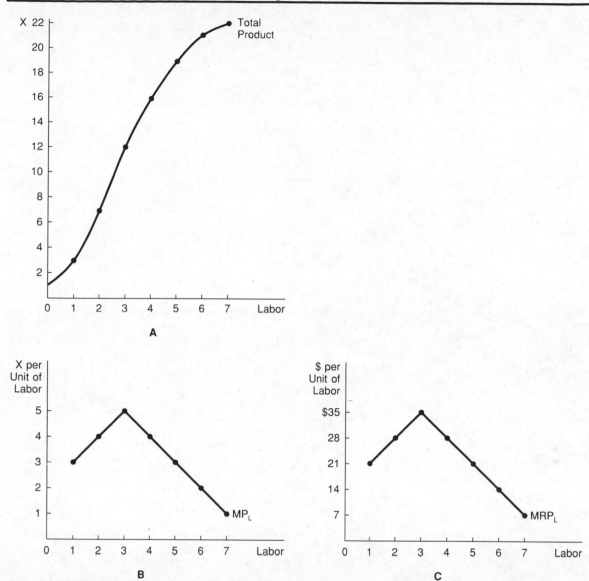

The total product and marginal product of labor (MP$_L$) curves are as in Exhibit 6–5. The marginal product of labor increases until diminishing marginal returns set in at L = 3, and it decreases thereafter. If the firm is competitive and sells its output at $7 per unit, then the marginal revenue product of labor (MRP$_L$) is given by

$$MRP_L = \$7 \times MP_L.$$

Thus the MRP$_L$ curve can be constructed from the MP$_L$ curve by simply changing the units on the vertical axis, as shown in panel C.

Exhibit 14–2   The Market for Labor and the Market for Output

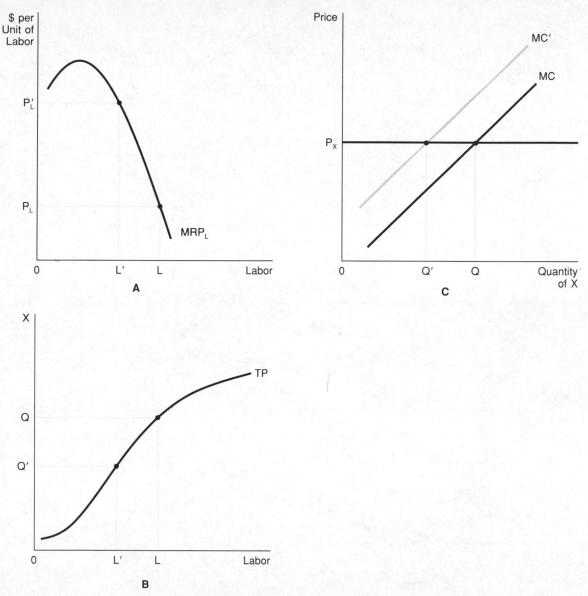

The marginal cost curve, MC, in panel C is derived from knowledge of the wage rate of labor, P_L, and the total product of labor curve, TP, in panel B. The derivation was given in Chapter 6. Thus each graph contains some information that is also encoded in the other graphs.

To see the interrelations, notice that when the wage rate is P_L, panel A shows that the firm hires L units of labor, panel B shows that L units of labor will produce Q units of output, and panel C confirms that the firm's output is Q. If the wage rate rises to P_L', the marginal cost curve rises to MC'. Now panel A shows that the firm hires L' units of labor, panel B shows that the firm produces Q' units of output, and panel C confirms this.

Exhibit 14–3 A Rise in the Price of Output

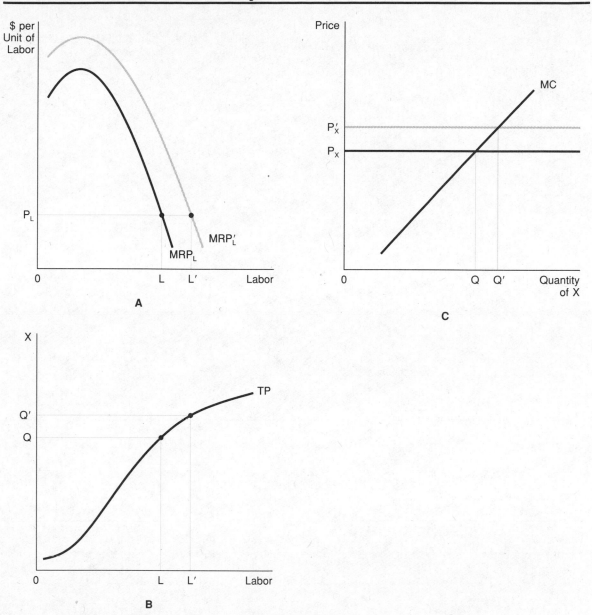

A

B

C

Initially, the price of output is P_X and the wage rate of labor is P_L. The firm hires L units of labor and produces Q units of output. When the price of output rises to P'_X, the MRP_L curve shifts out to MRP'_L, employment rises to L', and output increases to Q'.

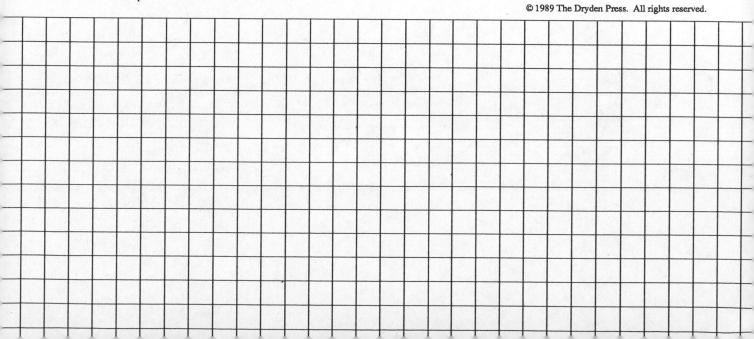

Exhibit 14–5 Constructing a Point on the Labor Demand Curve

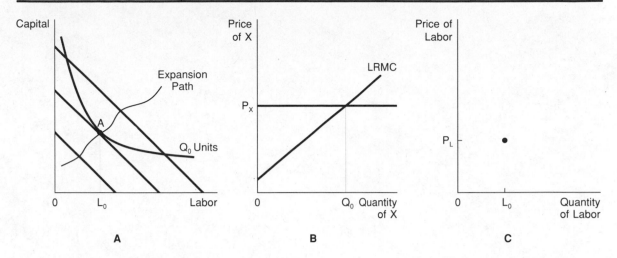

The graphs illustrate the construction of a single point on the firm's demand curve for labor, shown in panel C. The isoquant in panel A and the output price, P_x, shown in panel B are given and are independent of the wage rate. Now we assume a wage rate P_L. This enables us to draw the isocosts in the first panel, which have slope $-P_L/P_K$. These in turn determine the expansion path, also shown in panel A. Using panel A, we can derive the firm's long-run marginal cost (= long-run supply) curve, LRMC, using the methods of Section 6.3. Panel B determines the firm's output, which is Q_0. We now return to panel A to see that when the firm produces the quantity Q_0, it chooses the basket of inputs A, and this basket contains L_0 units of labor. Finally, we conclude that the wage rate P_L corresponds to the quantity of labor L_0, and we record this fact in panel C.

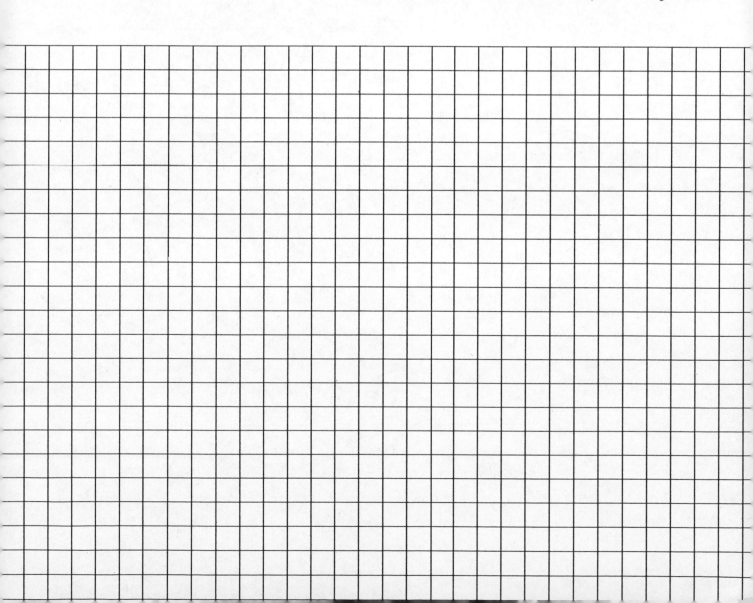

Exhibit 14–6   A Rise in the Wage Rate

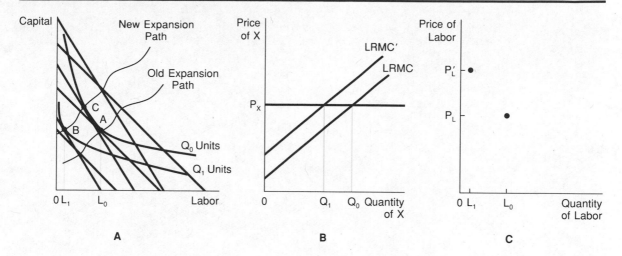

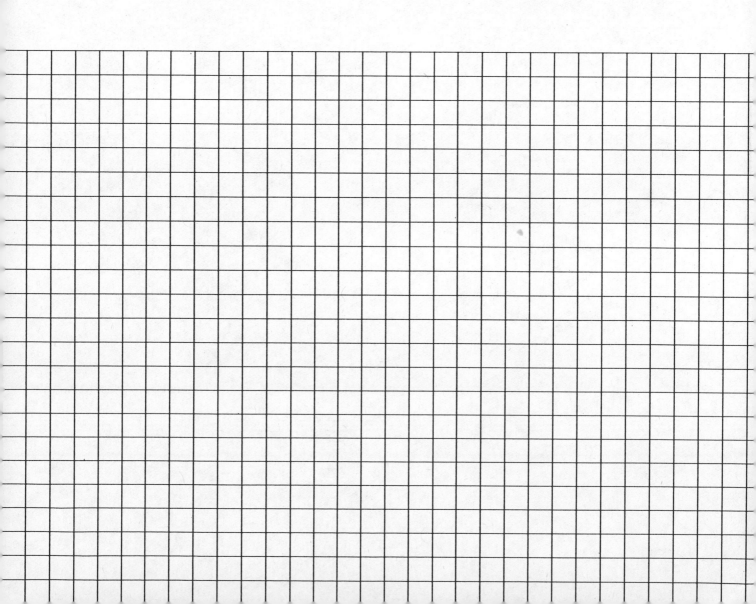

Beginning with the situation in Exhibit 14–5, we assume that the wage rate now rises from P_L to P_L'. The new curves are the colored ones. First we get new isocosts (with slope $-P_L'/P_K$) and a new expansion path in panel A. This yields a new marginal cost curve, LRMC', and a new quantity of output, Q_1, in panel B. The firm chooses a point on its expansion path where it can produce Q_1 units of output, namely, B in panel A. Thus it hires L_1 units of labor, generating the new point on the demand curve that is shown in panel C.

Exhibit 14–8 A Rise in the Wage of a Regressive Factor

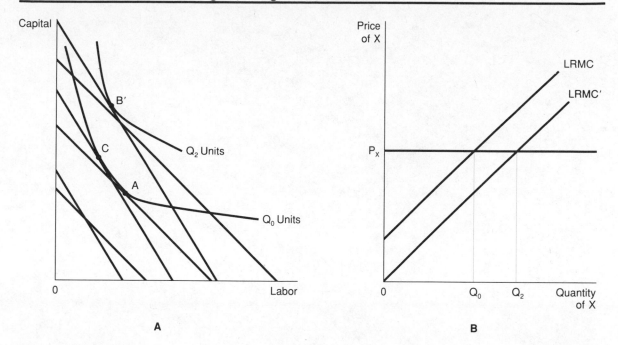

A

B

If labor is a regressive factor, than a rise in the wage rate leads to a fall in marginal cost and an increase in output, from Q_0 to Q_2. Therefore the firm moves from point A on the Q_0-isoquant to point B' on the higher Q_2-isoquant. The move can be decomposed into a substitution effect (the move from A to C) and a scale effect (the move from C to B').

Exhibit 14–9 Labor Demand in the Short Run and the Long Run

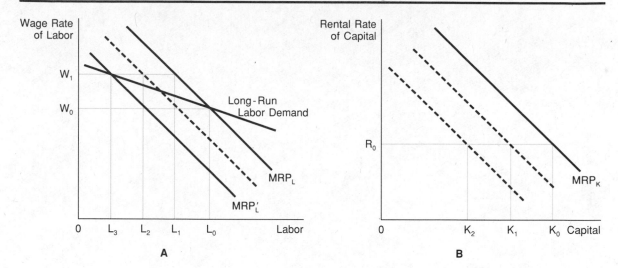

Initially, the wage rate of labor is W_0 and the rental rate on capital is R_0. The firm hires L_0 units of labor and K_0 units of capital.

Now the wage rate rises to W_1. In the short run the firm reduces its employment of labor to L_1, read off the MRP_L curve. Assuming that capital and labor are complements in production, this causes the MRP_K curve to fall to the level of the middle curve in panel B. The firm reduces its capital employment to K_1.

The reduced capital employment lowers the MRP_L curve to the level of the dashed curve in panel A, causing labor employment to fall to L_2. This lowers the MRP_K still further, causing capital employment to fall to K_2, and the process repeats. Eventually the MRP_L curve settles at the new level MRP'_L. Here the firm hires L_3 units of labor. Thus the long-run labor demand curve (in black) shows that a wage of W_1 corresponds to the quantity L_3 of labor employed.

Exhibit 14–10 Monopsony

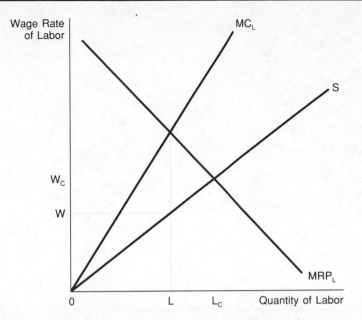

A monopsony demander of labor faces an upward-sloping labor supply curve (S) and a marginal cost of labor (MC_L) curve that lies everywhere above S. He hires L units of labor (where $MRP_L = MC_L$) and pays the wage W that he reads off the supply curve at that quantity.

In an industry with many firms, the going price for labor would be W_C, and each firm would face a flat supply curve at this price. L_C units of labor would be hired.

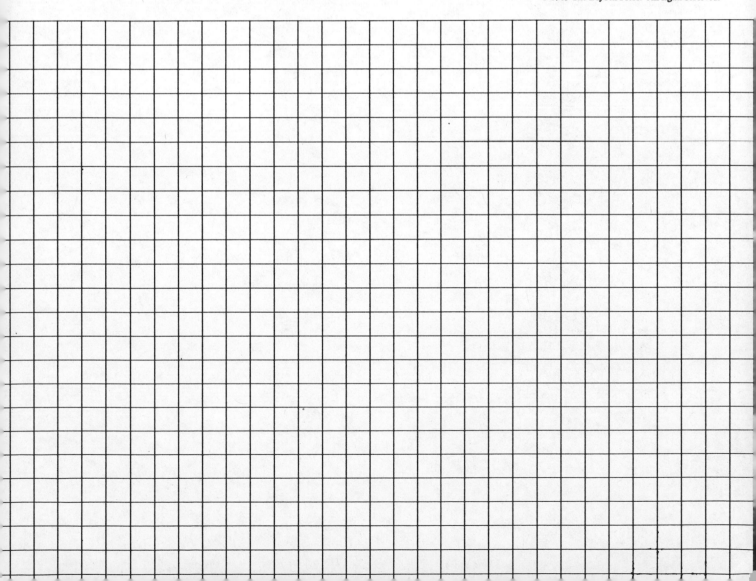

Exhibit 14–12　The Distribution of Rent

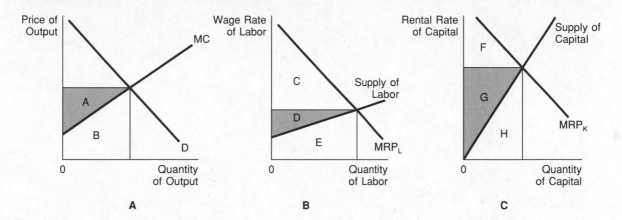

In long-run zero profits equilibrium, the industry's total revenue (given by A + B = C + D + E = F + G + H) is paid out to factors. Since labor's total wages are D + E and the total rental payments to capital are G + H, we have A + B = (D + E) + (G + H). Producers' surplus in the industry is equal to A, of which workers get D and owners of capital get G. Therefore A = D + G.

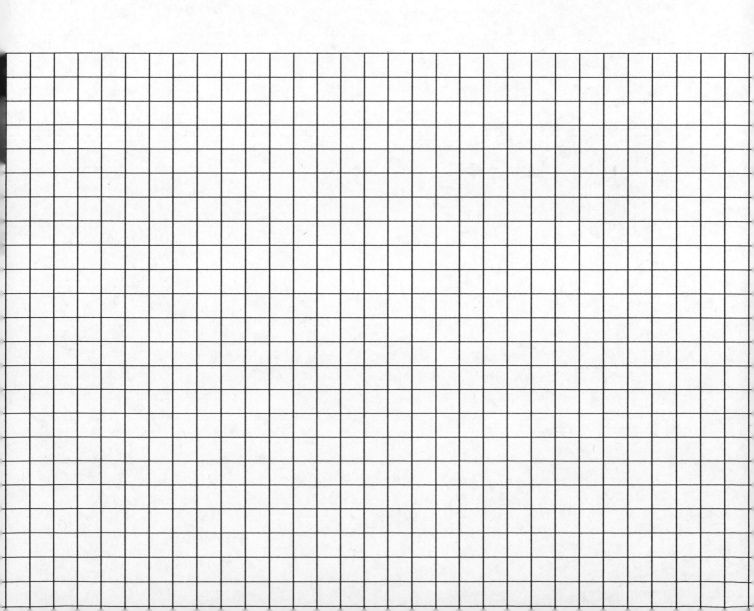

Exhibit 15–3 An Increase in Nonlabor Income

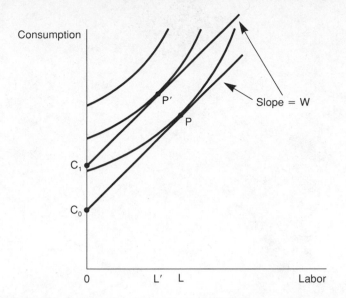

When nonlabor income increases from C_0 to C_1, the worker's budget line shifts upward parallel to itself. The new optimum is at point P'. If consumption and leisure are both normal (as opposed to inferior) goods, then P' lies above and to the left of P. Thus an increase in nonlabor income leads to increased consumption and less labor supplied. The quantity of labor that this worker supplies falls from L to L'.

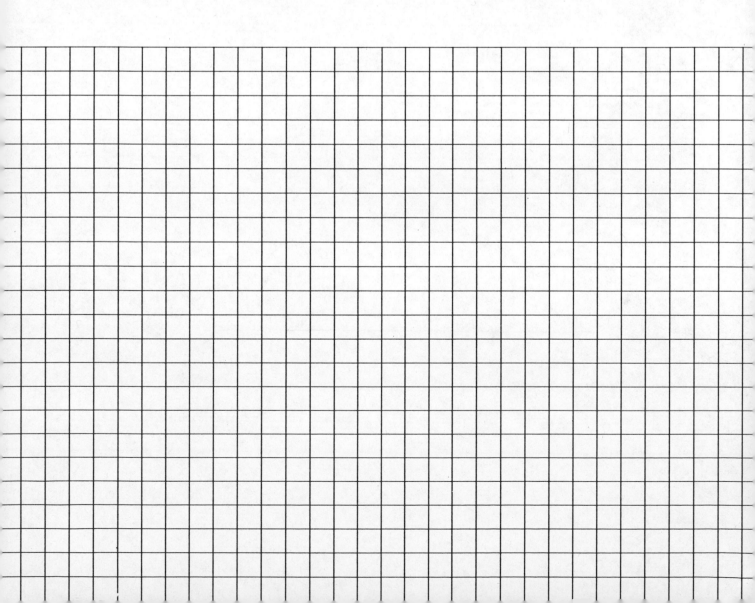

Exhibit 15–4   A Rise in the Wage Rate

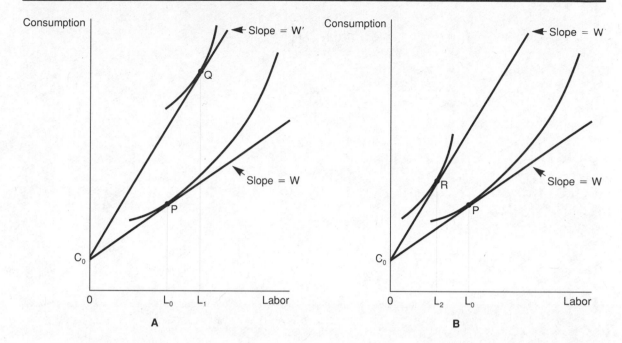

An increase in the wage, from W to W', causes the budget line to swing counterclockwise around the intercept C_0. Depending on the slope of the indifference curves, the new optimum could be at a point like Q, where more labor than before is supplied, or at a point like R, where less labor is supplied.

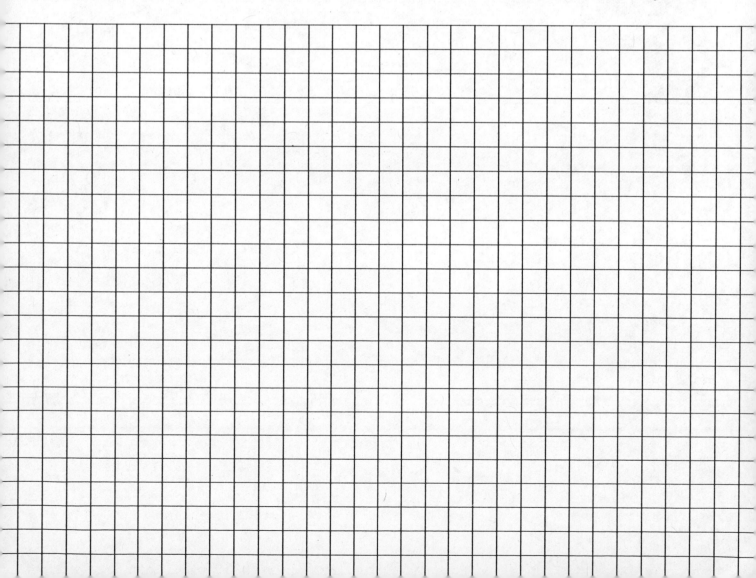

Exhibit 15–5   Income and Substitution Effects

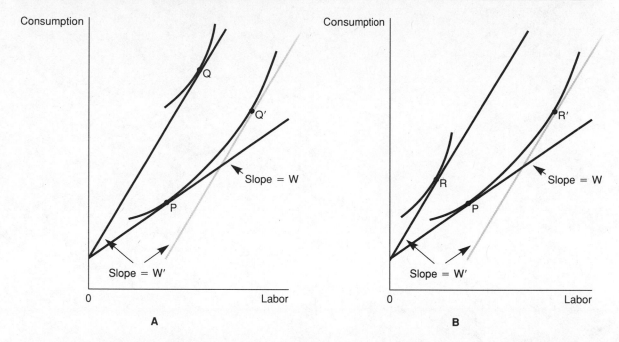

The effect of a wage increase can be decomposed into a substitution effect followed by an income effect.

When the wage goes up, we pretend that the worker loses just enough nonlabor income to keep him on his original indifference curve. In either panel this yields the light-colored budget line. The substitution effect is from P to Q' in panel A or from P to R' in panel B; it is a movement along the indifference curve and leads to more labor supplied.

The income effect is from Q' to Q in panel A or from R' to R in panel B. It leads to less labor supplied.

In panel A the substitution effect dominates the income effect, so that more labor is supplied after the wage increase. In panel B the opposite is true.

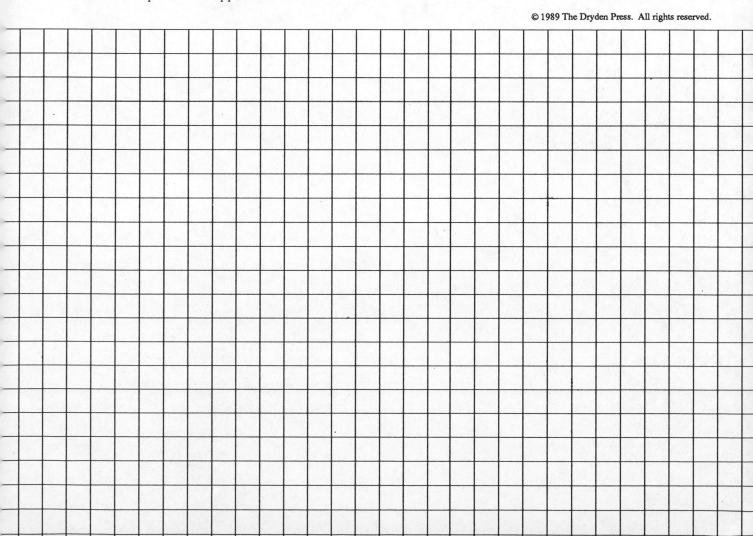

Exhibit 15–6   The Individual's Labor Supply Curve

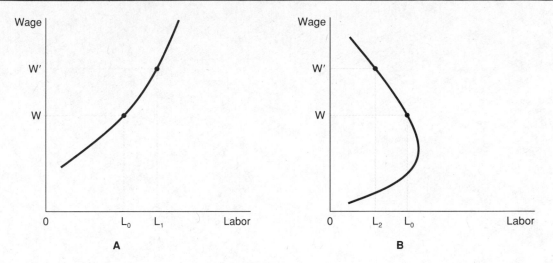

The graphs show the labor supply curves of the two individuals whose indifference curves are depicted in Exhibit 15–4. The enlarged points here are derived from the points P, Q, and R in that exhibit.

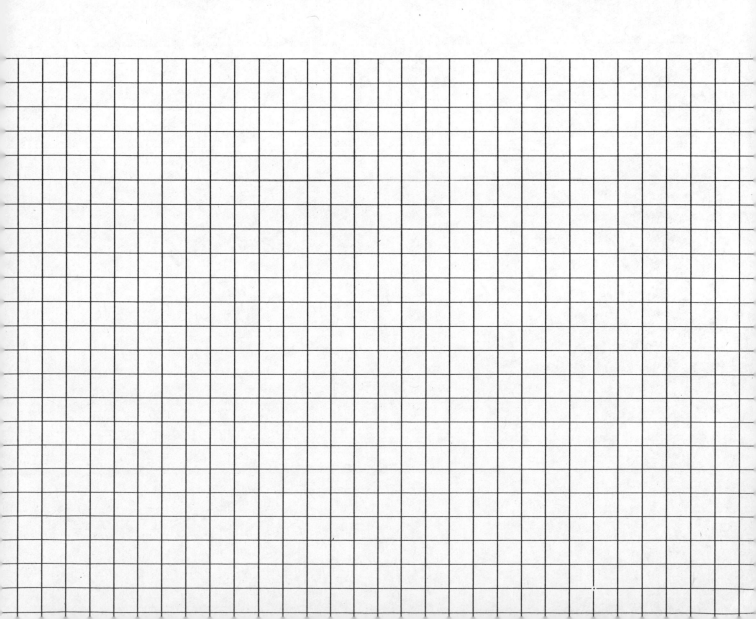

Exhibit 15–8 Valuing a Productive Asset

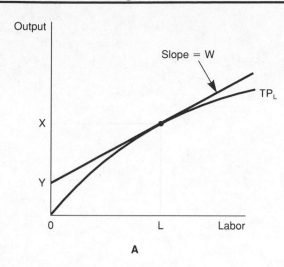

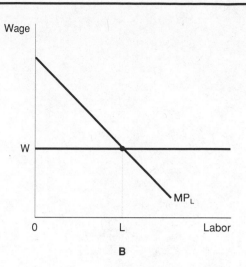

A

B

The graphs show how to determine the value of a given farm. Associated with the farm is a total product of labor curve TP_L, which shows how much output (say, wheat) the farm can produce for any given amount of labor. The marginal product of labor curve, MP_L, is derived from the TP_L curve in the usual way.

If the going wage rate is W, then the farmer hires L units of labor (where the wage is equal to the marginal product). This enables him to produce X bushels of wheat (read off the TP_L curve). He must pay his workers $W \times L = X - Y$ bushels, so that he is left with Y bushels for himself. Thus by owning the farm, the farmer earns Y bushels of wheat. The value of the farm in terms of wheat is Y bushels.

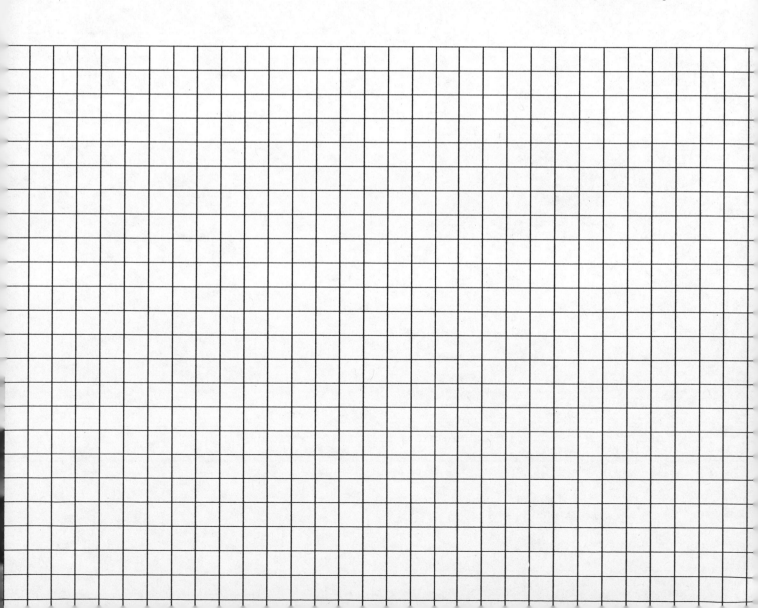

Exhibit 15–10   Labor Supply by Three Farmers

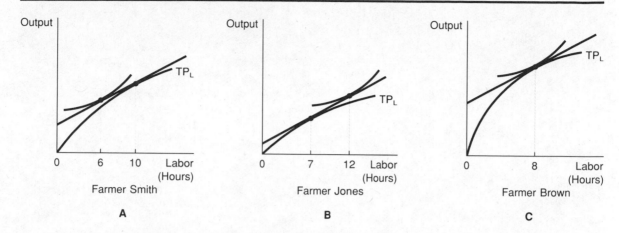

Each farmer owns a farm with a different production function, and each farmer has different indifference curves. All farmers face the same wage rate W. For each farmer we draw a straight line tangent to his production function, with slope W. This line intersects the vertical axis at a point representing the farmer's nonlabor income, so it is the farmer's budget line. Each farmer then chooses a point where his budget line is tangent to an indifference curve. The horizontal coordinate of this point shows how much labor the farmer supplies.

Each farmer hires labor until its marginal product is equal to the wage W. That is, he hires labor up to the point of tangency between his production function and his budget line. Farmer Smith demands more labor than he supplies, Farmer Jones supplies more labor than he demands, and Farmer Brown supplies and demands exactly the same amounts of labor.

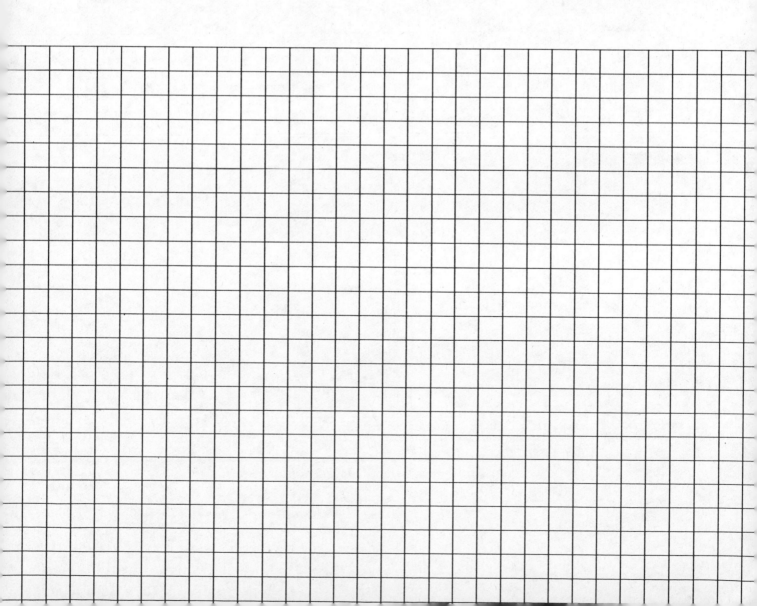

Exhibit 15–11   Deriving the Labor Supply Curve

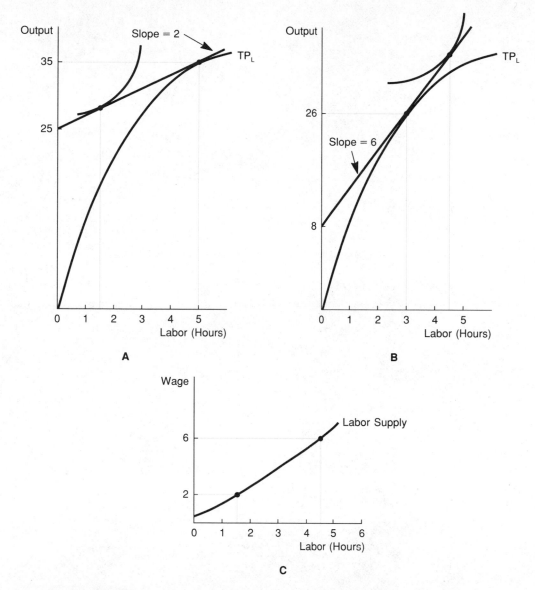

Panel A and panel B each give the derivation of a single point on the labor supply curve in panel C.

We begin by assuming that the wage is 2 units of output per unit of labor. The worker employs labor at his farm (or in association with whatever other productive asset he owns) until its marginal product is equal to the wage. This occurs where the total product curve has a slope of 2, at 5 units of labor. This enables him to produce 35 units of output. His wage bill is $2 \times 5 = 10$ units of output, so that he earns $35 - 10 = 25$ units of output in income from his farm. His budget line is the straight line in panel A. He selects the point of tangency with an indifference curve, where he supplies 1½ units of labor. Thus in panel C a wage of 2 corresponds to 1½ units of labor supplied.

Exhibit 15-12 Manna from Heaven

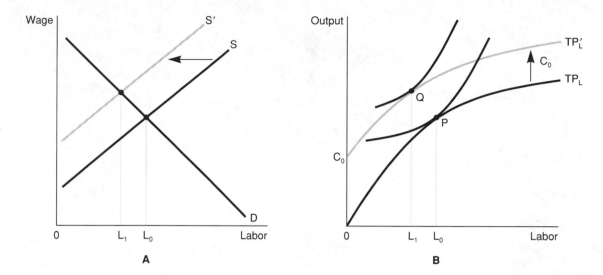

If manna falls from heaven, there is no change in the marginal product of labor, and hence no change in the labor demand curve. However, total product rises by the amount of manna that falls. This is a parallel shift upward in the total product curve, as shown in panel B. People are wealthier and therefore demand more leisure, causing the supply curve of labor to shift to the left in panel A.

The new equilibrium in panel A corresponds to the point Q in panel B. By looking at either panel, we can see that employment falls. Panel A makes it easy to see that the wage increases, and panel B makes it easy to see that consumption increases.

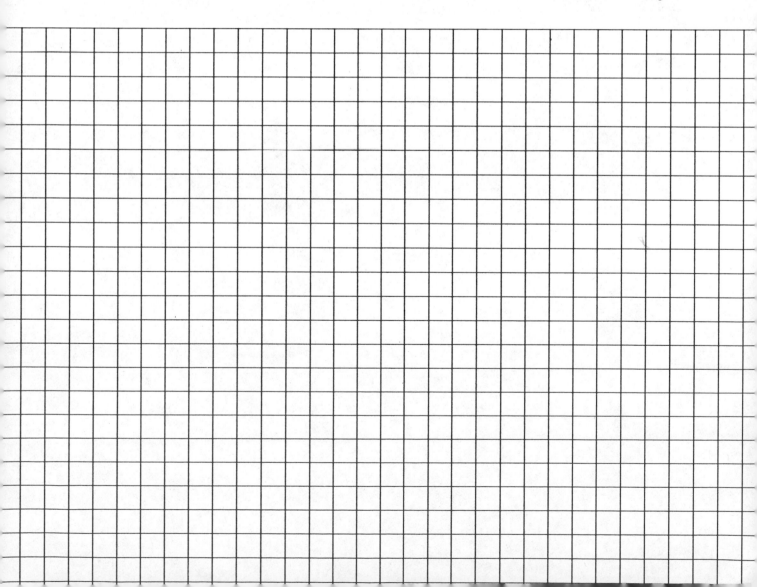

Exhibit 15–13   A Technological Improvement

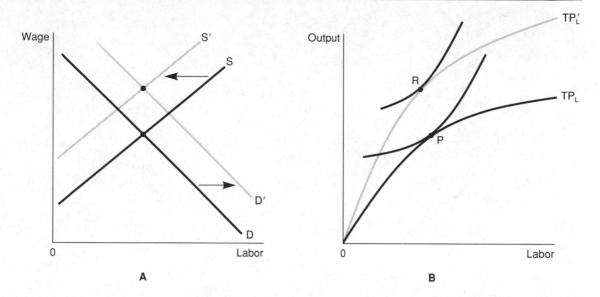

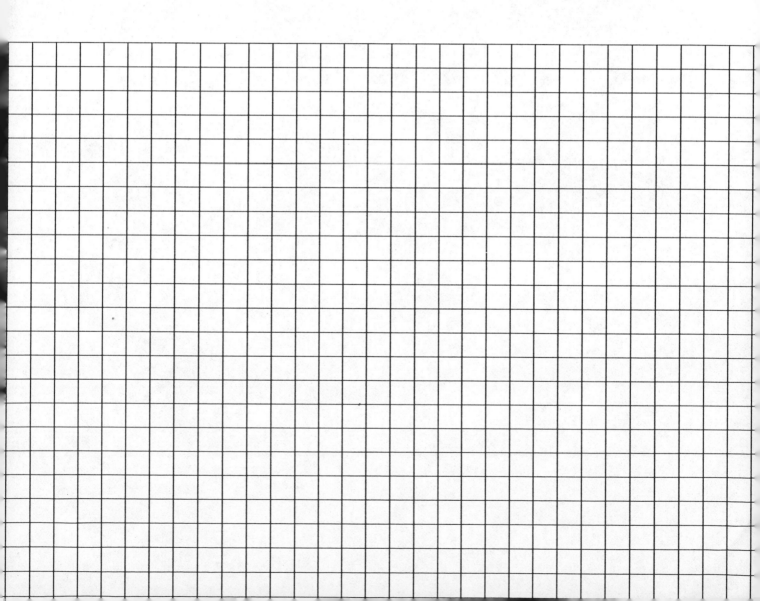

Exhibit 16–2   The Consumer's Choice

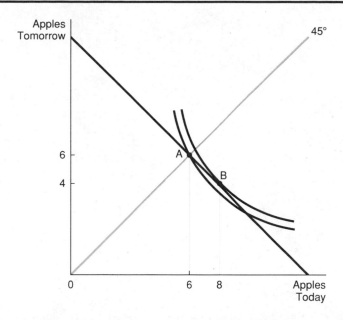

Starting from his endowment at A, Ken is given the opportunity to trade apples today for apples tomorrow (or vice versa) at a relative price of 1 for 1. This enables him to move to any point on the budget line shown, which has slope −1. Since Ken starts with equal numbers of apples today and tomorrow, we expect that he will trade to have more apples today and fewer tomorrow. Thus his optimum, B, is below and to the right of point A.

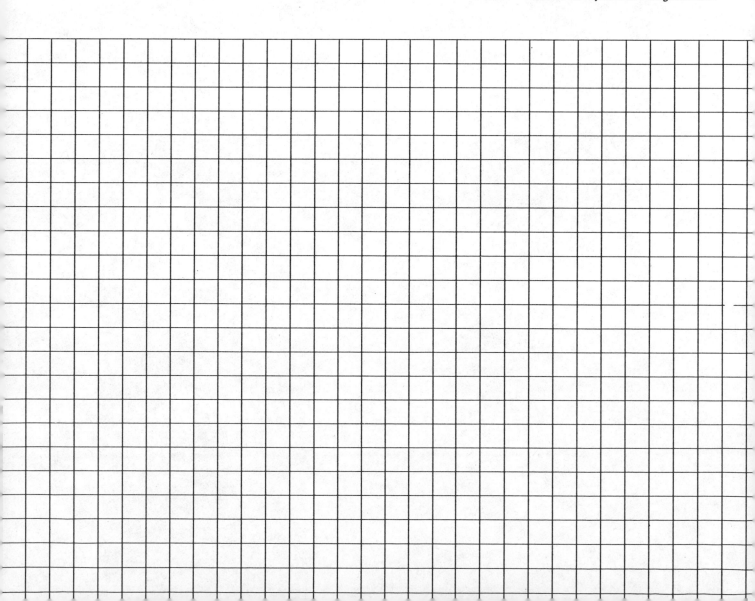

Exhibit 16–3 The Demand Curve for Current Consumption

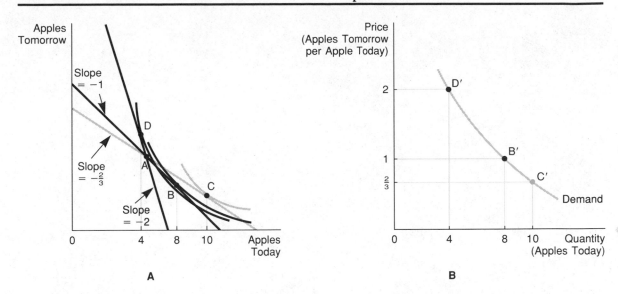

Ken's indifference curves, shown in panel A, can be used to derive his demand curve for apples today, shown in panel B. At a relative price of 1, Ken has the black budget line, chooses point B, and consumes 8 apples today. This is recorded by point B'. At a relative price of ⅔, Ken has the gray budget line, chooses point C, and consumes 10 apples today. This is recorded by point C'. At a relative price of 2, Ken has the blue budget line, chooses point D, and consumes 4 apples today. This is recorded by point D'.

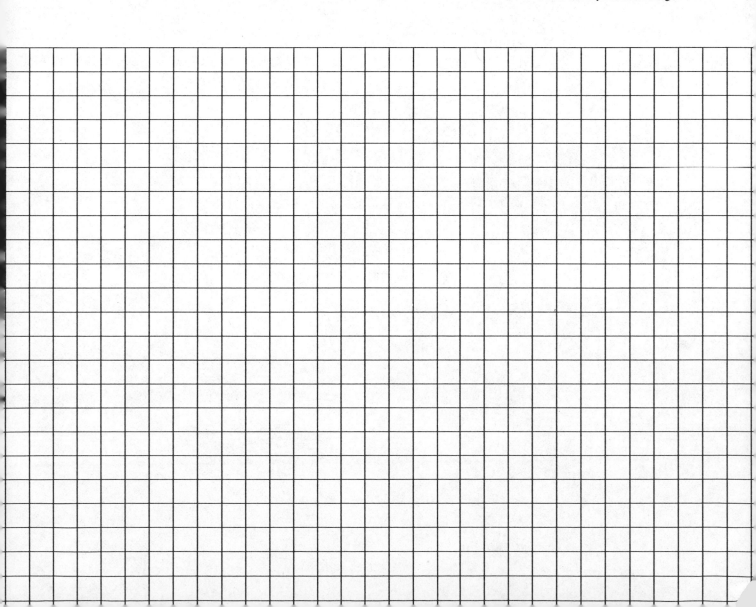

Exhibit 16–4   **Equilibrium in the Market for Current Consumption**

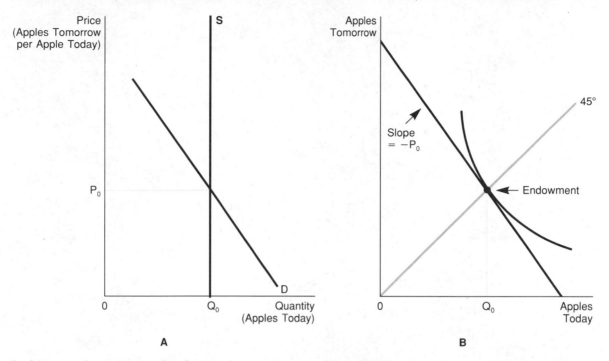

A

B

In this example we assume that there is no way to increase the supply of apples and no use for apples other than current consumption. Thus there is a given number of apples today, Q_0, and all of these will be supplied to the marketplace. It follows that the supply curve for apples is vertical.

The equilibrium price for apples today is P_0 apples tomorrow per apple today. Because this is the equilibrium price, the representative agent (that is, the "typical" or "average" consumer) must demand and supply the same quantities. In order for this to be so, the representative agent must choose to consume exactly her endowment, as in panel B.

Exhibit 16–5   An Increase in the Future Apple Supply

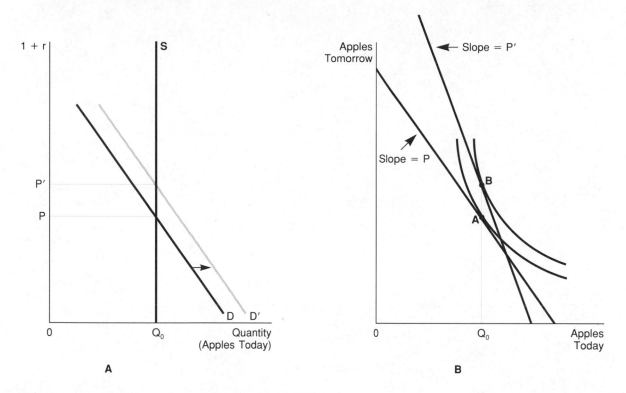

A

B

An increase in the future apple supply moves the representative agent from point A to point B in panel B, increasing wealth and hence increasing the demand for all noninferior goods, including apples today. The demand curve shifts outward in panel A and the equilibrium price rises from P to P′. The interest rate rises from r = P − 1 to r′ = P′ − 1.

The representative agent's budget line shifts from the black line (with slope P) to the blue line (with slope P′). The fact that the blue line is steeper confirms the observation that P′ is greater than P.

Exhibit 16–6 An Increase in the Current Apple Supply

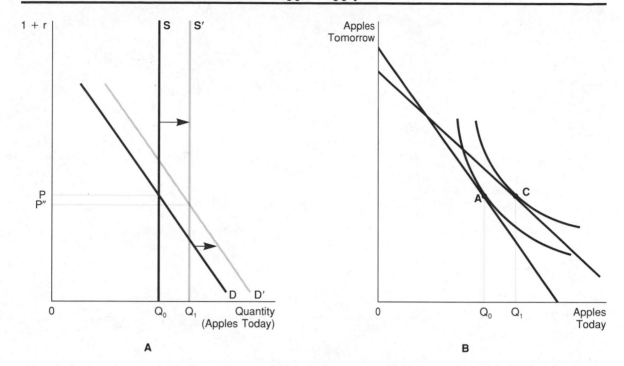

A

B

Because people are wealthier when the current apple supply increases, demand increases as well. The supply and demand graph in panel A does not reveal whether the new equilibrium price, P'', is greater or less than the old price, P. However, we can make this determination on the basis of Rebecca Representative's indifference curves. Her endowment moves from point A to point C, so her budget line changes from the black line to the shallower blue line. As the slope of the budget line is the same as the equilibrium price, we conclude that the equilibrium price (and hence the interest rate) falls.

Exhibit 16–7 The Gross Marginal Product of Capital

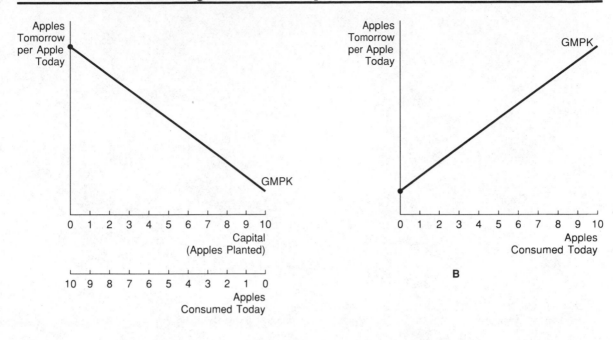

A

B

The gross marginal product of capital (GMPK) is the number of apples produced tomorrow by an apple planted today. Due to diminishing marginal returns, the GMPK curve is downward-sloping.

The number of apples planted is determined by the number of apples eaten. If there are 10 apples altogether, then the "apples eaten" axis is as shown in blue below the "apples planted" axis. When the "apples eaten" axis is drawn from left to right, as in panel B, the curve is reversed and appears upward-sloping.

Exhibit 16–10   **An Increase in Today's Apple Crop**

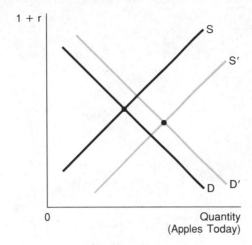

An increase in today's apple crop increases both the demand and the supply for current consumption. But demand increases by less than supply does, so the interest rate must fall.

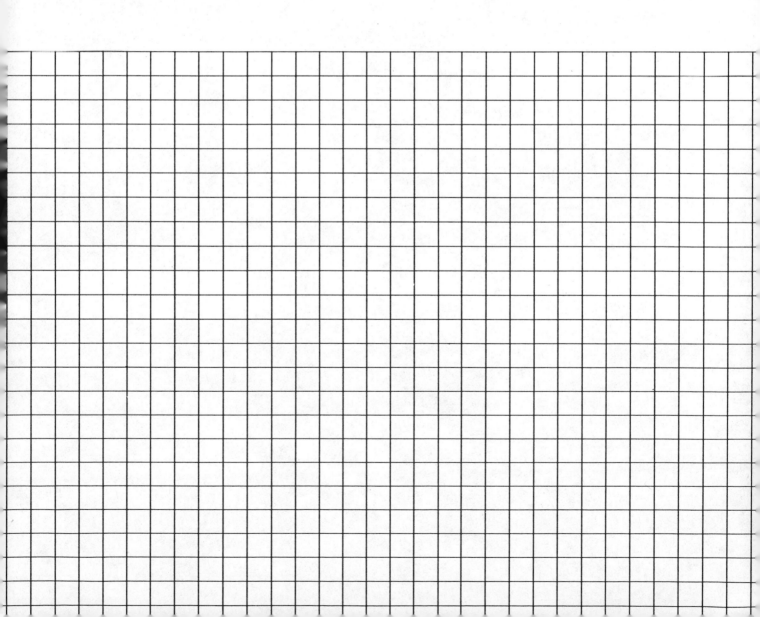

Exhibit 16–12   **The Effect of Government Borrowing**

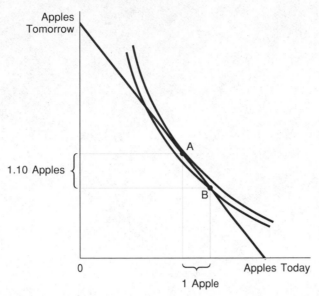

Terry Taxpayer faces an interest rate of 10% and hence a budget line with slope −1.10. He chooses the optimum point A. If the government borrows an apple so as to reduce Terry's taxes by 1 apple, then he has an additional apple today but will have 1.10 fewer apples tomorrow, when he will be taxed to pay the government debt. Thus the government borrowing moves him from point A to point B. But Terry will not stay at B. He will return to his old optimum at A, by lending an apple. Thus the government borrowing has no effect on Terry's demand for current consumption.

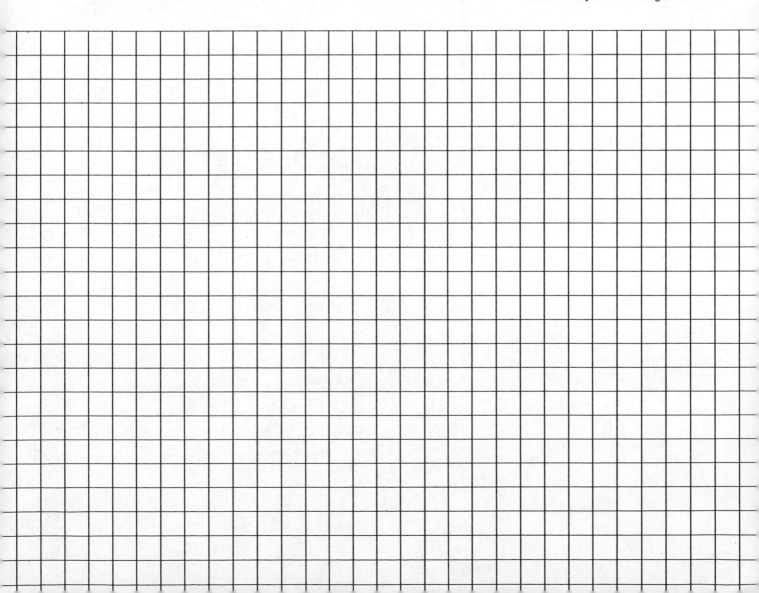

Exhibit 16–13   Default Risk and Government Borrowing

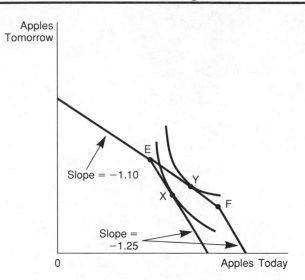

Terry Taxpayer has endowment point E. He can lend at the market rate of 10%, but he can borrow only at 25%. Thus his budget constraint is the black broken line. Along this constraint he chooses point X.

Now suppose that the government borrows an apple at the rate of 10%, cutting Terry's taxes by 1 apple at the same time. Then Terry gains 1 apple today but incurs a future tax burden of 1.10 apples. This moves his endowment to point F, which was not previously available, and makes all of the baskets on the blue broken line available. Given his new opportunities, Terry chooses basket Y. Thus the government borrowing increases Terry's demand for current consumption.

Exhibit 17–4 **Risk Neutrality**

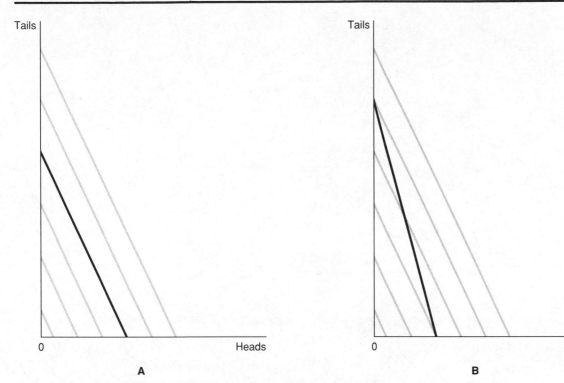

A risk-neutral individual has indifference curves that coincide with the iso-expected value lines, shown in gray in both panels. When he is offered fair odds, his budget line coincides with one of the indifference curves, as in panel A. In that case the individual is indifferent among all of the options available to him. When he is offered any odds other than fair odds, his budget line has a different slope than his indifference curves, like the black budget line in panel B. In that case he will always choose a corner and bet everything he has on one outcome or the other.

Exhibit 17–5   **Risk Aversion**

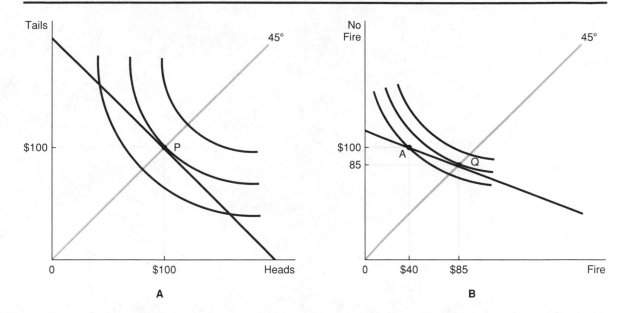

The two panels illustrate the indifference curves of individuals facing fair odds. In panel A the individual has initial wealth of $100 and is offered the opportunity to bet at even odds on the toss of a fair coin. His endowment is at point P, which is already on the 45° line. This is also his optimum, so he places no wager.

In panel B the individual has initial wealth of $100, which will be reduced to $40 in the event of a fire. His endowment is at point A. We assume that the probability of "no fire" is 3 times as great as the probability of "fire." Thus the fair odds for an insurance policy are 3 to 1, and we assume that such a policy is available. This gives the illustrated budget line, which crosses the 45° line at (85, 85). Since he is risk-averse, his optimum is at Q. He achieves this point by purchasing $15 worth of insurance.

Exhibit 17–8 Gambling at Favorable Odds

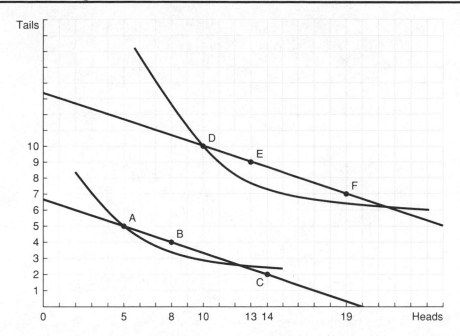

The indifference curves are those of a risk averter facing the opportunity to bet on the toss of an unbiased coin. His initial wealth is $5, so that point A is his endowment. Because he is risk-averse, the absolute slope of the indifference curve at A must reflect the fair odds of 1 to 1; in other words, it has an absolute slope of 1.

This individual is invited to bet on heads at the favorable odds of 3 to 1. By betting $1, he moves to point B, which he prefers to point A. If he bet $3, he would move to point C, which he likes less than point A. Thus if he is allowed to place the small bet of $1, he will do so, but if he must place the large bet of $3, he will decline.

Suppose that this individual has an increase in wealth, to $10. Then his endowment moves to point D. From point D a $1 bet moves him to point E, and a $3 bet moves him to point F. Either of these is an improvement over point D, and if offered either option, he will accept it. With greater initial wealth, he is willing to accept the $3 bet that he previously considered too large. However, he will continue to reject much larger bets.

Exhibit 17–10 **Insurance with Moral Hazard**

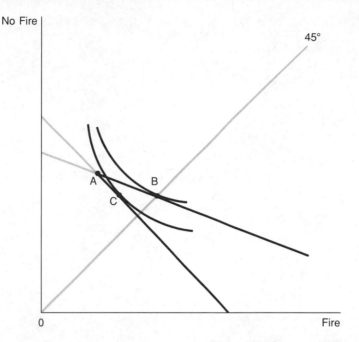

Although the initial probability of fire is .25, the insurance company knows that this will change after the homeowner is insured. Therefore it offers insurance at 1 to 1 odds, rather than 3 to 1. The homeowner's budget line is shown in blue. He chooses point C, where he is partially but not fully insured.

If the insurance company could require the homeowner not to change his behavior after the policy is issued, then it could offer insurance at 3 to 1 odds and the homeowner could achieve the preferred point B.

Exhibit 17–11 Adverse Selection

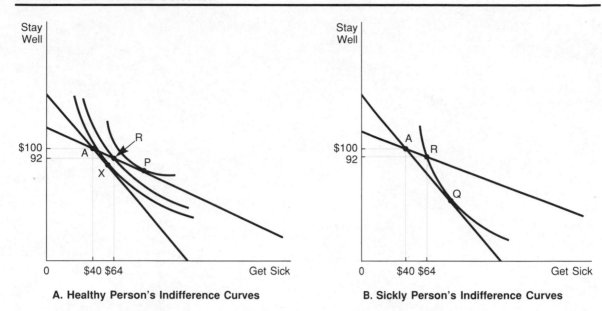

A. Healthy Person's Indifference Curves

B. Sickly Person's Indifference Curves

Healthies and Sicklies both have endowment point A. For Healthies the probability of illness is .25, so that the fair odds for insurance are 3 to 1, which would yield the black budget line. For Sicklies, the probability of illness is .50, so that the fair odds for insurance are 1 to 1, which would yield the blue budget line.

Because the company cannot distinguish Sicklies from Healthies, it cannot forbid Sicklies to buy 3–1 insurance. Thus it adopts a strategy that leads the Sicklies to choose 1–1 insurance voluntarily.

The strategy is to allow anyone to purchase any amount of 1–1 insurance, but to limit each customer to just under $8 worth of 3–1 insurance. Healthies can achieve either point X or point R, and they choose point R. (Actually they achieve a point slightly to the left of R.) Sicklies can achieve point Q or a point slightly to the left of R and choose point Q. Thus the Healthies and Sicklies each voluntarily select the policy that offers them fair odds.

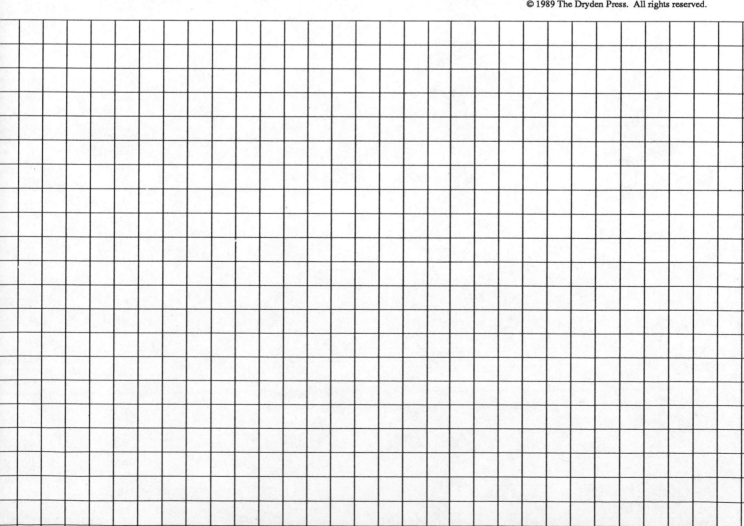

Exhibit 17–12   **Speculation**

Case 1: Speculator Right

Without speculator:
February welfare: A + B + D
March welfare: F + I + M + N
Total: A + B + D + F + I + M + N

With speculator:
February welfare: A + B + C + D + E
March welfare: F + I + M
Total: A + B + C + D + E + F + I + M

Gain due to speculator: C + E − N

Case 2: Speculator Wrong

Without speculator:
February welfare: A + B + D
March welfare: F + G + H + I + J + K + L + M + N
Total: A + B + D + F + G + H + I + J + K + L + M + N

With speculator:
February welfare: A + B + C + D + E
March welfare: F + G + I + J + M
Total: A + B + C + D + E + F + G + I + J + M

Loss due to speculator: H + K + L + N − C − E

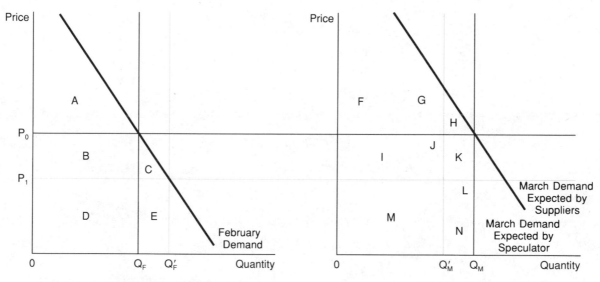

A. Supply and Demand for February Grain

B. Supply and Demand for March Grain

The February demand curve for grain is shown in panel A. Suppliers expect the March demand curve to be the dark blue curve in panel B. Thus they supply Q_F bushels in February and Q_M bushels in March, where these quantities are chosen to make the prices equal. The price in either month is P_0.

Now a speculator arrives on the scene, believing that the March demand curve will be the light blue curve in panel B. Thus he offers to sell March futures contracts, driving down the price of March grain and leading suppliers to sell more in February and less in March. The quantities adjust to Q_F' and Q_M'.

The table shows the welfare analysis, first when the speculator proves to be right and then when he proves to be wrong. In each case we must use the appropriate March demand curve—the light blue one if the speculator is right and the dark blue one if he is wrong. If the speculator is right, his arrival increases welfare, and if the speculator is wrong, his arrival decreases welfare.

Exhibit 17–14   **The Geometry of Portfolios**

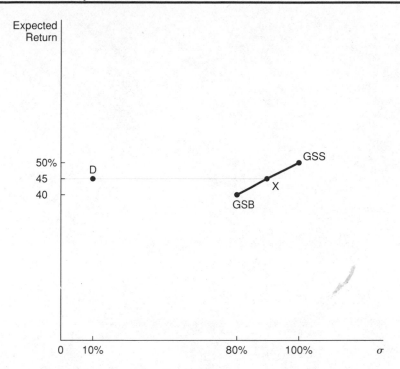

Every stock, and every portfolio, is represented by a point in the diagram. The points GSS and GSB represent General Snowshoes and General Surfboards, which are described in Exhibit 17–13.

The point X, which is midway between the stocks GSS and GSB, represents an asset with the average of their expected returns and the average of their standard deviations. The portfolio containing GSS and GSB has the average expected return but a smaller standard deviation. Thus it is represented by a point directly to the left of X, namely D.

Exhibit 17-15 The Efficient Set

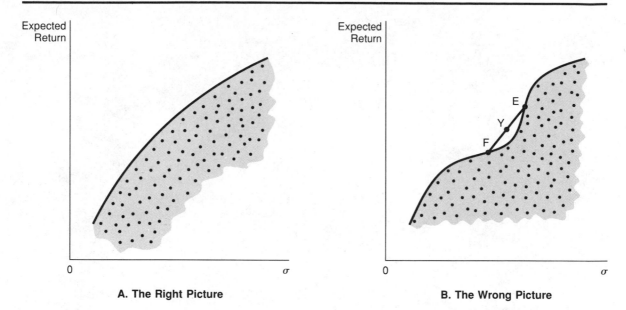

A. The Right Picture

B. The Wrong Picture

The dots represent the stocks available in the marketplace, and the shaded region represents all of the portfolios that can be constructed from those stocks. The picture must look like panel A and cannot look like panel B. In panel B the portfolio that combines portfolios E and F must be located at Y or to the left of Y, where the picture shows no portfolios. Therefore the picture is wrong.

In panel A, which is the correct picture, the northwest boundary of the shaded region is the efficient set. No investor would choose a portfolio that is not in the efficient set.

Exhibit 17–16 The Investor's Choice

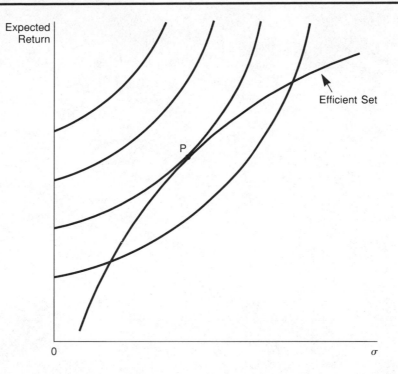

Because the investor views expected return as good and standard deviation as bad, his indifference curves are shaped as shown. Of the portfolios in the efficient set, he selects the one on the "highest" (most northwesterly) indifference curve, which is at the tangency P.

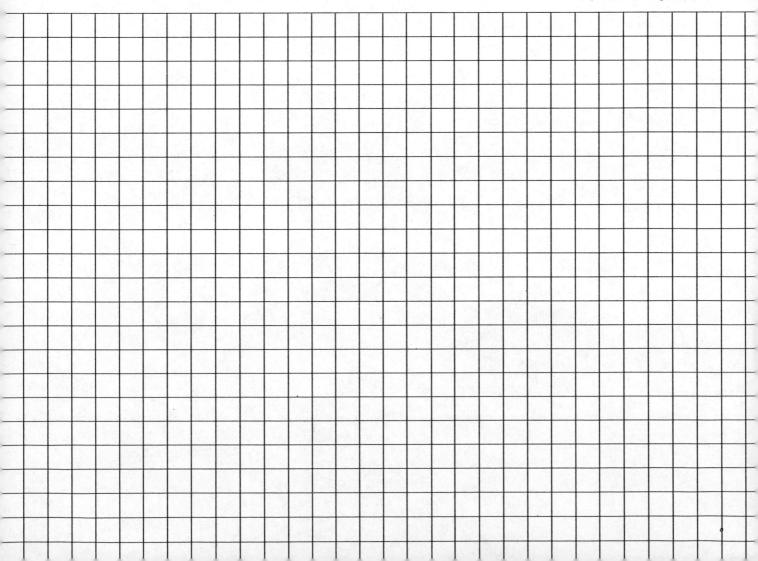

Exhibit 17–17 A Risk-Free Asset

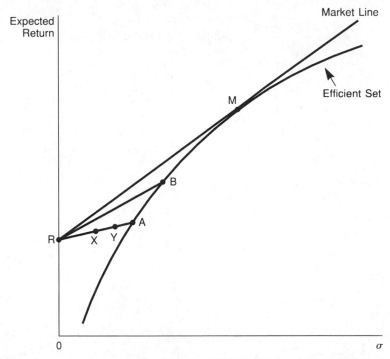

Point R represents a risk-free asset, possibly a Treasury bill. The investor can achieve any point along the illustrated line segments by combining R with portfolios such as A, B, and M. For example, combining R and A in equal amounts yields point X. The line connecting R and M contains the most desirable possibilities; it is called the market line. If R can be held in negative amounts (say by borrowing), then it is possible to move beyond point M along the market line.

No investor would ever want to be off the market line. Therefore every investor wants to hold a portfolio consisting partly of R and partly of a market portfolio M.

Exhibit 17–18 The Investor's Choice Revisited

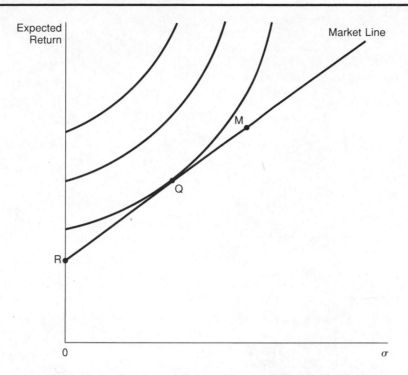

When there is a risk-free asset, the investor is no longer restricted to the old efficient set. He can now reach any point on the market line by combining the risk-free asset with the market portfolio in appropriate proportions. This investor chooses proportions that enable him to reach point Q.

The investor can never do better than to be on the market line. Thus his portfolio of risky assets will always be the market portfolio. There is never any reason to hold any other portfolio of risky assets.

Exhibit 17–19   Expectations and Supply

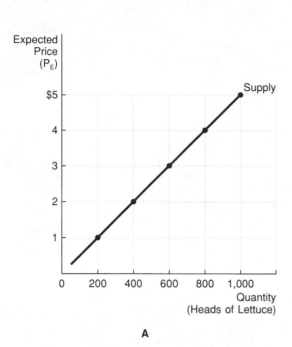

A

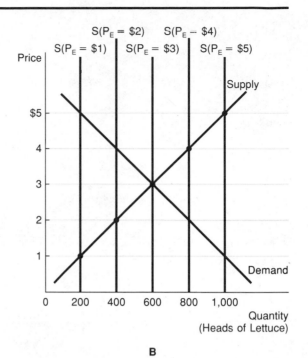

B

The curve in panel A shows how much lettuce the farmers bring to market at each expected price. It is like a supply curve, except that it depends on expected price rather than actual price.

When the farmers arrive at the market, the supply curve is vertical. The position of the vertical supply curve depends on the farmers' expectation of the price. Panel B shows the supply curve from panel A superimposed on several possible vertical supply curves. The actual price depends on the expected price (which determines the vertical supply curve) and the actual demand.

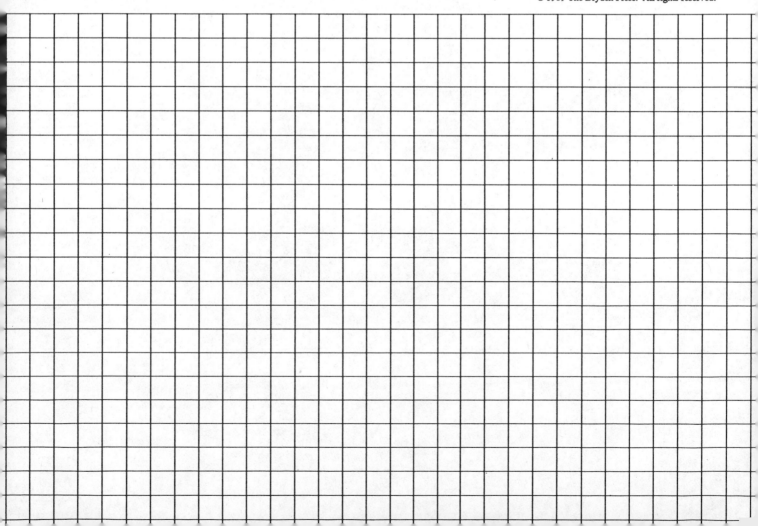

Exhibit 17–21 Lumberjacks' Income and the Price of Lettuce

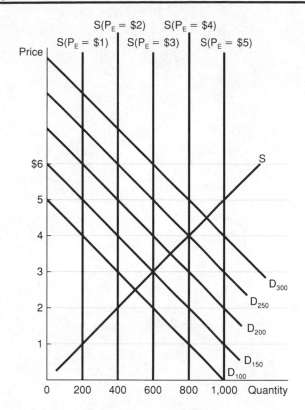

The demand curve for lettuce depends on the lumberjacks' income. When their income is $100, the demand curve is D_{100}; when their income is $150, the demand curve is D_{150}; and so on. Initially, the lumberjacks earn $150 on average. Thus the rational expectation of the price is $3 (where D_{150} crosses the upward-sloping supply curve), so farmers supply 600 heads of lettuce. When the lumberjacks really do earn $150, the rational expectation is fulfilled. On days when the lumberjacks earn $250, the price of lettuce is $5.

Now a paper mill arrives, raising the lumberjacks' income to $250 on average. The new rational expectation for the price is $4. Farmers bring 800 heads of lettuce to market. On the average day the lumberjacks earn $250 and the price of lettuce is $4.

An econometrician extrapolating from past experience would predict that on days when the lumberjacks earn $250, the price of lettuce is $5. Thus he would predict that when the paper mill arrives, the price of lettuce will go up to $5 on average. But he is wrong, because past experience is no longer relevant. When farmers have rational expectations, the additional lettuce that they bring to market invalidates the old relationship between the lumberjacks' income and the price of lettuce.

Exhibit 18–3 A Subsidy to Holding Money

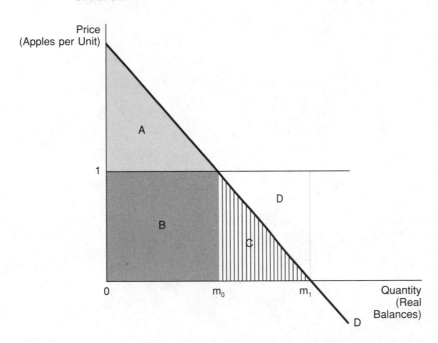

	Before Subsidy	After Subsidy
Consumer Surplus	A	A + B + C
Gains to Neighbors	B	—
Social Gain	A + B	A + B + C

The private cost of holding real balances is 1 apple per unit and the social cost is zero apples per unit. Therefore the consumer holds m_0 units, even though the social optimum is m_1 units. The consumer earns a surplus equal to area A. By forgoing m_0 apples, he makes this many more apples available to his neighbors and thus conveys a positive externality equal to area B.

Now suppose that the government subsidizes money holdings by rewarding each consumer with 1 apple per unit of real balances held. The private marginal cost drops to zero, and the consumer holds m_1 units of real balances. His consumer's surplus increases to A + B + C. The positive externality increases to B + C + D, but this is exactly offset by the fact that the neighbors who benefit from the externality must also pay the subsidy. Thus the increase in social gain is area C, as can be seen in the table.

Exhibit 18–5   Inflation

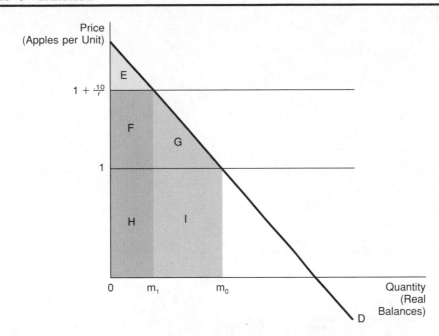

Initially, the money supply is stable at M_0, the price level is P_0, and people hold $m_0 = M_0/P_0$ units of real balances.

Now the authorities institute a policy of increasing the money supply by 10% per year. The price level must eventually also increase by 10% per year. This increases the cost of holding real balances from 1 apple per unit to $1 + .10/r$ apples per unit, where r is the real rate of interest. As a result, people reduce their real balance holdings from m_0 to m_1. This requires an initial period in which the price level grows faster than the money supply so that real balances can fall. The initial period is known as a period of overshooting.

The inflation reduces social welfare from $E + F + G + H + I$ to $E + F + H$, causing a deadweight loss of $G + I$.

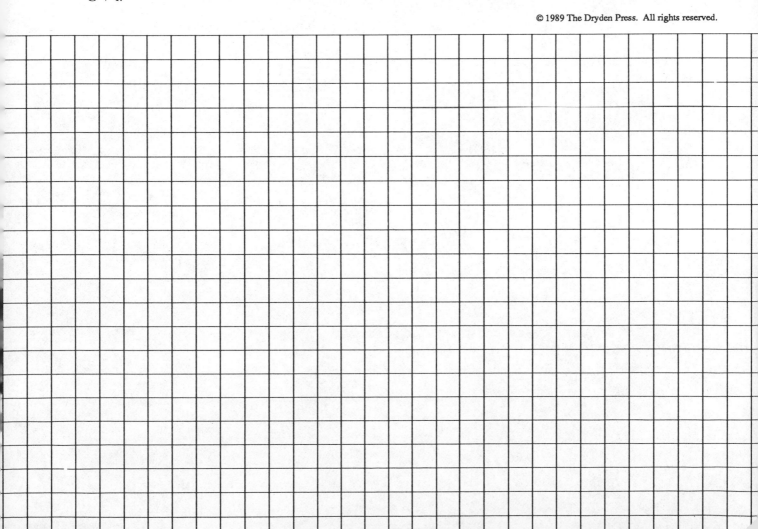

Exhibit 19–3 **Rats as Rational Consumers**

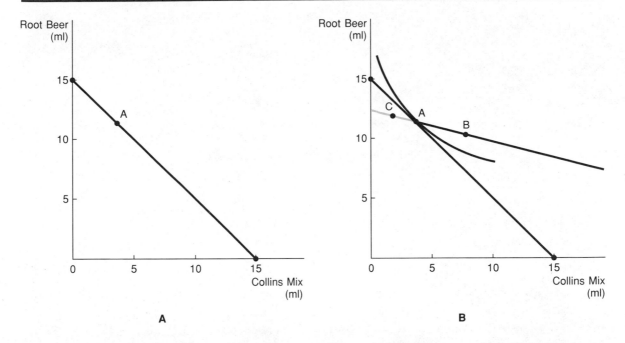

In panel A a rat with the black budget line chose point A. Prices and his income were then adjusted so that he now had the colored budget line in panel B. According to economic theory, the rat must now choose a point like B (on the darker part of the new line) rather than a point like C (on the lighter part). The reason is that if an indifference curve were tangent at C, it would have to cross the original indifference curve. In fact, the rat chose point B, confirming the economic prediction.

Exhibit 19–4   Pigeons and Labor Supply

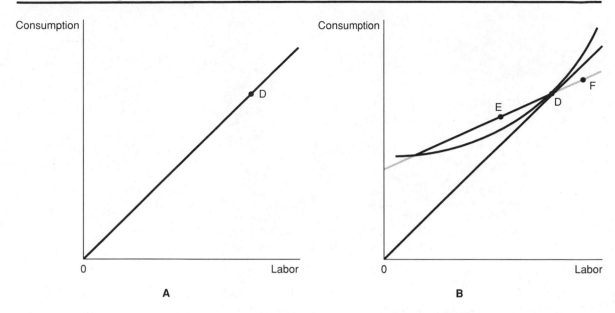

In panel A a pigeon with the black budget line chose point D. His wage and his nonlabor income were then adjusted so that he had the colored budget line. According to economic theory, the pigeon must now choose a point like E (on the darker part of the new line) rather than a point like F (on the lighter part). The reason is that if an indifference curve were tangent at F, it would have to cross the original indifference curve. In fact, the pigeon chose point E, confirming the economic prediction.

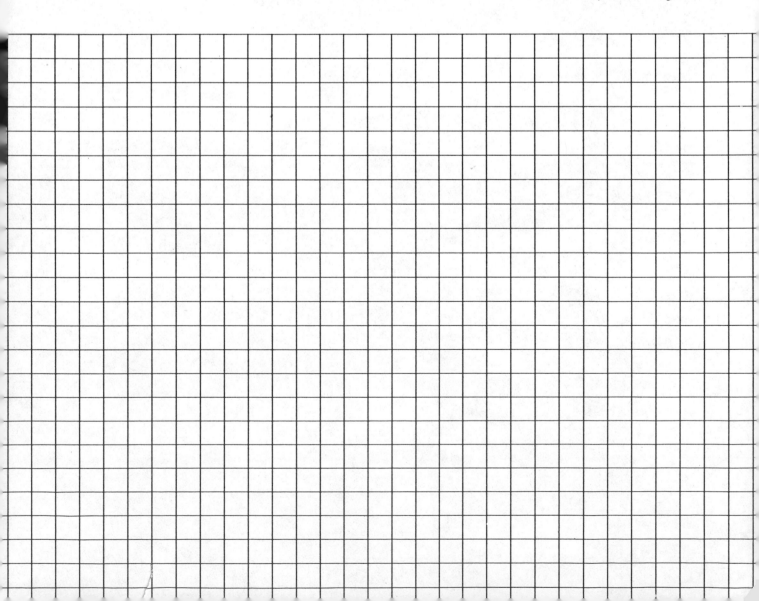